New Developments
in Productivity Analysis

Studies in Income and Wealth
Volume 63

National Bureau of Economic Research
Conference on Research in Income and Wealth

New Developments in Productivity Analysis

Edited by **Charles R. Hulten,
Edwin R. Dean, and
Michael J. Harper**

The University of Chicago Press

Chicago and London

CHARLES R. HULTEN is professor of economics at the University of Maryland, a research associate of the National Bureau of Economic Research, and chairman of the Conference on Research in Income and Wealth. EDWIN R. DEAN was formerly associate commissioner for productivity and technology, Bureau of Labor Statistics, U.S. Department of Labor. He is currently adjunct professor in the Department of Economics at The George Washington University, Washington, D.C. MICHAEL J. HARPER is a member of the staff of the Office of Productivity and Technology of the U.S. Bureau of Labor Statistics.

The University of Chicago Press, Chicago 60637
The University of Chicago Press, Ltd., London
© 2001 by the National Bureau of Economic Research
All rights reserved. Published 2001
Printed in the United States of America
10 09 08 07 06 05 04 03 02 01   1 2 3 4 5
ISBN: 0-226-36062-8 (cloth)

Library of Congress Cataloging-in-Publication Data

New developments in productivity analysis / edited by Charles R. Hulten, Edwin R. Dean, and Michael J. Harper
  p.   cm.—(Studies in income and wealth ; v. 63)
  Includes bibliographical references and index.
  ISBN 0-226-36062-8 (cloth : alk. paper)
  1. Industrial productivity—Congresses. 2. Economic development—Congresses. I. Hulten, Charles R. II. Dean, Edwin. III. Harper, Michael J. IV. Series.
  HC79.I52 N477   2001
  338'.06—dc21   00-053245

⊗ The paper used in this publication meets the minimum requirements of the American National Standard for Information Sciences—Permanence of Paper for Printed Library Materials, ANSI Z39.48-1992.

National Bureau of Economic Research

Officers

Carl F. Christ, *chairman*
Kathleen B. Cooper, *vice-chairman*
Martin Feldstein, *president and chief executive officer*
Robert Mednick, *treasurer*
Susan Colligan, *corporate secretary*
Kelly Horak, *controller and assistant corporate secretary*
Gerardine Johnson, *assistant corporate secretary*

Directors at Large

Peter C. Aldrich
Elizabeth E. Bailey
John H. Biggs
Andrew Brimmer
Carl F. Christ
Don R. Conlan
Kathleen B. Cooper
George C. Eads
Martin Feldstein
Stephen Friedman
George Hatsopoulos
Karen N. Horn
Judy C. Lewent
John Lipsky
Leo Melamed
Michael H. Moskow
Rudolph A. Oswald
Robert T. Parry
Peter G. Peterson
Richard N. Rosett
Kathleen P. Utgoff
Marina v.N. Whitman
Martin B. Zimmerman

Directors by University Appointment

George Akerlof, *California, Berkeley*
Jagdish Bhagwati, *Columbia*
William C. Brainard, *Yale*
Glen G. Cain, *Wisconsin*
Franklin Fisher, *Massachusetts Institute of Technology*
Saul H. Hymans, *Michigan*
Marjorie B. McElroy, *Duke*
Joel Mokyr, *Northwestern*
Andrew Postlewaite, *Pennsylvania*
Nathan Rosenberg, *Stanford*
Michael Rothschild, *Princeton*
Craig Swan, *Minnesota*
David B. Yoffie, *Harvard*
Arnold Zellner, *Chicago*

Directors by Appointment of Other Organizations

Marcel Boyer, *Canadian Economics Association*
Mark Drabenstott, *American Agricultural Economics Association*
Gail D. Fosler, *The Conference Board*
A. Ronald Gallant, *American Statistical Association*
Robert S. Hamada, *American Finance Association*
Robert Mednick, *American Institute of Certified Public Accountants*
Richard D. Rippe, *National Association for Business Economics*
John J. Siegfried, *American Economic Association*
David A. Smith, *American Federation of Labor and Congress of Industrial Organizations*
Josh S. Weston, *Committee for Economic Development*
Gavin Wright, *Economic History Association*

Directors Emeriti

Moses Abramovitz
Thomas D. Flynn
Lawrence R. Klein
Franklin A. Lindsay
Paul W. McCracken
Bert Seidman
Eli Shapiro

Since this volume is a record of conference proceedings, it has been exempted from the rules governing critical review of manuscripts by the Board of Directors of the National Bureau (resolution adopted 8 June 1948, as revised 21 November 1949 and 20 April 1968).

Contents

	Prefatory Note and Acknowledgments	ix
	Introduction Charles R. Hulten, Edwin R. Dean, and Michael J. Harper	xi
1.	**Total Factor Productivity: A Short Biography** Charles R. Hulten *Comment:* Jack E. Triplett	1
2.	**The BLS Productivity Measurement Program** Edwin R. Dean and Michael J. Harper	55
3.	**Which (Old) Ideas on Productivity Measurement Are Ready to Use?** W. Erwin Diewert	85
4.	**Dynamic Factor Demand Models and Productivity Analysis** M. Ishaq Nadiri and Ingmar R. Prucha *Comment:* Dale W. Jorgenson *Reply to Dale W. Jorgenson*	103
5.	**After "Technical Progress and the Aggregate Production Function"** Robert M. Solow	173
6.	**Accounting for Growth** Jeremy Greenwood and Boyan Jovanovic *Comment:* Barry Bosworth	179

7.	**Why Is Productivity Procyclical? Why Do We Care?** Susanto Basu and John Fernald *Comment:* Catherine J. Morrison Paul	225
8.	**Aggregate Productivity Growth: Lessons from Microeconomic Evidence** Lucia Foster, John Haltiwanger, and C. J. Krizan *Comment:* Mark J. Roberts	303
9.	**Sources of Productivity Growth in the American Coal Industry: 1972–95** Denny Ellerman, Thomas M. Stoker, and Ernst R. Berndt *Comment:* Larry Rosenblum	373
10.	**Service Sector Productivity Comparisons: Lessons for Measurement** Martin Neil Baily and Eric Zitzewitz *Comment:* Robert J. Gordon	419
11.	**Different Approaches to International Comparison of Total Factor Productivity** Nazrul Islam *Comment:* Charles I. Jones	465
12.	**Whatever Happened to Productivity Growth?** Dale W. Jorgenson and Eric Yip	509
13.	**Productivity of the U.S. Agricultural Sector: The Case of Undesirable Outputs** V. Eldon Ball, Rolf Färe, Shawna Grosskopf, and Richard Nehring *Comment:* Robin C. Sickles	541
14.	**Total Resource Productivity: Accounting for Changing Environmental Quality** Frank M. Gollop and Gregory P. Swinand *Comment:* William Pizer	587
15.	**A Perspective on What We Know About the Sources of Productivity Growth** Zvi Griliches	609
	Contributors	613
	Author Index	617
	Subject Index	625

Prefatory Note

This volume contains revised versions of most of the papers and discussions presented at the Conference on Research in Income and Wealth entitled "New Directions in Productivity Analysis," held in Silver Spring, Maryland, on 20–21 March 1998. It also contains some material not presented at that conference.

Funds for the Conference on Research in Income and Wealth are supplied by the Bureau of Labor Statistics, the Bureau of Economic Analysis, the Federal Reserve Board, and the Bureau of the Census; we are indebted to them for their support. This conference was supported by the National Science Foundation under grant SBR-9730608.

We thank Charles R. Hulten, Edwin R. Dean, and Michael J. Harper, who served as conference organizers and editors of the volume, and the NBER staff and NBER and University of Chicago Press editors for their assistance in organizing the conference and editing the volume.

Executive Committee, July 2000
Ernst R. Berndt
Carol S. Carson
Carol A. Corrado
Edwin R. Dean
Robert C. Feenstra
John Greenlees
John C. Haltiwanger
Charles R. Hulten, chair
Lawrence F. Katz
J. Steven Landefeld
Robert H. McGuckin III

Brent R. Moulton
Matthew Shapiro
Robert Summers

Volume Editors' Acknowledgments

The editors of this volume, who also served as the organizing committee for the CRIW conference that took place on 20–21 March 1998, gratefully acknowledge the financial support of the National Science Foundation through grant SBR-9730608. We thank Kirsten Foss-Davis and other members of the NBER conference department for their work in making the conference possible. In preparing these proceedings for publication, we relied greatly on the expert assistance of Helena Fitz-Patrick and other members of the NBER editorial staff as well as staff members of the University of Chicago Press. Finally, we thank two anonymous referees for their comments on the volume.

Introduction

Charles R. Hulten, Edwin R. Dean, and Michael J. Harper

The Conference on Research in Income and Wealth (CRIW) last met to discuss "new developments" in productivity analysis in November 1975 at a meeting organized by John W. Kendrick and Beatrice N. Vaccara. Discussions of productivity were dominated at that time by the methodological debate between Edward Denison, on the one hand, and Dale Jorgenson and Zvi Griliches, on the other. While many of the positions of Jorgenson and Griliches have been widely accepted—notably through the 1983 launch of the multifactor productivity program by the Bureau of Labor Statistics (BLS)—other issues have surfaced. The proceedings of the 1975 conference make no mention of the productivity slowdown that commenced in the early 1970s, but this slowdown became the central concern of productivity analysts over the next two decades.

The focus has shifted again in recent years as the prolonged economic expansion has offered up another conundrum: Why has measured productivity failed to keep up with the boom in a period notable for major innovations in information technology? The New Economy explanation of the recent boom assigns central importance to unmeasured gains in productivity arising from index number issues and from the failure to measure improvements in product quality. The potential importance of these issues is underscored by the recent revisions of government productivity statistics.

Charles R. Hulten is professor of economics at the University of Maryland and a research associate of the National Bureau of Economic Research and chairman of the Conference on Research in Income and Wealth. Edwin R. Dean was formerly associate commissioner for Productivity and Technology, Bureau of Labor Statistics, U.S. Department of Labor. He is currently adjunct professor in the Department of Economics at The George Washington University, Washington, D.C. Michael J. Harper is a member of the staff of the Office of Productivity and Technology of the U.S. Bureau of Labor Statistics.

Data on real gross domestic product (GDP) were revised in 1996 to use an annually chained Fisher Ideal Index number formula. The primary empirical impact of this was to assign the proper historical weights to computer hardware in calculating real GDP. In 1999 a second round of GDP revisions introduced computer software, improved the measures of banking output, and utilized price data that were developed using improved index number methods at the most detailed levels of aggregation. This second round of changes resulted in productivity estimates in the nonfarm business sector that reveal a smaller slowdown in the 1970s and more rapid growth since the mid-1990s. Advocates of the New Economy viewpoint may applaud these data improvements.

The perception that productivity statistics have a systematic downward bias is not universally shared. Environmentalists have argued that the bias may go in the opposite direction, because the measures of output and inputs used in conventional productivity calculations do not account adequately for the depletion of natural resources or damage to the environment. A recent publication by the National Research Council, "Nature's Numbers," suggests major changes in the national accounts to address this problem.

The theory of productivity measurement discussed at the 1975 conference was based on a view of economic growth that evolved largely from research published in the 1950s and early 1960s. The last twenty-five years have seen some basic shifts in the paradigm of growth. One shift emphasizes the endogeneity of macroeconomic productivity change and the importance of market structure. Another emphasizes the investigation of productivity growth at the firm and plant levels of detail, using large-scale microdata sets.

The CRIW met in March 1998 to discuss these developments; the fifteen papers in this volume reflect these deliberations. The first four papers present a summary of the history and the current state of play in the field. The paper by Charles R. Hulten is a biography of the total factor productivity (TFP) residual. It provides an overview of the evolution of nonparametric productivity analysis; discusses the main problems that currently beset the field, such as the difficulty in accounting for quality change; and presents an overall assessment of the strengths and weaknesses of the TFP residual as a tool for understanding the factors underlying long-term trends in economic growth. The paper, which is intended to serve as an introduction to the conference proceedings, provides an illuminating analysis of the survival of the residual as the main workhorse of empirical growth analysis. The paper by Edwin R. Dean and Michael J. Harper provides an overview of the BLS productivity measurement program, the development of which was one of the major milestones in the evolution of the field. This program publishes the official U.S. government productivity statistics. The paper shows that the adoption of theoretical advances by the BLS measurement program often required interesting judgment calls. A paper by W. Erwin Diewert then discusses which ideas are ready to be adopted by government statistical measurement programs. A paper by M. Ishaq Nadiri and Ingmar R. Prucha rounds out the section by reviewing developments in the econometric analysis of production, with a focus on dynamic interrelated factor demand models. The authors critically examine models based on restrictive simplifying assumptions and simple econometric specifications. They also provide a Monte Carlo study showing the magnitude of the errors that may arise from using simpler econometric specifications when the structure of production exhibits great complexity.

In a luncheon address, Robert M. Solow, whose seminal 1957 paper laid the conceptual foundations for TFP measurement, provided remarks assessing both progress in the field and potential future directions. He recommended that more emphasis be placed on his vintage model, an alternative framework for analyzing the role of capital in productivity, which he proposed in 1959.

The next two papers deal with new theoretical developments. The paper by Jeremy Greenwood and Boyan Jovanovic explores alternative models of productivity change. It compares the conventional model of disembodied technical change developed by Solow and by Jorgenson and Griliches with a variety of possibilities organized around the model of embodied technical change, which is extended to include learning and diffusion effects, plant heterogeneity, capital-skill complementarity, R&D, and worker-machine matching. Susanto Basu and John Fernald take up another theoretical issue that has challenged productivity analysis: the problem of short-run procyclical productivity fluctuations. Conventional analysis regards these fluctuations as a nuisance that obscures long-run movements in total factor productivity (also referred to as multifactor productivity.) This paper treats them as potentially interesting macroeconomic variables that need to be understood in their own rights. Several competing explanations are studied, including procyclical technology shocks, the effects of imperfect competition with increasing returns to scale, variable utilization of inputs over the business cycle, and resource reallocations over the cycle.

The next set of papers deals with another major theme in modern productivity analysis: the perception that the answer to productivity puzzles is to be found at the level of firms and plants, rather than at high levels of aggregation. The paper by Lucia Foster, John Haltiwanger, and C. J. Krizan explores this issue in the context of panel data on plant-level production (notably, the U.S. Bureau of the Census's LRD database). Productivity growth at the industry or economy level of aggregation arises from two general sources: productivity improvement at the plant level and the reallocation of resources among plants of different efficiencies. The first effect captures technological and organizational innovations, as well as other factors related to productivity, whereas the reallocation effect captures the interaction of productivity effects with other factors determining market share. Both are important for understanding the sources of productivity change.

The paper by Denny Ellerman, Thomas M. Stoker, and Ernst R. Berndt also emphasizes the importance of disaggregated productivity measures, but the focus here is on a specific industry: coal mining. Official statistics do not present an accurate picture of technical innovation because they abstract from the heterogeneity of the technologies, production scale, and coal quality. The paper illustrates the importance of industry-specific factors in interpreting and measuring productivity trends.

Martin Neil Baily and Eric Zitzewitz take the most disaggregated view of all. They report on the results of projects carried out by McKinsey and Company with data from client firms. Their focus is on one of the chronic problem areas of productivity analysis: the service sector. They present results for five service industries: the banking sector, telecommunications, retail trade, public transportation, and airlines. A key issue in each area is how to define and measure the output of the industry, which is a necessary step in calculating a productivity ratio. The authors argue that another necessary step in correctly measuring output is to understand the industry from the inside out.

The next two papers deal with international issues. A paper by Nazrul Islam examines alternative approaches to international comparisons of productivity. This is an issue that has occupied productivity specialists for years (see, for example, the paper by Laurits Christensen, Diane Cummings, and Dale W. Jorgenson in the Kendrick-Vacarra volume cited in Islam's paper). However, it has received increased attention in recent years in the literatures on the international convergence of growth rates, the debate over the nature of the East Asian Miracle, and the question of whether capital accumulation or assimilation of technology is the principle engine of growth. Then, a paper by Dale W. Jorgenson and Eric Yip uses the TFP framework and international data to challenge the notion that we have entered a new era of more rapid productivity growth. It is generally believed that productivity improvements are a necessary condition for long-run improvements in living standards, and it is also widely believed that productivity improvements support the recent prosperity in financial markets. The future prosperity of the United States will depend, fundamentally, on how fast productivity can grow.

The final two papers deal with environmental issues. Most conventional analyses of productivity growth make no allowance for production-related environmental factors such as pollution and resource depletion. This has clearly been an active policy issue, and it raises interesting conceptual problems for productivity theory—namely, how to treat outputs and inputs whose prices and quantities cannot be measured, and how to deal with multiple outputs, some of which are "bads" rather than "goods." The paper by V. Eldon Ball, Rolf Färe, Shawna Grosskopf, and Richard Nehring takes up this problem using a technique not used in conventional studies: distance functions. This approach gives rises to Malmquist indexes that incorporate environmental "bads." The authors apply this approach to pesticides and fertilizer runoff in the U.S. agricultural sector. Frank M. Gollop and Gregory P. Swinand show how to deal with environmental issues within the conventional TFP model. The central issue is to specify production and utility functions correctly in order to include the full environmental consequences of economic activity. Like the authors of the preceding paper, they apply their framework to the farm sector.

Zvi Griliches opened the conference with some brief remarks. Later, he prepared a written version of these remarks, and these are presented as the final paper in this volume. In this paper, Griliches comments on how well his 1967 paper with Jorgenson has held up over the years, and he provides insight into difficult measurement problems that are presently retarding progress in understanding productivity trends. Sadly, Zvi passed away on 4 November 1999. He was one of the seminal intellectual forces of the productivity research community, and he will be greatly missed. This volume is dedicated to the remembrance of his many contributions both to this research area and to others.

1
Total Factor Productivity
A Short Biography

Charles R. Hulten

1.1 Introduction

Colonial Americans were very poor by today's standard of poverty. On the eve of the American Revolution, GDP per capita in the United States stood at approximately $765 (in 1992 dollars).[1] Incomes rose dramatically over the next two centuries, propelled upward by the Industrial Revolution, and by 1997, GDP per capita had grown to $26,847. This growth was not always smooth (see fig. 1.1 and table 1.1), but it has been persistent at an average annual growth rate of 1.7 percent. Moreover, the transformation wrought by the Industrial Revolution moved Americans off the farm to jobs in the manufacturing and (increasingly) the service sectors of the economy.

Understanding this great transformation is one of the basic goals of economic research. Theorists have responded with a variety of models. Marxian and neoclassical theories of growth assign the greatest weight to productivity improvements driven by advances in the technology and the organization of production. On the other hand, the New Growth Theory and another branch of neoclassical economics—the theory of capital and investment—attach primary significance to the increase in investments in human capital, knowledge, and fixed capital.

The dichotomy between technology and capital formation carries over to empirical growth analysis. Generally speaking, the empirical growth

---

Charles R. Hulten is professor of economics at the University of Maryland, a research associate of the National Bureau of Economic Research, and chairman of the Conference on Research in Income and Wealth.

1. Estimates of real GDP per capita and TFP referred to in this section are pieced together from Gallman (1987), *Historical Statistics of the United States, Colonial Times to 1970,* and the 1998 *Economic Report of the President.*

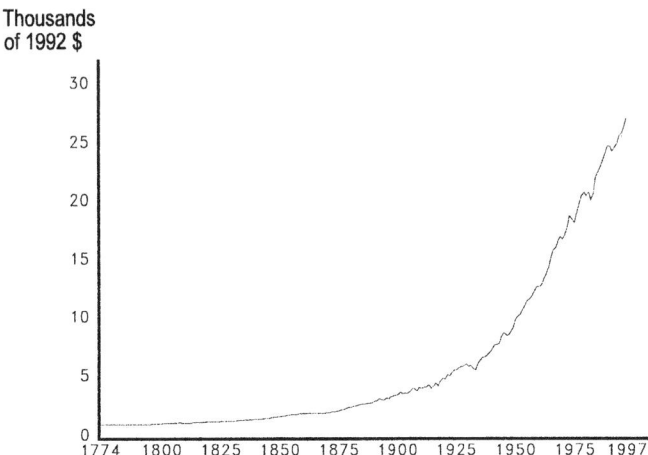

Fig. 1.1 Real GNP/GDP per capita in the United States.

economist has had two main tasks: first, to undertake the enormous job of constructing historical data on inputs and outputs; and second, to measure the degree to which output growth is, in fact, due to technological factors ("productivity") versus capital formation. This last undertaking is sometimes called "sources of growth analysis" and is the intellectual framework of the TFP residual, which is the organizing concept of this survey.

A vast empirical literature has attempted to sort out the capital technology dichotomy, an example of which is shown in table 1.2, but no clear consensus has emerged. Many early studies favored productivity as the main explanation of output growth (see Griliches 1996), and this view continues in the "official" productivity statistics produced by the U.S. Bureau of Labor Statistics (BLS). However, Jorgenson and Griliches (1967) famously disagreed, and their alternative view finds support in subsequent work (e.g., Young 1995) and in the New Growth literature.

In recent years, attention has turned to another issue: the slowdown in productivity that started in the late 1960s or early 1970s. This issue has never been resolved satisfactorily, despite significant research efforts. This, in turn, has been supplanted by yet another mystery: Why has the widely touted information revolution not reversed the productivity slowdown? In a review in the *New York Times* (12 July 1987, p. 36), Robert Solow puts the proposition succinctly: "We can see the computer age everywhere but in the productivity statistics." Recent research seems to have located some of the missing effect (Oliner and Sichel 2000; Jorgenson and Stiroh 2000) as the productivity pickup of the late 1990s has correlated well with the IT revolution. However, Nordhaus (1997) reminds us that the "Solow Par-

Table 1.1 Historical Growth Rates of Output per Person and Total Factor Productivity in the United States (by decade)

	Real GNP/GDP per Capita	TFP	Contribution of TFP (percent)
1779–1789	−0.002	n.a.	
1789–1799	−0.008	n.a.	
1799–1809	0.007	0.006	73.5
1809–1819	−0.009	0.006	64.4
1819–1829	0.008	0.006	69.7
1829–1839	0.012	0.006	44.0
1839–1849	0.018	0.007	38.4
1849–1859	0.016	0.007	45.1
1859–1869	0.004	0.007	161.7
1869–1879	0.023	0.007	30.7
1879–1889	0.017	0.007	42.7
1889–1899	0.023	0.003	12.6
1899–1909	0.018	0.002	13.5
1909–1919	0.019	0.003	16.3
1919–1929	0.024	0.002	7.7
1929–1939	0.016	0.003	16.6
1939–1949	0.026	0.003	9.6
1949–1959	0.034	0.002	6.2
1959–1969	0.027	0.003	12.0
1969–1979	0.023	n.a.	
1979–1989	0.017	n.a.	
1989–1997	0.009	n.a.	
1799–1979	0.018	0.005	26.0
Private Business Economy Only			
1948–1973	0.033	0.021	64
1973–1979	0.013	0.006	46
1979–1990	0.012	0.002	17
1990–1996	0.011	0.003	27
1948–1996	0.023	0.012	52

Sources: Gallman (1987), U.S. Department of Commerce, Bureau of the Census (1975), and the 1998 *Economic Report of the President*. Data for "Private Business Economy Only" are from the Bureau of Labor Statistics, miscellaneous press releases subsequent to Bulletin 2178 (1983).

Note: n.a. = not available.

adox" is not limited to computers. Based on his study of the history of lighting, he argues that official price and output data "miss the most important technological revolutions in economic history" (Nordhaus 1997, 54). Moreover, the Advisory Commission to Study the Consumer Price Index (1996) assigns an upward bias of 0.6 percentage points per year in the Consumer Price Index (CPI) as a result of missed quality improvement, with a corresponding understatement of quantity.

In this New Economy critique of productivity statistics, the growth path

Table 1.2 Sources of Growth in the U.S. Private Business Sector (selected intervals)

	Real Output	Labor Input	Capital Services	TFP
1948–1996	3.4	1.4	3.7	1.2
1948–1973	4.0	1.0	3.8	2.1
1973–1996	2.7	1.9	3.5	0.3
1973–1979	3.1	1.8	4.1	0.6
1979–1990	2.7	2.0	3.8	0.2
1990–1996	2.4	1.9	2.5	0.3

Source: Bureau of Labor Statistics miscellaneous press releases subsequent to Bulletin 2178 (1983).

evident in figure 1.1, impressive as it may seem, seriously understates the true gains in output per person occurring over the last two centuries. However, there is another New Economy paradox that has been largely overlooked: If the missed quality change is of the magnitude suggested by the figure, then the quality of the goods in past centuries—and the implied standard of living—must have been much lower than implied by official (and allegedly quality-biased) statistics (Hulten 1997). Indeed, taken to its logical extreme, the correction of figure 1.1 for quality bias would result in a quality-adjusted average income in 1774 that is dubiously small.[2]

A second line of attack on the New Economy view comes from environmentalists, who argue that GDP growth overstates the true improvement in economic welfare because it fails to measure the depletion of natural resources and the negative spillover externalities associated with rapid GDP growth. This attack has been broadened to include what are asserted to be the unintended consequences of the Industrial Revolution: poverty, urban decay, crime, and loss of core values, among others. This view is represented by a statement that appeared on the cover of *Atlantic Monthly:* "The gross domestic product (GDP) is such a crazy mismeasure of the economy that it portrays disaster as gain" (Cobb, Halstead, and Rowe 1995).

In other words, conventional estimates of productivity growth are either much too large or much too small, depending on one's view of the matter. The truth undoubtedly lies somewhere between the two extremes, but where? This essay attempts to illuminate, if not answer, this question. Its

---

2. If all prices (not just the CPI prices) grew at a rate that was actually 0.6 percent lower than official price statistics, the corresponding quantity statistics would have an offsetting downward bias. If this bias occurred all the way back to 1774, real GDP per capita would have been $202 in that year, not $765.

first objective is to explain the origins of the growth accounting and productivity methods now under attack. This explanation, a biography of an idea, is intended to show which results can be expected from the productivity framework and which cannot. The ultimate objective is to demonstrate the considerable utility of the idea, as a counterweight to the often erroneous and sometimes harsh criticism to which it has been subjected. The first part of the essay is a critical bibliography of the research works that have defined the field. The second part consists of a somewhat personal tour of recent developments in the field and includes tentative answers to some of the unresolved issues.

1.2 The "Residual": A Critical Bibliography to the Mid-1980s

1.2.1 National Accounting Origins

Output per unit input, or TFP, is not a deeply theoretical concept. It is, in fact, an implicit part of the circular income flow model familiar to students of introductory economic theory. In that model, the product market determines the price, p_t, and quantity, Q_t, of goods and services sold to consumers. The total value of these goods is $p_t Q_t$ dollars, which is equally the expenditure of consumers and the revenue of producers. The factor markets determine the volume of the inputs (labor, L_t, and capital, K_t), as well as the corresponding prices, w_t and r_t. The payment to these inputs, $w_t L_t + r_t K_t$, is a cost to the producer and the gross income of consumers. The two markets are connected by the equality of revenue and cost, on the producer side, and gross income and expenditure, on the consumer side, leading to the fundamental GDP accounting identity

$$(1) \qquad p_t Q_t = w_t L_t + r_t K_t .$$

This is, in effect, the budget constraint imposed on an economy with limited resources of capital, labor, and technology.

However, GDP in current prices is clearly an unsatisfactory metric of economic progress. Economic well-being is based on the quantity of goods and services consumed, not on the amount spent on these goods. Because the volume of market activity as measured by equation (1) can change merely because prices have risen or fallen, it can be a misleading indicator of economic progress. What is needed is a parallel accounting identity that records the volume of economic activity that holds the price level constant—that is, a revision of equation (1) using the prices of some baseline year for valuing current output and input.

The construction of a parallel constant-price account is a deceptively simple undertaking. If constant dollar value of output is equal to the constant dollar value of input in any one year, the equality cannot hold in the following year if an improvement in productivity allows more output to be obtained from a given quantity of inputs.[3] To bring the two sides of the constant dollar account into balance, a scaling factor, S_t, is needed. The correct form of the constant-price identity is thus

$$(2) \qquad p_0 Q_t = S_t[w_0 L_t + r_0 K_t].$$

The scaling factor has a value of 1 in the base year 0 but varies over time as the productivity of capital and labor changes. Indeed, if both sides of equation (2) are divided by $w_0 L_t + r_0 K_t$, it is apparent that the scaling factor S_t is the ratio of output to total factor input.

Growth accounting is largely a matter of measuring the variable S_t and using the result to separate the growth of real output into both an input component and a productivity component. Griliches (1996) credits the first mention of the output per unit input index to Copeland (1937), followed by Copeland and Martin (1938). The first empirical implementation of the output per unit input index is attributed to Stigler (1947).

Griliches also observes that Friedman uncovered one of the chronic measurement problems of productivity analysis—the index number problem—in his comment on the research by Copeland and Martin. The problem arises because, with some rearrangement, equation (2) can be shown to be a version of the fixed weight Laspeyres index:

$$(3) \qquad \frac{S_t}{S_0} = \frac{\dfrac{Q_t}{Q_0}}{\dfrac{w_0 L_t + r_0 K_t}{w_0 L_0 + r_0 K_0}}.$$

This is a widely used index formula (e.g., the CPI) and was employed in early productivity literature (e.g., Abramovitz 1956). However, the substitution bias of the Laspeyres index is also well known (and was recently pointed out by the Advisory Commission [1996] in its analysis of the CPI). Substitution bias arises when relative prices change and agents (producers or consumers, depending on the context) substitute the relatively cheaper item for the more expensive. The problem can sometimes be reduced by the use of chained (i.e., frequently reweighted) Laspeyres indexes, and both Kendrick (1961) and Denison (1962) endorse the use of chain-indexing procedures, although they primarily use fixed weight procedures.

---

3. The basic problem is illustrated by the following situation. Suppose that output doubles from one year to the next while labor and capital remain unchanged. If the accounting is done in the constant prices of the first year, the left-hand side of the constant price identity doubles while the right-hand side remains unchanged, violating the adding-up condition.

A more subtle problem arises in the interpretation of the ratio S_t. The basic accounting identities shown in equations (1) and (2) can be read from the standpoint of either the consumer or the producer. Virtually all productivity studies have, however, opted for the producer-side interpretation, as witnessed by terms like "output per unit input" and "total factor productivity." Moreover, discussions about the meaning of S_t have typically invoked the rationale of the production function (see, e.g., the long discussion in Kendrick 1961). However, the consumer-welfare side has lurked in the background. The early literature tended to regard S_t as an indicator of the welfare benefits of innovation, with the consequence that "real" national income, or real net national product, was preferred to output measured gross of real depreciation when calculating the numerator of the TFP ratio.[4] This preference was based on the argument that an increase in gross output might be achieved by accelerating the utilization (and thus deterioration and retirement) of capital, thereby increasing TFP without conveying a long-run benefit to society. This argument had the effect of commingling consumer welfare considerations with supply-side productivity considerations. This introduced a fundamental ambiguity about the nature of the TFP index that has persisted to this very day in a variety of transmuted forms.

1.2.2 The Production Function Approach and the Solow Solution

Solow (1957) was not the first to tie the aggregate production function to productivity. This link goes back at least as far as Tinbergen (1942). However, Solow's seminal contribution lay in the simple, yet elegant, theoretical link that he developed between the production function and the index number approach. Where earlier index number studies had interpreted their results *in light* of a production function, Solow *started* with the production function and deduced the consequences for (and restrictions on) the productivity index. Specifically, he began with an aggregate production function with a Hicksian neutral shift parameter and constant returns to scale:

$$(4) \qquad Q_t = A_t F(K_t, L_t).$$

---

4. The concept of depreciation has been a source of confusion in the productivity and national income accounting literatures, and elsewhere (Hulten 1990; Triplett 1996). Depreciation is a price concept that refers to the loss of capital *value* because of wear, tear, obsolescence, and approaching retirement. The loss of productive capacity as a piece of capital ages is not, strictly speaking, depreciation. The capital stock loses capacity through in-place deterioration and retirement.

The following terminology will be adopted in this paper: The net value of output is the difference between the gross value and depreciation; real net output is the difference between constant-price (real) gross output and a constant-price measure of depreciation; net capital stock is the difference between the gross stock and deterioration.

In this formulation, the Hicksian A_t measures the shift in the production function at given levels of labor and capital. It is almost always identified with "technical change," although this generally is not an appropriate interpretation.[5]

Once the production function is written this way, it is clear that the Hicksian A_t and the ratio of output per unit input S_t of the preceding section are related. The terms of the production function can be rearranged to express relative Hicksian efficiency, A_t/A_0, as a ratio with Q_t/Q_0 in the numerator and with the factor accumulation portion of the production function, $F(K_t, L_t)/F(K_0, L_0)$, in the denominator. The indexes A_t and S_t are identical in special cases, but A_t is the more general indicator of output per unit input (TFP). In the vocabulary of index number theory, the Laspeyres S_t is generally subject to substitution bias.

Solow then addressed the key question of measuring A_t using a nonparametric index number approach (i.e., an approach that does not impose a specific form on the production function). The solution was based on the total (logarithmic) differential of the production function:

$$(5) \qquad \frac{\dot{Q}_t}{Q_t} = \frac{\partial Q}{\partial K} \frac{K_t}{Q_t} \frac{\dot{K}_t}{K_t} + \frac{\partial Q}{\partial L} \frac{L_t}{Q_t} \frac{\dot{L}_t}{L_t} + \frac{\dot{A}_t}{A_t}.$$

This expression indicates that the growth of real output on the left-hand side can be factored into the growth rates of capital and labor, both weighted by their output elasticities, and the growth rate of the Hicksian efficiency index. The former growth rates represent movements along the production function, whereas the latter growth rate is the shift in the function.

The output elasticities in equation (5) are not directly observable; but if each input is paid the value of its marginal product, that is, if

$$(6) \qquad \frac{\partial Q}{\partial K} = \frac{r_t}{p_t} \text{ and } \frac{\partial Q}{\partial L} = \frac{w_t}{p_t},$$

then relative prices can be substituted for the corresponding marginal products. This, in turn, converts the unobserved output elasticities into observable income shares, s^K and s^L. The total differential in equation (5) then becomes

---

5. The difference between the Hicksian shift parameter, A_t, and the rate of technical change arises for many reasons. The most important is that the shift parameter captures only costless improvements in the way an economy's resources of labor and capital are transformed into real GDP (the proverbial manna from heaven). Technical change that results from R&D spending will not be captured by A_t unless R&D is excluded from L_t and K_t (which it generally is not). A second general reason is that changes in the institutional organization of production will also shift the function, as will systematic changes in worker effort. I will emphasize these and other factors at various points throughout this paper.

(7) $$\Re_t = \frac{\dot{Q}_t}{Q_t} - s_t^K \frac{\dot{K}_t}{K_t} - s_t^L \frac{\dot{L}_t}{L_t} = \frac{\dot{A}_t}{A_t}.$$

$\Re_t$ is the Solow residual—the residual growth rate of output not explained by the growth in inputs. It is a true index number in the sense that it can be computed directly from prices and quantities. The key result of Solow's analysis is that $\Re_t$ is, in theory, equal to the growth rate of the Hicksian efficiency parameter.

This is the theory. In practice, $\Re_t$ is a "measure of our ignorance," as Abramovitz (1956) put it, precisely because $\Re_t$ is a residual. This ignorance covers many components, some wanted (such as the effects of technical and organizational innovation), others unwanted (such as measurement error, omitted variables, aggregation bias, and model misspecification).

1.2.3 A Brief Digression on Sources of Bias

The unwanted parts of the residual might cancel if they were randomly distributed errors, leaving the systematic part of the residual unbiased. However, New Economy and environmentalist complaints arise precisely because the errors are thought to be systematic; these issues are addressed in the second half of this paper. Three other general criticisms will, however, be addressed here, in part because they involve challenges to the basic assumptions of the Solow model, and in part because they inform the evolution of the residual described in the next few sections.

First, there is the view that the Solow model is inextricably linked to the assumption of constant returns to scale. This view presumably originated from the close link between the GDP accounting identity shown in equation (1) and the production function. If the production function happens to exhibit constant returns to scale *and* if the inputs are paid the value of their marginal products as in equation (6), then the value of output equals the sum of the input values. This "product exhaustion" follows from Euler's Theorem and implies that the value shares, s^K and s^L, sum to 1. However, there is nothing in the sequence of steps in equations (4) to (7), leading from the production function to the residual, that requires constant returns (see Hulten 1973). Constant returns are actually needed for another purpose: to estimate the return to capital as a residual, as per Jorgenson and Griliches (1967). If an independent measure of the return to capital is used in constructing the share weights, the residual can be derived without the assumption of constant returns.

A second general complaint against the residual is that it is married to the assumption of marginal cost pricing (i.e., to the marginal productivity conditions shown in equation [6]). When imperfect competition leads to a price greater than marginal cost, Hall (1988) shows that the residual yields a biased estimate of the Hicksian shift parameter, A_t. There is, unfortunately, no way around this problem within the index number approach proposed by Solow, which is by nature nonparametric, meaning that it produces estimates of A_t directly from prices and quantities. The essence of the Solow method is to use prices to estimate the slopes of the production function at the observed input-output configurations, without having to estimate the shape of the function at all other points (i.e., without the need to estimate all the parameters of the technology). The residual is thus a parsimonious method for getting at the shift in the production function, but the price of parsimony is the need to use prices as surrogates for marginal products.

A third issue concerns the implied nature of technical change. In general, the Hicksian formulation of the production function shown in equation (7) is valid if innovation improves the marginal productivity of all inputs equally. In this case, the production function shifts by the same proportion at all combinations of labor and capital. This is clearly a strong assumption that may well lead to biases if violated. A more general formulation allows (costless) improvements in technology to augment the marginal productivity of each input separately:

$$(4') \qquad Q_t = F(a_t K_t, b_t L_t).$$

This is the "factor augmentation" formulation of technology. It replaces the Hicksian A_t with two augmentation parameters, a_t and b_t. If all the other assumptions of the Solow derivation are retained, a little algebra shows that the residual can be expressed as

$$(7') \qquad \Re_t = s_t^K \frac{\dot{a}_t}{a_t} + s_t^L \frac{\dot{b}_t}{b_t}.$$

The residual is now the share weighted average of the rates of factor augmentation, but it still measures changes in TFP. Indeed, when the rates of factor augmentation are equal, and the sum of the shares is constant, we effectively return to the previous Hicksian case.

Problems may arise if the rates of factor augmentation are not equal. In this situation, termed "Hicks-biased technical change," it is evident that productivity growth depends on the input shares as well as on the parameters of innovation. A change in the income shares can cause output per unit input (TFP) to increase, even if the underlying rate of technical change remains unchanged. This reinforces the basic point that productivity growth is not the same thing as technical change.

Some observers have concluded that the bias in technical change translates into a measurement bias in the residual. This is true only if one insists on identifying TFP with technical change. However, the productivity residual does not get off free and clear: Factor-biased technical change may not lead to measurement, but it does generally lead to the problem of path dependence, discussed in the following section.

1.2.4 The Potential Function Theorem

Solow's derivation of the residual deduces the appropriate index number formulation from the production function and, as a by-product, shows that it is not the Laspeyres form. But what type of index number is it? It was soon noted that equation (7) is the growth rate of a Divisia index (e.g., Richter 1966), a continuous-time index related to the discrete-time chain index mentioned above. This linkage is important because it allows Solow's continuous formulation to be implemented using discrete-time data, while preserving the theoretical interpretation of the residual as the continuous shift in an aggregate production function.

However, this practical linkage has one potential flaw. Solow showed that the production function shown in equation (4) and the marginal productivity conditions shown in equation (6) lead to the growth rate form in equation (7). He did *not* show that a researcher who starts with equation (7) will necessarily get back to the shift term A_t in the production function. Without such a proof, it is possible that the calculation in equation (7) could lead somewhere besides A_t, thus robbing the index of its conventional interpretation.

This issue was addressed in my 1973 paper, which shows that the Solow conditions are both necessary and sufficient. The expression in equation (7) yields a unique index only if there is a production function (more generally, a potential function) whose partial derivatives are equal to the prices used to compute the index. The production function (cum potential function) is the integrating factor needed to guarantee a solution to equation (7), which is in fact a differential equation. If there is no production function, or if it is nonhomothetic, the differential equation (7) cannot be (line) integrated to a unique solution. This problem is called "path dependence."[6]

The Potential Function Theorem imposes a good deal of economic structure on the problem in order to avoid path dependence. Unfortunately, these conditions are easily met. First, aggregation theory demonstrates that the necessary production function exists only under very restrictive assumptions (Fisher 1965), essentially requiring all the micro-production units in the economy (plants, firms, industries) to have production functions that are identical up to some constant multiplier (see also Diewert 1980). If the aggregation conditions fail, a discrete-time ver-

---

6. The problem of path dependence is illustrated by the following example. Suppose that there is a solution to the Divisia line integral, but only for a particular path of output and input Γ_1 between points A and B. If a different path between these two points, Γ_2, gives a different value, then path dependence arises. If the Divisia index starts with a value of 100 at point A and the economy subsequently moves from A to B along Γ_1, and then back to A along Γ_1, the Divisia index will not return to 100 at A. Because the path can cycle between A and B along these paths, the index can, in principle, have a purely arbitrary value.

sion of the Divisia index might still be cobbled together, but the resulting numbers would have no unique link to the efficiency index A_t. Indeed, the theoretical meaning of A_t itself is ambiguous if the aggregation conditions fail.[7]

When the Divisia index is path independent, Solow's procedures yield an estimate of the productivity residual that is uniquely associated with the shift in the production function. This result carries the important implication that the residual must be given a capacity interpretation, in this case, rather than a welfare interpretation. Or, more accurately, any welfare interpretation must be consistent with this main interpretation.

The Potential Function Theorem also sheds light on the debate over net versus gross measures of output and capital. The theorem requires the units of output or input selected for use in equation (7) to be consistent with the form of the production function used as the integrating factor. To choose net output for computing the Solow residual, for example, is to assert that the production process generates net output from capital and labor, and that factor prices are equal to the *net* value of marginal product rather than to the gross value of standard theory. This is an unusual view of real-world production processes, because workers and machines actually make gross units of output and the units of output emerging from the factory door are not adjusted for depreciation. Nor do we observe a price quoted for net output. Similar reasoning leads to the use of a net-of-deterioration concept of capital.

1.2.5 Jorgenson and Griliches versus Denison

The 1967 paper by Jorgenson and Griliches is a major milestone in the evolution of productivity theory. It advanced the hypothesis that careful measurement of the relevant variables should cause the Solow measure of total factor productivity to disappear. This is an intellectually appealing idea, given that the TFP index is a residual "measure of our ignorance." Careful measurement and correct model specification should rid the residual of unwanted components and explain the wanted ones.

Jorgenson and Griliches then proceeded to introduce a number of measurement innovations into the Solow framework, based on a strict application of the neoclassical theory of production. When the renovations were

---

7. Path dependence also rises if the aggregate production function exists but fails to satisfy any of the basic assumptions: namely, marginal productivity pricing, constant returns to scale, and Hicksian technical change. This statement must, however, be qualified by the remarks of the preceding section. If an independent estimate of the return of capital is used when constructing the share weight of capital, s^K, then the Divisia productivity index is path independent even under nonconstant returns to scale (Hulten 1973). Moreover, if costless technical change is Harrod neutral, line integration of the residual $\Re$ is subject to path dependence, but integration of the ratio $\Re/s^L$ is not, and leads to a path-*in*dependent index of the labor augmentation parameter, b_t, shown in equation (7'). The Divisia residual is more versatile than is commonly believed.

complete, they found that the residual had all but disappeared. This result stood in stark contrast to contemporary results, which found that the residual did make a sizeable contribution to economic growth. However, this attack on (and, indeed, inversion of) the conventional wisdom was answered by Denison, whose own results were consistent with the prevailing wisdom.

Denison (1972) compared his procedures with those of Jorgenson and Griliches and found that part of the divergence was caused by a difference in the time periods covered by the two studies and that another part was due to a capacity-utilization adjustment based on electricity use. The latter indicated a secular increase between equivalent years in the business cycle; and when this was removed, and the two studies put in the same time frame, Denison found that the Jorgenson-Griliches residual was far from zero.

The debate between Denison (1972) and Jorgenson and Griliches (1967, 1972) focused attention on the bottom line of empirical growth analysis: how much output growth can be explained by total factor productivity (manna from heaven), and how much had to be paid for capital formation. However, the debate obscured the true contribution of the Jorgenson-Griliches study, which was to cement the one-to-one link between production theory and growth accounting. For Solow, the aggregate production function was a parable for the measurement of TFP; for Jorgenson and Griliches it was the blueprint. Implementing this blueprint led to a number of important innovations in the Solow residual—a sort of productivity improvement in the TFP model itself.

One of the principal innovations was to incorporate the neoclassical investment theory developed in Jorgenson (1963) into productivity analysis. The first step was to recognize that the value of output in the accounting identity in equation (1) is the sum of two components: the value of consumption goods produced, $p^C C$, and the value of investment goods produced, $p^I I$ (hence, $pQ = p^C C + p^I I = wL + rK$). The price of the investment good was then assumed to be equal to the present value of the rents generated by the investment (with an adjustment for the depreciation of capital). This present value is then solved to yield an expression for the user cost of capital, $r = (i + \delta)P^I - \Delta P^I$. The problem, then, is to find a way of measuring r or its components. Direct estimates of the user cost are available for only a small fraction of the universe of capital goods (those that are rented). The alternative is to estimate the components of r. The investment good price, P^I, can be obtained from national accounts data, and the depreciation rate, δ, can be based on the Hulten-Wykoff (1981) depreciation study. The rate of return, i, can be estimated in two ways. First, it can be estimated independently from interest rate or equity return data. This is somewhat problematic because of the multiplicity of candidates and the need to pick a rate that reflects the risk and opportunity cost of the capital good. Jorgenson and Griliches suggest a second way: Impose constant returns to scale and find the implied i that causes the accounting equation $pQ = wL + rK$ to hold.[8] It is only at this point that constant returns are required for the measurement of TFP.

The quantity of capital, K_t, and the quantity of new investment, I_t, are connected (in this framework) by the perpetual inventory method, in which the stock is the sum of past investments adjusted for deterioration and retirement. The resulting concept of capital is thus defined net of deterioration, in contrast with the concept of undeteriorated "gross" stock used in some studies.

On the other hand, Jorgenson and Griliches recognized that output must be measured gross of depreciation if it is to conform to the accounting system implied by the strict logic of production theory. This put them in conflict with Denison, who advocated a concept of output net of depreciation, and Solow, who used gross output in his empirical work but preferred net output on the theoretical grounds that it is a better measure of welfare improvement arising from technical progress. The debate over this point with Denison thus seemed to pivot on the research objective of the study, not on technical grounds. However, as we have seen, the Potential Function Theorem, published after the 1967 Jorgenson and Griliches study, links their gross output approach to the A_t of conventional production theory, implying that the competing views of output cannot be simultaneously true (except in very special cases).

Another major contribution of the Jorgenson-Griliches study was to disaggregate capital and labor into their component parts, thereby avoiding the aggregation bias associated with internal shifts in the composition of the inputs (e.g., the compositional bias due to a shift from long-lived structures to shorter-lived equipment in the capital stock, or the bias due to the shift toward a more educated work force). The Divisia index framework was applied consistently to the aggregation of the individual types of capital and labor into the corresponding subaggregate, and applied again to arrive at the formulation in equation (7). However, because data are not continuous over time but come in discrete-time units, Jorgenson and Griliches introduced a discrete-time approximation to the Divisia derived from the Törnqvist index.[9]

In sum, Jorgenson and Griliches tied data development, growth ac-

---

8. The implied value of i is then $[P^C C + P^I I - \delta P^I K - \Delta P^I K]/P^I K$. When there are several types of capital goods, a different δ and P^I is estimated for each type, but arbitrage is assumed to lead to a common i for all assets. Hall and Jorgenson (1967) extended the user cost model to include parameters of the income tax system.

9. In the Tornqvist approximation, the continuous-time income shares s_t^K and s_t^L in equation (7) are replaced by the average between-period shares. Capital's discrete-time income share is $(s_t^K + s_{t-1}^K)/2$. Continuous-time growth rates are also replaced with differences in the natural logarithm of the variable. The growth rate of capital, for example, is $\ln(K_t) - \ln(K_{t-1})$.

counting, and production theory firmly together. The three are mutually dependent, not an ascending hierarchy as is commonly supposed. These linkages were developed further by Christensen and Jorgenson (1969, 1970), who developed an entire income, product, and wealth accounting system based on the mutuality principle.

1.2.6 Diewert's Exact and Superlative Index Numbers

The continuous-time theory of the residual developed by Solow provides a simple yet elegant framework for productivity measurement. Unfortunately, data do not come in continuous-time form. One solution, noted earlier, is to find reasonable discrete-time approximations to the continuous-time model. In this approach, the choice among competing approximation methods is based largely on computational expediency, with the implication that the discrete-time approximation is not derived as an organic part of the theory, thereby weakening the link between theory and measurement.

Herein lies the contribution of Diewert (1976). He showed that the Tornqvist approximation to the Divisia index used by Jorgenson and Griliches was an exact index number if the production function shown in equation (4) had the translog form developed by Christensen, Jorgenson, and Lau (1973). In other words, the Tornqvist index was not an approximation at all, but was actually exact under the right conditions. Moreover, because the translog production function could also be regarded as a good second-order approximation to other production functions, the discrete-time Tornqvist index was a sensible choice even if the "world" was not translog. In this event, the degree of exactness in the index number depends on the closeness of the translog function to the true production function. Diewert used the term "superlative" to characterize this aspect of the index.

What Diewert showed, in effect, was that the translog specification of the production function served as a potential function for the discrete Tornqvist index in the same way that the continuous production function served as a potential function for the continuous Divisia index. One important consequence of this result is that the index number approach of the Solow residual is not entirely nonparametric. There is a parametric production function underlying the method of approximation if the discrete-time index is to be an exact measure of Hicksian efficiency. However, the values of the "inessential" parameters of the translog—that is, those other than the Hicksian efficiency parameter—need not be estimated if the Solow residual is used.

1.2.7 Dispelling the "Measure of Our Ignorance" with Econometrics

If a specific functional form of the technology must be assumed in order to obtain an exact estimate of the efficiency parameter, why not go ahead and estimate all the parameters of that function using econometric techniques? That is, why not estimate the translog relation between Q_t, K_t, L_t, and A_t directly? For one thing, this avoids the need to impose the marginal productivity conditions of the index number approach.[10] Moreover, it gives a full representation of the technology: all the parameters (not just the efficiency term), and every possible path (not just the path actually followed). Moreover, noncompetitive pricing behavior, nonconstant returns, and factor-augmenting technical change can be accommodated, and embellishments like cost-of-adjustment parameters can be incorporated into the analysis to help "explain" the residual. Why settle for less when so much more can be obtained under assumptions that must be made anyway—for example, that the production function has a particular functional form like the translog?

The answers to these questions are familiar to practitioners of the productivity art. There are pitfalls in the econometric approach, just as there are with nonparametric procedures. For example, estimation of the translog (or another flexible) function can lead to parameter estimates that imply oddly shaped isoquants, causing practitioners to place a priori restrictions on the values of these parameters. There is often a question about the robustness of the resulting parameter estimates to alternative ways of imposing restrictions. Even with these restrictions, the abundance of parameters can press on the number of data observations, requiring further restrictions. Additionally, there is the question of the econometric procedures used to obtain the estimates. The highly complicated structure of flexible models usually requires nonlinear estimation techniques, which are valid only under special assumptions, and there are questions about the statistical properties of the resulting estimates. Finally, because the capital and labor variables on the right-hand side of the regression depend in part on the output variable on the left-hand side, there is the danger of simultaneous equations bias.

In other words, the benefits of the parametric approach are purchased at a cost. It is pointless to debate whether benefits outweigh those costs, simply because there is no reason that the two approaches should be viewed as competitors. In the first place, the output and input data used in the econometric approach are almost always index numbers themselves (there are simply too many types of output and input to estimate separately). Thus, the question of whether or when to use econometrics to measure productivity change is really a question of the stage of the analysis at which index number procedures should be abandoned. Secondly, there is no reason for there to be an either-or choice. Both approaches can be

---

10. The marginal productivity conditions can be avoided in the direct estimation of the production function. However, the marginal productivity conditions are used in the estimation of the "dual" cost and profit functions that form an essential part of the productivity econometrician's tool kit.

implemented simultaneously, thereby exploiting the relative simplicity and transparency of the nonparametric estimates to serve as a benchmark for interpreting the more complicated results of the parametric approach. The joint approach has an added advantage of forcing the analyst to summarize the parameters of the translog (or other) function in a way that illuminates their significance for TFP growth (i.e., for the dichotomy between the shift in the production function and factor-driven movements along the function).

Moreover, by merging the two approaches, econometrics can be used to disaggregate the TFP residual into terms corresponding to increasing returns to scale, the cost of adjusting the factor inputs, technical innovation, an unclassified trend productivity, and measurement error. Denny, Fuss, and Waverman (1981) were the first to start down this path, and it has grown in importance in recent years. The power of this approach is illustrated by the 1981 paper of Prucha and Nadiri on the U.S. electrical machinery industry. Their version of the TFP residual grew at an average annual rate of 1.99 percent in this industry from 1960 to 1980. Of this amount, 35 percent was attributed to technical innovations, 42 percent to scale economies, and 21 percent to adjustment cost factors, with only 2 percent left unexplained.

This development addresses the measure-of-our-ignorance problem posed by Abramovitz. It also provides a theoretically rigorous alternative to Denison, who attempted to explain the residual with informed guesses and assumptions that were above and beyond the procedures used to construct his estimates of the residual. It also speaks to the Jorgenson-Griliches hypothesis that the residual ought to vanish if all explanatory factors can be measured.

1.2.8 Digression on Research and Development Expenditures

Another contribution made by Jorgenson and Griliches (1967) was their recognition that aggregate measures of capital and labor included the inputs used in research and development programs to generate technical innovations. Thus, some part of the rate of innovation that drove the TFP residual was already accounted for in the data. As a result, if the social rate of return to the R&D expenditures buried in the input data is equal to the private return, the effect of R&D would be fully accounted for, and the innovation component of the residual should disappear. On the other hand, if there is a wedge between the social and private rates of return, then the innovation component of the residual should reflect the externality. This is a harbinger of the New Growth Theory view of endogenous technical innovation.

The important task of incorporating R&D expenditures explicitly into the growth accounting framework has, unfortunately, met with limited success. Griliches (1988) pointed out a key problem: Direct R&D spending is essentially an internal investment to the firm, with no observable "asset" price associated with the investment "good" and no observable income stream associated with the stock of R&D capital. As a result, there is no ready estimate of the quantity of knowledge capital or its growth rate, nor of the corresponding share weight, which are needed to construct a Divisia index. Moreover, much of the R&D effort of any private firm goes toward improving the quality of the firm's products, not the productivity of its production process (more on this later).

There is, of course, a huge literature on R&D and the structure of production, but it is almost entirely an econometric literature (see Nadiri 1993 and Griliches 1994 for reviews). A satisfactory account of this literature is well beyond the scope of a biography of the nonparametric residual.

1.2.9 The Comparison of Productivity Levels

The TFP residual defined earlier is expressed as a rate of growth. The TFP growth rate is of interest for intertemporal comparisons of productivity for a given country or region at different points in time, but it is far less useful for comparing the relative productivity of different countries or regions. A developing country may, for example, have a much more rapid growth in TFP than a developed country, but start from a much lower level. Indeed, a developing country may have a more rapid growth in TFP than a developed country *because* it starts from a lower level and is able to import technology. This possibility is discussed in the huge literature on convergence theory.

The first translog nonparametric estimates of TFP levels were developed by Jorgenson and Nishimizu (1978) for the comparison of two countries. This innovation was followed by an extension of the framework to include the comparison of several countries simultaneously by Christensen, Cummings, and Jorgenson (1981) and Caves, Christensen, and Diewert (1982a). Moreover, in a contemporaneous paper, Caves, Christensen, and Diewert (1982b) apply a different approach—the Malmquist index—to the comparison of relative productivity levels.

The Malmquist index asks simple questions: How much output could country A produce if it used country B's technology with its own inputs? How much output could country B produce if it used country A's technology with its inputs? The Malmquist productivity index is the geometric means of the answers to these two questions. If, for example, the output of country A would be cut in half if it were forced to use the other country's technology, while output in country B would double, the Malmquist index would show that A's technology is twice as productive.[11] When the produc-

---

11. Formally, let $Q_A = F(X_A)$ be the production function in country A and $Q_B = G(X_B)$ in country B. The Malmquist approach estimates how much output Q_A^* would have been produced in A if the technology of B had been applied to A's inputs; that is, $Q_A^* = G(X_A)$. The ratio Q_A/Q_A^* is then a measure of how much more (or less) productive is technology A com-

tion functions differ only by the Hicks-neutral efficiency index, A_A and A_B, respectively, the Malmquist index gives the ratio A_A/A_B. This is essentially the Solow result in a different guise. Moreover, when the technology has the translog form, Caves, Christensen, and Diewert (1982b) show that the Tornqvist and Malmquist approaches yield the same result.

However, the two approaches may differ if efficiency differences are not Hicks neutral or if there are increasing returns to scale. In these situations, the relative level of technical efficiency will depend on the input levels at which the comparison is made. If, by some chance, other input levels had occurred, the Malmquist index would have registered a different value, even though the production functions in countries A and B were unchanged. This is the essence of the path dependence problem in index number theory.

Malmquist indexes have been used in productivity measurement mainly in the context of nonparametric frontier analysis (e.g., Färe et al. 1994). Frontier analysis is based on the notion of a best-practice level of technical efficiency that cannot be exceeded, and which might not be attained. An economy (or industry or firm) may be below its best-practice level for a variety of reasons: obsolete technology, poor management, constraints on the use of resources, and so on. A measured change in the level of efficiency may therefore reflect an improvement in the best-practice technology or in the management of the prevailing technology. Sorting out which is which is an important problem in productivity analysis.

Frontier analysis tackles this problem by using linear programming techniques to "envelope" the data and thereby locate the best-practice frontier. The main advantages of frontier analysis are worth emphasizing. First, frontier techniques allow the observed change in TFP to be resolved into changes in the best-practice frontier and in the degree of inefficiency. Second, the technique is particularly useful when there are multiple outputs, some of whose prices cannot be observed (as when, for example, negative externalities such as pollution are produced jointly with output). The principal drawback arises from the possibility that measurement errors may lead to data that are located beyond the true best-practice frontier. There is a danger that the outliers will be mistakenly enveloped by frontier techniques (though stochastic procedures may help here), resulting in an erroneous best-practice frontier.

1.2.10 Capital Stocks and Capacity Utilization

Production functions are normally defined as a relation between the flow of output on the one hand, and the flows of capital and labor services on

---

pared to technology B at A's input level. A similar calculation establishes the ratio Q_B^*/Q_B, which measures how much more productive technology B is when compared to that of A at the input level prevailing in country B. The Malmquist index is the geometric mean of the two ratios.

the other. If the residual is to be interpreted as the shift in an aggregate production function, the associated variables must be measured as flows. This is not a problem for output and labor because annual price and quantity data are available. Nor would it be a problem for capital goods if they were rented on an annual basis, in which case there would be little reason to distinguish them from labor input. Capital goods are, however, most often used by their owners. Thus, we typically observe additions to the stock of goods, but not to the stock itself or to the services flowing from the stock. Stocks can be imputed using the perpetual inventory method (the sum of net additions to the stock), but there is no obvious way of getting at the corresponding flow of services.

This would not be a problem if service flows were always proportional to the stock, but proportionality is not a realistic assumption. As economic activity fluctuates over the business cycle, periods of high demand alternate with downturns in demand. Capital stocks are hard to adjust rapidly, so periods of low demand are typically periods of low capital utilization. A residual calculated using capital stock data thus fluctuates procyclically along with the rate of utilization. These fluctuations tend to obscure the movements in the longer-run components of the residual and make it hard to distinguish significant breaks in trend. The dating and analysis of the productivity slowdown of the 1970s form an important case in point.

Jorgenson and Griliches address this problem by adjusting capital stock for a measure of utilization based on fluctuations in electricity use. The form of this adjustment became part of the controversy with Denison, but the real problem lay with the use of any externally imposed measure of capital utilization. Any such measure leads to a theoretical problem: How does a direct measure of capital utilization enter the imputed user cost? Indeed, shouldn't the opportunity cost of unutilized capital be zero?

Berndt and Fuss (1986) provide an answer to these questions. They adopt the Marshallian view that capital stock is a quasi-fixed input in the short run, the income of which is the residual after the current account inputs are paid off. In terms of the fundamental accounting identity, the residual return to capital is $rK = pQ - wL$, where K is the stock of capital (not the flow) and r is the ex post cost of using the stock for one period. Fluctuations in demand over the business cycle cause ex post returns to rise or fall relative to the ex ante user cost on which the original investment was based. The key result of Berndt and Fuss is that the ex post user cost equals the actual (short-run) marginal product of capital, and is thus appropriate for use in computing the TFP residual. Moreover, since the ex post user cost already takes into account fluctuations in demand, no separate adjustment is, in principle, necessary.

On the negative side, it must be recognized that the Berndt-Fuss revisions to the original Solow residual model fail, in practice, to remove the procyclical component of the residual. This failure may arise because the amended framework does not allow for the entry and exit of firms over the business cycle (and, indeed, is only a partial theory of capital adjustment). Indeed, fluctuations in capital utilization are not just a nuisance factor in productivity measurement, but have an interesting economic life of their own (see Basu and Fernald, chapter 7 in this volume). Additionally, this approach to utilization does not generalize to multiple capital goods. However, the Berndt-Fuss insight into the nature of capital utilization, and its relation to the marginal product of capital, is a major contribution to productivity theory: It clarifies the nature of capital input and illustrates the ad hoc and potentially inconsistent nature of externally imposed utilization adjustments.[12]

1.3 Recent Developments and the Paths Not Taken

The 1980s were a high-water mark for the prestige of the residual, and a watershed for nonparametric productivity analysis as a whole. The Bureau of Labor Statistics (BLS) began publishing multifactor productivity (their name for TFP) estimates in 1983; major contributions also continued outside the government, with the articles already noted and with books by Jorgenson, Gollop, and Fraumeni (1987) and Baumol, Blackman, and Wolff (1989). There has also been an interest in applying growth accounting to explain international differences in growth (e.g., Dowrick and Nguyen 1989); the controversy triggered by Young (1992, 1995); and literature on infrastructure investment inspired by Aschauer (1989). However, the tide had begun to turn against the aggregative nonparametric approach pioneered by Solow, Kendrick, Jorgenson-Griliches, and Denison. Several general trends are discernible:

1. the growing preference for econometric modeling of the factors causing productivity change;
2. the shift in attention from the study of productivity at the aggregate and industry levels of detail to study at the firm and plant levels;
3. a shift in emphasis from the competitive model of industrial organization to noncompetitive models;
4. the effort to endogenize R&D and patenting into the explanation of productivity change; and
5. a growing awareness that improvements in product quality are potentially as important as process-oriented innovation that improve the productivity of capital and labor.

There were several reasons for this shift in focus. The explosion in computing power enabled researchers to assemble and analyze larger sets of

---

12. The dual approach to the Berndt-Fuss utilization model is explored in Hulten (1986). This papers clarifies the links between average cost, TFP, and the degree of utilization.

data. High-powered computers are so much a part of the current environment that it is hard to remember that much of the seminal empirical work done in the 1950s and early 1960s was done by hand or on mechanical calculating machines (or, later on, by early mainframe computers that were primitive by today's standards). Anyone who has inverted a five-by-five matrix by hand will know why multivariate regressions were not often undertaken. The growth of computing power permitted the estimation of more sophisticated, multiparametered production and cost functions (like the translog) and created a derived demand for large data sets like the U.S. Bureau of Census's Longitudinal Research Database (LRD), which came into play in 1982.

The arrival of the New Growth Theory was a more evident factor behind the shift in the research agenda of productivity analysis. New Growth Theory challenged the constant-returns and perfect-competition assumptions of the TFP residual by offering a view of the world in which (a) markets were noncompetitive; (b) the production function exhibited increasing returns to scale; (c) externalities among microunits were important; and (d) innovation was an endogenous part of the economic system. This shift in perspective gave an added push to the investigation of microdata sets and to the interest in R&D as an endogenous explanation of output growth.

These factors would have sufficed to redirect the research agenda of productivity analysis. However, it was the slowdown in productivity growth, which started sometime between the late 1960s and the 1973 OPEC oil crisis, that settled the matter. Or, more accurately, conventional productivity methods failed to provide a generally accepted explanation for the slowdown, which virtually guaranteed that the assumptions of the conventional analysis would be changed and that explanations would have to be sought elsewhere.[13] The residual was, after all, still the "measure of our ignorance," and the New Growth paradigm and the large-scale microproductivity data sets arrived just in time to fill the demand for their existence.

The directions taken by productivity analysis in recent years are not easy to summarize in a unified way. I will, however, offer some comments on recent developments in the field in the remaining sections. They reflect, to some extent, my own research interests and knowledge, and make no pretense of being an exhaustive survey.

---

13. The literature on the productivity slowdown is voluminous, and still growing (see, e.g., Denison 1979; Berndt 1980; Griliches 1980; Maddison 1987; Baily and Gordon 1988; Diewert and Fox 1999; and Greenwood and Jovanovic in chap. 6, this vol.). Many different explanations have been offered, from the failure to measure output correctly (particularly in the service sector) to the lag in absorbing and diffusing the IT revolution. No single explanation has decisively vanquished the others; nor has a consensus emerged about the relative importance of the various competing alternatives.

1.4 Productivity in the Context of Macrogrowth Models

1.4.1 The "Old" Growth Theory

The TFP model produces an explanation of economic growth based solely on the production function and the marginal productivity conditions. Thus, it is not a theory of economic growth because it does not explain how variables on the right-hand side of the production function—labor, capital, and technology—evolve over time. However, Solow himself provided an account of this evolution in a separate and slightly earlier paper (1956). He assumed that labor and technology were exogenous factors determined outside the model, and that investment is a constant fraction of output. Then, if technical change is entirely labor augmenting and the production function is well-behaved, the economy converges to a steady-state growth path along which both output per worker and capital per worker grow at the rate of technical change. Cass (1965) and Koopmans (1965) arrive at essentially the same conclusion using different assumptions about the saving-investment process.

Both of these "neoclassical" growth models produce a very different conclusion from that of the TFP model about the importance of technical change in economic growth. In the neoclassical growth models, capital formation explains *none* of the long-run, steady-state growth in output because capital is itself endogenous and driven by technical change: Technical innovation causes output to increase, which increases investment, which thereby induces an expansion in the stock of capital. This induced capital accumulation is the direct result of TFP growth and, in steady-state growth, *all* capital accumulation and output growth are due to TFP. While real-world economies rarely meet the conditions for steady-state growth, the induced-accumulation effect is present outside steady-state conditions whenever the output effects of TFP growth generate a stream of new investment.

What does this mean for the measurement of TFP? The residual is a valid measure of the shift in the production function under the Solow assumptions. However, because the TFP residual model treats all capital formation as a wholly exogenous explanatory factor, it tends to overstate the role of capital and understate the role of innovation in the growth process.[14] Since some part of the observed rate of capital accumulation is a TFP-induced effect, it should be counted along with TFP in any assessment of the impact of innovation on economic growth. Only the fraction of capital accumulation arising from the underlying propensity to invest

---

14. This was pointed out in Hulten (1975, 1978) in the context of the neoclassical model, and by Rymes (1971) and Cas and Rymes (1991) in a somewhat different context.

at a constant rate of TFP growth should be scored as capital's independent contribution to output growth.[15]

The distinction between the size of the residual on the one hand and its impact on growth on the other has been generally ignored in the productivity literature. This oversight has come back to haunt the debate over "assimilation versus accumulation" as the driving force in economic development. A number of comparative growth studies have found that the great success of the East Asian Tigers was driven mainly by the increase in capital and labor rather than by TFP growth (Young 1992, 1995; Kim and Lau 1994; Nadiri and Kim 1996; Collins and Bosworth 1996). With diminishing marginal returns to capital, the dominant role of capital implies that the East Asian Miracle is not sustainable and must ultimately wind down (Krugman 1994). However, these conclusions do not take into account the induced capital accumulation effect. The role played by TFP growth (assimilation) is actually larger, and the saving/investment effect is proportionately smaller.

Exactly how much larger is hard to say, because the induced-accumulation effect depends on several factors, such as the bias in technical change and the elasticity of substitution between capital and labor. I proposed a correction for this effect in my 1975 paper and estimated that the conventional TFP residual accounted for 34 percent of U.S. output growth over the period 1948 to 1966 (annual output growth was 4.15 percent and the residual was 1.42 percent). When the induced capital accumulation effect formation was taken into account, technical change was actually responsible for 64 percent of the growth in output. This is almost double the percentage of the conventional view of the importance of TFP growth.

A closely related alternative is to use a Harrod-Rymes variant of the TFP residual instead of the conventional Hicksian approach. The Harrodian concept of TFP measures the shift in the production function along a constant capital-output ratio, instead of the constant capital-labor ratio of the conventional Hicks-Solow measure (A_t) of the preceding sections. By holding the capital-output ratio constant when costless innovation occurs, the Harrodian measure attributes part of the observed growth rate of capi-

---

15. This point can be illustrated by the following example. Suppose that an economy is on a steady-state growth path with a Harrod-neutral rate of technical change of 0.06 percent per year. If capital's income share is one-third of GDP, a conventional TFP sources-of-growth table would record the growth rate of output per worker as 0.06 and allocate 0.02 to capital per worker and 0.04 to TFP. Observed capital formation seems to explain one-third of the growth in output per worker. However, its true contribution is zero in steady-state growth. The 0.06 growth rate of Q/L should be allocated in the following way: 0 to capital per worker and 0.06 to technical change.

A more complicated situation arises when technical change is also embodied in the design of new capital. In this case, the rate of investment affects the rate of technical change and creates a two-way interaction with TFP growth.

tal to the shift in the production function. Only capital accumulation in excess of the growth rate of output is counted as an independent impetus to output growth. The Harrodian approach thus allows for the induced-accumulation effect, and when the innovation happens to be of the Harrod-neutral form, the accounting is exact (Hulten 1975). Otherwise, the Harrodian correction is approximate.

When applied to the East Asian economies studied by Young, the Harrodian correction gives a very different view of the role of TFP growth (Hulten and Srinivasan 1999). Conventional Hicksian TFP accounts for approximately one-third of output growth in Hong Kong, South Korea, and Taiwan over the period 1966–1990/91. With Harrodian TFP, this figure rises to nearly 50 percent. Again, although the conventional Hicksian TFP residual is a valid measure of the shift in the production function, a distinction must be made between the magnitude of the shift and its importance for output growth.

1.4.2 The New Growth Models

Neoclassical growth models assume that innovation is an exogenous process, with the implication that investments in R&D have no systematic and predictable effect on output growth. But, can it really be true that the huge amount of R&D investment made in recent years was undertaken without any expectation of gain? A more plausible approach is to abandon the assumption that the innovation is exogenous to the economic system and to recognize that some part of innovation is, in fact, a form of capital accumulation.

This is precisely the view incorporated in the endogenous growth theory of Romer (1986) and Lucas (1988). The concept of capital is expanded to include knowledge and human capital and is added to conventional fixed capital, thus arriving at total capital. Increments of knowledge are put on an equal footing with all other forms of investment, and therefore the rate of innovation is endogenous to the model. The key point of endogenous growth theory is not, however, that R&D and human capital are important determinants of output growth. What is new in endogenous growth theory is the assumption that the marginal product of (generalized) capital is constant—not diminishing as in the neoclassical theories. It is the diminishing marginal returns to capital that bring about convergence to steady-state growth in the neoclassical theory; and, conversely, it is constant marginal returns that cause the induced-accumulation effect on capital to go on ad infinitum.[16]

Endogenous growth theory encompasses a variety of different models.

---

16. Barro and Sala-i-Martin (1995) provide a good overview of the various growth models (see also Easterly 1995). Not all relevant models involve increasing returns to scale, since technical change is endogenized by investment in R&D per se.

We will focus here on one that is perhaps the main variant in order to illustrate the implications of endogeneity for the measurement and interpretation of the productivity residual. Suppose that the production function in equation (4) has the Cobb-Douglas production function prevalent in that literature, and that (generalized) capital has two effects: Each 1 percent increase in capital raises the output of its owner-users by β percent but also spills over to other users, raising their output by a collective α percent. Suppose, also, that $\alpha + \beta = 1$, implying constant returns to scale in the capital variable across all producers, while labor and private capital are also subject to constant returns ($\beta + \gamma + 1$). This leads to

(8) $\qquad Q_t = A_0 K_t^\alpha [K_t^\beta L_t^\gamma], \quad \alpha + \beta = 1, \quad \beta + \gamma = 1.$

This production function exhibits increasing returns to scale overall, but it is consistent with equilibrium because each producer operates under the assumption of constant returns to the inputs that the producer controls.

What does this new formulation imply for the residual, computed as per the "usual" equation (7)? The residual is derived from the Hicksian production function shown in equation (4), and the formulation in equation (8) is a special case of this function in which the output elasticities are constant (Cobb-Douglas) and the efficiency term $A_0 K_t^\alpha$ replaces the Hicksian efficiency parameter A_t. The associated residual, analogous to equation (7), is thus equal to the growth rate of capital weighted by the spillover effect. The endogenous TFP residual continues to measure costless gains to society—the "manna from heaven"—from innovation. But now this manna is associated with the externality parameter α instead of the Hicksian efficiency parameter A_t. Thus, in the New Growth view, the residual is no longer a nonparametric method for estimating a fixed parameter of the production function, but is actually the reflection of a process. Moreover, there is no reason for the residual to disappear.[17]

The endogenous growth residual adds structure to the problem of interpreting the TFP residual, but does this new interpretation help explain the productivity slowdown? The endogenous growth view, in the increasing returns form set out previously, points either to a slowdown in the growth rate of (comprehensive) capital or to a decline in the degree of the externality α as possible causes of the slowdown. Unfortunately, neither possibility is supported by the available evidence. Investment in R&D as a percent of GDP has been relatively constant, and the proportion of industrial R&D has increased. The growth in fixed capital does not correlate with

17. These conclusions assume that the spillover externality augments the return to labor and "private" capital equally (an implication of the Cobb-Douglas form). All is well if labor continues to be paid the value of its marginal product. However, endogenous growth theory is part of a more general view of growth that stresses the importance of imperfect competition, and it is possible that the presence of spillover externalities may lead to a wedge between output elasticities and factor shares.

the fall in the residual. Moreover, the evidence does not provide support for a decline in the externality or spillover effect (Nadiri 1993; Griliches 1994), although this is debatable. It therefore seems reasonable to conclude that we must look elsewhere in the emerging growth literature, perhaps at the learning and diffusion mechanisms described in the Greenwood-Jovanovic survey, to explain fluctuations in the rate of productivity change.

1.4.3 Data on Quality and the Quality of Data

The production function–based models of TFP described in the preceding sections are based on a *process-oriented* view of technical change, one in which productivity growth occurs through improvements in transforming input into output. No explicit mention has been made of another important dimension of innovation: improvements in the quality of products and the introduction of new goods. Both present consumers and producers with a new array of products and, over time, completely transform the market basket (automobiles replace horses, personal computers replace typewriters, etc.). Much of the welfare gain from innovation comes from the production of better goods, not just from the production of more goods (i.e., by moving up the "quality ladder" [Grossman and Helpman 1991]). Unfortunately, the TFP residual is intended to measure only the production of more goods—this is what a shift in the production function means—and only the costless portion at that. Innovation that results in better goods is not part of the TFP story.

One way to handle this issue is to treat the two types of innovation as separate measurement problems and restrict use of the TFP residual to its proper domain. Unfortunately, the two types of innovation are not easily segregated, as the following example shows. First, imagine two economies, both of which have the same technology and start with 100 units of input, so that both produce 100 physical units of output. Suppose, now, that some ingenious person in economy A discovers a way to double the amount of output that the 100 units of input can produce. At the same time, an innovator in economy B discovers a way to double the utility of the 100 physical units of output that are produced (that is, inhabitants of B gladly exchange two units of the old output for one unit of new output). A measure of TFP based entirely on physical units will double in A but remain flat in B, even though the inhabitants of both countries are equally well off as a result of their respective innovations.

Is this the right result? In a sense, it is. The production function for physical units of output shifted in economy A but not in B. However, this judgment reflects a particular conception of output—that is, that physical units are the appropriate unit of measure. This convention obviously provides an unfavorable view of economy B because it defines away the true gains made in B. An alternative approach would be to measure output in units of consumption efficiency—that is, in units that reflect the marginal rate of substitution between old and new goods. In this efficiency-unit approach, both A and B experience a doubling of output, albeit for different reasons, and measured TFP reflects the increase. In other words, the TFP model does service in measuring both process and product innovation when output is measured in efficiency units.

The efficiency approach to productivity measurement has proceeded along two general lines. First, the 1950s saw the theoretical development of the model of capital-embodied technical change (Johansen 1959; Salter 1960; Solow 1960). In this model, technical innovation is expressed in the design of new machines, with the implication that different vintages of capital may be in service with different degrees of marginal productivity. When expressed in efficiency units, one physical unit of new capital represents more capital than one physical unit of an older vintage. The total "size" of this capital stock is the number of efficiency units it embodies, and the growth in this stock is the results of two factors: the arrival of more investment and the arrival of better investment. Moreover, the implied rate of productivity growth depends on the rate of investment.

Though theoretically plausible, the capital-embodiment model met initially with limited empirical success. Moreover, it was dismissed as unimportant by one of the leading productivity analysts, Denison (1964). However, the issue did not disappear entirely and has returned to prominence with the hedonic price study by Cole et al. (1986), who used price data to show that official investment-price statistics had essentially missed the computer revolution, overstating price and understating quantity (measured in efficiency units).[18] This finding led the Bureau of Economic Analysis (BEA) to switch to an efficiency-unit convention for investment in computers in the U.S. national income and product accounts (but only for computers). This analysis was extended by Gordon (1990), who adjusted the prices of a wide range of consumer and producer equipment for changes in quality. Gordon also found systematic overstatement of official price statistics and a corresponding understatement of efficiency-adjusted quantity investment output and the resulting capital input.

The CPI is another area in which price data are routinely adjusted for quality change. A variety of procedures is used in the adjustment process, including price hedonics, but the Advisory Commission (1996) concluded that they were not adequate and that the CPI was biased upward by 0.6

---

18. In the hedonic price model, a product is viewed as a bundle of constituent characteristics. The more there is of each characteristic, the more there is of the good. Computers, for example, are seen in terms of CPU speed, memory speed and capacity, storage capacity, and so on. The hedonic model estimates a "price" for each characteristic and thereby derives an implied price for the whole bundle. This also yields a "quantity" of the good measured in terms of efficiency. Embodied technical change is naturally seen as an increase in the efficiency units via an increase in the characteristics. See Triplett (1983, 1987) for more on the hedonic price model.

percentage points per year. In other words, the growth in efficiency price of consumption goods was overstated, and the corresponding quantity was understated. The BLS is currently undertaking revisions in its procedures, including increased reliance on price hedonics, to address the quality problem.

The fundamental problem with the efficiency approach is that improvements in product quality, or the advent of entirely new consumer goods, are essentially subjective. Physical units can be observed, however imperfectly, but when characteristic-efficiency units are involved, there is no direct observational check to the imputed amount of product. It is all too easy to misstate the true quantity of efficiency units, and there is little intuitive basis for rejecting the misstatement (exactly how much more utility do you feel you get from a Pentium III processor?).[19] It is worth recalling the words of Adam Smith, "Quality . . . is so very disputable a matter, that I look upon all information of this kind as somewhat uncertain."

The subjective nature of the efficiency approach leads to a more subtle problem. Because the quantity of efficiency units is determined by imputation of the relative marginal utility between old and new products, the very definition of product quantity becomes a matter of utility and consumer choice (Hulten 2000). This tends to blur the boundary between the supply-side constraint on growth, the production function, and the objective of growth, which is the province of the utility function. We will return to such boundary issues in the following sections.

1.4.4 Quality Change and the TFP Residual

Most of the TFP studies that have incorporated product-oriented innovation into the residual have focused on capital-embodied technical change. Nelson (1964) expressed the residual as a function of the rate of embodiment and the average age of the capital stock. Domar (1963) and Jorgenson (1966) observed that capital is both an input and an output of the production process, and the failure to measure capital in efficiency units causes two types of measurement error: one associated with the mismeasurement of capital input and one with the mismeasurement of invest-

---

19. The mismeasurement of quality in improved products is particularly difficult regarding nondurable consumer goods, where reliable overlapping prices of old and new models are harder to obtain. Moreover, the measurement problems posed by "quality" are not limited to product-oriented innovation. There are also myriad problems in the definition of output that involves a quality dimension without reference to innovation. Griliches (1994) speaks of the "hard to measure" sectors of the economy—largely the service sector—and notes that these sectors in particular have grown over time. For example, the bank revenues can be measured with some precision, but what exactly are the units of output? How would one measure these units in principle and account for differences in the quality of service that is characteristic of competition among banks? Unless the nature of the output can be defined precisely, it is impossible to determine its rate of growth and to confront questions about the impact of quality-enhancing innovations like automatic teller machines.

ment good output. Surprisingly, the two errors exactly cancel in Golden Rule steady-state growth, leaving the residual unbiased.[20]

The actual size of the input and output embodiment errors depends on the rate at which embodied efficiency increases and on the average embodied efficiency of the older vintages of capital stock. These cannot be estimated within the residual's index number framework, but in an earlier paper (1992b), I use data from Gordon (1990) to estimate the net embodiment effect for the U.S. manufacturing industry. The net embodiment effect was found to account for about 20 percent of the TFP residual over the time period 1949–83. Wolff (1996) reports an effect that is roughly twice as large for the economy as a whole for the same years. Greenwood, Hercowitz, and Krusell (1997) propose a variant of the embodiment model in which the total value of investment is deflated by the price of consumption rather than investment. The resulting estimate of the embodiment effect accounts for 58 percent of the aggregate residual, per the period 1954–90.

These studies deal with capital-embodied technical change. Productivity analysis has paid less attention to quality change in consumption goods. The example of the economies A and B from the preceding section suggests that this neglect results in an understatement of true output and TFP growth (recall the situation in economy B). However, the problem is even more complicated than that example suggests, because of another problem that has lurked in the background of productivity analysis: the cost of achieving technical innovations. A variant of our example illustrates the problem. Economies A and B each start with 100 units of input and the same technology, and produce 100 physical units of output. Economy A now invests half its workforce in research and is able to quadruple the output of the remaining 50 workers. Output and TFP thus double. In economy B, on the other hand, the 50 are diverted to research and manage to invent a new good that is four times as desirable (that is, inhabitants of B gladly exchange four units of the old output for one unit of new), but only 50 units of physical output are produced. Physical output and TFP fall by half in B, even though innovation has made the inhabitants of B as well off as those in A. The failure to measure output in efficiency units

---

20. This point is often overlooked in econometric studies of embodied technical change. If both capital input and investment output are correctly measured in efficiency units, the economy-wide TFP residual should be invariant to changes in the rate of capital embodiment. If input and output are not adjusted for quality, aggregate TFP is still invariant along the optimal growth path. Off the optimal path, there is the Hall (1968) identification problem: the exponential part of capital-embodied technical change cannot be distinguished from the equivalent rate of disembodied technical change given price or quantity data on age, vintage, and time. Only deviations from the exponential path can be identified. Finally, it is well to remember that the residual can only measure the costless part of innovation, embodied or otherwise.

thus gives the appearance of technical regress even though progress has occurred.

These considerations can be parameterized and embedded into the standard TFP model by introducing a simple type of quality ladder (Hulten 1996, 2000). Suppose that product-oriented technical change proceeds at a rate θ (essentially the marginal rate of substitution between old goods and new goods of superior quality), and the cost of achieving this rate of quality change is $\mu\theta$. Costless innovation occurs when μ equals zero. In a simplified world in which capital and labor are fixed, it can be shown that the TFP residual falls at the rate $\mu\theta$ when output is measured in physical units, but grows at a rate of $(1 - \mu)\theta$ when efficiency units are used. In the first case, an increase in the rate of innovation θ will actually cause the residual to decrease, resonating with the New Economy critique that the problem with productivity statistics is its failure to count improvements in product quality.[21]

1.4.5 Capacity versus Welfare Interpretations of the Residual: The Problem of Sustainable Consumption

Once it is recognized that product quality adjustments allow consumer welfare parameters to creep into the TFP residual, the boundary between the supply-side conception of the residual and the demand-side interpretations is blurred. If welfare considerations are permitted inside one region of the supply-side boundary (and they must be, if the quality dimension of output is to make sense), perhaps they should be permitted in other boundary areas, such as the net-versus-gross output controversy, where welfare arguments have also been made. After all, a high rate of real GDP growth, and hence a large gross-output productivity residual, can be sustained in the short run by depleting unreproducible resources at the expense of long-run welfare. Net output solves this problem by controlling for depreciation and environmental damage; some believe that it thus provides a more accurate picture of sustainable long-run economic growth. Does it not follow that a separate TFP residual based on net output is the appropriate indicator of the contribution of costless technical innovation to sustainable growth?

The short answer is "no." Changes in social welfare can be shown to depend on the standard gross-output concept of TFP, with no need to define a net-output variant of TFP. The result follows from the optimal growth model studied by Cass (1965) and Koopmans (1965), as augmented by Weitzman (1976), in which the intertemporal utility function

---

21. There is another possibility. Even if output is correctly measured in quality units, the residual can fall if the rate of innovation θ is pushed beyond its cost-effective optimum. In other words, research "booms" can lower TFP if pushed too far.

$U(C_0, \ldots, C_t)$ is maximized (C_t is the amount of consumption t years from the present time). For present purposes, it is useful to assume that prices are proportional to marginal utilities and to express the intertemporal welfare problem as one of maximizing the present value equation

$$(9) \qquad W_0 = \sum_{t=0}^{\infty} \frac{p_t C_t}{(1 + i)^{t+1}},$$

subject to the production function $C_t + I_t = A_t F(K_t, L_t)$ and the accumulation condition $K_t = I_t + (1 - \delta)K_{t-1}$ (here, we revert to the assumption that Hicksian efficiency and labor growth are exogenously determined). The economic problem of contemporary society, at each point in time, is to determine the optimal division of current output between consumption and investment.

This problem was studied by Weitzman (1976), who demonstrated that the optimal consumption path (C_t^*) satisfies the condition $p_t C_t^* + p_t \Delta K_t^*$. But this is really nothing more than the Hicksian definition of income: the maximum amount of output that could be consumed each year without reducing the original amount of capital, or, equivalently, "sustainable" consumption. This is the welfare indicator appropriate for the annualized measurement of increments to consumer welfare.

This welfare indicator of output is not the same as GDP. According to the fundamental accounting identity in equation (1), GDP is equal to the gross payments to capital and labor (as well as $p_t Q_t$). With some algebraic manipulation based on the Hall-Jorgenson user cost formula, it can be shown that Hicksian income is equal to net factor income or net national product in nominal prices, which differs from gross output by the amount of depreciation (Hulten 1992a):

$$(10) \qquad p_t C_t^* + p_t \Delta K_t^* = i_t p_t K_t + w_t L_t < p_t Q.$$

This identity may encourage some to suppose that net national product (NNP) should be used in productivity analysis instead of GDP because it is associated with maximum intertemporal welfare. However, the two output concepts are complements, not substitutes. The growth in real GDP indicates the expansion of the supply-side constraint in any year, and the residual computed using real GDP measures the change in the efficiency of production as represented by A_t (the shift in production constraint). The growth in NNP cum Hicksian income reveals the extent to which growth has improved society's welfare. These are separate issues and must be kept separate, and it is important to recognize that the gross-output TFP residual fits into the welfare-maximization problem via the production constraint.

This result does raise the question of how the gross-output residual is related to changes in economic welfare. This is a complicated issue that involves treating capital as an intertemporal intermediate product, and linking labor input and technology directly to the attainable consumption path (Hulten 1979). If the optimal consumption path (C_t^*) is chosen—that is, the one that maximizes equation (9)—an intertemporal consumption-based residual can be derived that is the weighted sum of the TFP residuals:

$$\Omega_{0,T} = \sum_{t=0}^{T} \omega_t \frac{\dot{A}_t}{A_t}. \tag{11}$$

The individual weights in this expression, ω_t, are the respective annual ratios of GDP to total wealth, W_0. They are the intertemporal counterparts of the weights used by Domar (1961) and Hulten (1978) to aggregate the sectoral gross-output residuals in the presence of intermediate inputs.

The $\Omega_{0,T}$ residual indicates the increase in optimal consumption associated with changes in the annual (gross-output) TFP residuals. It is not a substitute for these residuals, but a complement. It is clear, once again, that the appropriate welfare-based analysis is separate from, and complementary to, the GDP-based analysis of productive efficiency.

1.4.6 The Boundaries of Productivity Analysis

We have seen that the boundary between welfare and capacity is not as straightforward as one might wish. However, two general boundary principles are clear enough: A distinction must be maintained between ends (welfare improvement) and means (production); and a distinction must also be maintained between the impulse to save (i.e., defer consumption) and the impulse to invent (productivity). This section deals with yet another boundary: the line between what should be counted as output and input and what should not. This "comprehensiveness" boundary is central to the debate about the desirability of a "Green GDP" raised by environmentalists and discussed in Nordhaus and Kokkelenberg (1999).

A complete set of economic accounts would include information on the price and quantity of every variable that enters into the production or utility function of every agent in the economy. The required list of variables would extend far beyond the boundaries of the market economy. Goods produced in the household sector would be an important part of the complete accounting system, including work around the home, leisure, and education. Those public goods produced in the government sector and distributed free of direct charge (or at a price that does not reflect marginal cost) must also be part of the accounts, including national defense, public infrastructure, and so on. Also necessary are goods held in common for private use (such environmental variables as clean air and water, parks, forests, and mineral deposits), as well as spillover externalities, such as knowledge and congestion, and so on.

This is an impossibly large order to fill. The boundaries of a complete accounting system would include everything that correlates with the production of goods and services and affects economic welfare. Thus, for example, the effects of urbanization and materialism that are alleged correlates of the modern capitalist system could force their way into the complete accounts on the grounds that the breakdown of welfare-enhancing institutions (such as family and religion) are the results of these effects. The boundaries of a complete set of economic accounts may thus be extended to include statistics on crime, drug abuse, divorce, and so on.

Boundaries drawn this broadly go far beyond the limits of the current national economic accounts, and probably far beyond the comfort limits of most economists. This reinforces the current national income-accounting practice of relying primarily on market transactions to generate data. Market transactions, though flawed and incomplete, do provide an objective yardstick for measuring the volume of economic activity, as well as prices and quantities. Market data are also relatively easy to collect. These benefits are, unfortunately, purchased at a price: Narrow focus on products exchanged for money leads to the exclusion of many goods the data for which are harder to obtain. This, in turn, can lead to a distorted picture of the true production possibilities facing an economy. Productivity, in any of its many forms, is essentially a ratio of output to input and will be affected by the omission of any element of the numerator or denominator.

This dilemma can be illustrated by the following simplified example. Suppose that an industry produces a good Q_t, which it sells at marginal cost in the marketplace for price P_t. It produces the good using input X_t, which it purchases in the factor market for w_t, but also uses a good Z_t which is available without cost to the firm. The item Z_t might be a common good (e.g., clean air), an externality associated with another agent's behavior (e.g., technical knowledge appropriated from other firms in the industry), or self-constructed capital produced in an earlier year (the firm's stock of technical know-how). In any event, the statistician who looks only at market data will record the accounting identity $P_t Q_t = w_t X_t$, and the analyst will reckon productivity to be Q_t/X_t. The true nature of things is, of course, different. The correct accounting identity is $P_t^* Q_t = w_t X_t + \rho_t Z_t$, where P^* is the marginal social cost of the good, as opposed to the private cost, P_t, and ρ_t is the implicit cost to using the "free" input Z_t. The true productivity ratio is $Q_t/F(X_t, Z_t)$. The example could be complicated further by supposing that the firm generates an externality as it produces Q_t.[22]

---

22. There are many candidates for the role of "significant omitted variable." One in particular deserves mention because of its relation to the productivity of the computer revolution. The advent of computers has allowed firms to reduce the number of employees, often resulting in productivity gains to the firm. But this has often come at the expense of the consumer, who must substitute his/her own time for that of the departed employee. Anyone who has been on hold for a telephone connection to a human voice, or suffered through seemingly interminable menu-driven options, understands this problem.

In order for the statistician to "get it right," the variable Z_t, must be recognized and measured, and imputations must be made for the shadow prices P^* and ρ_t. The latter is particularly hard. Some imputations can be made using technical procedures like price hedonics, but many must be approached with controversial techniques such as "willingness-to-pay" criteria (e.g., see the discussion in Nordhaus and Kokkelenberg 1999). It is even harder for the statistician to proceed when imputation involves a politically sensitive issue such as the public's health, the preservation of the environment, or worker or product safety. Partisans with different points of view often impute vastly different amounts to the value of life or protection of the environment. In these cases, the imputation process is thus as likely to reflect partisan agendas as to reflect the true nature of productivity growth.

Some imputations are made in practice in the national accounts (e.g., owner-occupied housing), and quasi-imputations for government "output" are used. However, the bulk of unpriced goods is not included. This seems the safe path to follow, at least for the time being. Although the omission of important variables may limit the generality of conclusions that can be drawn from productivity statistics, at least the results are not subject to the changing winds of ideology or special interests. Nor is the direction of the "boundary bias" clear.[23]

1.5 The Total Factor Productivity Residual for Firms and Industries

1.5.1 The View from the Top Down

A TFP residual can, in principle, be computed for every level of economic activity, from the plant floor to the aggregate economy. These residuals are not independent of each other because, for example, the productivity of a firm reflects the productivity of its component plants. Similarly, industry residuals are related to those of the constituent firms, and productivity in the aggregate economy is determined at the industry level. As a result, productivity at the aggregate level will increase if productivity in each constituent industry rises, or if the market share of the high productivity industry increases (and so on, down the aggregation hierarchy).[24] A

---

23. The debate over boundaries has generally failed to recognize that the omission of environmental spillovers from official data does not necessarily mean that they are unnoticed. The public feel their effects regardless of whether they appear in the data, and, indeed, rational citizens should make their own corrections to flawed data (Hulten 2000). A great deal of pro-environment legislation has been informed by the "biased" statistics, and it is unclear whether fixing the bias would have led to a superior outcome.

24. The significance of shifting sectoral shares for explaining productivity growth has received much attention (see particularly Denison 1967 and Baumol 1967). The shift in resources out of agriculture is often held to be a cause of accelerating productivity growth, and the shift out of manufacturing industry into the service sectors is a potential explanation of slowing productivity. The Baumol stagnation hypothesis holds that a slowdown is inevi-

complete picture of the industrial dynamics of an economy would include a *mutually consistent* measure of the TFP residuals at each level in the hierarchy and of the linkages used to connect levels.

The task of constructing this hierarchy of residuals can be approached from the top down, in a process that can be likened to unpeeling an onion in order to reach lower layers of structure. Domar (1961) was the first to work out the problem of "unpeeling" the TFP residual, and to recognize the complication introduced by the presence of intermediate goods. This complication arises because plants and firms in each sublayer produce goods and services that are used as inputs in the production processes of the plants and firms. As each layer is unpeeled, the magnitude of these intermediate deliveries grows. For example, there are no intermediate goods in the aggregate economy because there is only one industry at this level of aggregation, and all interindustry flows cancel out.

However, these interindustry flows "uncancel" in passing to the one-digit industry level of detail. The iron ore delivered to the steel industry is counted in the gross output of the extractive industries, and is counted again as part of the gross output of the manufacturing industry. The sum of the one-digit industry gross output is therefore larger than total aggregate output.

The nature of this problem can be made more precise by observing that the total output of an industry (plant, firm) is composed of deliveries to final demand plus deliveries of the industry's output to the other industries that use the good. On the input side, the firm uses not only labor and capital, but also intermediate goods purchased from other industries. This leads to the accounting identity

$$(12) \qquad p_i D_i + p_i \Sigma_i M_{i,j} = w_i L_i + r_i K_i + \Sigma_j p_{j,i} M_{j,i}.$$

The summation term on the left-hand side of this expression is the value of the deliveries of the *i*th industry's output, and D_i denotes deliveries to final demand (time subscripts have been omitted for clarity of exposition). The summation on the right-hand side is the value of intermediate goods purchased from other industries, and the remaining terms on the right-hand side constitute the value added by the industry, $w_i L_i + r_i K_i$.

There is an expression like equation (12) for each industry (firm, etc.) in the economy. Summing them all up to the aggregate level gives the identity

$$(13) \qquad \Sigma_i p_i D_i + \Sigma_i w L_i + \Sigma_i r K_i = wL + rK.$$

(It is assumed here that competition equates wages and capital cost across sectors.) This is a variant of the fundamental accounting identity with

---

table in an economy in which the output demand for the low-productivity growth sector is inelastic. A large literature on this subject has evolved, but space limitations prevent a more detailed treatment of the various strands and criticisms.

which we started, but here we have total deliveries to final demand as the output measured on the left-hand side, and total value added on the right-hand side.

Total factor productivity residuals can be obtained from both expressions—industry residuals from equation (12) and the aggregate residual from equation (13) cum equation (1). Domar (1961) showed that the aggregate residual is the weighted sum of the industry residuals, where the weights are the ratio of industry gross output to total deliveries to final demand (GDP). His results are generalized in Hulten (1978) to

$$(14) \qquad \frac{\dot{A}_t}{A_t} = \sum_{i=1}^{N} \frac{p_{i,t} Q_{i,t}}{\Sigma_i p_{i,t} D_{i,t}} \frac{\dot{A}_{i,t}}{A_{i,t}}.$$

The unusual feature of this expression is that the weights sum to a quantity greater than 1 to account for the presence of the intermediate goods. Thus, for example, a uniform 1 percent rate of increase in productivity at the industry level may translate into, say, a 1.5 percent increase in productivity at the aggregate level. This inflation in the aggregate number is needed to account for the fact that, although an increase in industry-level productivity augments the production of intermediate goods, these intermediate goods have subsequently disappeared in the process of aggregation.[25]

The production function underlying the residual in equation (14) is the second unusual feature of the analysis. Whereas Solow assumed that the aggregate production function could be expressed as $Q = AF(K, L)$, the technology underlying equation (14) is a production possibility frontier of the following form: $F(Q_1, \ldots, Q_n; K, L, A_1, \ldots, A_n) = 0$. The left-hand side of equation (14) is the shift in the frontier, holding capital and labor constant. The right-hand side indicates that this shift can be "unpeeled" into separate components: the growth rates of industry-level productivity (A_i), and the sectoral share weights, which may change with the reallocation of GDP among sectors with different TFP levels and growth rates. There is no guarantee that the aggregate productivity index is path independent when the component A_i grow at different rates.

The chief difficulty with this unpeeling process lies in the nature of intermediate goods. The quantity gross output and intermediate goods in any industry are greatly affected by mergers and acquisitions. The merger of firms can transform what were once interfirm flows of goods into intrafirm flows, thereby extinguishing some amount of gross output. This has led some researchers to use real value added, a concept of industry output that is immune to this problem.

---

25. It is no accident that equation (14) looks very much like equation (11), the welfare equivalent of the Solow residual. The welfare residual is based on the intertemporal optimization of consumption, and capital is treated as an intermediate good in that model. Moreover, "years" are formally equivalent to industries in the conventional intermediate goods model described in this section.

The productivity analyst's job would be made easier if intermediate goods could be netted out directly in the identity shown in equation (12), leaving industry final demand equal to value added (i.e., $p_i D_i = w_i L_i + r_i K_i$). However, this will generally not happen, since the value of intermediate goods produced in an industry need not equal the amount used. One solution is to focus on the right-hand side of this expression and define industry output as the "real," or constant-price, part of $w_i L_i + r_i K_i$. Industry value added sums to total value added (GDP), and the relation between the two is not affected by intermediate goods. A variant of the TFP residual can be based on this concept of industry "output" by applying the original Solow formula. The result can be weighted up to the aggregate level using value added weights.

There are, however, two problems with this approach. First, there is nothing in the real world that resembles real value added. Do plants actually make things in units of real value added? Second, it is well known that real value added works only when innovation enhances the productivity of capital and labor but not intermediate inputs—that is, the industry-level production function has the form $Q_i = F[M_i, A_i G(K_i, L_i)]$. Thus, the productivity analyst is confronted with a dilemma: Use the gross output approach and become a prisoner of the degree of vertical and horizontal industrial integration, or use the implausible value added approach. Moreover, there is no guarantee that the production functions underlying either approach are suitable potential functions for the path-independent line integration required in equation (14), and many other problems are encountered at the industry level of analysis (Gullickson and Harper 1999).

1.5.2 The View from the Bottom Up

The preceding remarks take the top-down view of sectoral productivity analysis, in which the aggregate TFP residual is the point of reference. The bottom-up approach to productivity measurement starts from a very different perspective. It takes the universe of plants or firms as the fundamental frame of reference and does not impose the restrictive aggregation assumptions needed to achieve a consistent measure of overall productivity. Instead, it stresses the basic heterogeneity of the microproduction units. An important goal of this approach is to explain the observed heterogeneity of plant productivity in terms of factors such as R&D spending or patenting, or of differences in the financial or industrial structure.[26]

The literature on this approach is huge and can be treated with only a cursory overview. Early contributions were made by Griliches, Mansfield, and others (see Griliches 1994), and the work of Nelson and Winter explic-

---

26. See Bartelsman and Doms (2000) for a recent survey of this area, and the paper by Foster, Haltiwanger, and Krizan (chapter 8 in this volume).

itly focused on heterogeneity. This line of investigation was greatly aided by the development of microdata sets like the LRD in 1982, and by the enormous increase in computing power, which enabled researchers to analyze increasingly large data sets with ever more sophisticated econometric techniques. The R&D work of Griliches and Mairesse (1984) and B. Hall (1993) is noteworthy in this regard, as are the seminal contributions of Davis and Haltiwanger (1991).

The heterogenous plant/firm approach has much to recommend it because it permits a detailed examination of the factors that actually determine microproductivity. However, its very success is also its chief problem: It is hard to generalize the lessons learned from the microanalysis. This is due in part to the inherent heterogeneity of the data, but it is also due to the diverse (and often contradictory) findings of different econometric studies, although this is not an uncommon problem with large and complex data sets.

Several studies have attempted to link the micro and macro levels of analysis. Baily, Hulten, and Campbell (1992) used data from the LRD to examine the internal dynamics of industry-level residuals. This study found, among other things, that the representative agent model, which is often considered the conceptual link between macro and micro levels of analysis, is not supported by the data. When industry-level residuals were resolved into the weighted sum of the plant-level residuals, it was found that the plants with rising TFP levels and plants with high preexisting TFP levels were the main contributors to productivity growth. Firms with low preexisting TFP levels and declining firms were a drag on productivity. The persistence of firms with both high and low levels of productivity suggests a more complex view of industrial organization than the simple representative agent model used to motivate the aggregate TFP residual. The microdata also suggest a more complex productivity dynamic in which the entry and exit of firms, as well as their expansion and contraction, are important dimensions.

Many advances have been made in subsequent research. However, it remains true that a compelling link between the micro and macro levels has yet to be forged. This is one of the greatest challenges facing productivity analysts today. This challenge is all the more daunting because it must confront this problem: Industries are composed of heterogenous firms operated under conditions of imperfect competition, but the theoretical aggregation conditions required to proceed upward to the level of macroeconomy rely on perfect competition.

1.6 Conclusion

Any respectable biography must end with a summary judgment of the subject at hand; and, above all, the true character of the subject should be revealed. This is particularly important in the case of the TFP residual, the true character of which has often been misunderstood by friends and critics alike. The portrait painted in this paper reveals these essential features:

1. The TFP residual captures changes in the amount of output that can be produced by a given quantity of inputs. Intuitively, it measures the shift in the production function.

2. Many factors may cause this shift: technical innovations, organizational and institutional changes, shifts in societal attitudes, fluctuations in demand, changes in factor shares, omitted variables, and measurement errors. The residual should *not* be equated with technical change, although it often is.

3. To the extent that productivity is affected by innovation, it is the costless part of technical change that it captures. This "manna from heaven" may reflect spillover externalities thrown off by research projects, or it may simply reflect inspiration and ingenuity.

4. The residual is a nonparametric index number designed to estimate one parameter in the larger structure of production, the efficiency shift parameter. It accomplishes this by using prices to estimate marginal products.

5. The various factors comprising TFP are not measured directly but are lumped together as a "left-over" factor (hence the name "residual"). They cannot be sorted out within the pure TFP framework, and this is the source of the famous epithet, "a measure of our ignorance."

6. The Divisia index must be path independent to be unique. The discrete-time counterpart of the Divisia index, the Tornqvist approximation, is an exact index number if the underlying production function has the translog form. The problem of path dependence is one of uniqueness, and this is not the same thing as measurement bias.

7. The conditions for path independence are (a) the existence of an underlying production function and (b) marginal productivity pricing. Neither constant returns to scale nor Hicksian neutrality are absolutely necessary conditions, although they are usually assumed for convenience of measurement.

8. When the various assumptions are met, the residual is a valid measure of the shift in the production function. However, it generally understates the importance of productivity change in stimulating the growth of output because the shift in the function generally induces further movements along the function as capital increases.

9. The residual is a measure of the shift in the supply-side constraint on welfare improvement, but it is not intended as a direct measure of this improvement. To confuse the two is to confuse the constraint with the objective function.

This is the essential character of our subject. As with any portrait that is examined closely, flaws are detected and the final judgment is usually mixed with praise and criticism.

Much of the praise is deserved, but so is much of the criticism. The assumptions needed for the TFP model to work perfectly are stringent; much is left out of the analysis, and the pure TFP approach did not provide a consensus explanation of the productivity slowdown. However, alternative approaches are not immune to these criticisms, and a fair judgment must go beyond these criticisms and address a more fundamental question: To what extent are the perceived failures inherent in the character of the residual, and to what extent are the problems inherent in the data to which the residual technique is applied? If data on prices and quantities do not accurately reflect quality improvement, or if the boundaries of the data set are drawn too closely, attacking TFP is rather like shooting the messenger because of the message. If the data are the real source of complaint, other methods (e.g., econometrics) will not fare much better than the simple residual. Bad data are bad data regardless of how they are used.

The positive value of the TFP residual greatly outweighs the negatives. The residual has provided a simple and internally consistent intellectual framework for organizing data on economic growth, and has provided the theory to guide economic measurement. Moreover, it teaches lessons that are still not fully appreciated by mainstream economics and national income accounting: An empirically testable theory places restrictions on the way data must be collected and organized, and choices about the measurement procedures are often implicit choices about the underlying theory.

The residual is still, after more than forty years, the workhorse of empirical growth analysis. For all the residual's flaws, real and imagined, many researchers have used it to gain valuable insights into the process of economic growth. Thousands of pages of research have been published, and more are added every year (for, example, the TFP residual is central to the recent debate over the role of computers in stimulating economic growth). Total factor productivity has become a closely watched government statistic. Not bad for a forty-year-old.

References

Abramovitz, Moses. 1956. Resource and output trends in the United States since 1870. *American Economic Review* 46 (2): 5–23.
Aschauer, David A. 1989. Is public expenditure productive? *Journal of Monetary Economics* 23:177–200.
Baily, Martin N., and Robert J. Gordon. 1988. Measurement issues, the slowdown, and the explosion of computer power. *Brookings Papers on Economic Activity*, issue no. 2: 347–420. Washington, D.C.: Brookings Institution.

Baily, Martin N., Charles R. Hulten, and David Campbell. 1992. Productivity dynamics in manufacturing plants. *Brookings Papers on Economic Activity, Microeconomics:* 187–249. Washington, D.C.: Brookings Institution.

Barro, Robert J., and Xavier Sala-i-Martin. 1995. *Economic growth.* New York: McGraw-Hill.

Bartelsman, Eric J., and Mark Doms. 2000. Understanding productivity: Lessons from longitudinal micro data. *Journal of Economic Literature* 37 (3): 569–94.

Baumol, William J. 1967. Macroeconomics of unbalanced growth: The anatomy of urban crisis. *Journal of Political Economy* 57:415–26.

Baumol, William J., Sue A. B. Blackman, and Edward N. Wolff. 1989. *Productivity and American leadership: The long view.* Cambridge, Mass.: MIT Press.

Berndt, Ernest R. 1980. Energy price increases and the productivity slowdown in U.S. manufacturing. *The decline in productivity growth,* Conference Series no. 22, 60–89. Boston: Federal Reserve Bank of Boston.

Berndt, Ernest R., and Melvyn A. Fuss. 1986. Productivity measurement with adjustments for variations in capacity utilization, and other forms of temporary equilibrium. *Journal of Econometrics* 33:7–29.

Cas, Alexandra, and Thomas K. Rymes. 1991. *On concepts of multifactor productivity.* New York: Cambridge University Press.

Cass, David. 1965. Optimum growth in an aggregative model of capital accumulation. *Review of Economic Studies* 32 (July): 233–40.

Caves, Douglas W., Laurits R. Christensen, and W. Erwin Diewert. 1982a. Multilateral comparisons of output, input, and productivity using superlative index numbers. *Economic Journal* 92 (March): 73–86.

———. 1982b. The economic theory of index numbers and the measurement of input, output, and productivity. *Econometrica* 50 (6): 1393–1414.

Christensen, Laurits R., Diane Cummings, and Dale W. Jorgenson. 1981. Relative productivity levels, 1947–1973: An international comparison. *European Economic Review* 16:61–94.

Christensen, Laurits R., and Dale W. Jorgenson. 1969. The measurement of U.S. real capital input, 1929–1967. *Review of Income and Wealth* 15 (December): 293–320.

———. 1970. U.S. real product and real factor input, 1929–1969. *Review of Income and Wealth* 16 (March): 19–50.

Christensen, Laurits R., Dale W. Jorgenson, and Lawrence J. Lau. 1973. Transcendental logarithmic production frontiers. *Review of Economics and Statistics* 55 (February): 28–45.

Cobb, Clifford, Ted Halstead, and Jonathan Rowe. 1995. If the GDP is up, why is America down? *Atlantic* 276 (4): 59–78.

Cole, Rosanne, Y. C. Chen, J. A. Barquin-Stolleman, E. Dullberger, N. Helvacian, and J. H. Hodge. 1986. Quality-adjusted price indexes for computer processors and selected peripheral equipment. *Survey of Current Business* 66 (January): 41–50.

Collins, Susan M., and Barry P. Bosworth. 1996. Economic growth in East Asia: Accumulation versus assimilation. *Brookings Papers on Economic Activity,* issue no. 2: 135–91.

Copeland, Morris A. 1937. Concepts of national income. *Studies in Income and Wealth.* Vol. 1, 3–63. New York: National Bureau of Economic Research.

Copeland, Morris A., and E. M. Martin. 1938. The correction of wealth and income estimates for price changes. *Studies in Income and Wealth.* Vol. 2, 85–135. New York: National Bureau of Economic Research.

Davis, Steven J., and John C. Haltiwanger. 1991. Wage dispersion between and

within U.S. manufacturing plants, 1963–86. *Brookings Papers on Economic Activity,* issue no. 1: 115–20.
Denison, Edward F. 1962. *The sources of economic growth in the United States and the alternatives before us.* New York: Committee for Economic Development.
———. 1964. The unimportance of the embodiment question. *American Economic Review* 79 (5): 90–94.
———. 1967. *Why growth rates differ: Postwar experiences in nine western countries.* Washington, D.C.: Brookings Institution.
———. 1972. Some major issues in productivity analysis: An examination of the estimates by Jorgenson and Griliches. *Survey of Current Business* 49 (5, part 2): 1–27.
———. 1979. Explanations of declining productivity growth. *Survey of Current Business* 59 (August): 1–24.
Denny, Michael, Melvyn Fuss, and Leonard Waverman. 1981. The measurement and interpretation of total factor productivity in regulated industries, with an application to Canadian telecommunications. In *Productivity measurement in regulated industries,* ed. T. Cowing and R. Stevenson, 179–218. New York: Academic Press.
Diewert, W. Erwin. 1976. Exact and superlative index numbers. *Journal of Econometrics,* 4:115–45.
———. 1980. Aggregation problems in the measurement of capital. In *The measurement of capital,* ed. Dan Usher, 433–528. Studies in Income and Wealth, vol. 45. Chicago: University of Chicago Press.
Diewert, W. Erwin, and Kevin J. Fox. 1999. Can measurement error explain the productivity paradox? *Canadian Journal of Economics* 32 (April): 251–80.
Domar, Evsey D. 1961. On the measurement of technical change. *Economic Journal* 71:710–29.
———. 1963. Total factor productivity and the quality of capital. *Journal of Political Economy* 71 (December): 586–88.
Dowrick, Steven, and Duc-Tho Nguyen. 1989. OECD comparative economic growth 1950–85: Catch-up and convergence. *American Economic Review* 79 (5): 1010–30.
Easterly, William. 1995. The mystery of growth: Shocks, policies, and surprises in old and new theories of economic growth. *Singapore Economic Review* 40 (1): 3–23.
Färe, Rolf, Shawna Grosskopf, Mary Norris, and Zhongyang Zhang. 1994. Productivity growth, technical progress, and efficiency change in industrialized countries. *American Economic Review* 84 (1): 66–83.
Fisher, Franklin. 1965. Embodied technical change and the existence of an aggregate capital stock. *Review of Economic Studies* 32:326–88.
Gallman, Robert E. 1987. Investment flows and capital stocks: U.S. experience in the 19th century. In *Quantity and quiddity: Essays in U.S. economic history in honor of Stanley Lebergott,* ed. Peter Kilby, 214–54. Middletown, Conn.: Wesleyan University Press.
Gordon, Robert J. 1990. *The measurement of durable goods prices.* Chicago: University of Chicago Press.
Greenwood, Jeremy, Zvi Hercowitz, and Per Krusell. 1997. Long-run implications of investment-specific technical change. *American Economic Review* 87 (3): 342–62.
Griliches, Zvi. 1980. R&D and the productivity slowdown. *American Economic Review* 70 (2): 343–48.

———. 1988. Research expenditures and growth accounting. In *Technology, education, and productivity,* ed. Zvi Griliches, 249–67. New York: Blackwell.
———. 1992. The search for R&D spillovers. *Scandinavian Journal of Economics* 94:29–47.
———. 1994. Productivity, R&D, and the data constraint. *American Economic Review* 84 (1): 1–23.
———. 1996. The discovery of the residual: A historical note. *Journal of Economic Literature* 34 (September): 1324–30.
Griliches, Zvi, and Jacques Mairesse. 1984. Productivity and R&D growth at the firm level. In *R&D, patents, and productivity,* ed. Zvi Griliches, 339–73. Chicago: University of Chicago Press.
Grossman, Gene M., and Elhanan Helpman. 1991. *Innovation and growth in the global economy.* Cambridge, Mass.: MIT Press.
Gullickson, William, and Michael J. Harper. 1999. Possible measurement bias in aggregate productivity growth. *Monthly Labor Review* 122 (2): 47–67.
Hall, Bronwyn H. 1993. Industrial research during the 1980s: Did the rate of return fall? *Brookings Papers on Economic Activity, Microeconomics:* 289–330.
Hall, Robert E. 1968. Technical change and capital from the point of view of the dual. *Review of Economic Studies* 35:34–46.
———. 1988. The relation between price and marginal cost in U.S. industry. *Journal of Political Economy* 96:921–47.
Hall, Robert E., and Dale W. Jorgenson. 1967. Tax policy and investment behavior. *American Economic Review* 57:391–414.
Hicks, John. 1946. *Value and capital.* London: Oxford University Press.
Hulten, Charles R. 1973. Divisia index numbers. *Econometrica* 41:1017–25.
———. 1975. Technical change and the reproducibility of capital. *American Economic Review* 65 (5): 956–65.
———. 1978. Growth accounting with intermediate inputs. *Review of Economic Studies* 45 (October): 511–18.
———. 1979. On the "importance" of productivity change. *American Economic Review* 69:126–36.
———. 1986. Productivity change, capacity utilization and the source of efficiency growth. *Journal of Econometrics* 33:31–50.
———. 1990. The measurement of capital. In *Fifty years of economic measurement,* ed. Ernst R. Berndt and Jack E. Triplett, 119–52. Studies in Income and Wealth, vol. 54. Chicago: University of Chicago Press.
———. 1992a. Accounting for the wealth of nations: The net versus gross output controversy and its ramifications. *Scandinavian Journal of Economics* 94 (supplement): S9–S24.
———. 1992b. Growth accounting when technical change is embodied in capital. *American Economic Review* 82 (4): 964–80.
———. 1996. Quality change in capital goods and its impact on economic growth. NBER Working Paper no. 5569. Cambridge, Mass.: National Bureau of Economic Research, May.
———. 1997. Comment on "Do real output and real wage measures capture reality? The history of lighting suggests not." In *The Economics of New Goods.* Vol. 58, Studies in Income and Wealth, ed. Timothy Bresnahan and Robert J. Gordon, 66–70. Chicago: University of Chicago Press.
———. 2000. Measuring innovation in the New Economy. University of Maryland, Manuscript.
Hulten, Charles R., and Sylaja Srinivasan. 1999. Indian manufacturing industry: Elephant or tiger? NBER Working Paper no. 5569. Cambridge, Mass.: National Bureau of Economic Research, October.

Hulten, Charles R., and Frank C. Wykoff. 1981. The estimation of economic depreciation using vintage asset prices. *Journal of Econometrics* 15:367–96.
Johansen, Leif. 1959. Substitution versus fixed production coefficients in the theory of economic growth: A synthesis. *Econometrica* 27 (April): 157–76.
Jones, Charles I. 1995a. R&D-based models of economic growth. *Journal of Political Economy* 103 (August): 759–84.
———. 1995b. Times series tests of endogenous growth models. *Quarterly Journal of Economics* 110 (2): 495–525.
Jorgenson, Dale W. 1963. Capital theory and investment behavior. *American Economic Review* 53 (2): 247–59.
———. 1966. The embodiment hypothesis. *Journal of Political Economy* 74 (February): 1–17.
Jorgenson, Dale W., Frank M. Gollop, and Barbara M. Fraumeni. 1987. *Productivity and U.S. economic growth*. Cambridge, Mass.: Harvard University Press.
Jorgenson, Dale W., and Zvi Griliches. 1967. The explanation of productivity change. *Review of Economic Studies* 34 (July): 349–83.
———. 1972. Issues in growth accounting: A reply to Edward F. Denison. *Survey of Current Business* 52:65–94.
Jorgenson, Dale W., and Mieko Nishimizu. 1978. U.S. and Japanese economic growth, 1952–1974: An international comparison. *Economic Journal* 88 (December): 707–26.
Jorgenson, Dale W., and Kevin J. Stiroh. 2000. Raising the speed limit: U.S. economic growth in the information age. *Brookings Papers on Economic Activity*, issue no. 2: pp. 125–211.
Kendrick, John. 1961. *Productivity trends in the United States*. New York: National Bureau of Economic Research.
Kim, Jong-Il, and Lawrence J. Lau. 1994. The sources of economic growth of the East Asian newly industrialized countries. *Journal of Japanese and International Economies* 8:235–71.
Koopmans, T. C. 1965. On the concept of optimal economic growth. *Pacifica Academia Scientiarus* (Rome):276–79.
Krugman, Paul. 1994. The myth of Asia's miracle. *Foreign Affairs* 73 (6): 62–77.
Lucas, Robert E., Jr. 1988. On the mechanics of economic development. *Journal of Monetary Economics* 22:3–42.
Maddison, Angus. 1987. Growth and slowdown in advanced capitalist economies: Techniques and quantitative assessment. *Journal of Economic Literature* 25 (2): 649–98.
Nadiri, M. Ishaq. 1970. Some approaches to the theory and measurement of total factor productivity: A survey. *Journal of Economic Literature* 8 (December): 1137–77.
———. 1993. *Innovations and technological spillovers*. NBER Working Paper no. 4423. Cambridge, Mass.: National Bureau of Economic Research, August.
Nadiri, M. Ishaq, and Seongjun Kim. 1996. R&D, production structure, and productivity growth: A comparison of U.S., Japan, and Korean manufacturing sectors. RR no. 96-11, C. V. Starr Center for Applied Economics, New York University, March.
Nelson, Richard R. 1964. Aggregate production functions and medium-range growth projections. *American Economic Review* 54:575–606.
Nordhaus, William D. 1997. Do real output and real wage measures capture reality? The history of lighting suggests not. In *The economics of new goods*, ed. Timothy Bresnahan and Robert J. Gordon, 29–66. Studies in Income and Wealth, vol. 58. Chicago: University of Chicago Press.
Nordhaus, William D., and Edward C. Kokkelenberg, eds. 1999. *Nature's numbers:*

Expanding the national economic accounts to include the environment. Washington, D.C.: National Research Council, National Academy Press.
Oliner, Stephen D., and Daniel E. Sichel. 2000. The resurgence of growth in the late 1990s: Is information technology the story? *Journal of Economic Perspectives,* 14 (4), 3–22.
Prucha, Ingmar R., and M. Ishaq Nadiri. 1981. Endogenous capital utilization and productivity measurement in dynamic factor demand models: Theory and an application to the U.S. electrical machinery industry. *Journal of Econometrics* 15:367–96.
Richter, Marcel K. 1966. Invariance axioms and economic indexes. *Econometrica* 34:739–55.
Romer, Paul M. 1986. Increasing returns and long-run growth. *Journal of Political Economy* 94 (5): 1002–37.
Rymes, Thomas K. 1971. *On concepts of capital and technical change.* Cambridge, Mass.: Cambridge University Press.
Salter, W. E. G. 1960. *Productivity and technical change.* Cambridge: Cambridge University Press.
Solow, Robert M. 1956. A contribution to the theory of economic growth. *Quarterly Journal of Economics* 70 (February): 65–94.
———. 1957. Technical change and the aggregate production function. *Review of Economics and Statistics* 39 (August): 312–20.
———. 1960. Investment and technical progress. In *Mathematical methods in the social sciences 1959,* ed. K. Arrow, S. Karlin, and P. Suppes, 89–104. Stanford: Stanford University Press.
Stigler, George J. 1947. *Trends in output and employment.* New York: National Bureau of Economic Research.
Tinbergen, Jan. 1942. Zur theorie der langfristigen wirtschaftsentwick lung. *Weltwirtschaftliches Archiv* 55 (1): 511–49.
Törnqvist, L. 1936. The Bank of Finland's consumption price index. *Bank of Finland Monthly Bulletin* 10:1–8.
Triplett, Jack E. 1983. Concepts of quality in input and output price measures: A resolution of the user value-resource cost debate. In *The U.S. national income and product accounts: Selected topics,* ed. Murray F. Foss, 296–311. Studies in Income and Wealth, vol. 47. Chicago: University of Chicago Press.
———. 1987. Hedonic functions and hedonic indexes. In *The new Palgrave dictionary of economics,* vol. 2, ed. John Eatwell, Murray Milgate, and Peter Newman, 630–34. New York: Macmillan Press Limited.
———. 1996. Depreciation in production analysis and economic accounts. *Economic Inquiry* 31 (1): 93–115.
U.S. Advisory Commission to Study the Consumer Price Index. 1996. *Toward a more accurate measure of the cost of living.* Final Report to the Senate Finance Committee. 4 December.
U.S. Department of Commerce, Bureau of the Census. 1975. *Historical statistics of the United States, colonial times to 1970.* Washington, D.C.: GPO.
U.S. Department of Labor, Bureau of Labor Statistics. 1983. *Trends in multifactor productivity, 1948–81,* Bulletin 2178. Washington, D.C.: GPO, September.
Weitzman, Martin L. 1976. On the welfare significance of national product in a dynamic economy. *Quarterly Journal of Economics* 90:156–62.
Wolff, Edward N. 1996. The productivity slowdown: The culprit at last? Follow-up on Hulten and Wolff. *American Economic Review* 86 (5): 1239–52.
Young, Alwyn. 1992. A tale of two cities: Factor accumulation and technical change in Hong Kong and Singapore. In *NBER macroeconomics annual*

1992, ed. Olivier Blanchard and Stanley Fischer, 13–53. Cambridge, Mass.: MIT Press.

———. 1995. The tyranny of numbers: Confronting the statistical realities of the East Asian experience. *The Quarterly Journal of Economics* 110 (3): 641–80.

Comment   Jack E. Triplett

Charles R. Hulten has given us what he calls "a biography of an idea." It is, as we expect from Hulten, a valuable biography, a contribution that one would assign to graduate students as an introduction to the productivity literature. My comments amplify some of Hulten's points.

Measuring Productivity and Explaining It

Hulten states as an organizing principle that the productivity paradigm seeks to determine how much economic growth originates from productivity improvement (improvements in technology) and how much from increasing inputs (he says capital inputs, but per capita growth can also increase because of improvements in labor quality). Hulten uses this input-productivity or input-technology dichotomy as an organizing principle not only because it is theoretically appropriate (the theory of capital, for example, provides a framework for thinking about the capital input), but also because the available data and the relevant empirical work are both organized around the same dichotomy.

Useful as this dichotomy is, sometimes it cannot be implemented. One example, discussed in section 1.4, occurs when new technology is embodied in new machinery. A second, related problem is the distinction between innovations that are costly (brought about by investment in R&D, for example), and those that are in some sense or other "costless." I would add another: At the margins, the dichotomy depends on whether a particular innovating activity is paid for, and not just whether the innovation is costly. An anecdote illustrates.

A number of years ago I toured a machine-tool manufacturing plant. This establishment made very high-tech, advanced machine tools, but the factory in which these machines were made had been built in the nineteenth century and was originally water powered. Its manager told me that the employees had always brought the purchased materials in on the ground floor, carried out subassemblies on the second, and completed final assembly on the third floor. As the machines became larger and more complex, it proved ever more difficult to get them down from the third floor. Someone suggested sending the materials to the third floor so final as-

Jack E. Triplett is a visiting fellow at the Brookings Institution.

sembly could take place on the ground, an idea that resulted in an immediate improvement in the plant's productivity.

How does the input-productivity dichotomy deal with such new ideas? Suppose the suggestion had come from a (paid) management consulting firm, and then suppose the contract had called for the consulting firm to be paid the discounted value of the expected stream of marginal cost savings from its suggestion. Then, the change in the plant's productive arrangements would be fully attributed to an input, and we would record no multifactor productivity (MFP).

Suppose, on the other hand, that the suggestion came from an employee and that the company did not pay the employee the full marginal product of the suggestion. Then there is no compensated input. The dichotomy attributes the improvement entirely to MFP.[1]

Few suggestions, I suspect, will be paid for fully, because of uncertainty about their ultimate value if for no other reason. Many real productive improvements bridge, uncomfortably, the input-productivity dichotomy, especially when we try to implement the dichotomy empirically with fairly aggregative data. The example suggests that the conceptual framework that divides economic growth into input growth and MFP—often called "the residual"—carries us only so far, useful as the framework is. Hulten makes related points; I am emphasizing this problem only because others have overlooked it.

The Productivity Slowdown and Mismeasurement
of Economic Variables

Hulten notes, now only in passing, that the "mismeasurement hypothesis" is a very popular one among economists for explaining the post-1973 productivity slowdown. Though the hypothesis may ultimately be confirmed, there is enormous confusion within the profession about the hypothesis. When the mismeasurement hypothesis is properly understood, there is very little evidence in its behalf.

As I have noted elsewhere (Triplett 1997, 1998) the mismeasurement hypothesis is a hypothesis about *differential* mismeasurement. It is a statement that mismeasurement is more severe after 1973 than before.[2]

The evidence most often cited in behalf of the mismeasurement hypothesis consists of findings that some variable or other is currently mismeasured. For example, the Boskin Commission estimated that the Consumer Price Index (CPI) was upwardly biased by about 1.1 percentage points per year in the 1990s.

---

1. If the employee got the idea from some other firm, which, in turn, had paid the management consultant, this case would parallel spillovers from R&D.

2. It is also a statement that the effects of mismeasurement go predominantly in the same direction—that price increases are overstated by mismeasurement, and that growth rates of real variables, especially those of output, are understated.

However, the Boskin Commission provided no evidence that the CPI has been *differentially* mismeasured. For Boskin-type bias to explain the productivity slowdown, the CPI must have been measured more accurately in "the old days," before 1973. Yet, in 1961 the Stigler Committee pointed to almost exactly the same list of CPI defects that were identified by the Boskin Commission, and it recorded a professional consensus that the CPI was upwardly biased *then* (though the Stigler Committee never made a point estimate of the CPI bias). It should be evident that CPI measurement error did not begin in 1973; neither did the defects in the CPI cited by the Boskin Commission commence in the post-1973 period. The Boskin Commission estimate, therefore, does not by itself provide any evidence in favor of the mismeasurement hypothesis.

Indeed, convincing evidence is lacking that a major part of the productivity slowdown has its origins in differential mismeasurement. Differential mismeasurement implies one or more of several things: that statistical agencies are now worse than they used to be at adjusting for quality change and measuring the hard-to-measure services; that the amount of quality change is greater than it used to be; that measuring services is for some reason more difficult than it used to be (perhaps because the nature of services has changed); or that the sectors where mismeasurement exists have become more important than they were before 1973.

Additionally, the mismeasurement hypothesis implies that the measurement changes must have been abrupt because the productivity slowdown was abrupt. Though there is some debate about whether it really started in 1973, or whether signs of it were visible in the United States around 1968, the slowdown was not a gradual reduction in the rate of productivity improvement. If mismeasurement is to account for the productivity slowdown, then we must find some fairly abrupt change in measurement practices, or an abrupt increase in measurement problems, or an abrupt increase in the size of the poorly measured sectors of the economy. There is little evidence on this, but introspection weighs against abruptness in these changes.

Finally, the mismeasurement hypothesis implies measurement changes in many countries, because the productivity slowdown affected most industrialized economies at about the same time and in roughly similar magnitudes. Even if one thought that the U.S. Bureaus of Labor Statistics (source of U.S. price indexes and productivity measures) and Economic Analysis (the compilers of GDP) did things better in the "old days" (which seems implied by the views of some U.S. economists who subscribe to the mismeasurement hypothesis), how could economic statisticians in all countries "forget" in concert?[3]

---

3. I have discussed the evidence on the mismeasurement hypothesis in Triplett (1997, 1998, 1999).

Table 1C.1   Top Computer-Using Industries, 1992 Capital Flow

	Computers ($ millions)	Computers and Peripherals ($ millions)
Financial services	2,270	6,677
Wholesale trade	1,860	4,874
Business services[a]	1,383	3,598
Miscellaneous equipment rental and leasing	1,233	3,200
Communications services	873	2,299
Insurance services	738	1,875
Top four businesses	6,746	18,349
Percentage of top four industries of total	42.6	42.1
Top six industries	8,357	22,523
Percentage of top six industries of total	52.8	51.7

Source: Bonds and Aylor (1998).
[a]Excludes miscellaneous equipment rental and leasing.

I believe that the productivity slowdown is real, that it is not primarily a chimera caused by mismeasurement.

A Different Mismeasurement Story

Mismeasurement in economic statistics exists, however, and it is a problem for understanding productivity and technical change in exactly the portions of our economy—high technology and services—that are its rapidly expanding and dynamic sectors.

Computers are nearly the essence of the technology of our time. Consider where computers go, and where they are most used. Four industrial sectors—financial services, wholesale trade, miscellaneous equipment renting and leasing, and business services—account for more than 40 percent of computer investment in the 1992 capital flow table (Bonds and Aylor 1998). Add in two more sectors—insurance and communications—and the share exceeds 50 percent (see table 1C.1). Only in miscellaneous renting and leasing does the share of computer investment in total equipment investment approach half; these computer-using sectors are not necessarily computer intensive.

These six computer-using industries share several important characteristics. First, they are all services industries, broadly defined.

Second, *measured* productivity in these computer-using industries has been declining. Table 1C.2 presents the available numbers.[4]

---

4. Data in table 1C.2 do not incorporate the revisions to the industry accounts released in mid-2000.

Table 1C.2   **Multifactor Productivity and Labor Productivity, Selected Service Industries**

	Multifactor Productivity		Labor Productivity (GPO per hour)	
	1947–63	1977–93	1960–73	1973–97
Financial services				
Banks (SIC 60, 61)	n.a.	−2.9[a]	0.2	−0.3
Insurance services				
Insurance carriers	n.a.	−2.2	1.9	−0.1
Insurance agents	n.a.	−2.7	0.2	−0.8
Wholesale trade	n.a.	1.3	3.2	2.9
Business services (SIC 73)	n.a.	−0.4[b]	−0.2[c]	−0.4[c]
Communications services	2.5	1.8	5.0	3.9

Sources: Multifactor productivity figures are from Gullickson and Harper (1999). Labor productivity figures are from Triplett and Bosworth (2001).
Note: n.a. = not available.
[a]Also includes holding companies.
[b]Includes miscellaneous repair services (SIC 76).
[c]Also includes professional services (SIC 87).

New MFP estimates for services industries are in a BLS study by Gullickson and Harper (1999). Multifactor productivity is the ratio of gross output to capital and labor inputs. Additionally, value added per hour can be computed from BEA's gross product originating (GPO) series. Statistical information for services industries is often less complete than for the goods-producing sectors, as the "n.a." entries in table 1C.2 indicate.

Even though gross output MFP and value-added labor productivity do not always agree—and indeed, they shouldn't—the general picture for these computer-using services industries is the same, no matter which measure is used: Productivity growth has slowed remarkably since 1973, compared with the earlier postwar years. Additionally, table 1C.2 is filled with negative productivity numbers. In fact, among the computer-intensive services industries, only communications and wholesale trade show upward trends. Negative productivity numbers are always puzzling.

Third, with the possible exception of communications, the outputs of all these computer-intensive services industries are hard to measure.[5] As Zvi Griliches (1994, 1997) has repeatedly emphasized, if we do not know how to measure the output of an industry, then we do not know how to measure its productivity. And if the available productivity numbers, measured as best the statistical agencies can, show negative productivity, per-

---

5. How does one measure the output of banking and finance? This is an old, contentious issue in national accounts (see Triplett 1992 for a summary). A similar controversy concerns the output of the insurance industry. Furthermore, how do we measure the output of business services? For example, what is the output of an economics consulting firm? What is its price index? How would we compute its productivity?

haps the reason is that economic statistics are missing part of the output that these industries produce.

The relevance of this mismeasurement point is underscored by communications, which has positive productivity growth. Communications output is probably measured better than is the output of the computer-using services industries that have negative productivity. For example, even though evidence suggests that new communications products, such as cellular phones (Hausman 1997), do not get into the data fast enough, economic statistics are probably better at measuring telephone calls than consulting services. It may be no coincidence that communications is the computer-intensive industry with the strongest positive productivity growth. Those other negative productivity numbers might be suspicious.

Even if the output of computer-intensive services industries is mismeasured, this is not evidence for mismeasurement of *aggregate* productivity. Most of the output of these computer-using industries is intermediate, not final. By definition, all of business services (except for exports) and all of wholesale trade are intermediate products. Equipment renting and leasing is also largely an intermediate activity (consumer renting is in the retail sector in the old U.S. SIC system, and computer, aircraft, and vehicle leasing are not classified in this industry). Although finance, insurance, and communications contribute to final output in their sales to consumers (and in contributions to net exports),[6] much of their output goes to other business. Roughly two-thirds of communications and half of insurance are intermediate inputs to other industries. Thus, half of computer investment in the United States goes to six industries that primarily produce intermediate output.

The outputs of intermediate products net out in aggregate productivity measures, such as BLS's private nonfarm MFP. If computers are revolutionizing wholesale trade, as anecdotes suggest, their impact on wholesale trade will show up in the aggregate productivity numbers in the downstream industries that consume the output of the wholesale trade sector, mainly retail trade. If U.S. economic statistics measure correctly the price indexes and output of the retail trade sector (and that is a big "if"), then the contribution of computer investment in wholesale trade will already be incorporated into the aggregate productivity numbers, no matter how wholesale trade output is measured. Similarly, the causes of the great expansion of business services in the U.S. economy are not clear; but if business services are doing something to raise aggregate productivity, then their contribution is to the downstream-using industries.[7] Even if productivity growth in these computer-using industries were tremendous, it could not affect aggregate productivity directly, because in aggregate productivity,

---

6. Insurance has negative net exports.
7. Except for exports of business services, which have been growing rapidly.

as in GDP, the contributions of intermediate-producing industries cancel out in the totals.

Having no effect on aggregate productivity numbers does not mean, however, that possible mismeasurement in computer-intensive, intermediate services industries is unimportant. To understand the role of technology in a high-tech economy, to understand the impact of the computer on the U.S. economy, we ought to be looking at the impact of the computer at the industry level, to ask how computers have been contributing to industry growth and productivity, and how those industry growth patterns affect other industries and their uses of resources. At the industry level, however, our economic statistics do not appear adequate to analyze the effect of the computer, because much computer investment goes to sectors of the economy where even the concept of output is not well defined, and the existing measures of output in these computer-using sectors seem questionable. If the output measures and the productivity measures are inadequate, we lack the statistical basis on which to determine the impact of technology on industry performance. For a technological country, that is a great informational lacuna.

I conclude by stating that this is a good paper that deserves wide readership.

References

Bonds, Belinda, and Tim Aylor. 1998. Investment in new structures and equipment in 1992 by using industries. *Survey of Current Business* 78 (12): 26–51.
Griliches, Zvi, ed. 1992. Output measurement in the service sector. Studies in Income and Wealth, vol. 56. 71–108. Chicago: University of Chicago Press.
———. 1994. Productivity, R&D, and the data constraint. *American Economic Review* 84 (1): 1–23.
———. 1997. Paper read at the Simon Kuznets Memorial Lectures, 30 October, at Yale University, New Haven, Connecticut.
Gullickson, William, and Michael J. Harper. 1999. Possible measurement bias in aggregate productivity growth. *Monthly Labor Review* 122 (2): 47–67.
Hausman, Jerry. 1997. Valuing the effect of regulation on new services in telecommunications. *Brookings Papers on Economic Activity, Microeconomics:* 1–38.
Triplett, Jack E. 1992. Banking output. In *The new Palgrave dictionary of money and finance,* vol. 1, ed. Peter Newman, Murray Milgate, and John Eatwell, 143–46. New York: Stockton.
———. 1997. Measuring consumption: The post-1973 slowdown and the research issues. *Review of the Federal Reserve Bank of St. Louis* 79 (3): 9–42.
———. 1998. The mismeasurement hypothesis and the productivity slowdown. Paper presented at *International Conference on Information and Communications Technologies, Employment and Earnings.* 22–23 June, *Sophia Antipolis, France.*
———. 1999. The Solow productivity paradox: What do computers do to productivity? *Canadian Journal of Economics* 32 (2): 309–34.
Triplett, Jack E., and Barry Bosworth. 2001. Productivity in the services sector. In *Services in the International Economy,* ed. Robert M. Stern. Ann Arbor: University of Michigan Press. Forthcoming.

2   The BLS Productivity Measurement Program

Edwin R. Dean and Michael J. Harper

2.1   Introduction

Productivity measurement has long been an important activity of the U.S. Bureau of Labor Statistics (BLS). This program has evolved over the years, stimulated by changes in data availability, by new developments in the economics literature, and by the needs of data users. The program's first major activity was the publication of industry measures. Following the development of the National Income and Product Accounts (NIPA) at the U.S. Department of Commerce, the BLS introduced productivity measures for the aggregate U.S. economy. More recently, BLS has developed measures of multifactor productivity (MFP).

This paper discusses the current status of the BLS program, with emphasis on the data development work done in recent years. By way of background, we first review the status of the BLS program as of the mid-1970s (section 2.2) as well as some important advances in the economics literature that had occurred by that time (section 2.3). The paper then describes the development of MFP measures for the private business and private nonfarm business sectors—these were first published in 1983—as well as recent work to expand and improve these measures (section 2.4). It also describes recent extensions and improvements to measures for the manufacturing sector and for more detailed industries both within and

Edwin R. Dean is former associate commissioner for productivity and technology, Bureau of Labor Statistics, U.S. Department of Labor. He is currently adjunct professor of economics at The George Washington University, Washington, D.C.
Michael J. Harper is chief of the division of productivity research of the Bureau of Labor Statistics.

outside manufacturing (section 2.5). Finally, it provides comments on the potential for further improvements in the measures (section 2.6).

2.2 Background on the Industry and Aggregate Labor Productivity and Cost Measures

2.2.1 The Early BLS Productivity Program

The BLS was calculating productivity data for some industries by the 1920s. These measures compared the number of goods produced to the number of people needed to produce them. The immediate consequence of a productivity improvement can be the displacement of workers. The problem of displacement was the stimulus for the BLS productivity measurement program. According to Goldberg and Moye (1984, 168), "In 1935, the Bureau applied to the WPA for funds to conduct studies of productivity in 50 industries." In 1941, after initial studies were published, Congress appropriated funds for a program of continuing studies of productivity and technology. The BLS focused initially on measures of productivity and unit labor costs for manufacturing industries. The concern about worker displacement affected the methodology selected. It was believed that the preferred weights for aggregating outputs for the computation of an ideal productivity index were labor requirements. Essentially, productivity gains were weighted by the associated job losses.

In addition to publishing measures of productivity, the BLS productivity and technology program prepared qualitative information on technological developments in various industries. According to Goldberg and Moye (1984, 169), these were "for the use of U.S. agencies and those of allied governments." These qualitative reviews were abandoned in 1994 due to budget cuts.

2.2.2 The Development of Aggregate Measures of Labor Productivity and Costs

The Great Depression and World War II each played a role in shaping the NIPAs upon which BLS (1959) would base its aggregate productivity measures. Keynes' description of aggregate demand and Leontief's input-output models became central elements in the NIPAs. As Berndt and Triplett (1990) reminded us, the Conference on Research in Income and Wealth (CRIW) was also an influential part of this process. Using the Accounts, BLS (1959) introduced annual indexes of real product per manhour for the total private economy and for the private nonagricultural economy. (Measures for total manufacturing had been introduced in 1955.) The aggregate measures were developed under the supervision of Jerome A. Mark. Before long, the Bureau was publishing these measures quarterly.

The BLS aggregate output per hour series involved the matching of employment and hours collected in BLS surveys to output measures for selected NIPA sectors. Any difference in coverage can introduce a bias into the productivity trend. In limiting the measures to the total private sector, BLS (1959, 1) recognized that "there is no satisfactory method of measuring the goods and services provided by the government." In part, government output in the NIPAs was measured using data on labor inputs, which implies no productivity change.

Since 1976, BLS has published quarterly indexes of labor productivity, compensation per hour, and unit labor costs for the following sectors: business, nonfarm business, manufacturing (and its durable and nondurable goods–producing subsectors), and nonfinancial corporations.[1] Table 2.1 presents trends in output per hour, unit labor costs, hourly compensation, and real hourly compensation.

The data in table 2.1 indicate that there was a slowdown in productivity after 1973 in all six sectors. Since 1979, output per hour trends have recovered in manufacturing, due mainly to exceptional strength in durable manufacturing. Since 1990, output per hour growth has recovered partially in business and nonfarm business—though rates have remained well below their pace in the pre-1973 period. For nonfinancial corporations, the post-1990 recovery has been complete. Unit labor costs rose sharply after 1973, but since 1990 they have risen more slowly than in the pre-1973 years. Finally, real hourly compensation (compensation per hour deflated by the consumer price index [CPI]) has generally risen more slowly than output per hour, and the difference has been especially large since 1979.

2.3 Advances in Production Theory and Their Implications for Productivity Measurement

2.3.1 Developments in the Economic Literature on Productivity

By the mid-1970s, there was a significant accumulation of research relevant to productivity measurement that had not yet been reflected in government measures. The idea of using production functions as a means of analyzing aggregate economic activity was pioneered by Paul Samuelson (1947). The function, f, reflects the maximum amount of output that can be produced by various combinations of inputs of labor, L, and capital, K, given the technology available at time t:

---

1. In addition to excluding general government, the business sector also excludes the following components of GDP: private households, nonprofit institutions, and the NIPA imputation of the rental value of owner occupied dwellings. Like government, households and institutions are excluded because they are measured with labor inputs. Owner occupied housing is excluded because no corresponding labor hours data are available.

Table 2.1 Measures of Labor Productivity, Unit Labor Costs, Hourly Compensation, and Real Hourly Compensation for Major Sectors

Sector and Measure	Annual Change (%)				
	1947–99	1947–73	1973–79	1979–90	1990–99	1998–99
Business sector						
Output per hour of all persons	2.5	3.3	1.4	1.5	2.0	3.2
Unit labor costs	3.2	2.3	7.7	4.2	1.7	1.8
Hourly compensation	5.8	5.7	9.2	5.7	3.8	5.0
Real hourly compensation	2.0	3.0	1.0	0.6	1.3	2.8
Nonfarm business sector						
Output per hour of all persons	2.2	2.9	1.2	1.3	2.0	3.0
Unit labor costs	3.4	2.5	7.9	4.3	1.7	1.6
Hourly compensation	5.6	5.5	9.2	5.7	3.7	4.7
Real hourly compensation	1.8	2.7	1.0	0.6	1.2	2.6
Manufacturing sector[a]						
Output per hour of all persons	2.8	2.6	2.1	2.6	4.1	6.4
Unit labor costs	2.7	2.7	7.4	3.0	−0.4	−1.4
Hourly compensation	5.6	5.3	9.7	5.6	3.7	5.0
Real hourly compensation	1.8	2.6	1.5	0.5	1.2	2.8

Durable manufacturing sector[a]					
Output per hour of all persons	3.2	2.6	2.1	2.9	5.8	9.6
Unit labor costs	2.3	2.7	7.5	2.6	-2.2	-4.2
Hourly compensation	5.6	5.4	9.7	5.6	3.5	5.0
Real hourly compensation	1.8	2.7	1.4	0.5	1.0	2.9
Nondurable manufacturing sector[a]						
Output per hour of all persons	2.4	2.8	2.1	1.9	2.4	2.5
Unit labor costs	3.1	2.2	7.4	3.9	1.6	2.3
Hourly compensation	5.6	5.0	9.6	5.9	4.0	4.8
Real hourly compensation	1.7	2.3	1.4	0.7	1.5	2.7
Nonfinancial corporate sector[b]						
Output per employee-hour	2.1	2.6	1.2	1.5	2.5	4.0
Unit labor costs	3.3	2.5	7.6	3.9	1.0	0.8
Hourly compensation	5.4	5.2	8.9	5.4	3.5	4.9
Real hourly compensation	1.2	2.2	0.8	0.3	1.1	2.8

[a] Measures begin in 1949.
[b] Measures begin in 1958.

$$Y = f(K, L, t).$$

Robert Solow (1957) used a production function to show the role of capital in labor productivity trends. By assuming a production function and perfect competition in input factor markets, we can calculate the rate at which the production function is shifting:

$$\frac{d \ln f}{dt} = \frac{d \ln Y}{dt} - s_L \frac{d \ln L}{dt} - s_K \frac{d \ln K}{dt},$$

where s_L and s_K are the shares of labor and capital, respectively, in total cost. We call the rate at which the function is shifting the growth rate of MFP; MFP is also referred to as total factor productivity, or the "Solow residual." Solow showed that the rate of growth of labor productivity depends on the growth rate in the capital-labor ratio (weighted by capital's share) and the growth rate of MFP:

$$\frac{d \ln\left(\frac{Y}{L}\right)}{dt} = s_K \frac{d \ln\left(\frac{K}{L}\right)}{dt} + \frac{d \ln f}{dt}.$$

Solow argued that MFP is a better measure of technological change than labor productivity, but he also acknowledged that MFP reflects many other influences, because it is calculated as a residual.

The usefulness of aggregate production models and of aggregate capital stock measures had been debated in the literature during the 1950s. At issue was the validity of assuming that microeconomic relationships applied to aggregate data, as well as the validity of aggregating capital. The literature of the 1960s reflected an effort to build aggregate measures from increasingly detailed data using less restrictive assumptions about aggregation. Evsey Domar (1961) demonstrated how a system of industry and aggregate production functions could be used to compare industry productivity measures to the aggregate measures. A paper by Dale Jorgenson and Zvi Griliches (1967) showed how detailed data could be used to construct a capital aggregate without making strong assumptions about the relative marginal products of dissimilar assets. Also, it was recognized that commonly used index number formulas could introduce bias into the aggregation process. Diewert (1976) showed how production functions could be used as a basis for determining which index number formulas were least restrictive.

In the literature on productivity measurement, the Tornqvist (1936) index is the changing-weight index that has been used most frequently. The Tornqvist index employs as weights an average of the cost shares for the two periods being compared. The index number, X, is computed in logarithmic form:

$$\ln X_t - \ln X_{t-1} = \sum_i [s_i(\ln x_{it} - \ln x_{it-1})],$$

where x_i designates inputs, n inputs $(1 \ldots i \ldots n)$ are being considered, the two time periods are t and $t-1$, and the cost share weights, si, are computed as

$$s_i = \frac{1}{2}\left\{ \left[\frac{c_{it}x_{it}}{\sum_i(c_{it}x_{it})}\right] + \left[\frac{c_{it-1}x_{it-1}}{\sum_i(c_{it-1}x_{it-1})}\right]\right\}.$$

Here c_i is the unit cost of the input. An index number time series is retrieved by "chaining" these logarithmic differences and by using the exponential function.

The literature on the theory of index numbers has shown that the Tornqvist index of inputs has several desirable properties. In particular, Diewert (1976) demonstrated that the Tornqvist index is consistent with the flexible translog production function.

2.3.2 The panel to review productivity statistics

By the mid-1970s it was recognized that productivity growth trends had slowed dramatically. A flurry of research studies aimed at explaining the slowdown. Much of the analysis relied on concepts that went beyond labor productivity. The researchers often had to compile their own data sets to address the specific issues that interested them.

The Committee on National Statistics of the National Academy of Sciences (NAS) appointed a Panel to Review Productivity Statistics. The panel, chaired by Albert Rees, wrote a report (NAS 1979) making twenty-three recommendations to government statistical agencies; many of these recommendations were directed to the BLS productivity measurement program. Among these were that the BLS should develop a "survey of hours at the workplace" (recommendation 8), that BLS should study "the use of weighted labor input measures" (recommendation 9), and that the BLS should "experiment with combining labor and other inputs into alternative measures of multi-factor productivity" (recommendation 15). The report made specific mention of capital, weighted labor, and intermediate purchased inputs for inclusion in the MFP work. Many of the other recommendations were aimed at improving the scope and accuracy of productivity statistics by expanding source data on outputs, prices, and labor.

2.4 The Development of Major Sector Multifactor Productivity Measures

Following the NAS recommendations, BLS launched an intensive effort to develop additional input measures suitable for publication with its productivity measures. This effort was facilitated by additional funding for MFP measurement, provided by Congress beginning in 1982.

2.4.1 The Development of Aggregate Measures of Capital Service Inputs

The first project was to construct capital measures that would be comparable to the output per hour measures for aggregate sectors. Among the issues faced by BLS were what to include in capital and how best to aggregate detailed data on investment by vintage and by asset type.

A review of "the domain of definition of capital" issue in the context of productivity measurement was provided to the CRIW by Diewert (1980). After reviewing precedents, including Christensen and Jorgenson (1969), Denison (1974), and Kendrick (1976), Diewert recommended that capital measures include "structures, land, natural resources, machinery and other durable equipment, and inventory stocks used in the private business sector" (1980, 480–85). Diewert emphasized that the omission of either land or inventories would bias estimates of the contribution of capital to productivity. Financial assets and other intangible assets were excluded, mainly due to unresolved measurement issues.

An important result of production theory is that it is desirable to aggregate capital goods in terms of their marginal products in current production as distinct from the marginal costs of producing the capital goods. This leads to two fundamental steps that have been adopted in the BLS capital work: aggregation of vintages based on "relative efficiency," and aggregation of different types of assets using "rental prices."

The perpetual inventory method (PIM) is used to aggregate a time series of real investment.[2] The PIM involves an assumption about the deterioration of investment goods as they age.[3]

Hall (1968) showed that the rental price is the relevant margin on which to aggregate capital goods of different types. The rental price, c, reflects the price of new capital goods, p, the nominal discount rate, r, the rate of economic depreciation, δ, and the rate at which goods prices appreciate, Δp:

$$c = pr + p\delta - \Delta p.$$

Jorgenson and Griliches (1967) used implicit rental price estimates to aggregate the *services* of assets of different types. Another innovation in aggregation procedures attributable to Jorgenson and Griliches was the use of chained Tornqvist indexes to aggregate capital assets of different types. The growth rate of total capital input, $\Delta \ln K_T$, between successive

---

2. Real investment is created by dividing a nominal investment series by a price index, $p_{a,t}$.
3. The process of deterioration is usually modeled with an age-efficiency schedule. The capital stock is then the sum of weighted past real investments, the weights coming from this schedule.

periods ($t-1$ and t), was computed as a weighted sum over asset types, a, of the growth rates of asset stocks, $\Delta \ln k_a$. The weights were the arithmetic means of the shares, in the two periods, of the implicit "rents" generated by the respective assets in total rents. This procedure led to the following:

$$\Delta \ln K_T = \Sigma_a \Delta d \ln k_a \left\{ \frac{1}{2} \left[\left(\frac{k_{a,t} c_{a,t}}{\Sigma_i k_{i,t} c_{i,t}} \right) + \left(\frac{k_{a,t-1} c_{a,t-1}}{\Sigma_i k_{i,t-1} c_{i,t-1}} \right) \right] \right\}.$$

Most of the data needed to estimate rental prices are readily available. Jorgenson and Griliches estimated the discount rate as an "internal rate of return." This involved assuming that implicit rents in each time period account for the total of "property income," Ψ_t, in each period. Property income was assumed to be the residual derived by subtracting labor costs from nominal value added in the sector under study. Thus they solved for a single, r_t, for each sector, such that

$$\Psi_t = \Sigma_a k_{a,t} c_{a,t} = \Sigma_a k_{a,t} [p_{a,t} r_t + p_{a,t} \delta_a - (p_{a,t} - p_{a,t-1})].$$

Empirically, the main effect of using these techniques is to place relatively larger weights on assets that are depreciating quickly, compared to the weights that would result from a direct aggregation of stocks. The rationale for placing more weight on short-lived assets is the following: Investors must collect more rents on a dollar's worth of short-lived assets to compensate for their higher depreciation costs. Hall and Jorgenson (1967) formulated the rental prices to reflect the effects of tax laws. In the United States, tax laws have tended to favor shorter-lived assets, and account should be taken of this effect in a model that implicitly allocates property income to asset rents.

These and related advances in the literature strongly influenced the BLS approach to capital measurement. The BLS uses Tornqvist aggregation, formulating rental prices with Hall-Jorgenson type tax parameters and a Jorgenson-Griliches type internal rate of return, computed using property income data from the NIPA.

The BLS built its capital measures on earlier work by the Bureau of Economic Analysis (BEA). The BEA had begun measuring capital stocks in the 1960s in an effort to improve the NIPA estimates of capital consumption allowances (CCA). BEA used capital stocks, which were based on historical investment data, to adjust its CCA estimates, which were based on tabulations of business tax returns. The capital stock approach to CCA estimation was deemed preferable because, unlike the tax returns, it used consistent accounting conventions. The BEA capital stock work was reported to the CRIW by Young and Musgrave (1980).

As BLS developed its capital measures, a series of papers were prepared for discussion with other productivity researchers. The first set of capital measures completed was presented by Norsworthy and Harper (1981; henceforth NH).[4] Their approach to coverage, detail, and methods of aggregation was fairly similar to the study by Christensen and Jorgenson (1970).

The NH study went on to address the issue of aggregation of stocks of assets of different types. In this area, the study closely followed the procedures of Jorgenson and Griliches (1967) described earlier. Implicit rental prices were estimated for each of five asset types, and these were used to construct chained Tornqvist indexes of capital inputs. The resulting capital input measures grew about 0.2 percent per year faster than comparable "directly aggregated" capital stocks.

The same capital measures were used in a broader study of factors affecting productivity by Norsworthy, Harper and Kunze (1979; henceforth NHK). This paper contained a discussion of the issue of vintage aggregation. The available options were to use either the BEA gross or net stocks of capital. The BEA gross stocks assumed there were discards, but no depreciation; the BEA net stocks assumed there was straight line depreciation. Denison (1974) had used a 3:1 weighted average of gross and net stocks in his growth accounting work.[5]

NHK extended the scope of the MFP analysis beyond capital to look at other quantifiable influences on productivity. These included the effects of changing labor composition (to be discussed shortly), the effects of expenditures on pollution abatement equipment, and the effects of cyclical factors. NHK presented the MFP measures in terms of an equation similar to the one used by Solow (1957). This equation, which was derived from a production function, helps explain the differences between labor productivity and MFP. If y, l, k, and a are the growth rates of output, labor, capital, and MFP respectively, then

$$(y - l) = a + s_k(k - l)$$

---

4. This work was first reported in a January 1979 BLS working paper. The NH study worked with BEA net capital stock measures for three major subsectors of the private business sector: manufacturing, farm, and nonfarm-nonmanufacturing. For each sector, NH obtained BEA stocks of nonresidential structures and equipment and of residential capital owned and rented by private businesses. (Rented residential capital was included to ensure that the domain of the capital measures matched the data on labor hours and outputs used in the study.) The NH study also made estimates of inventories and land. The five asset categories included in the estimates (structures, equipment, rented residential capital, inventories, and land) were fairly close to the domain of capital measures recommended by Diewert for productivity work. The present BLS measures still cover this same domain.

5. The NH and NHK studies elected to use the BEA net stocks, although it was noted that "there is evidence that the net capital stock understates and the gross stock overstates real capital input" (NHK, 399).

where s_k is the share of capital income in the nominal value of output. Thus, labor productivity grows because of "shifts in the production function," a, and also because of increases in capital intensity. The NHK paper presented tables that illustrated this equation. BLS (2000) has continued to present its long-term MFP trends using tables like these (to be discussed later in this section, table 2.4).

2.4.2 The First Measures of Capital Formally Published by BLS: New Asset-Type Detail and New Assumptions about Vintage Aggregation

Soon after the MFP work was funded, BLS 1983 issued a formal publication presenting new BLS data series on MFP. This publication presented series on output per unit of combined labor and capital inputs for private business, private nonfarm business, and manufacturing. This work was summarized by Jerome Mark and William Waldorf (1983), who directed the project. Although similar in coverage and technique to the NHK study, this first formal publication of MFP numbers reflected more-detailed data work than had been done for the earlier research.

Rather than simply use the BEA net stocks of equipment and structures, BLS (1983) applied the rental price and Tornqvist aggregation techniques to more detailed categories of asset types.[6] In its estimation of capital consumption allowances, BEA had recognized that it is important to take account of changes in the mix of assets, because there is wide variation in the useful lives of assets. BLS recognized that the rental prices implied by different service lives would be quite different, and so the use of rental prices in aggregation from this amount of detail had the potential to reveal an important new dimension of capital composition change. It did indeed, as the new capital services input measure grew 0.8 percent per year faster than a corresponding directly aggregated capital stock! The comparable figure in the NH study, when only the five broad classes were used, was 0.2 percent. Thus, by applying the rental price and Tornqvist index techniques to the greater asset detail, changing capital composition contributed four times as much as it had when only the five broad asset classes had been considered.

The published BLS (1983) work, unlike earlier work by BLS researchers, did not make use of the BEA net stocks. With the cooperation of BEA, BLS obtained the asset-type detail underlying the BEA investment totals. Rather than use net stocks, BLS ran its own PIM calculations of stocks for detailed asset types. Harper (1983) had examined the issue of what to

---

6. BEA derived its net stock of equipment by adding together stock estimates for about twenty detailed types of assets. Similarly, BEA made separate stock estimates for fourteen types of nonresidential structures and ten categories of residential assets, each with its own service life.

assume about the way that weights for investments decline as assets age. As mentioned earlier, it was clear from the literature that the appropriate weights for vintage aggregation would reflect the relative marginal products of the capital goods.

This posed a dilemma because, although there was some evidence on economic depreciation of sales prices, the BLS researchers could find only limited empirical evidence on the deterioration of capital services as a function of age. The mileage that trucks were driven declined only gradually during the first few years of their service lives, and then more rapidly later.[7] BLS also consulted with people on its business and labor research advisory committees for their insights into patterns of deterioration. BLS adopted "age-efficiency" functions which declined gradually during the first few years of an asset's life and then more rapidly as the asset aged. BLS used a "hyperbolic" formula to represent the services, s_τ, of a τ-year-old asset:

$$s_\tau = \frac{L - \tau}{L - \beta\tau} \quad \text{for } \tau < L,$$

$$s_\tau = 0 \quad \text{for } \tau < L,$$

where L is the asset's service life and β is a shape parameter. For $\beta = 1$, this formula yields a gross stock. For $\beta = 0$, it yields a straight-line deterioration pattern. For $0 < \beta < 1$, the function declines slowly at first, and then more quickly later. BLS assumed $\beta = 0.5$ for equipment and $\beta = 0.75$ for structures. The formula was implemented assuming BEA's service-life estimates and assuming a discard process similar to the one used by BEA.[8]

2.4.3 Reformulation of Capital Measures at the Two-Digit Industry Level

Since their introduction, BLS capital measures have undergone several improvements, including reformulation at about the two-digit industry level. BEA completed a major data development project, reported by Gorman et al. (1985), to make investment data available for two-digit NIPA industries.[9] BLS began work to apply the rental price and Tornqvist aggregation techniques to detailed asset-type data at the two-digit industry level. In this work, the nominal rate of return, r, was computed as a single

---

7. In addition, Ball and Harper (1990) studied cows as a capital asset in conjunction with measures of MFP being developed by the U.S. Department of Agriculture. They found that the output of a cow actually increases between the first and second years of her "service life."

8. With these assumptions, the BLS stocks were bounded by BEA's gross and net stocks. The BLS approach is effectively quite similar to that of Denison (1974).

9. This study made use of capital flow tables, developed as part of the BEA input-output work, to allocate industry investment control totals to approximately the same asset-type detail that had been available earlier at the sectoral level. The control totals were based on the BEA plant and equipment survey and quinquennial economic censuses with adjustments for NIPA conventions.

Table 2.2 Early Experimental Rental Prices for Miscellaneous Manufacturing Industries

	Rental Price
1971	0.2997
1972	0.3518
1973	0.5535
1974	−0.4473
1975	0.1898
1976	0.3425
1977	0.4006
1978	0.6294
1979	2.0676
1980	1.2731
1981	0.4075

rate of return within each two-digit industry. This work made it possible to develop two-digit level measures of capital and MFP. After an initial set of calculations, it was discovered that rental prices for some asset types in some two-digit industries were quite volatile from one year to the next. The problems appeared to be linked to large variations in the revaluation terms, $\Delta p_a = p_{a,t} - p_{a,t-1}$, of the rental price equations. The problems were most serious from the middle 1970s to the early 1980s, a period when inflation rates accelerated. Some rental prices were even negative. As an example, rental prices were experimentally calculated by BLS in 1986 for metalworking machinery in miscellaneous manufacturing industries. These prices, based on the new data and the earlier methodology, are presented in table 2.2. The volatility of individual asset rental prices led to instability of the shares in the Tornqvist aggregation of capital assets within some industries. This, in turn, led to some erratic movements in the aggregate index of capital inputs for these industries.

A research project was initiated to determine why the model did not work properly under these circumstances. Harper, Berndt, and Wood (1989, 336; hereafter HBW) pointed out that the implicit rental-price formula is "based on the assumed correspondence between the purchase price of an asset and the discounted value of all future capital services derived from that asset." Because the discounted value is dependent on the future, it is a function of investors' expectations. Changing expectations could account for the observed variations in the revaluation terms, $p_{a,t} - p_{a,t-1}$. HBW noted that theory provides no guidance on how best to measure either expected revaluation, (Δp_a), or the discount rate, r. HBW then described various alternative means that had been used in the literature to estimate the rates of return and revaluation.

Following the recommendations of HBW, BLS decided to use a three-year moving average of prices, $(p_{a,t} - p_{a,t-3})/3$, to estimate expected revaluation. BLS also decided to continue to calculate internal rates of return, except for a few instances in which the problem of volatile rental prices remained.[10]

2.4.4 Empirical Evidence on Deterioration and Depreciation

While the BLS (1983) had adopted a hyperbolic formula to represent the capital decay process, it had used the service life estimates developed by BEA. However, there was very little evidence in the literature on service lives, rates of decay, or economic depreciation rates. There was some evidence on the economic depreciation of structures developed by Hulten and Wykoff (1981), but relatively little on equipment. BLS began an effort to find additional evidence. As part of that effort, Berndt and Wood (1984) examined data on automobile depreciation, and Hulten, Robertson, and Wykoff (1989) examined machine tools prices.

Evidence has continued to accumulate.[11] At a CRIW workshop on capital stock measurement, Triplett (1992) recommended that U.S. government agencies use the evidence already available while putting a priority on gathering additional evidence. BEA developed a plan for revising its service life estimates and depreciation measures. The available evidence was evaluated by Barbara Fraumeni (1997) and used by Arnold Katz and Shelby Herman (1997) to recalculate the BEA capital stocks. Rather than assume straight-line depreciation, BEA now assumes geometric depreciation of most asset types in computing its net stocks.

Detailed data associated with this new BEA work became available by September 1997. Using these data, BLS (1998) reestimated the two-digit capital input measures by type of asset. Because the productivity measures require a model of the deterioration of efficiency with age rather than one of economic depreciation, BLS continues to use its hyperbolic age-efficiency formula. However, BLS did adopt new service lives, based on the new information on depreciation published by BEA.

2.4.5 Changes in the Composition of the Labor Force and Its Effects on Productivity

The labor input data used in many studies of productivity are direct aggregates of hours worked or hours paid. However, worker skills are heterogenous and so some hours contribute more to economic production than do others. Hence, changes in the composition of the labor force can

---

10. In these cases, property income estimates in the NIPA were so low in some years that rates of return were negative. For these cases, BLS decided to assume a 3.5 percent rate of return on all assets, while deducting nothing for expected revaluation. The result is that BLS effectively assumes a 3.5 percent "real" rate of return for industries for which the three-year moving average fails.

11. For example, Ellen Dulberger (1989) and Stephen Oliner (1993) have studied depreciation of computers and their components.

account for part of output growth. For many years, Dale Jorgenson and his colleagues, and (using a different approach) Edward Denison, prepared estimates of the impact on output of changes in the composition of the labor force.[12] After considerable study, BLS researchers developed their own approach to this problem, culminating in a bulletin, *Labor Composition and U.S. Productivity Growth, 1948–90* (BLS 1993). This introduced a methodology for measuring labor composition change. Since 1993, the BLS major sector MFP data have been measured net of the effects of changes in labor force composition.

The BLS approach can be described, very broadly, along the following lines. The approach builds on the insight that each worker possesses a unique set of skills that are matched in varying degrees to a firm's needs. Labor hours are differentiated to take account of some of the primary differences in skills among workers, in particular those skill differences that can be captured by differences in years of schooling and work experience. The methods developed to measure these skill differentials make use of the assumption, fundamental for productivity analysis, that factor inputs are paid the values of their marginal products. Within this framework, labor input is defined as a weighted average of the growth rates of groups of hours, and the groups of hours are defined by reference to specific levels of education and experience. Because labor input is inclusive of labor composition changes, the BLS measures of labor productivity and MFP can be related directly to these compositional changes.

One major task faced by the BLS researchers was to determine which worker characteristics reflect underlying skill differences. In developing the theory of human capital, Becker and Mincer (e.g., Becker 1975) examined the roles of education and on-the-job training in the acquisition of skills and earnings, with skills being the ultimate source of worker productivity. Education and training are the means of acquiring additional skills beyond innate abilities, and the economic incentives to invest in skills yield a direct relationship between earnings and education/training. However, data on training are rarely available in the form required by a macroeconomic productivity measurement effort, so on-the-job training is not a practical basis for differentiating workers. Mincer (1974) attacked this problem by developing a wage model that related training investments to the length of work experience.

The BLS methodology took advantage of Mincer's model by developing time series on work experience and relating these data to other human capital variables. The BLS study cross-classifies hours of work by education and work experience for each sex. The choice of work experience, instead of commonly used variables such as age or the number of

---

12. Among the many studies of this impact by these two sets of researchers were Jorgenson, Gollop, and Fraumeni (1987) and Denison (1985).

years since leaving school, is dictated by the close relationship between work experience and the amount of time that a worker can learn through working.

The BLS approach to these issues was developed not only by the examination of human capital theory and its implications for productivity measurement, but also by a close study of previous productivity research related to the measurement of labor input. Dale Jorgenson, Frank Gollop, and Barbara Fraumeni (1987; hereafter JGF) disaggregated the labor input of all employed persons into cells, cross-classified by several characteristics of labor and by several dimensions of the structure of the economy. Further, Edward Denison (1985) provided data on the contribution to changes in output of each of several pertinent characteristics of labor. In both cases, information on the earnings of labor—fundamentally, information on the prices of the different types of labor—was used to provide weights for combining heterogenous labor inputs.[13] This use of earnings data reflects the common assumption that earnings of different types of labor reflect their respective marginal value products. One unique aspect of the BLS study was to develop labor market prices for each characteristic rather than to use average earnings data for bundles of traits.[14]

The labor composition series was introduced in a BLS (1993) bulletin, prepared mainly by Larry Rosenblum. This followed earlier work by Kent Kunze [1979]; William Waldorf, Kunze, Rosenblum, and Michael Tannen (1986); Edwin Dean, Kunze, and Rosenblum (1988); and Rosenblum, Dean, Mary Jablonski, and Kunze (1990).

2.4.6 The Construction of the BLS Labor Composition Series

To implement the methodology just described, estimates of the prices of each relevant type of labor are obtained from annually fitted hourly earnings functions. BLS then accepts the coefficients for schooling and experience as good approximate measures of the contribution of the skills associated with schooling and experience to both earnings and worker productivity.

The wage model is specified as

$$\ln(W_{ijk}) = a + bS_i + cX_j - dX_j^2 + fZ_k$$

The log of the wage, W_{ijk}, is a function of i years of schooling, S; j years of experience, X; and the kth bundle of other traits, Z. In line with the JGF approach and much of the human-capital literature, separate equations are estimated for men and women. In this equation, the parameters b, c, and

---

13. The BLS methodology includes the aggregation of different types of labor using Tornqvist indexes, consistent with the procedure introduced by Jorgenson and his colleagues. This aggregation approach is consistent with production theory and permits the incorporation of worker heterogeneity by modelling differences in workers' marginal products.

14. For a discussion of similarities and differences between the BLS approach and the approaches of JGF and Denison, see appendices F and A of BLS (1993).

d measure the roles of education and experience in determining wages for men and women. First- and second-order experience terms are included to capture the observed parabolic pattern of earnings with experience. Although the full equation is estimated, only the differences in earnings by education and experience are used directly to estimate changes in labor composition. However, the average effect over all other characteristics, $\overline{Z}$, is added to the intercept.[15]

To estimate the wage equations, hourly earnings are constructed from data available in the March supplement to the Current Population Survey (along with information from the decennial censuses for years before 1967). The education variable is defined for seven schooling groups, with zero through four years of schooling as the lowest schooling group and seventeen years or more as the highest.

Labor-force experience in this equation is not the commonly used "potential experience"—that is, age minus years of schooling minus 6. Instead, actual quarters of work experience are estimated. The estimating equations make use of actual quarters of work experience reported to the Social Security Administration.[16] Although the amount of work experience assigned to each type of worker does not change over time, shifts in the distribution of workers among categories do occur annually, allowing for changes in the average amount of work experience.

Table 2.3 shows estimated average annual growth rates of labor input, hours, and labor composition change for the private non-farm business sector. Growth rates for total labor input are produced by combining the changes in hours and labor composition.

Several results of this computation of labor input are noteworthy. First, because labor input rose more rapidly than did the direct aggregate of hours, there is a decrease in the estimated growth rate of MFP. Increases in skills, as measured by the labor composition shifts, led to faster labor input growth and slower MFP growth.[17]

---

15. For a full discussion of the estimating equation used, see appendices A and E of BLS (1993).

16. Estimated work experience is developed as a function of potential experience, a set of schooling dummy variables, the interaction of potential experience and schooling variables, other work experience variables, and selected demographic variables. For women, the estimating equations make use of number of children and marital status. The experience equation was estimated using detailed information for 1973 from an exact-match file linking Social Security data with Current Population Survey and Internal Revenue Service records. For each type of worker, the coefficients from the 1973 equation are used to estimate work experience. To implement the equation, it was necessary to construct annual matrices of hours worked by each age-experience-sex group. These matrices have 504 cells for men and 4,032 cells for women.

17. Note, however, that the contributions of labor composition change are smaller than the figures presented in table 2.3. The calculation of this contribution must take into account an estimate of the elasticity of output with respect to labor input; the best estimate of this elasticity is provided by labor's share of input, roughly two-thirds at the macro level. For further information on the contribution of labor composition change, see tables 2.4 and 2.5 and the accompanying text.

Table 2.3 Labor Input, Hours, and Labor Composition Change in Private Nonfarm Business, Average Annual Growth Rates for Selected Time Periods, 1948–98

Year	Labor Input	Hours of All Persons	Labor Composition
1948–98	1.8	1.5	0.3
1948–73	1.5	1.2	0.2
1973–98	2.1	1.7	0.4
1973–79	2.0	1.9	0.0
1979–90	2.1	1.6	0.5
1990–98	2.3	1.7	0.6

Note: Hours of all persons plus labor composition may not sum to labor input due to rounding.

A second noteworthy result is that between 1962 and 1979, the growth rate of labor composition declined to zero. This period coincided with both the entrance of the baby boom generation into the labor market and the rapidly rising labor participation rates for women. This decline contributed to the post-1973 slowdown in overall growth in output per hour.

A third important result is that the growth rate of labor composition change increased after 1979 and, for the first time, is about one-third as large as the growth in the direct aggregate of hours worked, in the private non-farm business sector.

A fourth result is not shown in table 2.3, but is presented in the bulletin that introduced these data. The researchers who undertook the labor composition study attempted to find a method for determining the contribution of the separate workforce traits—education, experience, and gender—to the overall trend in labor composition. The research concluded that exact measures of the separate traits would require a set of highly unlikely assumptions. Among other problems, an hour of work must be divisible into separate service flows for each trait. Consequently, no study of labor composition change is likely to produce an exact decomposition.[18]

Recently, Linda Moeller (1999) completed a study aimed at updating the experience equation using the Survey of Income and Program Participation (SIPP). BLS plans to integrate this work into its procedures for measuring labor composition.

---

18. See BLS (1993, Appendix H) and Rosenblum et al. (1990). Nonetheless, Rosenblum and his colleagues attempted to provide plausible estimates of the separate contributions of the various traits, by making heroic assumptions within the framework of the BLS labor composition model (BLS 1993, appendix H). Two of the results of this exercise can be described as follows. First, it appeared that the long-term increasing trend in labor composition was due predominantly to rising educational levels. Second, the turning points in labor composition trends between subperiods (such as the increased growth after 1979) were apparently due to changes in work experience.

2.4.7 Hours at Work

The actual input of labor into the production process is more closely approximated by hours at work than by hours paid. Yet the Current Establishment Survey, the main source of the hours data used in the BLS productivity program, is collected as hours paid. The NAS panel (1979, 125) recognized that this situation was unsatisfactory.

The BLS's Hours at Work Survey[19] has been used to convert the paid hours of nonagricultural production and nonsupervisory employees to an hours-at-work basis. This work is described by Jablonski, Kunze, and Otto (1990) and in BLS (1997). Hours at work exclude all forms of paid leave, but include paid time for travel between job sites, coffee breaks, and machine downtime. Hence, labor productivity in the BLS major sector work is essentially measured as the ratio of output to hours at work. Labor input in the MFP major sector series and the KLEMS manufacturing series (the acronym is explained in section 2.5.1) is also measured as hours at work.

2.4.8 Fisher Indexes for Output in Major Sectors

Earlier, this paper examined the introduction of superlative indexes into the BLS multifactor productivity measures in 1983. However, until February 1996, BLS used the BEA constant-dollar output data for its major sector productivity series.

In 1992, the BEA first introduced two new indexes of real GDP and its major components, both based on the Fisher index method, as alternatives to its constant-dollar indexes. One of these two new indexes was presented in annually chained form—the chain-type annual-weighted index. In 1996, BEA adopted the chain-type annual-weighted series as its featured measure for GDP and its major components, and BLS incorporated this type of output measure into its major sector labor-productivity series.[20]

2.4.9 Trends in Major Sector Multifactor Productivity

BLS updates the MFP study about once a year. The aim of this work is to examine some of the sources of economic growth. Table 2.4 shows the results through 1998. The trend in output per hour is attributable to growth in capital intensity (as in Solow's equation, which we discussed earlier), labor composition, and MFP. In addition, effects of expenditures

---

19. This survey of about 5,500 establishments has collected annual ratios of hours at work to hours paid since 1981. Ratios are developed for each two-digit SIC industry within manufacturing and for each one-digit industry outside manufacturing. Unpublished data and other survey information have been used to extend the annual ratios back to 1947 as well as to develop ratios for nonproduction and supervisory workers.

20. This means that all input indexes and most output indexes used in the BLS productivity measurement program are Törnqvist indexes, while some output indexes are Fisher indexes. This difference is not regarded as significant. For further discussion, see Dean, Harper, and Sherwood (1996); Dean, Harper, and Otto (1995); and Gullickson (1995).

Table 2.4 Compound Average Annual Rates of Growth in Output per Hour of All Persons, the Contributions of Capital Intensity, Labor Composition, and MFP, by Major Sector, 1948–98 and Subperiods

Item	1948–98	1948–73	1973–79	1979–90	1990–98[a]
Private business[b]					
Output per hour of all persons	2.5	3.3	1.3	1.6	1.9
Contribution of capital intensity[c]	0.8	1.0	0.7	0.7	0.6
Contribution of labor composition[d]	0.2	0.2	0.0	0.3	0.4
Multifactor productivity[e]	1.4	2.1	0.6	0.5	0.9
Private nonfarm business[b]					
Output per hour of all persons	2.2	2.9	1.2	1.4	1.8
Contribution of capital intensity[c]	0.8	0.9	0.7	0.8	0.6
Contribution of labor composition[d]	0.2	0.2	0.0	0.3	0.4
Multifactor productivity[e]	1.2	1.9	0.4	0.3	0.9
Contribution of R&D to MFP	0.2	0.2	0.1	0.2	0.2

Note: The sum of MFP and the contributions may not equal labor productivity due to independent rounding.

[a]Because 1990–98 is not a completed business cycle, comparison of trends with earlier periods may be misleading.
[b]Excludes government enterprises.
[c]Growth rate in capital services per hour × capital's share of current dollar costs.
[d]Growth rate of labor composition (the growth rate of labor input less the growth rate of hours of all persons) × labor's share of current dollar costs.
[e]Output per unit of combined labor and capital inputs.

on research and development are estimated using methods published by BLS (1989) based on work by Leo Sveikauskas (1986).

The post-1973 productivity slowdown is clearly evident in table 2.4. A slowdown in capital intensity made a modest contribution to the labor productivity slowdown. While labor composition effects contributed 0.2 to the slowdown during the 1973–1979 period, these effects have actually boosted labor productivity since 1979. The dominant source of the slowdown, however, is MFP. Since MFP is calculated as a residual and reflects many factors, the major factors underlying the slowdown are not evident in the BLS measurement model. The causes of the slowdown have been the subject of intensive investigation.

As we have seen, the BLS procedures involve a number of elements designed to ensure consistency of the measures with production theory. These involve aggregating labor, capital, and output from detailed data using value share weights and superlative index numbers. In table 2.5 we compare the BLS "production theory" measures (bold print) to alternatives based on more traditional measurement techniques. (Note that table

2.5 is reproduced from Dean, Harper, and Sherwood 1996 and does not contain the latest BLS data. It is not feasible to update some of the results in this table.) Since 1979, production theory based MFP has grown very little. Although MFP itself is not a traditional measure, if it were put together from output, labor, and capital data that were measured using traditional techniques, we would find MFP growing 0.8 percent per year from 1979 through 1990 and 1.8 percent during the period 1990–1994.

2.5 Industry Productivity Work

BLS found guidance for its work on aggregate capital measurement and labor composition measurement in the economics literature. The literature provides additional guidance on industry productivity measurement and on the issue of comparing industry and aggregate productivity measures.

Table 2.5 Output and Inputs: Measures Based on Production Theory Compared to Traditional Measures

	1948–73	1973–79	1979–90	1990–94
Output				
Production theory	**4.1**	**2.9**	**2.6**	**2.1**
Traditional (constant 87$)	3.8	2.4	2.7	2.9
Difference	0.3	0.5	−0.1	−0.8
Less weighted labor input[a]				
Production theory	**1.0**	**1.4**	**1.5**	**1.2**
Traditional	0.8	1.4	1.1	0.6
Difference	0.2	0.0	0.4	0.6
Effects of education	0.2	0.3	0.3	0.4
Effects of experience	−0.1	−0.3	0.1	0.2
Other effects	0.0	0.0	0.0	0.0
Less weighted capital input[a]				
Production theory	**1.2**	**1.2**	**1.2**	**0.6**
Traditional	0.9	0.9	0.9	0.5
Difference	0.3	0.3	0.3	0.1
Multifactor productivity				
Production theory	**1.9**	**0.3**	**0.0**	**0.3**
Traditional[b]	2.1	0.1	0.8	1.8
Difference	−0.2	0.2	−0.8	−1.5

Source: Dean, Harper, and Sherwood 1996.

Notes: Estimation of MFP growth in the private nonfarm business sector. The "private nonfarm business" sector excludes government enterprises, while these enterprises are included in the "nonfarm business" sector. Note also that the sums presented in this table may not equal the totals due to rounding.

[a] For each pair of successive years, the growth rate of each input is multiplied by that input's average share in the value of output for the two years. The data reported are averages of this result over the time period.

[b] The MFP trend based on production theory minus the "difference" associated with output plus the sum of the two "differences" associated with labor and capital.

This literature stresses the importance of taking account of the goods and services sold by one industry to another. These transactions are included in gross output measures. In computing MFP, these intermediate transactions should be reflected in input measures. Estimates of real value-added output treat the issue of intermediates in a restrictive way. The literature also stresses the importance of using nonrestrictive index number formulas at the industry level.

In this section we discuss the development of measures of MFP for the manufacturing sector and its two-digit level subsectors. We then describe recent improvements in the BLS program to measure labor productivity and MFP for more detailed industries.

2.5.1 Expansion of Multifactor Productivity Measures for Manufacturing to Include Intermediate Inputs

The NAS (1979) report recommended that BLS produce measures of intermediate inputs, as well as capital and labor inputs. Frank Gollop, in one section of the NAS report (Gollop 1979) and in a subsequent revised treatment of the same issues (Gollop 1981), discussed the role of intermediate inputs in the measurement of MFP. The correct treatment of MFP varies depending on whether the MFP measurement task is at a highly aggregate level or at the level of detailed industries. At a highly aggregate level, the analyst's interest may appropriately be focused on final product. This is because gross domestic product excludes intermediate inputs in order to avoid double counting. Aggregate production functions, including the work of Solow (1957) on productivity, described the entire economy and so included measures of final product.

For industry-level work, however, Gollop and others explained that it was a mistake to ignore intermediate inputs—those purchased from other industries. A different concept of output is also appropriate. Gross outputs, defined as total shipments adjusted for inventory change, should be compared to measures of labor, capital, and intermediate input. This approach was implemented by Berndt and Wood (1975) when they used Census of Manufactures data to estimate MFP for two-digit manufacturing industries.

As with capital measurement, the BLS work on manufacturing proceeded in several stages. In BLS (1983), measures of manufacturing MFP compared net outputs to labor and capital inputs. Data from the NIPA on real "gross product originating" (GPO) in manufacturing were used to measure net output. GPO data are net in the sense that intermediate inputs are subtracted from gross output. In concept, they are closely akin to value added.

At the same time, BLS was experimenting with a data set for total manufacturing that compared gross output to capital, labor, energy, and materials. Such data were used in research by Norsworthy and Harper (1981) and by Norsworthy and Malmquist (1983).

When capital measurement at the two-digit industry level became feasible, BLS began work on an MFP series for two-digit manufacturing industries that included intermediate inputs. In building these measures, BLS made use of definitions proposed by Domar (1961). Domar had used production functions to develop a structure for relating industry and aggregate MFP measures. The key was to define the output of any industry or sector to include intermediate products it ships *to other sectors* while defining inputs to include intermediates purchased *from other sectors.* At the same time, intermediate transactions occurring between establishments within the industry or sector were to be excluded from both outputs and inputs. Gollop (1979) referred to measures conforming to these definitions as "sectoral" outputs and inputs and recommended that BLS use them.[21]

A new BLS data set on MFP for manufacturing and two-digit manufacturing industries compared sectoral outputs to inputs of capital and labor as well as to three categories of intermediate inputs: energy, nonenergy materials, and purchased business services. More or less borrowing letters from each input, BLS refers to these as KLEMS measures.[22] In a 1986 conference paper, Harper and Gullickson discussed the interpretation of trends in these input series for manufacturing and manufacturing industries, cautioning that changes in factor proportions were linked, in theory, to changes in relative factor prices. MFP measures from this data set were formally presented as new BLS measures in Gullickson and Harper (1987). More recently, BLS (1996) began publishing the new KLEMS MFP measures for total manufacturing in place of the initial comparisons of GPO to capital and labor inputs. In addition, the annual "sectoral output" series has replaced BEA's "gross product originating" as the basis for annual movements in output for the output per hour measures for manufacturing that BLS publishes each quarter.[23] These changes in the quarterly series were described by Dean, Harper, and Otto (1995).

2.5.2 Improvements in the Productivity Measurement Program for Detailed Industries

For many years, BLS has developed, maintained, and published industry productivity measures at the three- and four-digit industry level. The

---

21. This approach had been used in many studies by Jorgenson and his associates, such as Jorgenson, Gollop, and Fraumeni (1987).
22. Sectoral output was based on four-digit level shipment data from the Census of Manufactures. Shipments were adjusted for inventory changes and for the exclusion of "intrasectoral" flows of intermediates, then deflated with price indexes. A Tornqvist index of five types of fuels was derived from data from the U.S. Department of Energy. The annual series on nonenergy materials and services were derived from data from the BLS Office of Employment Projections. These, in turn, were based on BEA's benchmark input-output tables. Deflation was accomplished with NIPA price indexes.
23. The Industrial Production Indexes of the Federal Reserve Board are still used to estimate quarterly movements in this series.

literature cited previously in the discussion of improvements in the data series for major sector and two-digit manufacturing industry measures has also been examined for its implications for these detailed industry data. In particular, the work of Solow, Domar, Jorgenson, and Diewert suggests that particular methods are appropriate to the development of such measures. This work suggests (1) the use of the sectoral output concept in developing MFP series; (2) aggregation from detailed product information using superlative indexes, such as the Tornqvist index; and (3) development of major sector productivity measures by aggregation of industry input and output data.

2.5.3 Implementation of the Improvements

As of the mid-1970s, the BLS industry measurement program could be described along the following lines. Output indexes were calculated by a fixed weight formula, with the weights changed (in most cases) every five years. Production indexes for detailed types of output were produced by one of two methods. The indexes in most industries were computed from information on physical quantities produced. In other industries, time series on nominal output data for detailed types of goods or services were divided by corresponding price indexes. The price indexes reflected price changes relative to a specific year, the base year. The detailed output indexes computed by one of these two procedures were then weighted, using base-year weights, and added to produce an aggregate index of output of the industry. With each new economic census—generally, every five years—new weights were introduced and the resulting series were linked. The types of weights used varied: for some series, unit value weights—or, roughly, price weights—were used; for other series, employment weights or other weights were used. The resulting output indexes were then divided by indexes of hours, generally developed from establishment surveys. For details on this measurement methodology, see Dean and Kunze (1992).

As of 1975, only fifty-three measures were prepared and published annually. The program was producing only labor productivity, or output per hour, measures. No MFP series were produced.

The improvements in the BLS productivity measurement program for detailed industries can be best explained by describing four separate activities that were undertaken between the mid-1970s and the year 2000.

First, a rapid expansion of BLS's original industry productivity measures was undertaken. While the number of annually published industry productivity measures in 1975 was fifty-three, by 1985, the BLS was publishing 140 measures. In addition, the number of measures based on deflated nominal data was expanded greatly and the measures based on physical quantity data became a small proportion of the total.

Second, development by BLS of MFP measures at the three-digit industry level began with measures for steel (Standard Industrial Classification

[SIC] 331) and automobiles (SIC 371) constructed by Sherwood and his BLS colleagues (as explained by Sherwood, 1987). As of 2000, data for ten industries are regularly published.[24] As noted earlier, MFP measures are prepared for total manufacturing and for 20 two-digit manufacturing industries. Both the three-digit and the two-digit manufacturing series are prepared using sectoral output and inputs of capital, labor, and intermediate purchased inputs. Tornqvist indexes are used to aggregate inputs as well as outputs.

Third, in 1995, most of the output measures for the labor productivity series were converted from fixed weight indexes, with the weights periodically updated, to Tornqvist indexes. Relative revenue weights were used to aggregate detailed product indexes in place of employment weights. At the same time, most of the output indexes were converted from gross output to sectoral output measures. This work was described by Kunze, Jablonski, and Klarqvist (1995).

The fourth stage of improvement of the industry productivity measures has yielded a very substantial increase in the number of labor productivity measures for detailed industries in manufacturing, as well as for service-producing and other nonmanufacturing industries. Output, hours, and output per hour series were developed for all three- and four-digit industries in manufacturing and in retail trade. Coverage was expanded substantially, mostly at the four-digit level, in transportation, communications, utilities, and mining industries. By 2000, BLS was publishing labor productivity measures for about 500 industries. In addition, BLS introduced hourly compensation and unit labor cost series for detailed industries. By 2000, BLS was publishing these series for 173 industries, mostly at the three-digit level.

This new expanded industry data set will prove useful in developing new insights into productivity trends in service-producing and other industries and in the ongoing effort to improve output and productivity series for service-producing industries.

2.6 Summary and Conclusions

For the past twenty years, the main thrust of the BLS productivity program has been to develop measures of multifactor productivity. These measures have been presented in a context of explaining the sources of growth in output per hour. Therefore, the BLS approach resembles that of Ed Denison, who sought to attribute output growth to specific sources. However, BLS has rationalized its work, using the Solow equation and using measurement techniques developed by Jorgenson and others. It would

---

24. Examples of the additional industries are railroad transportation (SIC 40) and cotton and synthetic broadwoven fabrics (SIC 221 and 222).

be accurate to say that BLS has focused on explanations that meet the following criteria: (1) They can be based on index number formulations. (2) They can be firmly based on simple assumptions about how firms would operate in equilibrium. (3) They can be supported with adequate data from the marketplace.

By basing the explanations on a particular body of theory, BLS does impose a number of assumptions that affect the conclusions. However, a theory-based approach has an important advantage over a more ad hoc approach: The assumptions are made explicitly and it is therefore clear what is being assumed. Another advantage is that a theory-based approach is often useful in consistently guiding the many choices that must be made in preparing data on output, prices, and productivity.

Nevertheless, the criteria have ruled out inclusion of many sorts of explanations of productivity. As a result, BLS publications include shorter lists of explanatory factors than did the many books written by Denison. The BLS publications also have cautioned readers that productivity trends reflect "the joint influences on economic growth of technological change, efficiency improvements, returns to scale, reallocation of resources due to shifts in factor inputs across industries, and other factors" (see, for example, BLS 2000).

Most of the papers presented at this conference have explored alternatives or supplements to the BLS approach. These include econometric specifications (in addition to the index number approach), the use of vintage capital models (rather than the Solow residual approach), departure from the equilibrium assumptions, the use of firm-specific data (instead of aggregate data), and the introduction of environmental variables.

These approaches might yield additional information about the sources of productivity change. Each of these approaches departs, in one or more ways, from the traditional BLS criteria. It appears such departures are essential to gain insight into various issues. For example, econometric methods can be used to estimate more complicated specifications of production than index number methods can. This can allow a more realistic description of behavior and the investigation of a longer list of explanations of productivity change. As another example, analysis of data on individual firms can lead to explanations of productivity change that do not emerge from aggregate data, such as effects of the entry of new firms.

BLS already has done some research along the lines of some of these alternative approaches. It appears to us that it may be valuable to pursue some of these directions further. Ideally, data would emerge from this work that could be tied in to the Solow framework. More likely than not, this will prove difficult. We may need to present such work in supplementary articles and tables. Pursuit, by BLS, of any of the alternative approaches will have other drawbacks. Some are resource intensive, some are narrow in scope, and some involve tenuous assumptions or limited data. This type of work will be valuable, nonetheless, if it allows attention to be focused on additional sources of productivity. BLS intends to pursue at least some of these alternative approaches.

Recently, a major distraction from exploring new explanations of productivity change has been questions about the output measures themselves. There have been growing concerns that the government may be underestimating productivity, particularly in service industries. BLS has recognized the importance of this issue, and recently three articles (by Dean 1999, Eldridge 1999, and Gullickson and Harper 1999) investigating this issue appeared in the *Monthly Labor Review*. It could not be conclusively demonstrated that productivity trends have been understated. Nevertheless, evidence was found to indicate that output and productivity trends were understated in several industries, including banking and construction.

In the meantime, we expect to pursue some of the suggested additional approaches to analyzing productivity. However, we also expect that the aggregate MFP measures will continue to constitute one of our most important products. For policy purposes, it is important to have data on the general characteristics of the economy.

References

Ball, V. Eldon, and Michael J. Harper. 1990. *Neoclassical capital measures using vintage data: An application to breeding livestock.* Washington, D.C.: Bureau of Labor Statistics.
Becker, Gary. 1975. *Human capital.* New York: Columbia University Press.
Berndt, Ernst R., and Jack E. Triplett, eds. 1990. *Fifty years of economic measurement.* Chicago: University of Chicago Press.
Berndt, Ernst R., and David O. Wood. 1975. Technology, prices, and the derived demand for energy. *Review of Economics and Statistics* 57 (3): 259–68.
———. 1984. Energy price changes and the induced revaluation of durable capital in U.S. manufacturing during the OPEC Decade. MIT Energy Lab Report no. 84-003. Cambridge: MIT.
Bureau of Labor Statistics. 1959. *Trends in output per man-hour in the private economy, 1909–1958.* Bulletin 1249. GPO.
———. 1983. *Trends in multifactor productivity, 1948–81.* Bulletin 2178. GPO.
———. 1989. *The impact of research and development on productivity growth.* Bulletin 2331.
———. 1993. *Labor composition and U.S. productivity growth, 1948–90.* Bulletin 2426. GPO.
———. 1996. *Multifactor productivity trends, 1994.* News Release no. 95-518. Washington, D.C.: U.S. Department of Labor.
———. 1997. *BLS handbook of methods.* Bulletin 2490. GPO.
———. 1998. *Revisions to capital inputs for the BLS multifactor productivity measures.* March 6. Washington, D.C.: Bureau of Labor Statistics, Office of Productivity & Technology.

———. 2000. *Multifactor productivity trends, 1998.* News Release no. 00-267, 21 September. Washington, D.C.: U.S. Department of Labor.

Christensen, Laurits R., and Dale W. Jorgenson. 1969. The measurement of U.S. real capital input, 1929–1967. *Review of Income and Wealth* ser. 15, no. 4 (December): 293–320.

Dean, Edwin R. 1999. The accuracy of the BLS productivity measures. *Monthly Labor Review* 122 (2): 24–34.

Dean, Edwin R., Michael J. Harper, and Phyllis F. Otto. 1995. Improvements to the quarterly productivity measures. *Monthly Labor Review* 118 (10): 27–32.

Dean, Edwin R., Michael J. Harper, and Mark K. Sherwood. 1996. Productivity measurement with changing weight indices of output and inputs. In *Industry productivity: International comparison and measurement issues,* 183–215. Paris: Organization for Economic Cooperation and Development.

Dean, Edwin R., and Kent Kunze. 1992. Productivity measurement in service industries. In *Output Measurement in the Service Sectors,* ed. Zvi Griliches, 73–101. Chicago: University of Chicago Press.

Dean, Edwin R., Kent Kunze, and Larry S. Rosenblum. 1988. Productivity change and the measurement of heterogeneous labor inputs. Paper presented at Conference on New Measurement Procedures for U.S. Agricultural Productivity. 31 March–1 April. Available from Bureau of Labor Statistics, Washington, D.C.

Denison, Edward F. 1974. *Accounting for U.S. economic growth, 1929–1969.* Washington, D.C.: Brookings Institution.

———. 1985. *Trends in American economic growth, 1929–1982.* Washington, D.C.: Brookings Institution.

Diewert, W. Erwin. 1976. Exact and superlative index numbers. *Journal of Econometrics* 4 (4): 115–45.

———. 1980. Aggregation problems in the measurement of capital. In *The measurement of capital,* ed. Dan Usher, 433–528. Chicago: University of Chicago Press.

Domar, Evsey D. 1961. On the measurement of technical change. *Economic Journal* 71 (284): 709–29.

Dulberger, Ellen R. 1989. The application of a hedonic model to a quality-adjusted price index for computer processors. In *Technology and capital formation,* ed. D. W. Jorgenson and R. Landau, 37–75. Cambridge: MIT Press.

Eldridge, Lucy P. 1999. How price indexes affect BLS productivity measures. *Monthly Labor Review* 122 (2): 35–46.

Fraumeni, Barbara M. 1997. The measurement of depreciation in the U.S. national income and product accounts. *Survey of Current Business* 77 (7): 7–23.

Goldberg, Joseph P., and William T. Moye. 1984. *The first hundred years of the Bureau of Labor Statistics.* Bulletin 2235. GPO.

Gollop, F. M. 1979. Accounting for intermediate input: The link between sectoral and aggregate measures of productivity. In *Measurement and interpretation of productivity,* 318–33. Washington, D.C.: National Academy of Sciences.

———. 1981. Growth accounting in an open economy. Boston College Department of Economics, Working Paper, March.

Gorman, John A., John C. Musgrave, Gerald Silverstein, and Kathy A. Comins. 1985. Fixed private capital in the United States. *Survey of Current Business* 65 (7): 36–59.

Gullickson, William. 1995. Measurement of productivity growth in U.S. manufacturing. *Monthly Labor Review* 118 (7): 13–28.

Gullickson, W., and Michael J. Harper. 1987. Multifactor productivity in U.S. manufacturing, 1949–83. *Monthly Labor Review* 110 (10): 18–28.

———. 1999. Possible measurement bias in aggregate productivity growth. *Monthly Labor Review* 122 (2): 47–67.
Hall, Robert E. 1968. Technical change and capital from the point of view of the dual. *Review of Economic Studies* 35 (1): 35–46.
Hall, Robert E., and Dale W. Jorgenson. 1967. Tax policy and investment behavior. *American Economic Review* 57 (3): 391–414.
Harper, Michael J. 1983. The measurement of productive capital stock, capital wealth, and capital services. Bureau of Labor Statistics Working Paper no. 128. Washington, D.C.: BLS.
Harper, Michael J., Ernst R. Berndt, and David O. Wood. 1989. Rates of return and capital aggregation using alternative rental prices. In *Technology and capital formation,* ed. D. W. Jorgenson and R. Landau, 331–72. Cambridge: MIT Press.
Harper, Michael J., and William Gullickson. 1986. Cost function models and accounting for growth. Paper presented at annual meeting of the American Economic Association. 28–30 December, New Orleans, La. Available from the Bureau of Labor Statistics, Washington, D.C.
Hulten, Charles R., James W. Robertson, and Frank C. Wykoff. 1989. Energy, obsolescence, and the productivity slowdown. In *Technology and capital formation,* ed. D. W. Jorgenson and R. Landau, 225–58. Cambridge: MIT Press.
Hulten, Charles R., and Frank C. Wykoff. 1981. The estimation of economic depreciation using vintage asset prices: An application of the Box-Cox power transformation. *Journal of Econometrics* 15:367–96.
Jablonski, Mary, Kent Kunze, and Phyllis F. Otto. 1990. Hours at work: A new base for BLS productivity statistics. *Monthly Labor Review* 113 (2): 17–24.
Jorgenson, Dale W., Frank M. Gollop, and Barbara M. Fraumeni. 1987. *Productivity and U.S. economic growth.* Cambridge: Harvard University Press.
Jorgenson, Dale W., and Zvi Griliches. 1967. The explanation of productivity change. *Review of Economic Studies* 34 (99): 249–83.
Katz, Arnold, and Shelby Herman. 1997. Improved estimates of fixed reproducible tangible wealth, 1929–95. *Survey of Current Business* 77 (5): 69–92.
Kendrick, John W. 1976. *The formation and stocks of total capital.* New York: Columbia University Press.
Kunze, Kent. 1979. Evaluation of work force composition adjustment. *Measurement and Interpretation of Productivity:* 334–62. Washington, D.C.: National Academy of Sciences.
Kunze, Kent, Mary Jablonski, and Virginia Klarqvist. 1995. BLS modernizes industry labor productivity program. *Monthly Labor Review* 118 (7): 3–12.
Mark, Jerome A., and William Waldorf. 1983. Multifactor productivity: A new BLS measure. *Monthly Labor Review* 106 (12): 3–13.
Mincer, Jacob. 1974. *Schooling, experience and earnings.* New York: Columbia University Press.
Moeller, Linda. 1999. A second decade of slower U.S. productivity growth: Prototype labor composition indexes based on the SIPP. Washington, D.C.: BLS Office of Productivity and Technology.
National Academy of Sciences. 1979. *Measurement and interpretation of productivity.* Washington, D.C.: National Academy of Sciences.
Norsworthy, J. Randolph, and Michael J. Harper. 1981. The role of capital formation in the recent slowdown in productivity growth. In *Aggregate and industry-level productivity analyses,* ed. Ali Dogramaci and Nabil R. Adam, 122–48. Boston: Martinus Nijhoff.
Norsworthy, J. Randolph, Michael J. Harper, and Kent Kunze. 1979. The slow-

down in productivity growth: Analysis of some contributing factors. *Brookings Papers on Economic Activity,* issue no. 3:387–421.
Norsworthy, J. Randolph, and David Malmquist. 1983. Input measurement and productivity growth in Japanese and U.S. manufacturing. *American Economic Review* 73 (5): 947–67.
Oliner, Stephen D. 1993. Constant-quality price change, depreciation, and retirement of mainframe computers. In *Price measurements and their uses,* ed. M. F. Foss, M. E. Manser, and A. H. Young, 19–61. Chicago: University of Chicago Press.
Rosenblum, Larry, Edwin Dean, Mary Jablonski, and Kent Kunze. 1990. Measuring components of labor composition change. Paper presented at annual meeting of the American Economic Association. 28–30 December, Washington, D.C. Available from BLS.
Samuelson, Paul A. 1947. *Foundations of economic analysis.* Cambridge: Harvard University Press.
Sherwood, Mark K. 1987. Performance of multifactor productivity in the steel and motor vehicle industries. *Monthly Labor Review* (August): 22–31.
Solow, Robert M. 1957. Technical change and the aggregate production function. *Review of Economics and Statistics* 39 (3): 312–20.
Sveikauskas, Leo. 1986. The contribution of R&D to productivity growth. *Monthly Labor Review* 109 (3): 16–20.
Tornqvist, Leo. 1936. The Bank of Finland's consumption price index. *Bank of Finland Monthly Bulletin* 10:1–8.
Triplett, Jack E. 1992. Measuring the capital stock: A review of concepts and data needs. Paper presented at Workshop on Measurement of Depreciation and Capital Stock, of the Conference on Research in Income and Wealth. 5 June, Washington, D.C. Available from BLS.
Waldorf, William, Kent Kunze, Larry Rosenblum, and Michael Tannen. 1986. New measures of the contribution of education and experience to U.S. productivity growth. Paper presented at American Economic Association Meeting. 28–30 December, New Orleans, La. Available from BLS.
Young, Allan H., and John C. Musgrave. 1980. Estimation of capital stock in the United States. In *The measurement of capital,* ed. Dan Usher, 23–68. Chicago: University of Chicago Press.

3 Which (Old) Ideas on Productivity Measurement Are Ready to Use?

W. Erwin Diewert

3.1 Introduction

The organizers of this conference gave me two tasks: (1) to review the paper on the BLS productivity measurement program by Dean and Harper (ch. 2, this volume), and (2) to suggest which new ideas on productivity measurement are ready to be embraced by statistical agencies and implemented in the near future.

I was able to complete the first task with admirable efficiency: I could find absolutely nothing to criticize in the Dean and Harper paper. They describe the history of the BLS labor and multifactor productivity (MFP) programs and indicate where the work is going in the future in an accurate and entertaining fashion. Of course, the BLS has been the world leader among statistical agencies in developing MFP measures and in incorporating new theoretical developments as they become available.

I was not able to complete the second task so efficiently. I could not think of any *new* ideas on productivity measurement that were ready to be implemented, but I was able to think of many *old* ideas that perhaps are. Thus, the remainder of this chapter concentrates on my second task (with the word *new* replaced by the word *old*).

Before I jump into the content of this chapter, perhaps it would be useful to remind people of the definition of productivity. Productivity is the output of a production unit (establishment, firm, industry, economy) divided by the input used over a given time period. Productivity growth of a production unit is the rate of growth of its output divided by the rate of growth

---

W. Erwin Diewert is professor of economics at the University of British Columbia and a research associate of the National Bureau of Economic Research.

of its input used over two time periods. Partial productivity measures are obtained by including only a subset of all of the outputs produced and inputs utilized by the production unit. For example, labor productivity is output (or value added) divided by labor input, and is a partial productivity measure because it neglects the contributions of other inputs, such as capital and land. On the other hand, MFP (or total factor productivity) includes all outputs produced and inputs utilized by the production unit.

Although labor productivity does have its uses, MFP seems to me to be the more useful measure of productivity. A rapid growth in a partial productivity measure could be due to a rapid growth in an omitted input category and thus could be quite misleading. In the remainder of this chapter, I will concentrate on some of the difficulties involved in measuring MFP.

It turns out that many classes of outputs and inputs are still not being measured adequately by statistical agencies. Thus, the old main idea that I would like to suggest to statistical agencies is that more effort should be put into measuring the major classes of inputs and outputs that production units produce and use. In sections 3.2–3.8, I review the main classes of outputs and inputs that statistical agencies must measure in order to form accurate measures of MFP for production units, and I discuss some of the measurement difficulties associated with each class. In sections 3.9–3.11, more esoteric capital inputs are discussed. It would be desirable to measure these inputs as well, but perhaps the appropriate methodology is not yet available.

Section 3.12 comments on the "optimal" organization of a statistical system that would measure MFP with more accuracy. Section 3.13 looks at the difference between the efficiency of particular production units and the efficiency of the economy as a whole. Section 3.14 concludes with some observations on the difficulties facing statistical agencies in this time of rapid change.

3.2 Gross Outputs

In order to measure the productivity of a firm, industry, or economy, one needs information on the outputs produced by the production unit for each time period in the sample, along with the average price received by the production unit in each period for each of the outputs. In practice, period-by-period information on revenues received by the industry for a list of output categories is required along with either an output index or a price index for each output. In principle, the revenues received should not include any commodity taxes imposed on the industry's outputs, because producers in the industry do not receive these tax revenues. The preceding sentences sound very straightforward, but many firms produce thousands of commodities, so the aggregation difficulties are formidable. Moreover, many outputs in service-sector industries are difficult to measure conceptually: Think of the proliferation of telephone service plans and the difficulties involved in measuring insurance, gambling, banking, and options trading.

3.3 Intermediate Inputs

Again, in principle, one requires information on all the intermediate inputs utilized by the production unit for each time period in the sample, along with the average price paid for each of the inputs. In practice, period-by-period information on costs paid by the industry for a list of intermediate input categories is required, along with either an intermediate input quantity index or a price index for each category. In principle, the intermediate input costs paid should include any commodity taxes imposed on the intermediate inputs because these tax costs are actually paid by producers in the industry.

The major classes of intermediate inputs at the industry level are materials, business services, and leased capital.

The current input-output framework deals reasonably well in theory with the flows of materials but not with intersectoral flows of contracted labor services or rented capital equipment. The input-output system was designed long ago, when the leasing of capital was uncommon and when firms had their own in-house business services providers. Thus there is little or no provision for business service and leased capital intermediate inputs in the present system of accounts. With the exception of the manufacturing sector, even the intersectoral value flows of materials are largely incomplete in the industry statistics.

This lack of information means the current input-output accounts will have to be greatly expanded to construct reliable estimates of real value added by industry. At present, there are no surveys (to my knowledge) on the interindustry flows of business services or on the interindustry flows of leased capital. Another problem is that using present national accounts conventions, leased capital resides in the sector of ownership, which is generally the finance sector. This leads to a large overstatement of the capital input into finance and a corresponding underestimate of capital services into the sectors actually using the leased capital.

It should be noted that at the level of the entire market economy, intermediate inputs collapse down to only imports plus purchases of government and other nonmarket inputs. This simplification of the hugely complex web of interindustry transactions of goods and services explains why it may be easier to measure productivity at the national level than at the industry level.

3.4 Labor Inputs

Using the number of employees as a measure of labor input into an industry will not usually be a very accurate measure of labor input, due to the long-term decline in average hours worked per full-time worker and the recent increase in the use of part-time workers. However, even total hours worked in an industry is not a satisfactory measure of labor input if the industry employs a mix of skilled and unskilled workers. Hours of work contributed by highly skilled workers generally contribute more to production than do hours contributed by very unskilled workers. Hence, it is best to decompose aggregate labor compensation into its aggregate price and quantity components using index number theory. The practical problem faced by statistical agencies is: How should the various categories of labor be defined? Alternative approaches to this problem are outlined in Jorgenson and Griliches (1967), BLS (1983), Denison (1985), Jorgenson, Gollop, and Fraumeni (1987), and Jorgenson and Fraumeni (1989, 1992). Dean and Harper (ch. 2, this vol.) provide an accessible summary of the literature in this area.

Another important problem associated with measuring real labor input is finding an appropriate allocation of the operating surplus of proprietors and the self-employed into labor and capital components. There are two broad approaches to this problem. In the first, if demographic information on the self-employed is available along with hours worked, then an imputed wage can be assigned to those hours worked based on the average wage earned by employees of similar skills and training. Then an imputed wage bill can be constructed and subtracted from the operating surplus of the self-employed, and the reduced amount of operating surplus can be assigned to capital. In the second approach, if information on the capital stocks utilized by the self-employed is available, then these capital stocks can be assigned user costs and an aggregate imputed rental can be subtracted from operating surplus; the reduced amount of operating surplus can then be assigned to labor. These imputed labor earnings can then be divided by hours worked by proprietors to obtain an imputed wage rate.

The problems posed by allocating the operating surplus of the self-employed are becoming increasingly more important as this type of employment grows. As far as we can determine, little has been done in countries other than the United States to resolve these problems. Fundamentally, the problem appears to be that the current System of National Accounts (SNA) does not address this problem adequately.

3.5 Reproducible Capital Inputs

When a firm purchases a durable capital input, it is not appropriate to allocate the entire purchase price as a cost to the initial period when the asset was purchased. It is necessary to distribute this initial purchase cost across the useful life of the asset. National income accountants recognize this and use depreciation accounts to do the distribution of the initial cost over the life of the asset. However, national income accountants are reluctant to recognize the interest tied up in the purchase of the asset as a true economic cost. Rather, they tend to regard interest as a transfer payment. Thus the user cost of an asset (which recognizes the opportunity cost of capital as a valid economic cost) is not regarded by many national income accountants as a valid approach to valuing the services provided by a durable capital input. However, if a firm buys a durable capital input and leases or rents it to another sector, national income accountants regard the induced rental as a legitimate cost for the using industry. It seems very unlikely that the leasing price does not include an allowance for the capital tied up by the initial purchase of the asset; that is, market rental prices include interest. Hence, it seems reasonable to include an imputed interest cost in the user cost of capital even when the asset is not leased. Put another way, interest is still not accepted as a cost of production in the SNA, since it is regarded as an unproductive transfer payment. However, interest is productive; it is the cost of inducing savers to forego immediate consumption.

The treatment of capital gains on assets is even more controversial than the national accounts treatment of interest. In the national accounts, capital gains are not accepted as an intertemporal benefit of production, but if resources are transferred from a period in which they are less valuable to one in which they are more highly valued, then a gain has occurred; that is, capital gains are productive according to this view.

However, the treatment of interest and capital gains poses practical problems for statistical agencies. For example, which of the following interest rates should be used?

1. An ex post economy-wide rate of return, which is the alternative used by Christensen and Jorgenson (1969, 1970).

2. An ex post firm or sectoral rate of return. (This method seems appropriate from the viewpoint of measuring ex post performance.)

3. An ex ante safe rate of return, such as a Federal Government one-year bond rate. (This method seems appropriate from the viewpoint of constructing ex ante user costs that could be used in econometric models.)

4. An ex ante safe rate, adjusted for the risk of the firm or industry.

Because the ex ante user-cost concept is not observable, the statistical agency will have to make somewhat arbitrary decisions in order to construct expected capital gains. This is a strong disadvantage of the ex ante concept. On the other hand, the use of the ex post concept will lead to rather large fluctuations in user costs, which in some cases will lead to negative user costs, which in turn may be hard to explain to users. However, a negative user cost simply indicates that instead of the asset's declining in value over the period of use, it rose in value to a sufficient extent to offset deterioration. Hence, instead of the asset's being an input cost to the economy during the period, it becomes an intertemporal output. For further discussion of the problems involved in constructing user costs, see Diewert (1980, 470–86). For evidence that the choice of user cost formula matters, see Harper, Berndt, and Wood (1989).

The distinction between depreciation (a decline in value of the asset over the accounting period) and deterioration (a decline in the physical efficiency of the asset over the accounting period) is now well understood but still has received little recognition in the latest version of the SNA.

A further complication is that our empirical information on the actual efficiency decline of assets is weak. We do not have good information on the useful lives of assets. The U.K. statistician assumes that machinery and equipment in manufacturing last twenty-six years on average, while the Japanese statistician assumes machinery and equipment in manufacturing last eleven years on average, see OECD (1993, 13). The problems involved in measuring capital input are also being addressed by the Canberra Group on Capital Measurement, which is an informal working group of international statisticians dedicated to resolving some of these measurement problems.

A final set of problems associated with the construction of user costs is the treatment of business income taxes: Should we assume that firms are as clever as Hall and Jorgenson (1967) and can work out their rather complex tax-adjusted user costs of capital, or should we go to the accounting literature and allocate capital taxes in the rather unsophisticated ways that are suggested there?

3.6 Inventories

Because interest is not a cost of production in the national accounts and the depreciation rate for inventories is close to zero, most productivity studies neglect the user cost of inventories. This leads to misleading productivity statistics for industries such as retailing and wholesaling, in which inventories are large relative to output. In particular, rates of return that are computed neglecting inventories will be too high because the opportunity cost of capital that is tied up in holding the beginning of the period stocks of inventories is neglected.

The problems involved in accounting for inventories are complicated by the way that accountants and tax authorities treat inventories. These accounting treatments of inventories are problematic in periods of high or moderate inflation. A treatment of inventories that is suitable for productivity measurement can be found in Diewert and Smith (1994). These inventory accounting problems seem to carry over to the national accounts in that, for virtually all OECD countries, there are time periods in which the real change in inventories has the opposite sign to the corresponding nominal change in inventories. This seems logically inconsistent.

3.7 Land

The current SNA has no role for land as a factor of production, perhaps because it is thought that the quantity of land in use remains roughly constant across time and hence can be treated as a fixed, unchanging factor in the analysis of production. However, the quantity of land in use by any particular firm or industry does change over time. Moreover, the price of land can change dramatically, so that the user cost of land will also change over time; this changing user cost will, in general, affect correctly measured productivity.

Land ties up capital just as inventories do (both are zero-depreciation assets). Hence, when computing ex post rates of return earned by a production unit, it is important to account for the opportunity cost of capital tied up in land. Neglect of this factor can lead to biased rates of return on financial capital employed. Thus, industry rates of return and total factor productivity (TFP) estimates may not be accurate for sectors such as agriculture that are land intensive.

Finally, property taxes that fall on land must be included as part of the user cost of land. In general, it may not be easy to separate the land part of property taxes from the structures part. In the national accounts, property taxes (which are input taxes) are lumped together with other indirect taxes that fall on outputs, which is another shortcoming of the current SNA.

3.8 Resources

Examples of resource inputs include depletion of fishing stocks, forests, mines and oil wells; and improvement of air, land, or water environmental quality (these are resource "outputs" if improvements have taken place and are resource "inputs" if degradation has occurred).

The correct prices for resource depletion inputs are the gross rents (including resource taxes) that these factors of production earn. Resource rents usually are not linked up with the depletion of resource stocks in the national accounts, although some countries (including the United States and Canada), are developing statistics for forest, mining, and oil depletion; see Nordhaus and Kokkelenberg (1999).

The pricing of environmental inputs or outputs is much more difficult. From the viewpoint of traditional productivity analysis based on shifts in the production function, the "correct" environmental quality prices are marginal rates of transformation while, from a consumer welfare point of view, the "correct" prices are marginal rates of substitution; see Gollop and Swinand (ch. 14, this volume).

The environmental situation is somewhat analogous to the case of a government enterprise that is told to provide services at prices well below marginal cost. In this case, it is useful to have an addendum to the accounts that revalues the subsidized goods and services at market (i.e., consumer) prices; this treatment would also be useful in the case of environmental goods and services. The problem with this suggestion is that it is much more difficult to estimate the appropriate consumer or producer environmental prices than it is to estimate the market price of a state subsidised good such as housing. Some techniques that could perhaps be used to estimate appropriate environmental prices and quantities are engineering studies (for the determination of producer environmental prices); epidemiological studies (for the determination of consumer environmental prices); and econometric and statistical techniques (which may also be useful in determining these producer and consumer environmental prices).

It is likely that environmental prices constructed using the previous techniques would not satisfy a reproducibility test—that is, different resource economists and statisticians would not come up with the same prices. This means that statistical agencies will have to be cautious in providing environmental accounts.

The above seven major classes of inputs and outputs discussed in sections 3.2–3.8 represent a minimal classification scheme for organizing information to measure TFP at the sectoral level. Unfortunately, no country has yet been able to provide satisfactory price and quantity information on all seven of these classes. To fill in the data gaps, it would be necessary for governments to expand the budget of the relevant statistical agencies considerably. This is one area of government expenditure that cannot be readily filled by the private sector. Given the importance of productivity improvements in improving standards of living, the accurate measurement of productivity seems necessary.

There are also additional types of capital that should be distinguished in a more complete classification of commodity flows and stocks, such as knowledge or intellectual capital, working capital or financial capital, infrastructure capital, and entertainment or artistic capital. Knowledge capital, in particular, is important for understanding precisely how process and product innovations (which drive TFP) are generated and diffused. In the following sections, I will comment on some of the measurement problems associated with these more esoteric kinds of capital.

3.9 Knowledge Capital

It is difficult to define what is meant by *knowledge capital* and *innovation*. I attempt to define these concepts in the context of production theory.

We think in terms of a local market area. In this area, there is a list of establishments or production units. Each establishment produces outputs and uses inputs during each period that it exists. *Establishment knowledge* at a given time is the set of input and output combinations that a local establishment could produce during at that given time period t. It is the economist's period t production function or period t production possibilities set. *Establishment innovation* is the set of *new* input-output combinations that an establishment in the local market area could produce in the current period compared to the previous period; that is, it is the growth in establishment knowledge or the increase in the size of the current period production possibilities set compared to the previous period's set. Since the statistical agency cannot know exactly what a given establishment's production possibilities are at any moment in time, it will be difficult to distinguish between the *substitution* of one input for another within a given production possibilities set versus an *expansion* of the production possibilities set; that is, it will be difficult to distinguish between substitution along a production function versus a shift in the production function.

Note that both process and product innovations are included in this definition of establishment innovation. Product innovations lead to additions to the list of outputs; traditional index number theory is not well adapted to deal with these additions, but the shadow price technique introduced by Hicks (1940)[1] and implemented by Hausman (1997, 1999) could be used.

Note also that this definition of establishment innovation includes all technology transfers from outside the establishment. One could further decompose innovations into local ones or global ones. A *global innovation* is the invention of a new set of input-output coefficients for the first time in the world; that is, the invention of a brand new product, process, or method of organization. A *local innovation* to a given establishment is merely the application of a global innovation to the local marketplace. However, local innovations are just as important as global innovations. A global innovation developed somewhere else in the world is useless to a local business unit if the new technology is not transmitted or diffused to the local establishment. In my view, the diffusion of a new product or process to the local economy is at least as important as the actual creation of the new knowledge for the first time.[2]

---

1. Hicks (1969, 55–56) later described these index number difficulties as follows: "Gains and losses that result from price changes (such as those just considered) would be measurable easily enough by our regular index number technique, if we had the facts; but the gains which result from the availability of new commodities, which were previously not available at all, would be inclined to slip through. (This is the same kind of trouble as besets the modern national income statistician when he seeks to allow for quality changes.) . . . The variety of goods available is increased, with all the widening of life that that entails. This is a gain which quantitative economic history which works with index numbers of real income, is ill-fitted to measure or even describe."
2. This highlights the important role that business consulting firms can play in diffusing best-practice technology or organizational techniques into the local economy.

How can we measure knowledge capital? Given the definition of knowledge as time-dependent, firm-specific production possibilities sets, it is extremely difficult to measure knowledge and changes in it (innovation). Some of the possible input-output combinations that a production unit can produce are imbedded in its capital equipment and the accompanying manuals. Other possible combinations of inputs and outputs might be imbedded in its patents or the unpublished notes of the scientists that developed the patents; yet other combinations might be imbedded in the brains of its workers. However, certain stocks can be measured that will probably be positively correlated with the size of local knowledge stocks. A science and technology statistical system should concentrate on collecting information on these knowledge related stocks. Some possible candidates for data collection are

1. stocks of patents (How should these be valued, and what depreciation rate should be used?)
2. research and development expenditures (How should these be deflated and what depreciation rate should be used?)
3. education and training undertaken in the firm (How should this be valued?)
4. trade fairs and professional meetings (In the local area only, or should the fairs and meetings abroad attended by local employees also be counted?)
5. availability of universities and research labs in the local region
6. stocks of books, journals, blueprints within the firm
7. availability of local libraries
8. local availability of trade magazines, newspapers, and how-to books (i.e., availability of local bookstores)
9. availability of mail service
10. availability of Internet services
11. ease of access to business consultants who can tell firms what best-practice input-output coefficients look like, then help the business unit to achieve the best-practice technology
12. participation of the local community in business associations, clubs, and societies

Obviously, it is very difficult to pin down exactly how knowledge flows into the local economy. Government regulations can also cause valuable knowledge flows. For example, my local building code now specifies that a layer of plastic insulation must be placed below ground-level concrete floors when the building is being constructed. This is relatively inexpensive but is very valuable in preventing loss of heat through the floor. Also, local building contractors must be licensed. Firms that sell new technologies obtain mailing lists of contractors from the licensing authority, and the contractors then receive useful information on new products.

These considerations bring up the positive role of advertising and marketing in transmitting useful information about new products and technologies to other business units.

3.10 Infrastructure Capital

Examples of infrastructure capital inputs are roads, airports, harbors, water supply, electricity supply, sewage disposal, garbage disposal, and telephone, cable television, and Internet hookups. Many of these stocks will appear in the list of reproducible capital stocks if privately owned. However, it still may be useful to distinguish the various types of infrastructure capital from ordinary structures. Publicly owned roads present special problems: They provide valuable services to business users but their price to the users is zero. Here is another example of demand prices' being quite different from supply prices.

There is a connection of infrastructure capital with knowledge capital. From Adam Smith and Alfred Marshall, we know that the bigger the market, the more establishments can specialize (i.e., create new local commodities). Thus reduction of transportation costs within and outside the local region can widen the market and reduce the costs of importing knowledge.

Similarly, a reduction in communication costs can make international and interregional knowledge more accessible to local establishments. Thus it seems likely that regions that are "large" and have "good" infrastructure facilities will have easier access to knowledge stocks, which, in turn, should lead to higher rates of productivity growth.

3.11 Entertainment or Artistic Capital

Examples of this type of capital include movies, paintings, novels, and games. Hill (1999) deals with this type of artistic, literary, or cultural capital. As was the case with the previous three types of capital, the cost of producing a piece of entertainment capital can be quite unrelated to its eventual value as a consumer service. Again, we have difficult practical valuation problems (how much money will the movie *Titanic* eventually make?) and difficult conceptual valuation problems (how can we justify a consumer valuation of the movie when, for productivity purposes, we are supposed to use a cost-of-production valuation?).

Before moving on to other productivity related topics, I sum up the previous material on measuring inputs and outputs of a production unit. Note that most productivity studies use only the information associated with output category 1 (outputs) and input categories 2 (intermediate inputs), 3 (labor), and 4 (reproducible capital). Typically, labor productivity studies use information from only categories 1 and 3, while many TFP studies use information from only categories 1, 3, and 4. I believe that these productivity studies are of very limited use. A more meaningful productivity study would use information on all categories and use at least categories 1–6; however, the valuation problems in categories 7–10 are formidable, both from the practical and conceptual points of view.

3.12 Productivity and the Organization of the Statistical System

In this section, we comment on the difficulties that statistical agencies may have in piecing together information from very different sources in order to construct multifactor or total factor productivity estimates.

The basic problem is this: Every statistical agency uses different surveys to collect information on the outputs of an industry and on the various input components. Furthermore, every statistical agency uses different surveys to collect information on prices and values.

These separate data-collection surveys do not greatly impede the construction of reasonably accurate price and quantity aggregates for the components of final demand for the economy as a whole, but they do lead to extremely inaccurate estimates of prices and quantities for industries or smaller units such as firms or establishments. In particular, the firm- or industry-specific price indexes that are applied to the firm's or industry's value components (such as output, intermediate input, labor input, etc.) will typically be very inaccurate. Hence, the resulting firm or industry productivity measures will be virtually useless.

In the United States the situation is particularly acute, with one or more agencies collecting value information and another entirely separate agency collecting price information. The various agencies have separate sampling frames and, at present, are not allowed even to exchange microinformation! To an outside impartial observer (i.e., to me), this situation cries out for reform. The various statistical agencies should be reorganized and combined into Statistics USA.

Statistics Canada, under the leadership of Phillip Smith, is instituting a new microdata management plan to manage the data burdens for large firms. Each large firm will have its own Statistics Canada representative, who will act as the single point of reference for all survey information to be collected from that firm. This will reduce respondent burden; but it will also ensure that the survey information is coherent, so that, for example, price information is matched up with the corresponding value information. It should also be mentioned that the national tax authority in Canada (Revenue Canada) has introduced a single business number for each firm in Canada; Statistics Canada will also use this number. I believe that every statistical agency should monitor the outcome of this experiment, and if it is successful, should plan to introduce a similar program.

Many firms have taken advantage of the low cost of computing and have detailed data on all their financial transactions (e.g., they have the value of each sale and the quantity sold by commodity). This opens up the possibility of the statistical agency's replacing or supplementing their surveys on, say, prices of outputs, by firms' electronic submission to the statistical agency of their computerized transaction histories for a certain number of periods. This information would provide the industry or firm counterparts to the scanner data studies that have proved to be so useful in the context of the Consumer Price Index. This information would also lead to true microeconomic price and quantity indexes at the firm level and to accurate firm and industry productivity indexes.

I turn now to another topic that has not received the attention it deserves.

3.13 System-Wide versus Sectoral Productivity Measurement

Individual firms or establishments could be operating efficiently (i.e., could be on the frontiers of their production possibilities sets), yet the economy as a whole may not be operating efficiently. How can this be? The explanation for this phenomenon was given by Gerard Debreu (1951)[3]: there is a loss of system-wide output (or *waste,* to use Debreu's term) due to the imperfection of economic organization; that is, different production units, although technically efficient, face different prices for the same input or output, which causes net outputs aggregated across production units to fall below what is attainable if the economic system as a whole were efficient. In other words, a condition for system-wide efficiency is that all production units face the same price for each separate input or output that is produced by the economy as a whole. Thus, if producers face different prices for the same commodity and if production functions exhibit some substitutability, then producers will be induced to supply jointly an inefficient, economy-wide net output vector. What are sources of system-wide waste?

1. industry-specific taxes or subsidies that create differences in prices faced by production units for the same commodity; for example, an industry-specific subsidy for an output or a tax on the output of one indus-

---

3. Debreu (1951, 285) distinguished two other sources of waste in the allocation of resources: (1) waste due to the underemployment of available physical resources (e.g., unemployed workers), and (2) waste due to technical inefficiency in production. Obviously, the application of knowledge capital could be useful in diminishing waste (2). Waste (1) results from market imperfections between the aggregate production sector and the household sector of the economy.

try where that output is used as an input by other industries (an example of the latter is a gasoline tax)

2. tariffs on imports or subsidies, or taxes on exports

3. union-induced wage differentials across firms for the same type of labor service

4. monopolistic or monopsonistic markups on commodities by firms, or any kind of price discrimination on the part of firms

5. imperfect regulation

6. a source of commodity price wedges related to imperfect regulation: the difficulty that multiproduct firms have in pricing their outputs, particularly when there are large fixed costs involved in producing new (or old) products (see Romer 1994)

Diewert and Fox (1998, 1999) further explore the problems of pricing new products, particularly when there is high inflation and the historical cost-accounting techniques for pricing products break down.

On the problem of imperfect regulation, it is very difficult for government regulators to set "optimal" prices for the commodities that are regulated (recall my earlier discussion of the difficulties involved in determining what the appropriate prices for environmental "bads" should be). If the regulators are unable to determine the optimal prices for regulated commodities, the other producers that use the regulated outputs as inputs will generate system-wide waste. Examples of imperfect regulation might include marketing boards; telecommunications; airlines; environmental protection and health and safety regulations; regulation of labor markets, including the collective bargaining framework; regulation of the radio-television spectrum; and municipal zoning and building-code regulations. Another source of market imperfections between economic agents might be the legal system: Are property rights well defined and enforceable? If not, the resulting uncertainty prevents the market from assigning a definite value to the asset or resource under dispute and will generally prevent the asset from being utilized in its most profitable use.

A final source of price wedges between economic agents is the existence of widespread bribery and corruption. A bribe has roughly the same effect as an uncertain tax on a transaction, and will create distortion wedges between business units.

The main message I want to convey in this section is that even if an individual production unit is efficient, inefficient economic institutions, inappropriate government taxation policies, and monopolistic behavior on the part of firms or unions can create a system-wide loss of productive efficiency. Thus, in addition to the sources of productivity growth that are due to new knowledge and innovation and the diffusion of knowledge to the business units in the local marketplace, further sources of productivity gain can arise from the elimination of pricing wedges.

3.14 Additional Problems Statistical Agencies Face

Statistical agencies face increasingly difficult problems in providing indexes of real output and input, which are the basic ingredients for computing productivity growth.[4] The amount of resources devoted to research and the development of new products is probably greater than ever before. Moreover, improvements in communication mean that this new knowledge can diffuse into the local economy faster than ever before. Traditional index number theory assumes that the set of commodities being aggregated is constant and unchanging over time; thus, strictly speaking, traditional index number theory is not applicable in this New World of ever-increasing choice sets. There is a lack of comparability of the set of commodities that exist in the current period with the set that existed in the previous period.

Most OECD economies are experiencing an increase in self-employment and an increase in the formation of new business units. The entrance of new firms and the exit of old firms again create problems for productivity statistics: The traditional methodology assumes an unchanging set of business units.[5] Thus, again, there is a lack of comparability: The set of firms and business units that exists in the present period is different from the set of firms that existed in the previous period.

When one examines the range of individual commodities produced by different firms in the same industry, one is struck by the tremendous amount of heterogeneity in the composition of these outputs. This heterogeneity makes comparisons of real output and productivity across firms somewhat dubious because their outputs may not be comparable.

Finally, the existence of seasonal commodities, on the lists of both inputs and outputs, again makes it difficult to compare this month's output or productivity with the previous month's. If a commodity produced this month was not produced at all in the previous month, between-month comparisons of output and productivity become meaningless.[6]

Thus, statistical agencies increasingly face the problem of a lack of comparability when they construct their estimates of business real output, input, and productivity. In addition, in sections 3.2–3.11, we saw that statistical agencies face many difficult conceptual measurement problems, in which reasonable statisticians could come up with quite different answers to these problems. These difficulties mean that it is increasingly difficult

---

4. Boskin (1997) also makes this point (and many other interesting points as well).
5. There is also the associated problem of firms' changing their product mix enough to shift them from one industry to another. This makes it difficult, if not impossible, to calculate accurate productivity growth rates for the two affected industries over the period when the switch takes place.
6. For additional material on the difficulties that seasonal commodities create (particularly in high inflation situations), see Hill (1996) and Diewert (1998, 1999).

for agencies to construct reproducible estimates of real output, input, and productivity.[7] Unfortunately, I do not see any easy solution to these measurement problems on the horizon.

References

Boskin, M. J. 1997. *Some thoughts on improving economic statistics to make them more relevant in the Information Age.* Document prepared for the Joint Economic Committee, Office of the Vice Chairman, United States Congress, 22 October. Washington, D.C.: GPO.
Bureau of Labor Statistics (BLS). 1983. *Trends in multifactor productivity, 1948–81.* Bulletin 2178. Washington, D.C.: GPO.
Christensen, L. R., and D. W. Jorgenson. 1969. The measurement of U.S. real capital input, 1929–1967. *Review of Income and Wealth* ser. 15, no. 4 (December): 293–320.
———. 1970. U.S. real product and real factor input, 1929–1967. *Review of Income and Wealth* ser. 16, no. 1 (March): 19–50.
Debreu, G. 1951. The coefficient of resource utilization. *Econometrica* 19:273–92.
Denison, E. F. 1985. *Trends in American growth, 1929–1982.* Washington, D.C.: Brookings Institution.
Diewert, W. E. 1980. Aggregation problems in the measurement of capital. In *The measurement of capital,* ed. Dan Usher, 433–528. Chicago: University of Chicago Press.
———. 1998. High inflation, seasonal commodities and annual index numbers. *Macroeconomic Dynamics* 2:456–71.
———. 1999. Index number approaches to seasonal adjustment. *Macroeconomic Dynamics* 3:48–68.
Diewert, W. E., and K. J. Fox. 1998. The productivity paradox and mismeasurement of economic activity. Paper presented at Eighth International Conference, Monetary Policy in a World of Knowledge-Based Growth, Quality Change, and Uncertain Measurement. 18 June, Institute for Monetary and Economic Studies, Bank of Japan, Tokyo.
———. 1999. Can measurement error explain the productivity paradox? *Canadian Journal of Economics* 32:251–80.
Diewert, W. E., and A. M. Smith. 1994. Productivity measurement for a distribution firm. *Journal of Productivity Analysis* 5 (December): 335–47.
Hall, R. E., and D. W. Jorgenson. 1967. Tax policy and investment behavior. *American Economic Review* 57:391–414.
Harper, M. J., E. R. Berndt, and D. O. Wood. 1989. Rates of return and capital aggregation using alternative rental prices. In *Technology and capital formation,* ed. D. W. Jorgenson and R. Landau, 331–72. Cambridge: MIT Press.
Hausman, J. A. 1997. Valuation of new goods under perfect and imperfect competition. In *The economics of new goods,* ed. T. F. Bresnahan and R. J. Gordon, 209–37. Chicago: University of Chicago Press.

---

7. The reproducibility test for data construction states that every competent statistician would construct the same aggregate, given identical disaggregated information sets. The idea of this test dates back to the early accounting literature.

———. 1999. Cellular telephone, new products and the CPI. *Journal of Business and Economic Statistics* 17:1–7.

Hicks, J. R. 1940. The valuation of the social income. *Economica* 7:105–40.

———. 1969. *A theory of economic history.* Oxford: Oxford University Press.

Hill, P. 1996. *Inflation accounting: A manual on national accounting under conditions of high inflation.* Paris: Organization for Economic Cooperation and Development.

———. 1999. Tangibles, intangibles, and services: A new taxonomy for the classification of output. *Canadian Journal of Economics* 32:426–46.

Jorgenson, D. W., and B. M. Fraumeni. 1989. The accumulation of human and non-human capital, 1948–1984. In *The measurement of saving, investment and wealth,* ed. R. Lipsey and H. Tice, 227–82. Chicago: University of Chicago Press.

———. 1992. Investment in education and U.S. economic growth. *Scandinavian Journal of Economics* 94 (supplement): 51–70.

Jorgenson, D. W., F. M. Gollop, and B. M. Fraumeni. 1987. *Productivity and U.S. economic growth.* Cambridge: Harvard University Press.

Jorgenson, D. W., and Z. Griliches. 1967. The explanation of productivity change. *Review of Economic Studies* 34:249–83.

Nordhaus, W. D., and E. D. Kokkelenberg. 1999. *Nature's numbers: Expanding the national economic accounts to include the environment.* Washington, D.C.: National Academy Press.

Organisation for Economic Cooperation and Development (OECD). 1993. *Methods used by OECD countries to measure stocks of fixed capital, national accounts: Sources and methods,* vol. 2. Paris: OECD.

Romer, P. 1994. New goods, old theory and the welfare costs of trade restrictions. *Journal of Development Economics* 43:5–38.

4 Dynamic Factor Demand Models and Productivity Analysis

M. Ishaq Nadiri and Ingmar R. Prucha

4.1 Introduction

The traditional approach to productivity analysis is to use the Divisia index number methodology. This approach has the advantage of simplicity as well as the benefit of not requiring direct estimation of the underlying technology. Therefore, the often difficult tasks of econometric specification and estimation of structural models can be avoided. However, for the index number approach to provide meaningful estimates of technical change, fairly strong assumptions about the underlying technology and allocation decisions by the firm must be maintained. In particular, it is necessary to assume a constant returns to scale technology, competitive input and output markets, full utilization of all inputs, and instantaneous adjustment of all inputs to their desired demand levels. As a result, the productivity measures based on the index number approach will in general yield biased estimates of technical change, if any of these assumptions are violated.

Technical change is an integral feature of the production process. Changes in variable factor inputs, the accumulation of quasi-fixed factor inputs, and technical change are in general intertwined in that the demand for inputs and the supply of outputs depend on the rate of technical change, while technical change, in turn depends typically on the input and

---

M. Ishaq Nadiri is the Jay Gould Professor in Economics at New York University and a research associate of the National Bureau of Economic Research.
Ingmar R. Prucha is professor of economics at the University of Maryland, College Park.
We would like to thank, in particular, William Baumol and Dale Jorgenson, and the participants of the CRIW Conference on New Developments in Productivity Analysis for interesting comments. Das Debabrata and Michel Kumhof provided excellent research assistance. We are also grateful for the support received from the C. V. Starr Center for Applied Economics at New York University.

output mix. The traditional measure of total factor productivity (TFP) measures only technical change, but does not explain the complex and simultaneously determined process that governs the evolution of outputs, inputs, and technical change.

A rationale for a general structural econometric modeling approach is that it allows for the careful testing of various features of a postulated model, rather than to simply impose those features a priori. We note that any misspecification of the underlying technology of the firm will typically lead to inconsistent estimates of technical change and the determinants of the investment decisions. A simple illustration of misspecification is the case where the true technology is translog but the hypothesized model is Cobb-Douglas, or the case where the input adjustments involve considerable time lags but are ignored, or where the expectation process is not taken into account or not formulated correctly. In such cases, the estimates of the model parameters, including the estimates of technical change, will be inconsistent. Thus, if the objective is to obtain a consistent estimate of the true model parameters, choosing, for example, a simple model for convenience of presentation and estimation is not admissible empirical practice. The reason for considering a dynamic rather than a static factor demand model is to not impose a priori that all factors are in long-run equilibrium.

A general dynamic factor demand model, as considered in this paper, has a fairly elaborate structure, requires an extensive data set and poses considerable estimation challenges. However, there seem to be two important advantages to this approach: First, the model contains "simpler" models as special cases. In particular, it contains static factor demand models as special cases, but does not impose a priori the premise that all factors are in long-run equilibrium. As in case of static factor demand models, the analysis can be carried out by specifying the technology in terms of a production function, cost/profit function, or restricted cost/profit function, and the model can be estimated from a subset or the complete set of the factor demand equations. Of course, if the model is only estimated from the variable factor demand equations, then we do not have to formulate an intertemporal optimal control problem.

Second, the dynamic factor demand model generates a very rich set of critical information about the structure of production, sources of productivity growth, impact of technical change and effects of policy instruments and expectations on output supply, input demand, direction of technical change and productivity growth. Not only is it possible to calculate the components of traditional productivity measures but also the determinants of employment and investment decisions of the firm simultaneously.

More specifically, the advantages of the estimation of (dynamic) factor demand models—apart from providing for the possibility of testing various modeling hypotheses—may include the following:

1. In estimating the technology we obtain explicit information on the process that transforms inputs into outputs, and on changes of the technological frontier over time. In particular, we obtain estimates of technological characteristics such as, for example, technical change, scale, and scope. We may also gain estimates of the effects of R&D, spillovers, and so on. Furthermore, we can compute marginal products, elasticities of substitution among the inputs, and the like, to describe the underlying structure of production.

2. In estimating the demand for variable and quasi-fixed factors, we gain additional insight into the underlying dynamics of factor allocation and factor accumulation—short-run, intermediate-run, and long-run—as a function of the variables that are exogenous to the firm. The latter variables typically include (expected) factor prices, taxes, exogenous technical change, spillovers, and so on.

3. As a by-product of estimating dynamic factor demand equations, we may gain insight into the expectation formation process and the firms planning horizon, and how this process affects production decisions in general and investment decisions in particular.

4. Furthermore, given that we allow the depreciation rate of capital goods to be endogenously determined, we obtain an economic model for replacement investment and expansion investment. (We note, however, that the modeling framework also covers the case of an exogenous and constant depreciation rate.)

The paper is organized as follows. In section 4.2, we begin by precisely defining input- and output-based technical change on the primal (production) side in the presence of adjustment costs. We then discuss how those measures can be evaluated on the dual (cost) side. We also show how capacity utilization rates can be derived in the context of dynamic factor demand models. Next we discuss the conventional measure of TFP based on the Divisia index, and show how this measure can be biased (as a measure of technical change) if the assumptions underlying its derivation are not satisfied. The biases can, for example, be due to the presence of economies of scale, adjustment costs, and the difference between the shadow prices and long-run rental prices of the quasi-fixed inputs.

In section 4.3, we first specify a general class of dynamic factor demand models, which allows for several nonseparable quasi-fixed factors, for the utilization rate/depreciation rate of some of the quasi-fixed factors to be endogenously determined, and for expectations to be nonstatic. We then discuss the class of linear quadratic dynamic factor demand models in more detail. For this class of models we give explicit analytic expressions for the firm's optimal control solution, that is, for the firm's optimal factor inputs. Those expressions make clear the dependence of the firm's investment decisions on the expectations of future exogenous variables. We also discuss convenient ways of estimating such models based on a reparameterization. Since some of this material may be unfamiliar and technically involved, we have attempted to show step-by-step how the models are derived and estimated. After our discussion of linear quadratic dynamic factor demand models, we discuss several approaches towards the estimation of dynamic factor demand models in general. This includes the estimation of the Euler equations by the generalized method of moments approach, given rational expectations.

Section 4.4 reviews several empirical applications of dynamic factor demand models. Dynamic factor demand models have been widely employed to study the behavior of factor demands including investment and employment decisions, output supply behavior, profitability, nature of technical change, spillover effects of R&D investment, international technology spillovers, role of public investment, taxes and subsidies, and so on. The empirical examples are provided to illustrate the versatility of these models.

In section 4.5 we present briefly the results of a Monte Carlo study that explores the effects of misspecifications. The true data generating process corresponds to a general dynamic factor demand specification with nonseparable quasi-fixed factors, nonconstant returns to scale, and nonstatic expectations. The model and various implied characteristics including technical change are then estimated under the correct specification and under various forms of misspecification. This allows us to assess the degree of bias induced by various forms of misspecifications as when a simple model of the firm's technology is adopted for convenience of presentation and estimation instead of the true model. Concluding comments are given in section 4.6. A longer version of this paper is available as Nadiri and Prucha (1999), which contains many of the underlying mathematical derivations, and a more extensive list of references.

4.2 On the Conventional Approach to Productivity Analysis

As remarked in the Introduction, a focus of this paper is the presentation of recent developments in the dynamic factor demand literature and their application to estimation of technical change and output growth. To set the stage, we first give a brief review of the conventional Divisia index based approach to productivity analysis. To put the discussion on sound footing, we start with a formal definition of technical change.[1]

---

1. The subsequent discussion makes use of the following notational conventions (unless explicitly indicated otherwise): Let Z_t be some $l \times 1$ vector of goods in period t, then p_t^Z refers to the corresponding $l \times 1$ price vector; Z_{ti} and p_{ti}^Z denote the i-th elements of Z_t and p_t^Z, respectively. Furthermore, in the following we often write $(p_t^Z)'Z_t$ for $\sum_{i=1}^{l} p_{ti}^Z Z_{ti}$, where "'" stands for transpose.

4.2.1 Definition of Technical Change

The conventional Divisia index based measure of total factor productivity growth assumes, in particular: (1) that producers are in long-run equilibrium, (2) that the technology exhibits constant returns to scale, (3) that output and input markets are competitive, and (4) that factors are utilized at a constant rate.[2] The puzzle of the observed slowdown of productivity growth during the 1970s has initiated a critical methodological review of the conventional measure of productivity growth.[3]

The model considered in the following discussion relaxes these assumptions corresponding to the conventional measure of total factor productivity growth. In the following we define, within the context of that model, appropriate measures of technical change. More specifically, in defining technical change we first give such a definition on the (primal) production side. We then show how the measure of technical change so defined can be expressed alternatively on the (dual) cost side. To interpret the expressions on the cost side, we also discuss measures of capacity utilization.

The following discussion allows, in particular, for a technology with multiple outputs, allows for some of the factors to be quasi-fixed (and thus does not assume that the firm is in long-run equilibrium), and allows for nonconstant returns to scale.[4] Now let $Y_t = (Y_{t1}, \ldots, Y_{tk})'$ be the vector of output goods produced by a firm during period t, and let $V_t = (V_{t1}, \ldots, V_{tm})'$ and $X_t = (X_{t1}, \ldots, X_{tn})'$ be the vectors of variable and quasi-fixed inputs utilized during period t, respectively. We then assume that the technology can be represented by the following transformation function

(1) $$F(Y_t, V_t, X_t, \Delta X_t, T_t) = 0,$$

where the vector of first differences ΔX_t represent internal adjustment costs in terms of foregone output due to changes in the quasi-fixed factors, and T_t represents an index of (exogenous) technical change.

In the following it will also be useful to decompose the variable factors into $M_t = V_{t1}$ and $L_t = (V_{t2}, \ldots, V_{tm})'$, and to represent the technology in terms of the following factor requirement function

(2) $$M_t = M(Y_t, L_t, X_t, \Delta X_t, T_t).$$

---

2. The assumption of constant returns to scale is not necessary in cases where an independent observation of the rental price of capital is available.

3. See, e.g., Berndt and Fuss (1986, 1989), Bernstein and Mohnen (1991), Caves, Christensen, and Swanson (1981), Caves, Christensen, and Diewert (1982), Denny, Fuss, and Waverman (1981a), Hall (1988), Hulten (1986), Mohnen (1992a), Mohnen, Nadiri, and Prucha (1983), Morrison (1986, 1992a,b), Nadiri and Prucha (1986, 1990a,b), Nadiri and Schankerman (1981a,b), and Prucha and Nadiri (1996).

4. Generalizations that allow for variable factor utilization rates will be discussed later.

We can then think of the transformation function to be of the form

(3) $\quad F(Y_t, V_t, X_t, \Delta X_t, T_t) = M(Y_t, L_t, X_t, \Delta X_t, T_t) - M_t \equiv 0.$

For ease of notation, in the following we drop time-subscripts whenever those subscripts are obvious from the context.

Primal Measures of Technical Change

To define technical change formally, assume that the technology index T shifts by, say, δ. Now let $a = a(\delta, Y, V, X, \Delta X, T)$ be the proportionality factor by which all outputs Y can be increased, and let $b = b(\delta, Y, V, X, \Delta X, T)$ be the proportionality factor by which all inputs can be decreased corresponding to this shift in technology when the firm remains on its production surface, that is, $F(aY, V, X, \Delta X, T + \delta) = 0$ and $F(Y, bV, bX, b\Delta X, T + \delta) = 0$. Furthermore, let $c = c(\kappa, Y, V, X, \Delta X, T)$ be the proportionality factor by which all outputs Y can be increased corresponding to an increase in all inputs by a factor κ when the firm remains on its production surface, that is, $F(cY, \kappa V, \kappa X, \kappa \Delta X, T) = 0$. We can then give the following two definitions of technical change, λ^Y and λ^X, and returns to scale, ρ:

(4) $\quad \lambda^Y = \left.\dfrac{\partial a}{\partial \delta}\right|_{\delta=0} = -\dfrac{\partial F}{\partial T} \bigg/ \left[\sum_{i=1}^{k} \dfrac{\partial F}{\partial Y_i} Y_i\right],$

$\lambda^X = -\left.\dfrac{\partial b}{\partial \delta}\right|_{\delta=0} = \dfrac{\partial F}{\partial T} \bigg/ \left[\sum_{j=1}^{m} \dfrac{\partial F}{\partial V_j} V_j + \sum_{l=1}^{n} \dfrac{\partial F}{\partial X_l} X_l + \sum_{l=1}^{n} \dfrac{\partial F}{\partial \Delta X_l} \Delta X_l\right],$

$\rho = \left.\dfrac{\partial c}{\partial \kappa}\right|_{\kappa=1} = \lambda^Y / \lambda^X,$

where $F(\cdot)$ is evaluated at $(Y, V, X, \Delta X, T)$. We refer to λ^Y and λ^X, respectively, as the rates of output and input based technical change or productivity growth. For an explicit derivation of the above expressions see appendix A in Nadiri and Prucha (1999). We note that the definitions given above are consistent with those given, for example, in Caves, Christensen, and Swanson (1981) and Caves, Christensen, and Diewert (1982) for the case of technologies without explicit adjustment costs.

In case of a single output good, we can also represent the technology in terms of a production function, say,

(5) $\quad\quad\quad\quad Y = f(V, X, \Delta X, T).$

Input and output based technical change can then also be expressed as usual as[5]

---

5. See appendix A in Nadiri and Prucha (1999) for a derivation.

(6)
$$\lambda^Y = \frac{\partial f}{\partial T}\bigg/ Y,$$

$$\lambda^X = \frac{\partial f}{\partial T}\bigg/ \left[\sum_{j=1}^{m} \frac{\partial f}{\partial V_j} V_j + \sum_{l=1}^{n} \frac{\partial f}{\partial X_l} X_l + \sum_{l=1}^{n} \frac{\partial f}{\partial \Delta X_l} \Delta X_l\right].$$

Dual Measures of Technical Change

We next show how these measures can be evaluated from the cost side, using simple arguments of duality theory. We note that the expressions developed below are given in terms of a restricted or variable cost function. Expressions in terms of the (unrestricted) cost function are contained as a special case, in that for the case where all factors are variable the restricted cost function and the (unrestricted) cost function coincide.

Let p^L denote the price vector for the variable inputs L normalized by the price of the variable input M. The normalized variable cost is then given by $M(Y, L, X, \Delta X, T) + (p^L)'L$. The normalized variable cost function is obtained by minimizing this expression w.r.t. L. Assuming that the factor requirement function $M(\cdot)$ is differentiable and that a unique interior minimum exists, the corresponding first order conditions are given by

(7)
$$\frac{\partial M}{\partial L} + (p^L)' = 0.$$

Let $\hat{L}$ denote the minimizing vector. The normalized variable cost function is then given by

(8)
$$G(p^L, Y, X, \Delta X, T) = \hat{M} + (p^L)'\hat{L}$$

where

$$\hat{M} = M(Y, \hat{L}, X, \Delta X, T).$$

For duality results between factor requirement functions and normalized restricted cost functions $G(\cdot)$, see, for example, Diewert (1982) and Lau (1976). We assume that the function $G(\cdot)$ is twice continuously differentiable in all its arguments, homogeneous of degree zero in p^L, nondecreasing in Y, $|\Delta X|$, and p^L, nonincreasing in X, concave in p^L, and convex in X, and ΔX.

Differentiating equation (3) yields

(9)
$$\frac{\partial F}{\partial Z} = \frac{\partial M}{\partial Z} \text{ for } Z = Y, L, X, \Delta X, T.$$

Differentiating equation (8) and utilizing equation (7) yields

(10)
$$\frac{\partial G}{\partial Z} = \frac{\partial M}{\partial Z} \text{ for } Z = Y, X, \Delta X, T.$$

Consequently, we have

(11) $$\frac{\partial F}{\partial Z} = \frac{\partial G}{\partial Z} \text{ for } Z = Y, X, \Delta X, T.$$

From equation (9) with $Z = L$ and equation (7) we obtain

(12) $$\frac{\partial F}{\partial L} = -(p^L)'.$$

Furthermore, we have from equation (3)

(13) $$\frac{\partial F}{\partial M} = -1.$$

Given the variable inputs $V = [M, L']'$ are chosen optimally, that is, $L = \hat{L}$ and $M = \hat{M}$, it follows from equations (12) and (13), and from equation (8), that

(14) $$G(p^L, Y, X, \Delta X, T) = \hat{M} + (p^L)'\hat{L} = -\sum_{j=1}^{m} \frac{\partial F}{\partial V_j} V_j.$$

Substituting the expressions in equations (11) and (14) into equation (4) yields the following expressions for technical change and returns to scale in terms of the normalized restricted cost function G:

(15) $$\lambda^Y = -\frac{\partial G}{\partial T} \bigg/ \left[\sum_{i=1}^{k} \frac{\partial G}{\partial Y_i} Y_i \right],$$

$$\lambda^X = -\frac{\partial G}{\partial T} \bigg/ \left[G - \sum_{l=1}^{n} \frac{\partial G}{\partial X_l} X_l - \sum_{l=1}^{n} \frac{\partial G}{\partial \Delta X_l} \Delta X_l \right],$$

$$\rho = \lambda^Y / \lambda^X = \left[G - \sum_{l=1}^{n} \frac{\partial G}{\partial X_l} X_l - \sum_{l=1}^{n} \frac{\partial G}{\partial \Delta X_l} \Delta X_l \right] \bigg/ \left[\sum_{i=1}^{k} \frac{\partial G}{\partial Y_i} Y_i \right].$$

The total shadow cost (normalized by the price of the variable factor M) is defined as

(16) $$C = G(p^L, Y, X, \Delta X, T) - \sum_{l=1}^{n} \frac{\partial G}{\partial X_l} X_l - \sum_{l=1}^{n} \frac{\partial G}{\partial \Delta X_l} \Delta X_l,$$

where $-\partial G/\partial X_l$ and $-\partial G/\partial \Delta X_l$ denote the respective "shadow values." The above expressions for output based and input based technical change and returns to scale generalize those given in Caves, Christensen, and Swanson (1981) in that they allow explicitly for adjustment costs.[6]

---

6. We note that the mathematics used in deriving the expressions in equation (15) is analogous to that used by Caves, Christensen, and Swanson (1981). The expressions also generalize those previously given in Nadiri and Prucha (1990a,b) for single-output technologies with

Observe that substituting equation (16) into equation (15) yields the following expressions for input-based technical change and scale: $\lambda^X = -(\partial G/\partial T)/C$ and $\rho = 1/[\sum_{i=1}^{k}(\partial G/\partial Y_i)Y_i/C]$. In the case where all factors are variable we have $C = G$, and thus in the case of a single output good we have the following simplifications: $\lambda^Y = \rho^{-1}\lambda^X$ with $\lambda^X = -(\partial C/\partial T)/C$ and $\rho = 1/[(\partial C/\partial Y)Y/C]$.

Capacity Utilization and Technical Change

The issue of a proper measure of technical change, given the firm is in short-run or temporary equilibrium, but not in long-run equilibrium, has also been discussed, among others, by Berndt and Fuss (1986, 1989), Berndt and Morrison (1981), Hulten (1986), and Morrison (1986). Those authors discuss proper measures of technical change in terms of adjustments of traditional technical change measures by utilization rate measures. Berndt and Fuss (1986) and Hulten (1986) consider single output technologies with constant returns to scale. Morrison also considers single output technologies, but allows for (possibly) nonconstant returns to scale and explicitly takes into account adjustment costs. Berndt and Fuss (1989) consider multiple output technologies with (possibly) nonconstant returns to scale, but do not explicitly consider adjustment costs.

We now show that the measures for λ^Y and λ^X are consistent with the technical change measures of Berndt, Fuss, Hulten and Morrison by demonstrating that λ^Y and λ^X can also be viewed as having been obtained via a capacity utilization adjustment of conventional (long-run) measures of technical change. For this purpose, consider the following restricted total cost function (normalized by the price of the variable factor M):

$$(17) \quad C^+ = \hat{M} + (p^L)'\hat{L} + (c^X)'X$$
$$= G(p^L, Y, X, \Delta X, T) + (c^X)'X,$$

where c^X denote the vector of rental prices for the quasi-fixed factors X (normalized by the price of the variable factor M). Recall that in long-run equilibrium, or in the case where all factors are variable, we have shown above that input based technical change equals $-(\partial C/\partial T)/C$. Now suppose we attempt to measure technical change in terms of the total restricted cost function C^+ analogously by

$$(18) \quad \lambda_+^X = -(\partial C^+/\partial T)/C^+.$$

Observing that $\partial C^+/\partial T = \partial G/\partial T$ it follows immediately from equation (15) and equation (16) that

---

adjustment costs. A generalization of those expressions for multiple-output technologies with adjustment costs and variable factor utilization rates is given in Prucha and Nadiri (1990, 1996), and will be discussed shortly.

(19) $$\lambda^Y = \rho\lambda_+^X(C^+/C),$$
$$\lambda^X = \lambda_+^X(C^+/C).$$

Analogously to Berndt, Fuss, Hulten, and Morrison we can interpret

(20) $$CU = C/C^+$$

as a measure of capacity utilization and we can therefore interpret our input- and output-based measures for technical change as being derived from λ_+^X via an adjustment in terms of a capacity utilization measure to account for temporary equilibrium. Clearly, in long-run equilibrium C^+ equals C and hence in the long run λ_+^X equals λ^X. In general, however, λ_+^X differs from λ^X by the factor C^+/C.

4.2.2 Divisia Index Approach

In the productivity literature, technical change is often estimated as the difference between the growth rate of a measure of aggregate output minus the growth rate of a measure of aggregate input. This approach to estimate technical change in terms of a residual dates back to Solow (1957). In computing aggregate output and input, one of the most widely used methods of aggregation is Divisia aggregation. The conceptual justifications for Divisia aggregation were developed by Jorgenson and Griliches (1967), Richter (1966), Hulten (1973), and Diewert (1976), among others.[7] In the following we first define the conventional measure of total factor productivity based on the Divisia index formula. As remarked, the Divisia index approach is based on a set of particular assumptions concerning the technology and the inputs and output markets. If any one of those assumptions is violated, the measure of total factor productivity based on the Divisia index formula will in general yield biased estimates of technical change in that it may then include, for example, effects of scale economies or temporary equilibrium in addition to shifts in the production frontier.[8] In the following, we first develop a growth accounting equation for technical change. We then compare this expression with that for the conventional measure of total factor productivity, and based on this comparison discuss potential sources of bias in the latter measure. The subsequent discussion builds on Denny, Fuss, and Waverman (1981a), who consider a model where all factors are variable, but where scale is allowed to differ from unity. In the following discussion we take $T = t$.

The Conventional Measure of Total Factor Productivity

For ease of presentation, we start our discussion in continuous time. Recall that $V = [M, L']'$ denotes the vector of all variable factors, and let

---

7. See also the article by Hulten, chapter 1 in this volume.
8. The TFP measure based on the Divisia index may, however, be of interest.

Dynamic Factor Demand Models and Productivity Analysis   113

$p^V = [1, p^{L'}]'$ denote the corresponding price vector (normalized by the price of M). Furthermore, let p^Y denote the vector of output prices, and let c^X denote the vector of rental prices for the quasi-fixed factors X (normalized by the price of M). The Divisia index for aggregate output, say Y^a, is now defined by

$$(21) \qquad \frac{\dot{Y}^a}{Y^a} = \sum_{i=1}^{k} s_i^Y \frac{\dot{Y}_i}{Y_i}$$

where the s_i^Y's denote output shares in total revenue $R^+ = \sum_{i=1}^{k} p_i^Y Y_i$, i.e.,

$$(22) \qquad s_i^Y = \frac{p_i^Y Y_i}{R^+},$$

and where dots over variables denote derivatives w.r.t. time t. The Divisia index for aggregate input, say F^a, is analogously defined by

$$(23) \qquad \frac{\dot{F}^a}{F^a} = \sum_{j=1}^{m} s_j^V \frac{\dot{V}_j}{V_j} + \sum_{l=1}^{n} s_l^X \frac{\dot{X}_l}{X_l}$$

where the s_j^V's and s_l^X's denote input shares in total cost $C^+ = \sum_{j=1}^{m} p_j^V V_j + \sum_{l=1}^{n} c_l^X X_l$; that is,

$$(24) \qquad s_j^V = \frac{p_j^V V_j}{C^+}, \quad s_l^X = \frac{c_l^X X_l}{C^+}.$$

The conventional measure of total factor productivity, say, TFP, is now defined as the ratio of the Divisia index of aggregate output over the Divisia index of aggregate input, that is, TFP = Y^a/F^a, and thus

$$(25) \qquad \frac{\dot{\text{TFP}}}{\text{TFP}} = \frac{\dot{Y}^a}{Y^a} - \frac{\dot{F}^a}{F^a}$$

$$= \sum_{i=1}^{k} s_i^Y \frac{\dot{Y}_i}{Y_i} - \sum_{j=1}^{m} s_j^V \frac{\dot{V}_j}{V_j} - \sum_{l=1}^{n} s_l^X \frac{\dot{X}_l}{X_l}.$$

The above Divisia index based definition of total factor productivity growth is given in continuous time. Empirical data typically refer to discrete time points. For discrete data, the above formulae for the growth rates of aggregate output, aggregate input, and total factor productivity are typically approximated by the following Törnqvist approximations, where Δ denotes the first difference operator:

$$(26) \qquad \Delta \ln Y_t^a = \frac{1}{2} \sum_{i=1}^{k} [s_{ti}^Y + s_{t-1,i}^Y] \Delta \ln(Y_{ti}),$$

$$(27) \quad \Delta \ln F_t^u = \frac{1}{2}\sum_{j=1}^{m}[s_{tj}^V + s_{t-1,j}^V]\Delta \ln(V_{tj})$$

$$+ \frac{1}{2}\sum_{l=1}^{n}[s_{tl}^X + s_{t-1,l}^X]\Delta \ln(X_{tl}),$$

and

$$(28) \quad \Delta \ln \text{TFP}_t = \Delta \ln Y_t^a - \Delta \ln F_t^a = \frac{1}{2}\sum_{i=1}^{k}[s_{ti}^Y + s_{t-1,i}^Y]\Delta \ln(Y_{ti})$$

$$- \frac{1}{2}\sum_{j=1}^{m}[s_{tj}^V + s_{t-1,j}^V]\Delta \ln(V_{tj}) - \frac{1}{2}\sum_{l=1}^{n}[s_{tl}^X + s_{t-1,l}^X]\Delta \ln(X_{tl}).$$

Diewert (1976) has shown that the Törnqvist index is in fact exact if the underlying potential function has a translog form. We note further that a primary feature of the Divisia/Törnqvist index approach is that it can be implemented even if the number of inputs and outputs is large; see Diewert (1980).

Growth Accounting Equation for Technical Change

For ease of presentation we again start our discussion in continuous time. Consider the continuous time analog of equation (8),

$$(29) \quad G(p^L, Y, X, \dot{X}, t) = \hat{M} + (p^L)'\hat{L}.$$

Differentiation of the above equation w.r.t. t and observing that $L = \hat{L}$ and $M = \hat{M}$ yields

$$(30) \quad \left[\frac{\partial G}{\partial p^L}\right]\dot{p}^L + \left[\frac{\partial G}{\partial Y}\right]\dot{Y} + \left[\frac{\partial G}{\partial X}\right]\dot{X} + \left[\frac{\partial G}{\partial \dot{X}}\right]\ddot{X} + \left[\frac{\partial G}{\partial t}\right]$$

$$= \dot{M} + (p^L)'\dot{L} + (L)'\dot{p}^L.$$

By Shephard's lemma $L = (\partial G/\partial p^L)'$. Upon substitution of this expression into the above equation it is easily seen that

$$(31) \quad -\frac{\partial G}{\partial t} = \left[\frac{\partial G}{\partial Y}\right]\dot{Y} - \dot{M} - (p^L)'\dot{L} - \left[\frac{-\partial G}{\partial X}\right]\dot{X} - \left[\frac{-\partial G}{\partial \dot{X}}\right]\ddot{X}.$$

As implied by equation (15), input-based technical change is now obtained by dividing the above equation by the continuous time analog of the restricted total shadow cost defined in equation (16), that is, $C = G(p^L, Y, X, \dot{X}, t) - \Sigma_l(\partial G/\partial X_l)X_l - \Sigma_l(\partial G/\partial \dot{X}_l)\dot{X}_l$. Some simple algebra—and recalling that $V = [M, L']'$ and $p^V = [1, p^L']'$—then yields the following expression for input-based technical change:

(32) $$\lambda^X = -\frac{1}{C}\frac{\partial G}{\partial t}$$

$$= \sum_{i=1}^{k} \bar{g}_i \frac{\dot{Y}_i}{Y_i} - \sum_{j=1}^{m} \bar{s}_j^V \frac{\dot{V}_j}{V_j} - \sum_{l=1}^{n} \bar{s}_l^X \frac{\dot{X}_l}{X_l} - \sum_{l=1}^{n} \bar{s}_l^{\dot{X}} \frac{\ddot{X}_l}{\dot{X}_l}$$

with

$$\bar{g}_i = \frac{\partial G}{\partial Y_i}\frac{Y_i}{C}, \quad \bar{s}_j^V = \frac{p_j^V V_j}{C},$$

$$\bar{s}_l^X = \frac{-\partial G}{\partial X_l}\frac{X_l}{C}, \quad \bar{s}_l^{\dot{X}} = \frac{-\partial G}{\partial \dot{X}_l}\frac{\dot{X}_l}{C}.$$

For given "shadow values" $-\partial G/\partial X_l$ and $-\partial G/\partial \dot{X}_l$, we have $\partial G/\partial Y_i = \partial C/\partial Y_i$, and the $\bar{g}_i$s can be interpreted as the elasticities of the restricted total shadow cost C with respect to the output Y_i. Furthermore, $\bar{s}_j^V$, $\bar{s}_l^X$ and $\bar{s}_l^{\dot{X}}$ represent the input cost shares for, respectively, V_j, X_l and $\dot{X}_l$ in the restricted total shadow cost. An analogous expression to (32) for single output technologies is, for example, given in Morrison (1986, 1992a). Analogous expressions for models without explicit adjustment costs are given in, for example, Denny, Fuss, and Waverman (1981a) and Berndt and Fuss (1989). Generalizations that allow for endogenous factor utilization are given in Prucha and Nadiri (1990, 1996), and will be discussed in section 4.3.

For purposes of interpreting equation (32), observe that in light of equation (15), $\Sigma_{i=1}^{k} \bar{g}_i = 1/\rho$, where ρ denotes the scale elasticity. In case of single output good, the above expression for input based technical change simplifies to

(33) $$\lambda^X = \rho^{-1}\frac{\dot{Y}}{Y} - \sum_{j=1}^{m} \bar{s}_j^V \frac{\dot{V}_j}{V_j} - \sum_{l=1}^{n} \bar{s}_l^X \frac{\dot{X}_l}{X_l} - \sum_{l=1}^{n} \bar{s}_l^{\dot{X}} \frac{\ddot{X}_l}{\dot{X}_l}.$$

From this expression we see that in calculating input based technical change in case of increasing (decreasing) returns to scale, output growth is diminished (enhanced) before subtracting the growth in aggregate inputs. In case of a single output good, constant returns to scale, and in case all factors are variable, the growth accounting equation for technical change simplifies further to

(34) $$\lambda^X = \lambda^Y = \frac{\dot{Y}}{Y} - \sum_{j=1}^{m} \bar{s}_j^V \frac{\dot{V}_j}{V_j},$$

which corresponds to the expression developed by Solow (1957).

The above expressions for technical change were derived in continuous time. In appendix A in Nadiri and Prucha (1999), we derive the following discrete time approximation of equation (32):

$$(35) \quad \frac{1}{2}(\lambda_t^x + \lambda_{t-1}^x) = \frac{1}{2}\left(-\frac{1}{C_t}\frac{\partial G_t}{\partial t} - \frac{1}{C_{t-1}}\frac{\partial G_{t-1}}{\partial(t-1)}\right)$$

$$= \frac{1}{2}\sum_{i=1}^{k}[\bar{g}_{ti} + \bar{g}_{t-1,i}]\Delta \ln(Y_{ti})$$

$$- \frac{1}{2}\sum_{j=1}^{m}[\bar{s}_{tj}^V + \bar{s}_{t-1,j}^V]\Delta \ln(V_{tj})$$

$$- \frac{1}{2}\sum_{l=1}^{n}[\bar{s}_{tl}^X + \bar{s}_{t-1,l}^X]\Delta \ln(X_{tl})$$

$$- \frac{1}{2}\sum_{l=1}^{n}[\bar{s}_{tl}^{\Delta X} + \bar{s}_{t-1,l}^{\Delta X}]\Delta \ln(\Delta X_{tl})$$

with

$$\bar{g}_{ti} = \frac{\partial G_t}{\partial Y_{ti}}\frac{Y_{ti}}{C_t}, \quad \bar{s}_{tj}^V = \frac{p_{tj}^V V_{tj}}{C_t},$$

$$\bar{s}_{lt}^X = -\frac{\partial G_t}{\partial X_{lt}}\frac{X_{tl}}{C_t}, \quad \bar{s}_{lt}^{\Delta X} = -\frac{\partial G_t}{\partial X_{lt}}\frac{\Delta X_{tl}}{C_t}.$$

Sources of Bias in the Conventional Measure of Total Factor Productivity

We now compare the growth accounting expression for technical change with the conventional measure of TFP and explore sources of potential bias in the latter measure. For ease of presentation, we again start the discussion in continuous time. Consider the following alternative index for aggregate output, say Y^b, defined by

$$(36) \quad \frac{\dot{Y}^b}{Y^b} = \sum_{i=1}^{k}\bar{s}_i^Y \frac{\dot{Y}_i}{Y_i}$$

where

$$\bar{s}_i^Y = \frac{\bar{g}_i}{\sum_{i=1}^{k}\bar{g}_i} = \frac{(\partial G/\partial Y_i)Y_i}{R}$$

with $R = \sum_{i=1}^{k}(\partial G/\partial Y_i)Y_i$. Furthermore, consider the following index for aggregate input, say F^b, defined by

$$(37) \quad \frac{\dot{F}^b}{F^b} = \sum_{j=1}^{m}\bar{s}_j^V \frac{\dot{V}_j}{V_j} + \sum_{l=1}^{n}\bar{s}_l^X \frac{\dot{X}_l}{X_l} + \sum_{l=1}^{n}\bar{s}_l^{\dot{X}} \frac{\ddot{X}_l}{\dot{X}_l}.$$

Recalling that in light of equation (15), $\Sigma_{i=1}^{k} \bar{g}_i = 1/\rho$, where ρ denotes the scale elasticity, we can now write the growth accounting equation (32) for input-based technical change as

$$(38) \qquad \lambda^X = \rho^{-1} \frac{\dot{Y}^b}{Y^b} - \frac{\dot{F}^b}{F^b}.$$

As demonstrated in appendix A in Nadiri and Prucha (1999), comparing equations (25) and (38) yields the following decomposition of the conventional measure of total factor productivity growth in continuous time.

$$(39) \qquad \frac{\dot{\text{TFP}}}{\text{TFP}} = \lambda^X + (1 - 1/\rho)\frac{\dot{Y}^b}{Y^b} + \left(\frac{\dot{Y}^a}{Y^a} - \frac{\dot{Y}^b}{Y^b}\right) + \left(\frac{\dot{F}^b}{F^b} - \frac{\dot{F}^a}{F^a}\right)$$

with

$$(40) \qquad \frac{\dot{Y}^a}{Y^a} - \frac{\dot{Y}^b}{Y^b} = \sum_{i=1}^{k} \left(\frac{(p_i^Y - \partial G/\partial Y_i)Y_i}{R}\right)\left(\frac{\dot{Y}_i}{Y_i} - \frac{\dot{Y}^a}{Y^a}\right),$$

$$\frac{\dot{F}^b}{F^b} - \frac{\dot{F}^a}{F^a} = \sum_{l=1}^{n} \left(\frac{(-\partial G/\partial X_l - c_l^X)X_l}{C}\right)\left(\frac{\dot{X}_l}{X_l} - \frac{\dot{F}^a}{F^a}\right)$$

$$+ \sum_{l=1}^{n} \left(\frac{(-\partial G/\partial \dot{X}_l)\dot{X}_l}{C}\right)\left(\frac{\ddot{X}_l}{\dot{X}_l} - \frac{\dot{F}^a}{F^a}\right).$$

The first term in the above decomposition of $\dot{\text{TFP}}/\text{TFP}$ corresponds to actual (input-based) technical change. The remaining terms decompose the difference between $\dot{\text{TFP}}/\text{TFP}$ and technical change; that is, they reflect sources of potential bias of $\dot{\text{TFP}}/\text{TFP}$ as a measure of technical change. More specifically, the second term reflects scale effects. We note that under increasing returns to scale and positive output growth $\dot{\text{TFP}}/\text{TFP}$ will overestimate technical change. The third term reflects the effects of deviations from marginal cost pricing. The fourth term is due to the presence of adjustment costs. It consists of two effects: One effect stems from the difference in the marginal conditions for the quasi-fixed factors between short- and long-run equilibrium due to adjustment cost, that is, the difference between the shadow price and (long-run) rental price.[9] The other effect reflects the direct effect of adjustment costs in the sense that due to the presence of $\dot{X}$ in the transformation function the growth rates of those terms also enter the decomposition of the output growth rate.

Empirical data typically refer to discrete time points. Equations (26)–

---

9. Suppose the shadow price for a particular quasi-fixed factor exceeds the long-run price used in the computation of $\dot{\text{TFP}}/\text{TFP}$. In this case $\dot{\text{TFP}}/\text{TFP}$ will, ceteris paribus, overestimate the technical change effects given the growth rate of the quasi-fixed input exceeds that of the aggregate input index.

(28) provided Törnqvist approximations for the growth rates of the aggregate output Y^a, the aggregate input F^a, and total factor productivity TFP. Analogously, consider the following approximations for the growth rates of the aggregate output Y^b, and of the aggregate input F^b:

$$(41) \quad \Delta \ln Y_t^b = \frac{1}{2}\sum_{i=1}^{k}[\bar{s}_{ti}^Y + \bar{s}_{t-1,i}^Y]\Delta \ln(Y_{ti})$$

where

$$\bar{s}_{ti}^Y = \frac{g_{ti}}{\sum_{i=1}^{k} g_{ti}} = \frac{(\partial G_t/\partial Y_{ti})Y_{ti}}{R_t}$$

with $R_t = \sum_{i=1}^{k}(\partial G_t/\partial Y_{ti})Y_{ti}$, and

$$(42) \quad \Delta \ln F_t^b = \frac{1}{2}\sum_{j=1}^{m}[\bar{s}_{tj}^V + \bar{s}_{t-1,j}^V]\Delta \ln(V_{tj})$$

$$+ \sum_{l=1}^{n}[\bar{s}_{tl}^X + \bar{s}_{t-1,l}^X]\Delta \ln(X_{tl})$$

$$+ \sum_{l=1}^{n}[\bar{s}_{tl}^{\Delta X} + \bar{s}_{t-1,l}^{\Delta X}]\Delta \ln(\Delta X_{tl}).$$

As demonstrated in appendix A in Nadiri and Prucha (1999), it is then possible to decompose the Törnqvist index based approximation of the growth rate of the conventional measure of total factor productivity as follows:

$$(43) \quad \Delta \ln \text{TFP}_t = \frac{1}{2}(\lambda_t^X + \lambda_{t-1}^X) + \frac{1}{2}\sum_{\tau=t,t-1}(1 - 1/\rho_\tau)\Delta \ln Y_t^{b,\tau}$$

$$+ (\Delta \ln Y_t^a - \Delta \ln Y_t^b) + (\Delta \ln F_t^b - \Delta \ln F_t^a)$$

with

$$(44) \quad \Delta \ln Y_t^a - \Delta \ln Y_t^b$$

$$= \sum_{i=1}^{k}\left[\frac{1}{2}\sum_{\tau=t,t-1}\left(\frac{(p_{\tau i}^Y - \partial G_\tau/\partial Y_{\tau i})Y_{\tau i}}{R_\tau}\right)(\Delta \ln(Y_{ti}) - \Delta \ln Y_t^{a,\tau})\right],$$

$$\Delta \ln F_t^b - \Delta \ln F_t^a$$

$$= \sum_{l=1}^{n}\left[\frac{1}{2}\sum_{\tau=t,t-1}\left(\frac{(-\partial G_\tau/\partial X_{\tau l} - c_{\tau l}^X)X_{\tau l}}{C_\tau}\right)(\Delta \ln(X_{tl}) - \Delta \ln F_t^{a,\tau})\right]$$

$$+ \sum_{l=1}^{n}\left[\frac{1}{2}\sum_{\tau=t,t-1}\left(\frac{(-\partial G_\tau/\partial \Delta X_{\tau l})\Delta X_{\tau l}}{C_\tau}\right)(\Delta \ln(\Delta X_{tl}) - \Delta \ln F_t^{a,\tau})\right]$$

and

$$\Delta \ln Y_t^{a,\tau} = \sum_{i=1}^{k} s_{\tau i}^Y \Delta \ln(Y_{ti})$$

$$\Delta \ln F_t^{a,\tau} = \sum_{j=1}^{m} s_{\tau j}^V \Delta \ln(V_{tj}) + \sum_{l=1}^{n} s_{\tau l}^X \Delta \ln(X_{tl})$$

for $\tau = t, t-1$. This decomposition and its interpretation is analogous to the continuous time decomposition of TFP growth given in equations (39) and (40). It generalizes analogous expressions given in Denny, Fuss, and Waverman (1981a) for technologies without adjustment costs and in Nadiri and Prucha (1986, 1990a,b) for single output technologies with adjustment costs. Expressions that allow for endogenous factor utilization have been considered in Prucha and Nadiri (1990, 1996), and will be discussed in section 4.3. We note that variations of the decomposition equations (39) or (43) have also appeared in various other studies, including Nadiri and Schankerman (1981b), Bernstein and Mohnen (1991), and Mohnen (1992a).

4.3 Recent Developments in Modeling Dynamic Factor Demand

The recent dynamic factor demand literature rests on the seminal work of several contributors. Four advances in the theory and estimation methodology are of particular importance: The neoclassical theory of investment, the advances in flexible functional forms of the production (cost) functions, the development of duality theory, and the theoretical and empirical developments concerning adjustment costs. It is the confluence of these strands of literature that made the wide empirical applications of factor demand models possible.

First, in a seminal contribution Jorgenson (1963) laid the foundation of the neoclassical model of investment. He developed the concept of the user cost of capital, that included explicitly various taxes and incentives. Also, he modeled the lagged response of investment to changes in demand for capital by generalizing the Koyck (1954) geometric lag distribution to what is called the rational distributed lag; see Jorgenson (1966) and Jorgenson and Stephenson (1967). Many other facets of investment decisions such as the rate of depreciation and the distinction between net and replacement investment were explicitly considered in a series of papers dealing with theory and application of the neoclassical theory of investment; see Jorgenson (1996a,b) for a collection of this important body of work.

Building on the neoclassical model of investment Nadiri and Rosen (1969, 1973) introduced their interrelated disequilibrium model, whereby disequilibrium in one factor market was formally related to the extent of disequilibrium in other factor markets. As a result, short-run overshooting is possible, and the difference between short- and long-run price elasticities for a particular input depends not only on its own partial adjustment parameter, but also on all cross adjustment parameters of other inputs.

A second major advance in the literature has been the formulation of flexible functional forms for the description of the technology. The purpose was to avoid restrictive features inherent in, for example, the Leontief and Cobb-Douglas production functions. Flexible functional forms of cost and production functions have first been introduced in the economics literature in seminal papers by Christensen, Jorgenson, and Lau (1971, 1973) and Diewert (1971). These authors introduced the transcendental logarithmic and the generalized Leontief functional forms, respectively.[10] These functional forms do not impose a priori restrictive constraints such as homotheticity, constancy of elasticity of substitution, additivity, and so on. Another important flexible functional form has been proposed by McFadden (1978) and extended by Diewert and Wales (1987).

The third strand of literature contributing to advances in the theory of production was the development of duality theory. Fundamental contributions include Shephard (1953), Diewert (1971, 1982), Lau (1976), and McFadden (1978).[11] Of course, there was close interaction between the development of flexible functional forms and duality theory. Profit and cost functions (or restricted versions thereof) are widely used in empirical analysis. This may be explained in part by the following observation of McFadden (1978): "In econometric applications, use of the cost function as the starting point of developing models avoids the difficulty of deriving demand systems constructively from production possibilities, while at the same time insuring consistency with the hypothesis of competitive cost minimization" (4).

Fourth, in an effort to construct a dynamic framework capable of yielding a demand for investment Eisner and Strotz (1963) introduced adjustment cost into the neoclassical theory of the firm. Other important contributions include Lucas (1967a,b), Treadway (1969, 1974), and Mortenson (1973). These studies indicated that the multivariate flexible accelerator model can be justified theoretically as a solution of a dynamic optimization problem that incorporates adjustment cost for the quasi-fixed factors. The adjustment cost incurred in order to change the level of the quasi-fixed factors can take two forms. The first type is internal and reflects the fact that firms may have to make trade-offs between producing current

---

10. The transcendental logarithmic form has been used by Jorgenson with different associates to study the properties of the production structure and productivity analysis in a number of sectors in the U.S. and Japanese economies and to compare productivity growth among different countries; see Jorgenson (1995a,b).

11. For a detailed review of the literature and a collection of various other important contributions see Fuss and McFadden (1978).

output and diverting some of the resources from current production to accumulate capital for future production (e.g., Treadway 1974). The second type is external: As the firm adjusts its quasi-fixed factors it may face either a higher purchase price for these factors (e.g., Lucas 1967a,b) or a higher financing cost for the accumulation of these inputs (e.g., Steigum 1983).

Based on these theoretical development on cost of adjustments a number of dynamic factor demand models referred to as the "third generation models" have been estimated. For comprehensive reviews of this influential literature see Berndt, Morrison, and Watkins (1981) and Watkins (1991). Examples include Denny, Fuss, and Waverman (1981b), Morrison and Berndt (1981), Morrison (1986), and Watkins and Berndt (1992). Several features of the "third generation" dynamic factor demand models are important to note. First, those models are explicitly dynamic and provide the optimal path of investment from temporary to full long-run equilibrium. The dynamic path of adjustment to long-run equilibrium is based on economic optimization at each point in time; thus short-, intermediate-, and long-run are clearly defined. Second, the speed of adjustment of the quasi-fixed factors to their long-run equilibrium levels is allowed to be endogenous and time varying, rather than exogenous and fixed. Third, the short-run demand equations for variable inputs depend on, among other things, prices of variable inputs, output, and stocks of the quasi-fixed inputs. Variable inputs may in the short-run overshoot their long-run equilibrium values to compensate for the partial adjustment of the quasi-fixed factors.

Empirical applications of third generation dynamic factor demand models typically only allowed for one quasi-fixed factor, or, slightly more generally, for several separable quasi-fixed factors. As a consequence of the separability assumption the models did not allow for interactions between the optimal investment paths. The technical reason for maintaining separability between the quasi-fixed factors was that it facilitated a major simplification in the computation of the firm's optimal investment decision. More specifically, separability implies the absence of interaction between the difference equations describing the optimal investment paths of the respective quasi-fixed factors. As a consequence, each of those equations can be solved separately. Technically this entails the solving of a quadratic equation for each of the quasi-fixed factors—which, of course, can readily be done analytically. If, however, separability is not maintained, then rather than having to solve several quadratic scalar equations, one is confronted with a quadratic matrix equation. Analytic expressions for the solution of this quadratic matrix equation, and hence for optimal investment, are then generally not available.

Other characteristics of the empirical implementation of third generation dynamic factor demand models were that the underlying technology was modeled in a linear quadratic fashion, that expectations were typically modeled as static, and that factor utilization rates were assumed to be constant. Recent developments were aimed at a relaxation of those assumptions.

4.3.1 Theoretical Model Specification

Technology and Optimal Control Policy

For the subsequent discussion we generalize the setup of section 4.2, in that we consider a firm that combines the set of variable inputs V_t and the set of quasi-fixed inputs X_t to produce the set of outputs for current sale Y_t, as well as a set of capital inputs for future production. More specifically, in the generalized setup we allow the firm to also choose how much of the beginning-of-period stocks of some (but not necessarily all) of the quasi-fixed capital inputs will be left over at the end of the period. We note that this adopted modeling framework dates back to Hicks (1946), Malinvaud (1953), and Diewert (1980). In the empirical dynamic factor demand literature this framework was first adopted by Epstein and Denny (1980) and Kollintzas and Choi (1985) for the case of a single quasi-fixed factor. Prucha and Nadiri (1990, 1996) generalized the setup by allowing for more than one quasi-fixed factor. They also discuss measures of technical change and capacity utilization for the generalized modeling framework.[12] We note that the generalized modeling framework contains—as discussed in more detail later—the case where a constant fraction of the beginning-of-period stocks is left over at the end of the period as a special case.

In the following we use K_t to denote the vector of the stocks of the quasi-fixed capital inputs at the end of period t for which the firm chooses how much of the beginning-of-period stocks will be left over at the end of the period, and K_t^o to denote the vector of "old" stocks left over at the end of period t from the beginning-of-period stocks K_{t-1}. Of course, being able to choose the level of K_t^o by, for example, choosing appropriate levels of maintenance, is equivalent to being able to choose endogenously the rate of depreciation for those stocks, since we can always write $K_t^o = (1 - \delta_t^K) K_{t-1}$ and interpret δ_t^K as a diagonal matrix of depreciation rates. R_t is the vector of the end-of-period stocks of the quasi-fixed factors, whose depre-

---

12. On a theoretical level the generalized modeling framework has also been considered by Bernstein and Nadiri (1987). A special case of the model was implemented in Nadiri and Prucha (1996). Bischoff and Kokkelenberg (1987) adopt a related framework in which the depreciation rate is modeled as a function of capacity utilization. For other contributions to the dynamic factor demand literature that allows for the firm to operate at different levels of utilization, but are based on an alternative modeling framework, see, e.g., Abel (1981) and Shapiro (1986).

ciation rates are exogenous to the firm. We assume furthermore that all quasi-fixed factors become productive with a lag.[13] In the notation of section 4.2, we then have $X_t = [K'_{t-1}, R'_{t-1}]'$ and $\Delta X_t = [\Delta K'_t, \Delta R'_t]'$. Furthermore, as in section 4.2, we will decompose the variable inputs as $V_t = [M_t, L'_t]'$.

In more detail, we assume that the firm's technology can be represented by the following factor requirement function:

$$(45) \qquad M_t = M(Y_t, L_t, K^o_t, K_{t-1}, R_{t-1}, \Delta K_t, \Delta R_t, T_t).$$

This specification generalizes the factor requirement function considered in equation (2) in that it includes the vector of capital stocks left over at the end of the period K^o_t. The stocks K_t and R_t accumulate according to the following equations:

$$(46) \qquad K_t = I^K_t + K^o_t, \quad R_t = I^R_t + (I - \delta^R_t)R_{t-1},$$

where I^K_t and I^R_t denote the respective vectors of gross investment and δ^R_t denotes the diagonal matrix of exogenous depreciation rates (some of which may be zero).

The firm's cost in period t, normalized by the price of the variable factor M_t, is given by

$$(47) \qquad M_t + (p^L_t)'L_t + (q^K_t)'I^K_t + (q^R_t)'I^R_t,$$

where q^K_t and q^R_t denote the prices of new investment goods after taxes, possibly normalized by $1 - u_t$, where u_t denotes the corporate tax rate.[14] We assume that the firm faces perfectly competitive markets with respect to its factor inputs.

Suppose the firm's objective is to minimize the expected present value of its future cost stream.[15] Substitution of equations (45) and (46) into equation (47) then yields the following expression for the firm's objective function:

---

13. This assumption is made for simplicity of exposition. For a generalization where some of the quasi-fixed factors immediately become productive and some become productive with a lag see Prucha and Nadiri (1990, 1996).

14. As an illustration, suppose K is a scalar and corresponds to the stock of a certain capital good; then q^K may equal $[1 - c - u(1 - mc)B]p^{IK}/(1 - u)$, where p^{IK} denotes the price of new investment goods, u denotes the corporate tax rate, c is the rate of the investment tax credit, m is the portion of the investment tax credit which reduces the depreciable base for tax purposes, and B is the present value of depreciation allowances. We note that the appropriate expressions for the price of new investment goods after taxes are actually obtained by explicitly introducing taxes into the firm's objective function. As a result, the price of new investment goods after taxes will in general also depend on expectations on future tax variables. We have not chosen this route for simplicity of presentation.

15. We note that the subsequent theoretical discussion can be readily modified also to apply to the case of a profit maximizing firm.

(48) $\quad E_t \sum_{\tau=t}^{\infty} \{M(Y_\tau, L_\tau, K_\tau^o, K_{\tau-1}, R_{\tau-1}, \Delta K_\tau, \Delta R_\tau, T_\tau) + (p_\tau^L)' L_\tau - (q_\tau^K)' K_\tau^o$

$\qquad + (q_\tau^K)' K_\tau + (q_\tau^R)'[R_\tau - (I - \delta_\tau^R) R_{\tau-1}]\} \prod_{s=t}^{\tau} (1 + r_s)^{-1},$

where E_t denotes the expectations operator conditional on the set of information available in period t and r denotes the real discount rate (which may possibly also incorporate variations in the corporate tax rate).

Suppose the firm follows a stochastic closed loop feedback control policy in minimizing the expected present value of its future cost stream defined by equation (48). Then, in period t the firm will choose optimal values for its current inputs L_t, K_t, R_t, and for K_t^o. At the same time the firm will choose a contingency plan for setting L_τ, K_τ, R_τ, and K_τ^o in periods $\tau = t + 1, t + 2, \ldots$ optimally, depending on observed realizations of the exogenous variables and past choices for the quasi-fixed factors. Of course, for given optimal values for L_τ, K_τ, R_τ, and K_τ^o the optimal values for M_τ are implied by equation (45). Prices, output, and the discount rate are assumed to be exogenous to the firm's optimization problem.

Since L_τ and K_τ^o can be changed without adjustment costs the stochastic closed loop feedback control solution can be found conveniently in two steps. In the first step, we minimize the total (normalized) cost in each period $\tau = t, t + 1, \ldots$ with respect to L_τ and K_τ^o for given values of the quasi-fixed factors and the exogenous variables. Substitution of the minimized expressions into equation (48) then leads in the second step to an optimal control problem that only involves the quasi-fixed factors K_τ and R_τ.

The part of total cost that actually depends on L_τ and K_τ^o is given by

(49) $\quad M(Y_\tau, L_\tau, K_\tau^o, K_{\tau-1}, R_{\tau-1}, \Delta K_\tau, \Delta R_\tau, T_\tau) + (p_\tau^L)' L_\tau - (q_\tau^K)' K_\tau^o,$

that is, variable cost minus the value of the "old" stocks left over at the end of the period from the beginning of period stocks. Assuming that $M(\cdot)$ is differentiable and that a unique interior minimum of the above expression exists, the first order conditions for that minimum are given by

(50) $\qquad \dfrac{\partial M_\tau}{\partial L_\tau} + (p_\tau^L)' = 0, \quad \dfrac{\partial M_\tau}{\partial K_\tau^o} - (q_\tau^K)' = 0.$

Let $\hat{L}_\tau$ and $\hat{K}_\tau^o$ denote the minimizing vectors, then the minimum of the variable cost minus the value of the "old" stocks is given by

(51) $\qquad G_\tau = G(p_\tau^L, q_\tau^K, Y_\tau, K_{\tau-1}, R_{\tau-1}, \Delta K_\tau, \Delta R_\tau, T_\tau)$

$\qquad\qquad = \hat{M}_\tau + (p_\tau^L)' \hat{L}_\tau - (q_\tau^K)' \hat{K}_\tau^o,$

with $\hat{M}_\tau = M(Y_\tau, \hat{L}_\tau, \hat{K}_\tau^o, K_{\tau-1}, R_{\tau-1}, \Delta K_\tau, \Delta R_\tau, T_\tau)$. The function $G(\cdot)$ has the interpretation of a normalized variable cost function net of the value of the "old" stocks left over at the end of the period from the beginning of period stocks. Technically it can be viewed as the negative of a normalized restricted profit function. For duality, results between factor requirement functions and normalized variable profit functions see, for example, Diewert (1982) and Lau (1976). We assume that the function $G(\cdot)$ is twice continuously differentiable in all its arguments, homogeneous of degree zero in p^L and q^K, nondecreasing in Y, $|\Delta K|$, $|\Delta R|$ and p^L, nonincreasing in K_{-1}, R_{-1} and q^K, concave in p^L and q^K, and convex in K_{-1}, R_{-1}, ΔK and ΔR.

As indicated above, the stochastic closed loop optimal control solution for the quasi-fixed factors can now be found by replacing $M_\tau + (p_\tau^L)'L_\tau - (q_\tau^K)'K_\tau^o$ in (48) by $G(p_\tau^L, q_\tau^K, Y_\tau, K_{\tau-1}, R_{\tau-1}, \Delta K_\tau, \Delta R_\tau, T_\tau)$ defined in equation (51), and then by minimizing

$$(52) \quad E_t \sum_{\tau=t}^{\infty} \{G(p_\tau^L, q_\tau^K, Y_\tau, K_{\tau-1}, R_{\tau-1}, \Delta K_\tau, \Delta R_\tau, T_\tau)$$

$$+ (q_\tau^K)'K_\tau + (q_\tau^R)'[R_\tau - (I - \delta_\tau^R)R_{\tau-1}]\} \prod_{s=t}^{\tau} (1 + r_s)^{-1}$$

with respect to the quasi-fixed factors $\{K_\tau, R_\tau\}_{\tau=t}^{\infty}$ only. Standard control theory implies that the stochastic closed loop feedback control solution that minimizes (52), say $\{\hat{K}_\tau, \hat{R}_\tau\}_{\tau=t}^{\infty}$, must satisfy the following set of stochastic Euler equations ($\tau = t, t+1, \ldots$):[16]

$$(53) \quad -E_\tau \frac{\partial G_{\tau+1}}{\partial K_\tau}(1 + r_{\tau+1})^{-1} = (q_\tau^K)' + \frac{\partial G_\tau}{\partial \Delta K_\tau} - E_\tau \frac{\partial G_{\tau+1}}{\partial \Delta K_{\tau+1}}(1 + r_{\tau+1})^{-1},$$

$$(54) \quad -E_\tau \frac{\partial G_{\tau+1}}{\partial R_\tau}(1 + r_{\tau+1})^{-1} = (c_\tau^R)' + \frac{\partial G_\tau}{\partial \Delta R_\tau} - E_\tau \frac{\partial G_{\tau+1}}{\partial \Delta R_{\tau+1}}(1 + r_{\tau+1})^{-1},$$

where

$$c_\tau^R = E_\tau[q_\tau^R(1 + r_{\tau+1}) - (I - \delta_\tau^R)q_{\tau+1}^R]/(1 + r_{\tau+1})$$

can be viewed as a vector of rental prices. The firm's optimization decisions with respect to L_τ and K_τ^o are incorporated in the stochastic Euler equations via G_τ. (Recall from equation [51] that G_τ gives the minimal value of the variable cost net of the value of the "old" stocks for given values of the quasi-fixed factors and exogenous variables.) A detailed economic interpretation of the stochastic Euler equations is given in appendix B in Nadiri and Prucha (1999).

The optimal values for L_τ and K_τ^o can be found by differentiating G_τ with

---

16. Compare, e.g., Stokey, Lucas, and Prescott (1989, ch. 9), for a more detailed list of assumptions and a careful exposition of stochastic control theory, as well as for a discussion of the transversality condition.

respect to p_τ^L and q_τ^K and then making use of equation (50), that is, via Shephard's and Hotelling's lemma:[17]

$$\text{(55)} \qquad \hat{L}_\tau = \left(\frac{\partial G_\tau}{\partial p_\tau^L}\right)', \quad \hat{K}_\tau^o = -\left(\frac{\partial G_\tau}{\partial q_\tau^K}\right)'.$$

The derivatives on the r.h.s. of the above equations need to be evaluated at the optimal control solution for the quasi-fixed factors.

The formulation of a stochastic closed loop control policy generally requires knowledge of the entire distribution of the exogenous variables. Alternatively, one may postulate—as will be the case in the empirical application—that the firm formulates a certainty equivalence feedback control policy, which only requires knowledge of the first moment (mean) of the exogenous variables. In that case, the firm's objective function is given by equations (48) or (52) with the expectations operator moved next to each of the exogenous variables. The firm would now devise in each period t an optimal plan for its inputs in periods $t, t + 1, \ldots$ such that its objective function in period t is optimized, and then choose its inputs in period t accordingly. In each future period the firm will revise its expectations and optimal plan for its inputs based on new information. In case of a certainty equivalence feedback control policy, the first order conditions for the optimal plan in period t for the quasi-fixed factors would be given by equations (53) and (54) with all exogenous variables replaced by their expected values (conditional on information available at time t and the expectations operator in front of the respective derivatives suppressed). Equation (55) remains the same. If $G(\cdot)$ is linear quadratic, then the well-known certainty equivalence principle implies that the stochastic closed loop and the certainty equivalence feedback control policy are identical.[18]

Generalized Expressions for Technical Change and
Total Factor Productivity Decomposition

The discussion in section 4.2 considered the case where the depreciation rates of all of the quasi-fixed factors are exogenously given. In this section, we have allowed the depreciation rate of some of the quasi-fixed factors to be endogenously determined. Analogously to equations (4) and (15) in section 4.2.1, we can define primal and dual measures of input-based technical change λ^X, output-based technical change λ^Y, and scale ρ, and we can define measures of capacity utilization for the generalized technology considered in this section. Those expressions are given in Prucha and Na-

---

17. In case of a profit maximizing model we have furthermore the following condition for the output vector: $\partial G_\tau/\partial Y_\tau = p_\tau^Y + [\partial p_\tau^Y/\partial Y_\tau] Y_\tau$.

18. For general technologies input decisions corresponding to the latter policy may be viewed as first-order approximations to those of the former policy; see, e.g., Malinvaud (1969) on the principle of certainty and first-order certainty equivalence.

diri (1990, 1996), and are not repeated here in order to conserve space.[19] Analogously to equations (39), (40), (43), and (44), one can also obtain, respectively, a decomposition of the growth rate of total factor productivity and its Törnqvist index based approximation. A generalization of the decomposition in equations (39) and (40) of the growth rate of TFP in continuous time is given in appendix B in Nadiri and Prucha (1999). The generalization of the Törnqvist index–based approximation in equations (43) and (44) is analogous. For the case of a single output good, the latter generalization is also given in Prucha and Nadiri (1990, 1996).

Flexible Functional Forms of Restricted Cost Functions

Empirical specifications of dynamic factor demand models typically model the underlying technology in a "flexible" fashion. As discussed at the beginning of section 4.3, flexible functional forms of cost and production functions have first been introduced by Diewert (1971) and Christensen, Jorgenson, and Lau (1971, 1973). In the dynamic factor demand literature, the technology has often been modeled in terms of a normalized restricted cost function. In the following we discuss some of the functional forms used in the recent literature.[20]

Recall that in our notation K refers to the vector of quasi-fixed factors whose depreciation rate is endogenously determined, and R refers to the vector of quasi-fixed factors whose depreciation rates are exogenous. For ease of presentation, we focus the subsequent discussion on the case where the depreciation rates of all quasi-fixed factors are exogenous to the firm.[21] In this case the normalized restricted cost function equation given in (51) simplifies to

$$(56) \qquad G_\tau = G(p_\tau^L, Y_\tau, R_{\tau-1}, \Delta R_\tau, T_\tau)$$

given that we can now suppress K (and thus q^K). Also, we focus the discussion on the case of a single output good Y. Furthermore, for ease of presentation, we drop time subscripts in the following.

Observe that for linear homogeneous technologies we have

$$(57) \qquad G(p^L, Y, R_{-1}, \Delta R, T) = g(p^L, \frac{R_{-1}}{Y}, \frac{\Delta R}{Y}, T)Y.$$

The normalized restricted cost function introduced by Denny, Fuss, and Waverman (1981b) and Morrison and Berndt (1981) is of the form

---

19. There are some typos in Prucha and Nadiri (1996) in that between equations (3.4) and (3.6) c^K and c^R should read $\underline{c}^K$ and $\underline{c}^R$, and in equation (3.9) C^+ should read C.

20. For general surveys of functional forms in modeling the firm's technology see, e.g., Fuss, McFadden, and Mundlak (1978) and Lau (1986).

21. The discussion can readily be extended to the case where both types of quasi-fixed factors are present.

(58) $G(p^L, Y, R_{-1}, \Delta R, T)$

$$= Y\Big[\alpha_0 + (a_L)'p^L + (a_R)'\frac{R_{-1}}{Y} + (a_{\dot{R}})'\frac{\Delta R}{Y} + \alpha_T T$$

$$+ 0.5(p^L)'A_{LL}p^L + (p^L)'A_{LR}\frac{R_{-1}}{Y} + (p^L)'A_{L\dot{R}}\frac{\Delta R}{Y} + (a_{LT})'p^L T$$

$$+ 0.5\frac{R'_{-1}}{Y}A_{RR}\frac{R_{-1}}{Y} + \frac{R'_{-1}}{Y}A_{R\dot{R}}\frac{\Delta R}{Y} + (a_{RT})'\frac{R_{-1}}{Y}T$$

$$+ 0.5\frac{\Delta R'}{Y}A_{\dot{R}\dot{R}}\frac{\Delta R}{Y} + (a_{\dot{R}T})'\frac{\Delta R}{Y}T + 0.5\alpha_{TT}T^2\Big]$$

where α_0, α_T, α_{TT} are (scalar) parameters, a_L, a_R, $a_{\dot{R}}$, a_{LT}, a_{RT}, $a_{\dot{R}T}$ are conformably dimensioned parameter vectors and A_{LL}, A_{LR}, $A_{L\dot{R}}$, A_{RR}, $A_{R\dot{R}}$, $A_{\dot{R}\dot{R}}$ are conformably dimensioned parameter matrices. The normalized restricted cost function given in equation (58) can be viewed as having been obtained from a second order approximation of $g(p^L, R_{-1}/Y, \Delta R/Y, T)$. Following Denny, Fuss, and Waverman (1981b) and Morrison and Berndt (1981), the above normalized restricted cost function can be simplified by imposing parameter restrictions such that the marginal adjustment costs are zero at $\Delta R = 0$, i.e., $a_{\dot{R}} = 0$, $A_{L\dot{R}} = 0$, $A_{R\dot{R}} = 0$, $a_{\dot{R}T} = 0$.

Nadiri and Prucha (1990b) generalize this normalized restricted cost function to cover also homothetic technologies by replacing Y on the r.h.s. of equation (58) by $h(Y) = Y^{\phi_0 + \phi_1 \ln(Y)}$. This generalization is based on the observation that the normalized restricted cost function corresponding to homothetic technologies is of the following general form:

(59) $\qquad G(p^L, Y, R_{-1}, \Delta R, T) = g\left(p^L, \frac{R_{-1}}{H(Y)}, \frac{\Delta R}{H(Y)}, T\right)H(Y)$

where $H(Y)$ is some function of Y. We note that $h(Y)$ can—apart from a scaling factor—be viewed as a second-order translog approximation of $H(Y)$, assuming the latter function is sufficiently smooth.[22] Utilizing (15) it is readily seen that scale is given by $[(dH/dY)(Y/H)]^{-1}$. In the special case where $H(Y) = Y^{\phi_1}$ scale equals $1/\phi_1$.

A convenient feature of the normalized restricted cost function equation (58) and its generalization is that they allow for closed form solutions for the firm's optimal factor demand. However, the factor demand equations implied by these restricted cost functions are not symmetric in the sense that they are not invariant as to which of the variable factors is chosen as the numeraire. Thus different normalizations represent different specifications of the technology, which may seem arbitrary.

---

22. Suppose we approximate $H(Y)$ in terms of a second-order expansion in logs, then $\ln H(Y) = const + \phi_0 \ln Y + \phi_1(\ln Y)^2 = const + \ln h(Y)$, and therefore $H(Y) \alpha Y^{\phi_0 + \phi_1 \ln Y}$.

Recently Mohnen (1992a) introduced a new restricted cost function which treats all factors symmetrically, but also allows for closed form solutions for the firm's optimal factor demand. This cost function generalizes the symmetric Generalized McFadden cost function put forth by Diewert and Wales (1987) through the inclusion of quasi-fixed factors. The manner in which the quasi-fixed factors are introduced is analogous to that in equation (59).

A further restricted cost function which treats all factors symmetrically was suggested by Morrison (1990). This restricted cost function represents an extension of the Generalized Leontief restricted cost function introduced by Diewert (1971). Prucha (1990) points out, however, that Morrison's restricted cost function is not invariant to units of measurement. Thus different choices of the units of measurements represent different specifications of the technology, which may again seem arbitrary. Prucha (1990) suggests a modification of Morrison's restricted cost function such that the resulting function is invariant to units of measurement. Based on the observation in equation (59), he also suggests a generalization to cover homothetic technologies.

For all of the above discussed functional forms, the implied Euler equations form in essence a linear system of difference equations, which can be solved explicitly along the lines discussed next in section 4.3.2. The Euler equation estimation approach discussed in section 4.3.3 does not require an explicit solution of the Euler equations. A functional form that has been used widely in conjunction with this approach is the transcendental logarithmic functional form introduced by Christensen, Jorgenson, and Lau (1971, 1973).

4.3.2 Solution and Estimation of Dynamic Factor Demand Models in Case of Linear Quadratic Technologies

Section 4.3.1 provided a general discussion of recent vintages of dynamic factor demand models. In this section, we consider in more detail dynamic factor demand models in case the firm's optimal control problem is of a "linear quadratic" nature. In this case, it is possible to obtain explicit analytic solutions for the firm's optimal factor inputs. We start the discussion by considering a specific example. We then consider the solution and estimation of a general class of "linear quadratic" dynamic factor demand models. To keep this discussion widely applicable, we only specify the model in terms of a set of first order conditions, rather than in terms of a specific cost or profit maximization problem.

Illustrative Example with Endogenous Depreciation Rate

In this subsection, we illustrate the solution and estimation of dynamic factor demand models by considering in detail a specific example of the model considered in section 4.3.1. As our illustrative model we consider the model employed by Prucha and Nadiri (1990, 1996) in analyzing the production structure, factor demand, and productivity growth in the U.S. electrical machinery industry. More specifically, we consider a model with two variable inputs M_t, and L_t, two quasi-fixed factors K_t and R_t, and one output good Y_t. Following Prucha and Nadiri (1990, 1996), we may assume that M_t and L_t denote, respectively, material input and labor input, and K_t and R_t denote, respectively, the end of period stocks of physical capital and R&D, and Y_t denotes gross output. We allow for the firm to determine the depreciation rate of capital endogenously, in that we allow the firm to choose K_t^o, the level of "old" stocks left over at the end of period t from K_{t-1}. The depreciation rate of R&D δ^R is fixed. With p_t^L we denote the price of labor, and q_t^K and q_t^R denote the after tax acquisition price for capital and R&D normalized by the price of material goods. The real discount rate r is taken to be constant over time.

To model the technology, we specify (dropping subscripts t) the following functional form for the normalized variable cost function net of the value of the "old" stocks as

(60) $G(p^L, q^K, K_{-1}, R_{-1}, \Delta K, \Delta R, Y, T)$

$$= Y^{1/\rho}\left[\alpha_0 + \alpha_L p^L + \alpha_{LT} p^L T + \frac{1}{2}\alpha_{K^o K^o}(q^K)^2\right.$$

$$\left. + \alpha_{LK^o} p^L q^K + \frac{1}{2}\alpha_{LL}(p^L)^2\right]$$

$$+ \alpha_K K_{-1} + \alpha_R R_{-1} + \alpha_{KL} K_{-1} p^L + \alpha_{KK^o} K_{-1} q^K$$

$$+ \alpha_{RL} R_{-1} p^L + \alpha_{RK^o} R_{-1} q^K + \alpha_{KT} K_{-1} T + \alpha_{RT} R_{-1} T$$

$$+ Y^{-1/\rho}\left(\frac{1}{2}\alpha_{KK} K_{-1}^2 + \alpha_{KR} K_{-1} R_{-1} + \frac{1}{2}\alpha_{RR} R_{-1}^2\right.$$

$$\left. + \frac{1}{2}\alpha_{\dot{K}\dot{K}} \Delta K^2 + \frac{1}{2}\alpha_{\dot{R}\dot{R}} \Delta R^2\right).$$

We note that the adopted functional form is a special case of the linear quadratic restricted cost function specified in equation (58)—abstracting from the fact that for notational simplicity the specification in equation (58) was given only for the case where the depreciation rates for all quasi-fixed factors are exogenously given. In light of the above discussion, we note further that the technology specified by equation (60) is homogeneous of degree ρ. Also recall that by duality theory $G(\cdot)$ is convex in K, R, ΔK, ΔR and concave in p^L and q^K. This implies the following parameter restrictions: $\alpha_{KK} > 0$, $\alpha_{RR} > 0$, $\alpha_{KK}\alpha_{RR} - \alpha_{KR}^2 > 0$, $\alpha_{\dot{K}\dot{K}} > 0$, $\alpha_{\dot{R}\dot{R}} > 0$, $\alpha_{LL} < 0$, $\alpha_{K^o K^o} < 0$, $\alpha_{LL}\alpha_{K^o K^o} - \alpha_{LK^o}^2 > 0$.

Now suppose the firm's objective is to minimize the present value of its future cost stream. Suppose further that the firm determines its inputs according to a certainty equivalence feedback control policy, and holds static expectations on relative prices, output, and the technology. In this case the firm's objective function is given by the certainty equivalence analog of equation (52) with $G(\cdot)$ defined by equation (60). As discussed above, in each period t the firm establishes a plan for periods $t, t+1, \ldots$ of how to choose its inputs optimally by optimizing this objective function conditional on its expectations, and implements the plan for the current period t (only). The plan is revised every period as new information becomes available. For simplicity, we assume that expected (relative) prices equal current (relative) prices. The certainty equivalence analog of the Euler equations (53) and (54) is then given by ($\tau = 0, 1, \ldots$)

(61) $-\alpha_{\dot{K}\dot{K}}K_{t+\tau+1} + [\alpha_{KK} + (2+r)\alpha_{\dot{K}\dot{K}}]K_{t+\tau} - (1+r)\alpha_{\dot{K}\dot{K}}K_{t+\tau-1} + \alpha_{KR}R_{t+\tau}$

$= -[\alpha_K + \alpha_{KT}T_t + \alpha_{KL}p_t^L + q_t^K(1 + r + \alpha_{KK^0})]\hat{Y}_t^{1/\rho},$

$-\alpha_{\dot{R}\dot{R}}R_{t+\tau+1} + [\alpha_{RR} + (2+r)\alpha_{\dot{R}\dot{R}}]R_{t+\tau} - (1+r)\alpha_{\dot{R}\dot{R}}R_{t+\tau-1} + \alpha_{KR}K_{t+\tau}$

$= -[\alpha_R + \alpha_{RT}T_t + \alpha_{RL}p_t^L + q_t^R(r + \delta^R)]\hat{Y}_t^{1/\rho}$

where $\hat{Y}_t$ denotes expected output. In solving equation (61), we restrict the solution space to the class of processes that are of mean exponential order less than $(1 + r)^{1/2}$.[23] This rules out the unstable roots. (Of course, the unstable roots can also be ruled out by imposing the transversality condition.) As demonstrated in appendix B in Nadiri and Prucha (1999), solving equation (61) yields

(62) $\Delta K_t = m_{KK}(K_t^* - K_{t-1}) + m_{KR}(R_t^* - R_{t-1}),$

$\Delta R_t = m_{RK}(K_t^* - K_{t-1}) + m_{RR}(R_t^* - R_{t-1}),$

with

$$\begin{bmatrix} K_t^* \\ R_t^* \end{bmatrix} = -\begin{bmatrix} \alpha_{KK} & \alpha_{KR} \\ \alpha_{KR} & \alpha_{RR} \end{bmatrix}^{-1}$$

$$\times \begin{bmatrix} \alpha_K + \alpha_{KT}T_t + \alpha_{KL}p_t^L + q_t^K(1 + r + \alpha_{KK^0}) \\ \alpha_R + \alpha_{RT}T_t + \alpha_{RL}p_t^L + q_t^R(r + \delta^R) \end{bmatrix}\hat{Y}_t^{1/\rho}.$$

That is, the optimal quasi-fixed inputs can be described in terms of an accelerator model. The accelerator coefficients $M = (m_{ij})_{i,j=K,R}$ are shown to satisfy the following matrix equation:

---

23. A vector process, say, η_t is said to be of mean exponential order less than κ if there exist constants c and λ with $0 < \lambda < \kappa$ such that $E_t \| \eta_{t+j} \| \leq c\lambda^{t+j}$ for all t and $j > 0$.

(63) $$BM^2 + (A + rB)M - A = 0$$

with $A = (\alpha_{ij})_{i,j=K,R}$ and where B is the diagonal matrix with elements $\alpha_{\dot{K}\dot{K}}$ and $\alpha_{\dot{R}\dot{R}}$ in the diagonal. The matrix $C = (c_{ij})_{i,j=K,R} = -BM$ is seen to be symmetric and negative definite.

The firm's demand equations for the variable factors and the firm's optimal choice for the "old" stock (to be left over from the beginning-of-period capital stock) can be derived from equation (60)—using Shephard's and Hotelling's lemma—as $M_t = G_t - p_t^L L_t + q_t^K K_t^o$, $L_t = \partial G_t / \partial p_t^L$, and $K_t^o = -\partial G_t / \partial q_t^K$:

(64) $$M_t = \left[\alpha_0 - \frac{1}{2}\alpha_{K^o K^o}(q_t^K)^2 - \alpha_{LK^o}p_t^L q_t^K - \frac{1}{2}\alpha_{LL}(p_t^L)^2\right]\hat{Y}_t^{1/\rho}$$
$$+ \alpha_K K_{t-1} + \alpha_R R_{t-1} + \alpha_{KT} K_{t-1} T_t + \alpha_{RT} R_{t-1} T_t$$
$$+ \left[\frac{1}{2}\alpha_{KK}\Delta K_{t-1}^2 + \alpha_{KR} K_{t-1} R_{t-1} + \frac{1}{2}\alpha_{RR} R_{t-1}^2 + \frac{1}{2}\alpha_{\dot{K}\dot{K}}\Delta K_t^2\right.$$
$$\left. + \frac{1}{2}\alpha_{\dot{R}\dot{R}}\Delta R_t^2\right]/\hat{Y}_t^{1/\rho},$$
$$L_t = [\alpha_L + \alpha_{LT} T_t + \alpha_{LK^o} q_t^K + \alpha_{LL} p_t^L]\hat{Y}_t^{1/\rho} + \alpha_{KL} K_{t-1}$$
$$+ \alpha_{RL} R_{t-1},$$

and

(65) $$K_t^o = -[\alpha_{LK^o} p_t^L + \alpha_{K^o K^o} q_t^K]\hat{Y}_t^{1/\rho} - \alpha_{KK^o} K_{t-1} - \alpha_{RK^o} R_{t-1}.$$

Equation (65) provides an economic model for K_t^o and hence for the depreciation rate of capital δ_t^K; recall that the depreciation rate of capital is implicitly defined by $K_t^o = (1 - \delta_t^K)K_{t-1}$. Equation (65) explains K_t^o as a function of relative prices, output, and lagged stocks. The case of a constant and exogenously given depreciation rate is contained as a special case with $\alpha_{LK^o} = \alpha_{K^o K^o} = \alpha_{RK^o} = 0$ and $\alpha_{KK^o} = -(1 - \delta^K)$. We emphasize that by imposing those zero restrictions we can formally test whether or not the depreciation rate is constant.[24]

One difficulty we face in trying to estimate this model is that in general the quadratic matrix equation (63) cannot be solved for M in terms of A and B. The equation can, however, be solved for A in terms of M and B: $A = BM(M + rI)(I - M)^{-1}$. Since the real discount rate r was assumed to be constant, the matrix M is constant over the sample. Hence, instead

---

24. As discussed in more detail in section 4.4, Prucha and Nadiri (1996) cannot reject the hypothesis of a constant depreciation rate for physical capital in the U.S. electrical machinery industry.

of estimating the elements of A and B, we may estimate those of M and B.[25] To impose the symmetry of C we can also estimate B and C instead of B and M. Observe that $A = C - (1 + r)[B - B(C + B)^{-1}B]$ and hence

(66) $\quad \alpha_{KK} = c_{KK} - (1 + r)[\alpha_{\dot{K}\dot{K}} - (\alpha_{\dot{K}\dot{K}})^2(\alpha_{\dot{R}\dot{R}} + c_{RR})/f],$

$\quad \alpha_{RR} = c_{RR} - (1 + r)[\alpha_{\dot{R}\dot{R}} - (\alpha_{\dot{R}\dot{R}})^2(\alpha_{\dot{K}\dot{K}} + c_{KK})/f],$

$\quad \alpha_{KR} = c_{KR} - (1 + r)(\alpha_{\dot{K}\dot{K}}\alpha_{\dot{R}\dot{R}}c_{KR})/f,$

with

$$f = (\alpha_{\dot{K}\dot{K}} + c_{KK})(\alpha_{\dot{R}\dot{R}} + c_{RR}) - c_{KR}^2.$$

To reparameterize equation (62), it also proves helpful to define $D = (d_{ij})_{i,j=K,R} = -MA^{-1}$. Observe that $D = B^{-1} + (1 + r)(C - rB)^{-1}$. Hence, D is symmetric and its elements are given by

(67) $\quad d_{KK} = 1/\alpha_{\dot{K}\dot{K}} + (1 + r)[c_{RR} - r\alpha_{\dot{R}\dot{R}}]/e,$

$\quad d_{RR} = 1/\alpha_{\dot{R}\dot{R}} + (1 + r)[c_{KK} - r\alpha_{\dot{K}\dot{K}}]/e,$

$\quad d_{KR} = -(1 + r)c_{KR}/e,$

with

$$e = (c_{KK} - r\alpha_{\dot{K}\dot{K}})(c_{RR} - r\alpha_{\dot{R}\dot{R}}) - c_{KR}^2.$$

Given the definition of D we can rewrite equation (62) as

(68) $\quad \Delta K_t = d_{KK}[\alpha_K + \alpha_{KT}T_t + \alpha_{KL}p_t^L + q_t^K(1 + r + \alpha_{K^oK^o})]\hat{Y}_t^{1/\rho}$

$\quad + d_{KR}[\alpha_R + \alpha_{RT}T_t + \alpha_{RL}p_t^L + q_t^R(r + \delta^R)]\hat{Y}_t^{1/\rho}$

$\quad + [c_{KK}/\alpha_{\dot{K}\dot{K}}]K_{t-1} + [c_{KR}/\alpha_{\dot{K}\dot{K}}]R_{t-1},$

$\Delta R_t = d_{KR}[\alpha_K + \alpha_{KT}T_t + \alpha_{KL}p_t^L + q_t^K(1 + r + \alpha_{K^oK^o})]\hat{Y}_t^{1/\rho}$

$\quad + d_{RR}[\alpha_R + \alpha_{RT}T_t + \alpha_{RL}p_t^L + q_t^R(r + \delta^R)]\hat{Y}_t^{1/\rho}$

$\quad + [c_{KR}/\alpha_{\dot{R}\dot{R}}]K_{t-1} + [c_{RR}/\alpha_{\dot{R}\dot{R}}]R_{t-1}.$

The reparameterized factor demand equations are now given by equations (64), (65), and (68) with α_{KK}, α_{RR}, α_{KR}, d_{KK}, d_{RR}, and d_{KR} defined by equations (66) and (67). Once the model has been estimated in the reparameter-

---

25. This reparameterization approach was first suggested by Epstein and Yatchew (1985) for a somewhat different model with a similar algebra, and was further generalized by Madan and Prucha (1989). It will be discussed in more detail and within a generalized setting in the next subsection. For additional empirical studies utilizing the reparameterization approach, see, e.g., Mohnen, Nadiri, and Prucha (1986) and Nadiri and Prucha (1990a,b).

ized form, we can obtain estimates for the original model parameters via $A = C - (1 + r)[B - B(C + B)^{-1}B]$.

A further difficulty in estimating the factor demand equations is that

(69) $$K_t = I_t^K + K_t^o$$

is unobserved, since K_t^o depends on a set of unknown model parameters. (We note that K_t^o is unobserved even in the special case of a constant and exogenously given depreciation rate, that is, even in the case where $\alpha_{LK^o} = \alpha_{K^oK^o} = \alpha_{RK^o} = 0$ and $\alpha_{KK^o} = -(1 - \delta^K)$, as long as δ^K is estimated from the data.) We now assume, analogously to the approach taken by Epstein and Denny (1980), that equation (65) for K_t^o holds exactly. This assumption is clearly strong. However, it facilitates expression of the unobservable stocks K_t and K_t^o, at least in principle, as functions of observable variables and the unknown model parameters. More specifically, by solving equation (65) together with the identity $K_t = I_t^K + K_t^o$ recursively for K_t and K_t^o from some given initial capital stock, say K_0, we can express K_t as a function of $I_t^K, I_{t-1}^K, \ldots, K_0, R_{t-1}, R_{t-2}, \ldots$, the exogenous variables and the model parameters. Consequently, upon replacing K_t and K_{t-1} in the variable factor demand equation (64) and in the quasi-fixed factor demand equation (68) by the expressions so obtained we can, at least in principle, rewrite the system of factor demand equations as a dynamic system of equations that determines I_t^K, R_t, M_t, and L_t, and where in the so obtained system *all variables are observable.* (If the initial stock is unobserved we may treat it as an additional parameter.)

For purposes of estimation, we need to add stochastic disturbance terms to each of the factor demand equations (64) and (68). Those disturbances can be viewed as random errors of optimization, errors in the data, or as stemming from random shocks observed by the firm but not by the researcher; cp., for example, Epstein and Yatchew (1985). Assuming that the disturbances are not correlated with the variables in the firm's information set we can, for example, use those variables (and functions of them) as instruments in estimating the model by the generalized method of moments (GMM) approach. The GMM estimation approach was introduced by Hansen (1982) within the context of stationary data generating processes. To allow for (possibly unknown) correlation over time, we may estimate the variance covariance matrix of the moments with a heteroskedasticity and autocorrelation robust variance covariance matrix estimator. For a general discussion and recent results concerning the asymptotic properties of GMM estimators for (possibly) temporally dependent and nonstationary data generating processes, including a discussion and consistency results of heteroskedasticity and autocorrelation robust variance covariance matrix estimator, see, for example, Gallant and White (1988) and Pötscher and Prucha (1997).

Numerical algorithms for the computation of estimators that are defined as optimizers of some statistical objective function—as, for example, the generalized methods of moments estimator or maximum likelihood estimator—generally require the numerical evaluation of the statistical objective function for different sets of parameter values. We note that for the actual numerical computation of estimators of the model parameters it is not necessary to solve equations (65) and (69) analytically for K_t (and K_t^o). Rather we can first solve, for any given set of parameter values, equations (65) and (69) numerically for K_t (and K_t^o), and then employ the numerical solution for K_t (rather than the analytic solution) in evaluating the statistical objective function. This approach is, however, typically cumbersome in that it requires the programming of the estimation algorithm by the researcher. Recently Prucha (1995, 1997) suggested a more convenient approach based on a reformulation of the analytic solution. This approach can be performed with standard econometric packages such as TSP.

Solution and Estimation of a General Class of Models

The illustrative example presented in the previous subsection can be viewed as a special case of a more general class of models where the firm's optimization problem involves the computation of a stochastic closed loop optimal control solution and where the objective function is "linear quadratic." As discussed above, the stochastic closed loop optimal control solution can always be found in two steps. In the first step we optimize the firm's objective function in each period with respect to the variable factors, for given values of the quasi-fixed factors. Substitution of the optimized values for the variable factors back into the firm's objective function then yields a new optimal control problem that only involves the quasi-fixed factors, which can be solved in a second step. In the following, let X_t denote the, say, $n \times 1$ vector of quasi-fixed factors—that is, the vector of control variables for the second step.

For a wide class of linear quadratic optimal control problems, the optimal control solution will have to satisfy a set of linear second order difference equations (possibly after recasting a higher order difference equation system into a second order one). In particular, assume that the control variables satisfy the following set of difference equations ($\tau = t, t + 1, \ldots$):

$$(70) \qquad -\underline{B} E_\tau X_{\tau+1} + \underline{G} X_\tau - (1 + r)\underline{B}' X_{\tau-1} = E_\tau \phi_\tau$$

where $\underline{B}$ and $\underline{G}$ are $n \times n$ matrices, the ϕ_τs represent a set of forcing variables, r is the discount rate, and where the respective expectations are assumed to exist. Since the objective function is linear quadratic, certainty equivalence implies that solving equation (70) is equivalent to solving the difference equations ($\tau = t, t + 1, \ldots$):

$$(71) \qquad -\underline{B} X_{\tau+1} + \underline{G} X_\tau - (1 + r)\underline{B}' X_{\tau-1} = (1 + r)\underline{a}_\tau$$

with $\underline{a}_\tau = E_t \phi_\tau / (1 + r)$.

We note that while the methodology discussed here is presented within the context of dynamic factor demand models, it applies more generally to any rational expectations model where the data generating process X_t is determined in the preceding manner.[26] The literature on finding optimal control solutions and solving rational expectations models has a long history.[27] The aim of the methodology outlined below is not only to obtain a solution of equation (71) for the X_t, but to express the solution so that the estimation of the model can be performed by standard econometric packages (such as TSP).

We assume that $\underline{B}$ is nonsingular and restrict the solution space to the class of processes X_t that are of mean exponential order less than $(1 + r)^{1/2}$. The characteristic roots of the difference equation system (71) are defined as solutions of

$$(72) \qquad p(\lambda) = \det[-\underline{B}\lambda^2 + \underline{G}\lambda - (1 + r)\underline{B}'] = 0.$$

It is well known and not difficult to show that those characteristic roots come in pairs multiplying to $(1 + r)$. We assume that these roots are distinct. It then follows that there are exactly n roots that are less than $(1 + r)^{1/2}$ in modulus. Let Λ be the $n \times n$ diagonal matrix of these roots, and let V be the $n \times n$ matrix of solution vectors corresponding to those roots, that is,

$$(73) \qquad -\underline{B}V\Lambda^2 + \underline{G}V\Lambda - (1 + r)\underline{B}'V = 0.$$

As in Kollintzas (1986) and Madan and Prucha (1989), we assume that V is nonsingular, and define $M = I - V\Lambda V^{-1}$. Given the maintained assumptions, the following theorem follows, for example, from Madan and Prucha (1989):

THEOREM 1. *The solution for X_t of the difference equation system (70) (or, because of certainty equivalence, [71]) is uniquely given by the following accelerator model:*

$$(74) \quad X_t = MX_t^* + (I - M)X_{t-1}, \quad X_t^* = \underline{A}^{-1}J_t,$$

$$J_t = D\sum_{\tau=t}^{\infty}(I + D)^{-(\tau-t+1)}\underline{a}_\tau,$$

$$D = (1 + r)(I - M')^{-1} - I,$$

$$\underline{A} = (I - M')^{-1}(rI + M')\underline{B}M/(1 + r) = D\underline{B}M/(1 + r).$$

---

26. We note that the discussion also applies to processes described by a set of higher order difference equations, as long as that system can be rewritten as a second order difference equation system of the above form.

27. See, e.g., Epstein and Yatchew (1985), Hansen and Sargent (1980, 1981), Kokkelenberg and Bischoff (1986), Kollintzas (1985), and Madan and Prucha (1989). See also Binder and Pesaran (1995, 1997) for a recent review of rational expectations models and macroeconometric modelling.

The accelerator matrix M satisfies

(75) $\quad -\underline{B}(I - M)^2 + \underline{G}(I - M) - (1 + r)\underline{B}' = 0.$

Furthermore, $S = \underline{B}(I - M)$ is symmetric.

In the case of static expectations on the forcing variables we have $\underline{a}_\tau = \underline{a}_t$. In this case the above solution simplifies in that in this case $J_t = \underline{a}_t$.

Madan and Prucha's proof of the theorem is based on a decomposition of X_τ into a backward component, given by $(I - M)X_{\tau-1}$, and a forward component, given by $g_\tau = X_\tau - (I - M)X_{\tau-1}$, where M is determined by equation (75). This basic approach has recently also been used by Binder and Pesaran (1995, 1997) to solve rational expectations models, where, in our notation, $\underline{B}$ is allowed to be nonsingular. Binder and Pesaran refer to this approach as the quadratic determinantal equation (QDE) method.

The quadratic matrix equation (75) can generally not be solved for M in terms of the original parameter matrices $\underline{B}$ and $\underline{G}$, except in case X_t is a scalar; that is, $n = 1$. However, we can use equation (75) to express $\underline{G}$ in terms of M and $\underline{B}$, that is,

(76) $\quad \underline{G} = \underline{B}(I - M) + (1 + r)\underline{B}'(I - M)^{-1}.$

Thus, we can reparameterize the model in terms of M and $\underline{B}$, and estimate M and $\underline{B}$ rather than the original parameter matrices $\underline{G}$ and $\underline{B}$. As remarked above, this reparameterization approach was first suggested by Epstein and Yatchew (1985) within the context of a symmetric dynamic factor demand model where $\underline{B} = \underline{B}'$ (and $\underline{G} = \underline{G}'$). Madan and Prucha (1989) point out that this symmetry is, for example, typically violated if factors are allowed to become productive at different points in time—for example, if some factors become productive immediately and some with a lag—and/or if we allow for nonseparability between the adjustment cost terms and the inputs. Madan and Prucha (1989) then extend the reparameterization approach to nonsymmetric dynamic factor demand models with $\underline{B} \neq \underline{B}'$ (and $\underline{G} = \underline{G}'$). This approach is presented in more detail in appendix B in Nadiri and Prucha (1999).[28] The discussion in this appendix also considers an explicit specification of the stochastic process governing the forcing variables. In adopting a re-parameterization for the parameters describing that process, it is possible, as also demonstrated in this appendix, to obtain closed form analytic expressions for X_t in terms of the model parameters and the forcing variables. The advantage of the reparameterized model is that it can be estimated with standard econometric packages such as TSP.[29]

---

28. Both Epstein and Yatchew (1985) and Madan and Prucha (1989) consider matrices G with additional structure, which they utilize during the reparameterization. The discussion in this appendix shows that the reparameterization approach works even without additional structure on G.

29. The above discussion of the solution and estimation of dynamic factor demand models is given in form of a discrete time model. The reason for this is that empirical data typically

4.3.3 Estimation of Dynamic Factor Demand Models for General Technologies

The theoretical model specified in section 4.3.1 is quite general, and allows for the firm's technology and optimal control problem to be "non-linear quadratic." We note that in case the firm's optimal control problem is not of a linear quadratic nature, it is generally not possible to obtain an explicit analytic expression for the firm's stochastic closed loop feedback control solution. In the following, we discuss strategies for estimating non-linear quadratic dynamic factor demand models. Those strategies can, of course, also be applied in estimating linear quadratic dynamic factor demand models.

Before proceeding we reemphasize that while the model specification in section 4.3.1 is quite general, the discussion does not impose this generality. That is, the discussion also covers implicitly less general specifications as special cases. The specification in section 4.3.1 contains in particular the case where all factors are variable—and hence the firm is at each point in time in long-run equilibrium—or the case where the depreciation rates of all quasi-fixed factors are exogenously given as special cases.

Estimation of Variable Factor Demand Equations

In estimating a factor demand model we can, in principle, always attempt to estimate the unknown model parameters from only a subset rather than the entire set of factor demand equations. Statistically there are pros and cons for such a strategy: If the model is correctly specified, we will generally obtain more efficient estimates by utilizing the entire set of factor demand equations rather than a subset. However, if one or a subset of the factor demand equations is misspecified, then not only the parameters appearing in the misspecified equations, but in general all model parameters will be estimated inconsistently.

As is evident from the discussion in section 4.3.1, certain aspects of the model specification such as the nature of the optimal control policy and the expectation formation process only enter into the specification of the demand equations for the quasi-fixed factors. Consequently, in this sense the demand equations for the quasi-fixed factors are more susceptible to potential misspecification than the demand equations for the variable factors. In cases where the determinants of the demand for the quasi-fixed factors are not of real interest, but where one is especially concerned about the possibility of misspecification of the quasi-fixed factor demand equations, it may be prudent only to estimate the variable factor demand equa-

---

refer to discrete time points. Potential pitfalls in using formulas for the optimal factor inputs derived from a continuous time model for estimation from discrete data are considered in Prucha and Nadiri (1991). For a more detailed discussion see Nadiri and Prucha (1999).

tions. By estimating only the variable factor demand equations, we are typically also faced with a less complex estimation problem.

The variable factor demand systems can take various forms depending on the specification of the technology. For example, in case the technology is specified in terms of a translog restricted cost function the variable factor demand system is typically given by a system of share equations.[30] The model specified in section 4.3.1 allows depreciation rates of some of the quasi-fixed factors to be determined endogenously and to be modeled as a function of unknown parameters. As remarked above, as a result the stocks of those quasi-fixed factors are then unobserved. To estimate the system of variable factors, we may proceed analogously as outlined at the end of section 4.3.2, subsection "Illustrative Example with Endogenous Depreciation Rate"; for empirical applications see, for example, Epstein and Denny (1980) and Nadiri and Prucha (1996).

Euler Equation Estimation Approach

In section 4.3.1 we derived a general set of stochastic Euler equations that need to be satisfied by the stochastic closed loop feedback optimal control solution for the quasi-fixed factors without restricting the technology to be linear quadratic. Those stochastic Euler equations are given by equations (53) and (54). In section 4.3.2 we solved those equations explicitly for the case where the technology is, indeed, linear quadratic. In case the technology is non–linear quadratic, such an explicit solution is generally not available. In this case we may then adopt an alternative estimation approach due to Kennan (1979), Hansen (1982), Hansen and Sargent (1982), and Hansen and Singleton (1982).[31] In this approach all expectations of future variables are replaced by their observed values in future periods. More specifically, in this approach we would rewrite the stochastic Euler equations (53) and (54) as

$$(77) \quad -\partial G_{t+1}/\partial K_t \Big/ (1 + r_{t+1}) - (q_t^K)' - \frac{\partial G_t}{\partial \Delta K_t} + \frac{\partial G_{t+1}}{\partial \Delta K_{t+1}} \Big/ (1 + r_{t+1}) = v_t^K,$$

$$(78) \quad -\partial G_{t+1}/\partial R_t \Big/ (1 + r_{t+1}) - (c_t^R)' - \frac{\partial G_t}{\partial \Delta R_t} + \frac{\partial G_{t+1}}{\partial \Delta R_{t+1}} \Big/ (1 + r_{t+1}) = v_t^R.$$

---

30. The variable factor demand equations typically form a triangular structural system. Lahiri and Schmidt (1978) point out that the full information maximum likelihood (FIML) estimator and the iterative seemingly unrelated regressions (SUR) estimator are identical for triangular structural systems. This identity might be thought to imply that for such systems the variance covariance matrix estimator typically associated with the SUR estimator is a consistent estimator for the asymptotic variance covariance matrix. However, Prucha (1987) points out that this is generally not the case.

31. The approach has been used widely in empirical work. Early empirical implementations include Pindyck and Rotemberg (1983) and Shapiro (1986).

If expectations are truly formed rationally, we have $E_t v_t^K = 0$ and $E_t v_t^R = 0$, and equations (77) and (78) can then be estimated consistently by the GMM estimation approach.[32] Of course, the stochastic Euler equations (77) and (78) can be augmented by the demand equations for the variable factors. Recall that K_t denotes the vector of quasi-fixed factors for which the depreciation rates are determined endogenously and are modeled as a function of unknown parameters. Thus, as remarked, K_t is unobserved. In estimating the demand equations, we may again proceed analogously as outlined at the end of the "Illustrative Example" subsection.

The Euler equation estimation approach allows considerable flexibility in the choice of the functional form for the technology. Also, it does not require an explicit specification of the process that generates the variables exogenous to the firm's decision process or specific assumptions concerning the firm's planning horizon. However, it is generally not fully efficient in that it neglects information from the entire set of Euler equations (and, e.g., the transversality condition), which only comes into play by actually solving the Euler equations. In their comparison of alternative methods for estimating dynamic factor demand models, Prucha and Nadiri (1986) report that small sample biases and efficiency losses seem especially pronounced for parameters that determine the dynamics of the demand for the quasi-fixed factors. We note further that, although the Euler equation estimation approach does not require either an analytic or numerical solution for the firm's optimal demand for the quasi-fixed factors, such a solution—or some approximation to it—will be needed, for example, for tax simulations.[33]

4.3.4 Further Developments

There have been other important developments in addition to those described above. In particular, since the late 1970s there was a process of convergence between the investment literature based on Tobin's (1969) q and the investment literature with explicit adjustment costs. In Tobin's investment model the rate of investment is a function of q, defined as the ratio of the market value of capital to its replacement cost. Hayashi (1982) shows the equivalence of the two investment theories for a general class of models; see also Mussa (1977) and Abel (1983). The literature distinguishes between average q, defined as the ratio of the market value of existing capital to its replacement cost, and marginal q, defined as the ratio of the market value of an additional unit of capital to its replacement cost.

---

32. For references concerning the asymptotic properties of GMM estimators see the discussion at the end of section 4.3.2.
33. A further approach for modeling and estimating dynamic factor demand models that allows for "non–linear quadratic" technologies and nonstatic expectations, and is based on a finite horizon specification, was suggested in several papers by Prucha and Nadiri (1982, 1986, 1988, 1991); recent contributions include Gordon (1996) and Steigerwald and Stuart (1997). A more detailed discussion is given in Nadiri and Prucha (1999).

While average q is observable, marginal q, which is the quantity relevant for the firm's investment decision, is not observable. However, Hayashi (1982) also derives an exact relationship between average q and marginal q, which is important for a proper empirical implementation of the q theory of investment.

Another important development is an expanding literature that considers the effects of irreversibility combined with uncertainty and timing flexibility on the firm's investment decision. Irreversibility is another avenue that introduces a dynamic element into the investment decisions. The literature on irreversible investment dates back to Arrow (1968). The more recent literature utilizes option pricing techniques to determine the firm's optimal investment pattern under irreversibility. A survey of this literature and exposition of those techniques is given in Dixit and Pindyck (1994). One way to incorporate irreversibility into an adjustment cost model is to assume infinitely large adjustment costs for negative investment. This approach was, for example, taken by Caballero (1991). Another approach was explored by Abel and Eberly (1994). Their model incorporates Arrow's observation that the resale price of capital may be less than the purchase price of new capital, which includes the case where the resale of capital is impossible, corresponding to the extreme case of a resale price of zero. Additionally, their model includes adjustment costs as well as fixed costs and thus provides for an interesting integration of the irreversible investment and adjustment cost literature.

4.4 Applications

There are numerous applications of the factor demand models using different sets of data and answering important questions of theoretical, empirical, and policy interest. There is a vast literature showing the widespread use of factor demand models for empirical analysis.[34] The class of dynamic factor demand models considered in section 4.3 has been used to study a variety of subjects ranging from the analysis of the production structure of various industries, the rate of technical change, the impact of R&D investment and R&D spillovers, the convergence of productivity levels, the effect of public infrastructure on the private sector productivity, the impact of financial variables on production decisions, the cyclical behavior of utilization and markup of prices over costs, and so on. Here we will provide only a brief description of a few applications of dynamic factor demand models for illustrative purposes. To save space, we do not report on the formal structure of the models used in the studies.

As remarked above, besides analyzing productivity behavior, the dynamic factor demand methodology also addresses issues concerning the

---

34. See, e.g., Berndt, Morrison, and Watkins (1981), Jorgenson (1986, 1995a,b, 1996a,b), Watkins (1991), and Good, Nadiri, and Sickles (1997) for partial references.

structure of production such as substitution among factors of production in response to changes in relative prices; technological change; changes in public capital; international, interindustry, or interfirm spillovers due to R&D investment; and so on. The time path of the adjustment of different types of capital and the linkages between short-, intermediate-, and long-run behavior are explicitly modeled and estimated. Changes in capacity utilization rates and depreciation rates of different types of capital and their effects on the demand for other inputs can be estimated. Given estimates of the depreciation rates it is possible to decompose gross investment into replacement and net investments, and generate consistent measures of capital stocks within the framework of the dynamic factor demand model.

4.4.1 Tax Incentives, Financing, and Technical Change

The effect of taxes and other incentives on factor demand and output growth has been of a long and ongoing interest in the literature. The role of taxes as a component of the user cost of capital was made clear in seminal papers by Jorgenson (1963) and Hall and Jorgenson (1967, 1971). Jorgenson and his associates have examined the impact of tax incentives for business investment in the United States in a series of papers; see Jorgenson (1996b) for more detailed references. Hall and Jorgenson (1967, 1971) modeled the accelerated depreciation of the 1954 tax law and guidelines for asset lifetimes, the investment tax credit introduced in 1962, the reduction in corporate tax rate in 1964 and the suspension of the investment tax credit in 1966. These tax law changes were incorporated as elements of the user cost of capital. The general conclusion of this body of work was that investment incentives exert a considerable long-run effect on the rate of capital accumulation. Each major change in investment incentives was followed by an investment boom which in turn led to increases in the level of economic activity that induced further increases in investment. However, the lag between changes in investment incentives and investment expenditure was found to be fairly long.

As discussed in section 4.3, given the underlying intertemporal optimization framework, the notion of a user cost of capital or the after tax acquisition price is also present within the framework of the dynamic factor demand models reviewed in this paper. A general discussion of the effect of taxes and incentives within the context of dynamic factor demand models is, for example, provided by Bernstein and Nadiri (1987). We emphasize that in general the effect of any tax changes designed to affect a particular factor of production will influence also the demand for other inputs. This arises from the interrelatedness of factors. Early generations of dynamic factor demand models assumed separability between the quasi-fixed factors and hence could not fully capture such effects.

Tax policy operates through factor prices. The effect of changes in tax policy depends in general on the degree of substitutability or complementarity among factors of production. As discussed in section 4.2, technological change, if not neutral, depends on relative prices (as is, e.g., evident from its definition on the cost side). Hence, tax policy can also affect technological change. We note that in the short-run the effects of changes in tax policy on factor demands may be quite different from their effects in the long-run in that in the short-run the firm may find it advantageous to over-adjust some of its variable factors to lessen the effects of adjustment costs. The framework of a dynamic factor demand model also provides a natural setting for analyzing the effects of expectations about future tax policies.

As an illustration of the application of the dynamic factor demand models for tax analysis, consider the recent study by Bernstein (1994). The tax instruments considered are the corporate income tax (CIT), the investment tax allowances (ITA), and capital consumption allowance (CCA). A normalized variable profit function with quadratic adjustment costs for capital stock is formulated and the model is estimated using data for the Turkish electrical machinery, non-electrical machinery, and transportation equipment industries. The empirical results suggest the following findings:

1. The adjustment cost parameter estimates suggest that these industries are not in long-run equilibrium. The mean value of the speed of adjustment ranged between 0.33 to 0.36 for each of the industries, implying that about 35 percent of the capital stock adjustment occurs within the first year of capital accumulation.

2. The effects of taxes and incentives on production and investment decisions are transmitted though changes in the rental price of capital. The magnitudes of the input elasticities to changes in tax instruments differ in short-, intermediate-, and long-run due to the presence of adjustment costs. They also differ with respect to the various tax policy instruments, as well as across industries. The long-run elasticities of output and the inputs are quite small, but larger than the short- and intermediate-run elasticities. Another important point is that, because of the interdependence among production decisions embedded in the dynamic factor demand models, taxes and incentives targeted toward a particular input also have effects on the other inputs.

3. Productivity growth can be affected by the tax policies. This arises since productivity growth depends on the growth of output and inputs, which are affected by changes in factor prices. As noted above, the latter are in turn affected by changes in tax instruments.

As illustrated by the above discussion, dynamic factor demand models provide a powerful framework to trace the effects of various policy decisions, such as tax and incentive policies and financial decisions. It is possible to examine the impact of these decisions in the short, intermediate, and long run on the production decisions and productivity performance. Also, the effect of expectations can be examined in this framework.

4.4.2 R&D Investment, Production Structure, and TFP Decomposition

The role of R&D and the behavior of other factors of production in the United States, Japanese, and German manufacturing industries was explored by Mohnen, Nadiri, and Prucha (1983, 1986) based on a special case of the dynamic factor demand model considered in section 4.3. One of the results of the study was that the average net rates of return were similar for both R&D and capital in the manufacturing sectors of the three countries. However, the rate of return on R&D was greater than that on capital in each sector. A further finding was that it takes a considerably longer time for the R&D stock to adjust to its optimum value than for the physical capital stock. The average lag for capital was approximately three years in the three countries, while the average lag for R&D was about five years in the United States, eight years in Japan, and ten years in Germany. The patterns of own- and cross-price elasticities of the inputs varied considerably among countries. The own-price elasticities were generally higher than the cross-price elasticities. There was mostly a substitutional relationship between the inputs. The output elasticities of the inputs in the short and intermediate runs differed from each other and across countries. The materials input overshot in the short run its long-run equilibrium value to compensate for the sluggish adjustments of the two quasi-fixed inputs, capital, and R&D; the output elasticities of the capital stock were larger than those of R&D in the short and intermediate runs; also, there was evidence of short-run increasing returns to labor. The Japanese manufacturing sector seems to have higher elasticities than the U.S. manufacturing sector and to display more flexibility.

Nadiri and Prucha (1990b) explore the production structure of the U.S. Bell System before its divestiture.[35] They consider a model with two variable factors, labor and materials, and two quasi-fixed factors, physical and R&D capital. The technology is not assumed to be linear homogeneous, but is allowed to be homothetic of a general form. The estimated degree of scale was about 1.6. As a consequence, in decomposing the traditional TFP measure they find that almost 80 percent of the growth of TFP is attributable to scale. The conventional TFP measure, if it is considered as a measure of technical change, was thus seriously biased upwards. The estimated rate of technical change was only about 10–15 percent of the measured TFP. The most significant source of output growth was the growth of capital with a contribution of over 50 percent, while labor and material contributed about 15 percent, and the contribution of technical change

---

35. For an exploration of Bell Canada see, e.g., Bernstein (1989b) and Fuss (1994).

was about half as much. The growth of R&D contributed about 2 percent, which, given its small share in the production is fairly substantial. The rate of return on R&D, however, was much greater than that on plant and equipment investment. The net rate of return for R&D investment is about 20 percent in comparison to the net rate of return of about 7 percent for investment in physical capital.

The study by Nadiri and Prucha also considers alternative specifications of the length of the planning horizon and the expectation formation process. They find that the optimal plans for the finite horizon model converge rapidly to those of the infinite horizon model as the planning horizon extends. This observation suggests that additional planning costs will quickly exceed additional gains from extending the planning horizon, which may provide a rationale for why many firms plan only for short periods into the future. Parameter estimates differ in their sensitivity to alternative specifications of the expectation formation process. Estimates of parameters determining the adjustment path of capital and R&D turned out to be sensitive. On the other hand, estimates of other characteristics of the underlying technology such as scale seem to be insensitive to the specification of the expectation formation process.

Recently the dynamic factor demand framework has been used to explore the role of high-tech capital and information technology equipment, as well as human capital, on the production structure and productivity growth in U.S. manufacturing; see Morrison (1997) and Morrison and Siegel (1997). One finding is that high-tech capital expansion increases demand for most capital and non-capital inputs overall, but saves on material inputs.

4.4.3 Technological Spillovers and Productivity Growth

An important feature of R&D investment that distinguishes it from other forms of investment is that firms which undertake R&D investment are often not able to exclude others from freely obtaining some of the benefits; that is, the benefits from R&D investment spill over to other firms in the economy, and the recipient firms do not have to pay for the use of knowledge generated by the investing firms' R&D activity. R&D spillovers may affect the production structure and factor demand in several ways. In particular, R&D investment may shift the production function up (or the cost function downward). This is the direct productivity effect. Also, changes in the R&D spillover may cause factor substitution. In the language of the technological change literature, changes in R&D spillovers may cause factor biases, which may be either factor using or factor saving. Changes in the R&D spillovers may also affect the adjustment process of the quasi-fixed factors.

There are a number of empirical studies using the dynamic factor demand framework to measure the impact of technology spillover.[36] As an illustration, consider the Bernstein and Nadiri (1989) study which provides an example of intraindustry spillover effects among the U.S. instruments, machinery, petroleum, and chemical industries. Several interesting results are reported:

1. The adjustment process of the two quasi-fixed inputs were shown to be interdependent; that is, as the physical and R&D capitals adjust toward their equilibrium levels, the speed of adjustment of one is affected by the adjustment of the other. The estimates indicate that about 33–42 percent of the adjustment of the physical capital stock occurred within a single year. R&D capital adjustment is lower than that of physical capital; the estimates show that about 22–30 percent of the adjustment of R&D capital occurred in one year. The adjustment processes vary across the industries.

2. There are a number of effects associated with the intraindustry R&D spillover. First, costs decline as knowledge expands for the externality-receiving firms. Second, production structures are affected, as factor demands change in response to the spillover. Third, the rates of both physical and knowledge capital accumulation are affected by the R&D spillover. The results indicate that the short-run demand for R&D and physical capital decreased in response to an increase in the intraindustry spillovers. Both the variable and average costs for each industry declined in response to the intra-industry spillovers. Spillover-receiving firms gained a 0.05 percent, 0.08 percent, 0.11 percent, and 0.13 percent average cost reduction, respectively, in the instruments, machinery, petroleum, and chemical industries as a result of a 1 percent increase in the intraindustry spillover. Not surprisingly, the effect of spillovers on the factor inputs and cost was larger in the long run than in the short run.

3. The results also indicate that for all four industries the net social rate of return greatly exceeded the net private rate of return. However, there was significant variation across industries in the differential between the returns. For chemicals and instruments, the social rate of return exceeded the private rate of return by 67 and 90 percent, respectively. Machinery exhibited the smallest differential of about 30 percent, and the petroleum industry exhibited the greatest differential as the social rate exceeded the private rate by 123 percent.

---

36. In recent years there has been a considerable effort to model and estimate the role of R&D spillover. There are a number of different approaches that have been taken to specify and measure technical spillover effects. Recent studies on R&D spillovers within the framework of dynamic factor demand models other than those discussed in this section include papers by Bernstein (1989a), Bernstein and Nadiri (1988), Goto and Suzuki (1989), Mohnen (1992a), Mohnen and Lépine (1991), and Srinivasan (1995).

Bernstein's (1988) study of Canadian industries shows that spillovers occur between rival firms within the same industry and between firms operating in different industries. These spillovers, specially those associated with interindustry spillovers, caused unit costs to decline and the structure of production of the receiving industries to change as the spillovers induced factor substitution. The productivity effect of the spillovers and the gap between the private and social rates of return to R&D varied among the industries.

Mohnen (1992b) explored the question of possible cross-country R&D spillovers among the manufacturing sectors of the United States, Japan, France, and the United Kingdom. He used a cost function with quasi-fixed factors and adjustment cost based on the symmetric generalized McFadden functional form. The results indicated that foreign R&D yields greater cost reduction than own R&D, own R&D and foreign R&D are complementary and foreign R&D can explain part of the productivity convergence among the manufacturing sectors of the leading industrial countries. In the case of the Canadian manufacturing sector, Mohnen (1992a) reports surprisingly weak spillover effects for R&D undertaken in other major industrialized countries. Bernstein and Mohnen (1998) have developed a bilateral model of production between U.S. and Japanese economies and trace the effects of international R&D spillovers on production cost, traditional factor demands, the demand for R&D capital, and productivity growth in each country. Their results show that international spillovers increased U.S. productivity growth by about 15 percent, while productivity growth of the Japanese economy is increased by 52 percent. The R&D spillovers affect the structure of production in both countries, particularly the demand for labor in Japan.

4.4.4 Capital Utilization, Depreciation Rates, and Replacement Investment

In general, productivity growth may, at least in the short run, be influenced by whether various factors of production are fully utilized. Most of the studies of firm demand for factors of production assume a constant rate of utilization of inputs and ignore the fact that the firm can choose simultaneously the level and rate of utilization of its inputs. As discussed above, a model which allows for the capital utilization and depreciation rate to be determined endogenously, along the lines of the dynamic factor demand model considered in section 4.3, was first implemented empirically by Epstein and Denny (1980). Using only the demand equations for the variable factors, their model was estimated from U.S. manufacturing data, based on a data set developed by Berndt and Wood. Epstein and Denny report an average rate of depreciation of 0.126 for physical capital. The estimated depreciation rates vary between 0.11 and 0.145 over the sample. The model generates a capital stock series which is quite different from that implied by the Berndt and Wood data. Also, their model indicates substantial cross-price elasticities, showing the interrelated nature of the choice about capital usage and other inputs and outputs which would be ignored if a simpler framework is used to describe the firm's technology. Kollintzas and Choi (1985) and Bischoff and Kokkelenberg (1987) report estimates of 0.126 and 0.106 on average for the rate of depreciation of physical capital in the U.S. manufacturing sector.

Morrison (1992a) reports that a significant portion of cost declines in the U.S., Canadian, and Japanese manufacturing industries, resulting from fluctuations in capacity utilization and scale economies, has been erroneously attributed to technical change. Morrison (1992b) finds furthermore that the markups of prices over costs are significant and influence measured productivity. Galeotti and Schiantarelli (1998) have examined the counter-cyclical behavior of markups in U.S. two-digit manufacturing industries in the context of a dynamic optimization model. Their results show that markups are affected by both the level and growth of the demand facing an industry in the presence of cost of adjustment.

As discussed above, Prucha and Nadiri (1990, 1996) apply the dynamic factor demand model specified in section 4.3.2 to data for the U.S. electrical machinery industry for the period 1960–80. This study builds on an earlier study by Nadiri and Prucha (1990a) that is based on capital stock data from the Office of Business Analysis (OBA). They estimate two versions of the model. In the more general version of the model, K_t^o, the stock of capital left over at the end of the period from the beginning of period stock, or equivalently the depreciation rate of capital, is permitted to be determined as a function of output and relative prices; see equation (65). In the other version of the model the depreciation rate of capital is taken to be constant but unknown by imposing the parameter restrictions $\alpha_{LK^o} = \alpha_{K^oK^o} = \alpha_{RK^o} = 0$. We note that for both models the depreciation rate is estimated and the respective capital stocks are generated internally during estimation in a theoretically consistent fashion. The paper reports the following findings:

1. The depreciation rate of capital is estimated to be 0.038 as compared to 0.055 for the OBA capital stock series. This translates into a difference of 16 percent in magnitude between the implied capital stock series and the OBA capital stock series at the end of the sample period.

2. Based on their tests Prucha and Nadiri accept the model corresponding to a constant depreciation rate. This finding is interesting, since the assumption of a constant depreciation rate has a long history, but has also been the subject of considerable debate. The assumption of a constant depreciation rate was challenged by, among others, Feldstein and Foot (1971), Eisner (1972), Eisner and Nadiri (1968, 1970), and Feldstein

(1974). It was forcefully defended by Jorgenson (1974).[37] Among other things he pointed out that some of the earlier studies on replacement investment were not fully consistent, in that they employed capital stock data that were generated under a different set of assumptions than those maintained in those studies. Within the modeling framework discussed here the capital stocks are generated in an internally consistent fashion from gross investment data. Thus, as a by-product, a consistent decomposition of gross investment into replacement investment and net investment can be obtained. In particular, replacement investment I_t^{KR} is defined as the difference between the beginning of period stocks and what is left over from these stocks at the end of the period, that is, $I_t^{KR} = K_{t-1} - K_t^o$. Net investment I_t^{KE} is defined as the difference between gross investment and replacement investment, that is, $I_t^{KE} = I_t^K - I_t^{KR} = K_t - K_t^o$. For the entire sample period, net investment as a percent of gross investment was about 60 percent. As expected, this ratio exhibited cyclical patterns with a low of 41 percent in 1975. The ratio of net investment to gross investment based on the estimated model is much higher than the rates implied by the OBA capital stock series.

3. The study finds significant adjustment costs. The own accelerator coefficient for physical capital is approximately 0.20, while that for the R&D capital is 0.15. The cross accelerator coefficients are small (about 0.02). The total adjustment costs are about 15 percent of total gross investments for each of these two types of capital.

4. The pattern of output elasticities reveals that the variable factors of production, labor, and materials, respond strongly in the short run to changes in output; in fact, they overshoot their long-run equilibrium values in the short run. The output elasticities of the quasi-fixed factors, capital, and R&D, are small in the short run but increase over time. The long-run output elasticities suggest an estimate of economics of scale of approximately 1.2. The own price elasticities are, as expected, all negative. The results also suggest that the cross price elasticities of labor and capital may be sensitive to whether or not the rate of depreciation is endogenous.

5. The study also provides a decomposition of the sources of TFP growth. This decomposition is reproduced in table 4.1 for both versions of the model. It shows that the estimate of productivity growth based on the traditional TFP measure is approximately three times larger than the estimate of pure technical change generated by the econometric model. The main source of the difference is the scale effect which represents about 46 percent of the growth in the traditional TFP measure. The remainder of the difference is mainly due to the presence of adjustment costs, which accounts for almost 21 percent of total factor productivity growth. The

---

37. The validity of a constant depreciation rate has also been tested in several papers by Hulten and Wykoff; see, e.g., Hulten and Wykoff (1981a,b).

Table 4.1   Decomposition of TFP Growth in the U.S. Electrical Machinery Industry in Percentages, 1960–80

	Model (estimated capital stock)	
	Constant Depreciation Rate	Variable Depreciation Rate
Technical change	0.69	0.66
Scale effect	0.83	0.93
Adjustment cost effects		
Temporary equilibrium effect	0.42	0.39
Direct adjustment cost effect	0.02	0.02
Variable depreciation effect	0.00	0.02
Unexplained residual	0.03	−0.03
Total factor productivity	1.99	1.99

estimated pure technical change exhibits a very smooth pattern and increases over time.

Nadiri and Prucha (1996) employ a special case of the model in section 4.3—where the depreciation rates are modeled as constant but unknown—to estimate the depreciation rates of both physical and R&D capital for the U.S. total manufacturing sector. The depreciation rate of R&D capital was, in particular, estimated to be about 0.12, which is quite similar to the ad hoc assumption of the R&D depreciation rate used in many studies that use the R&D capital stock as an input in the production function.[38] Given estimates for the depreciation rates, gross investment can again be decomposed into net and replacement investment. For the entire sample period, net investment in R&D in the U.S. total manufacturing as a percent of gross investment was 16 percent. However, during the 1970s, this percentage declined to 5 percent, reflecting the near collapse of R&D investment in that period.

4.5 Effects of Misspecification: A Monte Carlo Study

In this section we briefly explore, by means of a Monte Carlo study, the effects of model misspecification on the estimation of important characteristics of the production process such as technical change, scale, and adjustment speed. The "true" model from which the data for the Monte Carlo study are generated has the same basic structure as the model for the U.S. electrical machinery sector considered in Prucha and Nadiri (1996), but

---

38. See, e.g., Griliches (1980), Bernstein and Nadiri (1988), and Mamuneas and Nadiri (1996).

differs in terms of the specification of the restricted cost function and in terms of the assumed expectation formation. The model considered by Prucha and Nadiri is discussed in detail in section 4.3.2. The restricted cost function for that model is given by equation (60), which is a linear-quadratic function in p^L, q^K, q^R, K_{-1}/Y^p, R_{-1}/Y^p, $\Delta K/Y^p$, $\Delta R/Y^p$, T, multiplied by Y^p, where we have maintained the notation of section 4.3.2. In contrast, the restricted cost function of the true model underlying this Monte Carlo study is linear quadratic in p^L, q^K, q^R, K_{-1}, R_{-1}, ΔK, ΔR, Y, T, which allows for an explicit analytic solution even under non-static expectations. In the following, we use the abbreviations LQR (short for "linear quadratic in ratios") and LQ (short for "linear quadratic") to denote the former and latter restricted cost function. The true model assumes that prices and output are generated by simple first order autoregressive processes and takes expectation to be rational (and thus nonstatic). Explicit expressions for the demand equations for the labor, materials, capital, and R&D of the true model and the equations for the forcing variables are given in appendix C in Nadiri and Prucha (1999).

The selection of the true model parameters for the Monte Carlo study was guided by fitting a static version of the model to the U.S. electrical machinery data used in the Prucha and Nadiri study, and by estimating first order autoregressive processes for the forcing variables from those data. The aim was to select the true model parameters such that the generated data exhibited properties consistent with those found in the study by Prucha and Nadiri. The selection of the variance and covariances of the disturbance processes was also guided by those empirical results, as well as by computational considerations to keep the computing time within practical limits. In analogy to the study by Prucha and Nadiri, the data were generated for the period 1960 to 1980, with the initial values taken from the data set for that study. Each Monte Carlo experiment consisted of 100 trials.[39]

The R^2 values (calculated as the squared correlation coefficient between the actual variables and their fitted values calculated from the reduced form based on true parameter values) for the factor demand equations were approximately 0.98; those for the forcing variables ranged from 0.93 to 0.85. Output-based technical change, λ_Y, and scale, ρ, are computed from equation (15). Their values depend on the input and output mix. The median value of λ_Y, computed from the Monte Carlo sample, corresponding to the true parameter values decreased in a smooth pattern from 1.53 in 1961 to 1.00 in 1976 and 0.94 in 1980. The median value of ρ corresponding to the true parameter values was 1.09 in 1961, 1.11 in 1976, and 1.12 in 1980. The true accelerator coefficients m_{KK}, m_{KR}, m_{RK}, and m_{RR} take

---

39. The number of Monte Carlo trials is small, but is reflective of the considerable computational complexities underlying this study.

Table 4.2 Description of Monte Carlo Experiments

Number	Basic Characteristics of Estimated Model			
	Cost Function	Expectation	Returns to Scale	Adjustment Costs
1A, 1B	LQ	Rational	Nonconstant	Nonzero
2A, 2B	LQ	Static	Nonconstant	Nonzero
3A, 3B	LQ	Static[a]	Nonconstant	Zero
4A, 4B	LQR	Static	Nonconstant	Nonzero
5A, 5B	LQR	Static	Constant	Nonzero

[a]Expectations do not come into play, since the adjustment costs are zero.

the values 0.22, −0.02, −0.01, 0.15. The true depreciation rate δ^K was for simplicity taken to be constant and assumed to be 0.038.

Table 4.2 gives a description of the respective Monte Carlo experiments. The first experiment reestimates the true model from the generated data. As discussed above, the true model is based on the LQ restricted cost function, takes expectations to be rational, allows for nonconstant returns to scale and for nonzero adjustment costs; the equations for the true model are given in appendix C in Nadiri and Prucha (1999). In our second experiment, we estimate the same model, except that expectations are misspecified in that they are taken to be static. The third experiment estimates again the same model, but imposes zero adjustment costs (and thus imposes incorrectly $m_{KK} = m_{RR} = 1$). Of course, with zero adjustment costs expectations do not come into play. In experiment four, we then misspecify the functional form of the restricted cost function. More specifically, we estimate the model discussed in section 4.3.2 based on the restricted cost function LQR. We also take expectations to be static. Experiment five is as experiment four, except that here also scale is incorrectly assumed to be equal to unity. For each of the experiments we run two variants. Variant "A" takes the stock of capital (or equivalently, the depreciation rate of capital) as observed. Variant "B" takes the stock of capital as unobserved and estimates the (constant) depreciation rate of capital δ^K jointly with the other model parameters. As an estimation procedure, we use 3SLS with lagged inputs, output, prices, and squares of those lagged values as instruments. The sample period is 1961 to 1980. The study was performed using TSP 4.4.

In tables 4.3 and 4.4 we report, respectively, on the estimation results obtained from the Monte Carlo experiments corresponding to variants A and B of the experiments. Rather than to report on all parameter estimates, we focus on estimates of the adjustment coefficients, and the parameters determining those coefficients, and on estimates of technical change λ_Y and scale ρ. As in the Prucha and Nadiri study, we report estimates for λ_Y and ρ in 1976. The estimated values in tables 4.3 and 4.4 are Monte

Table 4.3   **Estimates of Model Parameters, Technical Change, and Scale (capital stock observed)**

Parameter	True Value	Estimates for Monte Carlo Experiment Number				
		1A	2A	3A	4A	5A
α_{KK}	0.420	0.472 (0.214)	0.314 (0.298)	0.598 (1.703)	1.151 (1.457)	2.356 (5.941)
α_{KR}	−0.066	−0.096 (0.097)	−0.310 (0.091)	−0.336 (1.314)	−0.442 (0.839)	−1.232 (3.338)
α_{RR}	0.376	0.391 (0.138)	0.338 (0.177)	0.585 (1.534)	0.357 (0.632)	0.921 (1.987)
$\alpha_{\dot{K}\dot{K}}$	5.616	5.487 (2.323)	4.337 (2.978)	0.0	8.655 (4.842)	8.134 (4.573)
$\alpha_{\dot{R}\dot{R}}$	10.98	12.52 (6.487)	13.05 (4.870)	0.0	8.645 (7.204)	10.27 (10.37)
m_{KK}	0.217	0.226 (0.050)	0.217 (0.058)	1.0	0.268 (0.093)	0.332 (0.218)
m_{KR}	−0.021	−0.029 (0.031)	−0.012 (0.043)	0.0	−0.060 (0.078)	−0.183 (0.161)
m_{RK}	−0.011	−0.013 (0.013)	−0.004 (0.012)	0.0	−0.066 (0.164)	−0.131 (0.180)
m_{RR}	0.147	0.144 (0.024)	0.125 (0.034)	1.0	0.134 (0.177)	0.119 (0.199)
λ_Y	1.000 (0.167)	0.968 (0.287)	0.604 (0.490)	1.296 (0.217)	0.503 (0.454)	1.216 (0.323)
Scale	1.110 (0.084)	1.136 (0.121)	1.212 (0.194)	1.025 (0.115)	1.341 (0.152)	1.0

Carlo medians. The second column contains the true values for comparison. As a measure of spread of the respective estimates, we report in parenthesis their interquantile ranges.[40] In table 4.4 we also present estimates for the depreciation rate of capital δ^K.

The estimates based on the true model, which are reported under experiments 1A and 1B in tables 4.3 and 4.4 are, in general, close to the true values. We note that the interquantile ranges of the estimates are generally smaller for experiment 1A than for experiment 1B, reflecting the fact that in the latter experiment also δ^K is being estimated in addition to the other model parameters. It is also interesting to note that the interquantile ranges for the estimates of the adjustment cost coefficients $\alpha_{\dot{K}\dot{K}}$ and $\alpha_{\dot{R}\dot{R}}$ are comparatively large. This observation is consistent with a similar finding

---

40. Since λ_Y and ρ depend on the input and output mix, their values vary in respective Monte Carlo trials even if evaluated at the true parameter values. It is for that reason that we also report an inter-quantile range for the true values of λ_Y and ρ. The variability of the parameter estimates reflects the small sample size and the assumptions on the variances of the disturbance processes.

Table 4.4 Estimates of Model Parameters, Technical Change, and Scale (capital stock unobserved; capital depreciation rate estimated)

Parameter	True Value	Estimates for Monte Carlo Experiment Number				
		1B	2B	3B	4B	5B
α_{KK}	0.419	0.469	0.218	1.350	0.414	0.774
		(0.422)	(0.466)	(5.003)	(1.151)	(1.129)
α_{KR}	−0.066	−0.077	0.020	−0.035	−0.194	−1.596
		(0.149)	(0.134)	(0.955)	(0.587)	(0.898)
α_{RR}	0.376	0.414	0.362	0.375	0.408	0.477
		(0.178)	(0.214)	(0.614)	(0.719)	(1.001)
$\alpha_{\dot{K}\dot{K}}$	5.616	5.403	4.862	0.0	9.581	6.465
		(3.710)	(2.923)		(9.299)	(5.594)
$\alpha_{\dot{R}\dot{R}}$	10.98	12.84	13.68	0.0	12.26	13.09
		(7.048)	(5.796)		(5.541)	(7.689)
m_{KK}	0.217	0.224	0.194	1.0	0.165	0.246
		(0.110)	(0.171)		(0.249)	(0.157)
m_{KR}	−0.021	−0.024	0.010	0.0	−0.051	−0.164
		(0.038)	(0.058)		(0.087)	(0.147)
m_{RK}	−0.011	−0.010	0.004	0.0	−0.037	−0.067
		(0.018)	(0.020)		(0.078)	(0.092)
m_{RR}	0.147	0.141	0.121	1.0	0.119	0.090
		(0.023)	(0.043)		(0.127)	(0.111)
λ_Y	1.000	0.960	0.552	1.664	−0.003	0.816
		(0.167)	(0.405)	(0.688)	(0.823)	(1.872)	(0.982)
Scale	1.110	1.128	1.213	0.825	1.390	1.0
		(0.084)	(0.161)	(0.244)	(1.037)	(0.266)	
δ_K	0.038	0.036	0.033	0.117	0.004	0.015
		(0.018)	(0.039)	(0.070)	(0.058)	(0.037)

in an earlier Monte Carlo study by Prucha and Nadiri (1986). In experiments 2A and 2B expectations are misspecified as being static. The effect of this misspecification is to substantially decrease the estimates of technical change to 0.60 and 0.55, respectively, as compared to a true value of 1.00, and to increase the estimates of scale to 1.21, as compared to a true value of 1.11. If the model is further misspecified by assuming that adjustment costs are zero, the estimates for technical change increase to 1.30 and 1.66, as reported under experiments 3A and 3B. Scale falls to 1.02 and 0.82, respectively. This type of misspecification also has a considerable effect on the estimate of δ^K. The median estimate is 0.11 as compared to a true value of 0.038.

Misspecifying the functional form of the restricted cost function in terms of equation (60), and assuming static expectations, results in estimates of technical change of 0.5 and 0, as reported under experiments 4A and 4B, respectively. The estimate for scale increases to 1.30 and 1.39, respectively. The estimates of the accelerator coefficients and the depreciation rate of capital are also fairly sensitive to this form of misspecification. Imposing constant returns to scale, as in experiments 5A and 5B, results in less bias in the technical change estimates, and in estimates of m_{KK} and m_{RR} that are higher and lower than the true values. There is also substantial downward bias in the estimates of the depreciation rate of capital. These Monte Carlo results suggest that the estimates of model parameters and model characteristics may be quite sensitive to misspecification of the functional form, especially since the functional form misspecification imposed in this study may be considered as modest in that equation (60) can be viewed as a second-order approximation of the true restricted cost function.

4.6 Concluding Remarks

In this paper we have discussed some recent advances in modeling and in the estimation of dynamic factor demand, and have argued that this approach provides a powerful framework to analyze the determinants of the production structure, factor demand, and technical change. The basic message of this paper can be summarized briefly. The conventional index number approach will measure the rate of technical change correctly if certain assumptions about the underlying technology of the firm and output and input markets hold. Furthermore, the conventional index number approach is appealing in that it can be easily implemented. However, if the underlying assumptions do not hold, then the conventional index number approach will, in general, yield biased estimates of technical change.

The index number approach also does not provide detailed insight into the dynamics of the production process and the determinants of factor demand and factor accumulation. The dynamic factor demand modeling approach reviewed in this paper provides a general framework to estimate the structure of the underlying technology and to relate the investment decisions and variation of technical change. Of course, in this approach there is, as in any other econometric investigation, the danger of misspecification. However, the basic appeal of this modeling strategy is its flexibility, that enables it to incorporate and analyze in a consistent framework both theoretical considerations and institutional factors that influence technical change, and to test various hypothesis concerning the specification of the technology and the optimizing behavior of the firm.

The dynamic factor demand modeling framework described in this paper enables us to examine a number of issues of both basic research and policy interest. Using the model it is possible to identify the possible biases in the conventional measure of total factor productivity growth. These biases can result from scale effects, the difference between marginal products and long-run factor rental prices in temporary equilibrium due to adjustment costs, the direct effect of adjustment costs as they influence output growth, and the selection of the depreciation rate by the firm. The model presented in this paper can be used to estimate the structure of the underlying technology and to specify the magnitudes of these biases if they are present. If the biases are not isolated, relying on the conventional TFP measure will, for example, overestimate technical change in the presence of increasing returns to scale and positive output growth.

The model also provides an analytical framework for estimating the response of input demands to changes in relative prices, exogenous technical change, and other exogenous variables that may shift the production or cost function. Since a clear distinction is drawn between variable and quasi-fixed inputs due to the presence of adjustment costs, the short-, intermediate-, and long-run responses of output, factors of production, and productivity growth can be estimated. (Of course, the approach does not impose the existence of adjustment costs and quasi-fixity, but rather leaves that to be determined empirically.) The class of models reviewed also allows for non-static expectations and nonseparability among the quasi-fixed factors of production. It is therefore possible to estimate possible substitution or complementaries in the short, intermediate, and long runs among various types of capital such as physical, R&D, and human capital.

It is also possible to formulate and estimate an appropriate measure of capacity utilization consistent with the underlying production technology. Moreover, the model allows for the decision on depreciation rates of various quasi-fixed factors of production such as physical and R&D capital to be endogenous. We note, however, that models in which the depreciation rate is constant are included as special cases. The framework thus allows for the econometric testing of the constancy hypothesis. Estimating the depreciation rates permits generating consistent capital stock series which may differ from the official estimates. It also allows the decomposition of gross investments of various types of capital into the net and replacement investments. The time profiles of these two types of investment have important analytical and policy implications.

To illustrate the workings of the model, we have discussed briefly some empirical results from several studies based on the dynamic factor demand model. These examples indicate how it is possible to account for the influences of scale, relative price movements, the rate of innovation due to R&D efforts and R&D spillovers, and financial decisions concerning the level of debt and dividend payouts on the production structure and technical change. The overall conclusion reached from these examples is that the econometric modeling approach allows us to identify the contribution of a complex and often competing set of forces that shape productivity growth, and to test their significance statistically. Generally speaking, the empirical results based on dynamic factor demand models suggest that the estimated rate of technological change is often much smaller and smoother than the conventionally measured total factor productivity growth. Also, there is evidence of substantial degree of interrelatedness embedded in the production process of the firm that could not be captured using simple formulations of the firm's technology. The evidence from several studies suggests that some factors of production such as physical and R&D capital are quasi-fixed in the short run. Also, there is evidence that economies of scale characterizes the production process in some industries and that the elasticity of factor substitution is often much smaller than unity. Investment in R&D is an integral part of the production structure and often significantly contributes to a reduction in cost. In addition, R&D spillovers among firms, industries, and economies often reduce the cost of production of the recipient. Dynamic factor demand models also permit studying the production and financial decisions of the firm in a consistent framework and to analyze the effect of taxes and other exogenous policy instruments on these decisions.

To illustrate how estimates of important characteristics of the production process can be affected by various forms of misspecification, a Monte Carlo study was undertaken. The results suggest, in particular, that estimates of the rate of technical change are sensitive to misspecification of the expectation formation process, to misspecification regarding whether or not the firms is in temporary or long-run equilibrium, and to misspecifications of the functional form of the cost/production function including scale. The exhibited sensitivity of technical change (and other model characteristics) to misspecification suggests that adopting simple specifications for reasons of convenience may result in serious estimation biases. This points to the importance of specification testing in the estimation of the cost/production functions and derived factor demands. Dynamic factor demand models provide a general framework for carrying out specification tests, and yield important insights in the complexity of the production decisions.

However, estimation of dynamic factor demand models is often challenging. These models are often complex and the estimation of these models requires considerable effort. Nonetheless, in order to measure technical change properly and to capture the dynamics of the adjustment of factor demands, and to analyze effects of relative prices and other exogenous variables such as taxes, subsidies, R&D spillovers, and so on, on factor demand and productivity growth, the dynamic factor demand modeling framework presented in this paper is an important tool of analysis.

References

Abel, A. B. 1981. A dynamic model of investment and capacity utilization. *Quarterly Journal of Economics* 96:379–403.

———. 1983. Optimal investment under uncertainty. *American Economic Review* 73:228–33.
Abel, A. B., and J. C. Eberly. 1994. A unified model of investment under uncertainty. *American Economic Review* 84:1369–84.
Arrow, K. J. 1968. Optimal capital policy with irreversible investment. In *Value, capital and growth: Papers in honour of Sir John Hicks,* ed. J. N. Wolfe, 1–19. Edinburgh, Scotland: Edinburgh University Press.
Berndt, E. R., and M. A. Fuss. 1986. Productivity measurement with adjustments for variations in capacity utilization and other forms of temporary equilibrium. *Journal of Econometrics* 33:7–29.
———. 1989. Economic capacity utilization and productivity measurement for multiproduct firms with multiple quasi-fixed inputs. Working Paper no. 2932. Cambridge, Mass.: National Bureau of Economic Research.
Berndt, E. R., and C. J. Morrison. 1981. Capacity utilization measures: Underlying economic theory and an alternative approach. *American Economic Review* 71:48–52.
Berndt, E. R., C. J. Morrison, and G. C. Watkins. 1981. Dynamic models of energy demand: An assessment and comparison. In *Measuring and modeling natural resource substitution,* ed. E. R. Berndt and B. C. Fields, 259–89. Cambridge: MIT Press.
Bernstein, J. I. 1988. Costs of production, intra- and interindustry R&D spillovers: Canadian evidence. *Canadian Journal of Economics* 21:324–47.
———. 1989a. The structure of Canadian interindustry R&D spillovers and the rates of return to R&D. *Journal of Industrial Economics* 21:324–47.
———. 1989b. An examination of the equilibrium specification and structure of production for Canadian telecommunications. *Journal of Applied Econometrics* 4 (3): 265–82.
———. 1994. Taxes, incentives and production: The case of Turkey. *Journal of Development Economics* 45:55–79.
Bernstein, J. I., and P. Mohnen. 1991. Price cost margins, exports and productivity growth: With an application to Canadian industries. *Canadian Journal of Economics* 24:638–59.
———. 1998. International R&D spillovers between U.S. and Japanese R&D intensive sectors. *Journal of International Economics* 44:315–38.
Bernstein, J. I., and M. I. Nadiri. 1987. Corporate taxes and incentives and the structure of production: A selected survey. In *The impact of taxation on business activity,* ed. J. M. Mintz and D. T. Purves, 178–208. Kingston: John Deutsch Institute for the Study of Economic Policy.
———. 1988. Interindustry R&D spillovers, rates of return, and production in high-tech industries. *American Economic Review* 78:429–34.
———. 1989. Research and development and intra-industry spillovers: An empirical application of dynamic duality. *Review of Economic Studies* 56:249–67.
Binder, M., and M. H. Pesaran. 1995. Multivariate rational expectations models and macroeconometric modelling: A review and some new results. In *Handbook of Applied Econometrics,* vol. 1, ed. M. H. Pesaran and M. Wickens, 139–87. Oxford, England: Basil Blackwell.
———. 1997. Multivariate linear rational expectations models: Characterization of the nature of the solutions and their fully recursive computation. *Econometric Theory* 13:877–88.
Bischoff, C. W., and E. C. Kokkelenberg. 1987. Capacity utilization and depreciation-in-use. *Applied Economics* 19:995–1007.
Caballero, R. J. 1991. On the sign of the investment-uncertainty relationship. *American Economic Review* 81:279–88.

Caves, D. W., L. R. Christensen, and W. E. Diewert. 1982. The economic theory of index numbers and the measurement of input, output, and productivity. *Econometrica* 50:1393–1414.

Caves, D. W., L. R. Christensen, and J. A. Swanson. 1981. Productivity growth, scale economies, and capacity utilization in U.S. railroads, 1955–74. *American Economic Review* 71:994–1002.

Christensen, L. R., D. W. Jorgenson, and L. J. Lau. 1971. Conjugate duality and the transcendental logarithmic functions. *Econometrica* 39:255–56.

———. 1973. Transcendental logarithmic production frontiers. *Review of Economics and Statistics* 55:28–45.

Denny, M., M. A. Fuss, and L. Waverman. 1981a. The measurement and interpretation of total factor productivity in regulated industries, with an application to Canadian telecommunications. In *Productivity measurement in regulated industries,* ed. T. Cowing and R. Stevenson, 179–218. New York: Academic Press.

———. 1981b. Substitution possibilities for energy: Evidence from U.S. and Canadian manufacturing industries. In *Modeling and measuring natural resource substitution,* ed. E. R. Berndt and B. C. Field, 230–58. Cambridge: MIT Press.

Diewert, W. E. 1971. An application of the Shephard duality theorem: A generalized Leontief production function. *Journal of Political Economy* 79:481–507.

———. 1976. Exact and superlative index numbers. *Journal of Econometrics* 4: 115–45.

———. 1980. Aggregation problems in the measurement of capital. In *The measurement of capital,* ed. D. Usher, 433–528. Chicago: University of Chicago Press.

———. 1982. Duality approaches to microeconomic theory. In *Handbook of mathematical economics,* vol. 2, ed. K. J. Arrow and M. D. Intriligator, 535–99. Amsterdam: North Holland.

Diewert, W. E., and T. J. Wales. 1987. Flexible functional forms and curvature conditions. *Econometrica* 55, 43–68.

Dixit, A. K., and R. S. Pindyck. 1994. *Investment under uncertainty.* Princeton: Princeton University Press.

Eisner, R. 1972. Components of capital expenditures: Replacement and modernization versus expansion. *Review of Economics and Statistics* 54:297–305.

Eisner, R., and M. I. Nadiri. 1968. On investment behavior and neoclassical theory. *Review of Economics and Statistics* 50:369–82.

———. 1970. Once more on that "Neoclassical theory of investment behavior." *Review of Economics and Statistics* 52:216–22.

Eisner, R., and R. Strotz. 1963. Determinants of business investment. In *Impacts of Monetary Policy,* 60–338. Englewood Cliffs, N.J.: Prentice Hall.

Epstein, L. G., and M. Denny. 1980. Endogenous capital utilization in a short-run production model: Theory and empirical application. *Journal of Econometrics* 12:189–207.

Epstein, L. G., and A. J. Yatchew. 1985. The empirical determination of technology and expectations: A simplified procedure. *Journal of Econometrics* 27: 235–58.

Feldstein, M. S. 1974. Tax incentives, stabilization policy, and the proportional replacement hypothesis: Some negative conclusions. *Southern Economic Journal* 40:544–52.

Feldstein, M. S., and D. K. Foot. 1971. The other half of gross investment: Replacement and modernization expenditures. *Review of Economics and Statistics* 53:49–58.

Fuss, M. A. 1994. Productivity growth in Canadian telecommunications. *Canadian Journal of Economics* 27 (2): 371–92.

Fuss, M. A., and D. McFadden. 1978. *Production economics: A dual approach to theory and applications,* vols. 1 & 2. New York: North-Holland.

Fuss, M. A., D. McFadden, and Y. Mundlak. 1978. A survey of functional forms in the economic analysis of production. In *Production economics: A dual approach to theory and applications,* ed. M. A. Fuss and D. McFadden, 219–68. New York: North-Holland.

Galeotti, M., and F. Schiantarelli. 1998. The cyclicality of markups in a model with adjustment costs: Econometric evidence for US industry. *Oxford Bulletin of Economics and Statistics* 60:121–42.

Gallant, A. R., and H. White. 1988. *A unified theory of estimation and inference for nonlinear dynamic models.* New York: Basil Blackwell.

Good, D., M. I. Nadiri, and R. Sickles. 1997. Index number and factor demand approaches to the estimation of productivity. In M. H. Pesaran and P. Schmidt, eds., *Handbook of Applied Econometrics: Vol. 2. Microeconometrics.* Oxford, England: Basil Blackwell.

Gordon, S. 1996. How long is the firm's forecast horizon? *Journal of Economic Dynamics and Control* 20:1145–76.

Goto, A., and Suzuki, K. 1989. R&D capital, rate of return on R&D investment and spillover of R&D in Japanese manufacturing industries. *Review of Economics and Studies* 71:555–64.

Griliches, Z. 1980. Returns to research and development expenditures in the private sector. In *New developments in productivity measurement and analysis,* ed. J. Kendrick and B. Vaccara, 419–54. Chicago: University of Chicago Press.

Hall, E. R. 1988. The relation between price and marginal cost in the United States industry. *Journal of Political Economy* 96:921–47.

Hall, R. E., and D. W. Jorgenson. 1967. Tax policy and investment behavior. *American Economic Review* 57:391–414.

———. 1971. Application of theory of optimum capital accumulation. In *Tax Incentives and Capital Spending,* ed. G. Fromm, 9–60. Washington, D.C.: Brookings Institution.

Hansen, L. P. 1982. Large sample properties of generalized method of moments estimators. *Econometrica* 50:1029–54.

Hansen, L. P., and T. J. Sargent. 1980. Formulating and estimating dynamic linear rational expectations models. *Journal of Economic Dynamics and Control* 2:7–46.

———. 1981. Linear rational expectations models for dynamically interrelated variables. In *Rational Expectations and Econometric Practice,* vol. 1, ed. R. E. Lucas Jr. and T. J. Sargent, 127–56. Minneapolis: University of Minnesota Press.

———. 1982. Instrumental variables procedures for estimating linear rational expectations models. *Journal of Monetary Economics* 9:263–96.

Hansen, L. P., and K. J. Singleton. 1982. Generalized instrumental variables estimation of nonlinear rational expectations models. *Econometrica* 50:1269–86.

Hayashi, F. 1982. Tobin's marginal and average q: A neoclassical interpretation. *Econometrica* 50:213–24.

Hicks, J. R. 1946. *Value and capital.* 2nd ed. Oxford: Oxford University Press.

Hulten, C. R. 1973. Divisia index numbers. *Econometrica* 41:1017–26.

———. 1986. Productivity change, capacity utilization, and sources of efficiency growth. *Journal of Econometrics* 33:31–50.

Hulten, C. R., and F. C. Wykoff. 1981a. The measurement of economic depreciation. In *Depreciation, inflation, and the taxation of income from capital,* ed. C. R. Hulten, 81–125. Washington, D.C.: Urban Institute.

———. 1981b. The estimation of economic depreciation using vintage asset prices. *Journal of Econometrics* 15:367–96.

Jorgenson, D. W. 1963. Capital theory and investment behavior. *American Economic Review* 35:247–59.
———. 1966. Rational distributed lag functions. *Econometrica* 34:135–49.
———. 1974. The economic theory of replacement and depreciation. In *Essays in honor of Jan Tinbergen, economic theory and miscellaneous,* ed. W. Sellekaerts, 189–221. Amsterdam: North-Holland.
———. 1986. Econometric methods for modeling producer behavior. In *Handbook of econometrics,* vol. 3, ed. Z. Griliches and M. D. Intriligalator, 1841–1915. New York: Elsevier Science Publishers.
———. 1995a. *Productivity: Vol. 1. Postwar U.S. economic growth.* Cambridge: MIT Press.
———. 1995b. *Productivity: Vol. 2. International comparison of economic growth.* Cambridge: MIT Press.
———. 1996a. *Capital theory and investment behavior.* Cambridge: MIT Press.
———. 1996b. *Tax policy and the cost of capital.* Cambridge: MIT Press.
Jorgenson, D. W., and Z. Griliches. 1967. The explanation of productivity change. *Review of Economic Studies* 34:249–83.
Jorgenson, D. W., and J. A. Stephenson. 1967. The time structure of investment behavior in the United States. *Review of Economics and Statistics* 49:16–27.
Kennan, J. 1979. The estimation of partial adjustment models with rational expectations. *Econometrica* 47:1441–56.
Kokkelenberg, E. C., and C. W. Bischoff. 1986. Expectations and factor demand. *Review of Economics and Statistics* 68:423–31.
Kollintzas, T. 1985. The symmetric linear rational expectations model. *Econometrica* 53:963–76.
———. 1986. A non-recursive solution for the linear rational expectations model. *Journal of Economic Dynamics and Control* 10:327–32.
Kollintzas, T., and J.-B. Choi. 1985. A linear rational expectations equilibrium model of aggregate investment with endogenous capital utilization and maintenance. University of Pittsburgh Department of Economics. Mimeograph.
Koyck, L. M. 1954. *Distributed lags and investment analysis.* Amsterdam: North-Holland.
Lahiri, L., and P. Schmidt. 1978. On the estimation of triangular structural systems. *Econometrica* 46:1217–21.
Lau, L. J. 1976. A characterization of the normalized restricted profit function. *Journal of Economic Theory* 12:131–63.
———. 1986. Functional forms in econometric model building. In *Handbook of econometrics,* vol. 3, ed. Z. Griliches and M. D. Intriligator, 1515–66. New York: North-Holland.
Lucas, R. E. 1967a. Adjustment costs and the theory of supply. *Journal of Political Economy* 75:321–34.
———. 1967b. Optimal investment policy and the flexible accelerator. *International Economic Review* 8:78–85.
Madan, D. B., and I. R. Prucha. 1989. A note on the estimation of nonsymmetric dynamic factor demand models. *Journal of Econometrics* 42:275–83.
Malinvaud, E. 1953. Capital accumulation and the efficient allocation of resources. *Econometrica* 21:233–68.
———. 1969. First order certainty equivalence. *Econometrica* 37:706–19.
Mamuneas, T., and M. I. Nadiri. 1996. Public R&D policies and cost behavior of the U.S. manufacturing industries. *Journal of Public Economics* 63:57–81.
McFadden, D. 1978. Cost, revenue and profit functions. In *Production economics: A dual approach to theory and applications,* vol. 1, ed. M. Fuss and D. McFadden, 3–109. New York: North-Holland, 3–109.

Mohnen, P. A. 1992a. *The relationship between R&D and productivity growth in Canada and other industrialized countries.* Ottawa: Canada Communication Group.
———. 1992b. International R&D spillovers in selected OECD countries. Université du Québec à Montréal, Département des sciences économiques, Cahier no. 9208.
Mohnen, P., and N. Lépine. 1991. R&D, R&D spillovers and payments for technology: Canadian evidence. *Structural Change and Economic Dynamics* 2 (1): 213–28.
Mohnen, P. A., M. I. Nadiri, and I. R. Prucha. 1983. R&D, production structure, and productivity growth in the U.S., Japanese, and German manufacturing sectors. In *Proceedings of the Conference of Qualitative Studies of Research and Development in Industry.* Paris: Institute National de la Statistique et des Etudes Economiques, 173–221.
———. 1986. R&D, production structure, and rate of return in the U.S., Japanese and German manufacturing sectors: A nonseparable dynamic factor demand model. *European Economic Review* 30:749–71.
Morrison, C. J. 1986. Productivity measurement with non-static expectations and varying capacity utilization: An integrated approach. *Journal of Econometrics* 33:51–74.
———. 1990. Decisions of firms and productivity growth with fixed input constraints: An empirical comparison of U.S. and Japanese manufacturing. In *Productivity growth in Japan and the U.S.,* ed. C. R. Hulten, 135–67. Chicago: University of Chicago Press.
———. 1992a. Unraveling the productivity growth slowdown in the United States, Canada and Japan: The effects of subequilibrium, scale economies and markups. *The Review of Economics and Statistics* 74 (3): 381–93.
———. 1992b. Markups in U.S. and Japanese manufacturing: A short-run econometric analysis. *Journal of Business & Economic Statistics* 10 (1): 51–63.
———. 1997. Assessing the productivity of information technology equipment in U.S. manufacturing industries. *Review of Economics and Statistics* 79:471–81.
Morrison, C. J., and E. R. Berndt. 1981. Short-run labor productivity in a dynamic model. *Journal of Econometrics* 16:339–65.
Morrison, C. J., and D. Siegel. 1997. External capital factors and increasing returns in U.S. manufacturing. *Review of Economics and Statistics* 79:647–54.
Mortenson, D. T. 1973. Generalized costs of adjustment and dynamic factor demand theory. *Econometrica* 41:657–65.
Mussa, M. 1977. External and internal adjustment costs and the theory of aggregate and firm investment. *Economica* 44:163–78.
Nadiri, M. I., and I. R. Prucha. 1986. Comparison and analysis of productivity growth and R&D investment in the electrical machinery industries of the United States and Japan. NBER Working Paper no. 1850. Cambridge, Mass.: National Bureau of Economic Research.
———. 1990a. Comparison and analysis of productivity growth and R&D investment in the electrical machinery industries of the United States and Japan. In *Productivity growth in Japan and the U.S.,* ed. C. R. Hulten, 109–33. Chicago: University of Chicago Press.
———. 1990b. Dynamic factor demand models, productivity measurement, and rates of return: Theory and an empirical application to the U.S. Bell system. *Structural Change and Economic Dynamics* 2:263–89.
———. 1996. Estimation of the depreciation rate of physical and R&D capital in the U.S. total manufacturing sector. *Economic Inquiry* 34:43–56.

———. 1999. Dynamic factor demand models and productivity analysis. NBER Working Paper no. 7079. Cambridge, Mass.: National Bureau of Economic Research.
Nadiri, M. I., and S. Rosen. 1969. Interrelated factor demand functions. *American Economic Review* 59:457–71.
———. 1973. *A disequilibrium model of demand for factors of production.* New York: Columbia University Press.
Nadiri, M. I., and M. A. Schankerman. 1981a. Technical change, returns to scale, and the productivity slowdown. *American Economic Review* 71:314–19.
———. 1981b. The structure of production, technological change, and the rate of growth of total factor productivity in the U.S. Bell system. In *Productivity measurement in regulated industries,* ed. T. Cowing and R. Stevenson, 219–47. New York: Academic Press.
Pindyck, R. S., and J. J. Rotemberg. 1983. Dynamic factor demands under rational expectations. *Scandinavian Journal of Economics* 85:223–38.
Pötscher, B. M., and I. R. Prucha. 1997. *Dynamic nonlinear econometric models: Asymptotic theory.* New York: Springer Verlag.
Prucha, I. R. 1987. The variance-covariance matrix of the maximum likelihood estimator in triangular structural systems: Consistent estimation. *Econometrica* 55:977–78.
———. 1990. Comments on C. J. Morrison, Decisions of firms and productivity growth with fixed input constraints: An empirical comparison of U.S. and Japanese manufacturing. In *Productivity growth in Japan and the U.S.,* ed. C. R. Hulten, 167–72. Chicago: University of Chicago Press.
———. 1995. On the econometric estimation of a constant rate of depreciation. *Empirical Economics* 20:299–302.
———. 1997. Estimation of a variable rate of depreciation: A dummy variable approach. *Structural Change and Economic Dynamics* 8:319–25.
Prucha, I. R., and M. I. Nadiri. 1982. Formulation and estimation of dynamic factor demand equations under non-static expectations: A finite horizon model. NBER Technical Paper no. 26. Cambridge, Mass.: National Bureau of Economic Research. (Revised March 1994).
———. 1986. A comparison of alternative methods for the estimation of dynamic factor demand models under nonstatic expectations. *Journal of Econometrics* 33:187–211.
———. 1988. On the computation of estimators in systems with implicitly defined variables. *Economics Letters* 26:141–45.
———. 1990. Endogenous capital utilization and productivity measurement in dynamic factor demand models: Theory and an application to the U.S. electrical machinery industry. NBER Working Paper no. 3680. Cambridge, Mass.: National Bureau of Economic Research.
———. 1991. On the specification of accelerator coefficients in dynamic factor demand models. *Economics Letters* 35:123–29.
———. 1996. Endogenous capital utilization and productivity measurement in dynamic factor demand models: Theory and an application to the U.S. electrical machinery industry. *Journal of Econometrics* 71:343–79.
Richter, M. K. 1966. Invariance axioms and economic indices. *Econometrica* 34:739–55.
Shapiro, M. D. 1986. Capital utilization and capital accumulation: Theory and evidence. *Journal of Applied Econometrics* 1:211–34.
Shephard, R. W. 1953. *Theory of cost and production functions.* Princeton: Princeton University Press.

Solow, R. M. 1957. Technical change and the aggregate production function. *Review of Economics and Statistics* 39:312–20.
Srinivasan, S. 1995. *Estimation of own R&D, R&D spillovers and exogenous technical change effects in some U.S. high-technology industries.* Ph.D. diss. University of Maryland, Department of Economics.
Steigerwald, D. G., and C. Stuart. 1997. Econometric estimation of foresight: Tax policy and investment in the United States. *Review of Economics and Statistics* 79:32–40.
Steigum, E., Jr. 1983. A financial theory of investment behavior. *Econometrica* 51 (3): 637–45.
Stokey, N. L., R. E. Lucas, and E. C. Prescott. 1989. *Recursive methods in economic dynamics.* Cambridge: Harvard University Press.
Tobin, J. 1969. A general equilibrium approach to monetary theory. *Journal of Money, Credit and Banking* 1:15–29.
Treadway, A. B. 1969. On rational entrepreneurial behavior and the demand for investment. *Review of Economic Studies* 36:227–39.
———. 1974. The globally optimal flexible accelerator. *Journal of Economic Theory* 7:17–39.
Watkins, G. C. 1991. Short- and long-term equilibria. *Energy Economics* 13:2–9.
Watkins, G. C., and E. R. Berndt. 1992. Dynamic models of input demand: A comparison under different formulations of adjustment costs. In *Advances in the economics of energy and resources,* vol. 7, ed. J. Moroney, 159–88. Greenwich, Conn.: JAI Press.

Comment   Dale W. Jorgenson

This very ambitious and stimulating paper is organized around the concept of dynamic factor demand models. Quasi-fixed factors are characterized by internal costs of adjustment. The production possibility frontier depends on outputs and inputs, technology, economies of scale, and rates of change of the quasi-fixed factors.

Section 4.2 of the paper connects most directly with the topic of the conference, new developments in productivity analysis. The key result is contained in section 4.2.3. This productivity measure is given in continuous time in equation (39) and discrete time in equation (43).

Equation (39) decomposes the growth rate of productivity in a model that does not maintain the standard assumptions. These are constant returns to scale, competitive markets for inputs and outputs, and no internal costs of adjustment. Terms in the decomposition correspond to scale effects, deviations from marginal cost pricing, adjustment costs, and the effects of changes in the quasi-fixed factors.

The empirical issue is how to measure the effects of departures from the standard assumptions. The authors' proposal is to specify and fit a dy-

Dale W. Jorgenson is the Frederic E. Abbe Professor of Economics at Harvard University.

namic factor demand model. It is significant that there is no empirical example of the full implementation of this proposal. Nonetheless, it is very valuable to have a well-specified alternative to the production model that underlies the productivity measures generated by official statistical programs.

The production model that underlies the Törnqvist index of productivity used in official productivity measurements also gives rise to an econometric model of factor demand. As Nadiri and Prucha point out, this model is much more restrictive and could be tested within their dynamic factor demand model. However, there is an important issue of research strategy here. Is it best to relax all the assumptions of the standard model at once, while limiting the empirical analysis to time series data on outputs and inputs and their prices?

Let me discuss one example: namely, modeling economies of scale. This is one of the most fruitful areas for econometric modeling of production. The most satisfactory approach has been to study economies of scale in isolation from other departures from the standard assumptions. Cross-sectional and panel data, especially for regulated industries, have been modeled extensively and reported in the econometric literature.

Intercity telecommunications and electricity generation industries are characterized by increasing returns to scale, whereas transportation industries are characterized by constant returns. As a consequence of these findings, transportation has been largely deregulated. Regulatory reform in electricity generation and telecommunications has limited regulation to areas where economies of scale are significant.

Section 4.3 is the core of the paper and presents a framework that encompasses all the features of production enumerated in section 4.2. Section 4.3.1 considers minimization of the firm's expected present value of cost, subject to the production possibility frontier. This leads to an Euler equation for modeling the dynamics of factor demand.

A more restrictive dynamic factor demand model, based on a linear quadratic specification, is given in equation (27). This model is characterized by certainty equivalence and takes the form of a system of linear difference equations. This idea has been present in the economic literature for several decades and in the engineering literature for even longer.

Section 4.5 of the paper presents a Monte Carlo study of the effects of misspecification on measures of productivity and economies of scale. This compares the linear quadratic model shown in equation (16) and employed by Prucha and Nadiri (1996) with a "true" linear quadratic model that can be solved analytically under rational expectations. Table 4.3 shows that the departures from the assumptions of the true model have sizable impacts on measured TFP and economies of scale.

Section 4.4 of the paper summarizes empirical applications of dynamic factor demand models. The description of these models is necessarily brief, but I was unable to find evidence of a successful empirical application of the rational expectations approach featured in section 4.3. Nonetheless, the list of topics covered is impressive:

1. Tax incentives, financing, and technical change (section 4.4.1)
2. R&D investment, production structure, and TFP decomposition (section 4.4.2)
3. Technological spillovers and productivity growth (section 4.4.3)
4. Capacity utilization, depreciation rates, and replacement investment (section 4.4.4)

The conclusions are worth summarizing:

First, when taxes are evaluated in terms of their effectiveness, measured as investment expenditures per government revenue loss, specific tax instruments are substantially more effective than is the corporate income tax rate. This conclusion is familiar to readers of the literature on tax policy and investment behavior. However, the methodology of choice in this area of policy analysis is general equilibrium modeling, which leads to measures of the impact of policy changes on consumer welfare.

Second, emphasizing economies of scale, Nadiri and Prucha have modeled production in the U.S. Bell System. They find that economies of scale accounted for more than 80 percent of the impressive productivity growth in the Bell System, suggesting a serious bias in conventional measures of TFP. This was a part of the unsuccessful defense of the Bell System against the breakup that resulted from the Department of Justice antitrust case.

Third, studies of R&D investment have produced evidence of spillovers, defined as effects of investment by one firm, industry, or country on the productivity of other firms, industries, or countries. This literature is surveyed by Griliches and Nadiri. The predominant methodology has been the estimation of cross-sectional production functions, which was pioneered by Griliches and is the subject of its own very substantial literature.

Fourth, the final applications are to measures of depreciation rates from investment in fixed assets and R&D. This has been far less influential than research focusing on used asset prices. The studies of Hulten and Wykoff have provided the basis for the recent revision of the capital accounts that underly the U.S. income and product accounts. This is described by Fraumeni (1997).

What can one claim for the empirical literature on dynamic factor demand modeling? This methodology has generated an impressive literature on a wide range of issues. However, in each of the areas reviewed in section 4.4, competing methodologies isolate one of the issues. This has been a more successful research strategy and one that has had a major impact on official productivity measures and the underlying national accounting magnitudes, as well as on economic policy.

In concluding, it is important to emphasize that Nadiri and Prucha have very forcefully reminded us how much remains to be done. For example, an important challenge for empirical economists is to develop satisfactory measures of R&D outputs as opposed to the inputs. These will be required for any definitive assessment of the prospects for endogenizing productivity growth through R&D investment and spillovers across producing units, as Nadiri and Prucha have suggested.

References

Fraumeni, B. M. 1997. The measurement of depreciation in the U.S. national income and product accounts. *Survey of Current Business* 77 (7): 7–23.
Prucha, I. R., and M. I. Nadiri. 1996. Estimation of the depreciation rate of physical and R&D capital in the U.S. total manufacturing sector. *Economic Inquiry* 34:43–56.

Reply   M. Ishaq Nadiri and Ingmar R. Prucha

We thank Professor Jorgenson for his stimulating comments. In his own work Jorgenson has evidently not embraced dynamic factor demand models, which are the subject of our review. This sets the stage for a discussion of important issues of research strategy. Not surprisingly there is some disagreement. To respond to some of the questions raised by Jorgenson's comments, and to reemphasize the contributions of the vast dynamic factor demand literature surveyed in our paper, we focus our reply on three sets of issues related to (a) the treatment of the quasi fixity of some inputs, (b) estimation strategies, and (c) comments on specific empirical studies.

First, as documented in our paper, the dynamic factor demand modeling approach has attracted many eminent scholars and has generated a voluminous literature in the past three decades. We emphasize that the approach builds on seminal contributions by other eminent economists. In particular, the dynamic factor demand literature builds on Jorgenson's neoclassical theory of investment and production. By introducing (internal or external) adjustment costs explicitly into the firm's decision-making process, dynamic factor demand models yield optimal factor demands not only in the long run, but also in the short and intermediate run. The introduction of adjustment costs is seen by many as a natural extension of the neoclassical theory of investment and production that permits a consistent modeling framework for *both* temporary and long-run equilibrium. As such, dynamic factor demand models provide a formal framework for tracing the evolution of investment and productivity growth over the short, intermediate, and long run.

The major methodological difference between the modeling approach favored by Jorgenson and the dynamic factor demand modeling approach is the latter's incorporation of adjustment costs to explicitly account—within the firm's decision-making process—for the widely documented quasi fixity of some inputs, such as the physical capital stock. The quasi fixity of capital inputs was in fact recognized in Jorgenson's own empirical study of investment expenditures some thirty years ago via the specification of an accelerator model. We note that dynamic factor demand models provide a formal economic justification for accelerator models of investment. Apart from the treatment of adjustment costs, both approaches are similar: In empirical applications both have specified the production technology in a similar general fashion using flexible functional forms, and both have considered data sets of similar levels of aggregation. As is discussed in our paper, the use of flexible functional forms was pioneered by Diewert, Jorgenson, and Lau in the early seventies.

It is also worth pointing out that the dynamic factor demand literature has adopted various modeling approaches ranging from linear quadratic specifications with an explicit solution for variable and quasi-fixed factor demands, to quadratic and nonlinear quadratic specifications in which the demand for the quasi-fixed factors is only described in terms of the Euler equations, to specifications in which only the variable factor demand equations are used for estimation. Static equilibrium models are, of course, contained as a special case. In developing methodologies that cover both complex and simple specifications, the dynamic factor demand literature presents a menu of flexible modeling options to the empirical researcher. The development of methodologies for complex specifications should be interpreted not as a prescription but as an option that can be selected when such a choice is indicated empirically. Concerning the question whether complex specifications have been implemented successfully, we point out, as an example, the decomposition of the conventional measure of TFP in the U.S. electrical machinery industry given in table 4.1. This decomposition reports on all forms of possible biases considered in equations (39) and (43).

Second, Jorgenson also raises an important issue of research strategy, which is closely related to the points made above. In particular, he questions whether it is best to relax all the assumptions of the standard model at once. As remarked above, the dynamic factor demand literature considers both simple and complex specifications, and we agree that a full-fledged dynamic factor demand model may not be suitable in all situations. However, we do advocate that specification tests are necessary prior to imposing potentially restrictive assumptions such as constant returns to scale, zero adjustment costs, competitive input and output markets, and so on. Assuming away the complexity of the underlying production process may result—as is shown by many studies and illustrated by the Monte Carlo study in our paper—in substantial mismeasurement of the determinants of factor demand, technical change, and other characteristics of the production process. This mismeasurement is then likely to affect significantly the research findings in several areas of economic studies; for example, industrial organization, income distribution, business cycle analysis, and growth modeling. For example, in the recent endogenous growth theory, the form of the production function is typically assumed to be Cobb-Douglas or AK. If the underlying production function is more complex, the results of these models are likely to be quite different. In such cases, the potential loss due to misspecifications may substantially exceed the costs arising from the complexity of the analysis. Flexible functional forms, such as the translog production and cost functions developed by Christensen, Jorgenson, and Lau provide important protections against potential misspecifications. We believe that for analogous reasons it is also important to allow for the possibility of quasi fixity in some of the inputs.

As remarked earlier, one way of taking into account the quasi fixity of some inputs is to base the estimation only on the demand equations for the variable factors (derived, e.g., from a restricted cost or profit function). This approach allows for the consistent estimation of the "technology" parameters but does not provide full insight into the dynamics of the production process. Whether this approach is appropriate—abstracting from questions of efficiency—depends on whether the dynamics of the production process is a focus of the investigation.

We also note that dynamic factor demand models can be estimated from panel data subject to the usual cautions in the pooling of data. Of course, those cautions also apply to static factor demand models.

Third, Jorgenson also makes several comments on specific empirical studies. He points to alternative approaches toward the measurement of depreciation rates, to evaluate and measure the effects of tax policy, spillovers, and economies of scale. We disagree that those alternative approaches represent more successful research strategies. In a nutshell, we see the various methodologies mentioned by Jorgenson and those reviewed in our paper as complementary approaches and not as substitutes. For example:

(a) We fully agree that Hulten and Wykoff have made seminal contributions to the measurement of depreciation rates using prices of used assets. Unfortunately, however, these types of data are not available for many sectors of the economy and are limited in coverage. We hence believe there is room for various approaches. In fact, one can view Hulten and Wykoff's approach as modeling the demand side of used assets, whereas the approach discussed in our review, which dates back to Hicks, Malinvaud, and Diewert, models the supply side. It seems interesting to try to combine the two approaches in future research. Also, the dynamic factor demand literature has generated an extensive literature on capital and capacity utilization, which are allowed to affect the depreciation rate of capital. Thus, this literature speaks not only to the magnitude of the depreciation rate, but also to wider related issues. Also the dynamic factor demand models have been used to estimate the depreciation rate of R&D, which was otherwise typically assumed as given, for example, in the literature referred to in the comments.

(b) General equilibrium models are certainly useful for evaluating the effects of changes in tax policies. Obviously, one of the points of contention in putting together a general equilibrium model for tax simulations is the choice of appropriate parameter values. (One of the major sessions of the recent world congress of the econometric society was devoted to the contentious issue of calibration versus classical estimation. In one view calibration is an estimation method, though typically with unknown statistical properties.) In estimating a dynamic factor demand model we obtain estimates of important parameters using classical econometric techniques with known statistical properties.

(c) Empirical estimation of the degree of scale at the firm, industry, and even aggregate economy level is critical for an understanding of economic growth. A number of models have successfully examined the degree of scale in various sectors and industries. The focus of our study of the Bell system was to understand the dynamics of the capital and R&D investment process as well as the nature of the production frontier faced by the Bell system, including the magnitudes of returns to scale and exogenous technical change. The study was undertaken after the Bell breakup. It was undertaken to study "what is," and not to argue either on the side of the government or on that of the Bell system. Moreover, that dynamic factor demand models have generally been estimated using time series data at the industry level is due to the paucity of specific output and factor prices at the firm level.

(d) Dynamic factor demand models provide a general dynamic framework for studying the contributions of physical capital and R&D and the spillover effects of R&D among sectors and economies. This literature has provided explicit estimates of the magnitude of the R&D spillovers and their contribution to the growth of output and productivity; the convergence of growth rates among industries and economies; and the evolution of productivity growth over the short, intermediate, and long run. It is true, as Jorgenson has pointed out, that modeling spillover effects poses a substantial challenge. We believe that the dynamic factor demand modeling framework can serve as a starting point to understand this dynamic phenomenon.

In conclusion we note again that the dynamic factor demand literature builds, in particular, on Jorgenson's seminal contributions to the neoclassical theory of investment and production. The static equilibrium model, which is the underlying foundation of the conventional measure of TFP, is a special case of the dynamic factor demand model. We argue that imposing a priori restriction on the production structure for the sake of simplicity can seriously bias estimates of productivity growth and can lead to a misdiagnosis of the sources of economic growth, among other problems. The Monte Carlo results reported in our paper clearly substantiate this phenomenon. Hence, specification tests are essential as a justification for imposing potentially restrictive assumptions on the form of the production structure and its dynamic evolution. Dynamic factor demand models provide a framework for such tests and furthermore serve as the basis of a general approach to estimating the rate of technical changes and the dynamics of productivity growth.

5

After "Technical Progress and the Aggregate Production Function"

Robert M. Solow

My never-failing source of guidance on occasions like this is a telephone call that Paul Samuelson once made. He had agreed to be the lunch speaker at a meeting of some business group. Talking to the organizer, Paul asked: "Should I talk for 30 minutes?" The reply was, "Thirty minutes would be optimal. Twenty minutes would be better."

That 1957 paper of mine is now a little over forty years old, about the same age as my youngest child. Like my children, it has aged well, and has produced grandpapers. It is very nice of the organizers of this conference to take note of it and invite me to comment on developments since then, and perhaps still to come.

It goes without saying that a lot of effort, by many hands, has gone into whittling away at the residual. Progress is being made any time some part of the residual can be imputed to some measurable input, or to some adjustment of measured output. This process began very quickly with the work of Ed Denison, and it continues today, even at this conference. I hardly need to mention the important advances that have been made in this way, but they include the introduction of human capital as an explicit input (or the adjustment of hours worked to account for the varying mix of skills); the attempt to define and measure a stock of technological knowledge that could be entered in a production function along with stocks of tangible and human capital; the effort to get a better measure of the flow of capital services as distinct from the mere existence of a stock (in which connection I should mention the almost single-handed campaign of Murray Foss to get a grip on the length of the work-week or work-year

---

Robert M. Solow is Institute Professor of Economics, Emeritus, at the Massachusetts Institute of Technology.

of capital goods); and the need to include the depletion of natural resources either as an input to production or as a deduction from output. I am undoubtedly forgetting some lines of research that lead in this general direction.

Sometimes this kind of work has to focus on measurement difficulties as the main obstacle to progress. This is no trivial matter. Recent papers by Ruth Judson and by Peter Klenow and Andres Rodriguez-Clare have shown that alternative ways of measuring human capital can make a big-time difference in the plausible interpretation of economic growth, so it is really important to come to some scientific agreement on the best way to deal with human capital as an input (and as an output, don't forget) and then to implement it. When comparable attention comes to be paid to natural—including environmental—resources, similar subtleties may arise.

Sometimes, however, this process of whittling away at the residual runs up against obstacles that are not simply measurement problems, but are conceptual problems or modeling problems. I want to come to one or two of those in a few minutes, but first I just want to mention a couple of conceptual issues that are too complicated to discuss in a lunch talk. For instance, there is the question of how to deal with the quality of capital goods. I suppose that if you play fast and loose with this notion, you could get rid of most of total factor productivity in a hurry. I *think* that is what Zvi Griliches and Dale Jorgenson once proposed to do. That was too bad; there was a lot of important stuff in that paper, and some of it got hidden behind that one minor and misguided side issue. To go very far down that line you have to think you can identify the source of improved quality of capital goods. And to do that you have to have greater faith than I can muster that whoever gets to appropriate the benefits of improved quality is also the source of improved quality. I will come back to this quality-of-capital question in a moment, in a more restricted context where it can be dealt with clearly.

That leads directly to a broader conceptual issue that I want to mention but don't want to discuss seriously. In accord with the spirit of the time in economics, there is a tendency to embed the estimation of technical change and the aggregate production function in a general equilibrium model, usually a very special general equilibrium model. Not only does this fit in with the spirit of the time, but it also may provide relatively easy answers to otherwise difficult specification problems. I find I am suspicious of this way of proceeding.

You might say that I am partially responsible for starting that habit forty years ago by cheerfully using observed factor shares as estimates of elasticities. Yes; and it made me uncomfortable then. As the process goes further, my discomfort increases. The problem is not that I am hostile to general equilibrium theory, or even to competitive general equilibrium theory in its place. I am not. The generic problem is that any kind of empirical application then becomes a test of a very broad combined hypothesis, including the hypothesis that the whole economy behaves as if it were doing something very special. You never know how to interpret the results, whether they are good or bad.

I think I will spend the rest of my time talking about a couple of other conceptual issues that arise in the continuing project of analyzing productivity growth into its measurable components and the residual. The first is—to quote the title of a very relevant paper by Dale Jorgenson—the embodiment question.

In the year following my 1957 paper, I wrote another paper called "Investment and Technical Progress." It was done for a conference at Stanford and took two years to get into print, but I think it was actually written in 1958. It seemed to me then that the 1957 model might have grossly understated the importance of old-fashioned capital investment as a vehicle for bringing new technology into productive operation: No amount of clever jet-engine technology could affect productivity unless airlines bought jet aircrafts—that sort of thing. The new paper produced a clean model in which *all* new technology had to be embodied in new gross investment before it could have any influence on production or productivity.

I liked the idea, but it went nowhere. Nobody ever suggested that it wasn't entirely plausible. How could they? It *is* plausible, common sense even: If you don't like the jet-engine example, how about numerically controlled machine tools? (You see the connection to the quality-of-capital problem.) The problem was not plausibility; it was that embodiment seemed to cut no empirical ice at all, and if you couldn't find the embodiment effect leaving a significant trace in data, then it wasn't really so interesting.

There are simple reasons why it might not show up even if it were really there. For instance, a steady state with embodiment looks like a steady state without embodiment; embodiment works through changes in the average age of capital equipment, and in or near a steady state the average age of equipment will be just about constant. So, unless the rate of investment fluctuates substantially, you would not see the embodiment effect at work. Or, to look in a different direction, if a substantial part of new technology can be retrofitted to old capital at a small expense, then the embodiment effect can be unimportant, or it can be swamped by other influences. (I have been told that a lot of chemical engineering technology is actually designed to allow retrofitting.) Anyway, decades went by and embodiment languished. Sad. (Ed Wolff thought he saw it once, and more recently Larry Lau had a sighting; it occurred to me that if it could be connected to the Clinton family, Kenneth Starr would either find it or invent it, or at least leak it. The general impression remains: no dice.)

But now all of a sudden the whole idea has revived, under the influence of an entirely new approach, as you will all learn when you hear the Jovanovic-Greenwood paper this afternoon, which builds on earlier work by Chuck Hulten, Jeremy Greenwood, Zvi Hercovitz, Per Krusell, and no doubt others. I don't want to spoil their story. Think of what I am about to say as a preview of coming attractions.

Imagine a two-sector economy. In one sector capital goods are produced by labor alone. In the other sector already accumulated capital goods (or their services) combine with the remaining labor to produce consumer goods. I want to tell two different stories about this economy. In one story, technological progress steadily reduces the labor input required to produce a unit of capital goods in the investment sector. The capital goods don't change at all. They enter the production function for consumer goods in the same old way. They become cheaper relative to consumer goods as time goes by, for obvious reasons.

The second story is more complicated. Suppose that the investment sector continues to produce "machines" with the same labor requirement as at the beginning. You could perhaps hear that I put machines in quotation marks, because I want to suppose that newer machines are more productive than old ones when employed in the manufacture of consumer goods. In other words, there is capital-embodied technological progress. When I say that it takes the same old amount of labor to produce a machine, I must be measuring the output of machines crudely—say, by counting the number of legs and dividing by four. It will come out all right at the end. The output of consumer goods is calculated by imagining an efficient allocation of labor to machines of different vintages, and then adding up the output over surviving vintages. (This is the kind of model I produced in 1958.)

Now the interesting thing is that these two stories are essentially indistinguishable from the macroeconomic point of view, by which I mean you can't tell them apart if you look only at aggregates and price indexes. You can see why that might be so: In story number two newer machines are more productive than older machines. In story number one that is not literally true; but if you think of machines as congealed labor, newer investment-sector labor is more productive (of consumer goods) than is older investment-sector labor. Under any reasonable pricing rule, the relative price of machines will be falling in story number one because the labor cost of producing a machine is perpetually falling, and there are constant returns in the production of machines. In story number two, the labor cost of producing a machine (in quotation marks) is constant, but the machines get more productive. If you asked for the labor cost of producing a machine of constant quality, it would be falling. And it would be falling at the rate of embodied technical progress. (Of course, if you look closely you can see the difference between a jet and a propeller.)

The new approach talks of investment-specific technological progress, because that term is meant to cover both stories. In both stories, it is true that society can only take advantage of technical progress to the extent that it invests. That is what the whole idea is about, after all. And it then becomes fairly natural to *measure* the rate of investment-specific technical progress by looking at the rate at which the relative price of quality-adjusted capital goods falls. According to this scheme the rate of investment-specific technical change has averaged close to 4 percent a year during the postwar period. (Needless to say, this does not translate one-for-one into output growth—not nearly.) What is even more interesting is that there is no sign of a post-1973 slowdown in the investment-specific component of technical change. But I will leave all this to the paper by Greenwood and Jovanovic, which you can look forward to.

What I do want to call to your attention is that this body of research suggests and confirms the importance of two general points I have been trying to make. The first is the way conceptual issues and measurement issues get intertwined. In the case of embodiment, an awful lot hangs on our ability to estimate the price trend for quality-corrected, or productivity-corrected, capital goods. Bob Gordon's heroic campaign to do just that was an indispensable foundation for this new line of research. It has to be carried forward and extended, as the Bureau of Labor Statistics is now doing.

The second point is more worrisome: It is the way that empirical research gets tied up with complex hypotheses about pricing and other aspects of market behavior. The idea of a dichotomy between measuring and modeling is breaking down. This is not a remark about productivity research but about economic research, and maybe about research in general. Progress in measuring and understanding investment-specific or capital-embodied technical change will then be tied up with different stories about the way the economy functions. I said that this is worrying, but it's not such a big deal. I only want to urge that research not get tied to any one particular picture of the way the economy functions. It would be a good idea to try out some alternative theories of factor pricing, for example, so we can have an educated idea about how sensitive the measurement outcome is to additional assumptions about the market environment from which observations are presumed to arise.

I am coming to the end of the time I allowed myself. The last thing I want to do is to throw out another pet idea and hope that it can play a role in future research on productivity. Bits of experience and conversation have suggested to me that it may be a mistake to think of R&D as the only ultimate source of growth in total factor productivity. I don't doubt that it is the largest ultimate source. But there seems to be a lot of productivity improvement that originates in people and processes that are not usually connected with R&D. Some of it comes from the shop floor, from the ideas of experienced and observant production workers. This should probably be connected with Arrow's "learning by doing" or with the Japanese slogan about "continuous improvement." There is another part that seems to originate in management practices—in design, in the choice of product mixes, even in marketing. Notice that this is not just straightforward enhancement of productive efficiency. All this talk about value creation that one hears from business consultants may be more than a buzzword; it may even be important. We need to understand much more about how those kinds of values get reflected in measured real output, and whether they can be usefully analyzed by our methods.

This is an inexhaustible subject; but patience is a scarce resource. Thank you for yours.

6 Accounting for Growth

Jeremy Greenwood and Boyan Jovanovic

6.1 Introduction

The story of technological progress is the invention and subsequent implementation of improved methods of production. All models of growth incorporate this notion in some way. For example, the celebrated Solow (1956) model assumes that technological progress and its implementation are both free. Technological progress rains down as manna from heaven and improves the productivity of all factors of production, new and old alike.

Based on his earlier model, Solow (1957) proposed what has since become the dominant growth-accounting framework. Its central equation is $y = zF(k, l)$, where y is output, k and l are the quality-uncorrected inputs of capital (computed using the perpetual inventory method) and labor, and z is a measure of the state of technology. If k and l were homogenous, then this would be the right way to proceed. In principle, the framework would allow one to separate the contribution of what is measured, k and l, from what is not measured, z. Now, neither k nor l is homogenous in practice, but one could perhaps hope that some type of aggregation result would validate the procedure—if not exactly, then at least as an approximation.

The problem with this approach is that it treats all vintages of capital (or for that matter labor) as alike. In reality, advances in technology tend to be embodied in the latest vintages of capital. This means that new capital is better than old capital, not just because machines suffer wear and

---

Jeremy Greenwood is professor of economics at the University of Rochester. Boyan Jovanovic is professor of economics at New York University and the University of Chicago, and a research associate of the National Bureau of Economic Research.

The authors wish to thank Levent Kockesen for help with the research. The National Science Foundation and the C. V. Starr Center for Applied Economics at New York University are also thanked for support.

tear as they age, but also because new capital is better than the old capital was when the *latter* was new. It also means that there can be no technological progress without investment. If this is what the "embodiment of technology in capital" means, then it cannot be captured by the Solow (1956, 1957) framework, for reasons that Solow (1960, 90) himself aptly describes:

> It is as if all technical progress were something like time-and-motion study, a way of improving the organization and operation of inputs without reference to the nature of the inputs themselves. The striking assumption is that old and new capital equipment participate equally in technical progress. This conflicts with the casual observation that many if not most innovations need to be embodied in new kinds of durable equipment before they can be made effective. Improvements in technology affect output only to the extent that they are carried into practice either by net capital formation or by the replacement of old-fashioned equipment by the latest models . . .

In other words, in contrast to Solow (1956, 1957), implementation is not free. It requires the purchase of new machines. Moreover, it requires new human capital, too, because workers and management must learn the new technology. This will take place either through experience or through training, or both. This type of technological progress is labelled here as *investment specific;* you must invest to realize the benefits from it.

If this view is correct, growth accounting should allow for many types of physical and human capital, each specific at least in part to the technology that it embodies. In other words, accounting for growth should proceed in a vintage capital framework. This paper argues that a vintage capital model can shed light on some key features of the postwar growth experience of the United States. The well-known models of Lucas (1988) and Romer (1990) do not fit into this framework. In Lucas's model, all physical capital, new and old alike, "participates equally" in the technological progress that the human capital sector generates; and, as Solow's quote emphasizes, this does not fit in with casual observation about how technological progress works. In contrast, Romer's model *is* a vintage capital model. New capital goods are invented every period—but new capital isn't better than old capital. It simply is different and expands the menu of available inputs, and production is assumed to be more efficient when there is a longer menu of inputs available. Thus capital does not become obsolete as it ages—an implication that denies the obvious fact that old technologies are continually being replaced by new ones.

6.1.1 Summary of the Argument and Results

Different variants of Solow's (1960) vintage capital model are explored here. To begin, however, a stab is made at accounting for postwar U.S. growth using the standard Solow (1957) framework.

Why the Model y = zF(k, l) Is Unsatisfactory

Solow's (1957) model is the dominant growth-accounting framework, and section 6.2 uses it in a brief growth-accounting exercise for the postwar period. The bottom line is that this model is unable to deal with these four facts:

1. *The prolonged productivity slowdown that started around 1973.* To explain the slowdown the model insists that technological progress has been dormant since 1973! This, of course, is greatly at odds with casual empiricism: personal computers, cellular telephones, robots, and the Internet, inter alia.

2. *The falling price of capital goods relative to consumption goods.* This price has declined by 4 percent per year over the postwar period, and it is a symptom of the obsolescence of old capital caused by the arrival of better, new capital. This relative price decline of capital is not consistent with a one-sector growth model such as Solow's (1956, 1957).

3. *The productivity of a best-practice plant is much larger than that of the average plant.* They can differ by a factor of two, three, or more, depending on the industry. This is at odds with a model such as Solow's (1956, 1957), in which all firms use the same production function.

4. *The recent rise in wage inequality.* The framework is silent on this.

Why the Baseline Vintage Capital Model Is Unsatisfactory

Section 6.3 introduces the baseline vintage capital model of Solow (1960), in which technological progress is exogenous and embodied in the form of new capital goods. Using the price of new equipment relative to consumption, the technological improvement in equipment is estimated to be 4 percent per annum during the postwar period. This makes the effective capital stock grow faster than it does in conventional estimates. As a consequence, the implied productivity slowdown after 1973 is even bigger than the estimate obtained from the Solow (1957) framework! This spells trouble for frameworks that identify total factor productivity (TFP) as a measure of technological progress, a datum that Abramovitz once labelled "a measure of our ignorance." Can Solow's (1960) framework rationalize the slowdown?

Adding Diffusion Lags and Technology-Specific Learning to the Baseline Vintage Model

One adjustment to the vintage capital model that can produce a productivity slowdown is the introduction of a technology-specific learning curve on the part of users of capital goods. The effects of learning can be amplified further if spillovers in learning among capital goods users are added.

Another important adjustment is to include lags in the diffusion of new technologies. The analysis assumes that the vintage-specific efficiency of investment starts growing faster in the early 1970s with the advent of information technologies, and that the new technologies have steep learning curves. Furthermore, it is presumed that it takes some time for these technologies to diffuse through the economy. This leads to a vintage capital explanation of the "productivity slowdown" as a period of above-normal unmeasured investment in human capital specific to the technologies that came on-line starting in the early 1970s.

Implications for Wage Inequality

The productivity slowdown was accompanied by a rise in the skill premium. It is highly probable that the two phenomena are related, and section 6.5 explains why. There are two kinds of explanations for the recent rise in inequality. The first, proposed by Griliches (1969), emphasizes the role of skill in the *use* of capital goods, and is labelled "capital-skill complementarity." The second hypothesis, first proposed by Nelson and Phelps (1966), emphasizes the role of skill in *implementing* the new technology, and is labelled "skill in adoption." Both explanations can be nested in a vintage capital model.

Endogenizing Growth in the Vintage Model

Section 6.6 presents three models in which growth is endogenous, each based on a different engine of growth. Each engine requires a different fuel to run it. To analyze economic growth one needs to know what the important engines are; each one will have different implications for how resources should be allocated across the production of current and future consumptions.

Learning by doing as an engine. Section 6.6.1 describes Arrow's (1962) model of growth through learning by doing in the capital goods sector. Learning by doing is the engine that fits most closely with Solow's (1960) original vintage capital model because the technological growth that it generates uses no resources. That is, all employed labor and capital are devoted to producing either capital goods or consumption goods. As capital goods producers' efficiency rises, the relative price of capital goods falls.

Research as an engine. Section 6.6.2 highlights Krusell's (1998) model of R&D in the capital goods sector. Here each capital goods producer must decide how much labor to hire to increase the efficiency of the capital good he sells.

Human capital as an engine. Section 6.6.3 assumes that capital goods producers can switch to a better technology if they accumulate the requisite technology-specific expertise. The section extends Parente's (1994) model in which the cost of raising one's productive efficiency is the output foregone while the new technology is brought up to speed through learning.

What does the power system look like? These three models have a common structure: Each has a consumption-goods and a capital-goods sector, and each has endogenous technological progress in the capital goods sector only. This technological progress is then passed onto final output producers in the form of a "pecuniary external effect" transmitted by the falling relative price of capital. Each model focuses exclusively on one growth engine, however; and while this simplifies the exposition, it does not convey an idea of how much each engine matters to growth as a whole.

Unless its discovery was accidental, whenever a new technology appears on society's menu, society pays an invention cost. Then, society must pay an implementation cost—the cost of the physical and human capital specific to the new technology. Society needs to pay an invention cost only once per technology, whereas the implementation cost must be paid once per user.[1] After this, there are only the costs of using the technology—"production costs." Not surprisingly, then, society spends much less on research than it does on the various costs of implementing technologies. Even in the United States, Jovanovic (1997) has estimated that implementation costs outweigh research costs by a factor of about 20:1.

Because people must learn how to use new technologies, it follows that the learning costs associated with the adoption of such technologies—be they in the form of schooling, experience, or on-the-job training—are inescapable at the level of a country. Because the object of this exercise is accounting for growth in the United States, one can conclude that schooling, experience, and training are, in some combination, essential for growth to occur.[2] Research, on the other hand, clearly is not, because the majority of the world's nations have grown not by inventing their own technologies, but by implementing technologies invented by others. Presumably, the United States could do the same (assuming that other countries would then be advancing the frontiers of knowledge).

6.1.2 Why Models Matter for Growth Accounting

In its early days, the Cowles Commission's message was that aside from satisfying one's intellectual curiosity about how the world works, economic models would, on a practical level, (a) allow one to predict the consequences of out-of-sample variation in policies and other exogenous vari-

---

1. The average cost of implementation may, however, be declining in the number of users because of synergies in adoption.
2. Jovanovic and Rob (1998) compare Solow's (1956, 1960) frameworks against the backdrop of cross-country growth experience.

ables; (b) guide the measurement of variables; and (c) allow one to deal with simultaneity problems. These points apply to economic models generally, and they certainly relate to the value of models that explain growth. It is worth explaining why.

Policy analysis. Denison (1964, 90) claimed that "the whole embodied question is of little importance for policy in the United States." He based this assertion on his calculation that a one-year change in the average age of capital would have little impact on the output. This misses the point. Different models will suggest different growth-promoting policies. For instance, in the version of Arrow's (1962) learning-by-doing model presented here, there are industry-wide spillover effects in capital goods production, and a policy that subsidized capital goods production would improve welfare. In Parente's (1994) model, however, capital goods producers fully internalize the effects of any investment in technology-specific expertise. Such a world is efficient. Government policies may promote growth, but only at the expense of welfare. Other policy questions arise. Vintage capital models predict a continual displacement of old technologies by more efficient new ones. If a worker needs to train to work a technology, then as a technology becomes obsolete so does the worker. This may have implications for such things as unemployment. These considerations had, long ago, led Stigler to conclude that job insecurity is the price that society must pay for progress.[3]

The measurement of variables. Economic theory provides a guide about which things should be measured and how to measure them. For example, the baseline vintage capital model developed here suggests that the decline in the relative price of new equipment can be identified with the pace of technological progress in the equipment goods sector. It also provides guidance on how the aggregate stock of equipment should be measured—and this stock grows more quickly than the corresponding National Income and Product Accounts (NIPA) measure. More generally, in a world with investment-specific technological progress, new capital goods will be more productive than old ones. The rental prices for new and old capital goods are indicators of the amount of investment-specific technological progress. For example, the difference in rents between old and new office buildings (or the rent gradient) can be used to shed light on the amount of technological progress that there has been in structures.

Investment in physical capital is counted in the NIPA, whereas invest-

---

3. "We should like to have both a rapid increase in aggregate output and stability in its composition—the former to keep pace with expanding wants, and the latter to avoid the losses of specialized equipment of entrepreneurs and crafts of employees and creating 'sick' industries in which resources are less mobile than customers. It is highly probable that the goals are inconsistent" (Stigler 1947, 30).

ment in knowledge is not. Yet, investment in knowledge may increase output tomorrow in just the same way as investment in physical capital does. This is sometimes referred to as the unmeasured investment problem. In the United States, R&D spending amounts to about 3 percent of GDP. The costs of implementing new technologies, in terms of schooling, on-the-job training, and so on, may amount to 10 percent of GDP. The models of Krusell (1998) and Parente (1994) suggest that such expenditures are as vital to the production of future output as is investment in equipment and structures. In the NIPA such expenditures are expensed or deducted from a firm's profits, as opposed to being capitalized into profits as when a firm makes a new investment good. By this accounting, GDP would be 13 percent higher if these unmeasured investments were taken into account.

This, indeed, is one way the vintage capital model can perhaps explain the productivity slowdown—the vintage of technologies that arrived around 1974 was promising but was subject to a protracted learning curve and high adoption costs. The productivity slowdown took place, in other words, because there was a lot of unmeasured investment. Conventional growth accounting practices will understate productivity growth to the extent that they underestimate output growth due to these unmeasured investments. This might suggest that more effort should be put into collecting aggregate data on R&D and adoption costs.

Simultaneity problems. Conventional growth accounting uses an aggregate production function to decompose output growth into technological progress and changes in inputs in a way that uses minimal economic theory. Clearly, though, a large part of the growth in the capital stock—equipment and structures—is due to technological progress. The general equilibrium approach taken here allows for the growth in capital stock to be broken down into its underlying sources of technological progress. Furthermore, it links the observed decline in the price of new equipment with the rate of technological progress in the production of new equipment. More generally, models allow one to connect observed rent gradients on buildings to the rate of technological progress in structures, and they allow one to connect the long diffusion lags of products and technologies to the costs of adopting them. Models lead to more precise inferences about such simultaneities.

6.2 Solow (1957) and Neutral Technological Progress

In one of those rare papers that changes the courses of economics, Solow (1957) proposed a way of measuring technological progress. Suppose output, y, is produced according to the constant-returns-to-scale production function

(1) $$y = zF(k,l),$$

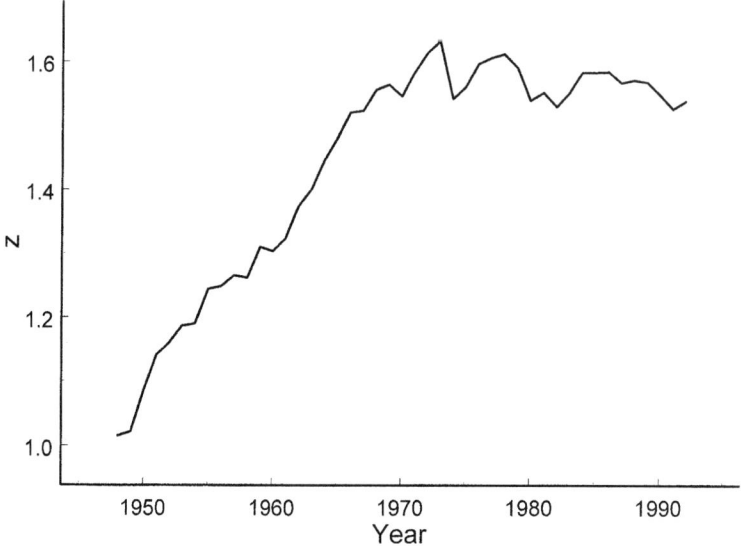

Fig. 6.1 Standard measure of neutral technological progress

where k and l are the inputs of capital and labor. The variable z measures the state of technology in the economy, and technological progress is neutral. Over time, z grows, reflecting technological improvement in the economy. Thus, for a given level of inputs, k and l, more output, y, can be produced.

For any variable x, let $g_x \equiv (1/x)(dx/dt)$ denote its rate of growth. If the economy is competitive, then the rate of technological progress can be measured by

$$(2) \qquad g_z = g_{y/l} - \alpha g_{k/l},$$

where α represents capital's share of income.

The rate of technological progress, g_z, can easily be computed from equation (2), given data on GDP, y, the capital stock, k, hours worked, l, and labor's share of income, $1 - \alpha$. Figure 6.1 plots z for the postwar period. Note that the growth in z slows down dramatically around 1973.[4] This is often referred to as the "productivity slowdown." Does it seem reasonable to believe that technological progress has been dormant since 1973? Hardly. Casual empiricism speaks to the contrary: computers, robots, cellular telephones, and so on.

Perhaps part of the explanation is that some quality change in output goes unmeasured so that g_y was understated. However, the above measures

---

4. In fact, over the whole period it grew on average at the paltry rate of 0.96 percent per year.

of k and l do not control for quality change, and this biases things in the other direction and makes the puzzle seem even larger. Is something wrong with the notion of technological progress in the Solow (1957) model? The remaining sections analyze vintage capital models in which technological progress is investment specific.

6.3 Solow (1960) and Investment-Specific Technological Progress

In a lesser-known paper, Solow (1960) developed a model that embodies technological progress in the form of *new* capital goods.

The production of final output. Suppose that output is produced according to the constant-returns-to-scale production function

(3) $$y = F(k,l).$$

Note that there is no neutral technological progress. Output can be used for two purposes: consumption, c, and gross investment, i. Thus, the economy's resource constraint reads: $c + i = F(k,l)$

Capital accumulation. Now, suppose that capital accumulation is governed by the law of motion

(4) $$\frac{dk}{dt} = iq - \delta k,$$

where i is gross investment and δ is the rate of physical depreciation on capital. Here q represents the current state of technology for producing new equipment. As q rises more new capital goods can be produced for a unit of forgone output or consumption. This form of technological progress is specific to the investment goods sector of the economy. Therefore, changes in q are dubbed *investment-specific* technological progress. Two important implications of equation (4) are:

1. In order to realize the gains from this form of technological progress there must be investment in the economy. This is not the case for neutral technological progress, as assumed in Solow (1957).
2. Efficiency units of capital of different vintages can be aggregated linearly in equation (3) using the appropriate weights on past investments: $k(t) = \int_0^\infty e^{-\delta s} q(t-s) i(t-s) ds.$[5]

The relative price of capital. In a competitive equilibrium the relative price of new capital goods, p, would be given by $p = 1/q$, because this shows

---

5. Benhabib and Rustichini (1991) relax this assumption and allow for a variable rate of substitution in production between capital stocks of different vintages.

how much output or consumption goods must be given up in order to purchase a new unit of equipment. Therefore, in the above framework it is easy to identify the investment-specific technological shift factor, q, by using a price series for new capital goods—that is, by using the relationship $q = 1/p$.

Growth accounting in the baseline model. Figure 6.2 shows the price series for new equipment and the implied series for the investment technology shock. Look at how much better this series represents technological progress. It rises more or less continuously throughout the postwar period; there is no productivity slowdown here.

So how much postwar economic growth is due to investment-specific versus neutral technological progress? To gauge this, assume that output is given by the production function

(5) $$y = zk_e^{\alpha_e} k_s^{\alpha_s} l^{1 - \alpha_e - \alpha_s},$$

where k_e and k_s represent the stocks of equipment and structures in the economy. Let equipment follow a law of motion similar to equation (4) so that

(6) $$\frac{dk_e}{dt} = qi_e - \delta_e k_e,$$

where i_e is gross investment in equipment measured in consumption units and δ_e is the rate of physical depreciation. Thus, equipment is subject to

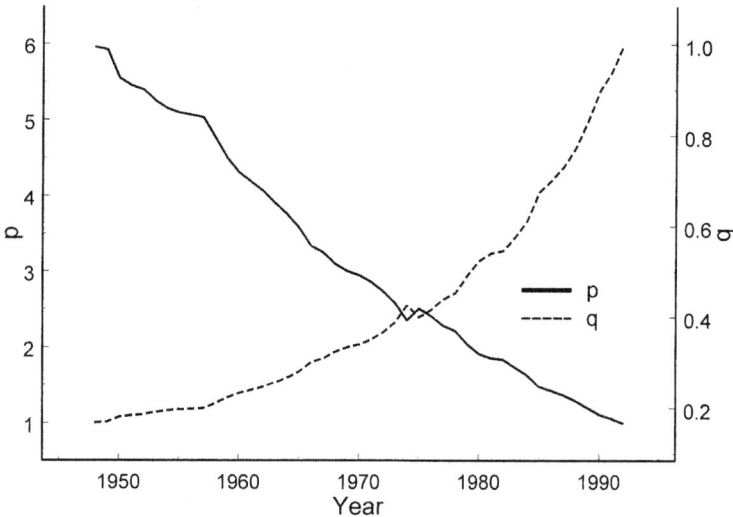

Fig. 6.2 **Relative price of equipment, p, and investment-specific technological progress, q**

investment-specific technological progress. The law of motion for structures is written as

$$\text{(7)} \qquad \frac{dk_s}{dt} = i_s - \delta_s k_s,$$

where i_s represents gross investment in structures measured in consumption units and δ_s is the rate of physical depreciation. The economy's resource constraint now reads[6]

$$\text{(8)} \qquad c + i_e + i_s = y.$$

It is easy to calculate from equation (5), in conjunction with equations (6)–(8), that along the economy's balanced path the rate of growth in income is given by

$$\text{(9)} \qquad g_y = \left(\frac{1}{1 - \alpha_e - \alpha_s}\right) g_z + \left(\frac{\alpha_e}{1 - \alpha_e - \alpha_s}\right) g_q.$$

To use this formula, numbers are needed for α_e, α_s, g_z, and q_q. Let $\alpha_e = 0.17$ and $\alpha_s = 0.13$.[7] Over the postwar period the rate of investment-specific technological progress averaged 4 percent per year, a fact that can be computed from the series shown for q in figure 6.2. Hence, $g_q = 0.04$. Next, a measure for z can be obtained from the production relationship in equation (5) that implies $z = (y/[k_e^{\alpha_e} k_s^{\alpha_s} l^{1-\alpha_e-\alpha_s}])$. Given data on y, k_e, k_s, and l the series for z can be computed. These series are all readily available, except for k_e. This series can be constructed using the law of motion in equation (6) and data for q and i_e. In line with NIPA, the rate of physical depreciation on equipment was taken to be 12.4 percent, so that $\delta_e = 0.124$. Following this procedure, the average rate of neutral technological advance was estimated to be 0.38 percent. Equation (9) then implies that investment-specific technological progress accounted for 63 percent of output growth, whereas neutral technological advance accounted for 35 percent.[8]

Why the baseline model is not adequate. All is not well with this model, however. With the quality change correction in the capital stock, it grows faster than did k in the Solow (1957) version. When this revised series is inserted into the production function for final goods, the implied produc-

---

6. Greenwood, Hercowitz, and Krusell (1997) have used this structure for growth accounting. Hulten (1992) employs a similar setup but replaces the resource constraint with $c + i_e q + i_s = y$. See Greenwood, Hercowitz, and Krusell (1997) for a discussion on the implications of this substitution.

7. This is what Greenwood, Hercowitz, and Krusell (1997) estimated.

8. The second part of the appendix works out what would happen if a growth accountant failed to incorporate investment-specific technological advance into his analysis.

tivity slowdown is even bigger than that arising from the Solow (1957) framework. How can this slowdown be explained? The introduction of lags in learning about how to use new technologies to their full potential, and lags in the diffusion of new technologies, seems to do the trick.

6.4 Adjusting the Baseline Solow (1960) Model

This section introduces lags in learning and diffusion of new technologies. The setting is necessarily one in which plants differ in the technologies they use. As will be seen, it turns out that aggregation to a simple growth model cannot be guaranteed in such settings. Some conditions on technology and the vintage structure that ensure Solow (1960) aggregation are presented.

6.4.1 Heterogeneity across Plants and the Aggregation of Capital

Notation. Some of the following variables are plant specific. Because plants of different ages, τ, will coexist at any date, one sometimes needs to distinguish these variables with a double index. The notation $x_\tau(t)$ will denote the value of the variable x at date t in a plant that is τ years old. The plant's vintage is then $v = t - \tau$. Variables that are not plant specific will be indexed by t alone. Moreover, the index t will be dropped whenever possible.

Production of final goods. Final goods are produced in a variety of plants. A plant is indexed by its vintage. Thus, the output of a plant of age τ is described by the production function

$$y_\tau = z_\tau k_\tau^\alpha l_\tau^\beta, \quad 0 < \alpha + \beta < 1,$$

where z_τ is the plant's TFP and k_τ and l_τ are the stocks of capital and labor that it employs. For now, z_τ is exogenous. A plant's capital depreciates at the rate δ and cannot be augmented once in place.

Investment-specific technological progress. Recall that g_q is the rate of investment-specific technological progress. Then, as before, an efficiency unit of new capital costs $1/q(t) = p(t) = e^{-g_q t}$ units of consumption in period t. The period t cost of the capital for new plant is therefore $k_0(t)/q(t)$.

Optimal hiring of labor. A price-taking plant of age τ will hire labor up to the point where the marginal product of labor equals the wage, w. Hence, $\beta z_\tau k_\tau^\alpha l_\tau^{\beta-1} = w$, so that

$$(10) \qquad l_\tau = \left(\frac{\beta z_\tau k_\tau^\alpha}{w}\right)^{1/(1-\beta)},$$

and

(11) $$y_\tau = \left(\frac{\beta}{w}\right)^{\beta/(1-\beta)} z_\tau^{1/(1-\beta)} k_\tau^{\alpha/(1-\beta)}.$$

Labor market clearing. Suppose that there are n_τ plants operating of age τ. If the aggregate endowment of labor is fixed at h, then labor market clearing requires that

$$\int_0^\infty n_\tau l_\tau d\tau = h.$$

Substituting equation (10) into the above formula then allows the following expression to be obtained for the market clearing wage

(12) $$w = \beta\left[\frac{\int_0^\infty n_\tau (z_\tau k_\tau^\alpha)^{1/(1-\beta)} d\tau}{h}\right]^{1-\beta}.$$

Plugging this into equation (11) yields the output of an age-τ plant as follows:

$$y_\tau = z_\tau^{1/(1-\beta)} k_\tau^{\alpha/(1-\beta)} \left[\frac{h}{\int_0^\infty n_\tau (z_\tau k_\tau^\alpha)^{1/(1-\beta)} d\tau}\right]^\beta.$$

Aggregate output. Aggregate output is the sum of outputs across all the plants: $y = \int_0^\infty n_\tau y_\tau d\tau$. It therefore equals

(13) $$y = \frac{h^\beta \int_0^\infty n_\tau z_\tau^{1/(1-\beta)} k_\tau^{\alpha/(1-\beta)} d\tau}{\left[\int_0^\infty n_\tau (z_\tau k_\tau^\alpha)^{1/(1-\beta)} d\tau\right]^\beta} = h^\beta \left(\int_0^\infty n_\tau z_\tau^{1/(1-\beta)} k_\tau^{\alpha/(1-\beta)} d\tau\right)^{1-\beta}.$$

Solow (1960) aggregation. This model is similar to the benchmark vintage capital model. In fact, it aggregates to it exactly if the following three assumptions hold:

1. Returns to scale are constant (so that $\alpha = 1 - \beta$).
2. Total factor productivity is the same in all plants (so that $z_\tau = z$).
3. The number of plants of each vintage does not change over time. That is, $n_{t-v}(t) = n_0(v)$, or equivalently, $n_\tau(t) = n_0(t - \tau)$, since $v = t - \tau$. In other words, all investment is in the current vintage plants, and plants last forever—only their capital wears off asymptotically.

In this situation, $y = zh^{1-\alpha}\mathbf{k}^\alpha$, where the aggregate capital stock $\mathbf{k}$ is defined by $\mathbf{k}(t) = \int_{-\infty}^t n_{t-v}(t) k_{t-v}(t) dv$. Now capital in each plant depreciates at the rate δ, which means that for any $v \leq t$,

$$\frac{dk_{t-v}(t)}{dt} = -\delta k_{t-v}(t).$$

Moreover, by assumption (3), $[dn_{t-v}(t)]/dt = 0$ for any $v \leq t$. Therefore,

$$\frac{d\mathbf{k}(t)}{dt} = -\delta \mathbf{k}(t) + q(t)i(t),$$

where $i(t) = [n_0(t)k_0(t)]/q(t)$ is gross investment (measured in consumption units).[9] If one identifies h and $\mathbf{k}$ with l and k in equations (3) and (4), the two models will have identical predictions.[10]

So, for the above vintage capital model to differ in a significant way from the benchmark model with investment-specific technological progress, some combination of assumptions (1), (2), and (3) must be relaxed. Without this, the model will be unable to resolve the productivity slowdown puzzle.

Lumpy investment assumption. Now, for the rest of section 6.4, suppose that the blueprints for a new plant at date t call for a *fixed* lump of capital, $k_0(t)$. Let $k_0(t)$ grow at the constant rate $\kappa \equiv g_q/(1 - \alpha)$ over time.[11] That is, the efficiency units of capital embodied by a new plant at date t are equal to $k_0(t) = e^{\kappa t}$. A plant built at date t then embodies $e^{\kappa t} \equiv (e^{g_q t})^{1/(1-\alpha)}$ efficiency units of capital. Thus, the consumption cost of building a new plant at date t is

(14) $$\frac{e^{\kappa t}}{q(t)} = e^{(\kappa - g_q)t} = (e^{g_q t})^{\alpha/(1-\alpha)}.$$

Therefore, the ratio of the capital stock between a new plant and a plant that is τ periods old will be given by $k_0/k_\tau = e^{(\kappa+\delta)\tau}$, where δ is the rate of physical depreciation on capital. Together with equation (11) this implies that $\lim_{\tau \to \infty} y_\tau/y_0 = 0$ so that, relative to new plants, old plants will wither away over time. In what follows, set $\delta = 0$.

6.4.2 Learning Effects

Established skills are often destroyed, and productivity can temporarily fall upon a switch to a new technology. In its early phases, then, a new

---

9. It makes sense that under constant returns to scale only the aggregate amount of investment matters, and not how it is divided among plants.

10. Even without these assumptions, the model will behave similarly in balanced growth. Assume for the moment that the number of plants is constant through time so that $n_\tau = n$ and z_τ grows at rate g_z. The supply of labor will be constant in balanced growth. Now, along a balanced growth path, output and investment must grow at a constant rate, g_y. This implies that $i = nk_0/q$ must grow at this rate, too. Therefore, k_0 must grow at rate $g_y + g_q$. Clearly, to have balanced growth, all of the k_τ's should grow at the same rate. Consequently, k_τ will grow at rate $g_y + g_q$. It is easy to deduce from equation (13) that the rate of growth in output will be given by $g_y = (1/y)(dy/dt) = [(1/1 - \alpha)g_z] + [(\alpha/1 - \alpha)g_q]$. This formula is identical in form to equation (9). (To see this, set $\alpha_s = 0$ and $\alpha_e = \alpha$ in equation [9]).

11. From note 10, it is known that along a balanced growth path, $k_0(t)$ must grow at rate $g_y + g_q$, where g_y is the growth rate of output and g_q is the growth rate of q. It is easy to check that $g_y + g_q = g_q/(1 - \alpha) \equiv \kappa$.

technology may be operated inefficiently because of a dearth of experience.

Evidence on learning effects. A mountain of evidence attests to the presence of such learning effects.

1. An interesting case study, undertaken by David (1975), is the Lawrence no. 2 cotton mill. This mill was operated in the U.S. antebellum period, and detailed inventory records show that no new equipment was added between 1836 and 1856. Yet, output per hour grew at 2.3 percent per year over the period. Jovanovic and Nyarko (1995) present a variety of learning curves for activities such as angioplasty surgery to steel finishing; see Argotte and Epple (1990) for a survey of case studies on learning curves.

2. After analyzing 2,000 firms from forty-one industries spanning the period 1973–86, Bahk and Gort (1993) find that a plant's productivity increases by 15 percent over the first fourteen years of its life due to learning effects.

The learning curve. A simple functional form for the learning curve will now be assumed. Suppose that as a function of its age, τ, a plant's time t TFP $z_\tau(t)$ does not depend on t per se, but only on τ, as follows:

$$z_\tau = (1 - z^* e^{-\lambda \tau})^{1-\beta}.$$

Thus, as a plant ages it becomes more productive, due (for example) to learning by doing. Observe that $z_0 = (1 - z^*)^{1-\beta}$, so that $1 - (1 - z^*)^{1-\beta}$ is the "amount to be learned." Moreover, z_τ is bounded above by one so that you can only do so much with any particular technology. Times of rapid technological progress are likely to have steeper learning curves. That is, z^* is likely to be positively related to the rate of investment-specific technological progress, g_q. The bigger g_q is, the less familiar the latest generation of capital goods will look, and the more there will be with which to get acquainted. Therefore assume that

(15) $$z^* = \omega g_q^\nu.$$

In what follows, assume that $\beta = 0.70$, $\lambda = 1.2$, $\omega = 0.3$, and $\nu = 12$. With this choice of parameter values, the learning curve shows a fairly quick rate of learning in that a plant's full potential is reached in about fifteen years (when g_q takes its postwar value of 0.04).

6.4.3 Diffusion Lags

Evidence. Diffusion refers to the spread of a new technology through an economy. The diffusion of innovations is slow, but its pace seems to be increasing over time. In a classic study Gort and Klepper (1982) examined forty-six product innovations, beginning with phonograph records in 1887 and ending with lasers in 1960. The authors traced diffusion by examining the number of firms that were producing the new product over time. On average, only two or three firms were producing each new product for the first fourteen years after its commercial development; then the number of firms sharply increased (on average six firms per year over the next ten years). Prices fell rapidly following the inception of a new product (13 percent a year for the first twenty-four years). Using a twenty-one-product subset of the Gort and Klepper data, Jovanovic and Lach (1997) report that it took approximately fifteen years for the output of a new product to rise from the 10 percent to the 90 percent diffusion level. They also cite evidence from a study of 265 innovations that found that a new innovation took forty-one years on average to move from the 10 percent to the 90 percent diffusion level. Grübler (1991) also presents evidence on how fast these products spread after they are invented. For example, in the United States the steam locomotive took fifty-four years to move from the 10 percent to the 90 percent diffusion level, whereas the diesel (a smaller innovation) took twelve years. It took approximately twenty-five years from the time the first diesel locomotive was introduced in 1925 to the time that diesels accounted for half of the locomotives in use, which occurred somewhere between 1951 and 1952.

Theories of diffusion lags. Diffusion lags seem to have several distinct origins:

1. *Vintage-specific physical capital.* If, in a vintage capital model, a firm can use just one technology at a time, as in Parente (1994), it faces a replacement problem. New equipment is costly, whereas old, inferior equipment has been paid for. Hence it is optimal to wait a while before replacing an old machine with a new, better one.[12] Furthermore, not everyone can adopt at the same time because the economy's capacity to produce equipment is finite. This implies some smoothing in adoption, and a smooth diffusion curve.

2. *Vintage-specific human capital.* The slow learning of new technologies acts to make adoption costly and slow it down, a fact that Parente (1994) and Greenwood and Yorukoglu (1997) emphasize. Adoption of a new technology may also be delayed because it is difficult at first to hire experienced people to work with them, as Chari and Hopenhayn (1991) emphasize.

---

12. For instance, David (1991) attributes the slow adoption of electricity in manufacturing during the early 1900s partly to the durability of old plants' use of mechanical power derived from water and steam. Those industries undergoing rapid expansion and hence rapid *net* investment—tobacco, fabricated metal, transportation, and equipment—tended to adopt electricity first.

3. *Second-mover advantages.* If, as Arrow (1962) assumes, the experience of early adopters is of help to those that adopt later, firms have an incentive to delay, and it is not an equilibrium for firms to adopt a new technology en masse; some will adopt right away, and others will choose to wait, as in models such as Jovanovic and Lach (1989) and Kapur (1993).

4. *Lack of awareness.* A firm may not be aware of any or all of the following: (a) that a new technology exists, (b) that it is suitable, or (c) where to acquire all the complementary goods. Diffusion lags then arise because of search costs, as in Jovanovic and Rob (1989) and Jovanovic and MacDonald (1994).[13]

5. *Other differences among adopters.* Given that origins 1–4 provide adopters a reason to wait, the optimal waiting time of adopters will differ simply because adopters "are different." For instance, the diffusion of hybrid corn was affected by economic factors such as the profitability of corn (relative to other agricultural goods) in the area in question, and the education of the farmers that resided there (Griliches 1957; Mansfield 1963; Romeo 1975).

Determining the number of entering plants, $n_0(t)$. To get a determinate number of plants of any vintage, the constant returns to scale assumption must be dropped. Suppose that there are diminishing returns to scale so that $\alpha + \beta < 1$. The profits from operating an age τ plant in the current period will be given by

$$\pi_\tau \equiv \max_{l_\tau}[z_\tau k_\tau^\alpha l_\tau^\beta - wl_\tau] = (1 - \beta)\left[\left(\frac{\beta}{w}\right)^\beta z_\tau k_\tau^\alpha\right]^{1/(1-\beta)}.$$

The present value of the flow of profits from bringing a new plant on line in the current period, t, will read

$$\int_0^\infty \pi_\tau(t + \tau)e^{-r\tau}d\tau - \frac{k_0(t)}{q(t)} - \phi(t),$$

where r denotes the real interest rate. From equation (14), $k_0(t)/q(t) = e^{[\alpha/(1-\alpha)]g_qt}$ is the purchase price of the newly installed capital, and $\phi(t) = \phi_0 e^{[\alpha/(1-\alpha)]g_qt}$ is the fixed cost of entry. If there is free entry into production, then these rents must be driven down to zero so that

(16) $$\int_0^\infty \pi_\tau(t + \tau)e^{-r\tau}d\tau - \frac{k_0(t)}{q(t)} - \phi(t) = 0.$$

---

13. The diffusion of technology has steadily gotten faster over the last century (Federal Reserve Bank of Dallas 1997, exhibit D). Search-theoretic models of technological advance naturally attribute this trend to the secular improvement in the speed and quality of communication.

This equation determines the number of new entrants $n_0(t)$ in period t. Although $n_0(t)$ does not appear directly in this equation, it affects profits because through equation (12) it affects the wage.

Choosing values for α and β. In the subsequent analysis, labor's share of income will be assumed to equal 70 percent so that $\beta = 0.70$. From the national income accounts alone it is impossible to tell how the remaining income should be divided up between profits and the return to capital. Assume that capital's share of income is 20 percent, implying that $\alpha = 0.20$, so that rents will amount to the remaining 10 percent of income. The real interest rate, r, is taken to be 6 percent.

A parametric diffusion curve. In what follows, a particular outcome for the diffusion curve for new inventions is simply postulated, as in Jovanovic and Lach (1997). Consider a switch in the economy's technological paradigm that involves moving from one balanced growth path, with some constant flow of entrants n^*, toward another balanced growth path, with a constant flow of entrants n^{**}. These flows of entrants should be determined in line with equation (16). Along the transition path there will be some flow of new entrants each period. Suppose that the number of plants adopting the new paradigm follows a typical S-shaped diffusion curve. Specifically, let

$$\frac{\int_0^\infty n_0(s)ds}{tn^{**}} = \frac{1}{1 + e^{(\Delta - \varepsilon t)}}.$$

The parameter Δ controls the initial number of users, or $n_0(0)$, while ε governs the speed of adoption. Assume that $\Delta = 3.5$ and $\varepsilon = 0.15$. With this choice of parameter values, it takes approximately twenty-five years to reach the 50 percent diffusion level, or the point at which about 50 percent of the potential users (as measured by tn^{**} have adopted the new technology.

Spillover Effects in Learning a Technology

Suppose that a new technological paradigm (for instance, information technology) is introduced at date $t = 0$, for the first time. Better information technologies keep arriving, but they all fit into the new paradigm, so as each new grade is adopted, the economy gains expertise about the entire paradigm. For someone who adopts a particular technological grade from this new paradigm, the ease of learning about this particular technological grade might be related to the cumulative number of users of the paradigm itself. The more users, the easier it is to acquire the expertise to run a new technological grade efficiently. In particular, let the starting point of the diffusion curve for a particular technological grade within the new paradigm depend positively on the number of plants that have already adopted a technology from the new paradigm. This number of adopters is an increasing function of time. Hence amend equation (15) to read

$$z^* = \omega g_q^\nu + \chi\left[1 - \frac{1}{1 + e^{(\Delta - \varepsilon t)}}\right]^\sigma,$$

where χ and σ are constants. Observe that z^* (a measure of the amount to be learned on one's own) is decreasing in t (the time elapsed since the first usage of the new paradigm in question). As $t \to \infty$ the spillover term vanishes. The strength of the spillover term is increasing in χ and decreasing in σ. In the subsequent analysis it will be assumed that $\chi = 0.4$ and $\sigma = 0.02$.

6.4.4 An Example: The Third Industrial Revolution

Now, imagine starting off along a balanced growth path where the rate of investment-specific technological progress is g_q^*. All of a sudden—at a point in time that will be normalized to $t = 0$—a new technological paradigm appears that has a higher rate of investment-specific technological progress, g_q^{**}. Because of the effect of g_q on learning, as specified in equation (15), learning curves become steeper once the new technological era dawns.

Perhaps the first balanced growth path could be viewed as the trajectory associated with the second industrial revolution. This period saw the rise of electricity, the internal combustion engine, and the modern chemical industry. The second event could be the dawning of the information age, or the third industrial revolution. What will the economy's transition path look like? How does this transition path depend on learning and diffusion?

For this experiment let $g_q^* = 0.035$ and $g_q^{**} = 0.05$. Figure 6.3 plots labor productivity for the economy under study. The straight line depicts what would have happened to productivity had information technology not been invented at all. The remarkable finding is how growth in labor productivity stalls during the nascent information age. Note that it takes productivity about thirty or so years to cross its old level.

The importance of learning is shown in figure 6.4, which plots the transition path when there are no learning effects. It now takes ten years less for productivity to cross its old trend path. Last, figure 6.5 shuts down the diffusion curve. There is still a productivity slowdown due to learning effects, but it is much weaker. The learning effects in the model are muted for two reasons. First, it takes no resources to learn. If learning required the input of labor, intermediate inputs, or capital, the effect would be strengthened. Second, in the model labor can be freely allocated across vintages. Therefore, less labor is allocated to the low productivity plants (such as

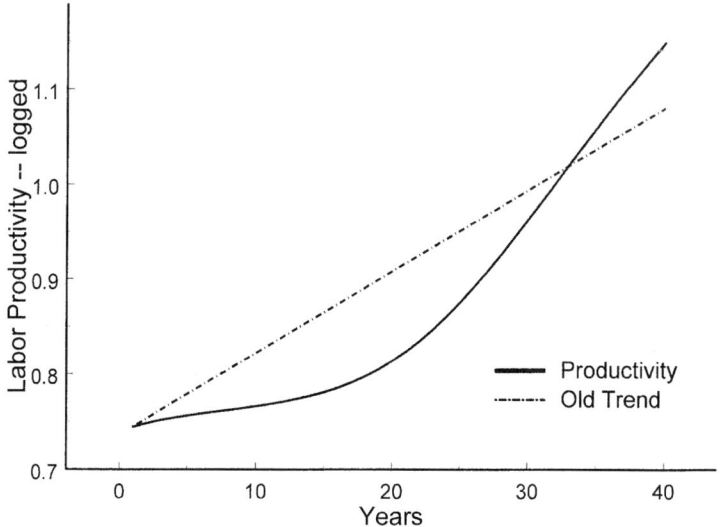

Fig. 6.3 Transitional dynamics

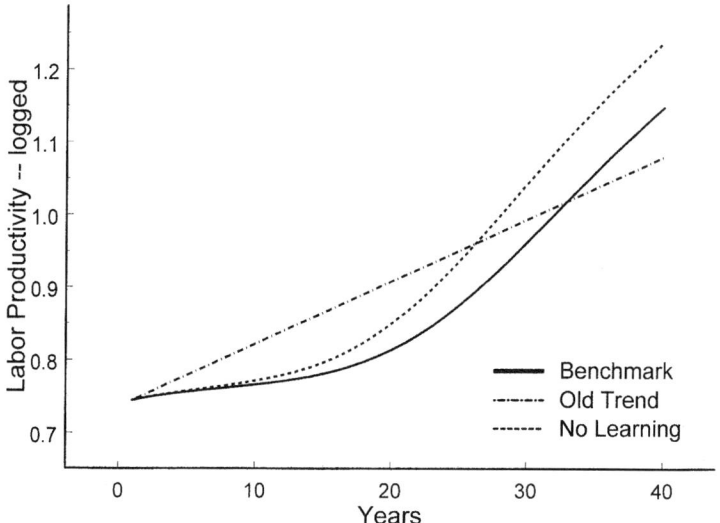

Fig. 6.4 Transitional dynamics (no learning)

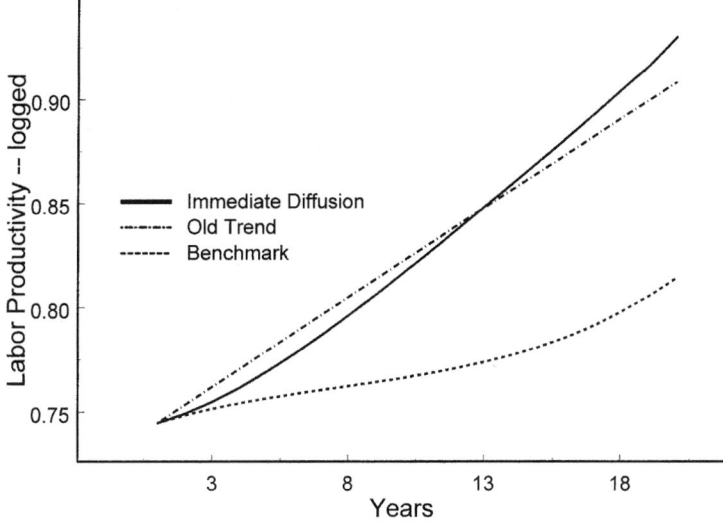

Fig. 6.5 Transitional dynamics (immediate diffusion)

the new plants coming on-line) and this ameliorates the productivity slowdown. If each plant required some minimal amount of labor to operate—another condition that would break Solow (1960) aggregation—then the learning effects would be stronger. Finally, a key reason for slow diffusion curves is high learning costs, and this channel of effect has been abstracted away from here. Learning and diffusion are likely to be inextricably linked and therefore difficult to separate, except in an artificial way, as was done here.

These figures make it clear that the vintage capital model can indeed explain the productivity slowdown if learning and diffusion lags matter enough, and the evidence presented here indicates that they do. Another appealing feature of the model is that it can also explain the concurrent rise in the skill premium, and this is the subject of the next section.

6.5 Wage Inequality

As labor-productivity growth slowed down in the early 1970s, wage inequality rose dramatically. Recent evidence suggests that this rise in wage inequality may have been caused by the introduction of new capital goods. For instance:

1. The era of electricity in manufacturing dawned around 1900. Goldin and Katz (1998) report that industries that used electricity tended to favor the use of skilled labor.

2. Autor, Katz, and Krueger (1998) find that the spread of computers may explain 30 to 50 percent of the growth in the demand for skilled workers since the 1970s.

3. Using cross-country data, Flug and Hercowitz (2000) discover that an increase in equipment investment leads to a rise both in the demand for skilled labor and in the skill premium. In a similar vein, Caselli (1999) documents, from a sample of U.S. manufacturing industries, that since 1975 there has been a strong, positive relationship between changes in an industry's capital-labor ratio and changes in its wages.

Theories of how skill interacts with new technology are of two kinds. The first kind of theory emphasizes the role of skill in the *use* of capital goods that embody technology. Here it is assumed that technology is embodied in capital goods. This is labelled the capital-skill complementarity hypothesis. The second hypothesis emphasizes the role of skill in *implementing* the new technology, referred to as skill in adoption.

6.5.1 Griliches (1969) and Capital-Skill Complementarity

The hypothesis in its original form. In its original form, the hypothesis fits in well with a minor modification of Solow (1956, 1957) that allows for two kinds of labor instead of one. Suppose, as Griliches (1969) proposed, that in production, capital is more complementary with skilled labor than with unskilled labor. Specifically, imagine an aggregate production function of the form

$$y = [\theta k^\rho + (1 - \theta)s^\rho]^{\alpha/\rho} u^{(1-\alpha)},$$

where s and u represent inputs of skilled and unskilled labor. Capital and skill are complements, in the sense that the elasticity of substitution between them is less than unity if $\rho < 0$. The skill premium, or the ratio of the skilled to unskilled wage rates, is just the ratio of the marginal products of the two types of labor:

$$\frac{\frac{\partial y}{\partial s}}{\frac{\partial y}{\partial u}} = \frac{\alpha(1 - \theta)}{1 - \alpha}\left[\theta\left(\frac{k}{s}\right)^\rho + (1 - \theta)\right]^{-1}\left(\frac{u}{s}\right).$$

Now, suppose that the endowments of skilled and unskilled labor are fixed. Then, the skill premium will rise whenever the capital stock increases, and so will labor's share of income.[14] Krusell et al. (2000) argue that an aggregate production function of this type fits the postwar experi-

---

14. Unskilled labor's share of income remains constant, whereas skilled labor's share increases.

ence well, provided that k is computed as in the benchmark vintage capital model of section 6.3: $k(t) = \int_0^\infty e^{-\delta s} q(t-s) i(t-s) ds$.

Shifts in the production structure. In Griliches's formulation, the skill premium depends on the supplies of the factors k, s, and u only. However, the premium will also change if the adoption of new technology is associated with a change in the economy's production structure. This is the tack that Goldin and Katz (1998) and Heckman, Lochner, and Taber (1998) take. For instance, suppose that the aggregate production function is

(17) $$y = [\theta u^\rho + (1-\theta) s^\rho]^{\alpha/\rho} k^{(1-\alpha)}.$$

Now, a change in k will not affect the skill premium, $(\partial y/\partial s)/(\partial y/\partial u)$, other things equal. But imagine that a new technology, say computers or electricity, comes along that favors skilled relative to unskilled labor. Heckman, Lochner, and Taber (1998) operationalize this by assuming that the production function shifts in such a way that θ drifts downwards.[15] This raises the skill premium. Note that equation (17) is an *aggregate* production function. Therefore, a decrease in θ affects new and old capital alike, and investment in new capital is *not* necessary to implement the technological progress.

A production structure that shifts toward skilled labor can easily extend to the case in which investment in new capital *is* required to implement new technologies. Suppose, as Solow (1960) does, that technological progress applies only to new capital goods, and write

$$y_v = A_v [\theta_v u_v^\rho + (1-\theta_v) s_v^\rho]^{\alpha/\rho} k_v^{(1-\alpha)},$$

where y_v, u_v, s_v, and k_v are the output and inputs of the vintage "v" technology, and θ_v is a parameter of the production that is specific to that technology. The newer vintage technologies are better, and so A_v is increasing in v. At each date, there will, in general, be a range of v's in use, especially if there is some irreversibility in the capital stock. Now suppose that θ_v is decreasing in v. That is, better technologies require less unskilled labor. The adoption of such technologies will raise the skill premium. In this type of model, the skill premium rises because of technological adoption and not directly because of a rise in the stock of capital.

Caselli (1997) suggests, instead, that each new technology demands its own types of skills, skills that may be easier or harder to acquire, relative to the skills required by older technologies. If the skills associated with a new technology are relatively hard to learn and if people's abilities to learn

---

15. They estimate that $[(1-\theta)/\theta]$ has grown at a rate of 3.6 percent since the 1970s. This yields roughly the right magnitude of the increase in the college-high school wage gap.

differ, a technological revolution may raise income inequality by rewarding those able enough to work with the new technology.

Matching Workers and Machines

Fixed proportions between workers and machines. The previous arguments presume that workers differ in skill, or in their ability to acquire it. A basic implication of the vintage capital model is that a range of vintages of machines will be in use at any date. Can one somehow turn this implication into a proposition that workers, too, will be different? If a worker could operate a continuum of technologies and if he could work with infinitesimal amounts of each of a continuum of machines of different vintages, the answer would be *no*, because each worker could operate the "market portfolio" of machines. As soon as one puts a finite limit to the number of machines that a worker can simultaneously operate, however, the model generates inequality of workers' incomes. To simplify, assume that the worker can operate just one machine at a time and, moreover, that each machine requires just one worker to operate it. In other words, there are fixed proportions between machines and workers. Under these assumptions, inequality in workers' skills will emerge because of differential incentives for people to accumulate skills, and it translates into a nondegenerate distribution of skills. The following is an outline of the argument.

1. *Production function.* Suppose that one machine matches with one worker. The output of the match is given by the constant-returns-to-scale production function $y = F(k, s)$, where k is the efficiency level of the machine, and s is the skill level supplied by the worker. Machine efficiency and skill are complements in that $\partial^2 F/\partial k \partial s > 0$.

2. *Growth of skills.* Let v be the fraction of his or her time that the worker spends working, and let h denote the level of his or her human capital. Then $s = vh$. Suppose that the worker can invest in raising h as follows: $dh/dt = \eta(1 - v)h$, where $1 - v$ is the fraction of his or her time spent learning.

3. *Growth of machine quality.* New machines, in turn, also get better. In other words, there is investment-specific technological progress. Suppose that anyone can produce a new machine of quality k according to the linearly homogenous cost function $C(k, \mathbf{k})$, where $\mathbf{k}$ is the average economy-wide quality of a newly produced machine.

4. *Balanced growth.* This setup produces a balanced growth path with some interesting features, as Jovanovic (1998) details. First, it results in nondegenerate distributions of machine efficiency and of worker skill. This can be true even if everybody was identical initially. It occurs because the scarcity of resources means that it is not optimal to give everyone the latest machine. The distributions over capital and skills move rightward over time. Second, because $\partial^2 F/\partial k \partial s > 0$, better workers match with the better

machines according to an assignment rule of the form $s = \Phi(k)$, with $\Phi' > 0$. Third, faster-growing economies should have a greater range over machine quality and skills.

6.5.2 Nelson and Phelps (1966) and Skill in Adoption

The previous subsection was based on the notion that skilled labor is better at *using* a new technology; the alternative view is that skilled labor is more efficient at *adopting* a technology and learning it. The original Nelson and Phelps (1966) formulation, and its subsequent extensions like Benhabib and Spiegel (1994), do not invoke the vintage-capital model. It will be invoked now.

Evidence on Adoption Costs and Their Interaction with Skill

When a new technology is adopted, output tends to be below normal while the new technology is learned. Indeed, output will often fall below that which was attained under the previous technology. In other words, the adoption of a new technology may carry a large foregone output cost incurred during the learning period. There is evidence that the use of skilled labor facilitates this adoption process.

1. Management scientists have found that the opening of a plant is followed by a temporary increase in the use of engineers whose job is to get the production process "up to speed" (Adler and Clark 1991).
2. Bartel and Lichtenberg (1987) provide evidence for the joint hypothesis that (a) educated workers have a comparative advantage in implementing new technologies, and (b) the demand for educated versus less educated workers declines as experience is gained with a new technology.
3. In a more recent study of 450 U.S. manufacturing industries from 1960 to 1990, Caselli (1999) finds that the higher an industry's nonproduction-production worker ratio was before 1975 (his measure of initial skill intensity), the larger was the increase in its capital-labor ratio over 1975 to 1990 period (a measure of the adoption of new capital goods).

Modelling the Role of Skill in Adoption

To implement the idea that skill facilitates the adoption process, let

$$y_\tau = z_\tau k_\tau^\alpha u_\tau^\beta$$

be the production function for the age τ technology, and k_τ and u_τ represent the amounts of capital and unskilled labor. Assume that the improvement in a plant's practice, $dz_\tau/d\tau$, depends upon the amount of skilled labor, s_τ, hired:

$$\frac{dz_\tau}{d\tau} = \vartheta(1 - z_\tau)s_\tau^\phi - \mu z_\tau.$$

There is an upper bound on the level of productivity that can be achieved with any particular vintage of capital. As the amount of unrealized potential $(1 - z_\tau)$ shrinks, it becomes increasingly difficult to effect an improvement. The initial condition for z, or its starting value as of when the plant is operational, is assumed to be inversely related to the rate of technological progress, g_q, in the following way:

$$z_0 = \psi g_q^{-\xi},$$

where ψ and ξ are positive parameters.

Such a formulation can explain the recent rise in the skill premium; the details are in Greenwood and Yorukoglu (1997). Suppose that in 1974 the rate of investment-specific technological progress rose, perhaps associated with the development of information technologies. This would have led to an increase in the demand for skill needed to bring the new technologies on line. The skill premium would then have risen, other things being equal.

6.6 Three Models of Endogenous Investment-Specific Technological Progress

It is simple to endogenize investment-specific technological progress. How? Three illustrations based on three different engines of growth will show the way:

1. Learning by doing, as in Arrow (1962).
2. Research in the capital goods sector à la Krusell (1998).
3. Human capital investment in the capital goods sector following Parente (1994).

6.6.1 Solow (1960) Meets Arrow (1962): Learning by Doing as an Engine of Growth

Arrow (1962) assumes that technological progress stems exclusively from learning by doing in the capital goods sector. There are no learning curves or diffusion lags in the sector that produces final output. In the capital goods sector, there are no direct costs of improving production efficiency. Instead, a capital goods producer's efficiency depends on cumulative aggregate output of the entire capital goods sector—or, what is the same thing, cumulative aggregate investment by the *users* of capital goods. Because each producer has a negligible effect on the aggregate output of capital goods, learning is purely external. The job of casting Arrow's notion of learning by doing in terms of Solow's vintage capital framework will now start.

Production of final goods and accumulation of capital. Population is constant; write the aggregate production function for final goods in per capita terms as $c + i = k^\alpha$, where c, i, and k are all per capita values, an innocuous normalization if returns to scale are constant. Physical capital accumulates as follows:

(18) $$\frac{dk}{dt} = iq - \delta k.$$

Once again, q is the state of technology in the capital goods sector: Anyone can make q units of capital goods from a unit of consumption goods.

Learning by capital goods producers. Suppose that at date t, q is described by

(19) $$q(t) = \nu \left[\int_0^\infty q(t - s) \mathbf{i}(t - s) ds \right]^{1-\alpha},$$

where $\mathbf{i}(t - s)$ denotes the level of industry-wide investment at date $t - s$ in consumption units, and $q(t - s)\mathbf{i}(t - s)$ is the number of machine efficiency units produced at $t - s$. In equation (19), as in Arrow's model, the productivity of the capital goods sector depends on economy-wide cumulative investment.[16]

Let λ be the mass of identical agents in this economy—the economy's "size" or "scale." Then, in equilibrium, $\mathbf{i} = \lambda i$, so that equation (19) becomes

(20) $$q(t) = \nu \lambda^{1-\alpha} \left[\int_0^\infty q(t - s) i(t - s) ds \right]^{1-\alpha}.$$

Endogenous balanced growth. Assume that consumers' tastes are described by

(21) $$\int_0^\infty e^{-\rho t} \ln c(t) dt.$$

Let g_x denote the growth rate of variable x in balanced growth. The production function implies that because population is constant, $g_y = \alpha g_k$. Along a balanced growth path, output of the capital goods sector, or $q\lambda i$, grows at rate g_k so that equation (20) implies that $g_q = (1 - \alpha)g_k$. Thus, the price of capital goods, $1/q$, falls as output grows.

---

16. In order to simplify things, Arrow's (1962) assumption that there are fixed, vintage-specific proportions between machines and workers in production is dropped. This assumption can lead to the scrapping of capital before the end of its physical life span. (In his analysis, capital goods face sudden death at the end of their physical life span, unless they are scrapped first, as opposed to the gradual depreciation assumed here.) Also, Arrow assumes that machine producers' efficiency is an isoelastic function of the cumulative number of machines produced, whereas here it is assumed to be an isoelastic function of the cumulative number of *efficiency units* produced.

LEMMA 1. *If a balanced growth path exists, g_k satisfies the equation*

(22) $$\underbrace{\rho + \delta + g_k}_{\text{Interest Rate}} = \underbrace{\alpha v \lambda^{1-\alpha}\left(1 + \frac{\delta}{g_k}\right)^{1-\alpha}}_{q \times MP_k}.$$

PROOF. First, from equation (18), $g_k = -\delta + qi/k$. Since g_k, and hence qi/k, must be constant, $g_k = g_q + g_i = g_q + g_y$, where the second equality follows from assuming that consumption and investment are constant fractions of income along the balanced growth path so that $g_i = g_c = g_y$. Second, consider the first-order condition of optimality for k. A forgone unit of consumption can purchase q units of capital that can rent for $\alpha k^{\alpha-1} q$. This must cover the interest cost, $\rho + g_y$, the cost of depreciation, δ, and the capital loss g_q, because capital goods prices are falling. This gives the efficiency condition $\alpha k^{\alpha-1} = (\rho + \delta + g_y + g_q)/q = (\rho + \delta + g_k)/q$. Third, in balanced growth, $q(t - s)i(t - s) = e^{-(g_q + g_i)s} q(t) i(t) = e^{-g_k s} q(t) i(t)$. Then, using equation (20), $q = v \lambda^{1-\alpha}(qi/g_k)^{1-\alpha}$, which yields $qk^{\alpha-1} = v \lambda^{1-\alpha}[(qi/k)/g_k]^{1-\alpha}$. Substituting the fact that $g_k = -\delta + (qi/k)$ into this expression gives $qk^{\alpha-1} = v \lambda^{1-\alpha}[(g_k + \delta)/g_k]^{1-\alpha} = v\lambda^{1-\alpha}(1 + \delta/g_k)^{1-\alpha}$. Recalling that $\alpha q k^{\alpha-1} = (\rho + \delta + g_k)$ yields equation (22). Q.E.D.

COROLLARY 2. *There exists a unique and positive solution to equation (22).*

PROOF. The left-hand side of equation (22) is positively sloped in g_k, with intercept $\rho + \delta$. The right-hand side is negatively sloped, approaching infinity as g_k approaches zero, and approaching $\alpha v \lambda^{1-\alpha}$ as g_k approaches infinity. Therefore, exactly one solution exists, and it is strictly positive. Q.E.D.

PROPOSITION 3. *Scale effect: A larger economy, as measured by λ, grows faster.*

PROOF. Anything that raises (lowers) the right-hand side of equation (22) raises (lowers) g_k. Anything that raises (lowers) the left-hand side of equation (22) lowers (raises) g_k.[17] Q.E.D.

Example 1. Set capital's share of income at 30 percent, the rate of time preference at 4 percent, and the depreciation rate at 10 percent. Hence, $\alpha = 0.3$, $\rho = 0.04$, and $\delta = 0.10$. Now, values are backed out for the parameters v and λ that will imply the existence of an equilibrium in which capital goods prices fall at 4 percent a year; that is, an equilibrium with $g_q = 0.04$. This leads to the capital stock's growing at rate $g_k = 0.04/(1 -$

---

17. It follows immediately that g_k is increasing in v, and decreasing in ρ.

0.3) = 0.057. To get this value of g_k to solve equation (22), it must transpire that v and λ are such that $v\lambda^{1-\alpha} = 0.32$.

Applying the model to information technology. The pace of technological progress in information technologies has been nothing short of incredible. Consider the cost of processing, storing, and transmitting information. Jonscher (1994) calculates that between 1950 and 1980 the cost of one MIP (millions of instructions per second) fell at a rate of somewhere between 27 and 50 percent per year. Likewise, the cost of storing information dropped at a rate of somewhere between 25 and 30 percent per year from 1960 to 1985. Last, the cost of transmitting information declined at a rate somewhere between 15 and 20 percent per year over the period 1974 to 1994.

Why such a precipitous fall in the cost of information technology? Arrow's model gives a precise answer. Information technology is a general purpose technology, usable in many industries. The scale of demand for the capital goods embodying it, and hence the cumulative output of these capital goods, has therefore been large, and this may well have led to a faster pace of learning and cost reduction.

A more specialized technology such as, say, new coal-mining machinery, would be specific to a sector (coal mining) and would, as a result, be demanded on a smaller scale. Its cumulative output and investment would be smaller, and so would its learning-induced productivity gains. In terms of the model, the value of λ for information technologies exceeds the value of λ for coal mining equipment. This amounts to a scale effect on growth. A higher λ hastens the decline in capital goods prices, a fact that proposition (3) demonstrates.

6.6.2 Solow (1960) Meets Krusell (1997): Research as an Engine of Growth

In Krusell's model, the improvement in capital goods comes about through research.

Final goods producers. The production function for final goods, y, is

(23) $$y = l^{1-\alpha}\int_0^1 k_j^\alpha dj,$$

where l is the amount of labor employed in the final output (or consumption) sector, and k_j is the employment of capital of type j. The consumption sector is competitive and rents its capital from capital goods producers each period.

Capital accumulation. Each type of capital, j, is produced and owned by a monopolist who rents out his stock of machines, k_j, on a period-by-period basis to users in the consumption goods sector. Technological progress occurs at the intensive margin; k_j grows as follows:

$$\frac{dk_j}{dt} = -\delta k_j + q_j x_j, \tag{24}$$

where x_j is spending by capital goods producer j, measured in consumption units, and q_j represents the number of type j machines that a unit of consumption goods can produce. In other words, q_j is the production efficiency of monopolist j.

Research by capital goods producers. Capital goods producer j can raise q_j by doing research. Because the markup the producer charges is proportional to q_j, he or she has the incentive to undertake research in order to raise q_j. If the producer hires h_j workers to do research, then monopolist j can raise his or her efficiency as follows:

$$\frac{dq_j}{dt} = q_j^\gamma \mathbf{q}^{1-\gamma} R(h_j), \tag{25}$$

where $R(\cdot)$ is an increasing, concave function. The term $\mathbf{q} = \int_0^1 q_j \, dj$ is the average level of productivity across all sectors, and γ is an index of the product-specific returns to R&D. This term affects incentives to do research (if $\gamma = 0$, no incentive exists), but it does not affect the growth accounting procedure as long as h_j lends itself to measurement.

Symmetric equilibrium. Consider a balanced growth path where each monopolist is a facsimile of another so that $k_j = k(t)$, $q_j = q(t)$, and $h_j = h(t)$, etc. The first three equations become

$$y = l^{1-\alpha} k^\alpha, \tag{26}$$

$$\frac{dk}{dt} = --\delta k + qx, \tag{27}$$

and

$$\left(\frac{1}{q}\right)\left(\frac{dq}{dt}\right) = R(h). \tag{28}$$

Then the capital stock can be represented as

$$k(t) = \int_{-\infty}^{t} e^{-\delta(t-s)} q(s) x(s) ds. \tag{29}$$

Equation (27) is of the same form as equation (4) of section 6.4, and the evolution of q now has a specific interpretation: Investment-specific technological progress is driven by research. Note from equation (27) that all new investment, $x(t)$, is in the frontier technology in the sense that it embodies $q(t)$ efficiency units of productive power per unit of consumption foregone.

Difficulties with research-based models. Although it captures features that section 6.2 argued were essential for understanding the U.S. growth experience, there are three problems with Krusell's model.

1. *A predicted secular increase in the growth rate.* Equation (28) implies that the rate of growth in the United States should have risen over time because in the U.S. data, and for that matter in most economies, h has trended upwards. Jones (1995) discusses the incongruity of these implications of research-based models with evidence.

2. *A positive scale effect.* To see this, take two identical economies and merge them into a single one that has twice as much labor and capital as the individual economies did. Now, hold the types of capital producers constant, because adding more types is tantamount to inventing new capital goods. If each agent behaves as previously described, then initially $y = 2l^{1-\alpha}k^\alpha$. Additionally, each firm could now use twice as much research labor so that q and k would grow faster. Alternatively, in this hypothetical experiment one could instead assume (realistically so perhaps) that the merged economy would have not a monopoly but a duopoly in each machine market. The consequences of such an assumption are not entirely clear, however, because the old allocation of labor to research would still not be an equilibrium allocation in the new economy. Competition in the machine market would lead to lower profits for the producers of machines, and this would reduce their incentives to do research and reduce growth. This would partially offset, and even reverse, the positive effect of scale on growth. These arguments make clear, moreover, that the scale problem in this model has nothing whatsoever to do with spillovers in research. The arguments go through intact even if $\gamma = 1$. The scale effect works through the impact that a larger product market has on firms' incentives to improve their efficiency.

3. *The resources devoted to research are small.* Most nations report no resources devoted to research, and only 3 percent or so of U.S. output officially goes to R&D. Because so much technology, even in the United States, is imported from other countries, research-based models make more sense at the level of the world than they do at the national level.

6.6.3 Solow (1960) Meets Parente (1994): Vintage Human Capital as an Engine of Growth

Parente (1994) offers a vintage human capital model without physical capital. This section adds a capital goods sector to his model. Once again, endogenous technological progress occurs in the capital goods sector only.

As in the Arrow and Krusell models, this technological progress is then passed onto consumption goods producers in the form of a beneficial "pecuniary external effect"—the falling relative price of capital.

Imagine an economy with two sectors of production: consumption and capital goods. The consumption goods sector is competitive and enjoys no technological progress. The productivity growth occurring in this sector arises because its capital input becomes less expensive over time relative to consumption goods and relative to labor.

The capital goods sector is competitive too, and its efficiency rises over time. A capital goods producer can, at any time, raise the grade of his technology, in the style of Zeckhauser (1968) and Parente (1994), but at a cost. The producer has an associated level of expertise at operating his grade of technology. This increases over time due to learning by doing. The profits earned by capital goods producers are rebated back each period to a representative consumer (who has tastes described by equation (21) and supplies one unit of labor).

Consumption goods sector. The production function for consumption goods is

$$(30) \qquad c = k^\alpha l^{1-\alpha},$$

where k and l are the inputs of capital and labor. This technology is unchanging over time.

Capital goods sector. Capital goods are homogeneous, but the technology for producing them can change at the discretion of the capital goods producer. A capital goods producer's technology is described by $o = Azh^{1-\alpha}$, where o is the producer's output of capital goods, A denotes the grade of the technology the producer is using, z represents the producer's level of expertise, and h is the amount of labor the producer employs. The price of capital is represented by p and the wage by w, both in consumption units. At any date the producer's labor-allocation problem is static and gives rise to flow profits given by

$$\max_h (pAzh^{1-\alpha} - wh) = \alpha \left[\frac{(1-\alpha)}{w} \right]^{(1-\alpha)/\alpha} (pAz)^{1/\alpha} \equiv \pi(A, z, p, w).$$

Learning by doing. Suppose that a producer's expertise on a given technological grade, A, grows with experience in accordance with

$$\frac{dz}{d\tau} = \lambda(1-z), \qquad \text{for } 0 \leq z \leq 1,$$

where τ is the amount of time that has passed since the producer adopted the technology. Observe that while $z < 1$, the producer learns by doing. In contrast to Arrow's assumptions, this rate does not depend on the volume of output, however, but simply on the passage of time. Eventually, the producer learns everything and $z \to 1$, which is the maximal level of expertise.[18]

Let z_τ represent the accumulated expertise of a producer with τ years of experience. With an initial condition $z_0 = \tilde{z} < 1$, the above differential equation has the solution

$$(31) \qquad z_\tau = 1 - (1 - \tilde{z})e^{-\lambda\tau} \equiv Z_\tau(\tilde{z})$$

for $\tau \geq 0$.

Upgrading. A capital goods producer can, at any time, upgrade the technology he or she uses. If the producer switches from using technology A to A' he or she incurs a switching cost of $\kappa + (\vartheta A')/A$, measured in terms of lost expertise. The idea is that the bigger the leap in technology the producer takes, the less expertise he can carry over into the new situation. Observe that

1. There is no exogenously specified technological frontier here. That is, A' is unconstrained,[19] and yet producers do not opt for an A' that is as large as possible.[20]

2. In sharp contrast to Arrow (and to Krusell, unless his $\gamma = 1$), there is no technological spillover in human capital accumulation across producers.

Figure 6.6 plots the evolution of TFP for a producer.

Balanced growth. The balanced growth path will be uncovered through a guess-and-verify procedure. To this end, suppose that the economy is in balanced growth at date zero. It seems reasonable to conjecture that con-

---

18. The functional form of the learning curve is taken from Parente (1994). Zeckhauser (1968) considers a wider class of learning curves.

19. One caveat on Parente's model: The choice of A' is constrained by the fact that the level expertise following an adoption z_0 cannot be negative. This constraint could be removed by choosing a different form for the loss of expertise caused by upgrading. An example of a functional form that would accomplish this is $z_0 = (A'/A)^\vartheta (z_T - \kappa)$, where $z_T > \kappa$ is the level of expertise just before the adoption and $\vartheta < 0$.

20. Chari and Hopenhayn (1991) and Jovanovic and Nyarko (1996) also focus on human capital–based absorption costs. These models provide a microfoundation for why switching costs should be larger when the new technology is more advanced. This implies that when a firm does switch to a new technology, it may well opt for a technology that is inside the frontier. This implication separates the human capital vintage models from their physical capital counterparts, because the latter all imply that all new investment is in frontier methods.

Search frictions can also lead firms to adopt methods inside the technological frontier. In the models of Jovanovic and Rob (1989) and Jovanovic and MacDonald (1994), it generally does not pay for firms to invest time and resources to locate the best technology to imitate.

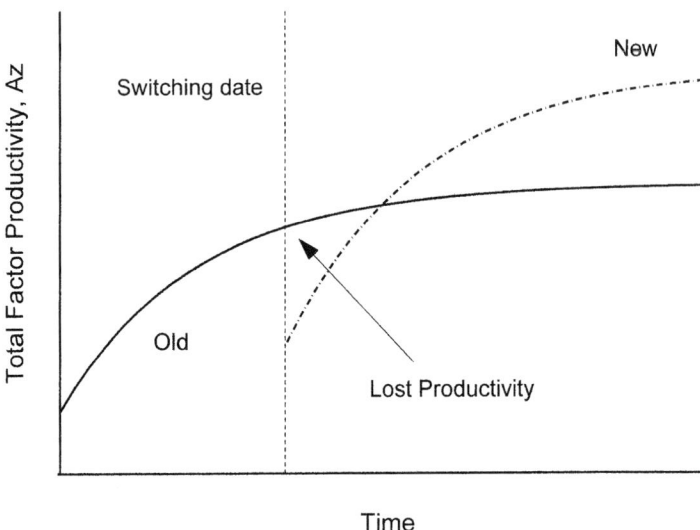

Fig. 6.6 Evolution of productivity

sumption, investment, aggregate output, and the stock of capital will all grow at constant rates, denoted as before by g_c, g_i, g_y, and g_k. If consumption and investment are to remain a constant fraction of income, then $g_c = g_i = g_y$. From equation (30), $g_y = \alpha g_k$.

Properties of the conjectured steady-state growth path.

1. Each capital goods producer will choose to upgrade A after interval T and by a factor ξ. Neither T nor ξ depends on time. Define g_A by $\xi = e^{g_A T}$. Then $g_A = (1/T) \ln \xi$ is the average growth rate of each producer's A.
2. At a point in time the age of the technologies in use are uniformly distributed over the interval $[0, T]$, with $1/T$ producers using each type of technology.
3. All producers using a technology of given grade have the same level of expertise.
4. z_0 solves the equation $z_0 = Z_T(z_0) - \kappa - \vartheta \xi$.

By properties 1 and 2, the distribution of technologies will be shifting continually to the right over time, and the maximal technological grade in use at time t, or $A_0(t)$, will grow exponentially: $A_0(t) = A_0(0) e^{g_A t}$. Let A_τ denote the level of technology that was upgraded τ periods ago. Then from the viewpoint of the producer that is using it, τ is the age of the technology A_τ. Then properties 1 and 2 also imply that $A_\tau(t) = A_0(t) e^{-g_A \tau}$. In a steady state, $(1/A_\tau[t])(dA_\tau[t]/dt) = g_A$ for all τ. The normalization $A_0(0) = 1$ will be employed in what follows.

By properties 3 and 4, $Z_\tau(z_0)$ is the level of expertise of each plant that uses the technology A_τ. By properties 2 and 3, the output of capital goods is

(32) $$\left(\frac{A_0}{T}\right)\int_0^T e^{-g_A\tau}Z_\tau(z_0)h_\tau^{1-\alpha}d\tau = \frac{i}{p},$$

where i is aggregate investment measured in consumption units and p is the price of capital in terms of consumption. The left-hand side of equation (32) implies that the output of capital goods grows at the rate $g_k = g_A$, given that h_τ is constant over time (a fact demonstrated below). In growth-rate form, equation (32) then reads $g_p = g_i - g_k$. If investment is to remain a constant fraction of income, $g_i = g_y$ must hold. Therefore, $g_p = g_y - g_k = -(1 - \alpha)g_A$.

It is easy to establish that distribution of labor remains constant across grades. That is, $h_\tau(t)$ will not depend on t. Optimal labor hiring in the consumption goods sector implies that $(1 - \alpha)(k/l)^\alpha = w$. If wages grow at the same rate as output, $g_y = \alpha g_k$, then l will be constant over time. Likewise, a capital goods producer using an age τ technology will hire labor according to the condition $(1 - \alpha)h_\tau^{-\alpha} = w/(pA_\tau z_\tau)$. Because $g_p = -(1 - \alpha)g_A$ and $g_A = g_k$, the right-hand side of this expression is constant over time, and, therefore, so is h_τ.

Producer's problem. In balanced growth, prices and wages grow at constant rates as a function of t, which therefore plays the role of the "aggregate state." To a capital goods producer, the state variables are his expertise, z, and his technological grade, A. Hence the Bellman equation pertaining to his decision problem is

$$V(A,z;t) = \max_{T',A'}\left\{\int_t^{t+T'}\Pi[A,Z_{s-t}(z);s]e^{-r(s-t)}ds\right.$$
$$\left. + e^{-rT'}V(A',Z_{T'}(z)) - \kappa - \vartheta\frac{A'}{A};t + T'\right\},$$

where $\Pi(A, Z_{s-t}(z); s) \equiv \pi[A, Z_{s-t}(z), p(s), w(s)]$. The interest rate r is presumed to be constant.

A stationary (s, S) upgrading policy. One still needs to verify that the balanced growth equilibrium has the property, conjectured in (1), that capital goods producers choose to upgrade A by a constant factor ξ, and after a constant waiting time, T. If so, then there exists an (s, S) policy on the interval $[z_0, z_T]$ so that z always starts from $z_0 \geq 0$ (just after a technological upgrade) and increases up to the point $z_T \leq 1$, which triggers the next upgrade, a return of z to z_0, and so on. To show that the balanced growth path is of this form, the following property of the profit function is helpful.

LEMMA 4. *Let* $a(t) \equiv A/A_0(t)$. *For* $s \geq t$, $\Pi(A, z; s) = e^{\alpha g_A t}\Phi[a(t), z, s - t]$.

PROOF. Because $g_p = -(1 - \alpha)g_A$ and $g_w = \alpha g_A$, it follows that profits for period s, $\Pi(A, z; s)$, can be expressed as $[\alpha(1 - \alpha)/w(s)]^{(1-\alpha)/\alpha}[p(s)Az]^{1/\alpha}$ $= e^{(1/\alpha)g_A t}a(t)^{(1/\alpha)}z^{(1/\alpha)} \times c(0)e^{-[(1-\alpha)/\alpha+1-\alpha]g_A s}$, where $c(0)$ is a constant whose value depends on some time-0 variables. Next, using the fact that $(1/\alpha) - [(1 - \alpha)/\alpha + 1 - \alpha] = \alpha$ allows the statement $\Pi(A, z; s) = e^{\alpha g_A t}a(t)^{(1/\alpha)}z^{(1/\alpha)} \times c(0)e^{-[(1-\alpha)/\alpha+1-\alpha]g_A(s-t)}$ to be written. Finally, the claim follows by setting $\Phi[a(t), z, s - t] = a(t)^{(1/\alpha)}z^{(1/\alpha)} \times c(0)e^{-[(1-\alpha)/\alpha+1-\alpha]g_A(s-t)}$. Q.E.D.

Let $a' = A'/A_0(t + T')$. Then because $A_0(t) = e^{g_A t}$ and $A'/A = [a'/a]$ $[A_0(t + T')/A_0(t)] = e^{g_A T'}(a'/a)$, the Bellman equation becomes

$$V(ae^{g_A t}, z; t) = e^{\alpha g_A t} \max_{T', a'} \left[\int_t^{t+T'} \Phi(a, Z_{s-t}(z), s - t)e^{-r(s-t)}ds \right.$$

$$\left. + e^{-rT' - \alpha g_A t}V(a'e^{g_A(t+T')}, Z_{T'}(z) - \kappa - \vartheta e^{g_A T'}\frac{a'}{a}; t + T') \right].$$

Now observe that after a change of variable $x = s - t$, $\int_t^{t+T'} \Phi(a, Z_{s-t}(z), s - t)e^{-r(s-t)}ds = \int_0^{T'} \Phi(a, Z_x(z), x)e^{-rx}dx$. Then, if one writes $B(a, z; t) \equiv e^{-\alpha g_A t}V(ae^{g_A t}, z, t)$, the Bellman equation becomes

(1') $$B(a, z; t) = \max_{T', a'} \left[\int_0^{T'} \Phi(a, Z_x(z), x)e^{-rx}dx \right.$$

$$\left. + e^{-(r-\alpha g_A)T'}B(a', Z_{T'}(z) - \kappa - \vartheta e^{g_A T'}\frac{a'}{a}; t + T') \right].$$

PROPOSITION 5. *The upgrading policy is stationary.*

PROOF. Consider equation (1'). For $\kappa > 0$, one can bound the optimal policy T' away from zero. Now, because αg_A is the growth of consumption, optimal savings behavior by consumers implies that $r - \alpha g_A > 0$.[21] Therefore, the operator is a contraction, and by starting an iteration with a function B that does not depend on t, one finds that the unique fixed point, $B(a, z)$ does not depend on t. Denote the optimal decision rules by $T'(a, z)$ and $a'(a, z)$. Since T' and a' do not depend on t, upgrading by each producer will be periodic and by the same multiple. This is all conditional on the existence of a balanced growth path. Q.E.D.

Definition of balanced growth. For a balanced growth path to exist there must be a triple (ξ, T, z_0) such that, for all t,

(33) $$T'(1, z_0) = T,$$

---

21. Suppose that tastes are described by equation (21). Then, along a balanced growth path, $r = \rho + g_y = \rho + \alpha g_k$. Hence, $r - \alpha g_k = \rho$.

(34)
$$a'(1, z_0) = 1,$$

and

(35)
$$z_0 = Z_T(z_0) - \kappa - \vartheta\xi.$$

In this case, output, consumption, and investment grow at the rate

$$\alpha g_A = \left(\frac{\alpha}{T}\right)\ln\xi.$$

Together, equations (33)–(35) imply that an economy that starts on the steady-state growth path described by properties 1–4, given earlier in section 6.6.3, remains on it. Equations (33) and (34) pertain to the optimal behavior of a producer right after he has upgraded his technology. Right after an upgrade, the producer has a technology $A = A_0(t)$ and hence $a = 1$. He must then choose to wait T periods (equation [33]) and, at that point, he must choose to upgrade A by a constant factor ξ (equation [34]). Finally, given the T and ξ that he has chosen, his expertise must be the same after each upgrade (equation [35]).

The changeover process. The above model generates a balanced growth path along which income grows and the relative price of capital falls. Technological progress in the capital goods sector is endogenous. At each point in time there is a distribution of capital goods producers, using a variety of production techniques. Each capital goods producer decides when to upgrade his technology. Because there is a cost of doing so, in terms of loss of expertise, he will economize on the frequency of doing this. In the real world such adoption costs may be quite high, implying that the changeover process will be slow.[22]

Salter (1966) noted some time ago that the changeover process at the plant level is slow. He quotes Hicks as stating that an "entrepreneur by investing in fixed capital equipment gives hostages to fortune. So long as the plant is in existence, the possibility of economizing by changing the method or scale of production is small; but as the plant comes to be renewed it will be in his interests to make a radical change" (4). The above model captures this process, but here the capital investment is in knowledge.

As evidence of the slow changeover process, consider table 6.1, compiled by Salter (1966). The first column presents labor productivity for plants using the best-practice or the most up-to-date techniques at the time. Average labor productivity across all plants is reported in the second column. As Salter (1966) notes,

---

22. This type of model may have some interesting transitional dynamics. Imagine starting off with some distribution of technologies where producers are bunched up around some particular technique. What economic forces will come to bear to encourage them not to all upgrade around the same date in the future? How long will it take for the distribution to smooth out?

Table 6.1 Best and Average Practice in the U.S. Blast Furnace Industry (tons of pig iron per man-hour, 1911–26)

Year	Best-Practice Plants	Industry Average
1911	0.313	0.140
1917	0.326	0.150
1919	0.328	0.140
1921	0.428	0.178
1923	0.462	0.213
1925	0.512	0.285
1926	0.573	0.296

Source: Salter (1966).

In this industry, average labor productivity is only approximately half best-practice productivity. If all plants were up to best-practice standards known and in use, labor productivity would have doubled immediately. In fact, a decade and a half elapsed before this occurred, and in the meantime the potential provided by best-practice productivity had more than doubled. (6)

Salter's (1966) findings have weathered time well, for, in a recent study of plants' TFP in 21 four-digit textile industries, Dwyer (1998) finds that average TFP among the second (from top) decile divided by the average TFP among the ninth-decile plants (a procedure that is relatively insensitive to outliers) falls between 2 and 3.

6.7 Conclusions: Solow (1956, 1957) versus Solow (1960)

Forty years ago, Solow wrote some classic papers on economic growth. In the classic Solow (1956) paper, technological progress rained down from heaven. The invention of new techniques and their implementation were free. Technological progress affected the productivity of all factors of production, capital and labor, both new and old, alike. By contrast, in Solow (1960) technological advance was embodied in the form of new capital goods. Its implementation is not free because one must invest to realize the benefits from it. This form of technological advance is dubbed investment specific.

So, which framework is better? It is argued here that the Solow (1960) vintage capital model is. First, over the postwar period there has been tremendous technological advance in the production of new capital goods. The relative price of capital goods has declined at about 4 percent per year. Second, the variation in productivity across plants in the United States is tremendous. It is hard to believe that some of this is not due to differences in capital goods employed. In fact, Bahk and Gort (1993) have found that a one-year change in the average age of capital is associated with a 2.5 to 3.5 percent change in a plant's output. Now, there is evidence suggesting that the pace of investment-specific technological progress has picked up since the 1970s with the advent of information technologies. Supposing that this is true, variants of the Solow (1960) framework, modified to incorporate implementation costs and skilled labor, can go some way in explaining the recent productivity slowdown and the rise in wage inequality.

Why does the source of technological progress matter? It may have implications for economic growth, unemployment, or other issues that society cares about. For example, if technological progress is embodied in the form of new capital goods, then policies that reduce the costs of acquiring new equipment (such as investment tax credits for equipment buyers or R&D subsidies for equipment producers) may stimulate growth.[23]

Appendix

Data Definitions and Sources

The sample period is 1948–92, and all data are annual. Real income, y, is defined as nominal GDP minus nominal gross housing product deflated by the implicit price deflator for personal consumption expenditure on nondurables and nonhousing services. The GDP series were obtained from the Bureau of Economic Analysis (STAT-USA website), and the prices series were taken from CITIBASE. Real private sector nonresidential net capital stock, k, and its equipment and structures components (k_e and k_s, respectively), were again downloaded from the BEA. Total private sector hours employed, l, is obtained from CITIBASE (series name LHOURS). Labor share, $1 - \alpha$, was constructed by dividing nominal total compensation of employees by nominal income minus nominal proprietor's income. The data are again from the BEA website. The (standard) rate of technological progress is calculated by using

$$\ln z_t - \ln z_{t-1} = \ln\left(\frac{y_t}{l_t}\right) - \ln\left(\frac{y_{t-1}}{l_{t-1}}\right) - \frac{(\alpha_t + \alpha_{t-1})}{2}\left[\ln\left(\frac{k_t}{l_t}\right) - \ln\left(\frac{k_{t-1}}{l_{t-1}}\right)\right],$$

so that

$$z_t = \exp\left[\sum_{j=1949}^{t} (\ln z_j - \ln z_{j-1})\right],$$

with $z_{1948} = 1$.

The price index for producer's durable equipment is taken from Gordon (1990, until 1983, and Krusell et al. 2000 after 1983). The relative price of

---

23. Stimulating growth does not necessarily improve welfare. The sacrifice in terms of current consumption may be prohibitively high.

equipment, p, is calculated by deflating this price index by the consumer price index. Investment-specific technological progress, q, is then just equal to $1/p$.

To calculate the k_e series used in section 6.3, a discrete approximation to equation (6) is used. The starting point for the equipment series was taken to be the value for k_e implied by the model's balanced-growth path for the year 1947 as taken from the relationship

$$k_e = \frac{qi_e}{(g_y + 1)(g_q + 1) - (1 - \delta_e)},$$

where i_e is nominal gross private domestic fixed investment in producer's durable equipment (from the BEA website) deflated by the price index for personal consumption expenditure on nondurables and non-housing services.

The Mismeasurement of Neutral Technological Progress in Traditional Growth Accounting

To simplify, assume that the labor force is constant. Now, suppose that a growth accountant failed to incorporate investment-specific technological progress into his analysis. He would construct his capital stock series according to

(A1) $$\frac{d\tilde{k}}{dt} = i - \delta\tilde{k}.$$

This corresponds to measuring the stock of capital at historical cost in output units. Using equation (2), he would obtain the following series describing neutral technological progress:

$$g_{\tilde{z}} = g_y - \alpha g_{\tilde{k}}.$$

Because by assumption all growth in output must derive from growth in the capital stock, it must transpire from equation (3) that $g_y = \alpha g_k$ so that

$$g_{\tilde{z}} = \alpha(g_k - g_{\tilde{k}}).$$

Hence, any change in the measured Solow residual arises solely from mismeasurement in the capital stock. To gain an understanding of this equation, suppose that the economy was gliding along a balanced growth path. From equations (4) and (A1), it is clear that in this situation, $g_k - g_{\tilde{k}} = g_q$, implying $g_{\tilde{z}} = \alpha g_q$. Although the growth accountant may have killed off investment-specific technological progress in his misspecification of the law of motion of capital, it has resurrected itself in the form of neutral technological progress.

The model demands that GDP should be measured in consumption units, the numeraire. Doing so is important. What would happen if the growth accountant used standard real GDP numbers? Specifically, let GDP be measured as

$$\tilde{y} = c + \bar{p}qi,$$

where $\bar{p}$ is some base year price for capital goods. Applying equation (2), the growth accountant would obtain

(A2) $\qquad g_{\tilde{z}} = g_{\tilde{y}} - \alpha g_k = g_{\tilde{y}} - g_y.$

The difference in the growth rates between the traditional measure of GDP, $\tilde{y}$, and the consumption based one, y, will be picked up as neutral technological progress. Now,

$$g_{\tilde{y}} = \left(\frac{c}{\tilde{y}}\right)g_c + \bar{p}\left(\frac{iq}{\tilde{y}}\right)g_i + \bar{p}\left(\frac{iq}{\tilde{y}}\right)g_q.$$

Along a balanced growth path $g_c = g_i = g_y$. Because q is growing, it must therefore transpire that $(c/\tilde{y}) \to 0$ and $(\bar{p}iq/\tilde{y}) \to 1$. Hence, asymptotically

$$g_{\tilde{y}} = g_i + g_q = g_y + g_q,$$

so that from equation (A2), $g_{\tilde{z}} = g_q$.

Once again, investment-specific technological progress has masqueraded itself as neutral technological progress.

References

Adler, Paul, and Kim Clark. 1991. Behind the learning curve: A sketch of the learning process. *Management Science* 37 (3): 267–81.
Argotte, Linda, and Dennis Epple. 1990. Learning curves in manufacturing. *Science* (247):920–24.
Arrow, Kenneth. 1962. The economic implications of learning by doing. *Review of Economic Studies* 29 (3): 155–73.
Autor, David, Lawrence Katz, and Alan Kruger. 1998. Computing inequality: Have computers changed the labor market? *Quarterly Journal of Economics* 113 (4): 1169–1213.
Bahk, Byong-Hyong, and Michael Gort. 1993. Decomposing learning by doing in new plants. *Journal of Political Economy* 101 (4): 561–83.
Bartel, Ann, and Frank Lichtenberg. 1987. The comparative advantage of educated workers in implementing new technology. *Review of Economics and Statistics* 69 (1): 1–11.
Benhabib, Jess, and Aldo Rustichini. 1991. Vintage capital, investment, and growth. *Journal of Economic Theory* 55 (2): 323–39.
Benhabib, Jess, and Mark Spiegel. 1994. The role of human capital in economic development: Evidence from aggregate cross country data. *Journal of Monetary Economics* 34 (2): 143–73.

Caselli, Francesco. 1999. Technological revolutions. *American Economic Review* 89 (1): 78–102.
Chari, V. V., and Hugo Hopenhayn. 1991. Vintage human capital. *Journal of Political Economy* 99 (6): 1142–65.
David, Paul. 1975. The "Horndahl" effect in Lowell, 1834–56: A short-run learning curve for integrated cotton textile mills. In *Technical choice, innovation and economic growth: Essays on American and British economic experience,* Paul David, 174–96. London: Cambridge University Press.
———. 1991. Computer and dynamo: The modern productivity paradox in a not-too-distant mirror. In *Technology and productivity: The challenge for economic policy,* 315–47. Paris: Organization for Economic Cooperation and Development.
Denison, Edward. 1964. The unimportance of the embodied question. *American Economic Review (Papers and Proceedings)* 54, no. 2, pt. 1: 90–93.
Dwyer, Douglas. 1998. Technology locks, creative destruction, and nonconvergence in productivity levels. *Review of Economic Dynamics* 1 (2): 430–73.
Federal Reserve Bank of Dallas. 1997. The economy at light speed. *Annual Report.*
Flug, Karnit, and Zvi Hercowitz. 2000. Some international evidence on equipment-skill complementarity. *Review of Economic Dynamics* 3 (3): 461–85.
Goldin, Claudia, and Lawrence Katz. 1998. The origins of technology-skill complementarity. *Quarterly Journal of Economics* 113 (3): 693–732.
Gordon, Robert. 1990. *The measurement of durable goods prices.* Chicago: University of Chicago Press.
Gort, Michael, and Stephen Klepper. 1982. Time paths in the diffusion of product innovations. *Economic Journal* 92 (367): 630–53.
Greenwood, Jeremy, Zvi Hercowitz, and Per Krusell. 1997. Long-run implications of investment-specific technological change. *American Economic Review* 87 (3): 342–62.
Greenwood, Jeremy, and Mehmet Yorukoglu. 1997. "1974." *Carnegie-Rochester Conference Series on Public Policy* 46 (June): 49–95.
Griliches, Zvi. 1957. Hybrid corn: An exploration in the economics of technological change. *Econometrica* 25 (4): 501–22.
———. 1969. Capital-skill complementarity. *Review of Economics and Statistics* 51 (4): 465–68.
———. 1979. Issues in assessing the contribution of research and development to productivity growth. *Bell Journal of Economics* 10 (1): 92–116.
Grübler, Arnulf. 1991. Introduction to diffusion theory. Chapter 1 in *Models, case studies and forecasts of diffusion.* Vol. 3 of *Computer integrated manufacturing,* ed. Robert Ayres, William Haywood, and Louri Tchijov. London: Chapman and Hall.
Heckman, James, Lance Lochner, and Christopher Taber. 1998. Explaining rising wage inequality: Explorations with a dynamic general equilibrium model of labor earnings with heterogeneous agents. *Review of Economic Dynamics* 1 (1): 1–58.
Hulten, Charles. 1992. Growth accounting when technical change is embodied in capital. *American Economic Review* 82 (4): 964–80.
———. 1997. Quality change, prices, and the productivity puzzle. University of Maryland, Department of Economics. Mimeograph.
Jaffe, Adam. 1986. Technological opportunity and spillovers of *R&D:* Evidence from firms' patents, profits, and market value. *American Economic Review* 76 (5): 984–1001.
Johansen, Leif. 1959. Substitution versus fixed production coefficients in the theory of economic growth. *Econometrica* 27 (2): 157–76.

Jones, Charles. 1995. Time series tests of endogenous growth models. *Quarterly Journal of Economics* 110 (2): 495–525.

Jonscher, Charles. 1994. An economic study of the information technology revolution. In *Information technology and the corporation of the 1990's*, ed. T. J. Allen and M. S. Scott Morton, 5–42. Oxford: Oxford University Press.

Jovanovic, Boyan. 1997. Learning and growth. In *Advances in economics*, vol. 2, ed. David Kreps and Kenneth Wallis, 318–39. New York: Cambridge University Press.

———. 1998. Vintage capital and inequality. *Review of Economic Dynamics* 1 (2): 497–530.

Jovanovic, Boyan, and Saul Lach. 1989. Entry, exit and diffusion with learning by doing. *American Economic Review* 79 (4): 690–99.

———. 1997. Product innovation and the business cycle. *International Economic Review* 38 (1): 3–22.

Jovanovic, Boyan, and Glenn MacDonald. 1994. Competitive diffusion. *Journal of Political Economy* 102 (1): 24–52.

Jovanovic, Boyan, and Yaw Nyarko. 1995. A Bayesian learning model fitted to a variety of learning curves. *Brookings Papers on Economic Activity, Microeconomics:* 247–306.

———. 1996. Learning by doing and the choice of technology. *Econometrica* 64 (6): 1299–310.

Jovanovic, Boyan, and Rafael Rob. 1989. The growth and diffusion of knowledge. *Review of Economic Studies* 56 (4): 569–82.

———. 1998. Solow vs. Solow. New York University. Mimeograph.

Kapur, Sandeep. 1993. Late-mover advantage and product diffusion. *Economics Letters* 43 (1): 119–23.

Krusell, Per. 1998. Investment-specific R&D and the decline in the relative price of capital. *Journal of Economic Growth* 3 (2): 131–41.

Krusell, Per, Lee Ohanian, Jose-Victor Rios-Rull, and Giovanni Violante. 2000. Capital-skill complementarity and inequality. *Econometrica* 68 (5): 1029–53.

Lucas, Robert E., Jr. 1988. On the mechanics of economic development. *Journal of Monetary Economics* 22 (1): 3–42.

Mansfield, Edwin. 1963. The speed of response of firms to new techniques. *Quarterly Journal of Economics* 77 (2): 290–311.

Nelson, Richard. 1964. Aggregate production functions and medium-range growth projections. *American Economic Review* 54 (5): 575–606.

Nelson, Richard, and Edmund Phelps. 1966. Investment in humans, technological diffusion, and economic growth. *American Economic Review* 56 (1–2): 69–75.

Parente, Stephen. 1994. Technology adoption, learning-by-doing, and economic growth. *Journal of Economic Theory* 63 (2): 346–69.

Romeo, Anthony. 1975. Interindustry and interfirm differences in the rate of diffusion of an innovation. *Review of Economics and Statistics* 57 (3): 311–19.

Romer, Paul. 1990. Endogenous technological change. *Journal of Political Economy* 98, no. 5, pt. 2: S71–S102.

Salter, Wilfred. 1966. *Productivity and technical change.* Cambridge: Cambridge University Press.

Solow, Robert. 1956. A contribution to the theory of economic growth. *Quarterly Journal of Economics* 70 (1): 65–94.

———. 1957. Technical change and the aggregate production function. *Review of Economics and Statistics* 39 (3): 312–20.

———. 1960. Investment and technological progress. In *Mathematical methods in the social sciences 1959,* ed. Kenneth Arrow, Samuel Karlin, and Patrick Suppes, 89–104. Stanford, Calif.: Stanford University Press.

Stigler, George. 1947. *Trends in output and employment.* New York: Herald Square Press.
Zeckhauser, Richard. 1968. Optimality in a world of progress and learning. *Review of Economic Studies* 35 (3): 363–65.

Comment   Barry Bosworth

This paper is a very coherent survey of a set of recent growth models that have attempted to extend Solow's contributions to growth theory. The authors are able to integrate within the framework of a formal model many of the ideas that have been put forth as explanations for the post-1973 productivity slowdown. They also develop a very interesting model in which they stress the role of embodied technical change.

They identify three issues that they believe cannot be fully explained within Solow's original one-sector growth model (1956): (a) the post-1973 slowdown, (b) the falling relative price of capital, and (c) the rising relative wage premium for skilled labor. They argue that the first is due to the high costs of implementing the new technologies and the second to rapid technical growth in the capital goods producing industry, and that the increased skill premium is a reflection of greater complementarity between the new capital and skilled labor. All of these conclusions are plausible and have been argued in various forms by others; but we suffer from a shortage not of possible explanations, but of evidence on which explanations are true. Let me address the authors' explanations in reverse order.

Wage Dispersion

The authors are certainly right to point to the sharp widening of wage inequality as a dramatic new feature of economic change over the last quarter century, and we can agree that technology is part of the explanation for a change in the distribution of labor demand by skill level, but its linkage to the productivity slowdown may be more tenuous. Nearly all industrial countries have had a productivity slowdown, but only a few have experienced a widening of the wage distribution. At the international level, it is interesting to note that countries with high growth rates seem to have narrower wage distributions. In addition, the dispersion of U.S. wage rates has increased in more dimensions than skill, suggesting that it is not only a reflection of an increased skill bias in technical change. Finally, if the dominant change were computers and similar technologies, I would expect it to rebound to the advantage of the young, who, it is said, find it easier to adapt; yet the age profile seems to have become more steep, and the widening of the wage distribution is concentrated among the young.

Barry Bosworth is a Senior Fellow in Economic Studies at the Brookings Institution.

Relative Price of Capital

The decline in the relative price of capital clearly indicates the need to use, at a minimum, a two-sector vintage model that distinguishes between capital and consumption goods to reflect sharply different rates of TFP growth between the two sectors.

In the discussion of embodiment, technical change is viewed as raising the quality and thus the real value of new capital. That is the perspective adopted with the introduction of the new price index for computers: a hedonic price index focused on computers of equivalent quality. What is TFP growth to the capital goods industry is rising capital inputs and slowing TFP growth to the consumption goods sector.

In the new national accounts data, total TFP growth is near zero, whereas the growth of manufacturing (read computers) TFP has returned to the high rates of the pre-1973 period. Hence, the growth of TFP in nonmanufacturing (services) must be negative. From the perspective of overall TFP, the new price index for capital is essentially a timing adjustment: first raising the TFP growth rate for manufacturing and then substituting a higher rate of growth of capital services for nonmanufacturing.

This is the same issue raised in a broader context by Gordon when he argued for much lower rates of price increase for equipment prices in the 1960s and 1970s. The authors of this paper make use of Gordon's price data to measure technical change; but normally that would require the construction of a new set of investment, capital, and output accounts, as was done with the introduction of the price deflator for computers. Again, the quality adjustment would raise the level of output in the capital goods industry; but, because it implies a higher future level of capital services, it lowers TFP growth in the consumption goods sector.

The authors avoid this process by defining a new measure of real output as nominal GDP deflated by the price index for consumption goods, neither of which is changed by the use of the Gordon data. The new price index changes only the real magnitude of the capital input. By their measure, the relative price of equipment declined to about one-sixth its 1950 level by 1990 (fig. 6.2). Using the price deflators of the current national accounts, the corresponding figure would be about two-thirds. Thus, the use of the Gordon data raises their concept of technological change roughly fourfold over the 1950–90 period. Although this is a dramatic story for the capital goods industry, we should wonder why the producers of consumer goods perform so poorly, given the large quantities of effective capital.

The Productivity Slowdown

The real puzzle is why the rate of TFP growth in the consumption sector (services) is near zero (or negative). The authors attribute this to the high costs of implementing the new technologies. I agree that the diffusion lags for formerly new technologies were surprisingly long, but we should distinguish between the lag due to the slow introduction of the technology—purchase of the machine—versus the costs and time required to learn to use them. Only the latter reduces productivity. I find it hard to believe that the second category of lag is so important that an acceleration of technological change has the perverse effect of reducing the growth of TFP. The post-1973 slowdown is extraordinarily broad across industries, including those that would seem to make little use of the new information technologies. I think the model is very interesting, but in the end it does not provide an answer; it changes the question.

7
Why Is Productivity Procyclical? Why Do We Care?

Susanto Basu and John Fernald

Productivity is procyclical. That is, whether measured as labor productivity or total factor productivity, productivity rises in booms and falls in recessions. Recent macroeconomic literature views this stylized fact of procyclical productivity as an essential feature of business cycles, largely because of the realization that each explanation for this stylized fact has important implications for the workings of macroeconomic models. In this paper, we seek to identify the empirical importance of the four main explanations for this stylized fact, and discuss the implications of our results for the appropriateness of different macroeconomic models.

Until recently, economists generally regarded the long-run *average* rate of productivity growth as important for growth and welfare; procyclical productivity, by contrast, seemed irrelevant for understanding business cycles. Economists presumed that high-frequency fluctuations in productivity reflected cyclical mismeasurement—for example, labor and capital worked harder and longer in booms—but these cyclical variations in utilization were not themselves important for understanding cycles.

In the past decade and a half, productivity fluctuations have taken center stage in modeling output fluctuations, and are now viewed as an essen-

Susanto Basu is associate professor of economics at the University of Michigan and a research associate of the National Bureau of Economic Research. John Fernald is senior economist at the Federal Reserve Bank of Chicago.

We are grateful for comments from Zvi Griliches, John Haltiwanger, Michael Horvath, Charles Hulten, Dale Jorgenson, Catherine Morrison, Plutarchos Sakellaris, and participants in the conference. Basu thanks the National Science Foundation and the Alfred P. Sloan Foundation for financial support. The views in this paper are solely the responsibility of the authors and should not be interpreted as reflecting the views of the Board of Governors of the Federal Reserve System or of any other person associated with the Federal Reserve System.

tial part of the cycle. Figure 7.2 (discussed later) charts the Solow residual for the aggregate U.S. economy. The figure also shows growth in output and growth in "inputs," defined as a weighted average of labor and capital growth (we discuss data sources and definitions in section 7.4). Mean productivity growth is positive, so that over time society's ability to produce goods or services that satisfy final demand is rising faster than its inputs. In addition, productivity growth is quite volatile. The volatility is not random, but is significantly procyclical: The correlation with output growth is about 0.8.

Macroeconomists have become interested in the cyclical behavior of productivity because of the realization that procyclicality is closely related to the impulses or propagation mechanisms underlying business cycles. Even the cyclical mismeasurement that was formerly dismissed as unimportant turns out to be a potentially important propagation mechanism.

There are four main explanations for high-frequency fluctuations in productivity. First, procyclical productivity may reflect procyclical technology. After all, under standard conditions, total factor productivity measures technology. If there are high-frequency fluctuations in technology, it is not surprising that there are high-frequency fluctuations in output as well. Second, widespread imperfect competition and increasing returns may lead productivity to rise whenever inputs rise. (Increasing returns could be internal to a firm, or could reflect externalities from the activity of other firms.) Figure 7.2 (discussed later) shows the key stylized fact of business cycles, the comovement of inputs and output. With increasing returns, the fluctuations in inputs then cause endogenous, procyclical fluctuations in productivity. Third, as already mentioned, utilization of inputs may vary over the cycle. Fourth, reallocation of resources across uses with different marginal products may contribute to procyclicality. For example, if different industries have different degrees of market power, then inputs will generally have different marginal products in different uses. Then aggregate productivity growth is cyclical if sectors with higher markups have input growth that is more cyclical. Alternatively, if inputs are relatively immobile or quasi-fixed, then marginal products may temporarily differ across uses; as these resources eventually shift, productivity rises.[1]

Why do economists now care about the relative importance of these four explanations? In large part, changes in the methodology of macroeconomics have raised the fact of procyclical productivity to the forefront. Macroeconomists of all persuasions now use dynamic general equilibrium (DGE) models, and it turns out that each of the four explanations has important implications for the workings of these models. Hence, answering

---

1. For examples of these four explanations, see, respectively, Cooley and Prescott (1995); Hall (1988, 1990); Basu (1996), Bils and Cho (1994), and Gordon (1993); and Basu and Fernald (1997a, 1997b).

why productivity is procyclical sheds light on the relative merits of different models of the business cycle.

First, if high-frequency fluctuations in productivity reflect high-frequency fluctuations in technology, then comovement of output and input (i.e., business cycles) are a natural byproduct. The DGE approach to business cycle modeling began with so-called real business cycle models, which explore the extent to which the frictionless one-sector Ramsey-Cass-Koopmans growth model can explain business cycle correlations. Real business cycle models use Solow's productivity residual—interpreted as aggregate technology shocks—as the dominant impulse driving the cycle (e.g., Cooley and Prescott 1995). Other impulses may affect output in these models, but technology shocks must dominate if the model is to match the key stylized fact of business cycles: the positive comovement of output and labor input.[2]

Second, recent papers show that increasing returns and imperfect competition can modify and magnify the effects of various shocks in an otherwise standard DGE model. In response to government demand shocks, for example, models with countercyclical markups can explain a rise in real wages while models with increasing returns can explain a rise in measured productivity. Perhaps most strikingly, if increasing returns are large enough, they can lead to multiple equilibria, in which sunspots or purely nominal shocks drive business cycles.[3] Furthermore, if firms are not all perfectly competitive, then it is not appropriate to use the Solow residual as a measure of technology shocks, since the Solow residual becomes endogenous. Taking the Solow residual to be exogenous thereby mixes impulses and propagation mechanisms.

Third, variable utilization of resources turns out to improve the propagation of shocks in DGE models. If firms can vary the intensity of factor use, then the effective supply of capital and labor becomes more elastic. Small shocks (to technology or demand) can then lead to large fluctuations.[4] If the model has sticky nominal prices, these elastic factor supplies greatly increase the persistence of the real effects of nominal shocks.

Fourth, reallocations of inputs, without any change in technology, may cause aggregate productivity to be procyclical. For example, in the sectoral

---

2. Barro and King (1984) provide an early discussion of this issue. Dynamic general equilibrium models without technology shocks can match this stylized fact with countercyclical markups of price over marginal cost, arising from sticky prices (as in Kimball, 1995) or from game-theoretic interactions between firms (as in Rotemberg and Woodford 1992). Models with an extreme form of increasing returns—increasing marginal product of labor—can also produce a positive comovement between output and labor input; see, for example, Farmer and Guo (1994).

3. See, for example, Rotemberg and Woodford (1992), Farmer and Guo (1994), and Beaudry and Devereux (1994). Rotemberg and Woodford (1995) survey dynamic general equilibrium models with imperfect competition.

4. See, for example, Burnside and Eichenbaum (1996); Dotsey, King, and Wolman (1997); and Wen (1998).

shifts literature (e.g., Ramey and Shapiro 1998 and Phelan and Trejos 1996), demand shocks cause differences in the marginal product of immobile factors across firms. Output fluctuations then reflect shifts of resources among uses with different marginal products. Basu and Fernald (1997a) provide a simple stylized example in which aggregation over constant-returns firms with different levels of productivity lead to the existence of multiple equilibria. Weder (1997) calibrates a DGE model where durables manufacturing firms have increasing returns while all other producers have constant returns (calibrated from results in Basu and Fernald 1997a), and shows that reallocations make multiple equilibria possible in that model. Of course, reallocations can also help propagate sector-specific technology shocks, as in Lilien (1982).

In this paper, we seek to identify the importance of the four explanations. Our approach builds on the seminal contributions of Solow (1957) and Hall (1990). We allow for imperfect competition and nonconstant returns to scale, as well as variations in the workweek of capital or the effort of labor that are unobservable to the econometrician. In the Solow-Hall tradition, we take the production function residual as a measure of sectoral technology shocks. We then aggregate over sectors, since our ultimate focus is on explaining movements in aggregate productivity.

Our empirical work relies primarily on the tools developed by Basu and Fernald (1997b) and Basu and Kimball (1997). Both papers allow for increasing returns to scale and markups of price over marginal cost. Basu and Fernald stress the role of sectoral heterogeneity. They argue that for economically plausible reasons—for example, differences across industries in the degree of market power—the marginal product of an input may differ across uses. Then aggregate productivity growth depends in part on which sectors change inputs.

Basu and Kimball stress the role of variable capital and labor utilization. Solow's original (1957) article presumed that variations in capacity utilization were a major reason for the procyclicality of measured productivity, a presumption widely held thereafter. (See, for example, Gordon 1993; Abbott, Griliches, and Hausman 1998). In essence, the problem is cyclical measurement error of input quantities: True inputs are more cyclical than measured inputs, so that measured productivity is spuriously procyclical.

Basu and Kimball use the basic insight that a cost-minimizing firm operates on all margins simultaneously—whether observed or unobserved—ensuring that the marginal benefit of any input equals its marginal cost. As a result, increases in observed inputs can proxy for unobserved changes in utilization. For example, when labor is particularly valuable, firms will work existing employees both longer (increasing observed hours per worker) and harder (increasing unobserved effort).

Our work on these issues follows the Solow-Hall tradition, which makes minimal assumptions and focuses on the properties of the resulting residual. An alternative literature, surveyed by Nadiri and Prucha (ch. 4, this volume), addresses issues of technology change by attempting to estimate an extensively parameterized production (or cost) function. That approach can address a wider range of issues because it imposes much more structure on the problem. If the problem is correctly specified and all necessary data are available, the more parametric approach offers clear theoretical advantages, since one can then estimate second-order properties of the production function such as elasticities of substitution. However, that approach is likely to suffer considerable practical disadvantages, such as the increased likelihood of misspecification and the necessity of factor prices being allocative period by period. We are skeptical that observed factor prices are always allocative—with implicit contracts, for example, observed wages need only be right on average, rather than needing to be allocative period by period. Hence, we argue in favor of an explicitly first-order approach when possible, since results are likely to be more robust.

Note that this production function literature sometimes claims to solve the capacity utilization problem (e.g., Morrison 1992a,b). Suppose, for example, that the capital stock cannot be changed instantaneously but that it is nevertheless used all the time. It can still be used more intensively by combining the fixed capital services with more labor and materials. As a result, the shadow value of this quasi-fixed capital stock may vary from its long-run equilibrium factor cost. Capital's output elasticity may also vary over time, reflecting variations in this shadow value. More generally, with quasi-fixity, quantities of inputs (and output) may differ from long-run equilibrium values; similarly, on the dual (cost) side, short-run variable cost may differ from long run variable cost at a given output level. If we equate full capacity with the firm's optimal long-run equilibrium point, then capacity utilization (defined by how far actual output or variable cost is from their appropriately-defined long-run equilibrium values) may vary over time.

For estimating the technology residual, the relevant feature of this literature is that it attempts to estimate the shadow value of quasi-fixed inputs in order to calculate the time variation in the output elasticities. The production function literature thus tries to control for time-varying output elasticities, while the capacity-utilization literature tries to measure factor quantities (i.e., the service flow) correctly.[5]

The enormous confusion between these two logically distinct ideas stems purely from the semantic confusion caused by both literatures claiming to address the capacity utilization problem. In particular, adherents of the time-varying elasticity approach often claim that their opti-

---

5. For our purposes, this is the only difference that matters. The structural literature also estimates a variety of other quantities, such as elasticities of substitution, that may be of independent interest.

mization-based methods obviate the need to use proxies that control for unobserved variations in capital workweek or labor effort, with the implication that the use of proxies is somehow ad hoc. This implication is wrong. The production function literature assumes that the quantities of all inputs are correctly measured; the capacity utilization literature devotes itself to correcting for measurement error in the inputs. The two address separate issues.

The easiest way to see the difference between the two concepts is to suppose that output is produced via a Cobb-Douglas production function. Then the output elasticities are constant, so for our purposes—for example, estimating returns to scale—the time-varying elasticity literature has nothing to add. But there is still a capacity utilization problem—for example, if workers work harder in a boom than in recessions, but this fact is not captured in the statistics on labor input. Formally, therefore, the problem of time-varying elasticities is a second-order issue—it relates to deviations from the first-order Cobb-Douglas approximation—but capacity utilization is a first-order issue, since it concerns the accurate measurement of the inputs.

After presenting empirical results, we discuss implications for macroeconomics. We discussed some of these implications above, in motivating our interest in procyclical productivity, so we highlight other issues. Normative productivity analysis emphasizes the welfare interpretation of the productivity residual. But what if productivity and technology differ because of distortions such as imperfect competition? Recent macroeconomic literature often seems to assume that we measure productivity in order to measure technology; any differences reflect mismeasurement. Although variable input utilization is clearly a form of mismeasurement, we argue that other distortions (such as imperfect competition) are not: Productivity has clear welfare implications, even in a world with distortions. A modified Solow residual—which reduces to Solow's measure if there are no economic profits—approximates to first order the welfare change of a representative consumer. Intuitively, growth in aggregate output measures the growth in society's ability to consume. To measure welfare change, we must then subtract the opportunity cost of the inputs used to produce this output growth. Input prices measure that cost, even when they do not measure marginal products. Hence, if productivity and technology differ, then productivity most closely indexes welfare.

Section 7.1 provides a relatively informal overview of the issues. We highlight key issues facing the empirical literature and make recommendations. That section will allow the reader to proceed to the data and empirical sections 7.4 and 7.5. However, some of our choices in section 7.1 require more formal treatment to justify fully; section 7.2 provides this treatment. Section 7.3 discusses aggregation from the firm to the economy-wide level. Section 7.4 discusses data, and section 7.5 presents results. Section 7.6 discusses several macroeconomic implications of our results. Section 7.7 concludes.

7.1 Methods of Estimating Technical Change: Overview

Why do macroeconomists care about fluctuations in productivity? First, and perhaps foremost, productivity yields information about the aggregate production of goods and services in the economy. Second, productivity analysis may provide information about firm behavior—for example, the markup and its cyclicality, the prevalence of increasing returns to scale, and the factors determining the level of utilization.

There are several possible approaches to empirical productivity analysis. Each has advantages and disadvantages. In this section, we assess these alternatives, and make recommendations about key decisions facing an empirical researcher. We summarize the microeconomic foundations of our preferred approach, which is in the spirit of Solow (1957) and Hall (1990). This discussion may satisfy the interests and needs of most readers, who can then proceed to the data and results. However, a full justification of our approach requires a somewhat more technical discussion. We present that technical discussion in sections 7.2 and 7.3.

Our ultimate goal is to understand the aggregate economy. At an aggregate level, the appropriate measure of output is national expenditure on goods and services, that is, GDP—the sum of consumption, investment, government purchases, and net exports. GDP measures the quantity of goods available to consume today or invest for tomorrow. GDP is intrinsically a value-added measure, since the national accounts identity assures us that when we aggregate firm-level value added (defined in nominal terms as total revenue minus the cost of intermediate inputs of materials and energy; in real terms, gross output with intermediate inputs netted out in some way, as discussed in section 7.3), aggregate value added equals national expenditure. The economy's resources for producing goods and services are capital and labor.

Nevertheless, despite our interest in macroeconomic aggregates, we should begin at the level where goods are actually produced: at the level of a firm or even a plant. The appropriate measure of output for a firm is gross output—shoes, books, computers, haircuts, and so forth. Firms combine inputs of capital, labor, and intermediate goods (materials and energy) to produce this gross output.

Our goal, then, is to explore how firm-level production of gross output translates into production of aggregate final expenditure. Macroeconomists often assume an aggregate production function that relates aggregate final expenditure (value added) to inputs of capital and labor. For many purposes, what matters is whether such a function provides at least a first-order approximation to the economy's production possibilities—even if an explicit aggregate function does not exist (as it rarely does). For example, in calibrating a dynamic general equilibrium model, one may care about how much aggregate output increases if the equilibrium quantity of labor increases, and a first-order approximation should give the right magnitude.[6] We argue that in a world without frictions or imperfections, aggregation is generally very clean and straightforward. However, with frictions and imperfections such as imperfect competition or costs of reallocating inputs, the assumption that an aggregate production function exists (even as a first-order approximation) generally fails—but the failures are economically interesting. These failures also help explain procyclical productivity.

7.1.1 The Basic Setup

We write the firm's production function for gross output, Y_i, in the following general form:

$$(1) \qquad Y_i = F^i(\tilde{K}_i, \tilde{L}_i, M_i, T_i)$$

Firms use capital services $\tilde{K}_i$, labor services $\tilde{L}_i$, and intermediate inputs of materials and energy M_i. We write capital and labor services with tildes to remind ourselves that these are the true inputs of services, which may not be observed by the econometrician. T_i indexes technology, which we define to include any inputs that affect firm-level production but are not compensated by the firm. For example, T_i comprises both standard exogenous technological progress and any Marshallian externalities that may exist; we take technology as unobservable. (For simplicity, we omit time subscripts.)

The services of labor and capital depend on both raw quantities (hours worked and the capital stock), and the intensity with which they are used. We define labor services as the product of the number of employees, N_i, hours worked per employee H_i, and the effort of each worker, E_i. We define capital services as the product of the capital stock, K_i, and the utilization of the capital stock, Z_i. (For example, K_i might represent a particular machine, whereas Z_i represents the machine's workweek—how many hours it is operated each period). Hence, input services are:

$$(2) \qquad \tilde{L}_i = E_i H_i N_i,$$

$$\tilde{K}_i = Z_i K_i.$$

We will generally assume that the capital stock and the number of employees are quasi-fixed, so firms cannot change their levels costlessly.

---

6. However, DGE models usually also need to relate changes in factor prices (e.g., wages) to changes in the quantities of inputs. For this purpose, the first-order approximation is not sufficient: One also needs to know the elasticities of substitution between inputs in production, which is a second-order property.

Let the firm's production function F^i be (locally) homogeneous of arbitrary degree γ_i in total inputs. Constant returns then corresponds to the case where γ_i equals 1. Formally, we can write returns to scale in two useful, and equivalent, forms. First, returns to scale equal the sum of output elasticities:

$$(3) \qquad \gamma_i = \frac{F^i_1 \tilde{K}_i}{Y_i} + \frac{F^i_2 \tilde{L}_i}{Y_i} + \frac{F^i_3 M_i}{Y_i},$$

where F^i_J denotes the derivative of the production function with respect to the Jth element (i.e., the marginal product of input J). Second, assuming firms minimize cost, we can denote the firm's cost function by $C_i(Y_i)$. (In general, the cost function also depends on the prices of the variable inputs and the quantities of any quasi-fixed inputs, although we omit those terms for simplicity here.) The *local* degree of returns to scale equals the inverse of the elasticity of cost with respect to output.[7]

$$(4) \qquad \gamma_i(Y_i) = \frac{C_i(Y_i)}{Y_i C'_i(Y_i)} = \frac{C_i(Y_i)/Y_i}{C'_i(Y_i)} = \frac{AC_i}{MC_i},$$

where AC_i equals average cost, and MC_i equals marginal cost. Increasing returns, in particular, may reflect overhead costs or decreasing marginal cost; both imply that average cost exceeds marginal cost. If increasing returns take the form of overhead costs, then $\gamma_i(Y_i)$ is not a constant structural parameter, but depends on the level of output the firm produces. As production increases, returns to scale fall as the firm moves down its average cost curve.

As equation (4) shows, there is no necessary relationship between the degree of returns to scale and the slope of the marginal cost curve. Indeed, increasing returns are compatible with increasing marginal costs, as in the standard Chamberlinian model of imperfect competition. One can calibrate the slope of the marginal cost curve from the degree of returns to scale only by assuming there are no fixed costs. An important point is that the slope of the marginal cost curve determines the slopes of the factor demand functions, which in turn are critical for determining the results of DGE models (for example, whether the model allows sunspot fluctuations). Several studies have used estimates of the degree of returns to scale to calibrate the slope of marginal cost; for a discussion of this practice, see Schmitt-Grohé (1997).

Firms may also charge a price P_i that is a markup, μ_i, over marginal cost. That is, $\mu_i \equiv P_i/MC_i$. Returns to scale γ_i is a technical property of the production function, whereas the markup μ_i is essentially a behavioral parameter, depending on the firm's pricing decision. However, from equation (4), the two are inextricably linked:

---

7. See Varian (1984, 68) for a proof.

(5) $$\gamma_i = \frac{C_i(Y_i)}{Y_i C_i'(Y_i)} = \frac{P_i}{C_i'(Y_i)} \frac{C_i(Y_i)}{P_i Y_i} = \mu_i(1 - s_{\pi i}),$$

where $s_{\pi i}$ is the share of pure economic profit in gross revenue. As long as pure economic profits are small (and in our data, we estimate the average profit rate to be at most 3 percent[8]), equation (5) shows that μ_i approximately equals γ_i. Large markups, for example, require large increasing returns. This is just what one would expect if free entry drives profits to zero in equilibrium—for example, in Chamberlinian monopolistic competition. Thus, although increasing returns and markups are not equivalent from a welfare perspective, they are forced to equal one another if competition eliminates profits. As a result, as we show in the next subsection, one can write the resulting wedge between output elasticities and factor shares in terms of either parameter. Given low estimated profits, equation (5) shows that strongly diminishing returns (γ_i much less than one) imply that firms consistently price output below marginal cost (μ_i less than one). Since price consistently below marginal cost makes no economic sense, we conclude that average firm-level returns to scale must either be constant or increasing. Increasing returns also require that firms charge a markup, as long as firms do not make losses.

7.1.2 The Solow-Hall Approach

Suppose we want to estimate how rapidly technology is changing. Solow's (1957) seminal contribution involves differentiating the production function and using the firm's first-order conditions for cost minimization. If there are constant returns to scale and perfect competition, then the first-order conditions (discussed below) imply that output elasticities are observed in the data by revenue shares. Hall (1988, 1990) extends Solow's contribution to the case of increasing returns and imperfect competition. Under these conditions, output elasticities are not observed, since neither returns to scale nor markups are observed. However, Hall derives a simple regression equation, which he then estimates. In this section, we extend Hall's approach by using gross-output data and taking account of variable factor utilization.

We begin by taking logs of both sides of equation (1) and then differentiating with respect to time:

(6) $$dy_i = \frac{F_1^i K_i}{Y_i} d\tilde{k}_i + \frac{F_2^i L_i}{Y_i} d\tilde{l}_i + \frac{F_3^i M_i}{Y_i} dm + dt_i.$$

Small letters denote growth rates (so dy, for example, equals $(1/Y)\dot{Y}$), and we have normalized the output elasticity with respect to technology equal to one for simplicity.

---

8. Rotemberg and Woodford (1995) also provide a variety of evidence suggesting that profit rates are close to zero.

As Solow (1957) and Hall (1990) show, cost minimization puts additional structure on equation (6), allowing us to relate the unknown output elasticities to observed factor prices. In particular, suppose firms charge a price P_i that is a markup, μ_i, over marginal cost. (The advantage of the cost minimization framework is that it is unnecessary to specify the potentially very complicated, dynamic profit maximization problem that gives rise to this price.) Perfect competition implies μ_i equals one. Suppose that firms take the price of all J inputs, P_{Ji}, as given by competitive markets. The first-order conditions for cost-minimization then imply that:

$$(7) \qquad P_i F^i_J = \mu_i P_{Ji}.$$

In other words, firms set the value of a factor's marginal product equal to a markup over the factor's input price. Equivalently, rearranging the equation by dividing through by μ_i, this condition says that firms equate each factor's marginal revenue product $(P_i/\mu_i)F^i_J$ to the factor's price.

The price of capital, P_{Ki}, must be defined as the *rental price* (or shadow rental price) of capital. In particular, if the firm makes pure economic profits, these are generally paid to capital, since the owners of the firm typically also own its capital. These profits should not be incorporated into the rental price. Equation (7) still holds if some factors are quasi-fixed, as long as we define the input price of the quasi-fixed factors as the appropriate *shadow* price, or implicit rental rate (Berndt and Fuss, 1986). We return to this point in section 7.2 where we specify a dynamic cost-minimization problem.

Using equation (7), we can write each output elasticity as the product of the markup multiplied by total expenditure on each input divided by total revenue. Thus, for example,

$$(8) \qquad \frac{F^i_1 Z_i K_i}{Y_i} = \mu_i \frac{P_{Ki} K_i}{P_i Y_i} \equiv \mu_i s_{Ki}.$$

(The marginal product of capital is $F^i_1 Z_i$, since the services from a machine depend on the rate at which it is being utilized; i.e., its workweek.) The shares s_{Ji} are total *cost* of each type of input divided by total *revenue*. Thus, the input shares sum to less than one if firms make pure profits.

We now substitute these output elasticities into equation (6) and use the definition of input services from equation (2):

$$\begin{aligned}
dy_i &= \mu_i[s_{Ki}d\tilde{k}_i + s_{Li}d\tilde{l}_i + s_{Mi}dm_i] + dt_i \\
&= \mu_i[s_{Ki}(dk_i + dz_i) + s_{Li}(dn_i + dh_i + de_i) + s_{Mi}dm_i] + dt_i \\
&= \mu_i[s_{Ki}dk_i + s_{Li}(dn_i + dh_i) + s_{Mi}dm_i] + \mu_i(1 - s_{Mi}) \\
&\quad \left[\frac{s_{Ki}dz_i + s_{Li}de_i}{(1 - s_{Mi})}\right] + dt_i
\end{aligned}$$

By defining dx as a share-weighted average of conventional (observed) input growth, and du as a weighted average of unobserved variation in capital utilization and effort, we obtain our basic estimating equation:

$$dy_i = \mu_i dx_i + \mu_i(1 - s_{Mi})du_i + dt_i. \tag{9}$$

Using equation (5), we could rewrite equation (9) in terms of returns to scale γ_i. In that case, the correct weights to calculate weighted average inputs are cost shares, which sum to one, rather than revenue shares, which might not. Hall (1990) used the cost-share approach, but there is no economic difference between Hall's approach and ours, and the data requirements are the same. In particular, once we allow for the possibility of economic profits, we must in any case estimate a required rental cost of capital. Writing the equation in terms of μ_i turns out to simplify some later derivations and also facilitates the welfare discussion in Section VI.

Suppose all firms have constant returns to scale, all markets are perfectly competitive, and all factor inputs are freely variable and perfectly observed. Then the markup μ_i equals one, du_i is identically zero (or is observed), and all factor shares are observed as data (since there are no economic profits to worry about). This case corresponds to Solow's (1957) assumptions, and we observe everything in equation (9) except technology change dt_i, which we can calculate as a residual. However, if Solow's conditions fail, we can follow Hall (1990) and treat equation (9) as a regression.

An alternative to the Solow-Hall approach involves estimating many more properties of the production function (equation [1])—Nadiri and Prucha (this volume) survey that approach. That approach requires much more structure on the problem. For example, one must usually postulate a functional form and specify the firm's complete maximization problem, including all constraints. If the problem is correctly specified and all necessary data are available, that approach offers clear theoretical advantages for estimating the second-order properties of the production function. However, the structural approach may suffer considerable practical disadvantages, such as the increased likelihood of misspecification and the need for all factor prices to be allocative period by period. In any case, for the first-order issues we focus on here, it should give similar results. (If it does not, our view is that the Solow-Hall approach is probably more robust).

Regarding equation (9) as an estimating equation, one immediately faces three issues. First, the econometrician usually does not observe utilization du directly. In particular, if capital and labor utilization vary, then growth rates of the observed capital stock and labor hours do not capture the full service flows from those inputs. In the short run, firms can vary their inputs of capital and labor only by varying utilization. In this case, the regression suffers from measurement error. Unlike classical measurement error, variations in utilization du are likely to be (positively) correlated with changes in the measured inputs dx, leading to an upward bias in estimated elasticities. Below, we draw on recent work in the literature on capacity utilization, when we attempt to control for variable service flow from inputs.

Second, should one take the output elasticities as constant (appropriate for a Cobb-Douglas production function or for a first-order log linear approximation), or time varying? That is, should one allow the markup and the share weights in equation (9) to change over time? If the elasticities are not truly constant over time, then treating them as constant may introduce bias. However, as we discuss later, attempting to estimate the time-varying shares may lead to more problems than it solves.

Third, even if the output elasticities are constant and all inputs are observable, one faces the "transmission problem" noted by Marschak and Andrews (1944): The technical change term, dt, is likely to be correlated with a firm's input choices, leading to biased OLS estimates. In principle, one can solve this problem by instrumenting, but the need to use instruments affects our choice of the appropriate technique for estimating equation (6). (One might expect technology improvements to lead to an expansion in inputs, making the OLS bias positive; Gali 1999 and Basu, Fernald, and Kimball 1999, however, argue that there are theoretical and empirical reasons to expect a negative bias.)

7.1.3 Empirical Implementation

We now discuss the empirical issues noted above, beginning with capacity utilization. In the estimating equation (9), we need some way to observe utilization growth du or else to control for the measurement error resulting from unobserved changes in utilization.

Our approach builds on the intuition that firms view all inputs (whether observed by the econometrician or not) identically. Suppose a firm wants more labor input but cannot instantaneously hire more workers. Then the firm should equate the marginal cost of obtaining more services from the observed intensive margin (e.g., working current workers longer hours) and from the unobserved intensive margin (working them harder each hour). If the costs of increasing hours and effort are convex, firms will choose to use both margins. Thus changes in an observed input—for example, hours per worker—provide an index of unobserved changes in the intensity of work. This suggests a regression of the form

$$(10) \qquad dy_i = \mu_t dx_i + a_t dh_i + dt_i,$$

where dh_i is the growth rate of hours per worker. Earlier work by Abbott, Griliches, and Hausman (1998) also runs this regression to control for utilization.

In section 7.2, we construct a dynamic model of variable utilization that provides complete microfoundations for this intuition. That model shows that the regression in equation (10) appropriately controls for variable effort. In addition, if the cost of varying the workweek of capital takes the form of a shift premium—for example, one needs to pay workers more to work at night—then this regression corrects for variations in utilization of capital as well as effort. (If the cost of varying capital's workweek is "wear and tear"—i.e., capital depreciates in use—then the regression is somewhat more complicated.)

Variable utilization of inputs suggests two additional problems in estimating regressions like equations (9) or (10), both of which make it difficult to observe "true" factor prices at high frequencies. First, firms will vary utilization only if inputs of capital and labor are quasi-fixed—that is, costly to adjust. Varying utilization presumably costs the firm something—for example, a shift premium. Thus, if firms could vary the number of machines or workers without cost, they would always adjust along these extensive margins rather than varying utilization. However, if inputs are costly to adjust, then the shadow price of an input to the firm may not equal its current market price. For example, investment adjustment costs imply that the return to installed capital may differ from its frictionless rental rate.

Second, varying utilization—especially of labor—is most viable when workers and firms have a long-term relationship. A firm may increase work intensity when demand is high, promising to allow workers a break in the next downturn. Such a strategy cannot be implemented if most workers are not employed by the firm when the next downturn comes. The existence of such long-term relationships suggests that wages may be set to be right "on average," instead of being the correct spot market wages in every period. Thus, both quasi-fixity and implicit labor contracts imply that we may not be able to observe factor prices at high frequencies.

This inability to observe factor prices period by period implies that we probably want to assume constant, rather than time-varying, elasticities. This is unfortunate, since the first-order equations (8) suggest that if factor shares vary over time, then output elasticities may vary as well. But if, because of quasi-fixity and implicit labor contracts, we do not observe the relevant shadow values, then observed shares do not tell us how the elasticities vary. For estimating the average markup, a first-order approximation may suffice, and may be relatively unaffected by our inability to observe factor prices at high frequency. Of course, if our goal were to estimate elasticities of substitution between inputs, then we would need to find some way to deal with these problems—we could not use a first-order approximation that simply assumes the elasticities are one.[9]

---

9. For example, Berman, Bound, and Griliches (1994) and others investigate the hypothesis that technological progress is skill-biased, and hence contributed to the increase in income inequality in the United States in recent decades; Jorgenson (1987) argues that part of the productivity slowdown of the 1970s and 1980s is due to energy-biased technical change.

With these considerations in mind, we now assess four methods of estimating the parameters in the production function. First, one can simply take equation (6) as an estimating equation and estimate the output elasticities directly. This approach, which essentially assumes that the production function is Cobb-Douglas, can be justified as a first-order approximation to a more general production function. But this procedure requires us to estimate three parameters (or more, if we include proxies for variable utilization) for the output elasticities using data that are often multicollinear, and also subject to differing degrees of endogeneity and hence differing OLS biases. The use of instrumental variables is not a complete solution, since most plausible instruments are relatively weak. The literature on weak instruments suggests that instrumental-variables methods have difficulty with multiple parameters; see, for example, Shea (1997).

Second, one can impose cost minimization and estimate equations (9) or (10), while still taking a first-order approximation. Cost minimization is a relatively weak condition, and seems likely to hold at least approximately. Imposing it allows us to move from estimating three parameters to estimating only one (the markup), thus increasing efficiency. (Of course, assuming a particular model of cost minimization, if it is inappropriate, can lead to specification error. For example, if firms are *not* price takers in factor markets—for example, if firms have monopsony power or, in general, face price-quantity schedules for their inputs rather than single prices—then cost-minimizing conditions, and hence the Hall equations [9] or [10], are misspecified.)

In this case, one simply assumes that the shares used in constructing dx_i are constant, as is the markup, μ_j. As with the first approach, if our interest is in first-order properties such as average markups or returns to scale, it can in principle give an accurate answer, although the omitted second-order terms may well be important. (Risk aversion is a second-order phenomenon, but there is an active insurance industry.) A substantial advantage of the first-order approach is that it does not require that observed factor prices (or rental rates) be allocative in every period. The average shares are likely to be close to the steady-state shares, so the approximation typically will be correct even with quasi-fixed inputs or implicit contracts.

Third, one could continue to estimate equations (9) or (10), but allow the shares to change period by period. If markups are constant, if factor prices are allocative period by period, and if there are no quasi-fixed factors, then this approach can, in principle, give a second-order approximation to any production function (Diewert 1976). If these conditions fail, then this approach in essence incorporates some second-order effects, but not others; it is unclear whether this is preferable to including none of them.

Fourth, one could estimate a flexible, general functional form along with Euler equations for the quasi-fixed inputs; as Nadiri and Prucha (this volume) discuss, this approach provides a complete second-order approximation to any production technology. If we properly parameterize the firm's problem, then the markup need not be constant, and factors can be quasi-fixed—the model provides estimates of the true shadow values. In principle, this full structural approach provides a complete characterization of the technology; one can then calculate elasticities of substitution, biases of technological change, and so forth. For some macroeconomic questions, these parameters are crucial.[10]

However, this general approach has the disadvantage that one needs to estimate many parameters (a translog production function for equation [1], for example, has twenty-five parameters before imposing restrictions, to say nothing of the associated Euler equations). Efficient estimation requires various restrictions and identifying assumptions, such as estimating the first-order conditions (equation [7]) along with the production function itself. Hence, results may be sensitive to misspecification. For example, if wages are determined by an implicit contract, and hence are not allocative period by period, then one would not want an approach that relies heavily on high-frequency changes in observed factor prices (and hence factor shares) for identification. The structural approach can be estimated either through the production or cost function—that is, from the primal or the dual side. Our concerns apply to both. We discuss these issues at greater length in section 7.2.3.

Since our primary interest is in measures of technical change, average returns to scale, and the average markup, in this paper we follow the second approach outlined above, using an explicitly first-order approximation. (In practice, this gives qualitatively similar results to the third approach, which allows the factor shares to vary over time). This second method is essentially the procedure of Hall (1990), generalized to include materials input and controls for variable factor utilization. Although this approach allows us to estimate the parameters governing firm-level technology and behavior, our ultimate interest is describing the evolution of aggregates. Thus, we must take one more step and aggregate output growth across firms.

7.1.4 Aggregation

So far, we have discussed production and estimation in terms of firm-level gross output. Our ultimate interest is in aggregate value added. In general, no aggregate production function exists that links aggregate output to aggregate inputs—but the relationship between these aggregates remains of interest. It turns out that aggregation across firms can introduce a significant new source of procyclical productivity.

---

10. For example, a recent strand of business-cycle theory emphasizes the cyclical properties of markups as important propagation mechanisms for output fluctuations; see, for example, Rotemberg and Woodford (1992, 1995). Time-series variation in the markup is a second-order property that can only be estimated with a second-order (or higher) approximation to the production function.

In section 7.3, we derive the following equation for aggregate output (value added) growth dv:

(11) $$dv = \bar{\mu}^V dx^V + du + R + dt^V.$$

$\bar{\mu}^V$ is the average "value added" markup across firms, du is an appropriately weighted average of firm-level utilization rates, R represents various reallocation (or aggregation) effects, and dt^V is an appropriately weighted average of firm-level technology. dx^V is an weighted average of the aggregate capital stock and labor hours. In all cases, the superscript V refers the fact that aggregate output is a value-added measure rather than a gross-output measure, which requires some minor changes in definitions. (As we discuss in section 7.3, for macroeconomic modeling it is the "value-added markup" that is likely to be of interest.)

The major implication of equation (11) is that output growth at the aggregate level is not completely analogous to output growth at the firm level. The firm-level equation (9) looks similar to equation (11). Firm-level output growth depends on input growth, the markup, variations in utilization, and technical change; aggregate output growth depends on aggregate input growth, the average markup, average variation in utilization, and average technical change. Equation (11), however, has a qualitatively new term, R.

The reallocation term reflects the effect on output growth of differences across uses in the (social) values of the marginal products of inputs. Output growth therefore depends on the distribution of input growth as well as on its mean: If inputs grow rapidly in firms where they have above-average marginal products, output grows rapidly as well. Thus, aggregate productivity growth is not just firm-level productivity growth writ large. There are qualitatively new effects at the aggregate level, which may be important both for estimating firm-level parameters and as powerful amplification and propagation mechanisms in their own right.

For example, suppose that some firms have large markups of price over marginal cost while others have low markups. Also suppose that all firms pay the same prices for their factors. Then resources such as labor have a higher marginal product in the firms with the larger markup, as shown by the first-order condition (equation [8]). Intuitively, because these firms have market power, they produce too little output and employ too few resources; hence, the social value of the marginal product of these inputs is higher. The reallocation term R captures the fact that aggregate output rises if resources shift from low- to high-markup firms.

To summarize this section, we argue in favor of the following approach to estimating technology change, controlling for utilization. First, interpret all results as first-order approximations, on the grounds that the data are probably insufficient to allow reliable estimation of second-order approximations. Second, estimate equation (10)—a Hall (1990)-style regression with a theoretically justified utilization proxy—at a disaggregated level. Take the residuals as a measure of disaggregated technology change. Third, use the aggregation equation (11)—which incorporates the disaggregated estimates of technology change, markups, and utilization—to identify the importance of the various explanations for procyclical productivity.

The casual reader is now well prepared to proceed to the data and empirical sections of this paper in sections 7.4 and 7.5. However, our discussion passed quickly over several technical details. To fully justify our choice of method, it is useful to address those issues in detail. We do so in sections 7.2 and 7.3.

7.2 The Meaning and Measurement of Capacity Utilization

Section 7.1 raised several issues with empirical implementation of the Solow-Hall approach to estimating technology, markups, and variations in utilization at a disaggregated level. First, we must decide what prices to use in calculating weights. With quasi-fixed inputs, the appropriate shadow price is not, in general, the observed factor price. In addition, even if factors are freely variable, the observed factor prices may not be allocative: For example, firms and workers may have implicit contracts. Second, we must decide whether to use a first- or second-order approximation to the continuous time equation (10). Third, we must find suitable proxies for du.

This section provides explicit microfoundations for our preferred approach. We specify a dynamic cost-minimization problem to provide appropriate shadow values. We then discuss the pros and cons of first- versus second-order approximations. Finally, we use the first-order conditions from the cost minimization problem to find observable proxies for unobserved effort and capital utilization.

We argue in favor of using an explicitly first-order approximation for the estimating equation, on the grounds that the data necessary for an appropriate second-order approximation are unavailable. We also argue for using growth in hours per worker to adjust for variations in effort and capital utilization. We also spend some time clarifying conceptual confusions over the meaning of capacity utilization. In particular, we argue that correcting for capacity utilization requires correcting quantities, not merely output elasticities.

7.2.1 A Dynamic Cost-Minimization Problem

We now specify a particular dynamic cost-minimization problem. Although the problem is relatively complicated, specifying it provides insight into several practical issues in attempting to estimate equation (10) in the previous subsection, and, in section 7.2.4, provides proxies for unobserved utilization.

We model the firm as facing adjustment costs in both investment and hiring, so that both the amount of capital (number of machines and buildings), K, and employment (number of workers), N, are quasi-fixed. We model quasi-fixity for two reasons. First, we want to examine the effect of quasi-fixity per se on estimates of production function parameters and firm behavior. Second, quasi-fixity is necessary for a meaningful model of variable factor utilization. Higher utilization must be more costly to the firm, otherwise factors would always be fully utilized. If there were no cost to increasing the rate of investment or hiring, firms would always keep utilization at its minimum level and vary inputs using only the extensive margin, hiring and firing workers and capital costlessly. Only if it is costly to adjust along the extensive margin is it sensible to adjust along the intensive margin, and pay the costs of higher utilization.[11]

We assume that the number of hours per week for each worker, H, can vary freely, with no adjustment cost. In addition, both capital and labor have freely variable utilization rates. For both capital and labor, the benefit of higher utilization is its multiplication of effective inputs. We assume the major cost of increasing capital utilization, Z, is that firms may have to pay a shift premium (a higher base wage) to compensate employees for working at night, or at other undesirable times.[12] We take Z to be a continuous variable for simplicity, although variations in the workday of capital (i.e., the number of shifts) are perhaps the most plausible reason for variations in utilization. The variable-shifts model has had considerable empirical success in manufacturing data, where, for a short period of time, one can observe the number of shifts directly.[13] The cost of higher labor utilization, E, is a higher disutility on the part of workers that must be compensated with a higher wage. We allow for the possibility that this wage is unobserved from period to period, as might be the case if wage payments are governed by an implicit contract in a long-term relationship.

Consider the following cost minimization problem for the representative firm of an industry:

---

11. One does not require *internal* adjustment costs to model variable factor utilization in an aggregative model (see, e.g., Burnside and Eichenbaum, 1996), because changes in input demand on the part of the representative firm change the aggregate real wage and interest rate, so in effect the concavity of the representative consumer's utility function acts as an adjustment cost that is *external* to the firm. However, if one wants to model the behavior of firms that vary utilization in response to idiosyncratic changes in technology or demand—obviously the case in the real world—then one is forced to posit the existence of internal adjustment costs in order to have a coherent model of variable factor utilization. (Both of these observations are found in Haavelmo's 1960 treatment of investment.)

12. Our model can be extended easily to allow utilization to affect the rate at which capital depreciates, as in Basu and Kimball (1997). We consider the simpler case for ease of exposition. Nadiri and Prucha (this vol.) show that their approach of estimating a second-order approximation to the production function can also accommodate variable depreciation, but do not consider either a shift premium or variable labor effort.

13. See, for example, Beaulieu and Mattey (1998) and Shapiro (1996).

(12) $$\min_{Z,E,H,M,I,A} C(Y) = \int_0^\infty e^{-\int_0^s r d\tau}[WNG(H,E)V(Z) + P_M M$$
$$+ WN\Psi(A/N) + P_I KJ(I/K)]ds$$

subject to

(13) $$Y = F(ZK, EHN, M, T)$$

(14) $$\dot{K} = I - \delta K$$

(15) $$\dot{N} = A$$

The production function and inputs are as before. In addition, I is gross investment, and A is hiring net of separations. $WG(H,E)V(Z)$ is total compensation per worker (compensation may take the form of an implicit contract, and hence not be observed period by period). W is the base wage; the function G specifies how the hourly wage depends on effort, E, and the length of the workday, H; and $V(Z)$ is the shift premium. $WN\Psi(A/N)$ is the total cost of changing the number of employees; $P_I KJ(I/K)$ is the total cost of investment; P_M is the price of materials; and δ is the rate of depreciation. We continue to omit time subscripts for clarity.

Using a perfect-foresight model amounts to making a certainty equivalence approximation. However, even departures from certainty equivalence should not disturb the key results, which rely only on intratemporal optimization conditions rather than intertemporal ones.

We assume that Ψ, and J are convex and make the appropriate technical assumptions on G in the spirit of convexity and normality.[14] It is also helpful to make some normalizations in relation to the normal or steady-state levels of the variables. Let $J(\delta) = \delta$, $J'(\delta) = 1$, $\Psi(0) = 0$. We also assume that the marginal employment adjustment cost is zero at a constant level of employment: $\Psi'(0) = 0$.

We use the standard current-value Hamiltonian to solve the representative firm's problem. Let λ, q, and θ be the multipliers on the constraints in equations (13), (14), and (15), respectively. Numerical subscripts denote derivatives of the production function F with respect to its first, second, and third arguments, and literal subscripts denote derivatives of the labor cost function G. The six intratemporal first-order conditions for cost-minimization are

(16) $$Z: \quad \lambda K F_1(ZK, EHN, M; T) = WNG(H, E)V'(Z).$$

(17) $$H: \quad \lambda ENF_2(ZK, EHN, M; T) = WNG_H(H, E)V(Z)$$

---

14. The conditions on G are easiest to state in terms of the function Φ defined by $\ln G(H, E) = \Phi(\ln H, \ln E)$. Convex Φ guarantees a global optimum; assuming $\Phi_{11} > \Phi_{12}$ and $\Phi_{22} > \Phi_{12}$ ensures that optimal H and E move together.

(18) $\quad E: \quad \lambda HNF_2(ZK, EHN, M; T) = WNG_E(H, E)V(Z)$

(19) $\quad M: \quad \lambda F_3(ZK, EHN, M; T) = P_M$

(20) $\quad A: \quad \theta = W\Psi'(A/N)$

(21) $\quad I: \quad q = P_I J'(I/K).$

The Euler equations for the capital stock and employment are

(22) $\quad \dot{q} = (r + \delta)q - \lambda Z F_1 + P_I[J(I/K) - (I/K)J'(I/K)]$

(23) $\quad \dot{\theta} = r\theta - \lambda EHF_2 + WG(H, E)V(Z)$
$\quad\quad + W[\Psi(A/N) - (A/N)\Psi'(A/N)].$

Since λ is the Lagrange multiplier associated with the level of output, one can interpret it as marginal cost. The firm internally values output at marginal cost, so λF_1 is the marginal value product of effective capital input, λF_2 is the marginal value product of effective labor input, and λF_3 is the marginal value product of materials input.[15] We defined the markup, μ, as the ratio of output price, and P, to marginal cost, so λ equals

(24) $$\lambda = C'(Y) = \frac{P}{\mu}.$$

Note that equation (24) is just a definition, not a theory determining the markup. The markup depends on the solution of the firm's more complex profit maximization problem, which we do not need to specify.

Equations (22) and (23) implicitly define the shadow (rental) prices of labor and capital:

(25) $\quad \lambda Z F_1 = (r + \delta)q - \dot{q} + P_I[J(I/K) - (I/K)J'(I/K)] \equiv P_K$

(26) $\quad \lambda EHF_2 = r\theta - \dot{\theta} + WG(H, E)V(Z)$
$\quad\quad + W[\Psi(A/N) - (A/N)\Psi'(A/N)] \equiv P_L.$

As usual, the firm equates the marginal value product of each input to its shadow price. Note that with these definitions of shadow prices, the atemporal first-order condition in equation (7) holds for all inputs. For some intuition, note that equation (25) is the standard first-order equation from a q-model of investment. In the absence of adjustment costs, the value of installed capital q equals the price of investment goods P_I, and the "price" of capital input is then just the standard Hall-Jorgenson cost of capital $(r + \delta)P_I$. With investment adjustment costs, there is potentially

---

15. For the standard static profit-maximization problem, of course, marginal cost equals marginal revenue, so these are also the marginal revenue products.

an extra return to owning capital, through capital gains $\dot{q}$ (as well as extra terms reflecting the fact that investing today raises the capital stock, and thus lowers adjustment costs in the future).

The intuition for labor in equation (26) is similar. Consider the case where labor can be adjusted freely, so that it is not quasi-fixed. Then adjustment costs ψ are always zero. So is the multiplier θ, since the constraint in equation (15) does not bind. In this case, as we expect, equation (26) says that the shadow price of labor input to the firm—the right side of the equation—just equals the (effort adjusted) compensation $WG(H, E)V(Z)$ received by the worker. Otherwise, the quasi-fixity implies that the shadow price of labor to a firm may differ from the compensation received by the worker.

7.2.2 First-Order Approximations

We now turn to issues of estimation. This subsection discusses how to implement our preferred first-order approximation; the next subsection compares this approach with second-order approximations.

Equations (6) and (9) hold exactly in continuous time, where the values of the output elasticities adjust continuously. In discrete time, we can interpret these equations as first-order approximations (in logs) to any general production function if we assume the elasticities are constant. For a consistent first-order approximation to equation (9), one should interpret it as representing small deviations from a steady-state growth path, and evaluate derivatives of the production function at the steady-state values of the variables. Thus, to calculate the shares in equation (9), one should use steady-state prices and quantities, and hence treat the shares as constant over time. The markup is then also taken as constant.

For example, in the first order approach, we want the steady-state output elasticity for capital, up to the unknown scalar μ. Using asterisks to denote steady-state values, we use equations (21) and (25) and our normalizations to compute the steady-state output elasticity of capital:

$$(27) \quad \frac{F_1^* Z^* K^*}{Y^*} = \mu * \frac{P_K^* K^*}{P^* Y^*} \equiv \mu * \frac{(r^* + \delta) P_I^* K^*}{P^* Y^*}.$$

Note that the steady-state user cost of capital is the frictionless Hall-Jorgenson (1967) rental price.[16] Since quasi-fixity matters only for the adjustment to the steady state, in the steady state $q = P_I$ and $\dot{q} = 0$. Operationally, we calculate the Hall-Jorgenson user cost for each period and take the time average of the resulting shares as an approximation to the steady-state share. We proceed analogously for the other inputs. In the final esti-

---

16. In practice, one would also include various tax adjustments. We do so in the empirical work, but omit them in the model to keep the exposition simple.

mating equation for equation (9), we use logarithmic differences in place of output and input growth rates, and use steady-state shares for the weights.

Thus, we can construct the index of observable inputs, dx, and take the unknown μ^* multiplying it as a parameter to be estimated. We can use a variety of approaches to control for the unobserved du; we discuss some of them in section 7.2.4. Alternatively, under the heroic assumption that du is always zero or is uncorrelated with dx, we can estimate equation (9) while simply ignoring du. Hall (1988, 1990) and Basu and Fernald (1997a) follow this second procedure.

In any case, we have to use instruments that are orthogonal to the technology shock dt, since technology change is generally contemporaneously correlated with input use (observed or unobserved).[17]

7.2.3 Second-Order Approximations

The first-order approach of constant weights is, of course, equivalent to assuming that for small, stationary deviations from the steady-state balanced growth path, we can treat the production function as Cobb-Douglas. Parameters such as the average markup or degree of returns to scale are first-order properties, so the bias from taking a first-order approximation may not be large.

Nevertheless, the Cobb-Douglas assumption is almost surely not literally true. In principle, using a second-order approximation allows us to eliminate some of the bias in parameter estimates from using Cobb-Douglas and eliminate approximation errors that end up in the residual. It also allows us to estimate second-order properties of production functions, such as separability and elasticities of substitution. (Nadiri and Prucha, this volume) discuss the benefits of the second-order approach.) Unfortunately, the second order approach suffers severe practical disadvantages—particularly the increased likelihood of misspecification. Our view is that these sizeable disadvantages outweigh the potential benefits.

We begin this discussion with a simplest case where one obtains an appropriate second-order approximation to equation (9) simply by using weights that change period by period. Suppose the production function takes a more general form than Cobb-Douglas, for example, translog. With a more general production function, output elasticities will typically vary over time if relative factor prices are not constant. Also suppose the markup is constant, and that all factor shadow values (i.e., input prices) are observed, as will be the case if observed prices are allocative and there are no costs of adjusting inputs. With a translog function (which provides a flexible approximation to any functional form), the discrete-time Tornqvist

---

17. Olley and Pakes (1996) propose an insightful alternative to the usual instrumental-variables approach; see Griliches and Mairesse (1998) for an excellent discussion of the pros and cons.

approximation to the continuous time equation (9) turns out to be exactly correct.[18] This approximation requires replacing growth rates with log differences and replacing the continuous-time input shares with average shares in adjacent periods. Thus, for example, the output elasticity for capital is approximated by $(1/2)(s_{Kt} + s_{Kt-1})$, and is multiplied by the capital change term ($\ln K_t - \ln K_{t-1}$). In this case, using a Tornqvist index of input use allows a correct second-order approximation.

A major potential shortcoming with using changing shares is that observed factor prices may not be allocative period by period because of implicit contracts or quasi-fixity. Then observed factor shares might not be proportional to output elasticities period by period, and the Tornqvist index is misspecified.

A large literature has focused on the problem of quasi-fixity of capital and labor, while largely ignoring the concern about implicit contracts. We briefly review that approach to estimating second-order approximations. As discussed in the introduction, the time-varying elasticity literature—for example, Berndt and Fuss (1986), Hulten (1986), and the much more parametric literature surveyed in Nadiri and Prucha (this volume)—tries explicitly to deal with quasi-fixity. Quasi-fixity may lead to large variations in input shadow prices, which in turn may cause the output elasticities to vary over time.[19] The shadow prices may differ substantially from observed prices; in our cost-minimization setup of section 7.2.1, equations (25) and (26) show the relationship between shadow price and observed prices. For example, a firm may find that it has too many workers, so that the output elasticity with respect to labor is very low. If the firm cannot (or chooses not to) immediately shed labor, it will be forced to continue paying these workers. Then the observed labor share may be higher than the true output elasticity, since the shadow value of labor is less than the wage.

Hulten (1986) shows that even with quasi-fixity, if there are constant returns and perfect competition, then one can implement the Tornqvist approximation to equation (9) using observed input prices and output growth as long as there is only a single quasi-fixed input (e.g., capital). Under these conditions, the revenue shares sum to one. Since the observed input prices give the correct shares for all inputs other than capital, capital's share can be taken as a residual. (As we emphasize again below, this approach corrects only for variations in the shadow values of quasi-fixed inputs, not unobserved changes in the workweek of capital.)

18. This result follows from Diewert (1976), who shows that the Tornqvist index is "superlative"—that is, exact for functional forms such as the translog that are themselves flexible approximations to general functions—and shows that superlative indices have desirable index-number properties. For discussions of the concept of "flexibility" and its limitations, see Lau (1986) and Chambers (1988, ch. 5).

19. As our previous discussion indicates, the output elasticities will generally change whenever input prices (shadow values) change. Quasi-fixity is only one reason why shadow values change.

Multiple quasi-fixed inputs cannot be accommodated using the nonparametric approach of equation (9), but one can estimate the parameters of a structural cost function. Pindyck and Rotemberg (1983) and Shapiro (1986), for example, estimate particular parametric forms of the production function along with Euler equations for the quasi-fixed inputs, such as equations (22) and (23). As a by-product, this approach provides estimates of the shadow values of the state variables, and thus one can construct a measure of period-by-period shadow costs by valuing the input of each quasi-fixed factor at its shadow price.

The problem grows even more challenging when one allows for nonconstant returns to scale. Since one cannot estimate the scale elasticity from the first-order conditions for the cost shares (e.g., see Berndt 1991, chapter 9), one must estimate both the cost function and the share equations together. But output is a right-hand side variable in the cost function; since the error term is interpreted as technical change, output is clearly endogenous. Pindyck and Rotemberg (1983) deal with this problem by using lagged variables as instruments, but it is unclear to what extent this procedure alleviates the problem. For example, technical change—the error term in the cost function—can be (and usually is found to be) serially correlated. Finally, one can compute the markup from the estimates of returns to scale (in this context, a time-varying parameter) by using equation (5) and the observed prices and estimated shadow prices to construct a period-by-period estimate of economic profit.

Morrison (1992a,b) attempts to construct better instruments by estimating industry demand curves embodying shift variables and then imputes values of output using the simple, static, monopoly pricing formula for the markup. However, there are also major problems with this procedure. First and most importantly, it implies that μ is no longer identified from cost minimization conditions alone; one has to subscribe to a particular model of firm behavior and use profit maximization conditions as well. This change is a major loss in generality. Second, Morrison's specific model of firm behavior assumes that firms can collude perfectly in every period and that prices are completely flexible, and hence is misspecified if the degree of collusion varies (as stressed, e.g., by Rotemberg and Saloner 1986 and Green and Porter 1984), or if prices are sticky in the short run, leading the actual markup to deviate from the optimal markup (see, e.g., Ball and Romer 1990 and Kimball 1995).

The challenges raised by these issues suggest that misspecification is a serious concern. Even in the best of cases, where factor prices for variable factors are correctly observed and utilization does not vary, one needs to specify correctly the problem and constraints and then estimate a large number of parameters. This complexity makes misspecification harder to spot.

Of course, this best of cases is unlikely to hold, so misspecification is probably much worse. First, we have strong reasons to think that input prices observed by the econometrician may *not* be allocative period by period because of implicit contracts. Since many economic relationships are long term, it may not be worth recontracting explicitly period by period. Then the correct shadow price of a variable input may differ from its observed price. The shadow prices may satisfy the first-order conditions period by period, while the observed factor payments may satisfy the conditions only on average. With implicit contracts, the data that are available hinder accurate estimation of a second-order approximation—even if the full problem and constraints were correctly specified.[20]

Second, variations in capacity utilization—that is, in labor effort E and capital's utilization/workweek Z—also lead to misspecification. Since these utilization margins are not observed by the econometrician, they remain as omitted variables in estimating a fully parametric production function. Using the dual approach does not help. In specifying the cost function, one needs to specify what margins the firm can use to adjust—and at what price. But it is virtually impossible for the econometrician to correctly observe the "prices" of varying effort or shifts to a firm. For example, Bils (1987) discusses the importance of the premium paid for overtime work. The wage function $G(H, E)$ in section 7.2.1 incorporates any overtime premium. However, the fully parameterized dual approach generally prices labor at the average wage rather than the correct marginal wage. Hence, the fully parameterized production or cost functions are almost surely misspecified.

The misspecification arising from omitted capacity utilization is sometimes obscured by the parameterized second-order literature, in part because that literature sometimes claims to solve the utilization problem. They are addressing a different issue. That is, there are two distinct concepts of utilization in the literature: what we call capacity utilization, and the Berndt-Fuss concern that inputs may not always be at their steady-state levels.

The Berndt-Fuss notion of utilization addresses the possible time-variation in output elasticities caused by time-varying shadow prices of quasi-fixed inputs. Capacity utilization, on the other hand, refers to the much earlier idea that there is a particular type of measurement error in the inputs: Certain factors—again, notably capital and labor—have variable service flow per unit of observed input (the dollar value of machinery or the number of hours worked). Many commentators have explained the

---

20. Carlton (1983) also stresses that observed materials prices may not be allocative if firms use delivery lags to clear markets. A similar problem arises from labor composition changes. Solon, Barsky, and Parker (1994) find that the marginal worker in a boom is of relatively low quality—and hence relatively low paid—so that if labor data do not adjust for this composition effect, the wage will appear spuriously countercyclical. Cost-function estimation that uses spuriously cyclical wage data is, of course, misspecified.

procyclicality of productivity and the short-run increasing returns to labor (SRIRL) puzzle by arguing that variations in the workweek of capital and changes in labor effort increase effective inputs much more than observed inputs. In terms of equation (9), they argue that du is nonzero, and is positively correlated with dy and dx.

It is easy to see the difference between the two concepts in the case where F is actually known to be a Cobb-Douglas production function. Since the elasticities are truly constant over time, the first-order discrete-time implementation of equation (9) is exact. The *observed* factor shares might vary over time, but since we know that F is Cobb-Douglas, these variations would reflect the effects of quasi-fixity rather than changes in output elasticities. Quasi-fixity of inputs thus creates no problems for estimation, since one can observe and use the steady-state prices and shares. Indeed, the Berndt-Fuss approach would "correct" the time-varying shares, using constant shares instead. Despite this correction, variations in factor utilization remains a problem. If one cannot somehow control for du, then estimates of the markup or returns to scale will generally be biased.

Formally, therefore, the problems posed by quasi-fixity are second order. If the first-order approximation of Cobb-Douglas is actually exact, then quasi-fixity—or, more generally, time-varying elasticities—cannot matter for the estimation of μ. On the other hand, capacity utilization remains a first-order problem, since it concerns the measurement of the right-hand-side variables. It continues to pose a problem even if the Cobb-Douglas approximation holds exactly.

The two concepts are often confused because, as we argued above, quasi-fixity is a necessary condition for capacity utilization to vary. As a result, the shadow value of an extra worker will be high at exactly the same time that unobserved effort is high. Because of this relationship, some authors in the production-function literature assert that the capacity utilization problem can be solved by allowing elasticities to vary over time, or by using a dual approach and allowing shadow values to vary from long-run equilibrium levels. Many of these authors do not appear to realize that there are two separate problems, and allowing for quasi-fixity does not solve the problem that the workweek of capital or the effort of workers may vary over time.[21] That is, there is no reason that the shadow value computed from a misspecified variable cost function will necessarily capture all of the effects of variable utilization.

We conclude this section by returning to the first-order approach. In

---

21. The survey by Nadiri and Prucha (this vol.) does try to address both issues. They focus primarily on the issue of time-varying elasticities. However, they also allow capital's workweek to vary, where the cost of increasing capital utilization is "wear and tear"—capital depreciates faster. They do not consider either a shift premium or variable labor effort (or the consequent problem that observed wages may not be allocative).

particular, though estimation using second-order approximations is likely to be misspecified, the problems that approach addresses—such as quasi-fixity—are clearly concerns. So given these concerns, how robust is the first-order approach that ignores them?

It is plausible that the first-order approach is relatively robust. That is, ignoring quasi-fixity probably does not significantly affect estimates of markups and returns to scale. First, quasi-fixity affects only the period-by-period computation of input shares, not the growth rate of capital (or any other quasi-fixed input). Since these shares are constant to a first-order Taylor approximation, any errors caused by failure to track the movements of the shares is likely to be small. Second, quasi-fixity is likely to be most important for capital. (Shapiro 1986 finds that quasi-fixity is not important for production-worker labor, although it is present for nonproduction workers). But mismeasurement of the rental rate of capital affects only capital's share, and since the growth rate of capital is almost uncorrelated with the business cycle, errors in measuring capital's share are unlikely to cause significant biases in a study of cyclical productivity. Caballero and Lyons (1989) present simulations indicating that maximum biases from ignoring quasi-fixity of capital are likely to be on the order of 3 percent of the estimated coefficients. (However, capital utilization *is* cyclical, and it is also multiplied by capital's share.)

In sum, the second-order approach offers great theoretical advantages that, in practice, it cannot deliver. The failures are understandable, since the problems are difficult. Given these practical difficulties, we prefer the explicitly first-order approach to estimation. This has costs as well, such as ignoring quasi-fixity for estimation purposes and the inability to estimate elasticities of substitution, time variation in the markup, and other second-order properties. Nevertheless, results on first-order properties are likely to be relatively robust.

7.2.4 Capacity Utilization

Before we can estimate μ from equation (9), we need to settle on a method for dealing with changes in utilization, du. A priori reasoning—and comparisons between results that control for du and those that do not—argue that du is most likely positively correlated with dx; thus ignoring it leads to an upward-biased estimate of μ^*. Three general methods have been proposed. First, one can try to observe du directly using, say, data on shiftwork. When possible this option is clearly the preferred one, but data availability often precludes its use.[22] Second, one can impose a priori restrictions on the production function. Third, one can derive links

---

22. In the United States, shift-work data are available only for a relatively short time period, and solely for manufacturing industries. The only data set on worker effort that we know of is the survey of British manufacturing firms used by Schor (1987).

between the unobserved du and observable variables using first-order conditions like equations (16)–(21). Both the second and third approaches imply links between the unobserved du and observable variables, which can be used to control for changes in utilization.

The approach based on a priori restrictions basically imposes separability assumptions on the production function. For example, Jorgenson and Griliches (1967) use an idea going back at least to Flux (1913), and assume that effective capital input is a function of capital services and energy (this idea has recently been revived by Burnside, Eichenbaum, and Rebelo 1995; we henceforth refer to it as the Flux assumption). To clarify this idea, it will be useful to separate intermediate goods M into two components: the flow of energy inputs, W (mnemonic: Wattage); and all other intermediate inputs O (mnemonic: Other). Then the Flux assumption implies:

$$(28) \qquad F(\tilde{K}, EHN, W, O; T) = G[S(\tilde{K}, W), EHN, O; T].$$

Jorgenson-Griliches and Burnside and colleagues generally also assume that

$$(29) \qquad S(\tilde{K}, W) = \min[\tilde{K}, W],$$

so that energy input is a perfect index of capital input.[23]

Using this implication of equation (29) to substitute into equation (9), we have

$$(30) \quad \begin{aligned} dy &= \mu[s_K(dk + dz) + s_L(dn + dh + de) + s_W dw + s_o do] + dt \\ &= \mu[(s_K + s_W)dw + s_L(dn + dh) + s_o do] + \mu s_L de + dt. \end{aligned}$$

Note that under the maintained hypothesis of equation (28), electricity use proxies for changes in capital utilization, but does not capture variations in labor effort. (The same is true if one uses direct observations on utilization, like the number of shifts.) Electricity use is also a much more sensible proxy for the utilization of heavy machinery than for the services of structures or light machinery like computers, which are often left on day and night regardless of use. Thus, electricity use is probably a reasonable proxy only within manufacturing—and even there it does not capture variations in effort.

Basu (1996) attempts to control for both labor effort and capital utilization by using either of two different separability assumptions:

---

23. Burnside et al. (1995) also experiment with a CES functional form for H, and allow the ratio of capital to energy to change depending on their relative prices. The generalization to the CES does not affect their results significantly, but their measures of the rental price of capital services are questionable.

(31) $$F(ZK, EHN, W, O; T) = TG[V(ZK, EHN), S(W, O)],$$

or

(32) $$F(ZK, EHN, W, O; T) = TG[V(ZK, W, EHN), S(O)].$$

In both cases, he assumes that G takes the Leontief form:[24]

(33) $$G(V, S) = \min(V, S).$$

The basic intuition behind the separability assumption is the distinction between the materials inputs that are being used up in production and the inputs that are assembling the materials into final output. In the simplest case, equation (32), the estimating equation is just

(34) $$dy = \mu do + dt.$$

Under the maintained hypothesis of equation (33), variations in materials use capture changes in both capital and labor utilization.

A problem with separability-based methods of controlling for utilization is that they rely crucially on the assumption that the production function is homothetic (i.e., relative input demands do not depend on the level of output).[25] In other words, it is important that the function S in the Flux case or the functions V and S in the Basu case all be homogenous of degree one. Basu (1996) discusses this issue in detail, and argues that if homotheticity does not hold (or if one does not take additional steps), the estimated values of μ from equations (30) and (34) are likely to be biased downward. With this caveat, however, the intuitive approaches presented here offer relatively easy ways to control for changes in utilization.

Bils and Cho (1994), Burnside and Eichenbaum (1996), and Basu and Kimball (1997) argue that one can also control for variable utilization using the relationships between observed and unobserved variables implied by first-order conditions like equations (16)–(21). Our discussion follows Basu and Kimball.

They begin by assuming a generalized Cobb-Douglas production function,

(35) $$F(ZK, EHN, M; Z) = Z\Gamma[(ZK)^{\alpha_K}(EHN)^{\alpha_L}M^{\alpha_M}],$$

where Γ is a monotonically increasing function. In their case this assumption is not merely a first-order approximation, because they make use of the second-order properties of equation (35), particularly the fact that the ratios of output elasticities are constant. Although they argue that one can relax the Cobb-Douglas assumption, we shall maintain it throughout our discussion.

---

24. Basu also experiments with CES specifications for G, but allowing deviations from the Leontief assumption has little effect on his estimates.

25. See Chambers (1988) for a discussion of homotheticity.

Equations (17) and (18) can be combined into an equation implicitly relating E and H:

$$(36) \quad \frac{HG_H(H,E)}{G(H,E)} = \frac{EG_E(H,E)}{G(H,E)}.$$

The elasticity of labor costs with respect to H and E must be equal, because on the benefit side the elasticities of effective labor input with respect to H and E are equal. Given the assumptions on G, (36) implies a unique, upward-sloping E-H expansion path, so that we can write

$$(37) \quad E = E(H), \quad E'(H) > 0.$$

Equation (37) says that the unobservable intensity of labor utilization E can be expressed as a monotonically increasing function of the observed number of hours per worker H. This result also holds in growth rates; thus,

$$(38) \quad d\ln(EHN) = dn + dh + de = dn + (1 + \zeta)dh.$$

Finding the marginal product of labor from equation (35) and substituting into the first-order condition for hours per worker, equation (17), we find

$$(39) \quad WNH\, G_H(H,E)V(U) = \lambda \gamma \alpha_L Y.$$

Substituting the marginal product of capital and equation (39) into equation (16) yields

$$(40) \quad \lambda \gamma \alpha_K \frac{Y}{Z} = \lambda \gamma \alpha_L Y \frac{G(H,E)}{HG_H(H,E)} \frac{V'(Z)}{V(Z)}.$$

Define

$$(41) \quad g(H) = \frac{HG_H(H,E(H))}{G(H,E(H))}$$

and

$$(42) \quad v(Z) = \frac{ZV'(Z)}{V(Z)}.$$

$v(Z)$ is thus the ratio of the marginal shift premium to the average shift premium. Rearranging, we get

$$(43) \quad 1 = \frac{\alpha_L}{\alpha_K} \frac{v(Z)}{g(H)}.$$

The labor cost elasticity with respect to hours given by the function $g(H)$ is positive and increasing by the assumptions we have made on $G(H,E)$. The labor cost elasticity with respect to capital utilization given by the function $v(Z)$ is positive as long as there is a positive shift premium. We also assume that the shift premium increases rapidly enough with Z to make the elasticity increasing in Z.

First, define

$$\eta = \frac{H^*g'(H^*)}{g(H^*)}, \tag{44}$$

and

$$v = \frac{Z^*v'(Z^*)}{v(Z^*)}. \tag{45}$$

η indicates the rate at which the elasticity of labor costs with respect to hours increases. v indicates the rate at which the elasticity of labor costs with respect to capital utilization increases. Using this notation, the log-linearization of equation (45) is simply[26]

$$dz = \frac{\eta}{v}dh. \tag{46}$$

Thus, equations (46) and (38) say that the change in hours per worker should be a proxy for changes in both unobservable labor effort and the unmeasured workweek of capital. The reason that hours per worker proxies for capital utilization as well as labor effort is that shift premia create a link between capital hours and labor compensation. The shift premium is most worth paying when the marginal hourly cost of labor is high relative to its average cost, which is the time when hours per worker are also high.

Putting everything together, we have an estimating equation that controls for variable utilization

$$dy = \mu^*dx + \mu^*\left(\zeta s_L + \frac{\eta}{v}s_K\right)dh + dt. \tag{47}$$

This specification controls for both labor and capital utilization, without making special assumptions about separability or homotheticity. However, for our simple derivation, the Cobb-Douglas functional form is important. As we have noted before, our model can be generalized to allow depreciation to depend on capital utilization. This modification would introduce two new terms into the estimating equation (47), as in Basu and Kimball (1997).

---

26. This equation is where the Cobb-Douglas assumption matters. Basu and Kimball differentiate (35) assuming that α_L/α_K is a constant. Their theory allows for the fully general case where the ratio of the elasticities is a function of all four input quantities, but they argue that pursuing this approach would demand too much of the data and the instruments.

7.3 Aggregation over Firms[27]

Sections 7.1 and 7.2 emphasize production and estimation in terms of firm-level gross output. Section 7.1 also provided an overview of the relationship between firm-level gross output measures and aggregate value-added measures. In this section, we derive and interpret this relationship in greater detail. We aggregate in two steps. First, we relate firm-level gross output to value added. Second, we aggregate over firm-level value added. We then provide an economic interpretation of the various terms in the aggregation equation. We conclude by discussing how aggregation could spuriously generate apparent external effects across firms or industries.

The discussion highlights the potential pitfalls of using value added directly as a production measure. A long literature from the 1970s (see, for example, Bruno 1978) also argues against the use of value added, but on very different grounds. That literature emphasized the strong separability assumptions necessary for the existence of a stable value-added function. By contrast, our argument against value added does not rely on separability, which is a second-order property of the production function. Instead, we point out that value added is akin to a partial Solow residual, subtracting from gross output growth the growth in intermediates, weighted by their share in revenue. Firms equate revenue shares to output elasticities only with perfect competition. Hence, with imperfect competition, some of the productive contribution of intermediate inputs remains in measured value-added growth—a first-order issue that applies regardless of whether separability holds or fails.

7.3.1 The Conversion to Value Added

Measures of real value added attempt to subtract from gross output the productive contribution of intermediate goods. Hence, gross output is shoes, while value added is "shoes lacking leather, made without power" (Domar 1961, 716), or books without paper or ink.

Despite its unobservable and perhaps unintuitive nature at a firm level, we focus on value added for two reasons. First, discussing firm-level value added turns out to be a useful intermediate step in moving between firm-level gross output and aggregate value added. Second, many researchers use data on value added for empirical work, and the results in this section shed light on the (de)merits of that approach.

Nominal value added, $P^V V$, is defined unambiguously: $P^V V = PY - P_M M$. It is less clear how to decompose nominal value added into price and quantity: We must subtract real intermediate inputs from gross output in some way, but several methods are possible.

For the national accounting identity to hold, one must deflate nominal

---

27. The appendix contains detailed derivations of the equations in this section.

value added with the same method used to deflate nominal final expenditure (Sato 1976). Since the national accounts now use chain-linked indexes, we follow suit here. In particular, we use the continuous time analogue to a discrete-time chain-linked index, and define value added at a firm level, dv_i, using the standard Divisia definition[28]

$$(48) \qquad dv_i \equiv \frac{dy_i - s_{Mi} dm_i}{1 - s_{Mi}}.$$

After substituting input for output growth from equation (9), we can write this as

$$(49) \quad dv_i = \mu_i(dx_i^V + du_i) + (\mu_i - 1)\frac{s_{Mi}}{1 - s_{Mi}} dm_i + \frac{dt_i}{1 - s_{Mi}},$$

where primary input growth, dx_i^V, is defined analogously to aggregate primary input growth

$$(50) \qquad dx_i^V = \frac{s_{Ki}}{1 - s_{Mi}} dk_i + \frac{s_{Li}}{1 - s_{Mi}} dl_i \equiv s_{Ki}^V dk_i + s_{Li}^V dl_i,$$

The main implication of equation (49) is that value-added growth is not, in general, simply a function of primary inputs dx_i^V. Value-added growth is calculated by subtracting from gross output the revenue-share-weighted contribution of intermediate goods. With markups, however, the output elasticity of intermediate inputs ($\mu_i s_{Mi}$) exceeds its revenue share. Hence, some of the contribution of materials and energy is attributed to value added; that is, value-added growth does not subtract off the full productive contribution of intermediate inputs. This extra productive contribution affects value-added growth.

Of course, value-added growth could still be a function of primary-input growth alone, to the extent that intermediate inputs move together with primary inputs. To explore this possibility, it is useful to rewrite equation (49) in the following way (the appendix shows the algebra)

$$(51) \quad dv_i = \mu_i^V dx_i^V + (\mu_i^V - 1)\left[\frac{s_{Mi}}{1 - s_{Mi}}\right](dm_i - dy_i) + \mu_i^V du_i + dt_i^V,$$

where

---

28. See Sato (1976). Until recently, the national accounts used a Laspeyres index for the expenditure side of GDP. That is, each component is valued using base-year prices, and then components are added. The national accounts identity then implied that one needed a Laspeyres or double-deflated index for real value added: $V^{DD} = Y - M$, where gross output Y and intermediate inputs M are valued in base-year prices. The chain-linked index gives cleaner results for productivity analysis, although the basic conclusions are unchanged. See the appendix to Basu and Fernald (1995).

$$(52) \quad \mu_i^V \equiv \mu_i \left[\frac{1 - s_{Mi}}{1 - \mu_i s_{Mi}} \right]$$

$$(53) \quad dt_i^V \equiv \frac{dt_i}{1 - \mu_i s_{Mi}}.$$

A useful benchmark case is where intermediate inputs are used in fixed proportions to output; this assumption is implicit in most dynamic general equilibrium models with imperfect competition (see, e.g., Rotemberg and Woodford 1995). With fixed proportions, equation (52) shows that value-added growth is, indeed, a function of primary inputs alone. The "value-added markup" μ_i^V, defined by equation (52), includes the productive contribution of primary inputs as well as the extra contribution of intermediates. Hence, if μ_i is greater than one, the value-added markup μ_i^V exceeds the gross-output markup μ_i. Nevertheless, equation (51) makes clear that with imperfect competition, if the assumption of fixed proportions fails, then value-added growth depends on the growth rate of the ratio of intermediate inputs to output.

The value-added markup is plausibly the appropriate concept for calibrating the markup charged by the representative firm in a one-sector macroeconomic model (see Rotemberg and Woodford 1995). The reason is that small markups at a plant level may translate into larger efficiency losses for the economy overall, because of "markups on markups." That is, firms buy intermediate goods from other firms at a markup, add value, and again price the resulting good with a markup, generally selling some of it to another firm to use as an intermediate good. We explore this (and other) intuition in greater detail in the appendix.

That the intensity of intermediate-input use affects value-added growth underlies our argument that the right approach to estimating even the value-added markup is to use gross-output data. Without making any auxiliary assumptions about whether materials are used in fixed coefficients, one can estimate (a utilization-corrected) μ from equation (10), and then transform it into its value-added analogue using equation (52). (Note that value added remains appropriate as a national accounting concept, because the wedge between the cost and marginal product of intermediate inputs represents actual goods and services available to society—it's just that we cannot in general allocate its production to primary inputs of capital and labor.)

The firm's revenue-weighted, value-added productivity residual, dp_i, equals $dv_i - dx_i^V$. Hence,

$$(54) \quad dp_i = (\mu_i^V - 1)dx_i^V + (\mu_i^V - 1) \left[\frac{s_{Mi}}{1 - s_{Mi}} \right](dm_i - dy_i) + \mu_i^V du_i + dt_i^V.$$

A long literature in the 1970s explored whether a value-added function exists (see, e.g., Bruno 1978) and argued that the answer depends on separability properties of the production function. The equation above shows that with imperfect competition, taking value added to be a function only of primary inputs is generally misspecified regardless of whether the production function is separable between value added and intermediate inputs. Separability is a second-order property of a production function, so its presence or absence does not affect first-order approximations like equations (49) and (51). However, the fact that the output elasticity of materials is $\mu_i s_{Mi}$ instead of simply s_{Mi} is of first-order importance.

7.3.2 Aggregation

We define aggregate inputs as simple sums of firm-level quantities.

$$K \equiv \sum_{i=1}^{N} K_i$$

$$L \equiv \sum_{i=1}^{N} L_i$$

For simplicity, we assume that there is one type of capital and one type of labor. (This can be relaxed easily.)

In principle, different firms may face different shadow prices for a homogeneous input; this will generally be the case if some inputs are quasi-fixed. For any input J, let P_{Ji} be the shadow price it pays to rent or hire the input for one period; differences across firms in shadow prices could reflect factor-price differences or else adjustment costs, as in section 7.2. We define the aggregate (rental) prices of capital and labor as implicit deflators—that is, total factor payments divided by aggregate quantities.

$$(55) \qquad P_K \equiv \frac{\sum_{i=1}^{N} P_{Ki} K_i}{K}$$

$$(56) \qquad P_L \equiv \frac{\sum_{i=1}^{N} P_{Li} L_i}{L}$$

We use the standard Divisia definition of aggregate output. This measure weights goods by market prices and hence avoids substitution bias in the aggregate output and price indices. Divisia aggregates are defined most naturally in growth rates, and we denote the growth in aggregate output (equivalently, aggregate value added) by dv. From the national accounting identity, one can define aggregate output in terms of either production (aggregating value added over firms) or expenditure (aggregating sales for consumption, investment, government purchases, or export). Welfare (discussed in section 7.6) uses the expenditure side; production (emphasized so far) relates to the value-added side. From the production side, aggregate output is a Divisia index of firm-level value added. In growth rates

$$(57) \qquad dv = \sum_{i=1}^{N} w_i dv_i,$$

where w_i is the firm's share of nominal value added

$$w_i = \frac{P_i^V V_i}{P^V V}.$$

We can now substitute in from equation (51) for dv_i. Substantial algebraic manipulation (shown in the appendix) yields our basic aggregation equation

$$(58) \qquad dv = \bar{\mu}^V dx^V + du + R + dt^V,$$

where

$$(59) \qquad dx^V = \left(\frac{P_L L}{P^V V}\right) dl + \left(\frac{P_K K}{P^V V}\right) dk \equiv s_L^V dl + s_K^V dk,$$

$$\bar{\mu}^V = \sum_{i=1}^{N} w_i \mu_i^V,$$

$$du = \sum_{i=1}^{N} w_i \mu_i^V du_i, \text{ and}$$

$$dt^V = \sum_{i=1}^{N} w_i dt_i^V.$$

dx^V is growth in aggregate primary inputs, $\bar{\mu}^V$ is the average firm value-added markup, du is average firm utilization growth (weighted by markups), and dt^V is average value-added technology change. R represents various reallocation effects

$$(60) \qquad R = R_\mu + R_M + \bar{\mu}^V R_K + \bar{\mu}^V R_L,$$

where

$$(61) \qquad R_\mu = \sum_{i=1}^{N} w_i(\mu_i^V - \bar{\mu}^V) dx_i^V,$$

$$R_M = \sum_{i=1}^{N} w_i(\mu_i^V - 1)\left[\frac{s_{Mi}}{1 - s_{Mi}}\right](dm_i - dy_i),$$

$$R_K = \sum_{i=1}^{N} w_i s_{Ki}^V \left[\frac{P_{Ki} - P_K}{P_{Ki}}\right] dk_i, \text{ and}$$

$$R_L = \sum_{i=1}^{N} w_i s_{Li}^V \left[\frac{P_{Li} - P_L}{P_{Li}}\right] dl.$$

Note that aggregate utilization du from equation (59) is the weighted average of firm-level value-added utilization. It is a value-added measure, since it is a form of primary input, albeit one that is unobserved. Since it is multiplied by value-added returns to scale, it captures the full effect on aggregate output of a change in utilization, incorporating both the contribution of a change in the unobserved *quantity* of input, and the contribution of the markup. (As with primary inputs, we could have separated this into a term reflecting the "average" markup and a "reallocation of the markup" term, but since our main interest in utilization is on the total effect, it is simpler to keep them together.)

Aggregate productivity growth is the difference between the growth rates of aggregate output, dv, and aggregate inputs, dx^V

(62) $$dp \equiv dv - dx^V.$$

Note that this is a modified Solow residual, since the input weights in dx^V need not sum to one. The shares are factor payments in total nominal value added, and sum to one only if there are no economic profits. Thus

(63) $$dp = (\bar{\mu}^V - 1)dx^V + du + R + dt^V.$$

Equation (63) shows the distinction between aggregate productivity and aggregate technology. If all firms are perfectly competitive, pay the same price for factors (perhaps reflecting perfect factor mobility), and do not vary utilization, then all terms other than dt^V disappear: Productivity equals technology. However, with imperfect competition or frictions in product or factor markets, productivity and technology are not equivalent.[29]

7.3.3 Productivity Interpretation of Reallocation Terms

Aggregate output combines goods using market prices, which in turn measure consumers' relative valuations. Suppose we want to know how much consumers (and, therefore, usually society) value having a marginal input allocated to a particular firm (which we assume produces a single good). That valuation equals the good's price times the factor's marginal product: $P_i F_{Ji}$. The first-order condition in equation (7) shows that this valuation equals the firm's markup times the input price paid by the firm: $\mu_i P_{Ji}$. If markups or input prices differ across firms, then the marginal "social value" of inputs also differs across firms. R_μ, R_K, and R_L reflect shifts of resources among uses with different marginal social values.

Consider the markup-reallocation term, R_μ. By definition, the markup represents the wedge between the value consumers place on the good—that is, its price—and its marginal cost. Reallocating resources from low-

---

[29]. Jorgenson, Gollop, and Fraumeni (1987) derive an equation for the case of case of constant returns to scale and perfect competition, so they omit the terms other than R_K and R_L. They also allow for heterogeneity in capital and labor, which we have ignored for simplicity. With heterogeneity, our results generalize easily: For example, if R_{Kk} is the factor-price reallocation term for capital of type k, then $R_K = \Sigma_k R_{Kk}$.

to high-markup firms thus shifts resources towards uses where consumers value them more highly. If the variability of firms' inputs are correlated with their market power, then imperfect competition affects aggregate productivity even if the average markup is small. For example, Basu and Fernald (1997a) estimate that durable goods industries have larger returns to scale and markups than nondurable goods industries. Durable industries are more cyclical, and employ a larger share of the marginal inputs in a boom. This marginal reallocation thus contributes to the procyclicality of aggregate productivity.

Now consider the input-reallocation terms R_K and R_L. Shifting labor from firms where it has a low shadow value to firms where it has a high shadow value increases aggregate output. Why might shadow values (or wages) differ across firms? First, labor may not be instantaneously mobile across sectors; sectoral shifts may lead workers in, say, defense industries to have lower marginal products than they would in health-care.[30] Second, efficiency wage considerations may be more important in some industries than others, as emphasized by Katz and Summers (1989). Third, unions with monopoly power might choose to charge different wages to different firms. Whatever the reason, shifting labor to more productive uses increases aggregate output, even if total input does not change.

Note that the first reason, costly factor mobility, is completely consistent with constant returns and perfect competition. Differences in marginal products that reflect factor immobility should be temporary—that is, P_K as defined in equation (25) should not differ persistently from the Hall-Jorgenson cost of capital, and P_L as defined in equation (26) should not differ persistently from the firm's compensation payments (see Berndt and Fuss 1986). With costly factor adjustment, these shadow values may differ substantially; hence reallocation effects on output and productivity may be significant, even in a world with perfect competition and constant returns.[31]

The materials-reallocation term, R_M, reflects the extent to which measured real value added depends on the intensity of intermediate-input use. Firm-level value added is useful for national accounting, regardless of technology or market structure. However, with imperfect competition, value-added growth does not subtract off the full marginal product of intermediate inputs. Growth in primary inputs captures some of this productive contribution (which is why μ_i^V differs from μ_i), but some wedge may

---

30. Whether differences in labor's marginal product lead to differences in wages depends on whether the adjustment costs are paid by workers or firms.

31. The "sectoral shifts" literature takes this approach; see, for example, Phelan and Trejos (1996). Horvath (1995) also incorporates adjustment costs into a dynamic general equilibrium model, generating effects on aggregate productivity from input reallocations. Microeconomic productivity literature (e.g., Baily, Hulten, and Campbell 1992) finds that there are systematic productivity level differences across firms within narrowly defined industries; to the extent these productivity differences are not measurement error, they show up either as higher profits from a higher markup, and hence are reflected in R_μ, or higher factor payments, and hence are reflected in R_K and R_L.

remain. R_M equals the sum of these wedges. It represents real goods and services, and hence affects aggregate output and productivity.

Note that R_M depends on the size of markups in firms *using* materials. Consider an economy where some firms produce intermediate goods using capital and labor, and other firms assemble intermediate goods into final goods (e.g., Beaudry and Devereux 1994). The importance of R_M depends on the size (and heterogeneity) of markups in the *final goods* industry. This is important because firms may be able to negotiate multi-part prices with long-term suppliers of their inputs, and thus partially offset the inefficiencies resulting from imperfect competition in intermediate goods industries.[32] The inefficiency in R_M, however, depends on markups in firms *using* intermediate goods, not those *selling* such goods; multipart pricing for intermediate goods does not eliminate this inefficiency. (However, the inefficiency is larger in symmetric models, such as Basu (1995), where all output is also used as materials input.)

7.3.4 The Definition of Technology Change

Conceptually, aggregate technology change measures the change in aggregate output in response to firm-level technology shocks, holding primary inputs fixed. Under what conditions does this correspond to our measure dt^V?

With constant returns and perfect competition, Domar (1961) and Hulten (1978) show that our definition properly measures the outward shift in society's production possibilities frontier (PPF) when firm-level technology changes. In figure 7.1 this case corresponds to point A, where society allocates resources optimally.

In this case, all of the μ_i equal 1, so this "Domar weighted measure" of aggregate technology equals

$$(64) \qquad dt^V = \sum_i w_i \frac{dt_i}{1 - s_{Mi}}.$$

Conceptually, Domar weighting converts gross-output technology shocks to a value-added basis by dividing through by the value-added share, $-s_M$. These shocks are then weighted by the firm's value-added share.

Even with imperfect competition, the Domar weighted measure correctly shows how much final output (the sum of value added over firms) increases, if all of the increase in gross output goes to final sales, with primary and intermediate inputs remaining unchanged. With perfect competition and perfect factor mobility, Domar weighting is correct even if inputs adjust. That is, the consequences for aggregate output and technology are the same whether the firm sells all of its additional output for

---

32. We thank Robert Hall for this observation.

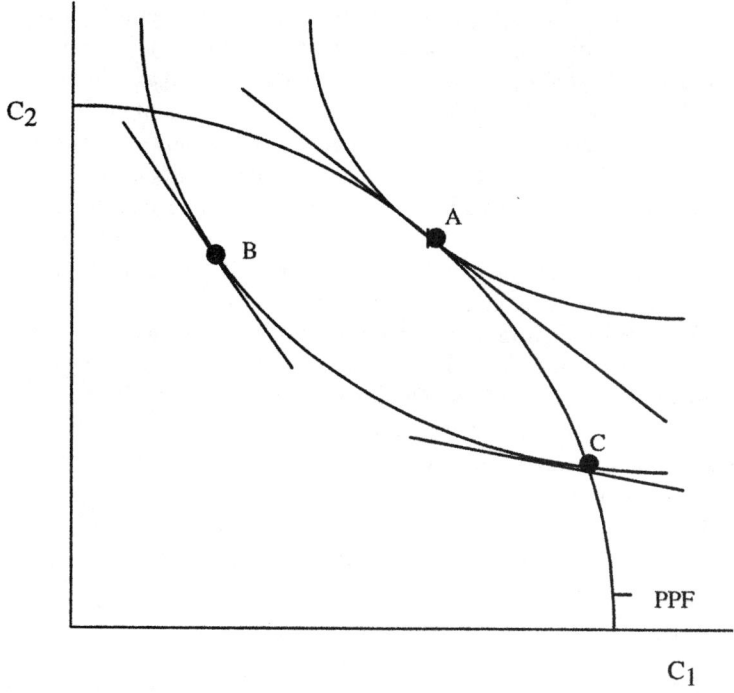

Fig. 7.1 Productivity and welfare

final consumption (with a valuation equal to its price), or instead sells the additional output to other producers, who in turn use the additional intermediate inputs (with a marginal product equated to the price) to produce goods for final consumption.

With imperfect competition, however, aggregate technology change is not unambiguously defined. The economy may produce inside its PPF, at a point like B in figure 7.1 or at an allocatively inefficient point on the PPF, like point C. At these points, the same firm-level technology shocks can affect the distribution of inputs across firms in different ways, and thus cause different changes in aggregate output. Imperfect competition or differences in factor payments across firms may lead the same factor to have a different social value for its marginal product in different uses. Hence, changes in the distribution of resources can affect aggregate output, even if there are no technology shocks and total inputs remain the same.

The definition in equation (59) is essentially a markup corrected measure. In terms of the gross-output shocks, it is equivalent to the following:

$$(65) \qquad dt^V = \sum_i w_i \frac{dt_i}{1 - \mu_i s_{Mi}}$$

This definition correctly measures the increase in aggregate output under standard conditions where an aggregate production function exists. Suppose there are no factor market frictions, and that all firms have the same separable gross-output production function, always use materials in fixed proportions to gross output, and charge the same markup of price over marginal cost. Under these assumptions, which are implicit or explicit in most dynamic general-equilibrium models with imperfect competition, there is a representative producer and an aggregate value-added production function (see, e.g., Rotemberg and Woodford 1995). In this case, aggregate technology change corresponds to our definition dt^V.

Qualitatively, the Domar weighted and markup corrected measures turn out to give very similar correlations between technology change and various business-cycle indicators. (One empirical note of caution is that concern the markup corrected measure is sometimes very sensitive to estimates of the markup. When we estimate μ_i for each sector, we hope that our estimates are unbiased. However, the estimate of value-added technology change in equation (53), $dt_i/(1 - \mu_i s_{Mi})$, is convex in μ_i. Hence, it overweights sectors where $\hat{\mu}_i$ exceeds μ_i, and underweights sectors where $\hat{\mu}_i$ is less than μ_i.)

7.3.5 Externalities

So far, we have discussed internal increasing returns but not Marshallian externalities. With such external effects, the economy might display aggregate increasing returns even if all firms produce with constant returns. Hence, one can model increasing returns without having to model imperfect competition. As a result, models of growth and business cycles use such externalities extensively (e.g., Romer 1986; Baxter and King 1991; Benhabib and Farmer 1994). Externalities are almost surely important for modeling economic growth, as suggested by the extensive R&D-spillover literature surveyed by Griliches (1992). High-frequency *demand* spillovers (as discussed in Cooper and John 1988) also seem eminently sensible. However, apart from Diamond (1982), few have proposed models of short-run *technological* spillovers that operate at high frequencies.

Caballero and Lyons (1992) argued, however, that a basic prediction of externality models is a robust feature of the data: Estimated returns to scale should rise at higher levels of aggregation, as the increasing returns become internalized. In other words, aggregate productivity should be more procyclical than would be implied by estimates of industry-level returns to scale. Thus, despite lacking a formal model of short-run external effects, they concluded that there is strong prima facie evidence for such externalities.

Caballero and Lyons (1990, 1992) proposed an empirical model to estimate any short-run externalities. They augmented a firm-level estimating equation like equation (10) with aggregate inputs as well as firm-level inputs. In practice, they used industry-level data on output and inputs, and added aggregate output to the estimating equation to capture any externalities that would otherwise be relegated to the error term, dt. They used NIPA data on real value added by industry. Thus, their basic estimating equation was essentially

$$dv_i = \mu_i^V dx_i^V + \beta dx^V + dt_i, \tag{66}$$

where i indexed a two-digit manufacturing industry, and dx^V was growth of aggregate capital and labor in manufacturing. (Their 1992 paper also included various utilization controls.) They found large, positive, and statistically-significant values of β in data from the United States and a number of European countries.

Numerous authors have questioned the interpretation and robustness of the Caballero-Lyons's results. For example, their results may reflect inappropriate data (Basu and Fernald 1995; Griliches and Klette 1996), incorrect econometric method (Burnside 1996), or inadequate utilization proxies (Sbordone 1997).

Nevertheless, even if one can dismiss their interpretation, the stylized fact remains that productivity is more procyclical at higher levels of aggregation. However, equation (63) suggests an alternative explanation of the Caballero-Lyons stylized fact. Aggregate productivity is more procyclical because the reallocation terms, R, are procyclical. Thus, we can explain the Caballero-Lyons stylized fact based only on firm-level heterogeneity, without invoking external effects that have questionable theoretical basis in the business cycle context. Indeed, we note that the one well-known economic model of short-run externalities, Diamond's (1982) search model, relies on increasing returns to scale in the "matching function" that produces new hires as a function of economy-wide vacancies and unemployment. Efforts to estimate this matching function directly (e.g., Blanchard and Diamond 1990), however, show that it exhibits approximately constant returns to scale, not large increasing returns. Thus, in the absence of any direct evidence for *short-run* externalities, we do not model them explicitly in this paper.[33]

7.4 Data and Method

7.4.1 Data

We now construct a measure of "true" aggregate technology change and explore its properties. As discussed in section 7.1, we estimate technology

---

[33]. The search for short-run spillovers remains an active area of ongoing research. See, for example, Bartelsman, Caballero, and Lyons (1994), Cooper and Johri (1997), and Paul and Siegel (1999).

change at a disaggregated level, and then aggregate using the theory in section 7.3. Our aggregate is the private U.S. economy, and our "firms" are thirty-three industries; for manufacturing, these industries correspond roughly to the two-digit Standard Industrial Classification (SIC) level.

Given that each industry includes thousands of firms, it may seem odd to take industries as firms. Unfortunately, no firm-level data sets span the economy. In principle, we could focus on a subset of the economy, using, say, the Longitudinal Research Database. However, narrowing the focus requires sacrificing a macroeconomic perspective, as well as panel length and data quality. By focusing on aggregates, our paper complements existing work that uses small subsets of the economy.[34]

We use data compiled by Dale Jorgenson and Barbara Fraumeni on industry-level inputs and outputs. These data comprise gross output and inputs of capital, labor, energy, and materials for a panel of thirty-three private industries (including twenty-one manufacturing industries) that cover the entire U.S. nonfarm private economy. These sectoral accounts seek to provide accounts that are, to the extent possible, consistent with the economic theory of production. (For a complete description of the dataset, see Jorgenson, Gollop, and Fraumeni 1987.) These data are available from 1947 to 1989; in our empirical work, however, we restrict our sample to 1950 to 1989, since our money shock instrument (described below) is not available for previous years.

We weight growth rates (measured as log changes) of capital, labor, and intermediate inputs using the *average* shares in revenue over the entire period. To compute capital's share, s_K, for each industry, we construct a series for required payments to capital. Following Hall and Jorgenson (1967) and Hall (1990), we estimate the user cost of capital C. For any type of capital, the required payment is then $CP_K K$, where $P_K K$ is the current-dollar value of the stock of this type of capital. In each sector, we use data on the current value of the fifty-one types of capital, plus land and inventories, distinguished by the BEA in constructing the national product accounts. Hence, for each of these fifty-three assets, indexed by s, the user cost of capital is

$$(67) \qquad C_s = (r + \delta_s)\frac{(1 - ITC_s - \tau d_s)}{(1 - \tau)}, \quad s = 1 \text{ to } 53.$$

r is the required rate of return on capital, and δ_s is the depreciation rate for assets of type s. ITC_s is the asset-specific investment tax credit, τ is the corporate tax rate, and d_s is the asset-specific present value of depreciation allowances. We follow Hall (1990) in assuming that the real required re-

---

34. See, for example, Baily et al. (1992), Haltiwanger (1997), Bartelsman and Dhrymes (1998), and Foster, Haltiwanger, and Krizan (this vol.). The aggregation theory in section 7.3 implies that our industry data include various intra-industry reallocation terms, including the analogous terms to R_μ, R_K, and R_L.

turn r equals the dividend yield on the S&P 500. Jorgenson and Yun (1991) provide data on ITC_s and d_s for each type of capital good. Given required payments to capital, computing s_K is straightforward.

As discussed in section 7.1, we require instruments uncorrelated with technology change. We use two of the Hall-Ramey instruments: the growth rate of the price of oil deflated by the GDP deflator and the growth rate of real government defense spending.[35] (We use the contemporaneous value and one lag of each instrument.) We also use a version of the instrument used by Burnside (1996): quarterly Federal Reserve "policy shocks" from an identified Vector Autoregression. We sum the four quarterly policy shocks in year $t - 1$ as instruments for year t.[36]

7.4.2 Estimating Technology Change

To estimate firm-level technology change, we estimate a version of equation (10) for each industry. Although we could estimate these equations separately for each industry (and indeed do so as a check on results), some parameters—particularly on the utilization proxies—are then estimated rather imprecisely. To mitigate this problem, we combine industries into four groups, estimating equations that restrict the utilization parameters to be constant within industry groups.

As discussed in section 7.2, this estimating equation corresponds to the special case where the cost of higher capital utilization is a shift premium. In that case, variations in hours per worker fully captures variations in capital utilization and effort. Thus, for each group we have

$$(68) \qquad dy_i = c_i + \mu_i dx_i + adh_i + dt_i.$$

The markup μ_i differs by industries within a group (Burnside 1996 argues for allowing this variation). The groups are durables manufacturing (eleven industries); nondurables manufacturing (ten); mining and petroleum extraction (four); and all others, mainly services and utilities (eight). To avoid the transmission problem of correlation between technology

---

35. We drop the third instrument, the political party of the President, because it appears to have little relevance in any industry. Burnside (1996) shows that the oil price instrument is generally quite relevant, and defense spending explains a sizeable fraction of input changes in the durable-goods industries.

36. The qualitative features of the results in section 7.3 appear robust to using different combinations and lags of the instruments. On a priori grounds, the set we choose seems preferable to alternatives—all of the variables have strong grounds for being included. In addition, the set we choose has the best overall fit (measured by mean and median F statistic) of the a priori plausible combinations we considered. Of course, Hall, Rudebusch, and Wilcox (1996) argue that with weak instruments, one does not necessarily want to choose the instruments that happen to fit best in sample; for example, if the "true" relevance of all the instruments is equal, the ones that by chance fit best in sample are in fact those with the largest small sample bias. That case is probably not a major concern here, since the instrument set we choose fits well for all industry groupings; for example, it is the one we would choose based on a rule of, say, using the instruments that fit best in durables industries as instruments for nondurables industries, and vice versa.

shocks and input use, we estimate each system using Three-Stage Least Squares, using the instruments noted above.

After estimating equation (68), we take the sum of the industry-specific constant c_i and residual $d\hat{t}_t$ as our measure of technology change in the gross-output production function. We then insert these industry estimates in the aggregation equation (63), derived in section 7.3. Note that this aggregation equation is an accounting identity. It allows us to decompose aggregate productivity into a technological component plus various non-technological components, including the effects of markups and various reallocations.

One problem in implementing the decomposition is that we may not, in fact, observe period-by-period the appropriate "shadow" factor prices P_{Li} and P_{Ki} defined by equations (25) and (26). We deal with this problem by taking an explicitly first-order approach to the estimating equation in equation (68), using fixed weights on capital and labor in constructing dx_i. (It is straightforward, though it requires some care, to ensure that the aggregation equation (63) remains an accounting identity with fixed weights.) This approach is unlikely to lead to major problems in estimating the markup and materials reallocation terms (R_μ and R_M) in the accounting identity, since those terms are driven primarily by changes in *quantities,* rather than changes in the weights (which, in turn, incorporate the shadow prices).

However, the inability to measure prices is a major problem for measuring the input reallocation terms (R_K and R_L), as those terms depend explicitly on differences in prices across sectors. Jorgenson, Gollop, and Fraumeni (1987) estimate these terms under the assumption that factor prices are allocative, and that there are zero profits in all sectors (so that they can "back out" capital's input P_K as a residual). Although we do not require these assumptions elsewhere, we will show summary statistics from Jorgenson and colleagues' estimates—we emphasize that these are meant to be suggestive only. Since the aggregation equation (63) is an accounting identity, changing our estimate of one component requires a change in other components as well. We then remove the effect of the input-reallocation terms from the average-markup term (a natural place to take it from, given appendix equation [A.17]). It is worth emphasizing that even if we mismeasure the input reallocation terms, this primarily affects our measurement of *other* nontechnological components of aggregate productivity. In particular, it does not directly affect our estimate of aggregate technology, which we built up from disaggregated residuals.

7.5 Results

We now investigate empirically why productivity is procyclical. We seek to identify the importance of (1) imperfect competition, (2) reallocations,

Table 7.1   **Descriptive Statistics for Technology Residuals**

	Mean	Standard Deviation	Minimum	Maximum
		A. Private Economy		
Solow residual	0.011	0.022	−0.044	0.066
Technology residual (no utilization correction)	0.012	0.016	−0.034	0.050
Technology residual (hours corrected)	0.013	0.013	−0.013	0.042
		B. Manufacturing		
Solow residual	0.023	0.035	−0.081	0.080
Technology residual (no utilization correction)	0.014	0.030	−0.085	0.072
Technology residual (hours corrected)	0.018	0.028	−0.030	0.082

Note: Sample period is 1950–89. The Solow residual is calculated using aggregate data alone. The two technology residuals are calculated by aggregating residuals from sectoral regressions of gross-output growth on input growth, as described in the text. The "hours corrected" residual corrects for variable utilization by including growth in hours per worker as a separate explanatory variable, in line with the theory developed in section 7.2.

and (3) variable utilization. Controlling for these influences allows us to move from aggregate productivity to aggregate technology. We then explore the cyclical properties of the "corrected" technology series.

We define aggregate productivity growth as the modified Solow residual defined in equation (62). This measure differs from the standard Solow residual since the revenue weights need not sum to one; the difference reflects economic profits or losses. However, we estimate that profits are small (about 3 percent on average, using our estimates of required payments to capital), so the results we report are essentially unchanged using the standard Solow residual instead.

Table 7.1 reports summary statistics for three series: the Solow residual; a series that makes no utilization corrections, but corrects only for aggregation biases; and a "technology" measure based on equation (68), which uses growth in hours per worker to correct for utilization. The first measure uses aggregate data alone. The other two are based on sectoral Solow-Hall–style regression residuals, as described in the previous section; these residuals are then aggregated using equation (63). Hence, aggregate technology change is the weighted sum of sectoral technology changes, as described in sections 7.1 and 7.3 (see equations [53] and [59]).

Panel A shows results for the entire nonfarm business economy. Our corrected series have about the same mean as the Solow residual. However, the variance is substantially smaller: The variance of the fully corrected series is less than one-third that of the Solow residual, so the standard deviation (shown in the second column) is only about 55 percent as large.

The reported minimums show that we do estimate negative technical change in some periods, but the lower variance of the technology series implies that the probability of negative estimates is much lower. For example, the Solow residual is negative in twelve out of forty years; the fully-corrected residual is negative in only five out of forty years.

Panel B gives results within manufacturing alone. Data within manufacturing (especially for output) are often considered more reliable than data outside manufacturing. In addition, some other papers (such as Burnside 1996) focus only on manufacturing, so these results provide a basis for comparison. The results are qualitatively similar to those for the aggregate economy.

Some simple plots and correlations summarize the comovement in our data: Output and inputs are strongly positively correlated, and all are positively correlated with the Solow residual. Figure 7.2 plots business cycle data for the nonfarm private economy: output (value-added) growth dv, primary input growth, dx^v, and the Solow residual dp (all series are demeaned). These series comove positively, quite strongly so in the case of dp and dv. Table 7.2 shows correlations for these three variables, as well as growth of total hours worked ($dh + dn$). Hours correlate more strongly with productivity than do total inputs, reflecting the low correlation of changes in the capital stock with the business cycle. The 95 percent confidence intervals show that all are significant.

Figure 7.3 plots our fully corrected technology series against these three variables. The top panel shows that technology fluctuates much less than

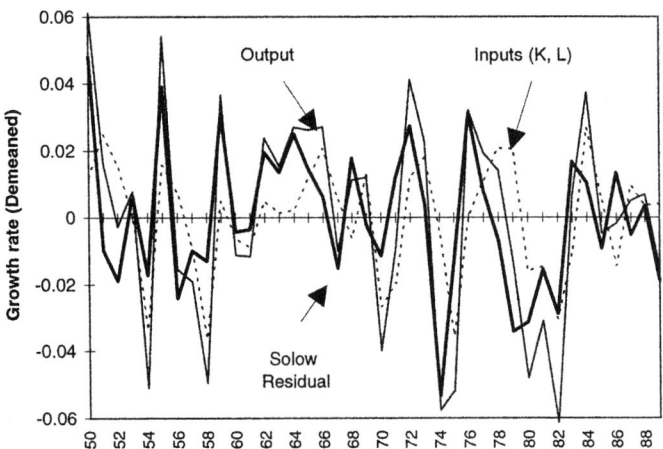

Fig. 7.2 Aggregate Solow residual, input growth, and output growth
Note: All series are demeaned. Sample period is 1950–89. Data is from Jorgenson, Gollop, and Fraumeni (1987). Inputs are a share weighted average of capital and labor growth.

Table 7.2 **Basic Data Correlations**

	Output Growth (dv)	Input Growth (dx^V)	Hours Growth ($dh+dn$)	Solow Residual
A. Private Economy				
Output growth (dv)	1			
Input growth (dx^V)	0.78	1		
	(0.62, 0.88)			
Hours growth ($dh+dn$)	0.80	0.91	1	
	(0.64, 0.89)	(0.83, 0.92)		
Solow residual	0.84	0.33	0.44	1
	(0.72, 0.91)	(0.02, 0.59)	(0.15, 0.66)	
B. Manufacturing				
Output growth (dv)	1			
Input growth (dx^V)	0.81	1		
	(0.66, 0.90)			
Hours growth ($dh+dn$)	0.86	0.98	1	
	(0.75, 0.92)	(0.96, 0.99)		
Solow residual	0.84	0.36	0.46	1
	(0.71, 0.91)	(0.05, 0.61)	(0.17, 0.68)	

Notes: 95 percent confidence intervals in parentheses, calculated using Fisher transformation. Sample period is 1950–89.

the Solow residual, consistent with intuition that nontechnological factors, such as variable input utilization, increase the volatility of the Solow residual. In addition, some periods show a phase shift: The Solow residual lags technology change by one to two years. This phase shift reflects the utilization correction. In our estimates, technology improvements are associated with low levels of utilization, thereby reducing the Solow residual relative to the technology series. The phase shift, in particular, appears to reflect primarily movements in hours per worker, which generally increase a year after a technology improvement. In the model from section 7.2, increases in hours per worker imply increases in unobserved effort, which in turn increase the Solow residual.

The middle panel plots aggregate value-added output growth (dv) against technology. There is no clear contemporaneous comovement between the two series although, again, the series appear to have a phase shift: Output comoves with technology, lagged one to two years.

Finally, the bottom panel plots the growth rate of primary inputs of capital and labor (dx^V) and the same technology series. These two series clearly comove negatively over the entire sample period.

Table 7.3 shows the correlations between our technology measures and business cycle variables. Panel A shows results for the aggregate private economy. With full corrections, the correlation of technology with output is about zero, and the correlations with inputs are strongly negative: −0.42

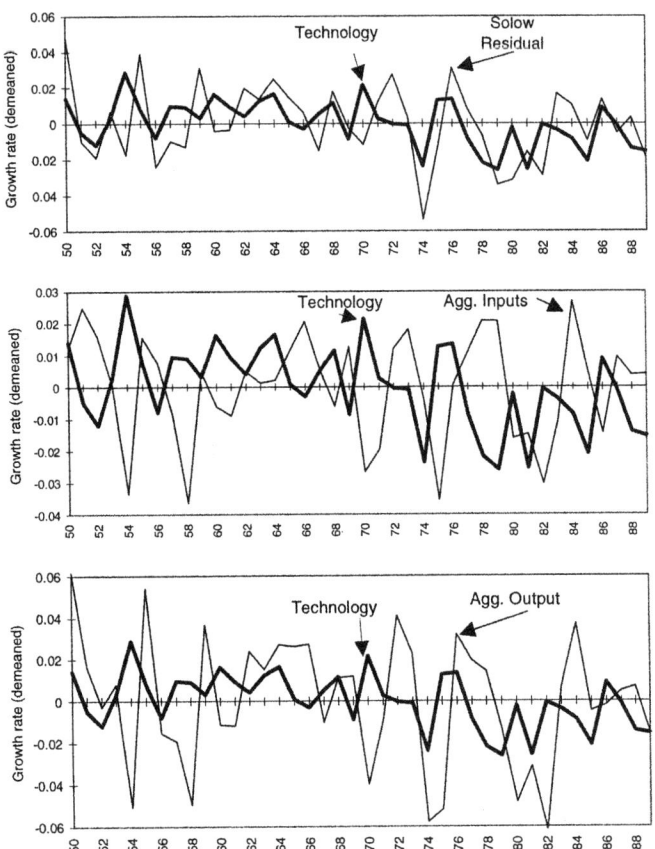

Fig. 7.3 Technology residual, Solow residual, output and input growth

Note: The technology series is the hours adjusted aggregate residual, which measures technology change (adjusted for variations in utilization) for the nonfarm business economy. Aggregate inputs are a share weighted average of capital and labor growth. All series are demeaned. Entries are log changes. Sample period is 1950–89.

for total primary inputs, and -0.44 for hours alone. Both correlations are statistically significantly negative at the 95 percent level.

The correlations with aggregate technology change differ sharply from those predicted by the usual RBC model (e.g., Cooley and Prescott 1995). In particular, in calibrated dynamic general equilibrium models with flexible prices, technology shocks generally cause a contemporaneous increase in both inputs and output. These kinds of standard, real business cycle models explore whether technology shocks lead to comovement that matches the stylized facts of business cycles. Given that the central stylized fact of business cycles is the comovement between inputs and output, if technology shocks drive the cycle then almost any sensible calibration implies that technology improvements increase inputs and output.

Table 7.3 Correlations of Technology Residuals with Basic Data

	Output Growth (dv)	Input Growth (dx^v)	Hours Growth ($dht+dn$)	Solow Residual
A. Private Economy				
Technology residual (no utilization correction)	0.46 (0.17, 0.68)	−0.12 (−0.41, 0.21)	−0.06 (−0.37, 0.26)	0.77 (0.63, 0.88)
Technology residual (hours corrected)	0.04 (−0.28, 0.35)	−0.42 (−0.65, −0.12)	−0.44 (−0.66, −0.14)	0.40 (0.10, 0.64)
B. Manufacturing				
Technology residual (no utilization correction)	0.42 (0.12, 0.65)	−0.14 (−0.44, 0.18)	−0.04 (−0.35, 0.28)	0.79 (0.63, 0.89)
Technology residual (hours corrected)	−0.40 (−0.64, 0.10)	−0.64 (−0.80, −0.41)	−0.62 (−0.78, −0.38)	−0.05 (−0.36, 0.27)

Notes: 95 percent confidence intervals in parentheses, calculated using Fisher transformation. Sample period is 1950–89. Technology residuals are calculated by aggregating residuals from sectoral regressions of gross-output growth on input growth, as described in the text. The "hours corrected" residual corrects for variable utilization by including growth in hours per worker as a separate explanatory variable.

Basu, Fernald, and Kimball (1999) explore the negative contemporary comovement between technology and input growth at length. They argue that this negative comovement is consistent with sticky price models. For example, suppose a firm's technology improves but the firm cannot change its price. If its demand curve does not change, then it cannot change its sales—but it can produce that same quantity with fewer inputs. Over time, of course, the firm (and economy) adjust to the technology change.

In terms of our accounting identities, what explains the movement away from a strong positive correlation? Figure 7.4 shows the our estimated utilization series—aggregated from the implicit utilization series for each industry using the equation for du from equation (59)—and our estimated reallocation series, both plotted against the Solow residual. Both utilization and reallocations are procyclical, as shown here by the positive comovement with the Solow residual. Each contributes about equally to generating the negative correlation. To see this, we first subtracted the

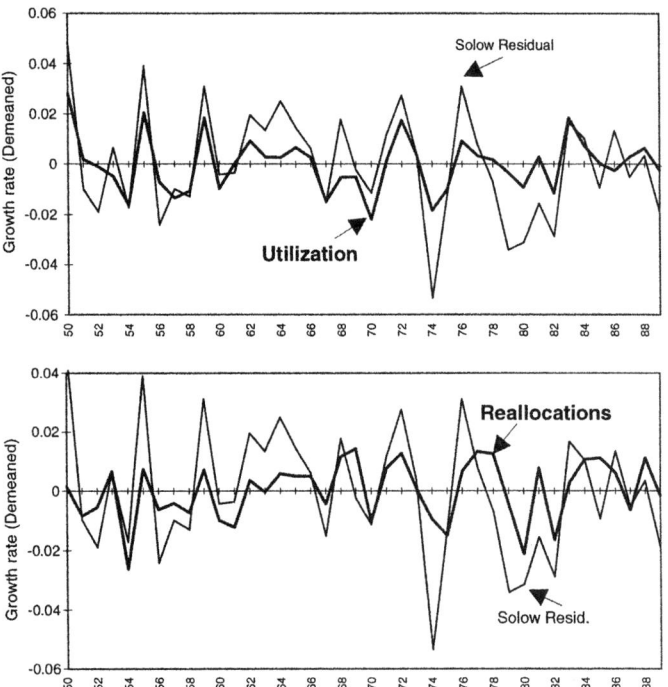

Fig. 7.4 Nontechnological adjustments to the Solow residual

Note: Aggregate utilization growth is a weighted average of estimated industry-level utilization growth (which includes the estimated markup for the industry). Estimated reallocations are the sum of R_μ (reallocations of inputs among industries with different markup estimates), R_M (reallocations of intermediate inputs), and R_K and R_L (reallocations of capital and labor among uses with different factor prices).

Table 7.4   Reallocation by Component, 1959–89 (instrumental variables estimates)

	R	R_μ	R_M	$\bar{\mu}^v R_K + \bar{\mu}^v R_L$
Mean	−0.11	−0.17	0.02	−0.03
Standard deviation	1.04	0.71	0.47	0.24
Minimum	−2.86	−2.05	−1.09	−0.51
Maximum	1.36	1.08	0.74	0.64

Notes: Entries are percentage points per year. R is the sum of the components shown in the columns to the right. R_μ is reallocations of inputs among industries with different markup estimates. R_M is reallocations of intermediate inputs. R_K and R_L are reallocations of capital and labor among uses with different factor prices, as calculated by Jorgenson and Fraumeni. See the text for further details.

estimated utilization change from the Solow residual; the correlation with inputs fell to about zero. Similarly, we then subtracted the estimated reallocation terms from the Solow residual; again, the correlation with inputs fell to about zero.

It is not surprising that utilization is procyclical. After all, utilization is a form of primary input, and inputs are procyclical. It is less obvious why reallocations are procyclical, as research at a highly disaggregated level—for example, using firms within a narrowly defined industry—finds that reallocations tend to be countercyclical.[37] Low productivity firms enter and expand disproportionately in booms, and contract or disappear disproportionately in recessions. Hence, within narrowly defined industries, reallocations appear to make aggregate productivity *less* cyclical, not more. (Because we use much more aggregated data on industries, these intra-industry reallocations will tend to appear as decreasing returns to scale or—given the close link between returns to scale and markups discussed in equation (5) of section 7.1—markups less than one.)

A different process clearly must be at work across aggregated industries. Table 7.4 presents summary statistics for the components of the reallocation terms from equation (61). (As discussed in the previous section, we obtained estimates of the capital and labor reallocation terms from Dale Jorgenson and Barbara Fraumeni.) None of these components has a sizeable mean, but they do have substantial standard deviations. R_μ and R_M are the most important components of the reallocation term. For the instrumented series, these terms have standard deviations of 0.72 and 0.51 respectively, compared with a total standard deviation of 1.11 for R. The sum of R_K and R_L is much less volatile. R_μ, in particular, comoves strongly with inputs, with a correlation of 0.7 with aggregate dx.

Why is R_μ so important over the cycle? Its variation reflects the fact that high-markup sectors tend to be more cyclical than average. Hence, in a boom, high-markup (and hence, high marginal product) firms produce a

---

37. See, for example, Foster, Haltiwanger, and Krizan, chapter 8 in this volume.

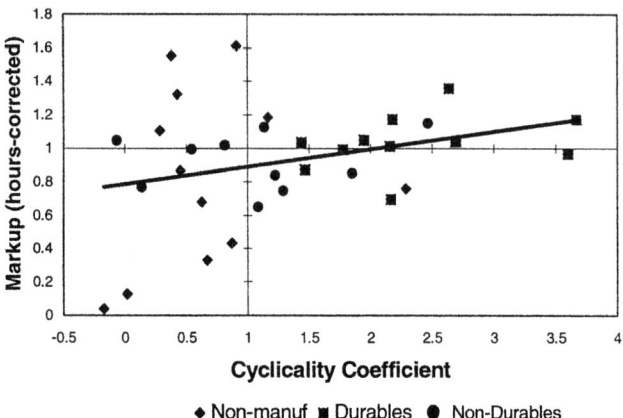

Fig. 7.5 Markups and cyclicality

Note: The horizontal axis shows the utilization corrected markup estimate by industry. The vertical axis shows the estimated cyclicality coefficient for the industry, estimated by regressing industry growth in primary inputs on aggregate growth in primary inputs.

disproportionate share of the marginal output. We can see this in figure 7.5, which shows estimates of the gross-output markup by industry, plotted against the relative cyclicality of the industry.[38] (The cyclicality was estimated by regressing $dx_i^V - dx^V$ on dx^V.) High markup industries tend to be durables manufacturing industries, which also tend to be the most cyclical. In a simulated DGE model, Basu, Fernald, and Horvath (1996) find that reallocations between durable and non-durable producers provide a significant propagation mechanism for shocks to the economy.

One might ask whether the reallocation effects we have identified represent the important gap between (utilization corrected) productivity and technology, or whether the difference between the two is still driven mostly by the "average markup" effect identified by Hall (1988, 1990). We compared our results to what we would have found had we used only the "average" correction, that is, that coming from the presence of the $(\bar{\mu}^V - 1)dx^V$ term. Using the correlations with dx^V as a benchmark, we found that the reallocation effects are the more important. For the OLS results, productivity corrected for the average effect would have yielded a correlation with input growth of 0.18, as opposed to 0.23 for the uncorrected series and 0.05 for our estimated technology series. For the section 7.4 results, the correlation would have been 0.12, as opposed to −0.13 for the estimated series. Thus, our reallocation effects are responsible for at least two-thirds

---

38. The mean markup in figure 7.5 is less than one. As Basu and Fernald (1997a) discuss, the average of sectoral estimates of gross-output markups is less than one, even though the average of value-added markups tends to be slightly greater than one. This primarily reflects the difference in weights used to aggregate the two.

of the correction. This result should not be surprising since, as we noted, the recent literature finds small average markups. Our results echo this finding: Without any utilization correction, we found $\overline{\mu}^V = 1.12$, for the hours-corrected case we found $\overline{\mu}^V = 1.05$. The surprising result is that even such small average markups are consistent with important differences between aggregate productivity and aggregate technology coming from reallocations across sectors.

7.6 Implications for Macroeconomics

7.6.1 Productivity as Welfare

Why is aggregate productivity growth interesting? The usual justification is Solow's (1957) proof that with constant returns to scale, perfect competition, and no frictions, it measures aggregate technology change. But in a world with distortions, is the Solow residual merely mismeasured technology?

In this section we summarize the argument of Basu and Fernald (1997b), who suggest that the answer is no. They show that productivity growth correctly computed from aggregate data (i.e., after eliminating the mismeasurement caused by changes in utilization) has a natural welfare interpretation, whether it also measures technology change. In particular, the modified aggregate Solow residual $(dp - dx^V)$ defined in section 7.3—which reduces to Solow's residual if there are no economic profits—measures welfare change for a representative consumer. This result holds even with imperfect competition in output markets and nonconstant returns to scale in production. Intuitively, growth in aggregate output measures the growth in society's ability to consume. To measure welfare change, we must then subtract the opportunity cost of the inputs used to produce this output growth. Input prices measure that cost, regardless of whether they also reflect marginal products. For example, increasing the stock of capital requires foregoing consumption, and the rental price of capital measures the consumer's opportunity cost of providing new capital, just as the wage measures the opportunity cost of providing extra labor. Proving our welfare result requires simply that consumers take prices parametrically. Hence, if productivity and technology differ, then it is productivity that most closely indexes welfare.

This conclusion is appealing for two reasons. First, it shows that productivity rather than, say, GDP, is the right measure of economic welfare under fairly general conditions. Second, it shows that even with distortions, policymakers can compute interesting quantities from aggregate data—we do not always need to calculate firm-level or aggregate technology change. In the short to medium run, productivity can change for reasons unrelated to technology change. Thus, even with distortions such as imperfect competition, when the aggregate Solow residual does not in general index technology change, it remains an excellent index of welfare change. Hence, it remains an appropriate target for policy, as well as a convenient indicator.

In section 7.3, we showed that aggregate technology change needs to be measured using disaggregated—ideally, firm-level—data. So why do aggregate data yield a meaningful measure of welfare change? The welfare properties of the Solow residual follow from the equality of relative market prices to the consumer's marginal rates of substitution (MRS) between goods; this includes the equality of the real wage to the MRS between goods and leisure. These equalities hold *even when market prices do not reflect the economy's marginal rate of transformation (MRT) between those goods.* Equivalently, we need only to investigate the expenditure side of the National Income and Product Accounts (NIPA) identity; we do not need to know the production technology of firms or the competitive structure of industries.

There are two qualifications to our argument. First, the ratio of factor prices may not equal the consumer's marginal rate of substitution: Taxes, for example, create a wedge between the two, since the wage paid by firms then differs from the wage received by households. The welfare interpretation of the residual requires factor prices received by households, but this modification is straightforward: All prices should be those perceived by the household. Second and more seriously, the representative-consumer assumption may fail. Consumers may have different marginal utilities of wealth or, as in standard efficiency-wage models or bargaining models, they may face different prices. In this case, one cannot compute aggregate welfare change from aggregate statistics alone. However, we do not claim that our proposed productivity measure is a completely general measure of welfare change, merely that it is one under much more general conditions than the usual Solow residual. It seems a particularly apt measure in the context of recent macroeconomic models with a representative consumer but with imperfect competition in product markets (e.g., Rotemberg and Woodford 1992, 1995), or with multiple sectors and costly factor reallocation (e.g., Ramey and Shapiro 1998).

Figure 7.1 shows the economic intuition underlying our argument. Suppose the economy produces two goods, both of which are consumed (and possibly also used as intermediate inputs). To keep the graph simple, assume that the supplies of capital and labor are fixed. The PPF depicts all feasible (C_1, C_2) pairs. An economy without distortions attains the social optimum at point A, supported by relative prices P_1/P_2. Now suppose there are distortions. Then the economy might be at an allocatively inefficient point on the PPF, like point B, or even within the PPF, like point C. As shown in figure 7.1, these outcomes can be supported by price ratios different from the MRT between C_1 and C_2.

Note that in all cases the consumer's budget line shows the economy's iso-output line, which aggregates heterogeneous output using market prices (regardless of whether these prices reflect technological tradeoffs.).[39] Thus, in this example welfare increases only if output increases. (This is a special case of our general result that welfare increases only if productivity increases, since in this example $dk = dl = 0$.) Hulten (1978) shows that under Solow's conditions—perfect competition and constant returns—aggregate productivity growth represents both technology improvement and welfare increase. In terms of figure 7.1, Hulten's result applies to an economy at point A: Output (productivity) can increase only if the PPF shifts out at point A, that is, if there is (local) technological improvement.

However, the same is not true at points B and C: Output (productivity) can increase without any change in technology, as long as distortions lessen. But these productivity improvements raise welfare, since output and inputs are weighted using prices that reflect the consumer's MRS between goods. Thus, Basu and Fernald's (1997b) finding generalizes Hulten's (1978) result to the case of imperfect competition and nonconstant returns, and clarifies the essence of his argument linking productivity and welfare.

7.6.2 Reallocations as Propagation Mechanisms

It is reasonable for practical macroeconomists to ask when and how they can avoid the perils posed by the nonexistence of an aggregate production function (even to a first-order approximation). It is also reasonable to ask whether the reallocation effects that lead to aggregation failures can also serve a positive function, by providing new amplification and propagation mechanisms in macro models. In this section we take a first pass at these large and difficult questions. Much of our intuition comes from the extended example of Basu and Fernald (1997a, section 5).

When can we ignore heterogeneity in production and act as if a representative firm produces all output? Doing so means modeling the production side of the economy using an aggregate production function for GDP. We ask three questions. First, is this procedure ever sensible if the world actually has significant heterogeneity? Second, what parameters should one use to calibrate the assumed aggregate production function? In particular, can one use estimates from aggregate data and ignore heterogeneity? Third, will the model with heterogeneity reproduce some of the interesting macroeconomic properties of the single-firm model it replaces?

We emphasize that in this subsection, as in the previous one, we abstract from variations in utilization. Capacity utilization is an important empirical issue, because it implies that certain inputs are unobserved by the econometrician. From the standpoint of theory, however, the possibility of changing utilization just changes the calibration of a model by changing

---

39. For a proof, differentiate the consumer's budget constraint holding income and prices fixed.

elasticities of supply and demand, but is not a qualitatively new effect. (For example, variable effort implies that the correct labor supply elasticity is larger than the usual data suggest; variable capital utilization implies that the labor demand curve is flatter than the standard production function would indicate.) In this section, by contrast, we ask whether reallocations of inputs constitute a qualitatively new propagation mechanism.

We now discuss whether a representative-firm model can capture the important features of a world where firms have approximately constant returns to scale, but where there are large reallocation effects. When it comes to fluctuations in output conditional on changes in aggregate inputs, the answer is often yes. The reason is that in many ways reallocations act like increasing returns to scale at a representative firm—in both cases, a one percent change in aggregate inputs is associated with a greater than one percent change in output. The major difference is that in the representative-firm economy, the degree of returns to scale is a structural parameter. In the economy with reallocations, however, the "effective returns to scale" depends on the nature of the reallocations induced by the driving shocks. Different shocks are likely to induce different degrees and types of reallocation, leading to variations in the effective returns to scale parameter under different circumstances—a classic example of the Lucas (1976) critique. However, this variation may actually prove an advantage under some circumstances. To the extent that the economy responds differently to shocks of different types, variable reallocation effects may help explain why. Basu, Fernald, and Horvath (1996) address this question, among others.

This answer to the first question that we posed at the beginning of this subsection also partially answers the second, on the issue of calibration. We believe that if any single summary statistic is useful, it is likely to be the degree of returns to scale (or markups) estimated from aggregate data without composition corrections. If the Lucas critique problem is not too severe, this parameter will correctly capture the procyclical behavior of aggregate output and productivity, but a one-sector model calibrated with the average of the firm-level parameters would be unable to replicate this behavior. But, as the discussion above indicated, a one-sector model can never be a perfect substitute for a multi-sector model if one wishes to understand the response to multiple shocks.

The final question—whether the model with heterogeneity reproduces some of the interesting macroeconomic properties of the single-firm model—is the hardest to answer. Indeed, the example of Basu and Fernald (1997a) shows that there are no general answers. Here we discuss one of many interesting issues, the possibility of positive-feedback loops that might magnify the effects of shocks, and in the limit give rise to multiple equilibria. The work on real rigidities (Ball and Romer 1990) and "indeterminacy" (e.g., Farmer and Guo 1994) has drawn attention to the importance of positive feedback as a propagation mechanism. Farmer and Guo show that a very strong form of increasing returns—increasing marginal product of inputs—provides such positive feedback. The intuition is simple. Suppose the labor demand curve is upward-sloping (due to increasing marginal product of labor) and steeper than the labor supply curve. Also suppose a shock increases lifetime wealth, causing workers to supply less labor at each real wage (without affecting labor demand). This leftward shift in the labor supply curve causes equilibrium labor supply to increase rather than decrease, as standard neoclassical theory predicts. If this effect is sufficiently strong, the increase in labor and output can be self-justifying. Workers expect higher real wages now and in the future, which reduces their marginal utility of wealth, which increases the equilibrium real wage—validating the initial expectation of higher lifetime wealth.[40]

An interesting question, then, is whether reallocation effects can create such positive-feedback loops. Note that positive feedback depends on changes in marginal factor prices, since these are the prices that are relevant for economic decisions (saving and labor supply). In fact, increasing returns in the normal sense is not sufficient to create positive feedback. As we discussed in Section I, returns to scale can come from fixed costs, and can be quite consistent with diminishing marginal products. Thus, we conjecture that reallocations coming from differences in markups, R_μ, and the failure of a value-added production function, R_M, will have a positive-feedback effect only if the increasing returns accompanying the markups take the form of diminishing marginal cost.[41]

Similar caveats apply to R_K and R_L. Recall that these terms capture differences in shadow prices of the same input across firms. If the variance in shadow prices comes only from adjustment costs, and adjustment costs are paid by the firm, then the differences in marginal product will not translate directly to differences in factor prices. (Of course, adjustment costs usually have general-equilibrium effects on both prices and quantities.) Again, the reallocations induced by quasi-fixity will typically affect the dynamics of aggregate output following a shock (as discussed by Ramey and Shapiro 1998).

However, if the R_K and R_L terms come from steady-state differences in factor payments across sectors, matters might be different. (In the case of labor, for example, these differences might come from efficiency wages or union wage premia.) If the wage differences are allocative for the firm—that is, if the firm equates the marginal product of labor to the above-market-clearing wage, as in Katz and Summers (1989), instead of the wage premium reflecting efficient bargaining—then these reallocations can have feedback effects. Even in this case, however, positive feedback is not guar-

40. In a dynamic model one also needs an increase in capital accumulation to increase the rate of return to capital.
41. As discussed in section 7.1, we believe on theoretical and empirical grounds that free entry eliminates long-run economic profits, forcing markups to approximately equal the degree of returns to scale.

anteed, because it is unclear what form of rationing rule supports long-run differences in wages for identical labor—that is, how high-paying jobs are restricted to a subset of workers. Basu and Fernald (1997a, Section V) show that the form of the rationing rule determines whether long-run wage premia that give rise to a non-zero R_L also generate positive feedback. Thus, the implications of reallocation for macroeconomic models are likely to be quite sensitive to institutional assumptions, including institutions that do not directly concern production and firm behavior.

The general point of this discussion is that reallocation effects are not just a "nuisance term"—they are potentially important propagation mechanisms for shocks, and in the limit can give rise to multiple equilibria. This is an important lesson, as recent empirical estimates (including those we provide above) suggest that average, firm-level returns to scale are approximately constant. We argue that this finding does not necessarily imply that one should reject macroeconomic parables in which increasing returns at a representative plant play a central role in explaining economic fluctuations. Ascertaining which paradigm provides better macroeconomic insights is an important, unresolved question, and the focus of on-going research.

7.7 Conclusions

In this paper, we explore the meaning and measurement of productivity in a world with frictions and distortions. In such a world, productivity growth might not estimate aggregate technology change. We provide a general accounting framework that relates growth in aggregate productivity and aggregate technology. We identify various nontechnological terms that reflect not only variations in utilization, but also changes in the allocation of factors across uses with different marginal products. Marginal products, in turn, can differ because of frictions or distortions in the economy. These reallocations affect aggregate output and productivity, without necessarily reflecting technology. Hence, computing aggregate technology change requires micro data.

The nontechnological components should not necessarily be considered "mismeasurement." Variable input utilization clearly constitutes mismeasurement, but reallocations do not. In fact, we argue in section 7.6 that even with distortions such as imperfect competition, a modified Solow residual appropriately measures welfare change. Thus, though much of the recent productivity literature emphasizes the use of micro data, in some circumstances welfare measurement requires only readily-available national income accounts data.[42]

Several existing studies provide models of fluctuations in economies that

---

42. In practice, of course, welfare depends on a broader measure of output than just GDP—for example, household production, investment in human capital, and changes in environmental policy. Unfortunately, these items are hard to measure.

deviate in a variety of ways from the standard one-sector model of production. In those models, the nontechnological sources of productivity fluctuations are not always clear, nor is the relationship to other models. Our general framework can aid in understanding and interpreting the fluctuations arising, for example, from sector-specific technology shocks, vintage capital effects, or imperfect competition with heterogeneity (see, respectively, Phelan and Trejos 1996, Gilchrist and Williams 1996, and Basu, Fernald, and Horvath 1996).

Applying our decomposition to the data raises several practical and methodological issues. We discuss the pros and cons of estimating first- and second-order approximations to the production function, and advocate an explicitly first-order approach. We use a model of a dynamically cost-minimizing firm to derive a proxy for unobserved variations in labor effort and the workweek of capital. We estimate aggregate technology change by aggregating industry-level shocks that are "purged" of the effects of variable utilization and imperfect competition.

Variable utilization and cyclical reallocations appear to explain much of the cyclicality of aggregate productivity. We find that in the short run, technology improvements significantly reduce input use while appearing to reduce output slightly as well. These results are inconsistent with standard parameterizations of RBC models, which imply that technology improvements raise input use at all horizons. However, Basu, Fernald, and Kimball (1999) argue that they *are* consistent with standard sticky-price models.

Finally, we discuss implications for macroeconomics. We conclude that reallocations are welfare-relevant, and hence not biases. We also conclude that while accounting for reallocation reduces the average markup and the average degree of returns to scale, an economy with strong reallocation effects can sometimes display the same behavior as an economy with large increasing returns. Hence, reallocations constitute a potentially-important propagation mechanism, which can be utilized in multi-sector dynamic models of business cycles.

Appendix

Derivations from Section 7.3

This appendix presents detailed derivations of the equations in section 7.3. We first derive the relationship between firm-level gross output and firm-level value added, and discuss the interpretation of the value-added equation. We then aggregate firm-level value-added growth to obtain aggregate output growth as a function of aggregate inputs, technology, utilization, and reallocations of resources.

As discussed in Section III, the Divisia definition of value-added growth is:[43]

$$(A.1) \quad dv_i = \frac{dy_i - s_{Mi}dm_i}{1 - s_{Mi}} = dy_i - \left[\frac{s_{Mi}}{1 - s_{Mi}}\right](dm_i - dy_i).$$

We now want to substitute in for output growth dy_i. In section 7.1, we obtained the following equation for output growth

$$dy_i = \mu_i dx_i + \mu_i(1 - s_{Mi})du_i + dt_i.$$

Inserting this equation using the definition of input growth dx_i gives

$$(A.2) \quad dy_i = \mu_i[s_{Ki}dk_i + s_{Li}(dn_i + dh_i) + s_{Mi}dm_i] + \mu_i(1 - s_{Mi})du_i + dt_i.$$

We can rewrite this equation as

$$(A.3) \quad dy_i = \mu_i(1 - s_{Mi})\left[\frac{s_{Li}}{(1 - s_{Mi})}dl_i + \frac{s_{Ki}}{(1 - s_{Mi})}dk_i\right]$$

$$+ \mu_i(1 - s_{Mi})du_i + \mu_i s_{Mi}dm_i + dt_i$$

$$= \mu_i(1 - s_{Mi})(dx_i^V + du_i) + \mu_i s_{Mi}dm_i + dt_i,$$

where primary-input growth, dx_i^V, is defined analogously to aggregate primary input growth

$$dx_i^V = \frac{s_{Ki}}{1 - s_{Mi}}dk_i + \frac{s_{Li}}{1 - s_{Mi}}dl_i \equiv s_{Ki}^V dk_i + s_{Li}^V dl_i.$$

Note that s_{Ki}^V and s_{Li}^V are shares of capital and labor costs in nominal value added.

Now subtract $\mu_i s_{Mi}dy_i$ from both sides of equation (A.3) and divide through by $(1 - \mu_i s_{Mi})$. This gives

$$dy_i = \left[\frac{\mu_i(1 - s_{Mi})}{1 - \mu_i s_{Mi}}\right](dx_i^V + du_i) +$$

$$\left[\frac{\mu_i s_{Mi}}{1 - \mu_i s_{Mi}}\right](dm_i - dy_i) + \frac{dt_i}{1 - \mu_i s_{Mi}}.$$

43. Double-deflation is an alternative method, where $V \equiv Y - M$, where Y and M are valued at base-year prices. By differentiating the double-deflated index, we can express the growth in double-deflated value added in a form completely parallel to equation (7A.1)—the only difference is that the intermediate share is calculated using *base-year* prices, rather than current prices. An implication of this difference is that just as substitution bias affects Laspeyres indices of aggregate expenditure, substitution bias affects double-deflated value added. Hence, as Basu and Fernald (1995, appendix) show, double-deflated value added suffers all of the biases we identify in this section for Divisia value-added, *plus* an additional substitution bias.

We can write this equation as

(A.4) $$dy_i = \mu_i^V(dx_i^V + du_i) + \mu_i^V\left(\frac{s_{Mi}}{1 - s_{Mi}}\right)(dm_i - dy_i) + dt_i^V,$$

where

(A.5) $$\mu_i^V \equiv \mu_i \frac{1 - s_{Mi}}{1 - \mu_i s_{Mi}}$$

(A.6) $$dt_i^V \equiv \frac{dt_i}{1 - \mu_i s_{Mi}}.$$

Equation (A.4) relates gross output growth to growth rates of primary inputs dx_i^V, utilization du_i, the intermediates-output ratio $dm_i - dy_i$, and technology. Growth in primary inputs and utilization are multiplied by a "value-added markup" μ_i^V, defined by equation (A.5). We provide an economic interpretation of μ_i^V below.

We can now substitute for dy_i from equation (A.4) into the definition of value-added growth (equation [A.1])

(A.7) $$dv_i = \mu_i^V dx_i^V + (\mu_i^V - 1)\left[\frac{s_{Mi}}{1 - s_{Mi}}\right](dm_i - dy_i) + \mu_i^V du_i + dt_i^V.$$

The firm's revenue-weighted value-added productivity residual, dp_i, equals $dv_i - dx_i^V$. Hence,

(A.8) $$dp_i = (\mu_i^V - 1)dx_i^V + (\mu_i^V - 1)\left[\frac{s_{Mi}}{1 - s_{Mi}}\right]$$

$$(dm_i - dy_i) + \mu_i^V du_i + dt_i.$$

It is obvious from equations (A.7) and (A.8) that value-added growth is not, in general, simply a function of primary inputs dx_i^V. A long literature in the 1970s (e.g., Bruno 1978) explored whether a "value-added function" exists, and argued that the answer depends on separability properties of the production function. The equation above shows that with imperfect competition, taking value added to be a function only of primary inputs is generally misspecified—regardless of whether the production function is separable between value added and intermediate inputs. Separability is a second-order property of a production function, so its presence or absence does not affect first-order approximations like equation (A.7). However, the fact that the output elasticity of materials is $\mu_i s_{Mi}$ instead of simply s_{Mi} is of first-order importance.

Nevertheless, it will be useful to make that further assumption of separability in order to provide a simple interpretation of value-added growth. In particular, suppose the production function is separable, as follows

(A.9) $\quad Y_i = F^i(\tilde{K}_i, L_i, M_i, T^V_i) = G^i[V^{Pi}(\tilde{K}_i, L_i, T^V_i), H^i(M_i)].$

The firm combines primary inputs to produce "productive value added," V^{Pi}, which it then combines with intermediate inputs to produce gross output. (Note that V^{Pi} does not necessarily correspond to the national-accounting measure of value added—that is, the sum of firm-level productive value added need not equal national expenditure.) We can break the cost-minimization problem into two stages: First, minimize the cost of using primary inputs to produce any level of V^{Pi}; second, minimize the cost of using productive value added and intermediate inputs to produce any level of gross output.

In the first stage, the logic from equation (15) implies that the "productive" value-added growth, dv^P, depends on the revenue-weighted growth in primary inputs dx^V, plus technology shocks (without loss of generality we normalize to one the elasticity of productive value added V^{Pi} with respect to technology)

(A.10) $\qquad\qquad\qquad dv^P_i = \mu^V_i dx^V_i + dt^V_i.$

In the second stage, the firm seeks to minimize the cost of using value added and intermediate inputs to produce gross output. The cost in the minimization problem is $MC^V_i V_i + P_{Mi} M_i$, where MC^V_i is the marginal cost of value added to the firm. The first-order condition is then $MC^V_i = P_i G^i_V / \mu_i$. Analogously to the problem in section 7.1, we can interpret the value-added markup μ^V_i as the ratio of the price of productive value added to the marginal cost of producing it: $\mu^V_i = P^V_i / MC^V_i$. Hence,

(A.11) $\qquad\qquad\qquad \dfrac{G_V V^{Pi}}{G} = \dfrac{\mu_i}{\mu^V_i} s_{Vi}.$

Note that s_{Vi} equals $P^V_i V_i / P_i Y_i = (P_i Y - P_{Mi} M_i)/P_i Y$, which equals $(1 - s_{Mi})$. However, without knowing more about the shape of the production function (and hence, the slopes of marginal cost of producing V^P and Y), we cannot make any general statements about the magnitude of the value-added markup μ^V_i.

To do so, we make the further substantive assumption that all returns to scale are in V^P, arising perhaps from overhead capital or labor. This requires that G be homogeneous of degree one in V^P and H, and that H be homogeneous of degree one in M. Under these assumptions, the left-hand-side of equation (A.11) equals $(1 - \mu_i s_{Mi})$. Equation (A.11) then reads

(A.12) $\qquad\qquad\qquad (1 - \mu_i s_{Mi}) = \dfrac{\mu_i}{\mu^V_i}(1 - s_{Mi}).$

Rearranging this equation verifies that the value-added markup μ^V_i is the same as we defined in equation (A.5). Hence, just as μ_i creates a wedge between an input price and the input's marginal product in terms of gross output, μ_i^V appropriately measures the wedge between the input price and the marginal product in terms of value added.

Note that for macroeconomic modeling, the value-added markup μ^V is likely to be the parameter of interest. Rotemberg and Woodford (1995), for example, make this point in a dynamic general-equilibrium model with imperfect competition. In their model, there are no factor-market frictions, all firms have the same separable gross-output production function, always use materials in fixed proportions to gross output, and charge the same markup of price over marginal cost. Under these assumptions (which are implicit or explicit in most other dynamic general-equilibrium models with imperfect competition), there is a representative producer and an aggregate value-added production function. Rotemberg and Woodford show that the correct aggregate markup corresponds to μ^V.

One source of economic intuition for μ^V is that under some circumstances, it correctly captures "economy-wide" distortions, as small markups at the plant level translate into larger efficiency losses for the economy overall. Suppose, for example, that final output is produced at the end of an infinite number of stages. At each stage a representative firm with markup μ uses all the output of the previous stage as intermediate input, and also uses primary inputs of capital and labor. Then the percent change in national income—the output of the last (nth) stage—is

$$dy_n = \mu(1 - s_M)dx_n^V + \mu s_M dy_{n-1}$$
$$= \mu(1 - s_M)dx_n^V + \mu s_M \mu(1 - s_M)dx_{n-1}^V + (\mu s_M)^2 dy_{n-2}.$$

We can substitute into this equation for dy_{n-j}, and let j go to infinity. Since each firm is identical, dx_i^V is the same for all i as for the aggregate. This gives an infinite sum

(A.13) $$dy_n \equiv dv = \mu(1 - s_M)dx^V \sum_{j=1}^{\infty} (\mu s_M)^j$$

$$= \mu(1 - s_M)dx^V \frac{1}{1 - \mu s_M} = \mu^V dx^V.$$

Thus, μ^V is plausibly the appropriate concept for calibrating the markup charged by the representative firm in a one-sector macroeconomic model.

Thus, μ^V correctly captures the idea that small deviations from perfect competition "cascade" in going from gross output to value added, because of the "markup on markup" phenomenon: Firms buy intermediate goods from other firms at a markup, add value, and again price the resulting good with a markup, generally selling some of it to another firm to use as an intermediate good. Nevertheless, this derivation shows that there is a limit to how much the effects can cascade or build up.

Even if we want this value-added markup, however, we still in general require data on intermediate inputs. The reason is that we do not observe

V^{Pi} directly, but must infer it from observable gross output and intermediate inputs.

Returning to equation (A.7), real value-added growth depends on primary input growth, changes in the materials-to-output ratio, variations in utilization of capital and labor, and technology. The first term shows that primary inputs are multiplied by the value-added markup. The second term reflects the extent to which the standard measure of value added differs from "productive" value added V^{Pi}, and hence does not properly measure the productive contribution of intermediate inputs. Intuitively, the standard measure of value added subtracts off intermediate input growth using revenue shares, whereas with imperfect competition the productive contribution of these inputs exceeds the revenue share by the markup. The third term shows that variations in utilization are also multiplied by the value-added markup. The fourth term is the value-added-augmenting technology shock.

We now aggregate over firms to get aggregate output growth as a function of technology, aggregate primary inputs growth, and the distribution of inputs. As in section 7.3, we define aggregate output growth dv as a share-weighted average of firm-level value-added growth

$$dv = \sum_{i=1}^{N} w_i dv_i,$$

where $w_i = P_i^V V_i / P^V V$. Substituting in from equation (A.7) for dv_i gives

(A.14) $\quad dv = \sum_{i=1}^{N} w_i \mu_i^V dx_i^V + \sum_{i=1}^{N} w_i(\mu_i^V - 1)\left[\dfrac{s_{Mi}}{1 - s_{Mi}}\right](dm_i - dy_i)$

$\qquad + \sum_{i=1}^{N} w_i \mu_i^V du_i + \sum_{i=1}^{N} w_i dt_i^V.$

As in the text, we will define

$$du = \sum_{i=1}^{N} w_i \mu_i^V du_i$$

$$R_M = \sum_{i=1}^{N} w_i(\mu_i^V - 1)\left[\dfrac{s_{Mi}}{1 - s_{Mi}}\right](dm_i - dy_i), \text{ and}$$

$$dt^V = \sum_{i=1}^{N} w_i dt_i^V.$$

Hence, equation (A.14) becomes

(A.15) $\quad dv = \sum_{i=1}^{N} w_i \mu_i^V dx_i^V + R_M + du + dt^V$

We now decompose the first term into the effects of the "average" value-added markup $\bar{\mu}^V$, and the distribution of the markup. Rearranging equation (A.15) gives

$$\text{(A.16)} \quad dv = \bar{\mu}^V \sum_{i=1}^{N} w_i dx_i^V + \sum_{i=1}^{N} w_i(\mu_i^V - \bar{\mu}^V)dx_i^V + R_M + du + dt^V$$

$$= \bar{\mu}^V \sum_{i=1}^{N} w_i dx_i^V + R_\mu + R_M + du + dt^V,$$

where

$$R_\mu = \sum_{i=1}^{N} w_i(\mu_i^V - \bar{\mu}^V)dx_i^V.$$

At this point, we are almost finished. However, we still need to relate the first term on the right-hand side of equation (A.16) to aggregate input growth. As in section 7.3, consider the case where there was only one type of capital and one type of labor.[44] Aggregate labor and capital are arithmetic sums across firms, so that $K = \sum_{i=1}^{N} K_i$ and $L = \sum_{i=1}^{N} L_i$. Aggregate primary input growth is the share-weighted growth in aggregate capital and labor growth

$$dx^V = s_K^V dk + s_L^V dl.$$

Using the definitions of s_{Ki}^V and s_{Li}^V, and differentiating the definitions of aggregate K and L, we can write this as

$$dx^V = \frac{P_K K}{P^V V} \sum_{i=1}^{N} \frac{K_i}{K} dk_i + \frac{P_L K}{P^V V} \sum_{i=1}^{N} \frac{L_i}{L} dl_i$$

$$= \sum_{i=1}^{N} \frac{P_i^V V_i}{P^V V} \frac{P_{Ki} K_i}{P_i^V V_i} \frac{P_K}{P_{Ki}} dk_i + \sum_{i=1}^{N} \frac{P_i^V V_i}{P^V V} \frac{P_{Li} L_i}{P_i^V V_i} \frac{P_L}{P_{Li}} dl_i.$$

Noting the definitions of w_i, s_{Ki}^V, and s_{Li}^V, we can write this as

$$\text{(A.17)} \quad dx^V = \sum_{i=1}^{N} w_i s_{Ki}^V \frac{P_K}{P_{Ki}} dk_i + \sum_{i=1}^{N} w_i s_{Li}^V \frac{P_L}{P_{Li}} dl_i$$

$$= \sum_{i=1}^{N} w_i(s_{Ki}^V dk_i + s_{Li}^V dl_i) - \sum_{i=1}^{N} w_i s_{Ki}^V \left(\frac{P_{Ki} - P_K}{P_{Ki}}\right) dk_i$$

$$- \sum_{i=1}^{N} w_i s_{Li}^V \left(\frac{P_{Li} - P_L}{P_{Li}}\right) dl_i = \sum_{i=1}^{N} w_i dx_i^V - R_K - R_L,$$

where

---

44. In general, suppose there are N firms, N_L types of labor, and N_K types of capital. For each type of capital K^k and labor L^l, the aggregate is an arithmetic sum across firms, so that $K^k = \sum_{i=1}^{N} K_i^k$ and $L^l = \sum_{i=1}^{N} L_i^l$. Aggregate capital and labor are then defined as a Divisia index across these types of capital, so that, for example, aggregate labor growth is $dl \equiv \sum_{l=1}^{N_L} P_L^l L^l / P_L L dl^l$, where $P_L^l L^l$ is total labor compensation to labor of type l. The derivations that follow extend easily to this general case, except that there is a separate input-reallocation term for each type of labor and capital. Jorgenson, Gollop, and Fraumeni (1987) derive this result explicitly.

$$R_K = \sum_{i=1}^{N} w_i s_{Ki}^V \left[\frac{P_{Ki} - P_K}{P_{Ki}} \right] dk_i,$$

$$R_L = \sum_{i=1}^{N} w_i s_{Li}^V \left[\frac{P_{Li} - P_L}{P_{Li}} \right] dl_i,$$

By substituting equation (A.17) into equation (A.16), we find

(A.18) $\quad dv = \overline{\mu}^V dx^V + du + R_\mu + R_M + \overline{\mu}^V R_K + \overline{\mu}^V R_L + dt^V$

$\quad\quad\quad = \overline{\mu}^V dx^V + du + R + dt^V.$

Since aggregate productivity equals $dv - dx^V$, it immediately follows that

(A.19) $\quad\quad\quad dp = (\overline{\mu}^V - 1) dx^V + du + R + dt.$

References

Abbott, Thomas A., Zvi Griliches, and Jerry Hausman. 1998. Short run movements in productivity: Market power versus capacity utilization." In *Practicing econometrics: Essays in method and application,* ed. Zvi Griliches, 333–42. Cheltenham, UK: Elgar.
Baily, Martin N., Charles Hulten, and David Campbell. 1992. Productivity dynamics in manufacturing plants. *Brookings Papers on Economic Activity (Microeconomics),* issue no. 1:187–267.
Ball, Laurence, and David Romer. 1990. Real rigidities and the non-neutrality of money. *Review of Economic Studies* 57:183–203.
Barro, Robert J., and Robert G. King. 1984. Time-separable preferences and intertemporal substitution models of business cycles. *Quarterly Journal of Economics* 99 (November): 817–39.
Bartelsman, Eric J., Ricardo J. Caballero, and Richard K. Lyons. 1994. Customer- and supplier-driven externalities. *American Economic Review* 84 (4): 1075–84.
Bartelsman, Eric J., and Phoebus Dhrymes. 1998. Productivity dynamics: U.S. manufacturing plants, 1972–1986. *Journal of Productivity Analysis* 9 (1): 5–34.
Basu, Susanto. 1995. Intermediate goods and business cycles: Implications for productivity and welfare. *American Economic Review* 85 (June): 512–31.
———. 1996. Cyclical productivity: Increasing returns or cyclical utilization? *Quarterly Journal of Economics* 111 (August): 719–51.
Basu, Susanto, and John G. Fernald. 1995. Are apparent productive spillovers a figment of specification error? *Journal of Monetary Economics* 36 (December): 165–88.
———. 1997a. Returns to scale in U.S. manufacturing: Estimates and implications. *Journal of Political Economy* 105 (April): 249–83.
———. 1997b. Aggregate productivity and aggregate technology. International Finance Discussion Paper no. 593. Federal Reserve System, Board of Governors.
Basu, Susanto, John G. Fernald, and Michael T. K. Horvath. 1996. Aggregate production function failures. Manuscript.
Basu, Susanto, John G. Fernald, and Miles S. Kimball. 1999. Are technology improvements contractionary? Manuscript.

Basu, Susanto, and Miles S. Kimball. 1997. Cyclical productivity with unobserved input variation. NBER Working Paper no. 5915. Cambridge, Mass.: National Bureau of Economic Research, February.

Baxter, Marianne, and Robert King. 1991. Productive externalities and business cycles. Discussion Paper no. 53. Federal Reserve Bank of Minneapolis, Institute for Empirical Macroeconomics.

Beaudry, Paul, and Michael Devereux. 1994. Monopolistic competition, price setting, and the effects of real and nominal shocks. Boston University, Department of Economics, Manuscript.

Beaulieu, John J., and Joseph Mattey. 1998. The workweek of capital and capital utilization in manufacturing. *Journal of Productivity Analysis* 10 (October): 199–223.

Benhabib, Jess, and Roger E. A. Farmer. 1994. Indeterminacy and increasing returns. *Journal of Economic Theory* 63 (1): 19–41.

Berman, Eli, John Bound, and Zvi Griliches. 1994. Changes in the demand for skilled labor within U.S. manufacturing: Evidence from the annual survey of manufactures. *Quarterly Journal of Economics* 109 (2): 367–97.

Berndt, Ernst R. 1991. *The practice of econometrics: Classic and contemporary.* Reading, Mass.: Addison Wesley.

Berndt, Ernst R., and Melvin A. Fuss. 1986. Productivity measurement with adjustments for variations in capacity utilization and other forms of temporary equilibrium. *Journal of Econometrics* 33 (October/November): 7–29.

Bils, Mark. 1987. The cyclical behavior of marginal cost and price. *American Economic Review* 77:838–55.

Bils, Mark, and Jang-Ok Cho. 1994. Cyclical factor utilization. *Journal of Monetary Economics* 33:319–54.

Blanchard, Olivier J., and Peter Diamond. 1990. The aggregate matching function. In *Growth/productivity/unemployment: Essays to celebrate Bob Solow's birthday,* ed. Peter Diamond, 159–201. Cambridge, Mass.: MIT Press.

Bruno, Michael. 1978. Duality, intermediate inputs, and value added. In *Production economics: A dual approach to theory and applications,* vol. 2, 3–16. ed. Melvyn Fuss and Daniel McFadden. Amsterdam: North-Holland.

Burnside, Craig. 1996. What do production function regressions tell us about increasing returns to scale and externalities? *Journal of Monetary Economics* 37 (April): 177–201.

Burnside, Craig, and Martin Eichenbaum. 1996. Factor-hoarding and the propagation of business-cycle shocks. *American Economic Review* 86:1154–74.

Burnside, Craig, Martin Eichenbaum, and Sergio Rebelo. 1995. Capital utilization and returns to scale. In *NBER Macroeconomics Annual 1995,* ed. Ben S. Bernanke and Julio J. Rotemberg, 67–110. Cambridge, Mass.: MIT Press.

Caballero, Ricardo J., and Richard K. Lyons. 1989. The role of external economies in U.S. manufacturing. NBER Working Paper no. 3033. Cambridge, Mass.: National Bureau of Economic Research.

———. 1990. Internal and external economies in European industries. *European Economic Review* 34:805–30.

———. 1992. External effects in U.S. procyclical productivity. *Journal of Monetary Economics* 29:209–26.

Carlton, Dennis W. 1983. Equilibrium fluctuations when price and delivery lag clear the market. *Bell Journal of Economics* 14 (2): 562–72.

Chambers, Robert G. 1988. *Applied production analysis: A dual approach.* Cambridge: Cambridge University Press.

Cooley, Thomas F., and Edward C. Prescott. 1995. Economic growth and business cycles. In *Frontiers of business cycle research,* ed. Thomas F. Cooley, 1–38. Princeton: Princeton University Press.

Cooper, Russell, and Andrew John. 1988. Coordinating coordination failures in Keynesian models. *Quarterly Journal of Economics* 103 (3): 441–63.

Cooper, Russell, and Alok Johri. 1997. Dynamic complementarities: A quantitative analysis. *Journal of Monetary Economics* 40 (1): 97–119.

Diamond, Peter A. 1982. Aggregate demand management in search equilibrium. *Journal of Political Economy* 90:881–94.

Diewert, Erwin. 1976. Exact and superlative index numbers. *Journal of Econometrics* 4:115–46.

Domar, Evsey D. 1961. On the measurement of technical change. *Economic Journal* 71 (December): 710–29.

Dotsey, Michael, Robert King, and Alexander Wolman. 1997. Menu costs, staggered price setting, and elastic factor supply. University of Virginia, Department of Economics, Manuscript.

Farmer, Robert, and Jang-Ting Guo. 1994. Real business cycles and the animal spirits hypothesis. *Journal of Economic Theory* 63:42–72.

Flux, A. W. 1913. Gleanings from the Census of Productions report. *Journal of the Royal Statistical Society* 76 (6): 557–85.

Gali, Jordi. 1999. Technology, employment, and the business cycle: Do technology shocks explain aggregate fluctuations? *American Economic Review* 89 (March): 249–74.

Gilchrist, Simon, and John Williams. 1996. Investment, capacity, and output: A putty-clay approach. Finance and Economics Discussion Series no. 1998–44. Federal Reserve System, Board of Governors.

Gordon, Robert J. 1993. Are procyclical productivity fluctuations a figment of measurement error? Northwestern University, Department of Economics, Mimeograph.

Green, Edward J., and Robert H. Porter. 1984. Noncooperative collusion under imperfect price information. *Econometrica* 52 (January): 87–100.

Griliches, Zvi. 1992. The search for R&D spillovers. *Scandinavian Journal of Economics* 94 (Supplement): 29–47.

Griliches, Zvi, and Tor Jacob Klette. 1996. The inconsistency of common scale estimators when output prices are unobserved and endogenous. *Journal of Applied Econometrics* 11 (July/August): 343–61.

Griliches, Zvi, and Jacques Mairesse. 1998. Production functions: The search for identification. In *Practicing econometrics: Essays in method and application,* ed. Zvi Griliches, 343–411. Cheltenham, U.K.: Elgar.

Haavelmo, Trygve. 1960. *A study in the theory of investment.* Chicago: University of Chicago Press.

Hall, Alastair R., Glenn D. Rudebusch, and David W. Wilcox. 1996. Judging instrument relevance in instrumental variables estimation. *International Economic Review* 37 (2): 283–98.

Hall, Robert E. 1988. The relation between price and marginal cost in U.S. industry. *Journal of Political Economy* 96 (October): 921–47.

———. 1990. Invariance properties of Solow's productivity residual. In *Growth/productivity/unemployment: Essays to celebrate Bob Solow's birthday,* ed. Peter Diamond. Cambridge, Mass.: MIT Press.

Hall, Robert E., and Dale W. Jorgenson. 1967. Tax policy and investment behavior. *American Economic Review* 57 (June): 391–414.

Haltiwanger, John C. 1997. Measuring and analyzing aggregate fluctuations: The importance of building from microeconomic evidence. *Review of the Federal Reserve Bank of St. Louis* (79) (3): 55–77.

Horvath, Michael T. K. 1995. Cyclicality and sectoral linkages: Aggregate fluctu-

ations from independent sectoral shocks. *Review of Economic Dynamics* 1 (4): 781–808.
Hulten, Charles. 1978. Growth accounting with intermediate inputs. *Review of Economic Studies* 45:511–18.
———. 1986. Productivity change, capacity utilization, and the sources of efficiency growth. *Journal of Econometrics* 33 (October/November): 31–50.
Jorgenson, Dale W. 1987. Productivity and postwar U.S. economic growth. *Journal of Economic Perspectives* 2 (4): 23–42.
Jorgenson, Dale W., Frank Gollop, and Barbara Fraumeni. 1987. *Productivity and U.S. economic growth.* Cambridge, Mass.: Harvard University Press.
Jorgenson, Dale W., and Zvi Griliches. 1967. The explanation of productivity change. *Review of Economic Studies* 34:249–83.
Jorgenson, Dale W., and Kun-Young Yun. 1991. *Tax reform and the cost of capital.* Oxford: Oxford University Press.
Katz, Lawrence F., and Lawrence H. Summers. 1989. Industry rents: Evidence and implications. *Brookings Papers on Economic Activity (Microeconomics)* (1): 209–90.
Kimball, Miles S. 1995. The quantitative analytics of the basic neomonetarist model. *Journal of Money, Credit, and Banking* 27 (November): 1241–77.
Lau, Laurence. 1986. Functional forms in econometric model building. In *Handbook of Econometrics,* vol. 3, ed. Zvi Griliches and Michael Intriligator, 1515–66. Amsterdam: North-Holland.
Lilien, David M. 1982. Sectoral shifts and cyclical unemployment. *Journal of Political Economy* 90 (August): 777–93.
Lucas, Robert E., Jr. 1976. Econometric policy evaluation: A critique. *Journal of Monetary Economics* (Suppl. Series): 19–46.
Marschak, Jacob, and William H. Andrews Jr. 1994. Random simultaneous equations and the theory of production. *Econometrica* 12 (3/4): 143–205.
Morrison, Catherine. 1992a. Markups in U.S. and Japanese manufacturing: A short-run econometric analysis. *Journal of Business and Economic Statistics* 10 (1): 51–63.
———. 1992b. Unraveling the productivity growth slowdown in the United States, Canada and Japan: The effects of subequilibrium, scale economies and markups. *Review of Economics and Statistics* 74 (3): 381–93.
Olley, G. Steven, and Ariel Pakes. 1996. The dynamics of productivity in the telecommunications equipment industry. *Econometrica* 64:1263–97.
Paul, Catherine J. Morrison, and Donald S. Siegel. 1999. Scale economies and industry agglomeration externalities: A dynamic cost function approach. *American Economic Review* 89 (1): 273–90.
Phelan, Christopher, and Alberto Trejos. 1996. On the aggregate effects of sectoral reallocation. *Journal of Monetary Economics* 45 (2): 249–68.
Pindyck, Robert S., and Julio J. Rotemberg. 1983. Dynamic factor demands and the effects of energy price shocks. *American Economic Review* 73 (December): 1066–79.
Ramey, Valerie A., and Matthew D. Shapiro. 1998. Costly capital reallocation and the effects of government spending. *Carnegie-Rochester Conference Series on Public Policy* 48 (June): 145–94.
Romer, Paul M. 1986. Increasing returns and long-run growth. *Journal of Political Economy* 94 (5): 1002–37.
Rotemberg, Julio J., and Garth Saloner. 1986. A supergame-theoretic model of price wars during booms. *American Economic Review* 76 (June): 390–407.
Rotemberg, Julio J., and Michael Woodford. 1992. Oligopolistic pricing and the

effects of aggregate demand on economic activity. *Journal of Political Economy* 100 (December): 1153–07.

———. 1995. Dynamic general equilibrium models with imperfectly competitive product markets. In *Frontiers of business cycle research,* ed. Thomas F. Cooley, 243–93. Princeton: Princeton University Press.

Sato, K. 1976. The meaning and measurement of the real value added index. *Review of Economics and Statistics* 58:434–42.

Sbordone, Argia M. 1997. Interpreting the procyclical productivity of manufacturing sectors: External effects or labor hoarding? *Journal of Money, Credit, and Banking* 29 (1): 26–45.

Schmitt-Grohé, Stephanie. 1997. Comparing four models of aggregate fluctuations due to self-fulfilling expectations. *Journal of Economic Theory* 72 (1): 96–147.

Schor, Juliet B. 1987. Does work intensity respond to macroeconomic variables? Evidence from British manufacturing, 1970–1986. Harvard University Department of Economics, Manuscript.

Shapiro, Matthew D. 1986. Capital utilization and capital accumulation: Theory and evidence. *Journal of Applied Econometrics* 1:211–34.

———. 1996. Macroeconomic implications of variation in the workweek of capital. *Brookings Papers on Economic Activity* issue no. 2:79–119.

Shea, John. 1997. Instrument relevance in multivariate linear models: A simple measure. *Review of Economics and Statistics* 79 (2): 48–52.

Solon, Gary, Robert Barsky, and Jonathan A. Parker. 1994. Measuring the cyclicality of real wages: How important is composition bias? *Quarterly Journal of Economics* 109 (February): 1–25.

Solow, Robert M. 1957. Technological change and the aggregate production function. *Review of Economics and Statistics* 39:312–20.

Varian, Hal. 1984. *Microeconomic analysis.* New York: W. W. Norton.

Weder, Mark. 1997. Animal spirits, technology shocks, and the business cycle. *Journal of Economic Dynamics and Control* 24 (2): 273–95.

Wen, Yi. 1998. Capacity utilization under increasing returns to scale. *Journal of Economic Theory* 81 (July): 7–36.

Comment Catherine J. Morrison Paul

My comments might be entitled, "Where Are the Microfoundations, and Do We Care?" In my view, yes, we do—or at least should—care. We care because the questions we are interested in asking, the explanatory power and interpretability we seek, and the implications for welfare and policy we pursue, all of which are crucial aspects of productivity analysis, are not effectively addressed or exhibited in the macro-oriented Basu-Fernald approach. In addition, it will not surprise anyone who knows of my own work over the past twenty years or so that I think this paper in a sense "reinvents the wheel." The paper raises numerous issues of technological,

Catherine J. Morrison Paul is professor of economics at the University of California, Davis.

market, and cross-market structure that are not novel, but have been addressed in various perspectives in a number of literatures and for a long time.

However, I must say that the macro literature on which the paper builds has been critical for both theoretical and conceptual development of productivity analysis. Also, the issues addressed are indeed important, and the many literatures in which these issues have been raised are not yet integrated. Perhaps this meeting may be used as a forum in which these different types of perspectives may begin to be aired and linked more effectively.

The different perspectives building the existing foundations of productivity analysis have been raised in the microproduction theory (parametric and nonparametric), efficiency, macro, "new growth," and "new IO" literatures, most of which have at least some representation in this gathering. The varying perspectives facilitate the creation of additional insights over any one viewpoint, and they are at least starting to converge.

The Basu and Fernald paper is an important case in point because it (implicitly) recognizes the importance of the microproduction theory literature to the macro issues addressed. It at least gives lip service to the basis of the theory of the firm—although the model developed is not really used for analysis—and recognizes the usefulness of a "bottom-up" approach. However, rather than building on the existing micro foundation, or synthesizing the different perspectives, this treatment primarily sweeps the existing literature under the rug, so rather than working together as the complements they have the potential to be, the different literatures become like two ships passing in the night. Perhaps a better analogy, given the contentious competition that sometimes rears its head between opposing camps, might be that of the *Andrea Doria,* where two massive ships crashed in thick fog without seeing each other.

So what is "new" here? Not much, I think. Important seminal work by Solow and later elaborations by Hall are extended to recognize issues raised already in the macro, as well as the micro, foundations literature. Bringing them together is a useful exercise, but I'm not sure exactly what we learn from it. I *am* left, however, contemplating a number of distinctions they make that are useful to think about in the context of the existing micro foundations literature, and the gap between this and the macro treatments. These distinctions will take the form of seven general points I wish to raise.

First-versus Second-Order Analysis

The authors emphasize that their analysis focuses on first-order effects, because that is mainly what is of interest for macroeconomic applications. However, most of the intriguing issues focused on in productivity analysis—including those raised in the paper about utilization, "biases," scale effects, externalities, and spillovers—are based fundamentally on second-order relationships.

For example, utilization has to do with over- or underuse of existing stocks of capital and labor (or increases or decreases in the service flow of these stocks) by differential use of substitutable and complementary inputs. This is a second-order phenomenon. Biases in input use (or output production if reallocation among outputs occurs) also have to do with second-order effects (although in the macro literature, biases are often raised in the context of statistical biases, rather than real biases with respect to technology or market valuation stemming from technological and market forces). Recognizing these relationships, as in the microproduction theory literature overviewed by Nadiri and Prucha in this volume, allows structural modeling and separate identification of their impacts rather than relying on instruments, proxies, and control variables to "back-out" these relationships. Without this, little interpretation of the results is forthcoming.

Top-Down versus Bottom-Up

The authors indicate that macro questions require a top-down perspective but also motivate their analysis via a bottom-up approach, which in this case means aggregating over two-digit industries.

I have sympathy for the industry-oriented approach, although I would have preferred it to stem from something like the four-digit level, which represents much more homogeneous industry divisions. A true micro (say, plant-level) approach sometimes tends to get lost in the immense heterogeneity within even the most homogeneous divisions (as is evident from the Ellerman, Stoker, and Berndt paper in this volume). Also, typical questions of interest about patterns observed within and across industries require an industry focus for analysis. Thus, beginning with an industry-level micro perspective has its merits. Again, though, more structured analysis of the technological and market structure is important. The simple first-order analysis here glosses over the determinants of utilization, scale effects, and other technological and market conditions of interest in the simple average relationships. Once these patterns are determined at the industry level, bottom-up analysis means to me that they are summarized across industries to obtain insights about overall patterns, rather than just lumped into one, or a very limited number of, parameters.

Mismeasurement versus Mismodeling

I am not speaking here of the data mismeasurement issues raised by Triplett and others, which focus on quality. However, one aspect of the quality issue that may be addressed in a more complete microproduction theory structural model that allows consideration of differential input and output patterns is (second-order) changes in input and output composition. In this context, for example, changes in the proportion of high-tech capital, or educational attainment levels for labor, as well as trends in output mix, may be incorporated.

The main question I am raising about mismeasurement instead has to do with the literature in which the Basu-Fernald piece falls, which refers to mismeasurement in terms of distortions. That is, productivity is considered a combination of technology and distortions. However, much of the technological and market structure underlying these distortions, such as utilization and scale patterns, can be identified separately in a microproduction theory structural model, which is in fact represented by the theory-of-the-firm model in their paper. This could potentially facilitate the interpretation and use of measures of these production characteristics, instead of collapsing them together as mismeasurement, as is done in the implementation for this macro treatment.

For example, basic micro theory provides us information about the distinction between capital stock and service flow resulting from fixity of the capital factors and thus fluctuations in the intensity of their use. Therefore, the resulting input use patterns may be evaluated in terms of this conceptual framework, rather than mismeasurement or a "measure of our ignorance." This in turn allows these impacts to be separated from what is left of the measure of our ignorance, which productivity analysis is designed to illuminate. This relates also to the next distinction.

Primal versus Dual

Although there are some conceptual differences between the (first-order) variable utilization and (second-order) capacity utilization concepts, they are inextricably linked. The authors suggest that the first concept focuses on the distinction between service flow and stock, and the latter on valuing the stock. However, in both cases the underlying question is the service flow. In the first case, it relies on a more primal notion—revising the measure of the capital or labor level to correspond to its service flow. In the second case it is somewhat more of a nuance. Additional services or effort from a given stock of capital (or labor) results from more intensive application of other inputs, which in turn affects its marginal valuation in terms of other inputs.

That is, if, given input prices, greater output demand causes more capital effort to be expended, this raises the amount of other inputs applied to production from a given amount of capital stock, increasing its marginal valuation. This revaluation embeds the utilization issue in the dual or price term of the price times quantity "total value" of the stock, rather than directly in the quantity measure. But the effect is the same: greater utilization implies a higher capital share. This primal/dual distinction allows different perspectives on the issue, but they are essentially mirror images. The dual perspective also provides a structure in which shadow values (of both inputs and outputs), which are alluded to many times in the Basu-Fernald paper, may be measured and analyzed, whereas this is not possible in the (first-order) primal model.

Technical versus Market Structure

In the Basu-Fernald treatment, the notions of imperfect competition and scale economies are often used nearly interchangeably. However, our micro structure, again learned from principles classes, emphasizes the different motivations and thus interpretations resulting from these production structure characteristics. Scale economies, which arise from technology, may be good in the sense of cost efficiency. Effective representation of the cost structure is therefore crucial for appropriate analysis of these effects. Market imperfections, which arise from the output demand structure, may be bad in the context of resource allocation. Recognition of the market structure, and what might be driving evidence of market power, is therefore important for justifiable interpretation and use of "markup" measures. They need to be separately distinguished, identified, and analyzed, which is not possible here.

External versus Internal Effects

Many production and market characteristics mentioned in the productivity literature, raised in this conference, and alluded to in the Basu-Fernald piece may have external or spillover, as well as internal, effects. These include, but are not restricted to, R&D, trade (import penetration or competition), high-tech capital investment (capital composition), and education (labor composition). They also may more generally be characterized as agglomeration effects. These externalities may generate scale effects, as emphasized by the endogenous growth literature. However, these external effects may not be disentangled within the simple first-order model used in the Basu-Fernald paper, and thus again collapse to just another component of the distortions, mismeasurement, or measure of our ignorance captured in the residual. Appropriate characterization of these effects must recognize their impact on the cost-output relationship, as external shift factors. Note also that the notion of the internalization of these effects at more macro levels of aggregation has a clear representation in this context; spillovers that are external at low aggregation levels will be internal at high levels.

Welfare versus Productivity versus Technical Change

This final distinction is a crucial one in terms of interpretation of measures. Although addressed by Basu and Fernald, I believe it again requires a microfoundations perspective for appropriate representation, because the different types of distortions or components of the productivity growth measure independent of technical change may be separately distinguished in such a framework. For example, returning to the scale economy/market power distinction, these different production and market structure characteristics have widely varying connotations in terms of welfare analysis and thus policy implications, which thus require separate identification for evaluation of welfare implications.

Therefore, many technological, market, and cross-market issues raised by Basu and Fernald, and in the many linked micro- and macroproductivity studies in this area, seem to require a more detailed structural microfoundations emphasis for effective implementation, interpretation, and use. The different components of the Solow residual ("measure of our ignorance") need to be independently captured, identified, and unraveled. There are disadvantages of a more complex approach to modeling these relationships for more microunits, and ultimately summarizing them across industries to obtain macro implications, because implementation is more complicated. However, such an exercise can provide useful guidance, or at least underpinnings, for the first-order, top-down macro perspective of these issues overviewed in the Basu and Fernald piece. Hopefully, these views or perspectives are converging. The complementary insights provided by the different approaches should be investigated and synthesized.

8

Aggregate Productivity Growth
Lessons from Microeconomic Evidence

Lucia Foster, John Haltiwanger, and C. J. Krizan

8.1 Overview

Recent research using establishment- and firm-level data has raised a variety of conceptual and measurement questions regarding our understanding of aggregate productivity growth.[1] Several key related findings are of interest. First, there is large-scale, ongoing reallocation of outputs and inputs across individual producers. Second, the pace of this reallocation varies over time (both secularly and cyclically) and across sectors. Third, much of this reallocation reflects within- rather than between-sector reallocation. Fourth, there are large differentials in the levels and the rates of growth of productivity across establishments within the same sector. The rapid pace of output and input reallocation along with differences in productivity levels and growth rates are the necessary ingredients for the pace of reallocation to play an important role in aggregate (i.e., industry) productivity growth. However, our review of the existing studies

---

Lucia Foster is an economist at the Bureau of the Census.

John Haltiwanger is professor of economics at the University of Maryland, a research associate at the Center for Economic Studies at the Bureau of the Census, and a research associate of the National Bureau of Economic Research.

C. J. Krizan is an economist at Fannie Mae and a research associate of the Center for Economic Studies at the Bureau of the Census.

We thank Tomas Dvorak for helpful research assistance. The analyses and results presented in this paper are attributable to the authors and do not necessarily reflect concurrence by the Bureau of the Census or Fannie Mae.

1. Empirical papers of relevance that focus on the connection between micro- and aggregate productivity growth include: (a) for the United States: Baily, Hulten, and Campbell (1992), Baily, Bartelsman, and Haltiwanger (1996, forthcoming), Bartelsman and Dhrymes (1998), Dwyer (1998, 1997), Haltiwanger (1997), and Olley and Pakes (1996); (b) for other countries: Tybout (1996), Aw, Chen, and Roberts (1997), Liu and Tybout (1996), and Griliches and Regev (1995).

indicates that the measured contribution of such reallocation effects varies over time and across sectors and is sensitive to measurement methodology. An important objective of this paper is to sort out the role of these different factors so that we can understand the nature and the magnitude of the contribution of reallocation to aggregate productivity growth.

These recent empirical findings have been developed in parallel with an emerging theoretical literature that seeks to account for the heterogeneous fortunes across individual producers and to explore the role of such micro-heterogeneity in aggregate productivity growth. This theoretical strand combined with the literature concerning the role of reallocation forms the theoretical underpinning of this paper. Of course, the idea that productivity growth in a market economy invariably involves restructuring and reallocation across producers is not new. For example, Schumpeter (1942, 83) coined the term "creative destruction," which he described as follows:

> The fundamental impulse that keeps the capital engine in motion comes from the new consumers' goods, the new methods of production and transportation, the new markets . . . [The process] incessantly revolutionizes from within, incessantly destroying the old one, incessantly creating a new one. This process of Creative Destruction is the essential fact of capitalism.

However, what is new in the emerging empirical literature is the growing availability of longitudinal establishment-level data that permit characterization and analysis of the reallocation across individual producers within narrowly defined sectors and, in turn, the connection of this reallocation to aggregate productivity growth.

In this paper, we seek to synthesize and extend this emerging literature on the connection between micro- and aggregate productivity growth dynamics. We focus primarily on the empirical findings and we find, as will become clear, that the measured quantitative contribution of reallocation to aggregate productivity growth varies significantly across studies. Our objective is to understand the sources of the differences in results across studies. We pursue this objective in two ways. First, we compare the results carefully across studies, taking note of differences on a variety of dimensions including country, sectoral coverage, time period, frequency, and measurement methodology. Second, we exploit establishment-level data for the U.S. manufacturing sector as well as for a few selected service sector industries to conduct our own independent investigation of the relevant issues. The inclusion of service sector results is of particular interest since the existing literature has focused almost exclusively on manufacturing industries.

The paper proceeds as follows. In section 8.2, we provide a summary of theories that can account for the observed heterogeneous fortunes across establishments in the same narrowly defined sector. In addition, we consider the related theoretical literature on creative destruction models of growth. This brief discussion of theoretical underpinnings is of considerable help in putting the results on the relationship between micro- and macroproductivity growth into perspective. In section 8.3, we present a review and synthesis of the recent literature. As already noted above, there are significant differences in the quantitative findings across studies. Section 8.4 presents a discussion of key measurement and methodological questions that can potentially account for these differences. In section 8.5, we present a sensitivity and robustness analysis of alternative measurement methodologies using establishment-level data for the U.S. manufacturing sector. Section 8.6 presents new evidence on the relationship between micro and aggregate productivity behavior using selected service sector industries. Section 8.7 provides concluding remarks.

8.2 Theoretical Underpinnings

This section draws together theories and evidence related to the reasons for cross-sectional heterogeneity in plant-level and firm-level outcomes. A pervasive empirical finding in the recent literature is that within-sector differences dwarf between-sector differences in behavior. For example, Haltiwanger 1999, table 1, shows that four-digit industry effects account for less than 10 percent of the cross-sectional heterogeneity in output, employment, capital equipment, capital structures, and productivity growth rates across establishments.

The magnitude of within-sector heterogeneity implies that idiosyncratic factors dominate the determination of which plants create and destroy jobs and which plants achieve rapid productivity growth or suffer productivity declines. An examination of the literature suggests that the following may account for plant-level heterogeneity: uncertainty; plant-level differences in managerial ability, capital vintage, location, and disturbances; and diffusion of knowledge. Starting with the first of these, one likely reason for heterogeneity in plant-level outcomes is the considerable uncertainty that surrounds the development, adoption, distribution, marketing and regulation of new products and production techniques. Uncertainty about the demand for new products or the cost-effectiveness of alternative technologies encourages firms to experiment with different technologies, goods, and production facilities (Roberts and Weitzman 1981). Experimentation, in turn, generates differences in outcomes (Jovanovic 1982; Ericson and Pakes 1992). Even when incentives for experimentation are absent, uncertainty about future cost or demand conditions encourages firms to differentiate their choice of current products and technology so as to position themselves optimally for possible future circumstances (Lambson, 1991).

Another possible reason is that differences in entrepreneurial and managerial ability lead to differences in job and productivity growth rates among firms and plants. These differences include the ability to identify and develop new products, to organize production activity, to motivate workers, and to adapt to changing circumstances. There seems little doubt that these and other ability differences among managers generate much of the observed heterogeneity in plant-level outcomes. Business magazines, newspapers, and academic case studies (e.g., Dial and Murphy 1995) regularly portray the decisions and actions of particular management teams or individuals as crucial determinants of success or failure. High levels of compensation, often heavily skewed toward various forms of incentive pay (Murphy 1999), also suggest that senior managers play key roles in business performance, including productivity and job growth outcomes.[2] A related idea is that it takes time for new businesses to learn about their own abilities.

Other factors that drive heterogeneity in plant-level productivity, output, and input growth outcomes involve plant- and firm-specific location and disturbances. For example, energy costs and labor costs vary across locations, as do the timing of changes in factor costs. Cost differences induce different employment and investment decisions among otherwise similar plants and firms. These decisions, in addition, influence the size and type of labor force and capital stock that a business carries into the future. Thus, current differences in cost and demand conditions induce contemporaneous heterogeneity in plant-level job and productivity growth, and they also cause businesses to differentiate themselves in ways that lead to heterogeneous responses to common shocks in the future. The role of plant-specific shocks to technology, factor costs, and product demand in accounting for the pace of job reallocation has been explored in Hopenhayn (1992), Hopenhayn and Rogerson (1993), and Campbell (1998).

Slow diffusion of information about technology, distribution channels, marketing strategies, and consumer tastes is another important source of plant-level heterogeneity in productivity and job growth. Nasbeth and Ray (1974) and Rogers (1983) document multiyear lags in the diffusion of knowledge about new technologies among firms producing related products. Mansfield, Schwartz, and Wagner (1981) and Pakes and Schankerman (1984) provide evidence of long imitation and product development lags.[3]

Part of the differences across plants may reflect the vintage of the in-

---

2. Many economic analyses attribute a key role to managerial ability in the organization of firms and production units. Lucas (1977), for example, provides an early and influential formal treatment.

3. Knowledge diffusion plays a key role in many theories of firm-level dynamics, industrial evolution, economic growth and international trade. See, for example, Grossman and Helpman (1991), Jovanovic and Rob (1989), and Jovanovic and MacDonald (1994).

stalled capital.[4] Suppose, for example, that new technology can be adopted only by new plants. Under this view, entering, technologically sophisticated plants displace older, outmoded plants and gross output and input flows reflect a process of creative destruction. A related idea is that it may not be the vintage of the capital but rather the vintage of the manager or the organizational structure that induces plant-level heterogeneity (see, e.g., Nelson and Winter 1982).

These models of plant-level heterogeneity are closely related to the theoretical growth models emphasizing the role of creative destruction. Creative destruction models of economic growth stress that the process of adopting new products and new processes inherently involves the destruction of old products and processes. Creative destruction manifests itself in many forms. An important paper that formalizes these ideas is Aghion and Howitt (1992). They consider a model of endogenous growth where endogenous innovations yield creative destruction. Specifically, the creator of a new innovation gets some monopoly rents until the next innovation comes along, at which point the knowledge underlying the rents becomes obsolete. The incentives for investment in R&D and thus growth are impacted by this process of creative destruction.[5]

An alternative but related type of creative destruction growth model mentioned above as a source of plant-level heterogeneity is the vintage capital model. One form of these models (Caballero and Hammour 1994; Campbell 1998) emphasizes the potential role of entry and exit. If new technology can be adopted only by new establishments, growth occurs only via entry and exit, and this requires output and input reallocation. An alternative view is that new technology is embodied in new capital (e.g., Cooper, Haltiwanger, and Power 1999), but that existing plants can adopt new technology by retooling. Under this latter view, both within-plant and between-plant job reallocation may be induced in the retooling process. If, for example, there is skill-biased technical change, the adoption of new technology through retooling will yield a change in the desired mix

---

4. See Aghion and Howitt (1992), Caballero and Hammour (1994, 1996), Campbell (1998), Stein (1997), Cooley, Greenwood, and Yorukoglu (1997), and Chari and Hopenhayn (1991).

5. Growth may be more or less than optimal since there are effects that work in opposite directions. On the one hand, appropriability and intertemporal spillover effects make growth slower than optimal. The appropriability effect derives from the fact that, in the Aghion and Howitt (1992) model, research on new innovations requires skilled labor as does the production of the intermediate goods where new innovations are implemented. A fixed supply of skilled labor implies that skilled labor earns part of the returns from new innovations. The inability of the research firms to capture all of the value from the innovations reduces their incentives to conduct research. The intertemporal spillover effect derives from the fact that current and future innovators derive benefits (i.e., knowledge) from past innovations but do not compensate past innovators for this benefit. The fact that private research firms do not internalize the destruction of rents generated by their innovation works in the opposite direction. This business-stealing effect can actually yield a too-high growth rate. Aghion and Howitt (1992) also find, however, that the business-stealing effect also tends to make innovations too small.

of skilled workers at an establishment. In addition, there may be an impact on the overall desired level of employment at the establishment.

In all of these creative destruction models, the reallocation of outputs and inputs across producers plays a critical role in economic growth. In these models, stifling reallocation in turn stifles growth. It is important to emphasize, however, that there are many forces that may cause growth and the pace of reallocation to deviate from optimal outcomes. As mentioned above in the context of Aghion and Howitt (1992), a generic problem is that agents (firms, innovators, workers) do not internalize the impact of their actions on others. In an analogous manner, Caballero and Hammour (1996) emphasize that the sunkness of investment in new capital implies potential ex post holdup problems that yield several harmful side effects. They explore the hold-up problem generated by worker-firm bargaining over wages after the firm's investment in specific capital.[6] A related point is that, even though reallocation may be vital for growth, there are clearly losers in the process. The losers include the owners of the outmoded businesses that fail as well as the displaced workers.

8.3 Review of Existing Empirical Evidence

The theoretical literature on creative destruction as well as the underlying theories of heterogeneity characterize technological change as a noisy, complex process with considerable experimentation (in terms of entry and retooling) and failure (in terms of contraction and exit) playing integral roles. In this section, we review the evidence from the recent empirical literature that has developed in parallel with the theoretical literature. We conduct this review in two parts: First, we provide a brief review of the micropatterns of output, input, and productivity growth; second, we consider the aggregate implications of these micropatterns. Our review of micropatterns is brief since we regard the results discussed in this section as well established, and excellent recent survey articles by Bartelsman and Doms (2000) and Caves (1998) cover much of the same material in more detail. Moreover, it is the aggregate consequences of these micropatterns that are more open to debate and, as we make clear, a number of measurement issues generate the variation that is found across studies on this dimension.

8.3.1 Brief Review of Key Micropatterns

We begin our review by briefly summarizing a few key patterns that have become well established in this literature. Virtually all of the findings refer to manufacturing; they are as follows.

---

6. Indeed, Blanchard and Kremer (1997) argue that for transition economies, such holdup problems are potentially severe enough that the restructuring process is better described as "disruptive destruction" rather than creative destruction.

Large-scale reallocation of outputs and inputs within sectors. The rate of within-sector reallocation of output and inputs is of great magnitude. Davis and Haltiwanger (1999) summarize much of the recent literature on gross job flows; they note that in the United States, more than one in ten jobs is created in a given year and more than one in ten jobs is destroyed every year. Similar patterns hold for many other market economies. Much of this reallocation reflects reallocation within narrowly defined sectors. For example, Davis and Haltiwanger (1999) report that across a variety of studies, only about 10 percent of reallocation reflects shifts of employment opportunities across four-digit industries.

Entry and exit play a significant role in this process of reallocation. For annual changes, Davis, Haltiwanger, and Schuh (1996) report that about 20 percent of job destruction and 15 percent of job creation is accounted for by entry and exit. For five-year changes, Baldwin, Dunne, and Haltiwanger (1995) report that about 40 percent of creation and destruction are accounted for by entry and exit, respectively.[7]

Persistent differences in levels of productivity. There are large and persistent differences in productivity across plants in the same industry (see Bartelsman and Doms 2000 for an excellent discussion). In analyzing persistence, many studies report transition matrices of plants in the relative productivity distribution within narrowly defined industries (see, e.g., Baily, Hulten, and Campbell 1992 and Bartelsman and Dhrymes 1998). These transition matrices exhibit large diagonal and near-diagonal elements, indicating that plants that are high in the distribution in one period tend to stay high in the distribution in subsequent periods. In contrast, establishment-level productivity growth *rates* exhibit an important transitory component. Baily, Hulten, and Campbell (1992) and Dwyer (1998) present strong evidence of regression to the mean effects in productivity growth regressions.

Low productivity helps predict exit. Many studies (e.g., Baily, Hulten, and Campbell 1992; Olley and Pakes 1996; Dwyer 1998) find that the productivity level helps predict exit. Low-productivity plants are more likely to exit even after controlling for other factors such as establishment size and age. A related set of findings is that observable plant characteristics are positively correlated with productivity, including size, age, wages, adoption of advanced technologies, and exporting (see, e.g., Baily, Hulten, and Campbell 1992; Doms, Dunne, and Troske 1996; Olley and Pakes 1996; Bernard and Jensen 1999). It has been more difficult to find correlates of changes

---

7. The calculations in Baldwin, Dunne, and Haltiwanger (1995) are an updated version of earlier calculations by Dunne, Roberts, and Samuelson (1989). The five-year gross flows and the shares accounted for by entry and exit are somewhat lower in the later work for equivalent periods, reflecting the improvement in longitudinal linkages in the Census of Manufacturers over time.

in productivity. For example, Doms, Dunne, and Troske (1996) find that plants that have adopted advanced technologies are more likely to be high-productivity plants, but that the change in productivity is only weakly related to the adoption of such advanced technologies.

8.3.2 Reallocation and Aggregate Productivity Growth

Empirical analysis of the implications of the pace of reallocation and restructuring for productivity dynamics has been recently provided by Baily, Hulten, and Campbell (1992), Olley and Pakes (1996), Bartelsman and Dhrymes (1998), Dwyer (1998, 1997) and Haltiwanger (1997), using plant-level manufacturing data from the United States; Aw, Chen, and Roberts (1997) using firm-level data from Taiwan; Tybout (1996) and Liu and Tybout (1996) using data from Colombia, Chile, and Morocco; and Griliches and Regev (1995) using data from Israel.[8] Virtually all of the studies consider some form of decomposition of an index of industry-level productivity:

$$(1) \qquad P_{it} = \sum_{e \in I} s_{et} p_{et}$$

where P_{it} is the index of industry productivity, s_{et} is the share of plant e in industry i (e.g., output share), and p_{et} is an index of plant-level productivity.

Using plant-level data, the industry index and its components can be constructed for measures of labor and multifactor productivity. Many studies have decomposed the time series changes in aggregate (i.e., industry-level) productivity into components that reflect a within component (holding shares fixed in some manner) and other effects that reflect the reallocation of the shares across plants, including the impact of entry and exit. Table 8.1 presents a summary of results from a variety of studies using different countries, time periods, frequency of measured changes, productivity concepts (i.e., multifactor vs. labor), and measurement methodologies.[9] The differences along these many dimensions make fine comparisons difficult so our objective in considering the alternative studies is to consider broad patterns. In the next section, we consider methodological issues in detail and then conduct our own sensitivity analysis. For now, we attempt to compare studies on dimensions that are relatively easy to compare.

One core aspect that is roughly comparable across studies is the contribution of the within plant contribution to aggregate productivity growth.

---

8. Baldwin (1995) presents some related analysis of the contribution of plant turnover to productivity growth for Canada, but his methodology differs sufficiently from the rest of the literature that it is not easy to integrate his work into this discussion.

9. In the case of Taiwan, a simple average (or simple median) of the industry-level results reported in the Aw, Chen, and Roberts (1997) paper is presented.

Table 8.1 A Comparison of Decompositions of Aggregate Productivity Growth

Country	Frequency	Sample Period	Sectoral Coverage	Weight Used to Calculate Within Plant Changes[a]	Average Fraction from Within Plant Changes	Fraction of Activity[b] from Entrants (t)	Fraction of Activity from Exits (t−k)	Relative Productivity of Births (t) to Deaths (t−k)	Study
				A. Multifactor Productivity Decompositions					
U.S.	Five-year	1972–87	Selected manufacturing industries (23)	Output (t−k)	0.37	n.a.	n.a.	n.a.	Baily, Hulten, and Campbell (1992)
U.S.	Five-year	1977–87	All manufacturing industries	Output (t−k)	0.23	0.08	0.10	1.05	Haltiwanger (1997)
U.S.	Ten-year	1977–87	All manufacturing industries	Output (t−k)	0.54	0.16	0.21	1.11	Haltiwanger (1997)
Taiwan[c]	Five-year	1981–91	Selected manufacturing industries (9)	Output (average of [t−k] and t)	0.94 (Median = 0.63)	n.a.	n.a.	n.a.	Aw, Chen, and Roberts (1997)
Colombia	Annual	1978–86	Selected manufacturing industries (5)	Input index[d] (average of [t−k] and t)	1.00	n.a.	0.05	1.05	Liu and Tybout (1996)
				B. Labor Productivity Growth Decompositions					
U.S.	Ten-year	1977–87	All manufacturing industries	Employment (t−k)	0.79	0.26	0.28	1.42	Baily, Bartelsman, and Haltiwanger (1996)
U.S.	Annual	1972–88	All manufacturing industries	Manhours (t−k)	1.20	0.01	0.02	1.03	Baily, Bartelsman, and Haltiwanger (forthcoming)
Israel	Three-Year	1979–88	All manufacturing industries	Employment (average of [t−k] and t)	0.83	0.08	0.06	1.20	Griliches and Regev (1995)

Note: n.a. = not available.

[a] Within contribution is measured as the weighted sum of plant-level productivity growth as a fraction of aggregate index of productivity growth. In all cases, output above refers to gross output.

[b] Activity is measured in the same units as weight (e.g., employment or output).

[c] Simple average (and simple median) of industry-based results reported.

[d] The input index is a geometric mean of inputs using estimated factor elasticities.

Even for this measure, there are differences in the methodology along a number of dimensions. These include whether the measure of productivity is multifactor or labor, whether the share is based on output or employment weights, and whether the share is based on the initial share at the base period or the average share (averaged over base and end period).

The fraction of within-plant contribution to multifactor productivity growth ranges from 0.23 to 1.00 across studies, while the fraction of the within-plant contribution to labor productivity growth ranges from 0.79 to 1.20 across studies. It is obviously difficult to draw conclusions even in broad terms about whether the within-plant contribution is large or small. The variation across countries may reflect a variety of factors. Nevertheless, careful examination of the individual studies indicates that this variation is due in part to there being considerable sensitivity to time period, frequency, and cross-industry variation.

To shed light on the sensitivity to business cycles and industry, table 8.2 presents a few selected results from different time periods and industries from the Baily, Hulten, and Campbell (1992) and Haltiwanger (1997) studies. For the 1977–82 period, the within-plant contribution for manufacturing in general is negative for both studies reflecting the fact that, while there is modest overall productivity growth over this period, its source is not the within-plant component. In contrast, for the 1982–87 period, the within-plant contribution is large and positive during a period of robust productivity growth. This apparent sensitivity to the business cycle (1982 was during a severe slump in U.S. manufacturing) is interesting in its own right. These results suggest that overall productivity is less procyclical than within-plant productivity. The inference is that reallocation effects tend to generate a countercyclical "bias," and thus recessions are times when the share of activity accounted for by less productive plants decreases either through contraction or exit.[10] The more general point in the current context is that the within-plant contribution varies substantially with the cycle.

Table 8.2 also shows that the results tend to vary dramatically by detailed industry. Steel mills (Standard Industrial Classification [SIC] 3312, blast furnaces) exhibit tremendous cyclicality in the behavior of productivity, while telecommunications equipment (SIC 3661, telephone and telegraph equipment) does not. Moreover, the fraction accounted for by within-plant changes is large and stable for telecommunications and very large and variable for steel mills.

Given the discussion of theoretical underpinnings in section 8.2 an obvious question is the contribution of plant entry and exit to these aggregate productivity dynamics. While many studies consider this issue, the precise measurement of the contribution of net entry and exit is quite sensitive to

---

10. Baily, Bartelsman, and Haltiwanger (forthcoming) provide a more extensive analysis of the role of reallocation for the cyclical behavior of productivity.

Table 8.2 Sensitivity of Decomposition Results to Business Cycle and Sector (five-year frequency)

Sectoral Coverage	1977–82		1982–87		Study
	Multifactor Productivity Growth	Fraction from Within Plant Changes	Multifactor Productivity Growth	Fraction from Within Plant Changes	
All manufacturing industries	2.43	−0.12	8.26	0.58	Haltiwanger (1997)
Selected manufacturing industries (23)	2.39	−0.46	15.63	0.87	Baily, Hulten, and Campbell (1992)
Blast furnaces (SIC = 3312)	−3.66	2.15	18.30	1.06	Baily, Hulten, and Campbell (1992)
Telephone and telegraph equipment (SIC = 3661)	14.58	0.78	13.19	0.86	Baily, Hulten, and Campbell (1992)

Notes: Weight for within calculation from both studies is initial gross output share for the plant in each industry. Results aggregated across industries are based upon weighted average with weight for this purpose equal to the average of nominal gross output for the industry.

the decomposition methodology that is used. This sensitivity, in turn, makes cross-study comparisons of the contribution of net entry especially difficult. Nevertheless, some aspects of the underlying roles of entry and exit can be directly compared across studies.

Returning to table 8.1, we see that one important factor is the horizon over which the productivity growth is measured. By construction, the share of activity accounted for by exits in the base year and entrants in the end year are increasing in the horizon over which the base and end year are measured. At an annual frequency, we observe that the share of employment accounted for by exits in the U.S. in the year $t - 1$ is only 0.02 and by entrants in year t is only 0.01. In contrast, at a ten-year horizon, the share of employment accounted for by plants in the United States in year $t - 10$ that ultimately exit over the ten years is 0.28 while the share of employment accounted for by plants in year t that entered over the ten years is 0.26. These results imply that the contribution of any differences in productivity between entering and exiting plants will be greater for changes measured over a longer horizon.

The influence of the horizon also is likely to impact the observed productivity differences between exiting plants in the base year and entering plants in the end year via selection and learning effects. That is, one-year-old plants are likely to have on average a lower productivity than ten-year-old plants because of selection and learning effects. Many studies (e.g., Olley and Pakes 1996; Liu and Tybout 1996; Aw, Chen, and Roberts 1997) present results suggesting that selection and learning effects play an important role. The results in table 8.1 reflect this in that the relative productivity of entering plants in the end year to exiting plants in the base year is increasing for changes measured over a longer horizon.[11]

Putting these results on entry and exit together helps account for the finding that studies that focus on high frequency variation (e.g., Baily, Bartelsman, and Haltiwanger forthcoming and Griliches and Regev 1995) tend to find a small contribution of net entry to aggregate productivity growth while studies over a longer horizon find a large role for net entry (e.g., Baily, Bartelsman, and Haltiwanger 1996; Haltiwanger 1997; and Aw, Chen, and Roberts 1997). We return to this theme in subsequent sections.

Overall, however, the fact remains that it is difficult to assess the contribution of reallocation to productivity growth by a simple comparison of results across studies. Obviously, part of the reason for this is that the results across studies are from different countries, time periods, frequencies, and sectoral coverage. Indeed, exploiting the variation along these

---

11. Although the earlier vintage arguments suggest that it may be that younger plants should have higher productivity. While such vintage effects may be present, the evidence clearly suggests that the impact of selection and learning effects dominate.

dimensions would be useful to shed light on the factors that yield variation in the contribution of reallocation to productivity growth. However, part of the reason for the differences across studies reflects differences in the decomposition methodology across studies. To disentangle these differences, we conduct our own analysis and consider in detail the sensitivity of results to alternative measurement methodologies. We now turn our attention to this sensitivity analysis.

8.4 Measurement and Methodological Issues

8.4.1 Alternative Decomposition Methodologies

To illustrate the sensitivity to measurement methodology, we consider two alternative decomposition methodologies. The first decomposition method (denoted method 1 in what follows) we consider is a modified version of that used by Baily, Hulten, and Campbell (1992) and is given by[12]

$$(2) \quad \Delta P_{it} = \sum_{e \in C} s_{et-1} \Delta p_{et} + \sum_{e \in C} (p_{et-1} - P_{it-1}) \Delta s_{et} + \sum_{e \in C} \Delta p_{et} \Delta s_{et}$$
$$+ \sum_{e \in N} s_{et}(p_{et} - P_{it-1}) - \sum_{e \in X} s_{et-1}(p_{et-1} - P_{it-1})$$

where C denotes continuing plants, N denotes entering plants, and X denotes exiting plants. The first term in this decomposition represents a within plant component based on plant-level changes, weighted by initial shares in the industry. The second term represents a between-plant component that reflects changing shares, weighted by the deviation of initial plant productivity from the initial industry index. The third term represents a cross (i.e., covariance-type) term. The last two terms represent the contribution of entering and exiting plants, respectively.

In this decomposition, the between-plant term and the entry and exit terms involve deviations of plant-level productivity from the initial industry index. For a continuing plant, this implies that an increase in its share contributes positively to the between-plant component only if the plant has higher productivity than average initial productivity for the industry. Similarly, an exiting plant contributes positively only if the plant exhibits

---

12. The first term in this decomposition (the "within component") is identical to that in Baily, Hulten, and Campbell (1992). They essentially combined the second two terms by calculating a term based upon the sum of changes in shares of activity weighted by ending period productivity. In addition, they did not deviate the terms in the between and net entry terms from initial levels. As Haltiwanger (1997) points out, this implies that even if all plants have the same productivity in both beginning and end periods, the between component and the net entry component in the Baily, Hulten, and Campbell decomposition will, in general, be nonzero. See Haltiwanger (1997) for further discussion.

productivity lower than the initial average, and an entering plant contributes positively only if the plant has higher productivity than the initial average.

This decomposition differs somewhat from others that have appeared in the literature in some subtle but important ways. Key distinguishing features of the decomposition used here are: (a) an integrated treatment of entry/exit and continuing plants; (b) separating-out within and between effects from cross/covariance effects. Some of the decompositions that appear in the literature are more difficult to interpret because they do not separate out cross/covariance effects. For example, some measure the within effect as the change in productivity weighted by average shares (in t and $t - k$—see method 2 below). While the latter method yields a seemingly cleaner decomposition, it also allows the within effect to reflect partially the reallocation effects, since it incorporates the share in period t. Another problem is in the treatment of net entry. Virtually all of the decompositions in the literature that consider net entry measure the contribution of net entry via the simple difference between the weighted average of entrants and exiting plants productivity. Even if there are no differences in productivity between entering and exiting plants, this commonly used method yields the inference that net entry contributes positively to an increase (decrease) in productivity growth if the share of entrants is greater (less than) the share of exiting plants. There are related (and offsetting) problems in the treatment of the contribution of continuing plants.

While this first method is our preferred decomposition, measurement error considerations suggest an alternative decomposition closely related to that used by Griliches and Regev (1995). Consider, in particular, the following alternative decomposition (denoted method 2 in the remainder of this paper):

$$(3) \quad \Delta P_{it} = \sum_{e \in C} \bar{s}_e \Delta p_{et} + \sum_{e \in C} (\bar{p}_e - \bar{P}_i) \Delta s_{et} + \sum_{e \in N} s_{et}(p_{et} - \bar{P}_i) - \sum_{e \in X} s_{et-1}(p_{et-1} - \bar{P}_i)$$

where a bar over a variable indicates the average of the variable over the base and end years. In this decomposition, the first term is interpretable as a within effect that is measured as the weighted sum of productivity with the weights equal to the average (across time) shares. The second is interpretable as a between effect where the changes in the shares are indexed by the deviations of the average plant-level productivity from the overall industry average. In a like manner, the net entry terms are such that entry contributes positively as long as entering plants are higher than the overall average and exiting plants are lower than the overall average.

This second decomposition method is a modification of the standard within/between decomposition that is often used for balanced panels. The disadvantage of this method is that the measured within effect will now reflect in part cross/covariance effects (as will the measured between effect). However, this second method is apt to be less sensitive to measurement error in outputs or inputs relative to the first method as shown in equation (2). Suppose, for example, we are considering labor productivity (e.g., output per man-hour) and that there is random measurement error in measured man-hours. Measurement error of this type will imply that plants in a given period with spuriously high measured man-hours will have spuriously low measured productivity. Such measurement error will yield a negative covariance between changes in productivity and changes in shares (measured in terms of man-hours) and a spuriously high within-plant effect under method 1. In a similar manner, consider the decomposition of multifactor productivity (MFP) using output weights. Random measurement error in output will yield a positive covariance between productivity changes and changes in shares and a spuriously low within-plant effect under method 1. In contrast, the measured within effect from method 2 will be less sensitive to random measurement error in output or inputs since the averaging across time of the shares will mitigate the influence of measurement error.[13]

An alternative cross-sectional decomposition methodology utilized by Olley and Pakes (1996) is of interest as well. Consider the following cross-sectional decomposition of productivity for an industry in period t (denoted method 3 in what follows):

(4) $$P_{it} = \bar{p} + \sum_{e}(s_{et} - \bar{s})(p_{et} - \bar{p})$$

where in this case a bar over a variable represents the *cross-sectional* (unweighted) mean across all plants in the same industry. The second term in this decomposition provides insights into whether activity (e.g., output or employment, depending on how shares are measured) is disproportionately located at high-productivity plants. In addition, by examining the time series pattern of each of the terms in this decomposition we can learn whether the cross-sectional allocation of activity has become more or less productivity enhancing over time. One advantage of this cross-sectional approach is that the cross-sectional differences in productivity are more persistent and less dominated by measurement error and transitory shocks. A related advantage is that this cross-sectional decomposition does not rely on accurately measuring entry and exit. Both of these problems potentially plague the time series decompositions using method 1 or method 2 (although method 2 has some advantages in terms of measure-

---

13. This discussion focuses on simple classical measurement error. There may be other forms of nonrandom measurement error that are important in this context.

ment error). Of course, examining the time series patterns of the cross-sectional decomposition does not permit characterizing the role of entry and exit.

Clearly each of these techniques has notable strengths and weaknesses. Given the measurement concerns we have raised and given the independent interest in each of these alternative methodologies, we present results from each of the three methods in the analysis that follows.

8.4.2 Measurement of Output, Inputs, and Productivity Using the Census of Manufactures

In the next section, we present evidence applying the alternative decomposition methodologies using plant-level data from the Census of Manufactures. A number of different but related versions of the decompositions are considered. First, we consider the decomposition of industry-level MFP where the shares (s_{et}) are measured using plant-level gross output. This weighting methodology is common in the recent literature investigating such MFP decompositions (see, e.g., Baily, Hulten, and Campbell 1992; Bartelsman and Dhrymes 1994; Olley and Pakes 1996; Aw, Chen, and Roberts 1997). Next, we consider a decomposition of industry-level labor productivity using both gross output and employment share weights. For labor productivity, the seemingly appropriate weight is employment (or man-hours) since this will yield a tight measurement link between most measures of labor productivity using industry-level data and industry-based measures built up from plant-level data. Both the Griliches and Regev (1995) and Baily, Bartelsman, and Haltiwanger (1996) papers use employment weights in this context. However, as we shall see, using gross output weights as an alternative provides useful insights into the relationship between multifactor and labor productivity decompositions and, in so doing, on the role of reallocation in productivity growth.

The index of plant-level multifactor productivity (MFP_{et}) used here is similar to that used by Baily, Hulten, and Campbell (1992). The index is measured as follows:

$$\ln \text{MFP}_{et} = \ln Q_{et} - \alpha_K \ln K_{et} - \alpha_L \ln L_{et} - \alpha_M \ln M_{et},$$

where Q_{et} is real gross output, L_{et} is labor input (total hours), K_{et} is real capital (in practice separate terms are included for structures and equipment), and M_{et} is real materials. Outputs and inputs are measured in constant (1987) dollars. Factor elasticities are measured via industry cost shares. The index of plant-level labor productivity is measured as the difference between log gross output and log labor input.[14] Using this mea-

---

14. We also performed the labor productivity analysis using value added per unit of labor. The results using this alternative measure in terms of the decompositions and relative productivity are very similar to those we report in the subsequent sections.

surement methodology with equation (1) yields industry-level growth rates in productivity that correspond closely to industry-level growth rates constructed using industry-level data.

The Census of Manufactures (CM) plant-level data used in the analysis include information on shipments, inventories, book values of equipment and structures, employment of production and nonproduction workers, total hours of production workers, and cost of materials and energy usage. For the most part, the measurement methodology closely follows that of Baily, Hulten, and Campbell (1992). The details of the measurement of output and inputs are provided in the appendix.

8.5 Results for the U.S. Manufacturing Sector

We begin by characterizing results on the U.S. manufacturing sector over the 1977 to 1987 period. We focus on this interval since it comes close to reflecting changes on a peak-to-peak basis. In the second subsection, we consider various five-year intervals which tend to be dominated more by cyclical variation in productivity. In the third subsection, we look at net entry in more detail. The last subsection summarizes the results.

8.5.1 Ten-year changes: Basic Decompositions

Table 8.3 presents estimates of the gross expansion and contraction rates of employment, output and capital (structures and equipment) over the 1977–87 period. The rates of output and input expansion (contraction) are measured as the weighted average of the growth rates of expanding (contracting) plants including the contribution of entering (exiting) plants using the methodology of Davis, Haltiwanger, and Schuh (1996).[15] The pace of gross output and input expansion and contraction is extremely large over the ten-year horizon. Expanding plants yielded a gross rate of expansion of more than 40 percent of outputs and inputs and contracting plants yielded a gross rate of contraction in excess of 30 percent of outputs and inputs. Net growth rate of output is higher than that of inputs (especially employment) reflecting the productivity growth over this period. A large fraction of the output and input gross creation from expanding plants came from entry and a large fraction of the output and input gross destruction came from exit.

Table 8.3 also includes the fraction of excess reallocation within four-digit industries in each of these industries. Excess reallocation is the sum of gross expansion and contraction rates less the absolute value of net

---

15. This methodology entails defining plant-level growth rates as the change divided by the average of the base and end-year variable. The advantage of this growth rate measure is that it is symmetric for positive and negative changes and allows for an integrated treatment of entering and exiting plants.

Table 8.3 Gross Reallocation of Employment, Output, Equipment, and Structures (ten-year changes from 1977–87)

Measure	Creation (Expansion) Rate	Share of Creation (Expansion) Due to Entrants	Destruction (Contraction) Rate	Share of Destruction (Contraction) Due to Exits	Fraction of Excess Reallocation within 4-Digit Industry
Real gross output	49.4	0.44	34.4	0.61	0.80
Employment	39.4	0.58	45.8	0.62	0.75
Capital equipment	46.1	0.42	37.1	0.51	0.71
Capital structures	44.9	0.44	48.4	0.42	0.69

Source: Tabulations from the CM.

Note: See text for details of construction of output, equipment, and structures measures.

change for the sector. Thus, excess reallocation reflects the gross reallocation (expansion plus contraction) that is in excess of that required to accommodate the net expansion of the sector. Following Davis, Haltiwanger, and Schuh (1996; see pages 52 and 53 for a description of the methodology), excess reallocation rates at the total manufacturing level can be decomposed into within- and between-sector effects. The far right column of table 8.3 indicates that most of the excess reallocation at the total manufacturing level reflects excess reallocation within four-digit industries. Thus, the implied large shifts in the allocation of employment, output, and capital are primarily among producers in the same four-digit industry.

The large within-sector reallocation rates motivate our analysis of productivity decompositions at the four-digit level. We apply the decompositions in equations (2) and (3) at the four-digit level. In most of our results, we report the results for the average industry. Following Baily, Hulten, and Campbell (1992), the weights used to average across industries are average nominal gross output, averaged over the beginning and ending years of the period over which the change is measured. The same industry weights are used to aggregate the industry results across all of the decompositions. The motivation for this is that the focus here is on within-industry decompositions and thus the results do not reflect changing industry composition.[16]

Consider first the decomposition of industry-level *multifactor* productivity reported in table 8.4 for the 1977–87 period. For method 1, the within-plant component accounts for about half of average industry productivity growth, the between-plant component is negative but relatively small, and the cross term is positive and large accounting for about a third of the average industry change. Net entry accounts for 26 percent of the average industry change. For method 2, the within component accounts for 65 percent of average industry productivity growth, the between component 10 percent, and net entry 25 percent.[17] The comparison across methods for MFP suggests that the impact of net entry is robust across methods but that inferences regarding the contribution of reallocation among continuing plants vary widely across methods. We return to considering the reasons for this below after we consider the labor productivity decompositions.

The decompositions of *labor* productivity are reported in table 8.4 as

---

16. Change in aggregate productivity from between-industry reallocation is an interesting topic in its own right, but the conceptual and measurement issues are potentially quite different. Our focus is on the noisy and complex process of industry growth with individual businesses in the same industry that are trying to find the best ways to produce and sell their goods and services given their own potentially idiosyncratic conditions. The resulting entry/exit as well as contraction and expansion of businesses in the same industry reflects the evolution of the idiosyncratic decisions and fortunes across businesses.

17. We look at method 3 at the end of this subsection.

Table 8.4   Decomposition of Multifactor and Labor Productivity Growth, 1977–87

Measure	Weight	Overall Growth	Within Share	Between Share	Cross Share	Net Entry Share
		A. Method 1				
Multifactor productivity	Gross output	10.24	0.48	−0.08	0.34	0.26
Labor productivity						
(per hour)	Gross output	25.56	0.45	−0.13	0.37	0.31
	Man-hours	21.32	0.77	0.08	−0.14	0.29
(per worker)	Employment	23.02	0.74	0.08	−0.11	0.29
		B. Method 2				
Multifactor productivity	Gross output	10.24	0.65	0.10	—	0.25
Labor productivity						
(per hour)	Gross output	25.56	0.64	0.06	—	0.31
	Man-hours	21.32	0.70	0.00	—	0.30
(per worker)	Employment	23.02	0.69	0.01	—	0.30

Source: Tabulations from the CM.
Note: Long dash = not applicable.

well. For labor productivity at the establishment level we consider two alternatives: output per man-hour and output per worker. In general, the results are very similar between these alternatives. To aggregate across establishments in the same industry, we consider two alternatives as well: output weights and labor input weights. When we use output weights, we only report the results for output per man-hour since the results are very similar to those for output per worker. In the discussion that follows we focus on the distinction between those results that use output weights and those that use labor weights (either employment or manhours).

Interestingly, whether one uses labor or output shares yields approximately the same overall average industry growth in labor productivity over this period. In addition, the contribution of net entry is quite similar whether labor or output shares are used or whether method 1 or method 2 is used. Thus, in either case, reallocation plays an important role (at least in an accounting sense) in labor productivity growth via net entry.

The biggest difference between the results using output and employment weights is associated with the continuing plants for method 1. The decomposition of labor productivity using gross output share weights looks very similar to the multifactor productivity decomposition in that the respective roles of within, between, and cross effects are quite similar. When labor shares are used as weights as opposed to output shares, the within-plant component of labor productivity growth is much larger. In addition, with labor weights, there is relatively little contribution from the between and covariance terms. This finding of a large within-plant contribution for labor productivity using labor weights is similar to the findings in Griliches and Regev (1995) and Baily, Bartelsman, and Haltiwanger (1996). The implication from the labor weighted results is that, for continuing plants, much of the increase in labor productivity would have occurred even if labor shares had been held constant at their initial levels.

For method 2, the differences between the results using labor or output weights are substantially diminished. Indeed, under method 2, the results using alternative productivity measures (multifactor or labor) or alternative weights (output, man-hours, or employment) are very similar. These results suggest that more than 60 percent of average industry productivity growth can be accounted for by within-plant effects, less than 10 percent by between-plant effects, and more than 25 percent by net entry.

An obvious question is what underlies the differences between method 1 and method 2? To shed light on the differences in results across methods, table 8.5 presents simple correlations of the plant-level growth rates in multifactor productivity, labor productivity, output, employment, equipment and structures. These correlations are based upon the 1977–87 changes for continuing plants. Multifactor productivity and labor productivity growth are strongly positively correlated. Not surprisingly, output growth and input growth are highly positively correlated (especially output and employment growth). Nevertheless, while output growth is strongly positively correlated with both multifactor and labor productivity growth, employment and capital growth are virtually uncorrelated with multifactor productivity growth. There is a positive correlation between capital growth and labor productivity growth and an even stronger positive correlation between capital intensity growth (the growth in capital per unit of labor) and labor productivity growth. The negative correlation between labor productivity growth and labor input growth underlie the negative cross terms in the decompositions of labor productivity using employment or man-hours weights. In an analogous manner, the positive correlations between productivity (multifactor or labor) growth and output growth underlie the positive cross terms in the decompositions using output weights.

A number of factors are at work in generating these patterns; analyzing these factors will help us disentangle the differences in the results between methods 1 and 2. The first potential factor is measurement error, the second factor concerns changes in factor intensities. As discussed in section 8.4, measurement error will generate a downward bias in the correlation between productivity growth and employment growth and an upward bias in the correlation between productivity growth and output growth. Likewise, measurement error will yield a spuriously low (high) within plant share for multifactor (labor) productivity growth using method 1. The patterns in tables 8.4 and 8.5 are consistent with such influences of measurement error. Moreover, the seemingly consistent results across productivity

Table 8.5 Correlation between Plant-Level Productivity, Output, and Input Growth, 1977-87 (continuing plants)

	Multifactor Productivity	Labor Productivity (per hour)	Labor Productivity (per worker)	Output	Employment	Manhours	Capital Equipment	Capital Structures
Multifactor productivity	1.00							
Labor productivity								
(per hour)	0.41	1.00						
(per worker)	0.38	0.93	1.00					
Output	0.24	0.47	0.52	1.00				
Employment	−0.03	−0.17	−0.17	0.76	1.00			
Man-hours	−0.04	−0.22	−0.12	0.75	0.96	1.00		
Capital equipment	−0.06	0.16	0.18	0.55	0.49	0.49	1.00	
Capital structures	−0.07	0.15	0.17	0.52	0.46	0.46	0.76	1.00
Capital intensity	−0.03	0.34	0.30	0.06	−0.16	−0.19	0.71	0.63

Source: Tabulations from the CM.

measures using method 2 suggests that method 2 is effective in mitigating these measurement error problems. Recall that method 2 uses averages across time to generate the appropriate aggregation "weights" for the changes in productivity and changes in activity shares and this averaging will tend to mitigate problems from measurement error.

While it is tempting to conclude that measurement error is driving the differences between methods 1 and 2 and thus method 2 should be preferred, there are alternative explanations of the observed patterns. First, the differences between methods 1 and 2 are systematic for alternative measures of productivity. In particular, the results for labor productivity per hour are very similar to those using labor productivity per worker. Since employment and shipments are measured relatively well (in comparison to, say, hours), the latter productivity measure should be the least affected by measurement error but we do not see a different pattern for this measure. In addition, and perhaps more importantly, there are a number of reasons that the patterns of labor productivity and multifactor productivity should be different. We now consider these issues briefly.

Recall that table 8.5 shows a strong positive correlation between labor productivity growth and capital intensity growth. Moreover, there is a positive correlation between plants with initially high labor shares and growth in capital intensity (their correlation is 0.14). These patterns suggest that changes in capital intensity may be associated with the large within-plant contribution for labor productivity under method 1. That is, plants with large changes in capital intensity also exhibited large changes in labor productivity and had large initial labor shares. These factors together contribute to a large within-plant share under method 1 for labor productivity. Note as well that changes in capital intensity need not be tightly linked to changes in MFP, which is indeed the case as seen in table 8.5. Viewed from this perspective, method 2 may be masking some important differences in the patterns of labor and multifactor productivity. Recall that the conceptual problem with method 2 is that the within term confounds changes in plant-level productivity with changes in shares of activity. The within-plant component for labor productivity is lessened because the change in labor productivity is aggregated using average instead of initial labor shares and thus mitigates the relationship between changes in capital intensity and labor productivity (and initial shares).

To help differentiate between the measurement error and productivity-enhancing changes in factor intensities, it is useful to consider evidence for some individual industries. Consider, for example, the steel industry (SIC 3312). As documented in Davis, Haltiwanger, and Schuh (1996), the steel industry underwent tremendous restructuring over the 1970s and the 1980s. A large part of this restructuring involved the shifting from integrated mills to mini-mills. While substantial entry and exit played a major role, the restructuring of the industry also involved the retooling of many continuing plants. Baily, Bartelsman, and Haltiwanger (1996) present evidence that continuing plants in the steel industry downsized significantly over this period of time and exhibited substantial productivity gains (i.e., there is a large negative covariance between employment changes and labor productivity changes among the continuing plants in the steel industry). As reported in Davis, Haltiwanger, and Schuh (1996), the average worker employed at a steel mill worked at a plant with 7,000 workers in 1980 and only 4,000 workers by 1985. Moreover, this downsizing was associated with large subsequent productivity gains in the steel industry (see, e.g., figure 5.8 in Davis, Haltiwanger, and Schuh 1996). These patterns are reflected in the decompositions we have generated underlying table 8.4. For SIC 3312, for example, we find that growth in labor productivity per hour is 29.7 for the 1977–87 period and the within component using method 1 accounts for 93 percent. Consistent with the view that the downsizing was productivity enhancing in this industry we find a negative cross term of 23 percent. In addition, capital intensity growth in the steel industry is positively correlated with changes in labor productivity at the plant level, with a correlation of 0.26. Taken together, these patterns paint a picture of many plants changing their factor intensities in dramatic ways and this in turn being reflected in the growth in labor productivity.[18]

As the discussion of the steel industry illustrates, the patterns we observe in the cross terms in the decompositions for method 1 using alternative weights are potentially driven by part of a within-plant restructuring process that yields substantial productivity gains. More generally, these results suggest that the connection between measured reallocation of inputs, outputs, and productivity growth is quite complex. Plants are often changing the mix of inputs at the same time they change the scale of production. Some technological innovations (e.g., mini-mills) may lead to substantial downsizing by plants that adopt the new technology. Alternatively, technological innovations may take the form of cost savings or product quality enhancements that enable successfully adopting plants to increase their market share with accompanying expansion.

Results using the cross-sectional decomposition (method 3) are reported in table 8.6. We conducted this decomposition separately for every four-digit industry using MFP with output weights, labor productivity per hour using man-hour weights, and labor productivity per worker using employment weights. The reported results are the average industry results where the weighted average across industries uses the same industry weights as those used in table 8.4. There is a positive second term for all productivity measures for all years indicating that plants with higher productivity have higher output and labor shares in their industry. For each of the measures,

---

18. It is worth noting, as well, that the within component using method 1 accounts for 87 percent of the growth in MFP in this industry.

Table 8.6   Cross-Sectional Decompositions of Productivity, by Year

Measure	Weight	1977			1987		
		Overall	$\bar{p}$	Cross	Overall	$\bar{p}$	Cross
Multifactor productivity	Gross output	1.62	1.57	0.05	1.73	1.67	0.06
Labor productivity							
(per hour)	Man-hours	4.12	4.01	0.11	4.37	4.21	0.15
(per worker)	Employment	4.80	4.67	0.13	5.06	4.90	0.16

Source: Tabulations from the CM.

the overall productivity increases between 1977 and 1987. The decomposition reveals that this reflects both an increase in the unweighted mean productivity across plants and an increase in the cross term for the average industry. This latter finding indicates that the reallocation of both outputs and labor inputs between 1977 and 1987 has been productivity enhancing.

8.5.2   Five-Year Changes: 1977–82, 1982–87, and 1987–92

For the five-year changes in industry-level productivity, we consider a subset of the exercises considered in the prior section. In particular, we consider the time series decompositions using methods 1 and 2 for the five-year changes measured from 1977 to 1982, 1982 to 1987, and 1987 to 1992. The productivity measures we consider are MFP using gross output weights in the decompositions and labor productivity per hour using man-hour weights in the decompositions.

The results of these decompositions are reported in table 8.7. Cyclical variation in productivity growth plays a dominant role in the overall patterns. Productivity growth is especially modest in the 1977–82 period and very strong in the 1982–87 period. Using method 1, the multifactor productivity and labor productivity decompositions yield quite different stories, especially for the periods that are roughly coincident with cyclical downturns. For example, for the 1977–82 period, the within share is actually negative for the multifactor productivity decomposition while the within share is above one for the labor productivity decomposition. Associated with these dramatically different within plant contributions are very different cross terms. For the MFP decomposition, the cross term is positive and relatively large (above 1) and for the labor productivity decomposition, the cross term is negative and relatively large (above 1 in absolute magnitude).

In contrast, method 2 yields results that are much less erratic across multifactor and labor productivity and across the alternative subperiods. Even here, however, the contribution of within-plant changes to MFP

Table 8.7 Decomposition of Multifactor and Labor Productivity Growth over Subperiods

Years	Measure	Weight	Overall Growth	Within Share	Between Share	Cross Share	Net Entry Share
			A. Method 1				
1977–82	Multifactor productivity	Gross output	2.70	−0.09	−0.33	1.16	0.25
	Labor productivity	Man-hours	2.54	1.22	0.85	−1.27	0.20
1982–87	Multifactor productivity	Gross output	7.32	0.52	−0.18	0.51	0.14
	Labor productivity	Man-hours	18.67	0.83	0.13	−0.15	0.19
1987–92	Multifactor productivity	Gross output	3.30	−0.06	−0.39	1.10	0.35
	Labor productivity	Man-hours	7.17	0.94	0.33	−0.49	0.21
			B. Method 2				
1977–82	Multifactor productivity	Gross output	2.70	0.49	0.26	—	0.25
	Labor productivity	Man-hours	2.54	0.59	0.21	—	0.20
1982–87	Multifactor productivity	Gross output	7.32	0.78	0.08	—	0.14
	Labor productivity	Man-hours	18.67	0.75	0.03	—	0.21
1987–92	Multifactor productivity	Gross output	3.30	0.49	0.17	—	0.34
	Labor productivity	Man-hours	7.17	0.70	0.08	—	0.22

Source: Tabulations from the CM.
Notes: Labor productivity is per hour. Long dash = not applicable.

Table 8.8   **Correlation between Plant-Level Productivity, Output, and Input Growth for Subperiods (continuing plants)**

	1977–82	1982–87	1987–92
A. Multifactor Productivity			
Output	0.29	0.23	0.24
Man-hours	−0.07	−0.08	−0.07
Capital intensity	0.07	−0.00	−0.08
Labor productivity (per hour)	0.45	0.41	0.40
B. Labor Productivity (per hour)			
Output	0.52	0.50	0.53
Man-hours	−0.25	−0.26	−0.27
Capital intensity	0.38	0.39	0.29

Source: Tabulations from the CM.

ranges from about 50 percent in cyclical downturns to about 80 percent in cyclical upturns.

What underlies these very different patterns? Table 8.8 sheds light on this issue by characterizing the simple correlations for continuing establishments. The correlation between productivity growth (either multifactor or labor) and output growth is large and positive while the correlation between labor productivity and man-hours growth is large and negative. These correlations and the implied patterns in the decompositions likely reflect a variety of cyclical phenomena and associated measurement problems. For example, cyclical changes in factor utilization will yield spurious changes in measured productivity to the extent that the changes in utilization are poorly measured.

In short, the high-frequency results are difficult to characterize since the contribution of various components is sensitive to decomposition methodology, the measurement of multifactor versus labor productivity, and to time period. However, a couple of patterns are robust. First, the contribution of net entry is robust to the alternative measurement methods. Second, while the contribution of net entry is sensitive to time period, the pattern is regular in the sense that the contribution of net entry is greater in cyclical downturns.[19] Third, using the method more robust to measure-

---

19. It is useful to note that the large contribution of net entry to productivity growth in 1977–82 and 1987–92 is not due to an especially large share of activity accounted for by entering and exiting plants, but rather by a large gap in productivity between entering and exiting plants relative to the overall growth in productivity. For example, for the 1987–92 period, the share of output of exiting plants in 1987 is only 0.13 and the share of output of entering plants in 1992 is only 0.12. However, the difference in productivity between entering and exiting plants is about 7 percent, which is substantially greater than the 3.3 percent overall growth in productivity over this time period.

ment error problems (method 2), the contribution of reallocation amongst continuing plants is also greater in cyclical downturns. Putting these pieces together yields the interesting inference that the contribution of reallocation to productivity growth tends to be greater during cyclical downturns.

8.5.3 The Role of Entry and Exit

As noted in the previous subsections, a robust result is the contribution of net entry. Whether we examine ten-year or five-year changes, net entry plays an important role in accounting for aggregate productivity growth. We begin our detailed examination of the roles of entry and exit by returning to the ten-year changes for 1977–87. The material under heading A of table 8.9 provides information about some of the underlying determinants of the role of net entry by reporting output and labor shares of entering and exiting plants and the weighted average of productivity levels for continuing, entering and exiting plants. The reported productivity indexes are relative to the weighted average for continuing plants in 1977. Entering plants tend to be smaller than exiting plants, as reflected in the generally smaller output and employment shares of entrants (relative to exiting plants). Entering plants in period t (here 1987) tend to have higher productivity than the level of productivity in period $t - k$ (here 1977) for exiting and continuing plants, but entrants exhibit slightly lower productivity than continuing plants in period t. Exiting plants from period $t - k$ tend to have lower productivity than continuing plants in period $t - k$.

One insight that emerges from comparing heading A of table 8.9 to the results of table 8.4 is that the contribution of entering plants displacing exiting plants to productivity growth is disproportionate relative to the respective contribution of entry and exit in accounting for activity. For example, the contribution of net entry to MFP is 25 percent while the share of output accounted for by exiting plants is 22 percent and the share of activity accounted for by entering plants is 21 percent. Similar patterns of disproportionality are observed for labor productivity. The disproportionate contribution of net entry reflects the fact that the gap in productivity between entering and exiting plants is larger than the gap across time among continuing plants. This finding is important because it indicates that the contribution of net entry is not simply an accounting result. That is, if entry and exit were just random and uncorrelated with productivity, then the contribution of net entry would simply reflect the share of activity accounted for by entering and exiting plants.

It is, of course, limiting to simply compare the relative productivity of entering plants in 1987 with exiting plants in 1977. The differences reflect many factors, including overall productivity growth and selection and learning effects. To begin shedding light on these issues, heading B of table 8.9 considers the relative productivity of the entering plants in 1987 based upon a cross classification of the year of entry. Given the availability of

Table 8.9 Relative Productivity for Continuers, Exiters, and Entrants, 1977–87

A. Output Shares and Relative Productivity

		Shares		Relative Productivity			
Measure	Weight	Exiting Plants $(t-k)$	Entering Plants (t)	Exiting Plants $(t-k)$	Entering Plants (t)	Continuing Plants $(t-k)$	Continuing Plants (t)
Multifactor productivity	Gross output	0.22	0.21	0.96	1.09	1.00	1.10
Labor productivity (per hour)	Man-hours	0.25	0.21	0.83	1.11	1.00	1.20
(per worker)	Employment	0.25	0.21	0.82	1.11	1.00	1.21

B. Relative Productivity of Plants in 1987 for Entrants by Entry Cohort

		Plants that entered between:	
Measure	Weight	1978–82	1983–87
Multifactor productivity	Gross output	1.10	1.07
Labor productivity (per hour)	Man-hours	1.16	1.04
(per worker)	Employment	1.16	1.05

Source: Tabulations from the CM.

economic census data in 1982, entry age can be measured for all entering establishments in terms of census cohorts (i.e., 1978–82 or 1983–87). For multifactor productivity, we find that in 1987 the relative productivity of the older cohort is higher (1.10) than the younger cohort (1.07). For labor productivity using man-hours or employment, a similar pattern is observed. These findings are consistent with the predicted impact of selection and learning effects but still are inadequate for understanding the underpinnings of the contribution of net entry. Following methodology used by Aw, Chen, and Roberts (1997), we can make a bit more progress in distinguishing between alternative factors using some simple regression analysis to which we now turn.

Table 8.10 presents regression results using the pooled 1977–87 data. Heading A of table 8.10 considers a simple regression of the (log) of productivity on a set of dummies indicating whether the plant exited in 1977 or entered in 1987; a year effect to control for average differences in productivity across the two years; and four-digit industry dummies (not reported).[20] The omitted group is continuing plants in 1977 so the coefficients can be interpreted accordingly. This first set of results simply confirms earlier results but helps in quantifying statistical significance: Exiting plants have significantly lower productivity (multifactor and labor) than continuing plants; plants in 1987 have significantly higher productivity (multifactor and labor) than plants in 1977; and entering plants in 1987 have lower *labor* productivity than the continuing plants in 1987. Note, however, that according to these regressions there is no statistical difference between continuing plants and entering plants in terms of MFP in 1987. Also reported in heading A is the F-test on the difference between entering and exiting plants, which is highly significant for all measures even after having controlled for year effects.

Heading B of table 8.10 is the regression analogue of heading B of table 8.9. Essentially the same specification as in the upper panel is used except that here we classify entering plants based on whether they entered between 1977 and 1982 or 1982 and 1987. The results indicate that there are significant differences between the cohorts of plants. The plants that en-

---

20. By pooling the data across industries, we are pursuing a slightly different approach than in prior decomposition exercises where we calculated the decomposition for each industry and then took the weighted average of the four-digit results. However, by controlling for four-digit effects and using analogous weights to those used in the decomposition exercises, these results are close to being the regression analogues of earlier tables. The results using unweighted regressions are qualitatively similar to those reported here with similar significance levels for the various tests on coefficients. Moreover, for MFP, the magnitudes of the coefficients are very similar using unweighted results. We suspect that this is because the typical entering and exiting plant is smaller and less capital intensive than the typical continuing plant. Since there is a positive relationship among size, capital intensity, and labor productivity, this will yield larger differences in average productivity levels among continuing, entering, and exiting plants using weighted as opposed to unweighted regressions.

Table 8.10   Regression Results Concerning Net Entry, 1977–87

A. Differences Between Continuing, Entering, and Exiting Plants

Measure	Exit Dummy in 1977 (β)	Entry Dummy in 1987 (δ)	1987 Year Effect	F-test on $\beta = \delta$ (p-value)
Multifactor productivity	−0.019 (0.002)	0.003 (0.002)	0.098 (0.001)	0.0001
Labor productivity				
(per hour)	−0.150 (0.003)	−0.075 (0.003)	0.191 (0.002)	0.0001
(per worker)	−0.162 (0.003)	−0.086 (0.003)	0.208 (0.002)	0.0001

B. Regression Results Distinguishing between Entering Cohorts

Measure	Entry Dummy in 1987 Interacted with Dummy for 1977–82 Cohort (η)	Entry Dummy in 1987 Interacted with Dummy for 1982–87 Cohort (μ)	F-test on $\eta = \mu$ (p-value)
Multifactor productivity	0.016 (0.002)	−0.010 (0.002)	0.0001
Labor productivity			
(per hour)	−0.020 (0.004)	−0.123 (0.004)	0.0001
(per worker)	−0.032 (0.004)	−0.132 (0.004)	0.0001

Notes: Results under heading A are based upon regression of pooled 1977 and 1987 data with dependent variable the measure of productivity (in logs) and the explanatory variables including four-digit industry effects, year effects, an exit dummy in 1977, and an entry dummy in 1987. The results under heading B use the same specification but interact the entry dummy with entering cohort dummies. Under heading B, the exit dummy and year effect dummy are not shown as they are the same as under heading A. All results are weighted regressions with gross output weights in regressions using multifactor productivity, hours weights in labor productivity per hour regressions, and employment weights in labor productivity per worker regressions. Standard errors in parentheses.

tered earlier have significantly higher productivity (multifactor or labor) than plants that entered later.

Heading B of table 8.10 still does not permit disentangling selection and learning effects. In table 8.11, we report results that shed some light on these different effects.[21] In table 8.11, we use a similar pooled specification with year effects, entry dummy, exit dummy, and four-digit effects. However, in this case we consider additional information about plants that entered between 1972 and 1977. By dividing this entering cohort into exiters and survivors, we can characterize selection and learning effects. In particular, we make three comparisons using this information. First, for exits, we distinguish among exits those who entered between 1972 and 1977 and those who did not (comparing α and γ). Second, we distinguish among the entering cohort those that exit and those that survive to 1987 (comparing α and θ). Finally, for the surviving 1972–77 cohort, we also examine productivity in 1977 (the entering year) and productivity ten years later (comparing θ and λ).

Plants that entered between 1972 and 1977 and then exited are significantly less productive in 1977 than continuing incumbents in 1977 (who are not from that entering cohort) whether productivity is measured in terms of multifactor or labor productivity ($\alpha < 0$). Of exiting plants, those that entered between 1972 and 1977 are less productive in 1977 than other exiting plants ($\alpha < \gamma$), although the results are not statistically significant for MFP. The exiting plants from this entering cohort are also less productive in 1977 than the surviving members of this cohort ($\alpha < \theta$), although the differences are not statistically significant for the MFP measure even at the 10 percent level. The latter findings are broadly consistent with selection effects since it is the less productive plants from the entering cohort that exit (although again this is not always highly significant).

Even the surviving members of the entering 1972–77 cohort are less productive than incumbents ($\theta < 0$). However, for the entering cohort, we observe significant increases in productivity over the ten years ($\theta < \lambda$), even though we are controlling for overall year effects. This pattern is consistent with learning effects playing an important role.

To conclude this section, we consider similar regression exercises for the five-year changes from 1977 to 1982, 1982 to 1987, and 1987 to 1992.[22] Tables 8.12 and 8.13 report regression results for these five-year intervals. Interestingly, the patterns for the five-year changes regarding the differ-

21. This specification is quite similar to various specifications considered in Aw, Chen, and Roberts (1997). Our results are qualitatively consistent with theirs in the sense that we find that both learning and selection effects contribute significantly to the observed plant-level productivity differentials.

22. All specifications include four-digit industry effects, year effects, and entry and exit dummies. Table 8.13 is analogous to table 8.11; we decompose some of these effects allowing for potentially different behavior of the most recent entering cohort.

Table 8.11 Regression Results Distinguishing between Selection and Learning Effects Using 1972–77 Entering Cohort

Measure	Exit Dummy in 1977 for Entering Cohort (α)	Exit Dummy in 1977 for Other Exiting Plants (γ)	Survival Dummy in 1987 for Entering Cohort (θ)	Survival Dummy in 1987 for Entering Cohort (λ)	F-test on $\alpha = \gamma$ (p-value)	F-test on $\alpha = \theta$ (p-value)	F-test on $\theta = \lambda$ (p-value)
Multifactor productivity	−0.024 (0.004)	−0.019 (0.002)	−0.017 (0.003)	0.018 (0.003)	0.238	0.184	0.0001
Labor productivity (per hour)	−0.182 (0.007)	−0.149 (0.003)	−0.058 (0.006)	−0.016 (0.005)	0.0001	0.0001	0.0001
Labor productivity (per worker)	−0.215 (0.007)	−0.158 (0.003)	−0.072 (0.006)	−0.017 (0.005)	0.0001	0.0001	0.0001

Source: Tabulations from the CM.

Notes: Results are based upon regression of pooled 1977 and 1987 data with dependent variable the measure of productivity and the explanatory variables including four-digit industry effects, year effects, an entry dummy, the exit dummy interacted with whether the plant is in the 1972–77 entering cohort, and a surviving dummy for the 1972–77 entering cohort interacted with the year effects. All results are weighted regressions with gross output weights in regressions using multifactor productivity, hours weights in labor productivity per hour regressions, and employment weights in labor productivity per worker regressions. Standard errors in parentheses.

Table 8.12 Regression Results on Differences between Continuing, Entering, and Exiting Plants

Measure	Exit Dummy in Beginning Year (β)	Entry Dummy in Ending Year (δ)	End Year Effect	F-test on $\gamma = \delta$ (p-value)
A. 1977–82				
Multifactor productivity	−0.047 (0.002)	0.005 (0.002)	0.021 (0.001)	0.0001
Labor productivity				
(per hour)	−0.164 (0.004)	−0.140 (0.004)	0.022 (0.002)	0.0001
(per worker)	−0.187 (0.004)	−0.131 (0.004)	−0.009 (0.002)	0.0001
B. 1982–87				
Multifactor productivity	−0.017 (0.002)	−0.005 (0.002)	0.071 (0.001)	0.0002
Labor productivity				
(per hour)	−0.193 (0.004)	−0.121 (0.004)	0.169 (0.002)	0.0001
(per worker)	−0.204 (0.004)	−0.130 (0.004)	0.211 (0.002)	0.0001
C. 1987–92				
Multifactor productivity	−0.056 (0.002)	0.009 (0.002)	0.025 (0.001)	0.0001
Labor productivity				
(per hour)	−0.179 (0.004)	−0.140 (0.004)	0.064 (0.002)	0.0001
(per worker)	−0.192 (0.004)	−0.126 (0.004)	0.083 (0.002)	0.0001

Note: Standard errors in parentheses.

ences between entering and exiting plants and the role of selection and learning effects mimic those for the ten-year changes. In table 8.12, we observe that entering plants have higher productivity than exiting plants even while controlling for year effects. In table 8.13, we examine the behavior of the entering cohorts for each of the five-year changes.[23] With one exception, for plants that exit the plants that are in the entering cohort have lower productivity than other plants ($\alpha < \gamma$). For the entering cohort, the productivity level in the year of entry is lower for those that immediately exit than those that survive ($\alpha < \theta$). For those that survive in the entering cohort, we observe significant increases in productivity even after controlling for average increases in productivity amongst all plants via year

---

23. That is, for the 1977–82 changes we consider the 1972–77 entering cohort; for the 1982–87 changes we consider the 1977–82 entering cohort; and for the 1987–92 changes we consider the 1982–87 entering cohort.

Table 8.13　Regression Results Distinguishing between Selection and Learning Effects Using Entering Cohort

Measure	Exit Dummy in Start for Entering (α)	Exit Dummy in Start for Other Exiting (γ)	Survival Dummy in Start for Entering (θ)	Survival Dummy in End for Entering (λ)	F-test on $\alpha = \gamma$ (p-value)	F-test on $\alpha = \theta$ (p-value)	F-test on $\theta = \lambda$ (p-value)
\multicolumn{8}{l}{A. 1977–82 (start = 1977, end = 1982)}							
Multifactor productivity	−0.050 (0.005)	−0.047 (0.003)	−0.011 (0.003)	0.023 (0.003)	0.662	0.0001	0.0001
Labor productivity							
(per hour)	−0.190 (0.008)	−0.164 (0.005)	−0.069 (0.005)	−0.035 (0.005)	0.005	0.0001	0.0001
(per worker)	−0.231 (0.008)	−0.184 (0.005)	−0.089 (0.005)	−0.032 (0.005)	0.0001	0.0001	0.0001
\multicolumn{8}{l}{B. 1982–87 (start = 1982, end = 1987)}							
Multifactor productivity	−0.039 (0.005)	−0.014 (0.002)	−0.017 (0.003)	0.001 (0.003)	0.0001	0.0001	0.0001
Labor productivity							
(per hour)	−0.306 (0.008)	−0.175 (0.004)	−0.063 (0.006)	−0.045 (0.005)	0.0001	0.0001	0.019
(per worker)	−0.313 (0.008)	−0.186 (0.004)	−0.061 (0.006)	−0.052 (0.005)	0.0001	0.0001	0.216
\multicolumn{8}{l}{C. 1987–92 (start = 1987, end = 1992)}							
Multifactor productivity	−0.049 (0.005)	−0.060 (0.003)	−0.017 (0.003)	0.043 (0.003)	0.048	0.0001	0.0001
Labor productivity							
(per hour)	−0.254 (0.008)	−0.170 (0.004)	−0.097 (0.005)	−0.057 (0.005)	0.0001	0.0001	0.0001
(per worker)	−0.274 (0.007)	−0.183 (0.004)	−0.101 (0.005)	−0.050 (0.005)	0.0001	0.0001	0.0001

Note: Standard errors in parentheses.

effects ($\theta < \lambda$). One interesting feature of these results is that the differences reflecting both selection and learning effects are highly significant for both multifactor and labor productivity measures.

In sum, we find that net entry contributes disproportionately to productivity growth. The disproportionate contribution is associated with less productive exiting plants being displaced by more productive entering plants. New entrants tend to be less productive than surviving incumbents but exhibit substantial productivity growth. The latter reflects both selection effects (the less productive amongst the entrants exit) and learning effects.

8.5.4 Summing Up the Results for Manufacturing

To sum up the results from this sensitivity analysis, our results suggest that reallocation plays a significant role in the changes in productivity growth at the industry level. While measurement error problems cloud the results somewhat, two aspects of the results point clearly in this direction. First, our time series decompositions show a large contribution from the replacement of less productive exiting plants with more productive entering plants when productivity changes are measured over five- or ten-year horizons. A key feature of these findings is that the contribution of net entry is disproportionate—that is, the contribution of net entry to productivity growth exceeds that which would be predicted by simply examining the share of activity accounted for entering and exiting plants. Second, the cross-sectional decompositions, which are less subject to measurement error problems, uniformly show that the reallocation of both output and labor inputs has been productivity enhancing over this same period.

Nevertheless, an important conclusion of this sensitivity analysis is that the quantitative contribution of reallocation to the aggregate change in productivity is sensitive to the decomposition methodology that is employed. Using a method that characterizes the within-plant contribution in terms of the weighted average of changes in plant multifactor (labor, when using labor weights) productivity using fixed initial weights yields a substantially lower (higher) within-plant contribution than an alternative method that uses the average time series share of activity as weights. The former method (method 1) arguably yields cleaner conceptual interpretations but is also more subject to measurement error. The latter method (method 2) yields results that are more consistent across multifactor and labor productivity measures. Examining the detailed components of the decompositions across multifactor and labor productivity measures yields results consistent with measurement error interpretations and, on this basis, favors method 2, which mitigates measurement error problems. However, some aspects of the patterns (in particular, the strong correlation between within-plant changes in labor productivity and capital intensity) suggest that there are likely important and systematic differences in the contribution of reallocation to labor and multifactor productivity.

8.6 Productivity and Reallocation in the Service Sector

8.6.1 Overview and Measurement Issues

All of the studies we have reviewed, as well as our analysis of the sensitivity of the results to alternative methodologies, have been based on productivity decompositions using manufacturing data. In this section, we consider the same issues in the context of changes in productivity in a service sector industry. We restrict our attention here to a small number of four-digit industries that account for the three-digit industry automotive repair shops (SIC 753). Our focus on this three-digit industry is motivated by several factors. First, since this is one of the first studies to exploit the Census of Service Industries establishment-level data at the Bureau of the Census, we wanted to conduct a study on a relatively small number of four-digit industries to permit careful attention to measurement issues.[24] Second, for this specific three-digit industry, we can apply procedures for measuring plant-level labor productivity (here measured as gross output per worker) in a manner that is directly comparable to official BLS methods. That is, for this specific industry, BLS generates four-digit output per worker measures by using gross revenue from the Census of Service Industries and then deflating the four-digit revenue using an appropriate four-digit deflator derived from the Consumer Price Index.[25] By obtaining the appropriate deflators, we can mimic BLS procedures here, which is especially important given our concerns about measurement issues.

A third reason that we selected this specific three-digit industry is that this industry has been subject to rapid technological change. Over the last decade or so, the automotive repair industry has experienced significant changes in the nature and complexity in both the automobiles that are being serviced and in the equipment used to do the servicing. According to Automotive Body Repair News (ABRN; 1997), " . . . vehicles are becoming more electronic and require more expensive diagnostic tools for successful troubleshooting." For example, ABRN reports that the percentage of automobiles with electronic transmissions has increased from 20 percent in 1990 to 80 percent in 1995 and is expected to increase to 95 percent by the year 2000. According to ABRN, "this growth in automotive electronics has not only changed the vehicle, it has altered significantly the technical requirements of the individuals who service" the automobiles.

Recent improvements in automobiles and in the manner in which they are repaired may interfere with our measurement of changes in output per worker. It is possible that we may not accurately characterize productivity changes in the industry because of changes in the quality of both the out-

---

24. Given that these data have not been widely used, the results reported here should be viewed as exploratory and interpreted with appropriate caution.
25. See the paper by Dean and Kunze (1992) on service sector productivity measurement.

puts and the inputs. While we recognize that this pervasive concern may be especially problematic in the service sector, we believe that these problems will be somewhat mitigated by several factors unique to this context. First, our (admittedly limited) research on changes in this industry indicate that process innovations dominate product innovations. That is, while both the parts and processes to repair automobiles have undergone substantial improvement, we believe that the improvements in repair technology are more important for our purposes. For example, some of the largest changes have taken place in the field of troubleshooting and have provided mechanics with the ability to diagnose repair problems more accurately and more quickly. Such improvements in diagnostics are appropriately reflected in our (and the official BLS) output per worker measures since establishments that are better at diagnosis will exhibit higher measured output per worker. Second, our focus is on the decomposition of productivity changes rather than the overall change itself. Mismeasured quality change will undoubtedly imply that the overall change in mismeasured, but it is less clear how it will distort the inferences about the contribution of reallocation to the overall change.

We conduct our analysis by exploiting the Census of Service Industries establishment-level data from 1987 and 1992. The Census of Service Industries data contain information on gross revenue and employment as well as a host of establishment-level identifiers. The data on gross revenue are deflated with an appropriate four-digit deflator to generate a measure of real gross output (in 1987 dollars). Combining the data on real gross output with the employment data allows us to generate measures of labor productivity that are fully comparable to those presented in section 8.5. A discussion of the method used to link establishments in the Census of Service Industries can be found in the appendix.

Before proceeding to our analysis of the microdata, it is useful to consider the official BLS productivity series for SIC 753. Figure 8.1 plots the index for output per worker produced by BLS. As is evident from the figure, this industry exhibits substantial cyclicality in labor productivity. This cyclicality likely influences our analysis since we focus on the Census of Service Industries microdata from 1987 to 1992. Figure 8.1 indicates that while recovery had begun in 1992 and 1992 labor productivity exceeds 1987 labor productivity, labor productivity was below the cyclical peak it had reached in 1989. Recall from the discussion in sections 8.3 and 8.4 that the role of reallocation in productivity growth appears to be cyclically sensitive for studies using manufacturing data. We need to keep the impact of cyclicality in mind, therefore, when considering the determinants of industry-wide productivity growth.

8.6.2 Decompositions of Industry Productivity Changes

We now turn our attention to an analysis of the decomposition of aggregate productivity growth for the automobile repair industry. To begin,

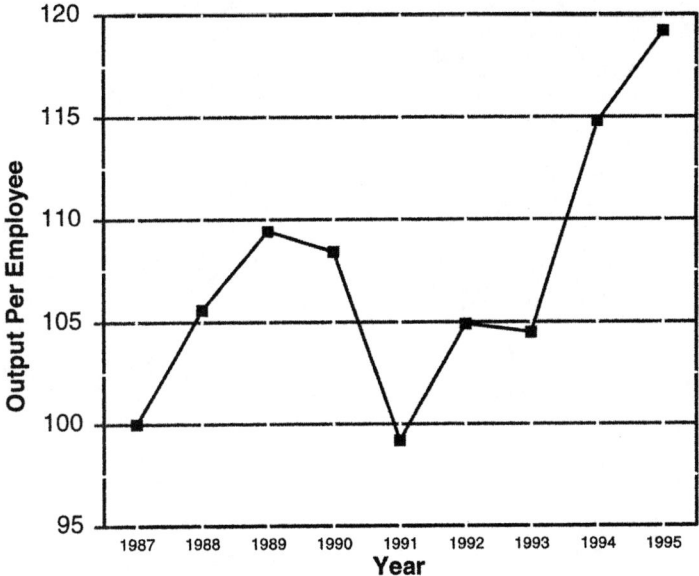

Fig. 8.1 Automotive repair shops (SIC 753; BLS productivity calculations)

table 8.14 presents gross expansion and contraction rates for employment and output for the overall three-digit industry and the underlying four-digit industries. The gross flows of employment and output are quite large in this industry with five-year gross expansion and contraction rates of approximately 50 percent. The implied five-year excess reallocation rates for each industry are often above 80 percent. These rates are quite large relative to the ten-year gross rates for manufacturing reported in table 8.3. Indeed, for manufacturing, five-year gross employment expansion and contraction rates are typically less than 30 percent (see, e.g., Dunne, Roberts, and Samuelson 1989 and Baldwin, Dunne, and Haltiwanger 1995). Thus, taken at face value, these rates suggest tremendous churning among automotive repair shops.[26]

In a related manner, the share of expansion accounted for by entrants and the share of contraction accounted for by exits are both extremely large. The entry and exit shares exceed 50 percent for all industries and in

---

26. Given the magnitude of establishment births and deaths on employment flows and productivity, and the newness of these data, we considered it prudent to try to find benchmarks for business failure from sources outside the Census Bureau. We contacted BABCOX Publications, publishers of several automobile service periodicals. BABCOX provides its publications free of charge to all companies in, among others, SIC 7532 (top, body, and upholstery repair shops and paint shops), and they believe that their mailing list includes almost all of the individual establishments in the industry. They find that about 10 percent of the businesses on their mailing list disappear each year. Over a five-year period, therefore, their attrition rate is similar to what we find.

Table 8.14 Gross Reallocation of Employment and Output for Automobile Repair Shops

Industry	Creation (Expansion) Rate	Share of Creation (Expansion) Due to Entrants	Destruction (Contraction) Rate	Share of Destruction (Contraction) Due to Exits	Excess Reallocation Within Industry
		A. Five-Year Changes from 1987–92, Employment			
Automobile repair shops (SIC = 753)	50.9	75.8	44.2	63.5	88.4
Top, body, and upholstery repair shops and paint shops (SIC = 7532)	44.2	69.3	42.9	59.1	85.8
Auto exhaust system repair shops (SIC = 7533)	46.0	69.5	37.1	55.3	74.2
Tire retreading and repair shops (SIC = 7534)	53.2	79.0	57.5	82.1	105.4
Automotive glass replacement shops (SIC = 7536)	60.3	79.6	38.9	51.7	77.8
Automotive transmission repair shops (SIC = 7537)	38.9	70.4	46.1	61.4	77.8
General automotive repair shops (SIC = 7538)	58.3	80.0	45.3	67.4	90.6
Automotive repair shops not elsewhere classified (SIC = 7539)	43.6	76.2	43.9	61.8	87.2

	B. Five-Year Changes from 1987–92, Output			
Automobile repair shops (SIC = 753)	51.8	75.8	40.3	61.3	80.6
Top, body, and upholstery repair shops and paint shops (SIC = 7532)	44.7	68.8	38.5	57.1	77.0
Auto exhaust system repair shops (SIC = 7533)	45.2	71.2	31.9	55.7	63.8
Tire retreading and repair shops (SIC = 7534)	53.6	79.7	51.2	80.3	102.4
Automotive glass replacement shops (SIC = 7536)	59.9	79.8	38.7	45.3	77.4
Automotive transmission repair shops (SIC = 7537)	37.9	74.5	42.7	57.5	75.8
General automotive repair shops (SIC = 7538)	59.9	79.3	41.2	65.4	82.4
Automotive repair shops not elsewhere classfied (SIC = 7539)	42.8	78.3	43.4	59.3	85.6

Source: Tabulations from Censuses of Service Industries.

some cases exceed 80 percent. To provide some perspective, Baldwin, Dunne, and Haltiwanger (1995) report that roughly 40 percent of five-year gross job flows in U.S. manufacturing are accounted for by entrants and exits.

Table 8.15 presents the gross contraction and expansion rates by establishment-size class along with information regarding the distribution of establishments by size class. The vast majority of automotive repair shops are very small, with fewer than ten employees. This helps account for the rapid pace of output and employment reallocation and the dominant role of entrants and exits. Many studies (see the survey in Davis and Haltiwanger 1999) have shown that the pace of reallocation as well as entry/exit rates are sharply decreasing functions of employer size.

Table 8.16 presents the decomposition of labor productivity (per worker) growth using method 1 (heading A) and method 2 (heading B) described in section 8.4. The components in these tables are reported directly (essentially the terms in equations [2] and [3]) rather than as shares of the total as in prior tables. We present them in this form to avoid confusion. The components exhibit considerable variation in both sign and magnitude so the shares of the total often exceed one.

For the overall three-digit industry, we find that the gain in productivity across the five-year period is approximately 2.4 percent. This is lower than the BLS estimate in figure 8.1 of approximately 4.9 percent. There are several possible explanations for this difference. First, our data on revenue and employment come exclusively from the economic censuses. While, according to Dean and Kunze (1992), BLS gets its employment data from a variety of sources including BLS's Establishment Survey, IRS's Statistics of Income, and the Census Bureau's Current Population Survey.[27] Furthermore, BLS attempts to adjust their industry output to account for businesses without payroll (e.g., sole proprietorships). By contrast, the economic census data we use cover only establishments with paid employees.

Next, note from table 8.16 that net entry plays a very large role regardless of the method used. Indeed, productivity growth from net entry actually exceeds the overall industry growth. Thus, the overall contribution of continuing establishments is negative. On the other hand, the decomposition of the effects of continuing establishments differs substantially across methods 1 and 2. The reason for this is that there is an extremely large negative cross effect with method 1. With method 1, the within and between effects are typically positive. In contrast, under method 2, the within effect is uniformly negative and the between effect is typically positive.

---

27. A joint BEA, BLS, and Bureau of the Census project currently underway is comparing the establishment data gathered by BLS and Census. One of its goals is to examine how mixing employment and revenue data from the two agencies may affect statistics such as industry productivity measurements.

Table 8.15 Gross Reallocation of Employment and Output by Size Class for Automobile Repair Shops

Establishment Average Employment	Number of Establishments	Average Number of Employees	Creation (Expansion) Rate	Share of Creation (Expansion) Due to Entrants	Destruction (Contraction) Rate	Share of Destruction (Contraction) Due to Exits	Net Job Flow Rate of Size Class	Net Output Flow Rate of Size Class
A. Five-Year Changes from 1987–92, Employment									
1–4	123,378	224,309	71.7	85.2	53.3	77.1	18.4	
5–9	22,163	145,528	36.5	63.1	36.5	51.3	0.0	
10–19	6,683	86,647	28.0	52.0	33.1	40.2	-5.1	
20–49	1,236	33,230	32.6	56.0	39.9	40.5	-7.3	
50+	88	7,624	54.6	65.3	66.6	61.9	-12.0	
B. Five-Year Changes from 1987–92, Output									
1–4	123,378	224,309	73.9	84.5	47.0	75.5		26.9
5–9	22,163	145,528	35.3	64.1	35.2	48.7		0.1
10–19	6,683	86,647	27.5	52.4	32.4	38.9		-4.9
20–49	1,236	33,230	34.3	52.1	34.9	40.5		-0.6
50+	88	7,624	44.1	58.8	50.8	54.5		-6.7

Source: Tabulations from Censuses of Service Industries.

Table 8.16 Decomposition of Labor Productivity Growth, 1987–92

Industry	Average Number of Employees	Overall Growth	Within Effect	Between Effect	Cross Effect	Total Continuer Effect	Net Entry Effect
			A. Method 1				
Auto repair shops (SIC = 753)	497,336	2.43	2.41	4.58	−7.29	−0.30	2.73
Top, body, and upholstery repair shops and paint shops (SIC = 7532)	163,302	4.16	3.24	5.81	−8.13	0.92	3.24
Auto exhaust system repair shops (SIC = 7533)	22,112	3.47	5.72	4.02	−9.80	−0.06	3.54
Tire retreading and repair shops (SIC = 7534)	12,874	−1.34	−2.99	5.23	−2.78	−0.54	−0.81
Automotive glass replacement shops (SIC = 7536)	19,816	−3.55	−0.43	1.50	−4.57	−3.50	−0.05
Automotive transmission repair shops (SIC = 7537)	24,507	0.79	1.26	4.93	−8.35	−2.16	2.96
General automotive repair shops (SIC = 7538)	213,768	2.36	2.38	3.90	−6.79	−0.51	2.87
Automotive repair shops not elsewhere classified (SIC = 7539)	40,956	−1.22	1.36	4.85	−7.67	−1.46	0.24

				B. Method 2		
Automobile repair shops (SIC = 753)	497,336	2.43	−1.24	1.01	—	−0.23	2.66
Top, body, and upholstery repair shops and paint shops (SIC = 7532)	163,302	4.16	−0.82	1.84	—	1.02	3.15
Auto exhaust system repair shops (SIC = 7533)	22,112	3.47	0.81	−0.73	—	0.08	3.39
Tire retreading and repair shops (SIC = 7534)	12,874	−1.34	−4.37	3.85	—	−0.52	−0.81
Automotive glass replacement shops (SIC = 7536)	19,816	−3.55	−2.72	−1.16	—	−3.88	0.33
Automotive transmission repair shops (SIC = 7537)	24,507	0.79	−2.92	0.76	—	−2.16	2.95
General automotive repair shops (SIC = 7538)	213,768	2.36	−1.02	0.59	—	−0.43	2.79
Automotive repair shops not elsewhere classfied (SIC = 7539)	40,956	−1.22	−2.48	0.99	—	−1.49	0.28

Source: Tabulations from Censuses of Service Industries.

Correlations for continuing establishments are reported in table 8.17. Underlying the cross terms in table 8.16 are the large positive correlation between labor productivity growth and output growth and the large negative correlation between labor productivity growth and employment growth.

Since the time series decompositions are sensitive to measurement error problems and longitudinal linkage problems, it is useful to also examine the Olley-Pakes style cross-sectional decompositions. Table 8.18 reports these cross-sectional decompositions for 1987 and 1992. The cross term for all industries is positive, indicating that the share of employment is greater at establishments with larger productivity. The relative importance of the cross term is especially large for the overall three-digit industry and also for its biggest single four-digit industry, general automotive repair shops (SIC 7538). In addition, for the overall three-digit industry as well as for general automotive repair shops there is an increase in the cross term, reflecting the fact that the reallocation of employment over this time has been productivity enhancing.

8.6.3 The Role of Entry and Exit

The results in the prior section indicate that in an accounting sense essentially all (indeed more than all) of the productivity growth in these industries comes from net entry. Table 8.19 illustrates the underlying determinants of the contribution of net entry. Several features of table 8.19 stand out. First, the shares of employment accounted for by exiting plants in 1987 and by entering plants in 1992 are very large. Second, continuing plants exhibit little overall change in productivity. Third, entering plants in 1992 actually have somewhat lower productivity than the incumbents had in 1987 but they have much larger productivity than the exiting plants had in 1987. Thus, the greatest impact comes from the large exodus of low-productivity plants.

In an analogous manner to the regression exercises in section 8.4, table 8.20 characterizes the differences between entering and exiting plants more formally. The specification includes year effects, four-digit industry effects (not shown), and entry and exit dummies. Even after controlling for year effects (and thus overall trends in productivity growth in the industry), exiting plants have significantly lower productivity than continuing plants, entering plants have significantly lower productivity than continuing plants, and entering plants have significantly higher productivity than exiting plants.

8.6.4 Summary of Service Sector Results

Since the Census of Service Industries microdata have not been widely used, this analysis and the findings should be viewed as exploratory. Nevertheless, taken at face value the results are quite interesting and clearly call

Table 8.17   Correlation among Plant-Level Productivity, Output, and Input Growth, 1987–92 (continuing plants; SIC = 753)

	Change in Labor Productivity (per worker)	Change in Output	Change in Employment	Employment in 1987	Employment in 1992
Change in labor productivity (per worker)	1				
Change in output	0.51	1			
Change in employment	−0.39	0.60	1		
Employment in 1987	0.06	−0.18	−0.24	1	
Employment in 1992	−0.10	0.11	0.21	0.72	1

Source: Tabulations from Census of Service Industries.

Table 8.18   Cross-Sectional Decompositions of Productivity, by Year

Industry	Year	Overall	P-Bar	Cross
Automotive repair shops (SIC = 753)	1987	3.92	3.69	0.23
	1992	3.95	3.69	0.25
Top, body, and upholstery repair	1987	3.75	3.68	0.07
shops and paint shops (SIC = 7532)	1992	3.77	3.69	0.08
Auto exhaust system repair shops	1987	3.96	3.95	0.01
(SIC = 7533)	1992	4.02	4.02	0.00
Tire retreading and repair shops	1987	3.96	3.95	0.01
(SIC = 7534)	1992	3.91	3.90	0.01
Automotive glass replacement shops	1987	3.95	3.95	0.01
(SIC = 7536)	1992	3.96	3.95	0.01
Automotive transmission repair shops	1987	3.67	3.66	0.01
(SIC = 7537)	1992	3.70	3.70	0.01
General automotive repair shops	1987	3.76	3.65	0.11
(SIC = 7538)	1992	3.77	3.63	0.13
Automotive repair shops not	1987	3.71	3.69	0.02
elsewhere classified (SIC = 7539)	1992	3.75	3.74	0.01

Source: Tabulations from Censuses of Service Industries.

for further analysis. First, there is tremendous reallocation of activity across these service establishments with much of this reallocation generated by entry and exit. Second, the productivity growth in the industry is dominated by entry and exit effects. The primary source of productivity growth between 1987 and 1992 for the automobile repair shop industry is accounted for by the exit of very low–productivity plants.

8.7 Concluding Remarks

In this study we have focused on the contribution of the reallocation of activity across individual producers in accounting for aggregate productivity growth. A growing body of empirical analysis reveals striking patterns in the behavior of establishment-level reallocation and productivity. First, there is a large ongoing pace of reallocation of outputs and inputs across establishments. Second, the pace of reallocation varies secularly, cyclically, and by industry. Third, there are large and persistent productivity differentials across establishments in the same industry. Fourth, entering plants tend to have higher productivity than exiting plants. Large productivity differentials and substantial reallocation are the necessary ingredients for an important role for reallocation in aggregate productivity growth. Nevertheless, a review of existing studies yields a wide range of findings regarding the contribution of reallocation to aggregate productivity growth.

In both our review of existing studies and our own sensitivity analysis, we find that the variation across studies reflects a number of factors. First, the contribution of reallocation varies over time (i.e., is cyclically sensitive)

Table 8.19   Employment Shares and Relative Labor Productivity, 1987–92

Industry	Shares		Relative Productivity		
	Exiting Plants $(t-k)$	Entering Plants (t)	Exiting Plants $(t-k)$	Entering Plants (t)	Continuing Plants $(t-k)$	Continuing Plants (t)
Automotive repair shops (SIC = 753)	0.39	0.32	0.84	0.93	1.00	1.00
Top, body, and upholstery repair shops and paint shops (SIC = 7532)	0.27	0.32	0.80	0.92	1.00	1.02
Auto exhaust system repair shops (SIC = 7533)	0.22	0.31	0.81	0.96	1.00	1.00
Tire retreading and repair shops (SIC = 7534)	0.49	0.48	0.86	0.85	1.00	0.99
Automotive glass replacement shops (SIC = 7536)	0.23	0.44	0.78	0.86	1.00	0.96
Automotive transmission repair shops (SIC = 7537)	0.28	0.30	0.80	0.90	1.00	0.97
General automotive repair shops (SIC = 7538)	0.38	0.45	0.86	0.94	1.00	1.00
Automotive repair shops not elsewhere classified (SIC = 7539)	0.30	0.35	0.90	0.92	1.00	0.98

Source: Tabulations from Censuses of Service Industries.

Table 8.20   Regression Results on Differences among Continuing, Entering, and Exiting Plants

Measure	Exit Dummy in Beginning Year (β)	Entry Dummy in Ending Year (δ)	End Year Effect	F-test on $\beta = \delta$ (p-value)
1987–92 for SIC = 753 Labor productivity (weighted by employment)	−0.153 (0.004)	−0.068 (0.003)	0.001 (0.003)	0.0001

Source: Tabulations from Censuses of Service Industries.
Note: Standard errors in parentheses.

and across industries. Second, the details of the decomposition methodology matter. Our findings suggest that measurement error interacts with the alternative decomposition methodologies in ways that affect the final results. Third, the contribution of net entry depends critically on the horizon over which the changes are measured. Small shares of the role of entrants and exits in high-frequency data (e.g., annual) make for a relatively small role of entrants and exits using high frequency changes. However, intermediate and longer run (e.g., five- and ten-year) changes yield a large role for net entry. Part of this is virtually by construction since the share of activity accounted for by entry and exit will inherently increase the longer the horizon over which changes are measured. Nevertheless, a robust finding is that the impact of net entry is disproportionate since entering plants tend to displace less productive exiting plants, even after controlling for overall average growth in productivity. The gap between the productivity of entering and exiting plants also increases in the horizon over which the changes are measured since a longer horizon yields greater differentials from selection and learning effects. Our findings confirm and extend others in the literature that indicate that both learning and selection effects are important in this context.

A novel aspect of our analysis is that we have extended the analysis of the role of reallocation in aggregate productivity growth to a selected set of service sector industries. Our analysis considers the four-digit industries that form the three-digit automobile repair shop sector. This sector has been experiencing dramatic changes over the last decade because of the greater technological sophistication of new automobiles and the accompanying advances in the equipment used to service them. We found tremendous churning in this industry with extremely high rates of entry and exit. Moreover, we found that productivity growth in the industry is dominated by entry and exit. In an accounting sense, the primary source of productivity growth in this industry over the 1987–92 period is the exit of very low–productivity plants. While these results should be viewed as exploratory given the limited use to date of the nonmanufacturing establishment data at Census, the results are quite striking and clearly call for further analysis.

While the precise quantitative contribution of reallocation varies along a number of systematic dimensions and is sensitive to measurement methodology, a reading of the literature and our own analysis of manufacturing and service sector industries clearly yield the conclusion that an understanding of the dynamics of *aggregate* productivity growth requires tracking the dynamics of *microeconomic* productivity growth. Indeed, the fact that the contribution of reallocation varies across sectors and time makes it that much more important to relate aggregate and microeconomic productivity dynamics.

Given this conclusion, a natural question is what the implications are for the existing official productivity measures from the Bureau of Labor

Statistics. Our findings of the importance of reallocation effects have implications for the *interpretation* of aggregate productivity measures rather than suggesting another potential source of *measurement* problems in the official aggregate productivity statistics per se. There are a number of well-recognized measurement challenges confronting the developers of the official statistics and there have been a number of associated proposals for improvements in the measurement of these statistics. These challenges include accounting for changes in quality in inputs and output, important technical issues on the ideal choice of an index, and the difficult conceptual and measurement problems in measuring output in the service sector. While there is a substantial literature on these topics, addressing these challenges requires further research as well as enhanced resources for data collection.[28] A related literature, of which our paper is a part, takes a different tack by focusing on the relationship between microeconomic productivity dynamics and aggregate productivity growth while taking the measurement methodology of aggregate productivity as given. Our results suggest that interpreting and understanding changes in the official aggregate productivity measures across time and across sectors would be significantly enhanced by relating the aggregate measures to the underlying microeconomic evidence.

Rather than a call for additional data, the implied recommendation of our work is a change in the collection and processing of data that would readily permit relating the aggregate and the microstatistics. Put differently, our results suggest that a comprehensive and integrated approach to the collection and processing of data on establishments is important. Ideally, we would like to measure outputs, inputs, and associated prices of outputs and inputs at the establishment level in a way that permits the analysis of aggregate productivity growth in the manner discussed in this paper. Current practices at statistical agencies are far from this ideal with many of the components collected by different surveys with different units of observation (e.g., establishments vs. companies) and indeed by different statistical agencies. Pursuing the approach advocated in this paper requires overcoming the legal data-sharing limitations that are currently part of the U.S. statistical system.

There are a large number of open conceptual and measurement issues that deserve further attention in pursuing the connection between micro- and aggregate productivity dynamics. One issue that we and most of the literature neglect is the role of within-sector price dispersion and related issues of product differentiation. Following the literature, we use four-digit deflators for shipments and materials in the construction of our productiv-

---

28. As examples of this extensive literature, see the following previous NBER Studies in Income and Wealth conference volumes: Griliches (1992), Berndt and Triplett (1990), Kendrick and Vaccara (1980).

ity measures. However, a limited number of studies (e.g., Roberts and Supina 1997) find considerable price dispersion across establishments even within narrow seven-digit product classes. If the price dispersion reflects quality differences across the products produced by different establishments, then the common procedures in the literature are such that measured productivity differences across establishments will reflect such quality differences. A related and more serious problem is the extent to which price dispersion reflects product differentiation implying that we need both a richer characterization of market structure and the information on this market structure to proceed appropriately.

Another problem is that much that we have discussed in this paper is simply accounting. To understand the role of reallocation in productivity growth, we need to provide better connections between the theoretical underpinnings in section 8.2 and the variety of empirical results summarized in the succeeding sections. For one thing, we need to come to grips with the determinants of heterogeneity across producers. There is no shortage of candidate hypotheses, but currently this heterogeneity is mostly a residual with several claimants. For another, we need to develop the theoretical structure and accompanying empirical analysis to understand the connection between output and input reallocation. The results to date suggest that this connection is quite complex, with restructuring and technological change yielding changes in the scale and mix of factors that are not well understood. A related problem is that there is accumulating evidence that the adjustment process of many of these factors is quite lumpy, so the dynamics are quite complicated. Developing the conceptual models of heterogeneity in behavior, reallocation, and lumpy adjustment at the micro level and, in turn, considering the aggregate implications, should be a high priority.

Appendix
Measuring Output and Inputs in the Manufacturing Sector

The Census of Manufactures (CM) plant-level data includes value of shipments, inventories, book values of equipment and structures, employment of production and nonproduction workers, total hours of production workers, and cost of materials and energy usage. Real gross output is measured as shipments adjusted for inventories, deflated by the four-digit output deflator for the industry in which the plant is classified. All output and materials deflators used are from the four-digit NBER Productivity Database (Bartelsman and Gray, 1996, recently updated by Bartelsman, Becker and Gray). Labor input is measured by total hours for production workers plus an imputed value for the total hours for nonproduction workers. The latter imputation is obtained by multiplying the number of nonproduction workers at the plant (a collected data item) times the average annual hours per worker for a nonproduction worker from the Current Population Survey. We construct the latter at the 2-digit industry level for each year and match this information to the CM by year and industry. The methodology for constructing this hours variable is discussed at length in Davis and Haltiwanger (1999).

We have also used an alternative estimate of total hours, like that in Baily, Hulten and Campbell (1992), which is total hours for production hours multiplied by the ratio of total payroll for all workers plus payments for contract work to payroll for production workers. The multiplication factor acts as a means for accounting for both hours of nonproduction and contract workers. The correlation between these alternative hours measures is 0.95 at the plant level. Moreover, the results for the aggregate decompositions and other exercises are very similar using the alternative measures. However, we did find that the use of this ratio adjusted hours measure yielded somewhat more erratic results in comparing results using only Annual Survey of Manufactures (ASM) cases to all Census of Manufactures (CM) cases. In particular, we found substantial differences in results between those generated from the full CM and the ASM when considering decompositions of labor productivity per hour. We did not have this type of deviation for any of the other measures (e.g., multifactor productivity and labor productivity per worker) including the CPS-based hours method.

Materials input is measured as the cost of materials deflated by the 4-digit materials deflator. Capital stocks for equipment and structures are measured from the book values deflated by capital stock deflators (where the latter is measured as the ratio of the current dollar book value to the constant dollar value for the two-digit industry from Bureau of Economic Analysis data). Energy input is measured as the cost of energy usage, deflated by the Gray-Bartelsman energy-price deflator. The factor elasticities are measured as the industry average cost shares, averaged over the beginning and ending year of the period of growth. Industry cost shares are generated by combining industry-level data from the NBER Productivity Database with the Bureau of Labor Statistics (BLS) capital rental prices.

The CM does not include data on purchased services (other than that measured through contract work) on a systematic basis (there is increased information on purchased services over time). Baily, Hulten, and Campbell used a crude estimate of purchased services based on the two-digit ratio of purchased services-to-materials usage available from the Bureau of Labor Statistics KLEMS data. They applied the two-digit ratio from the aggregate KLEMS data to the plant level data on materials. Because they reported that this adjustment did not matter much and it is at best a crude adjustment that will not provide much help in decomposing productivity growth *within four-digit* industries, this adjustment was not incorporated in the analysis.[29]

The data used are from the mail universe of the CM for 1977 and 1987. In the CM, very small plants (typically fewer than five employees) are excluded from the mail universe and denoted administrative record cases. Payroll and employment information on such very small establishments are available from administrative records (i.e., the Standard Statistical Establishment List) but the remainder of their data are imputed. Such administrative record cases are excluded from the analysis. In addition to the usual problems in using book-value data, for plants that were not in the Annual Survey of Manufactures (about 50,000–70,000 plants) but in the mail universe of the CM, book-value data are imputed in years other than 1987. We investigated this issue (and like Baily, Hulten, and Campbell) found little sensitivity on this dimension. This partly reflects the relatively small capital shares in total factor costs when materials are included. Nevertheless, for the exercises presented in section V, we considered results using both the full CM (less administrative records) and results generated from the ASM plants. Note that to do this properly, we used the CM files to identify entering, exiting and continuing plants and then considered the ASM subsample of each of those files and applied appropriate ASM sample weights. We only report the results for the full CM since the results are quite similar using the full CM and the ASM only cases. Part of the preference for the full CM in this context is that net entry plays an important role and the measure of the aggregate contribution of entry and exit is likely to be more reliable using the full CM.

Linking Establishments over Time for the Services Sector

Our first step in using the Census of Service Industries establishment-level data is to employ a flag used by the Census Bureau in their tabulation of the non-manufacturing censuses to identify observations containing inappropriate data (for example, out-of-scope establishments). These observations are excluded from tabulations for official Census publications and we eliminated them from our analysis as well. In addition, we excluded a small number of observations with duplicate permanent plant numbers (PPN) in each year that could not be matched with alternative matching routines. Our initial files closely approximated both the number of establishments and total employment contained in official Census Bureau publications.

The biggest challenge that we face in using the Census of Service Industries data for this effort is linking the establishment data over time and measuring the contribution of entry and exit to employment changes and productivity growth. To accomplish this, we match the micro data files

---

29. Siegel and Griliches (1992) also find a relatively modest role for purchased services in their study of manufacturing productivity growth.

using PPNs that the Bureau of the Census assigns to establishments. In principle, PPNs are supposed to remain fixed even during changes in organization or ownership. However, the actual assignment of PPNs is far from perfect. During the construction of the Longitudinal Research Database (LRD) which encompasses the CM and ASM, many PPN linkage problems were detected through analyses of the data by many different individuals (see the appendix of Davis, Haltiwanger and Schuh (1996) for more discussion on PPN linkage problems in the LRD).

Since the service sector data have not previously been linked together over time or analyzed in this manner, it is undoubtedly the case that initial attempts at linking the data that rely only on PPNs will leave a greater number of longitudinal linkage problems than remain in the LRD. Therefore, we took an additional step to improve the matches and used additional identifiers on the files (i.e., Census File Numbers and Employer Identification Numbers). Unfortunately, even after this step, an exploratory analysis of births and deaths for a specific zip code shows that a small but important fraction of the births and deaths reflected changes in ownership for an establishment that continued to operate at the same location in the same industry.

To overcome the remaining linkage problems, we use the name and address information in the files and a sophisticated matching software (Automatch) to improve the matches. Most data processing software takes a very literal approach to this sort of information, thus limiting its value for matching purposes. For example, if an establishment's name is 'K Auto Mart Inc.' in one file and has the exact same name in the other, the two records will match. However, if in the second year the establishment's name is 'K Auto Mart Incorporated' it will not match the previous record if linked using conventional software because the two entries are not exactly the same. Clearly, abbreviations, misspellings, and accidental concatenations can substantially reduce the usefulness of these fields for matching purposes if literal matches are required. However, the software we used is designed to recognize many alternative specifications for the same name and address. That is, it can recognize that abbreviations such as "St" that frequently appear in addresses may stand for "Saint" as in "St James Street" or "Street" as in "Saint James St." The software assigns probability-based weights to the set of potential matches and the user determines the cut-off value of the weights that gives him the best set of 'valid' matches.[30]

Heading A of table 8A.1 shows that by using this technique we are able to reduce the number of unmatched establishments in the 1987 file by

---

30. Two types of errors are unavoidable in this process. First, some "true" matches will not be made and some "false" matches will be. Our review of the individual records indicates that the overall error rate is, nevertheless, substantially diminished.

Table 8A.1   **Results of Using Automatch to Improve Longitudinal Linkages**

A. Summary Statistics

	Continuers Based on Original Linkages	Additional Continuers after Improved Linkages	Exits after Improved Linkages	Entrants after Improved Linkages
Number of establishments	59,011	9,447	44,281	61,649
Employment mean: 1987	5.2	5.1	3.7	
Employment mean: 1992	5.0	4.8		3.4

B. Impact on Gross Employment Flows

	Original Matched Files	File after Matching Name/Address	Change	Percentage Change
Employment at births	231,094	192,016	−39,078	−16.9
Employment at deaths	179,111	139,408	−39,703	−22.2
Job creation rate	56.2	50.9	−5.3	−9.4
Job destruction rate	49.3	44.2	−5.1	−10.3
Percent of creation from entry	82.6	75.8	−6.8	−8.2
Percent of destruction from exits	73	63.5	−9.5	−13.0
Net employment growth rate	6.9	6.7	−0.2	−2.9

Source: Tabulations from Censuses of Service Industries.

about 17.6% and the number of unmatched establishments in the 1992 file by about 13.3%. Notice also that the mean size (employment) of the additional matched establishments is much closer to that of the original matched cases than it is to the remaining unmatched establishments. Heading B of table 8A.1 shows the effects of the additional matches on the five-year gross employment flows statistics. Both the positive and negative flows are about 10% lower after using Automatch than when the only plant identifier numbers are used. This percentage decrease is less than the percent decrease in the number of unmatched establishments since matched establishments often generate positive or negative job flows, though obviously of a lesser magnitude than those generated by spurious entrants and exits. Overall, we consider the application of the matching software to be successful and this bodes well for future longitudinal database development using the non-manufacturing establishment data at Census.

References

Aghion, Philippe, and Peter Howitt. 1992. A model of growth through creative destruction. *Econometrica* 60 (2): 323–51.
Automotive Body Repair News. 1997. Automotive technology: The 21st century car. [http://www.abrn.com] 12 November.
Aw, Bee Yan, Xiaomin Chen, and Mark J. Roberts. 1997. Firm-level evidence on productivity differentials, turnovers, and exports in Taiwanese manufacturing. *Fondazione Eni Enrico Mattei Note di Lavoro* 69:28.
Baily, Martin Neil, Eric J. Bartelsman, and John Haltiwanger. 1996. Downsizing and productivity growth: Myth or reality? *Small Business Economics* 8:259–78.
———. forthcoming. Labor productivity: Structural change and cyclical dynamics. *Review of Economics and Statistics,* forthcoming.
Baily, Martin Neil, Charles Hulten, and David Campbell. 1992. Productivity dynamics in manufacturing plants. *Brookings Papers on Economic Activity, Microeconomics:* 187–249.
Baldwin, John R. 1995. Turnover and productivity growth. In *The dynamics of industrial competition,* ed. J. R. Baldwin, 208–38. Cambridge: Cambridge University Press.
Baldwin, John R., Tim Dunne, and John Haltiwanger. 1995. Plant turnover in Canada and the United States. In *The dynamics of industrial competition,* ed. J. R. Baldwin, 119–52. Cambridge: Cambridge University Press.
Bartelsman, Eric J., and Mark Doms. 2000. Understanding productivity: Lessons from longitudinal microdata. Finance and Economics Discussion Series no. 2000-19. Washington, D.C.: Board of Governors of the Federal Reserve System.
Bartelsman, Eric J., and Wayne Gray. 1996. The NBER manufacturing productivity database. NBER Technical Working Paper no. 205. Cambridge, Mass.: National Bureau of Economic Research, October.
Bartelsman, Eric J., and Phoebus J. Dhrymes. 1998. Productivity dynamics: U.S. manufacturing plants, 1972–1986. *Journal of Productivity Analysis* 9 (1): 5–34.

Bernard, Andrew B., and J. Bradford Jensen. 1999. Exceptional exporter performance: Cause, effect, or both? *Journal of International Economics* 47 (1): 1–25.

Berndt, Ernst R., and Jack E. Triplett, eds. 1990. *Fifty years of economic measurement.* Studies in Income and Wealth, vol. 54. Chicago: University of Chicago Press.

Blanchard, Olivier, and Michael Kremer. 1997. Disorganization. *Quarterly Journal of Economics* 112 (4): 1091–1126.

Caballero, Ricardo, and Mohamad Hammour. 1994. The cleansing effects of recessions. *American Economic Review* 84 (5): 1356–68.

———. 1996. On the timing and efficiency of creative destruction. *Quarterly Journal of Economics* 111 (3): 805–52.

Campbell, Jeffrey R. 1998. Entry, exit, embodied technology, and business cycles. NBER Working Paper no. 5955. *Review of Economic Dynamics* 1 (2): 371–408.

Caves, Richard E. 1998. Industrial organization and new findings on the turnover and mobility of firms. *Journal of Economic Literature* 36 (4): 1947–82.

Chari, V. V., and Hugo Hopenhayn. 1991. Vintage human capital, growth, and the diffusion of new technology. *Journal of Political Economy* 99 (6): 1142–65.

Cooley, Thomas F., Jeremy Greenwood, and Mehmet Yorukoglu. 1997. The replacement problem. *Journal of Monetary Economics* 40 (3): 457–99.

Cooper, Russell, John Haltiwanger, and Laura Power. 1999. Machine replacement and the business cycle: Lumps and bumps. *American Economic Review* 89 (4): 921–46.

Davis, Steven J., and John Haltiwanger. 1991. Wage dispersion between and within U.S. manufacturing plants, 1963–86. *Brookings Papers on Economic Activity (Microeconomics):* 115–20.

———. 1999. Gross job flows. In *Handbook of labor economics,* vols. 3 and 4, ed. Orley Ashenfelter and David Card, 2711–2805. New York: Elsevier Science.

Davis, Steven J., John C. Haltiwanger, and Scott Schuh. 1996. *Job creation and destruction.* Cambridge: MIT Press.

Dean, Edwin R., and Kent Kunze. 1992. Productivity measurement in service industries. In *Output measurement in the service sector,* ed. Zvi Griliches, 73–101. Chicago: University of Chicago Press.

Dial, Jay, and Kevin J. Murphy. 1995. Incentives, downsizing, and value creation at General Dynamics. *Journal of Financial Economics* 37:261–314.

Doms, Mark, Timothy Dunne, and Kenneth Troske. 1996. Workers, wages, and technology. *Quarterly Journal of Economics* 112:253–90.

Dunne, Timothy, Mark Roberts, and Larry Samuelson. 1989. Plant turnover and gross employment flows in the U.S. manufacturing sector. *Journal of Labor Economics* 7 (1): 48–71.

Dwyer, Douglas. 1997. Productivity races I: Are some productivity measures better than others? Center for Economic Studies Working Paper no. CES 97-2. New York: William M. Mercer.

———. 1998. Technology locks, creative destruction, and nonconvergence in productivity levels. *Review of Economic Dynamics* 1 (2): 430–73.

Ericson, Richard, and Ariel Pakes. 1992. An alternative theory of firm and industry dynamics. Yale Cowles Foundation Discussion Paper 1041:45.

Griliches, Zvi, ed. 1992. *Output measurement in the service sectors.* Studies in Income and Wealth, vol. 56. Chicago: University of Chicago Press.

Griliches, Zvi, and Haim Regev. 1995. Productivity and firm turnover in Israeli industry: 1979–1988. *Journal of Econometrics* 65:175–203.

Grossman, Gene M., and Elhanan Helpman. 1991. *Innovation and growth in the global economy.* Cambridge: MIT Press.

Haltiwanger, John. 1997. Measuring and analyzing aggregate fluctuations: The importance of building from microeconomic evidence. *Review of the Federal Reserve Bank of St. Louis* 79 (3): 55–78.
Hopenhayn, Hugo. 1992. Entry, exit, and firm dynamics in long run equilibrium. *Econometrica* 60 (5): 1127–50.
Hopenhayn, Hugo, and Richard Rogerson. 1993. Job turnover and policy evaluation: A general equilibrium approach. *Journal of Political Economy* 101 (5): 915–38.
Jovanovic, Boyan. 1982. Selection and the evolution of industry. *Econometrica* 50 (3): 649–70.
Jovanovic, Boyan, and Glenn M. MacDonald. 1994. Competitive diffusion. *Journal of Political Economy* 102 (1): 24–52.
Jovanovic, Boyan, and Rafael Rob. 1989. The growth and diffusion of knowledge. *Review of Economic Studies* 56 (4): 569–82.
Kendrick, John W., and Beatrice N. Vaccara, eds. 1980. *New developments in productivity and measurement analysis.* Studies in Income and Wealth, vol. 44. Chicago: University of Chicago Press.
Lambson, Val E. 1991. Industry evolution with sunk costs and uncertain market conditions. *International Journal of Industrial Organization* 9 (2): 171–96.
Liu, Lili, and James R. Tybout. 1996. Productivity growth in Chile and Columbia: The role of entry, exit and learning. In *Industrial evolution in developing countries: Micro patterns of turnover, productivity and market structure,* ed. M. J. Roberts and J. R. Tybout, 73–103. New York: Oxford University Press.
Lucas, Robert E. 1977. On the size distribution of business firms. *Bell Journal of Economics* 9 (Autumn): 508–23.
Mansfield, Edwin, Mark Schwartz, and Samuel Wagner. 1981. Imitation costs and patents. *Economic Journal* 91:907–18.
McGuckin, Robert H. 1995. Establishment microdata for economic research and policy analysis: Looking beyond the aggregates. *Journal of Economics and Business Statistics* 13 (1): 121–26.
Murphy, Kevin J. 1999. Executive compensation. In *Handbook of labor economics,* vol. 3B, ed. Orley Ashenfelter and David Card, 2485–2563. Amsterdam: North-Holland 1974.
Nasbeth, Lars, and George Ray, eds. 1974. *The diffusion of new industrial processes: An international study.* Cambridge: Cambridge University Press.
Nelson, Richard R., and Sidney G. Winter. 1982. *An evolutionary theory of economic change.* Cambridge: Harvard University Press.
Olley, G. Steven, and Ariel Pakes. 1996. The dynamics of productivity in the telecommunications equipment industry. *Econometrica* 64 (6): 1263–97.
Pakes, Ariel, and Mark Schankerman. 1984. The rate of obsolescence of patents, research gestation lags, and the private rate of return to research resources. In *R&D, patents, and productivity,* ed. Zvi Griliches, 73–88. Chicago: University of Chicago Press.
Roberts, Mark J., and Dylan Supina. 1997. Output price and markup dispersion in micro data: The roles of producer heterogeneity and noise. NBER Working Paper no. 6075. Cambridge, Mass.: National Bureau of Economic Research, June.
Roberts, Kevin, and Martin L. Weitzman. 1981. Funding criteria for research, development, and exploration projects. *Econometrica* 39:1261–88.
Rogers, Everett M. 1983. *Diffusion of innovations.* 3rd ed. New York: Free Press.
Schumpeter, J. A. 1942. *Capitalism, socialism, and democracy.* New York: Harper and Brothers.

Siegel, Donald, and Zvi Griliches. 1992. Purchased services, outsourcing, computers, and productivity in manufacturing. In *Output measurement in the service sector,* ed. Zvi Griliches, 429–58. Chicago: University of Chicago Press.

Stein, Jeremy. 1997. Waves of creative destruction: Firm-specific learning-by-doing and the dynamics of innovation. *Review of Economics and Statistics* 4 (2): 265–88.

Trager, Mitchell L., and Richard A. Moore. 1995. Development of a longitudinally-linked establishment based register, March 1993 through April 1995. U.S. Bureau of the Census Working Paper. Washington, D.C.

Tybout, James R. 1996. Heterogeneity and productivity growth: Assessing the evidence. In *Industrial evolution in developing countries: Micro patterns of turnover, productivity, and market structure,* ed. M. J. Roberts and J. R. Tybout, 43–72. New York: Oxford University Press.

Comment   Mark J. Roberts

Over the last decade economists have gained access to the firm- or plant-level data collected as part of the economic censuses conducted in many developed and developing countries. This has given rise to a large empirical literature on the patterns of producer dynamics that now spans the fields of industrial organization, macro, labor, and development economics. Two broad conclusions emerge from these studies. First, there is extensive heterogeneity across producers in virtually every dimension examined, but particularly in size and productivity. This heterogeneity exists across producers within the same industry and is not a purely transitory or measurement error phenomenon; rather, the micro-level differences can persist for long periods of time. Second, the entry, growth, and exit processes often generate large gross flows of employment or output among producers within the same industry, even when there is little net change in the total employment or output of the industry.

These findings raise the obvious question, to what extent does the underlying heterogeneity drive the patterns of producer turnover? In response, empirical studies for a number of countries have focused on the correlation between productivity and firm transitions in or out of operation. They have often used an accounting framework to ask if the aggregate or industry productivity changes we observe over time result from widespread changes in productivity at the micro level or from changes in the mix of producers—that is, the entry and expansion of higher productivity producers and the decline and exit of less efficient ones.

The paper by Foster, Haltiwanger, and Krizan covers three topics in

---

Mark J. Roberts is professor of economics at Pennsylvania State University and a research associate of the National Bureau of Economic Research.

this literature. First, the authors ask how differences in methodology alter the conclusions about the micro sources of aggregate productivity change in the U.S. manufacturing sector. They focus on the decisions that researchers must make concerning the measure of productivity (single factor or multifactor productivity), the way plants or firms are weighted to construct the productivity aggregate (output or input weights), and the time series decomposition of the aggregate into within-plant and between-plant movements in the components. Second, they use the microdata for U.S. manufacturing and compare the average productivity of entering, exiting, and continuing cohorts of plants to see if there are systematic differences that reflect market selection forces. Third, they provide one of the first analyses of the micro sources of industry productivity growth for a service sector industry, in this case the U.S. automobile repair industry. This service sector is interesting because it is characterized by very high rates of producer turnover and large micro-level differences in productivity, particularly between entering and exiting plants, that, together, are an important contributing factor to industry productivity change.

Decomposing Aggregate Productivity Change

I will begin with a discussion of some of the methodological issues raised in section 8.4 of their paper. Aggregate productivity is defined as a share-weighted sum of plant productivity levels. The aggregate can change over time as the productivity of individual plants changes, labeled the within-plant component; as the share weights shift among continuing plants, the between-plant component; or as entry and exit occur, the net entry component. For plants that continue in operation for several years, movements in their productivity and share weights are correlated over time, and the authors argue that it is useful to isolate this correlation from the within, between, and net entry components. The decomposition of aggregate productivity change, which they label "method 1," does this by breaking out a covariance term between the change in a plant's productivity and the change in its share weight. The authors label this the cross share. They compare this decomposition with one they label method 2, which is essentially the decomposition developed by Griliches and Regev (1995). In this second approach, the within-plant effect is constructed by weighting the change in plant productivity by the plant's average share in the beginning and ending period, rather than the beginning period share used in method 1. Comovements in the weights and productivity are thus both captured in the within-plant component. A similar distinction is made with the between-plant component of the two decompositions. The use of the method 1 decomposition represents a useful extension of the methods developed by Baily, Hulten, and Campbell (1992) and Griliches and Regev (1995) because it addresses the question of whether the plants that are improving their productivity are also responsible for an increasing or decreasing share of the resources that are reflected in the weights. If the shares are measured using plant output, we would expect that market competition, which reallocates production toward the least cost producers, would generate a positive cross share. This is what the authors find (the first two rows of table 8.4), and we see that productivity improvement in the continuing plants, evaluated at both their initial output shares and recognizing the contemporaneous increase in their market share, is a major source of aggregate productivity change.

The authors' comparison of decomposition methods 1 and 2 illustrates that real care in interpretation is needed. Terms that are superficially similar to the casual reader, and are often labeled the same, are not measuring the same resource flows. The different methods are related, however, and the terms can be sorted out. From the decompositions in table 8.4 we see that the within share in method 2 is equal to the within share in method 1 plus one-half the cross share. This holds as an identity. The other half of the method 1 cross share is allocated into both the between share and net entry share in method 2. In their particular application it is virtually all allocated to the between share, which leaves the net entry share with the same role regardless of decomposition method. I believe that the important question in the choice of decomposition method 1 or 2 is whether it is useful to measure the covariance term separately. I believe it is useful because the comovement of productivity and resource shares is a unique and potentially important source of dynamic adjustment.

Single versus Multifactor Productivity

One of the major differences revealed by the methodological comparisons in table 8.4 is the difference in the overall growth rates of multifactor and labor productivity. The authors calculate that between 1977 and 1987 the U.S. manufacturing labor productivity grew by 21.32 to 25.56 percent, depending on the measurement method, whereas TFP grew by 10.24 percent. This difference largely reflects differences in the growth rate of nonlabor inputs. The U.S. Bureau of Labor Statistics multifactor productivity calculations show that between 1977 and 1987 capital input in manufacturing grew 32.8 percent, and material input grew 9.9 percent, whereas labor hours declined by 2.4 percent. The substantial amount of input substitution that is reflected in these large changes in the capital-labor and material-labor ratios leads to the much higher growth in labor productivity and is a familiar argument for using measures of multifactor productivity instead of labor productivity.

Aggregating Plant Productivity

The second place where the methodology clearly has an effect on the results and their interpretation is the choice of aggregation weights. When plants are aggregated using their share of output, we observe a positive correlation between productivity growth, regardless of whether it is multifactor or labor productivity, and the change in the shares. Plants with rising productivity are accounting for a rising share of industry output, which generates the *positive* cross share observed in the first two rows of table 8.4. In contrast, when plant labor productivity is aggregated using the share of labor input as weights (rows 3 and 4 of the table) we observe a *negative* cross share and a larger within-plant share. This implies that plants that are increasing their (labor) productivity are reducing their share of industry labor input. The authors suggest that a combination of measurement error and changing input intensities is the likely explanation.

Transitory measurement errors in output can certainly produce the observed positive correlation between changes in output shares and changes in productivity. A plant with higher-than-normal output in year t as a result of measurement error will show a spurious increase in both productivity and market share between years $t-1$ and t. The changes will both be negative from year t to year $t+1$ as the plant's output returns to normal levels. Similarly, measurement errors in labor input can produce the negative correlation between changes in labor input shares and changes in labor productivity. What works against this measurement error explanation is the ten-year period over which the changes are calculated. As the time period increases, the effect of uncorrelated, transitory measurement errors on the output or employment levels should diminish, and the permanent, or at least long-term, changes in output and inputs should become more prominent. Thus the correlations between the change in productivity and the change in the aggregation weights are more likely to reflect long-term changes in plant size and production efficiency. Over a ten-year period, particularly one characterized by as much restructuring as the 1977–87 period for U.S. manufacturing, it is likely that changes in productivity and shares reflect more fundamental long-term changes in a plant's capital intensity and size. Plants that substitute capital and materials for labor over this decade would have large increases in labor productivity and could have large increases in TFP and their output share, while reducing their share of manufacturing labor use. (The latter depends on whether an increase in labor demand due to increases in size outweighs the substitution effect.) Input substitution is able to explain the signs of the cross shares and the differences in overall labor and TFP growth that we observe. It is also an important reason for the patterns that the authors cite for the steel industry.

In table 8.4, Foster, Haltiwanger, and Krizan provide a detailed comparison of the effect of using alternative productivity measures and aggregation weights on the sources of aggregate productivity change. It is still necessary for the researcher to choose among the methods, and here the economic theory of index numbers can provide some guidance. Diewert

(1980, section 8.5.3) shows that a change in industry productivity, which is defined as a proportional shift in the industry variable profit function over time, equals a weighted sum of the shifts in individual plant, or firm, variable profit functions. The appropriate weight for each micro unit in a competitive industry is their share of industry revenue, which is equivalent to their share of industry output. The construction of multifactor productivity indexes at the micro level and their aggregation with output weights, as the authors do in the first row of table 8.4, can be justified by this argument.

Index Numbers for Plant Productivity

An additional methodological issue concerns the measurement of multifactor productivity for the micro units. Diewert (1976) has established the linkages between the form of the index number used to measure productivity and the form of the underlying production function. His work provides the justification for superlative productivity indexes, such as the Tornqvist, which aggregate inputs using time varying input cost shares as weights, because they are consistent with more general production functions than are fixed weight input indexes. The multifactor productivity index used by Foster, Haltiwanger, and Krizan recognizes differences in input and output levels across producers but weights all inputs with their industry-level cost shares, thus not allowing any variation in factor prices or the marginal products of inputs across micro units.

The multilateral Tornqvist index numbers developed by Caves, Christensen, and Diewert (1982) provide a general basis for measuring productivity in microlevel panel data sets in a way that is consistent with general production functions. The productivity indexes they develop express the output and input levels of each micro observation as a deviation from a single reference point, the geometric mean of the output and input levels over all observations in the data. The use of this single reference point makes the index free of the units in which output and input are measured and preserves the transitivity of comparisons among observations. In the productivity index, the inputs for each micro observation are aggregated using information on the input cost shares for the micro unit, which will capture the effect of factor price differences across micro units on the input bundle used, and the average input cost shares across all observations. This blending of the microlevel and industry-level cost shares as input weights has the advantage of recognizing the substantial variation in input mix at the micro level while providing some smoothing of the weights across units. The use of microlevel input cost shares does raise the additional practical issue of how much of the observed factor price and input share variation is real and how much is due to measurement errors in the microdata. I do not believe this issue has been addressed in the productivity literature, and it is a difficult one to answer with the data that is typically collected in plant-level surveys or censuses conducted by most government statistical agencies.

Overall, a good methodological basis for microlevel productivity measurement and aggregation is provided by the economic theory of index numbers. The measurement of TFP at the micro level using a Tornqvist index number formula and aggregation to the industry or sector level using the plant's share of industry or sector output as a weight can be justified on fairly general grounds. This can provide a common starting point for the type of productivity measurements made by Foster, Haltiwanger, and Krizan, and by related papers in the literature. The disaggregation of changes in aggregate productivity into within-plant, between-plant, covariance, and entry-exit components using a decomposition like the authors' method 1 is a useful next step in accounting for the productivity changes at the micro level and for how they contribute to the aggregate growth.

The Importance of Entry and Exit

In the U.S. manufacturing data the authors find (first row of table 8.4) that continuing plant productivity gains, reallocation of market shares toward higher productivity plants, and turnover all contributed to the manufacturing sector gains over the 1977–87 period. Although not always defined in the same way, within-plant productivity improvements have virtually always been found in this literature to be an important source of aggregate productivity movements. The finding by Foster, Haltiwanger, and Krizan that entry and exit are a significant source of U.S. manufacturing productivity gain over the 1977–87 period is not true of many of the other studies using this type of accounting decomposition. As the authors point out, the time period over which entry and exit are measured is likely to be a key factor in their productivity contribution. What also appears to be important is the magnitude of demand or cost shocks that occur during the period. This paper covers a time period that includes one of the largest recessions experienced by the manufacturing sector. The two other papers that find an important role for entry and exit also covered time periods of major structural adjustments. Olley and Pakes (1996) study the U.S. telecommunications industry around the time of deregulation, and Aw, Chen, and Roberts (1997) study the Taiwanese manufacturing sector during the decade of the 1980s, a time period when real manufacturing output grew at an annual rate of 6.5 percent and the annual rate of net firm entry was 7.7 percent. Time periods that include substantial demand or supply shocks appear to generate a significant role for producer turnover to contribute to aggregate productivity movements.

Foster, Haltiwanger, and Krizan also document the average productivity differences among cohorts of entering, exiting, and continuing plants. A useful theoretical basis for these comparisons is provided by recent models of industry dynamics (Jovanovic 1982; Hopenhayn 1992; Ericson and Pakes 1995). These models begin with the assumption that producers differ in their productivity and are subject to idiosyncratic shocks or uncertainty about their efficiency. Differences in the evolution of their productivity over time, in turn, lead producers to make different decisions regarding entry, growth, and exit. As a result they provide a useful framework for organizing microlevel data on plant productivity and turnover.

A number of the empirical regularities reported by the authors in this paper are consistent with predictions that follow from these theoretical models. The models predict that exit will be concentrated among the least productive producers at each point in time. This occurs because a plant's current productivity is a determinant of its likely future productivity. Low-productivity plants are less likely to experience increases in future productivity and more likely to experience low future profit levels that will induce them to exit. As reported in table 8.11, the authors find that in 1977 the plants that do not survive until 1987 are less productive than the ones that do survive until 1987. They have, on average, TFP levels that are 1.9 percent below the survivors if they are old plants (entered prior to 1972) and 2.4 percent below if they are young plants (entered between 1972 and 1977). Also, if we just focus on the cohort of plants that first appear in the data in 1977, the ones that do not survive until 1987 are, on average, 0.7 percent less productive than the cohort members that do survive. The labor productivity differentials between exiting and surviving plants are even more substantial, likely reflecting the fact that exiting plants tend to be less capital intensive than survivors. The exiting plants have labor productivity (output per hour) levels that, depending on their age, are an average of 18.2 percent or 14.9 percent lower than survivors. Within the 1977 entry cohort the exiting plants are 12.4 percent less productive than the survivors.

On the entry side, the theoretical model by Hopenhayn (1992) predicts that under stable market demand the productivity distribution of older cohorts will stochastically dominate the productivity distribution of an entering cohort. This occurs because of market selection. Older plants will have had more opportunities to experience productivity levels low enough to induce exit, and thus as a cohort ages it will be increasingly composed of only the higher productivity members. The numbers presented in the lower half of table 8.10 are consistent with this. In 1987, plants that were zero to five years old were less productive, on average, than plants six to ten years old. However, this pattern is not very strong when comparing the whole group of new plants in 1987 with the whole group of incumbents. In this case there is no difference between the average TFP of entrants and incumbents (table 8.9, row 1).

One possible reason for this weak pattern is that the model predictions are based on assumptions of stable market demand and that entering plants have no knowledge of their individual productivity prior to entry. If instead there are cyclical movements in demand and producers have some knowledge of their likely productivity prior to entry, then the composition of the entering cohort would change over time. Only the highest productivity entrants would find it profitable to enter in low demand periods, and the average productivity of the entering cohort would move countercyclically. One result of the 1982 recession could be a relatively productive group of entrants that are first observed in 1987. Running counter to this trend would be the exit of large numbers of low-productivity incumbents during the recession, which would tend to raise the productivity of the older cohorts in the years following the recession. Further refinements of the comparison between the productivity of new and old cohorts may be useful in sorting out one pathway by which cyclical shocks can affect aggregate productivity.

In the paper the authors emphasize the broad conclusion that net entry plays a significant role in aggregate productivity growth in the period 1977–87. This is a combination of the facts that in 1977 the plants that were not going to survive were less productive than was the group of survivors, and that in 1987 the entrants were similar (or slightly lower) in productivity than were the incumbents in that year. As a result, the productivity difference between the entering group in 1987 and the exiting group in 1977 is larger than the productivity differential across the two years for the continuing plants. This productivity differential between entering and exiting plants plays a larger role in the automobile repair industry, which the authors analyze in the last section of the paper. In this case, the productivity of incumbent plants changes very little over time so that most industry productivity growth is due to the replacement of low-productivity exiting plants by higher productivity entrants.

The Role of Sunk Entry and Exit Costs

The theoretical models of industry evolution also suggest one reason that entry and exit play a larger role in the service industries. Hopenhayn (1992) demonstrates that the amount of producer turnover will be positively related to the magnitude of sunk entry or exit costs. If these costs are not too large, industry equilibrium will involve simultaneous offsetting flows of entering and exiting producers, and changes in the level of entry costs will affect the magnitude of these flows. An increase in the entry cost raises the level of discounted profits needed to make entry profitable, thus discouraging entry. An increase in these costs also lowers the minimum productivity level needed for incumbents to survive, thus lowering the amount of exit. High entry costs choke off both entry and exit. This can lead to a useful across-industry comparison. The authors find that plant turnover in the automobile repair service industry is very high when compared with the typical manufacturing sector. If service sector industries have lower entry costs because the scale of operation is smaller and the technology less capital intensive, for example, then we would expect higher rates of producer turnover and smaller productivity differentials to exist across producers.

Sunk entry costs may also be one reason why the results in the existing literature, which covers a very diverse group of countries, industries, and time periods, are so difficult to reconcile. If entry costs or other lump-sum costs of adjustment are important, then the level of current demand and cost are not sufficient to explain a plant's decision to be in operation. Demand conditions that generate profits sufficient to keep current producers in operation may not be sufficient to induce entry. Consider two time periods with the same level of demand. When entry costs are large, small demand fluctuations between the two periods will lead to little entry or exit. In contrast, if the intervening period is characterized by a large demand increase followed by a large decline in demand, this can cause a permanent increase in the number of producers or hysteresis in market structure. The magnitude of entry and exit flows will depend on the entire path of demand (or cost) shocks, not just the level at the beginning and end of the period of analysis, and the dependence on the path of demand will increase with the level of entry costs. Even comparing across two business cycle peaks is not sufficient to control for the role of demand changes in determining entry and exit. This suggests that attempts to reconcile the diverse findings on the sources of aggregate productivity growth, and particularly the role of entry and exit as a contributing factor, will need to separate industries, countries, or time periods by the importance of entry costs and the pattern of demand or cost shocks that are present over longer periods of time.

In this paper the authors have made substantial progress on a number of outstanding issues in the literature linking microlevel adjustments and aggregate productivity change. They have clarified several methodological issues that should help standardize the approach used by researchers in future work. They have also laid out a set of stylized facts for manufacturing that can be used as a basis for future comparisons and have extended the literature to the service sector. I completely agree with their assessment that developing a better understanding of the role of heterogeneity, reallocation, and lumpy adjustment at the micro level should be a top research priority for those interested in understanding firm dynamics and its implications for aggregate growth.

References

Aw, Bee Yan, Xiaomin Chen, and Mark J. Roberts. 1997. Firm-level evidence on productivity differentials, turnovers, and exports in Taiwanese manufacturing. NBER Working Paper no. 6235. Cambridge, Mass.: National Bureau of Economic Research.
Baily, Martin Neil, Charles Hulten, and David Campbell. 1992. Productivity dy-

namics in manufacturing plants. *Brookings Papers on Economic Activity (Microeconomics):* 187–249.

Caves, Douglas W., Laurits Christensen, and W. Erwin Diewert. 1982. Output, input, and productivity using superlative index numbers. *Economic Journal* (92): 73–96.

Diewert, W. Erwin. 1976. Exact and superlative index numbers. *Journal of Econometrics* (4): 115–45.

———. 1980. Aggregation problems in the measurement of capital. In *The measurement of capital,* ed. Dan Usher, 433–528. Chicago: University of Chicago Press.

Ericson, Richard, and Ariel Pakes. 1995. Markov-perfect industry dynamics: A framework for empirical work. *Review of Economic Studies* 62 (1): 53–82.

Griliches, Zvi, and Haim Regev. 1995. Productivity and firm turnover in Israeli industry: 1979–1988. *Journal of Econometrics* 65:175–203.

Hopenhayn, Hugo. 1992. Entry, exit, and firm dynamics in long run equilibrium. *Econometrica* 60 (5): 1127–50.

Jovanovic, Boyan. 1982. Selection and the evolution of industry. *Econometrica* 50 (3): 649–70.

Olley, G. Steven, and Ariel Pakes. 1996. The dynamics of productivity in the telecommunications equipment industry. *Econometrica* 64 (6): 1263–97.

9   Sources of Productivity Growth in the American Coal Industry 1972–95

Denny Ellerman, Thomas M. Stoker, and Ernst R. Berndt

9.1 Introduction

Aggregate productivity statistics succinctly and conveniently measure the efficiency with which resources are being used in a country or industry, but problems of measurement and aggregation in the inevitable presence of heterogeneity require that these statistics be interpreted carefully to avoid misleading results.

This paper exploits an unusual database to explore the differences between productivity trends as they appear at the aggregate level and as they may be experienced at the firm level. The Mine Safety and Health Administration (MSHA), as part of its mandated regulatory effort, has collected labor input and coal output information for every mine in the United States since 1972, along with data on site locations, operator identity, and mining techniques (U.S. Department of Labor, MSHA, "Part 50 Coal Mining Address/Employment and Accident/Injury Files"; henceforth USDOL, MSHA, Part 50). Thus, labor productivity can be observed for this industry at the lowest practicable level; and, based on this microdata, a national aggregate, as well as any number of subaggregates, can be formed from the bottom up. Working from microdata all the way up to the aggregate industry level not only supplements industry aggregate statistics but also permits an examination of the root causes of aggregate productivity change with greater clarity than is usually the case.

Denny Ellerman is executive director, Center for Energy and Environmental Policy Research, and senior lecturer at the Sloan School of Management, Massachusetts Institute of Technology. Thomas M. Stoker is the Gordon Y. Billard Professor of Applied Economics at the Sloan School of Management, Massachusetts Institute of Technology. Ernst R. Berndt is the Louis B. Seley Professor of Applied Economics at the Sloan School of Management,

9.2 The American Coal Industry

9.2.1 Postwar Output, Price, and Productivity Trends

Although the database for this paper limits analysis to 1972–95, a longer view helps to place these years, and particularly the extraordinary decade of the 1970s, in perspective. Figure 9.1 provides the essential aggregate statistics for the U.S. coal industry: the price and quantity of output and an index of total factor productivity (TFP) from the late 1940s until 1991 (Jorgenson, 1990, plus update). The year our microdata begins, 1972, is close to the year 1969, which according to anecdote as well as statistics, marked a turning point for the industry.

The Mine Safety and Health Act was passed in 1969, signaling the beginning of what was to be a decade of increasing regulation to address issues associated with the health, safety, and environmental aspects of coal mining. Perhaps not coincidentally, 1969 also marked the end of a long period of declining real price and moderately increasing productivity. The 1970s were to be characterized by sharply rising nominal and real prices for output and significant declines in coal mining productivity. Then, in

---

Massachusetts Institute of Technology, and director of the Program on Technological Progress and Productivity Measurement at the National Bureau of Economic Research.

This work has been made possible by the dedicated efforts of a succession of research assistants who have worked on the massive database underlying the research. We are particularly indebted to Susanne Schennach and Chiaming Liu, the most recent of these assistants and formerly graduate students in MIT's Department of Economics and Sloan School of Management, respectively, who performed much of the final regression and simulation analyses. Their work and this paper would not have been possible, however, without the earlier contributions of Frank Felder, Babu Bangaru, Kevin Wellinius, and Narasimha Rao, all former MIT graduate students who assembled the database that made this analysis possible.

Personnel at the Mine Safety and Health Administration in Denver, Colorado, the source of our data, have been extremely helpful in clarifying definitional and procedural issues concerning the data collection. Special thanks are due Alice Brown, chief of statistics, and Rhys Llewellyn, head of the data division.

This research has been funded chiefly by the Center for Energy and Environmental Policy Research through grants from a number of corporate sponsors supporting MIT research in energy and environmental economics. Early funding for this project was also provided by the Office of Coal, Uranium, and Renewable Fuels Analysis at the Energy Information Administration in the U.S. Department of Energy. To all, we are grateful.

This paper has benefited from comments and insights provided by a number of persons in the U.S. coal industry and participants in the NBER/CRIW conference at which this paper was first presented. Among coal industry personnel, particular gratitude is due William Bruno of Consolidation Coal Company, William Dix of the Pittsburg and Midway Coal Mining Company, and the senior management of both Cyprus Amax Coal Company and the Pittsburg and Midway Coal Mining Company. Among NBER/CRIW participants, we are especially indebted to our respondent, Larry Rosenblum, and to Dale Jorgenson and the late Zvi Griliches for insightful and encouraging comments. Responsibility for any errors is, however, solely ours.

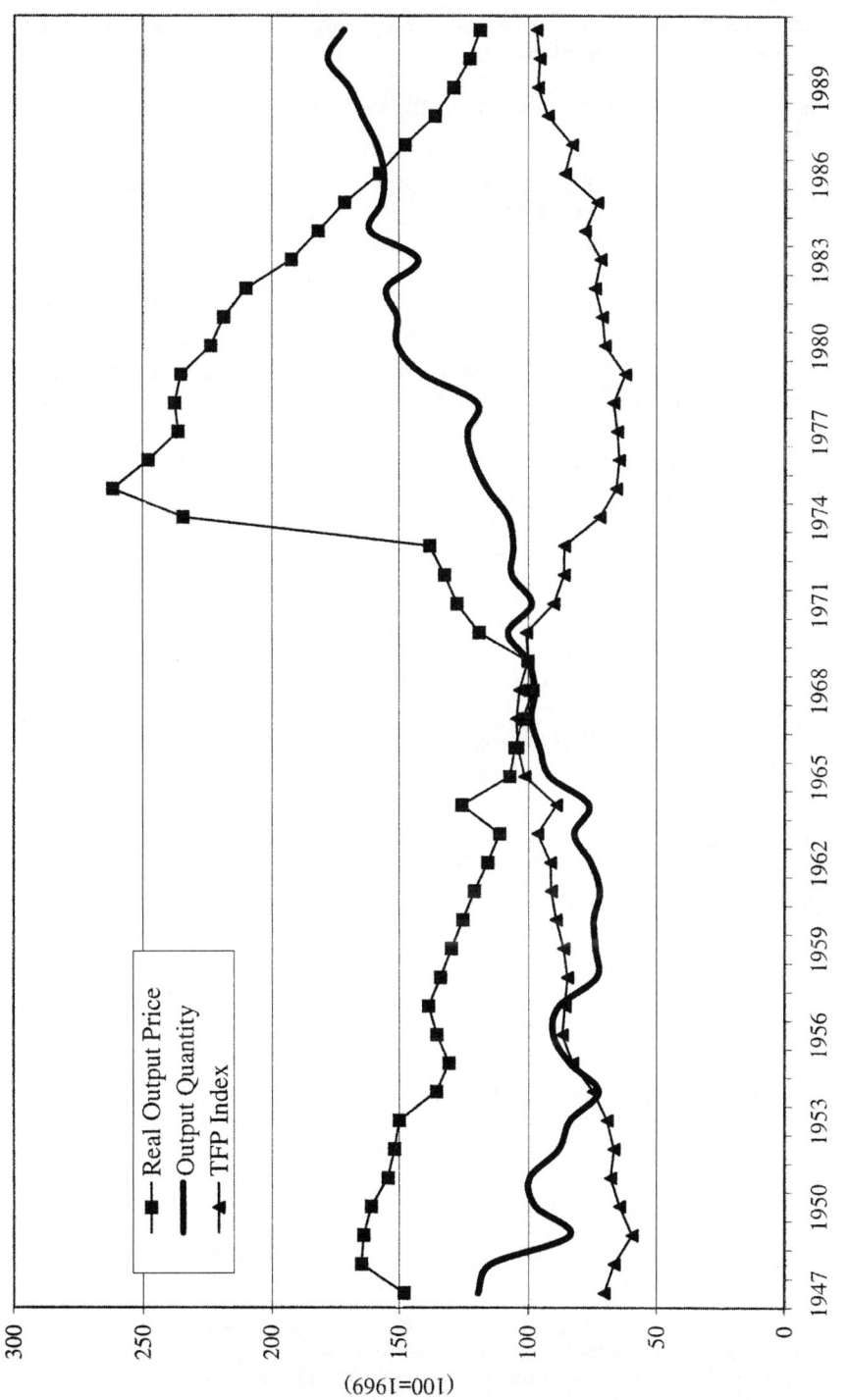

Fig. 9.1 Price, quantity, and TFP, U.S. coal industry

the 1980s and continuing to the present, the former trend of declining real price and rising productivity resumed, albeit at an accelerated pace.

9.2.2 Elements of Heterogeneity in the Industry

There are a number of reasons for approaching aggregate coal productivity statistics with caution. Coal is produced in many locations in the United States, from the Great Western Basin to the Appalachian Mountains, and labor productivity differs among coal-producing regions, whose shares of output have changed significantly over the past twenty-five years. In particular, coal from the Powder River Basin (PRB, in the northeastern corner of Wyoming and adjacent parts of Montana) increased from less than 1 percent of national production in 1970 to 25 percent in the mid-1990s. Although the PRB is located far from most coal markets, unusually favorable geology enables operations there easily to produce twenty to thirty tons of coal per hour of labor input. In contrast, eight to ten tons per hour is as much as the best mines in the Midwest or Appalachia can reasonably hope to achieve. Thus, even if there were no change in productivity within any region, the increasing PRB share would cause the national aggregate for labor productivity to increase.

Although quantity of output is conventionally measured in tons of production, the ultimate service sought by nearly all coal purchasers is heat content (measured in British thermal units, or Btu), which also varies considerably across regions. Again, the PRB requires special consideration: The Btu content of each ton of coal produced there is a third to a quarter less than the heat content of Midwestern or Appalachian coals. Thus, although the increase in PRB coal production has been great, however production is measured, statistics based on tons overstate the importance of the PRB and growth in aggregate national labor productivity. The same arguments apply for lignite (an even lower rank of coal than that produced in the PRB),[1] whose share of national output has also increased, though not as spectacularly as that for PRB coal.

Traditionally, coal mining has been an underground operation in which a shaft is sunk or tunnels are extended into the seam, from which coal is removed and transported to the surface. Underground mining techniques are further divided into two basic types: continuous and longwall mining. Continuous mines employ machines with giant bits mounted in front that advance into a seam to remove coal from the face and pass it back to a

---

1. Coal is conventionally classified by rank (from highest to lowest quality) as anthracite, bituminous, sub-bituminous, and lignite. Rank is determined by a number of characteristics, among which is Btu content. Most coal produced in the United States is of bituminous rank, which ranges from 21 to 28 million Btu (mmBtu) per short ton. Sub-bituminous coals, including that produced in the PRB, range from 16 to 23 mmBtu per ton, and Lignites have a heat content from 12 to 17 mmBtu/ton. Production of anthracite coal is insignificant and can be ignored for all practical purposes after the Second World War. For a more complete discussion of coal classifications, see U.S. DOE/EIA-0584(94), *Coal Industry Annual 1994,* table C1.

shuttle car or conveyer belt system to transport to the surface. Such systems require tunnels, and a portion of the coal must be left in place as pillars to support the roof. Longwall mining, on the other hand, involves an elaborate shearing device that operates along an extended face (hence the term *longwall*), an attached shield that supports the roof, and a conveyor belt to take the coal to the surface. The distinctive feature of longwall mining is that the whole device—shearer, roof shield, and conveyor system—advances into the face as coal is removed. The strata above the coal seam are then allowed to subside into the cavity created by the advancing longwall.[2] As a result, a higher percentage of the reserve can be removed by longwall mining than by continuous mining. The longwall shearer also separates a greater volume of coal from the seam per unit of time than does the continuous miner.

Coal lying close to the surface is mined by techniques in which the overburden is stripped away to expose the coal seam, after which the overburden is put back in place and the original surface condition is restored. Bulldozers, steam shovels, draglines, and trucks are employed in a giant earth-moving operation more akin to modern road building than to the underground mining that conjures traditional images of black-faced miners tunneling through the bowels of the earth. All three production techniques compete in most coal-producing regions, although some areas, such as the Powder River Basin and the lignite-producing areas of Texas and North Dakota, are mined exclusively by surface methods.

9.2.3 Eleven Relatively Homogeneous Subaggregates

In order to account for such geographical, geological, and technological heterogeneity, we assign each coal mine in the United States to one of eleven subaggregates, or groups. Table 9.1 lists these groups and the average heat content assumed for coal produced by each. In general, the western foothills of the Appalachian Mountains divide the Appalachian and Interior regions, and the Great Plains separate the Western and Interior regions. Coal quality generally diminishes westward from Appalachia. We separate Western surface mining into three groups: the PRB; lignite, produced only in North Dakota, Texas, and Louisiana and the only coal that is surface mined in these states; and all other Western surface mining (subsequently called Western Surface Ex or WSX). This latter group is extremely heterogeneous but not very important.

Labor productivity varies widely among the eleven subaggregates. As if to offset the tendency of coal quality to decline from east to west, the absolute level of labor productivity improves from east to west. In particular, the PRB enjoys levels that are from two to eight times greater than other regions. The two other Western surface regions also have labor pro-

---

2. The roof is supported in the conventional manner for a passage to provide entry and egress at one end of the advancing longwall face. See USDOE/EIA (1995) for more details.

Table 9.1 Characteristics of the Eleven Subaggregates

Geographic Region	Production Technology	Heat Content (mmBtu/short ton)
Appalachia	Underground/continuous	23
	Underground/longwall	23
	Surface	23
Interior	Underground/continuous	21
	Underground/longwall	21
	Surface	21
Western	Underground/continuous	22
	Underground/longwall	22
	Powder River Basin	17
	Lignite	13
	Other surface	20

ductivity higher than all groups excepting the PRB, although by the end of the period, Western longwall productivity had drawn equal to their level. Labor productivity has also varied over time. Labor productivity declined for all the subaggregates through the late 1970s or early 1980s, and improved thereafter. From 1972 to 1978, the national aggregate coal productivity declined from 45 to 37 mmBtu/h of labor input (2.0 to 1.6 standard tons),[3] and thereafter increased steadily to a value of 112 mmBtu/h (4.9 standard tons) in 1995.

The relative shares of Btu output by these eleven regions in terms of Btu output are given in figure 9.2. The three Appalachian regions are the bottom three bands, representing continuous, longwall, and surface production, respectively, followed by the three Interior regions, with the five Western regions at the top of the graph. Two points are notable. First, the contribution of Western coal has increased tremendously, from slightly less than 8 percent of coal Btu output in 1972 to 40 percent in 1995. In particular, the PRB has risen from 1.5 percent to 24 percent of the U.S. coal industry's Btu output. Second, despite a decline in share from 66 percent to 48 percent between 1972 and 1995, Appalachia remains the largest producer of Btu's from coal.

9.3 Aggregate Measures of Productivity Change

9.3.1 Labor and Total Factor Productivity

Though our purpose in this paper is not to address the difference between aggregate TFP and labor productivity growth, the two are closely

---

3. The unit of quality-adjusted output for these productivity figures is millions of Btu per hour (mmBtu). As noted in table 9.1, a standard (eastern) short ton of coal is equivalent to about 23 mmBtu.

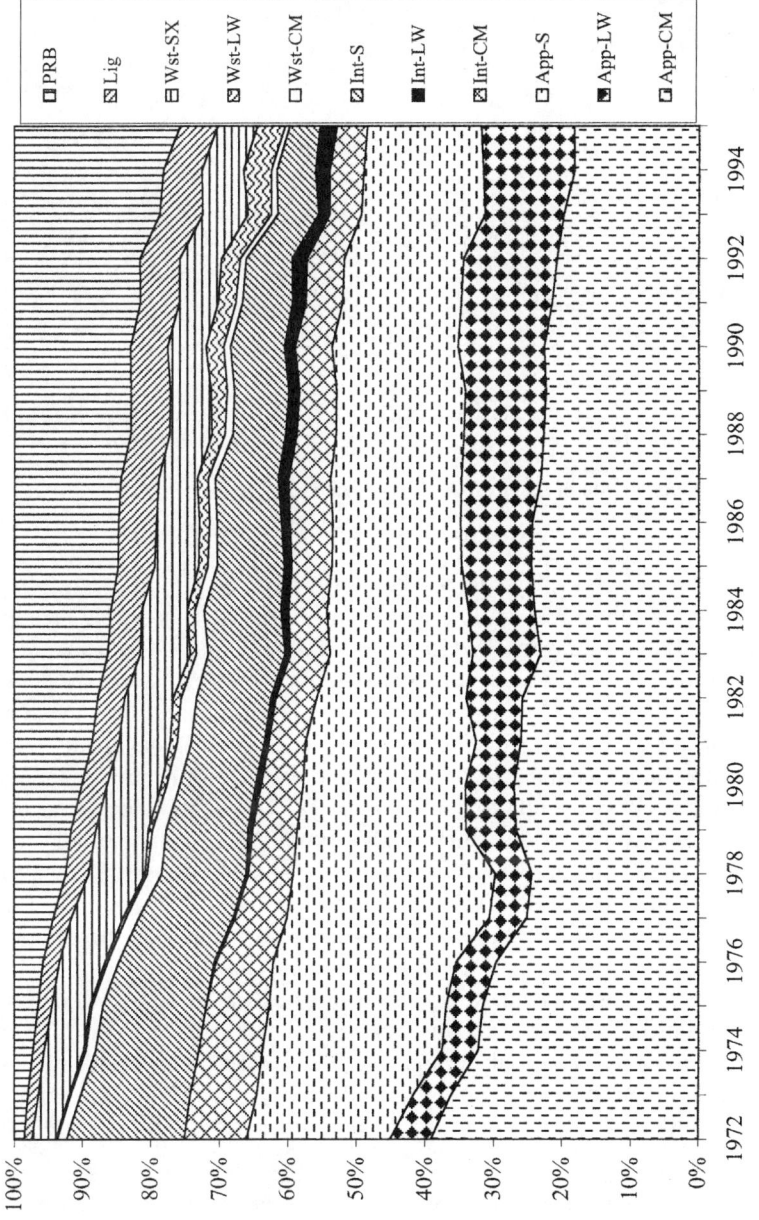

Fig. 9.2 Btu output shares by component, 1972–95

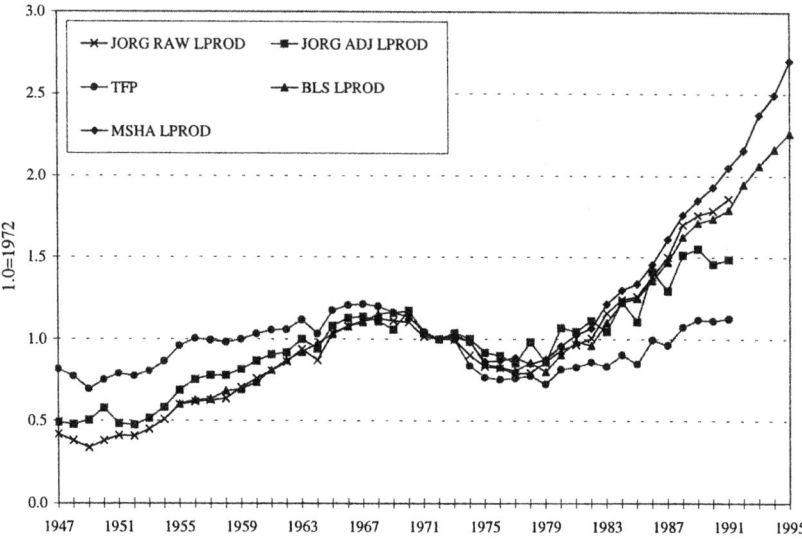

Fig. 9.3 Comparison of labor productivity with TFP

related. Figure 9.3 displays the total factor productivity (TFP) index, first introduced in figure 9.1, with various labor productivity indexes. Five indexes are shown, all normalized to the 1972 value. Three indexes, spanning the years 1947–1991, draw upon aggregate coal industry statistics developed by Jorgenson and associates:[4] output quantity divided by raw labor hours (Jorg Raw Lprod), labor productivity when labor hours are adjusted for quality differences (Jorg Adj Lprod),[5] and total factor productivity. The fourth index (BLS Lprod), extending from 1955 through 1995, is the Bureau of Labor Statistics' measure of labor productivity, which for all practical purposes coincides with Jorgenson's non–quality adjusted labor productivity index (USDOL, BLS, 1996). The last index (MSHA Lprod) is formed from the 1972–95 MSHA data by summing each year's production across all mines and dividing by the comparable sum for labor hours.

The close correspondence among the MSHA, BLS, and Jorgenson non–quality adjusted labor productivity indexes indicates that the same underlying phenomena—coal output and undifferentiated labor input hours—are being measured. Moreover, labor productivity and TFP move together, albeit at different rates. During the progressive periods, labor productiv-

---

4. The development of these aggregate statistics is described in Jorgenson, Gollop, and Fraumeni (1987) and Jorgenson (1990). Updated series through 1991 were kindly provided by Dale Jorgenson and Kevin Stiroh.

5. Output is treated as homogeneous, notwithstanding some notable differences in the quality of coal produced by different mines and regions. We address this issue in what follows.

ity improves at a rate greater than that for TFP; during the one period of regress, labor productivity does not fall as sharply as TFP. Earlier econometric work using Jorgenson's industry-level statistics suggests the coal industry has a strong labor-saving bias to technical change (Berndt and Ellerman 1996). This bias explains most of the difference between the rates of TFP and aggregate labor productivity improvement that can be observed in figure 9.3. That research also suggests that a more or less constant relation exists between rates of change in labor productivity and TFP.

Finally, labor constitutes the largest input value share in output for the coal industry. Approximate aggregate shares are labor, 40 percent; materials, 30 percent; and capital and energy, about 15 percent each, although in recent years there has been a slight tendency for the labor share to decline and for the materials share to increase. This suggests that observed changes in labor productivity can, with appropriate adjustment, be used as an indicator of change that is highly correlated with TFP.

Further support for viewing labor productivity as a proxy for TFP can be found in the relationship between output prices and labor productivity in different coal-producing regions. If factor proportions are more or less constant across regions, output prices would reflect, inversely, differences in absolute labor productivity. In fact, such an inverse relationship is observed. Coal produced in the extraordinarily productive PRB currently sells for $4–5 per ton at the mine, whereas lower-productivity coal produced in the Midwest sells at the higher price of $18–23 per ton, and still lower-productivity Appalachian coal sells for even more, $22–28 per ton (*Coal Markets,* various issues). These price relationships are roughly the inverse of average 1995 mmBtu/h productivity levels in these regions.

9.3.2 Decomposition of the National Aggregate

The national aggregate for coal labor productivity is the sum of output across the component mining groups or subaggregates divided by the analogous sum for labor input. As shown in equation (1), this aggregate is equivalent to an input weighted average of labor productivity in each mining group.

(1) $$\frac{Q}{L} = \frac{\sum_i Q_i}{\sum_i L_i} = \sum_i \frac{L_i}{\sum_i L_i} \frac{Q_i}{L_i}$$

In this equation, Q represents output and L labor hours, and subscripts denote components of the aggregate. The absence of a subscript indicates the aggregate for the respective variable. The aggregate rate of change can be decomposed into the sum of changes (denoted by d) in input shares and in productivity (Q/L) for each component, weighted by output:

(2) $$\frac{d\left(\frac{Q}{L}\right)}{\frac{Q}{L}} = \sum_i \frac{Q_i}{Q} \frac{d\left(\frac{Q_i}{L_i}\right)}{\frac{Q_i}{L_i}} + \sum_i \frac{Q_i}{Q} \frac{d\left(\frac{L_i}{L}\right)}{\frac{L_i}{L}}$$

The first term on the right-hand side of equation (2) can be used to form an index that would indicate average *output*-weighted productivity improvement. The second right-hand side term is a similarly weighted index of the change in *input* shares. It indicates the extent to which aggregate productivity is affected by reallocation of labor input resulting from both shifts in the geographical distribution of the demand for coal and differing rates of labor productivity improvement among the subaggregates. The easiest interpretation of this second term is that it indicates the extent to which a completely aggregated index of labor productivity (i.e., the left-hand side term) differs from the output weighted average of changes in labor productivity for the components of the aggregate (i.e., the first right-hand side term).[6] The first term on the right-hand side would be the appropriate aggregate measure of productivity change if production from the various components did not compete in the market.

Table 9.2 provides several aggregate measures of productivity change in the U.S. coal industry, based on the MSHA data. The top row in table 9.2 represents the conventional measure of aggregate labor productivity, where the numerator, output, is stated in tons of coal. The second row is the Btu corrected ("quality adjusted") expression of the same index, using the heat content assumptions listed in table 9.1. Treating all tons as if they were equal leads to a slight overstatement of productivity improvement: about a third of a percentage point in annual growth over the entire period. The bottom two rows represent Btu output-weighted indexes for labor productivity improvement, using two different decompositions.[7] The bottom line treats each of the eleven subaggregates as independent, noncompeting entities—obviously, a lower bound. A more nearly correct estimate is provided by the three-region index, in which the implicit assumptions are that coals produced by continuous, longwall, and surface techniques compete within the Appalachian, Interior, and Western regions, but not between these regions.

Table 9.2 also displays values at the key turning points for these indexes and the intervening annual rates of change. In both the 1970s and 1980s,

---

6. The second right-hand side term in equation (2) would sum to zero only if (a) labor productivity change were uniform across components and output shares were unchanged, or (b) output is increasing at the same rate as labor productivity for each component. Although not impossible, it is unlikely that either condition would occur.

7. In constructing these indexes, we use the Törnqvist approximation of the Divisia index, in which the share weights are the arithmetic average of the beginning and ending shares for each discrete, annual change.

Sources of Productivity Growth in the American Coal Industry 383

Table 9.2   Alternate Measures of Productivity Change

Index	1972	1978	1995	1972–78 (%)	1978–95 (%)	1972–95 (%)
Tons	1.00	.850	2.704	−2.71	+6.81	+4.32
Btu	1.00	.819	2.458	−3.33	+6.47	+3.90
Three regions	1.00	.756	1.963	−4.55	+5.77	+2.98
Eleven mining groups	1.00	.657	1.634	−7.00	+5.36	+2.14

the national aggregates, whether in tons or Btu's, provide a misleading picture of productivity change in the coal industry. Productivity declined during the 1970s, but the severity of the decline in the subaggregates is masked in these national aggregates by the increasing share of the higher-productivity Western regions. The Btu index suggests that labor productivity declined at a rate of about 3.3 percent per annum from 1972 through 1978, while the disaggregated index indicates that labor productivity was falling on average by more than twice that rate, or 7.0 percent per annum. During the subsequent period of rising productivity, the misstatement of the national aggregate (i.e., not taking into account compositional changes) is not as severe, but is still present. The national Btu aggregate indicates a rate of improvement from 1978 to 1995 of 6.5 percent per annum, whereas the production weighted average improvement in labor productivity in the constituent groups for these years is 5.4 percent per annum. Over the whole period from 1972 to 1995, labor productivity is not 2.7 times its 1972 level, but from 1.65 to 1.95 times that level, and the annual rate of improvement is about half of what it otherwise would appear to be.

9.3.3 Differing Trends among the Subaggregates

So far we have noted only the differences in absolute levels of labor productivity among the eleven subaggregates, and the changes of share among them. An equally, and perhaps more interesting, aspect is the very different rates of productivity improvement observed among these mining groups. Of particular note is that labor productivity of Western longwall mining was more than five times its 1972 level in 1995; its improvement is twice that of the mining group experiencing the next greatest improvement in labor productivity (Appalachian longwall mining). Moreover, four of the five surface mining subaggregates have labor productivity levels in 1995 very little different than in 1972, although better than in the late 1970s. The fifth surface mining region, the PRB, experienced more labor productivity improvement, but only as much as the least progressive underground mining subaggregates. By contrast, Western longwall mining is only the most outstanding of what is generally impressive productivity improvement for all underground mining. Another regularity is that for each of the three main regions, longwall mining is experiencing greater rates of productivity improvement than are continuous mines. Finally, there is a clear regional ordering in rates of productivity improvement by coal mining technology. Given the mining technique, labor productivity is highest in the West, followed by Appalachia, with the Interior region in last place.

9.4 Data and Methodology

9.4.1 Database Description

The Mine Safety and Health Act of 1969 requires each coal mine in the United States to report quarterly to the MSHA on accidents and incidents, as well as tons produced, employees, and hours worked (USDOL, MSHA, Part 50). Each mine is issued a unique mine identification number that is retained as long as the mine is active. In addition to accident data, the quarterly reports contain the following information:

current name of the mine and reporting address
location of the mine, by county and state
tons of coal produced for the quarter being reported
number of employees and employee hours associated with the mine
whether the coal is mined by underground or surface techniques[8]

Our study has summed the quarterly data to obtain annual observations, of which there are some 86,000 on 19,098 individual mines that reported production during at least one quarter from 1972 through the end of 1995.

Production is measured in "clean" tons produced. A clean ton is a ton that has been screened and washed to remove rock and dirt and is ready for shipment to the customer. Although the raw ton that comes from the mine is not clean, the factor to convert raw, run-of-mine coal to clean coal is well known and applied prospectively by operators for MSHA reporting purposes. This factor tends to be mine specific, reflecting the geology of the mine, but is not necessarily constant over time.

In order to identify longwall production, we had to add data to the MSHA database. The industry magazine *Coal Age* (now *Coal*) has conducted an annual longwall survey since the late 1970s (*Coal Age*, various issues). This survey lists every longwall mine for the given year and indicates, among other things, when the longwall panel was first installed. We use the name, location, and other information from the longwall survey and another industry publication (*Keystone Coal Industry Manual* 1996) to match each reported longwall mine with an underground MSHA mine

---

8. We defined surface techniques to include the small amounts of coal produced by augers and dredging and from culm banks.

identification number. Unless the industry survey indicates that a longwall has been removed, we consider all production at a mine since the installation of a longwall to be longwall production.[9]

Because output prices vary considerably by location, separate price indexes were created to correspond to the Appalachian, Interior, Western, Lignite, and PRB subaggregates. The Energy Information Administration of the U.S. Department of Energy collects and publishes nominal minemouth coal prices by state on an annual basis.[10] For the Appalachian, Interior, and Western regions, the prices reported for each coal-producing state within these regions are weighted by that state's quantity share of coal production for the region, as reported in the MSHA database, and summed to form a regional index of nominal coal prices.

Unlike coal output prices, labor markets are reasonably well integrated not only across coal-producing regions, but also with competing employment in construction and other related industries. Accordingly, we use a single national index for the wage rate in all regions: average hourly earnings for production workers in Standard Industrial Classification (SIC) number 12 (Coal Mining), as reported in the *Employment, Hours, and Earnings* series published by the Bureau of Labor Statistics. Finally, nominal prices for output and labor are deflated to real prices using the consumer price index. Further data details are spelled out in Ellerman, Stoker, and Berndt (1998, a more detailed version of the present chapter with tables appended).

9.4.2 Specification of the Model for Estimating Labor Productivity

The principal aim of our empirical analysis is to describe succinctly how labor productivity varies over individual mines in order to gain a better understanding of changes in aggregate coal productivity. In our panel data set, we incorporate fixed mine effects and time effects.

For coal mines, numerous geological features are essentially unique to each mine location and remain more or less constant over time. For instance, for underground mines, these features include seam height; roof conditions; width, length, and slope of the seam; and surface structures relevant to accessibility of various parts of the seam.

Other important features tend to change over time but affect all mines more or less equally in a given year. New advances in coal-mining technology tend to diffuse quickly across mines and raise labor productivity, but the precise impact on a given mine still varies with the mine's ability to

---

9. In fact, continuous miners used to prepare the longwall panels and ancillary passageways account for some of the production.

10. See USDOE/EIA, *Coal Production Annual* (now *Coal Industry Annual*) for various years since the 1970s. Prior to the formation of the U.S. Department of Energy and the Energy Information Administration in the 1970s, this data was collected by the Bureau of Mines and published in the *Minerals Yearbook*.

benefit from a particular advance in technology. Other time-varying factors are specific to particular years, such as strikes, which featured prominently in coal mining during the 1970s. Several prominent regulatory programs were also enacted and implemented during this decade, and these measures could be expected to affect coal-mining productivity in one year or over several years. Finally, although mine-mouth prices vary according to netback considerations involving location and coal transportation systems, those prices tend to move together from year to year within a given coal-producing region, moderated at some mines by long-term contract terms.

Annual output Q_{it} and labor (man-hours) input L_{it} is observed for each mine i for each year t that the mine produces, $i = 1, \ldots, N_{group}$ and $t = T_{1i}, \ldots, T_{Ti}$, where "producing" is defined as having positive observed output. Mines were classified into the eleven groups indicated in table 9.1: three broad geographic regions (Appalachia, Interior, and Western); three distinct mining technologies (surface, continuous, and longwall) for each of these regions; and two unique surface mining regions (Lignite and the PRB) located in the Western United States.

A standard modeling approach for productivity analysis assumes price-taking behavior for output and input prices at each mine, with optimal output levels chosen either when marginal profits became zero or when output reached the physical maximum capacity of existing production facilities. That is, labor productivity is implied by the optimal choices concerning output and inputs, given the price of coal (net of transportation costs) and prices of all associated inputs. The existing facilities and types of technology are chosen via a medium- to long-term planning process, based on geological features of the mine site and expectations of future prices.

We have not adopted this standard approach mostly because appropriate price information is not available and mine-specific capital cannot be observed. Moreover, output at most mines is produced under coal supply contracts of more than a year's duration that specify many features of the contracted supply, including the quantity to be produced. The duration and incidence of these contracts is less in the 1990s than in the 1970s, and the contracts have always been more prevalent in the West than in the East, but these contracts still largely define the conditions under which coal is produced for market (Joskow, 1987). Thus, in modeling labor productivity, we assume that output quantity is determined exogenously by contract, and that operators strive toward efficiency and higher labor productivity, conditional on output scale.[11]

---

11. In a related paper (Berndt, Ellerman, Schennech, and Stoker 1999), we carry out numerous statistical tests of the exogeneity of output and find no evidence that the estimates presented here would change substantially by relaxing this assumption.

For mines within each of the eleven group classifications, the basic model takes the form

$$(3) \qquad \ln\left(\frac{Q_{it}}{L_{it}}\right) = \tau_t + \alpha_i + F(\ln Q_{it}) + \varepsilon_{it}.$$

The parameters τ_t, $F(\cdot)$ and α_i vary by group classification in our analysis, although for simplicity the group distinction is omitted from the notation.

The mine-specific fixed effect α_i captures all time-invariant, mine-specific geological and technical attributes by establishing a base level of (log) labor productivity for each mine. The time effect τ_t represents the common impact of all year-specific changes, such as common technological advances, input price effects, and regulations for each classified group of mines. The disturbance ε_{it} is assumed to capture all other idiosyncratic features of productivity for each mine, to be normally distributed with mean zero and constant variance, and to be uncorrelated across mines and time periods.[12]

Estimation of the model, as well as numerous diagnostic tests, are covered in a related paper by Berndt and colleagues (1999). In the present paper, a brief description of the basic approach to estimation is given, and issues relating to interpretation of the model are discussed. The resulting estimates are presented in the following section.

Of particular interest is the way labor productivity varies with scale of operation; this is represented by the unknown function $F(\cdot)$ of (log) output Q_{it}. A nonparametric approach to the specification of $F(\cdot)$ is adopted on the assumption that it is well approximated by a polynomial in log output. Within the context of the panel model in equation (3), the order of the log output polynomial for each region is chosen by least squares cross validation.[13] The result is that all regions are adequately described by a cubic polynomial in log output:

$$(4) \qquad F(\ln Q_{it}) = \beta_1 \ln Q_{it} + \beta_2 (\ln Q_{it})^2 + \beta^3 (\ln Q_{it})^3.$$

Specifically, for six of the groups, a cubic polynomial is indicated; for three groups, a quadratic polynomial is indicated ($\beta_3 = 0$); and for two groups, a log linear function is indicated ($\beta_2 = 0$, $\beta_3 = 0$).

In the panel data format, time effects τ_t capture the impacts of all variables that are time varying but equal across mines during any given time period. In order to examine the relationship between coal productivity and

---

12. Little detailed information is available on mine features that vary across mines and time other than output and labor input. Seam height is reported; however, close inspection of this data showed that the values given were almost always constant over time, and thus part of the fixed effect for each mine.

13. We considered up to fifth-degree polynomials. For a general discussion of cross validation, see, among many others, Green and Silverman (1994).

prices, these time effects are related to real prices and wages, in a separate equation, as follows:

$$\tau_t = \kappa + \gamma_p \ln p_t + \gamma_w \ln w_t + \delta D_t + \eta_t \tag{5}$$

where $\ln p_t$ is the log of real coal price and $\ln w_t$ is the real wage rate. Here γ_p is the labor productivity elasticity with respect to real coal prices on common productivity levels and γ_w is the elasticity with respect to real wage changes. We include a test of the hypothesis that $\gamma_p = -\gamma_w$ for each region, which tests whether the time effects depend only on the coal price-wage ratio. The variable D_t is a dummy variable for 1972 and 1973, found to be empirically necessary to account for the change of regime in the outlook for coal that followed the four-fold increase in the price of oil associated with the Arab Oil Embargo in late 1973. On the basis of testing, we apply $\gamma_p = -\gamma_w$, to define a restricted form of equation (5) and set $\delta = 0$ for groups where those restrictions are not rejected. The remainder, η_t, gives the common log productivity level net of price and wage effects.

There are several important features to note from this structuring of the time effects. First, without additional assumptions on the structure of η_t, the price and wage effects are not identified, and equation (5) places no restriction on the panel equation (3). Consequently, we adopt a two-stage approach to estimation. The first stage is to estimate equation (3) by ordinary least squares (OLS), with fixed time and mine effects, giving a series of estimated time effects $\hat{\tau}_t$, $t = 1, \ldots, T$. The second stage is to estimate equation (5) using OLS with the estimated time effects $\hat{\tau}_t$ as dependent variables. This gives estimates of the price and wage elasticities, as well as the coefficient on the 1972–73 dummy variable. The estimated residuals from equation (5), $\hat{\eta}_t$, represent the remaining time effects after taking price effects into account (what we later term *residual time effects*). This is consistent with an assumption that the residual time effects are stochastic with zero mean, and

$$\text{cov}(\ln p_t, \eta_t) = 0; \quad \text{cov}(\ln w_t, \eta_t) = 0 \tag{6}$$

where covariance is taken over time periods. However, the structure of equations (5) and (6) is not imposed on equation (3) for the initial estimation, because of our interest in the overall level of time effects.

One way to view this procedure is that we are assuming equations (3)–(6) but using an inefficient two-stage estimation procedure. Another way is that we are not assuming equation (6), but are using OLS to define the split between price and wage effects, and residual time effects in equation (6) (imposing the empirical analogue of equation [6]).

The panel data approach gives a flexible empirical model for accounting for mine heterogeneity. Because of this flexibility, some interesting issues are difficult to study. Suppose one were interested in measuring linear depletion (or mine-specific learning) effects by including the age of the mine as a regressor. Age, however, is perfectly collinear with a linear combination of the mine and time effects. A model with the linear age effect has the same fitted values as a model without such an effect, with the estimated age effect not necessarily representative of the aging process (separate from the mine and time effects). If a specific nonlinear aging profile were available for representing depletion, then a depletion effect could be measured; however, we have no a priori reason for choosing a particular depletion profile.

Before proceeding with the discussion of empirical results, we comment briefly on the interpretation of our methodology. Although this approach for studying labor productivity is very flexible, it serves primarily as a method for describing mine-level changes in productivity over the past two decades. The approach is clearly reduced form in nature, in that the process under which particular innovations give rise to improvements in productivity with scale is not specified, nor is the way those innovations differentially impact mine types and regions. Our work is therefore best viewed as a cohesive description of general patterns of change in coal-mining productivity. Improving upon this would require a more detailed accounting of other factors involved in coal production and in the choice of mining technique.

Earlier we noted the importance of the assumed exogeneity of scale in our approach. A number of other potential sources of bias are avoided by our panel data format, in particular by the estimation of mine-level fixed effects. For instance, selection bias may arise from excluding nonoperating mines, so the estimates could commingle efficient production decisions with the decision whether to keep a mine in operation. In fact, the rate of coal mine turnover is quite pronounced. However, the impact of selection on our model would be to introduce a familiar (Mills ratio) bias term that would reflect the probability of a mine's continuing in operation. To the extent that this term does not vary substantially over time, it is included as a component of the fixed effect estimated for the mine. We view the decision to keep a mine in operation as strongly influenced by mine-specific factors, so the fixed effects adequately account for selection bias. If additional information that suggests a strong correlation between scale changes and exit (given mine-specific factors) were to arise, our scale structure could be subject to some bias in estimation. In that case, our scale estimates are interpretable as including those correlations relevant to the decision to continue mine operation.

9.4.3 Regression Results

Full sets of estimates of the panel equation (3) are attached as an appendix to Ellerman, Stoker, and Berndt (1998). As discussed earlier, the scale-labor productivity relationship in equation (3) is modeled as a polynomial in log output, of orders 1, 2, or 3, chosen on the basis of cross validation (cf. equation [4]). Estimates of these scale effects are presented in table 9.3 for underground mines and in table 9.4 for surface mines. Actual magnitudes of the coefficients are generally difficult to assess (because they are polynomial coefficients embedded in the model with firm and time effects); nonetheless, some common patterns can be discerned.

Underground continuous mines are characterized by clear estimated nonlinear patterns of log labor productivity increasing with scale. For underground longwall mines, two groups (Appalachia and Interior) are log linear with strong positive scale effects. Western longwall mines have an estimated structure with the same shape as that for underground continuous mines.

These estimates are all consistent with substantial economies of scale. For example, it is easy to verify that if the log linear models, Appalachia

Table 9.3 **Cubic Scale Coefficients: Underground Mines**

	Continuous			Longwall		
	Appalachia	Interior	Western	Appalachia	Interior	Western
ln Q	1.784	5.223	2.192	0.471	0.333	9.212
	(35.9)	(11.3)	(6.86)	(33.57)	(7.66)	(2.97)
$(\ln Q)^2$	−0.158	−0.411	−0.165			−0.731
	(−28.7)	(−10.0)	(−4.81)			(−2.863)
$(\ln Q)^3$	0.00519	0.0113	0.00467			0.0199
	(26.0)	(9.40)	(3.95)			(2.863)
Number of mines	8,339	173	128	111	14	29
N	38,100	1,295	902	1,216	106	224
R^2 within mines	0.335	0.634	0.556	0.774	0.923	0.573
R^2 overall	0.265	0.439	0.609	0.745	0.865	0.797

Notes: Polynomial order chosen by cross validation, and t-statistics in parentheses.

Table 9.4 **Cubic Scale Coefficients: Surface Mines**

	Appalachia	Interior	Western	Lignite	PRB
ln Q	1.686	1.502	1.207	1.178	1.801
	(24.6)	(7.93)	(15.93)	(13.70)	(14.204)
$(\ln Q)^2$	−0.128	−0.114	−0.0314	−0.0222	−0.0447
	(−17.2)	(−6.12)	(−9.24)	(−6.32)	(−9.366)
$(\ln Q)^3$	0.0037	0.00348			
	(14.0)	(5.802)			
Number of mines	9,019	1,260	87	40	30
N	37,161	5,219	789	506	450
R^2 within mines	0.302	0.391	0.673	0.767	0.828
R^2 overall	0.177	0.179	0.619	0.529	0.609

Notes: Polynomial order chosen by cross validation, and t-statistics in parentheses.

Table 9.5 **Relative Price Effects**

	Log Relative Price Effect	Log Relative Wage Effect	Dummy 1972–73	R^2	Test of General Equation (5) $\gamma_P = -\gamma_W$ (p-value)
Underground continuous mines					
Appalachia	−0.399 (−13.5)	−0.011 (−0.1)	−0.130 (−4.8)	0.923	0.0075
Interior	−0.759 (−6.8)	0.321 (0.8)	−0.287 (−4.0)	0.802	0.2098
Western	−1.071 (−4.2)	0.870 (1.1)	−0.079 (−0.6)	0.554	0.7477
Underground longwall mines					
Appalachia	−0.858 (−21.6)	0.202 (1.0)	−0.407 (−11.2)	0.968	0.0021
Interior	−1.449 (−8.9)	1.140 (1.9)	—	0.877	0.5341
Western	−1.432 (−3.2)	1.474 (1.1)	−0.735 (−3.3)	0.380	0.9691
Surface mines					
Appalachia	0.174 (3.3)	−0.500 (1.8)	0.389 (8.0)	0.742	0.2006
Interior	−0.252 (−1.6)	0.105 (0.2)	0.259 (2.6)	0.538	0.7561
Western	−0.110 (−0.4)	−0.379 (−0.5)	0.517 (4.1)	0.530	0.4330
Lignite	−0.617 (−9.0)	−0.360 (−1.6)	−0.031 (−0.6)	0.877	0.0001
Powder River Basin	−0.399 (−3.9)	0.002 (0.0)	0.263 (3.1)	0.688	0.4468

Notes: Each category: twenty-four time periods, and *t*-statistics in parentheses. Dash indicates no production prior to 1976.

and Interior longwall, arose from Cobb-Douglas technologies, the overall output elasticities implied by the estimates are 1.471 and 1.333, respectively, which are substantially greater than 1, the value associated with constant returns to scale.[14] The patterns of coefficient signs are uniform across regions and technologies with cubic scale effects, quadratic scale effects, and log linear scale effects.

Table 9.5 summarizes the results of regressing the time effects estimated

---

14. Berndt and colleagues (1999) examine returns to scale estimates under several alternative stochastic assumptions. While their estimates differ, they find virtually no evidence against the overall hypothesis of increasing returns to scale for each group.

with equation (3) on the log of real coal price and log real wage rate. The elasticity of coal price is expected to be negative, as higher coal prices call forth the employment of less productive labor. The estimates are in fact negative and significantly different from zero at ($p < 0.05$) for eight mining groups. The elasticity of labor productivity with respect to real wages is expected to be positive, but it is statistically insignificant for all mining groups in this estimation presumably because of the very slight variation in the real wage rate over the period of this study. The 1972–73 dummy is statistically discernible for eight of the ten mining groups for which it is applicable. The p-values for the test of the restricted form of equation (5) against the general equation (5) are reported for each mine group, and the equality is accepted for eight of the eleven subaggregates. On the whole, the degree of correlation between estimated time effects and log coal prices is quite high.

9.4.4 Indexes of Productivity Change by Source

We now decompose the aggregate change in labor productivity in U.S. coal mining into basic sources of productivity change in order to understand the roles of price, scale, time, and the features embodied in each mine. The data and model permit productivity indexes to be created for each mine group, as follows.

The measurement of sources of productivity growth follows the decomposition inherent to the basic equations (3) and (5). For each group, aggregate productivity at time t is given as

$$(7) \quad \frac{\sum_i Q_{it}}{\sum_i L_{it}} = \frac{\sum_i L_{it} \exp\left(\ln \frac{Q_{it}}{L_{it}}\right)}{\sum_i L_{it}} = \frac{\sum_i L_{it} \exp(\hat{\tau}_i) \exp(\hat{\alpha}_i + \hat{F}(\ln Q_{it}) + \hat{\varepsilon}_{it})}{\sum_i L_{it}}$$

using equation (3), where "hats" denote the use of the estimated parameter values. Using equation (5), this simplifies to

$$(8) \quad \frac{\sum_i Q_{it}}{\sum_i L_{it}} = \exp(\hat{\kappa} + \hat{\gamma}_p \ln p_t + \hat{\gamma}_w \ln w_t + \hat{\delta} D_t)$$

$$\exp(\hat{\eta}_t) \frac{\sum_i L_{it} \exp[\hat{\alpha}_i + \hat{F}(\ln Q_{it}) + \hat{\varepsilon}_{it}]}{\sum_i L_{it}}.$$

Equation (8) suggests the following definitions of productivity indexes. First, price impacts on productivity are indicated by the price effect index based on equation (5):

(9) $$P_t = \exp(\hat{\kappa} + \hat{\gamma}_p \ln p_t + \hat{\gamma}_w \ln w_t + \delta D_t).$$

The remaining common time effects, namely those net of prices, are indicated by the residual time effect index, based on the estimated residual in equation (5):

(10) $$R_t = \exp(\hat{\eta}_t).$$

The overall common time pattern is completed as the product, $P_t \cdot R_t$.

The remaining term in equation (8) captures elements that vary across mines within each time period. In general, this term does not cleanly decompose. The following approximate decomposition can be defined, consistent with the notion that fixed effects, scale effects, and residual (microheterogeneity) terms are independently distributed (in the labor weighted distribution of firms).

Scale effects are indicated by the scale effect index:

(11) $$SC_t = \frac{\sum_i L_{it} \exp[\hat{F}(\ln Q_{it})]}{\sum_i L_{it}}.$$

The mine-specific (initial) productivity levels for each mine are indicated by the fixed effect index:

(12) $$FE_t = \frac{\sum_i L_{it} \exp(\hat{\alpha}_i)}{\sum_i L_{it}}.$$

Finally, the remaining heterogeneity in labor productivity across mines is indicated by the residual microheterogeneity index:

(13) $$MR_t = \frac{\sum_i L_{it} \exp(\hat{\varepsilon}_{it})}{\sum_i L_{it}}.$$

The final term in equation (8) is not generally equal to the product of these three indexes because of correlation between estimated fixed effects and scale, or because of higher order moments between fixed effects, scale effects, and the residuals from the estimated equation (3). As a result, changes in observed aggregate labor productivity for each of the eleven mining groups will not be exactly replicated. Consequently, the predicted productivity index, defined as

(14) $$PR_t = SC_t \cdot FE_t \cdot MR_t \cdot P_t \cdot R_t,$$

will err to the extent that the scale effects, fixed effects, and residual microheterogeneity are not independent. The predicted index in equation (14) permits a ready decomposition of the change in aggregate labor productivity into five sources: price, time, scale, fixed mine-specific features, and residual microheterogeneity.

9.5 Sources of Productivity Change

We now report results obtained when the conceptual framework just described is implemented empirically.

9.5.1 Scale Effects

The panel data regression yields estimates of the effects of changing output on labor productivity; these effects are significant and positive for all eleven mining groups, as indicated by the results reported in tables 9.3 and 9.4. We refer to these effects as scale effects, but the term *scale* is being used in a very limited sense. It refers to the changing levels of output over time. Inputs into the production process other than labor are not observed, so we do not know whether the conventional definition of scale as a proportionate increase of all inputs would apply. Also, the relation between productivity and output is estimated only over time, and not across mines during the same time period. To the extent that there is a persistent cross-sectional relation between output and productivity, it would appear in equation (3) as a fixed effect.

The estimated value for the productivity-output elasticity varies according to the output level for those mining groups requiring a higher-order polynomial. The values of these productivity-output elasticities are remarkably uniform. All take positive values lower than unity, and most values fall in a range between 0.30 and 0.50. Even though the cubic specification permits great flexibility, a tendency toward uniformity by mining technique was found. The three typically large mine-size Western surface mining groups show declining elasticity with output, whereas the Eastern surface mining and continuous mining subaggregates show increasing elasticity with output. The longwall mining subaggregates form the exception to the general uniformity by mining technique. For two longwall regions, Appalachia and Interior, the quadratic and cubic terms drop out of the estimating equation so that the indicated scale elasticity is constant over the range of observed output. For Western longwalls, the full cubic specification is required and scale elasticity rises steadily and dramatically over the observed range. In fact, the value approaching unity, indicated for the largest output observed for this mining group, must be questioned because such values imply that labor has ceased to be an essential input.

The extent to which the productivity-output elasticity affects aggregate productivity depends in part upon the change in output level at mines that continue in production from one year to the next. Because entering and exiting mines would affect average size but not scale effects as defined here, average mine size is not a perfect indicator of the extent to which this elasticity matters. Nevertheless, it is an acceptable one for this data set because average mine size changes mostly as a result of changing output levels at continuing mines, not because entering or exiting mines are on average significantly larger or smaller than continuing mines.

National average mine size increased by about 2.5 times between 1972 and 1995, but the components exhibit tremendous diversity. Western mining groups increased steadily in average mine output over the period, whereas Interior and Appalachian subaggregates experienced a decline in average mine size during the 1970s and an increase thereafter. As of 1995, average mine size was larger than it was in 1972 for all subaggregates except Interior surface mining. The three largest increases were registered by three Western subaggregates—PRB, Lignite, and Western longwall mining—where average mine size rose 4.5–6 times over the 1972 levels.

The effect of changing output levels on labor productivity is represented by the scale effect indexes, computed as a scale elasticity weighted change in observed output at any given mine. Among the eleven mining groups, four subaggregates stand out: Appalachian longwall (App LW) mining and the three Western mining groups (the PRB, Lignite, and Western longwall mining). Our model indicates that if nothing else had changed, increases in output levels at continuing mines would have increased labor productivity from 1.7 (App LW) to 2.2 (Lignite) times the 1972 level. For the other seven subaggregates, the contributions of changing output levels to labor productivity were not particularly important. The 1995 indexes for these mining groups range from 0.85 (Interior surface) to 1.22 (Appalachian surface).[15]

9.5.2 Fixed Effects

As seen in equation (12), the fixed effect index is the labor-share weighted sum of the fixed effect coefficients for producing mines in each successive year. The average of fixed effect coefficients for all producing mines over all time periods is zero; however, the mean of fixed effect coefficients for any single year within the sample can differ from zero, and typically varies as individual mines with differing coefficients enter and exit. As such, it reflects the extent to which time-invariant, mine-specific features of producing mines are causing productivity to increase or decline.

One obvious and plausible interpretation of the fixed effect index is that it reflects the productivity-enhancing effects of the technology embodied

---

15. The scale effect index for Appalachian continuous mining is less than 1.0 in 1995, whereas average mine size is 30 percent larger than in 1972. This mining group is characterized by a short average mine life (four years) and a high degree of entry and exit. In this case, new mines tend to be bigger, but the output level at mines does not increase during their short average lives.

in each new vintage of mines. If capital equipment and other features of mine layout and design improve labor productivity with each successive vintage, then the mean of fixed effects coefficients would increase over time. As earlier noted, the index could be expected to increase if cross-sectional scale effects exist.

There are other interpretations for changes observed in the fixed effect index. Geological features are an important consideration in a minerals extraction industry such as coal mining. The successive development and depletion of the best prospects over time would contribute to a declining fixed effect index, although for coal, the ordering of mines for development does not necessarily follow geological criteria, since transportation cost can be as important as mining cost in determining economic viability.[16] It has also been suggested to us that, at least in Appalachia, the sale of coal reserves previously owned by integrated steel companies has led to the exploitation of better reserves during much of the period of this study. Finally, if unionized mines are characterized by lower labor productivity, as is asserted, then the increasing share of nonunion mines would increase the mean of the fixed effects coefficients. Considerably more analysis is required to distinguish among these various interpretations. For the present, we take the index to represent potentially all these influences on mine-level productivity.

We find that the fixed effect indexes for the eleven subaggregates have regional patterns that are almost the exact complement of what we found for the scale effect indexes. Five of the seven regions that were not particularly distinguished by scale effects now reveal steadily rising labor productivity due to the changing composition of mines. These five regions include all three continuous mining subaggregates and Appalachian and Interior surface mining. In contrast, the four regions experiencing a significant increase in the scale effect index show very little impact from fixed effects; one region, lignite, shows a marked decline. For two of these regions, the PRB and Western longwall mining, the fixed effect means are approximately the same in 1995 as they were in 1972, although the means declined markedly during the 1970s and rose at 2–3 percent per annum during the 1980s and 1990s. Rising fixed effect indexes are consistent with improving technology with each new mine vintage, but it is curious that this effect would occur consistently only with continuous mining in all regions and Appalachian and Interior surface mines.

These indexes' differences in behavior by mining group emphasize one important qualification to be remembered when interpreting the indexes: When the number of mines is small, as is the case in some mining groups during some years, a single mine's entry or exit can unduly influence the

---

16. The PRB illustrates the development of good geological prospects far from market on a national scale; the same effect could occur within any subaggregate.

Sources of Productivity Growth in the American Coal Industry 397

Table 9.6   Maximum (minimum) Number of Mines by Subaggregate

	Longwall Mines	Continuous Mines	Surface Mines
Appalachia	64	2,137	2,438
	(32)	(870)	(864)
Interior	9	65	382
	(1)	(36)	(93)
Western	15	58	47
	(2)	(16)	(20)
Lignite	n.a.	n.a.	26
			(13)
Powder River Basin	n.a.	n.a.	26
			(5)

Note: n.a. = not applicable.

index. Table 9.6 shows the maximum and minimum number of mines observed in any year for each subaggregate.

Only three of the subaggregates have a number of mines in all years sufficiently large that the yearly means would not be greatly affected by the entry or exit of a few mines, or even a single one. For the others, particularly for those with very small numbers, the changing composition of mines can have a large influence.

9.5.3 Residual Microheterogeneity

The residual microheterogeneity index also reflects the effects of changes in mine composition within a subaggregate. Microheterogeneity can be usefully compared to macroheterogeneity, which is captured in our analysis by decomposing the very heterogeneous national aggregate into eleven more homogeneous subaggregates. Although the mines within each of these groups are more alike than they are similar to mines in other groups, heterogeneity does not stop at the subaggregates. There is every reason to believe there are differences among mines within these groups that are not captured in the primary panel regression. The effect of these differences on labor productivity will manifest itself, along with measurement error and stochastic variance, in the error term for each mine-year observation. The labor input weighted error terms for each year are then formed into an index to indicate the extent to which such unexplained microdifferences affect labor productivity.

For many of the subaggregates, the residual microheterogeneity indexes remain close to the 1972 level throughout the twenty-four-year period; however, a few subaggregates remain consistently above or below the rest, indicating greater error between observed and predicted productivities at individual mines. The indexes for longwall, continuous, and surface mining in the West are always above their 1972 levels and comparable index levels for all the other subaggregates. At the other extreme, indexes for Lignite

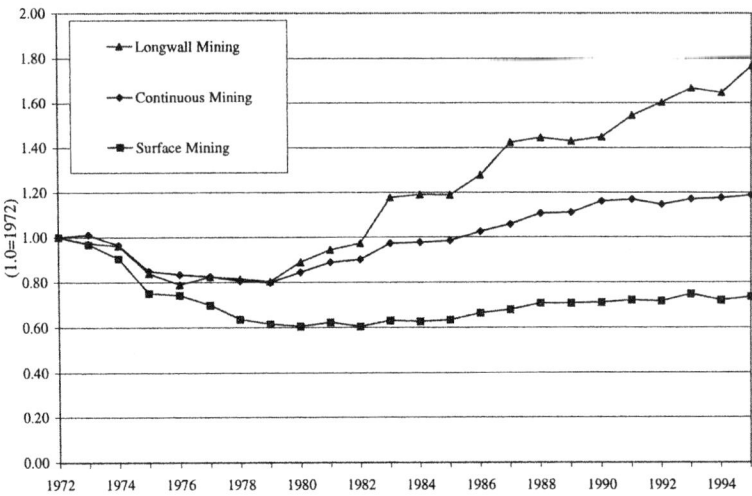

Fig. 9.4 Undifferentiated time effect indexes by mining technique

are consistently well below comparable indexes for all other subaggregates. These four mining groups—all in the West—are in fact the most heterogeneous of the eleven. Although there are differences within the Interior and Appalachian subaggregates, none are as great as those that occur in the West—for instance, between lignite mining in Texas and North Dakota, or between surface mines in New Mexico and Utah.

9.5.4 Time and Price Effects

The time coefficients from the primary panel regression create a very distinctive pattern of time effects in which two features stand out. First, the pattern is one of decline in the 1970s, regardless of technique or location, followed by a steady rise at varying rates of growth beginning in the late 1970s or early 1980s. Second, there is a definite clustering of these time effects by technology, as shown in figure 9.4.[17] In the middle and late 1970s, surface mining experienced a much greater time-related drop in labor productivity than did either of the underground mining techniques. Moreover, once the bottom was reached, the improvement in time-related effects was greatest for longwall mines (4.9 percent per annum), followed by continuous mining (2.5 percent), with surface mining showing the least improvement (1.4 percent). As a consequence of its deeper trough and slower recovery, surface mining's index of time-related productivity effects was only

---

17. The aggregate national indexes by mining technique are output-weighted products of the indexes for the constituent mining groups. Thus, the longwall index includes the Appalachian, Interior, and Western longwall mining groups. The Lignite and PRB mining groups are included in the surface mining index.

74 percent of the 1972 level in 1995, whereas the longwall and continuous mining indexes in the same year were 1.77 and 1.19 times the 1972 level, respectively. The explanation for these differing rates of change by technique lies in untangling several time related influences.

One of the most significant features of the American coal industry since 1970 is the dramatic change in the evolution of real output prices. As is shown in figure 9.1, the real price index for coal output more than doubled during the early 1970s and peaked in 1975. Real output prices in some regions peaked later; however, by the early 1980s, real output prices were falling in all regions, and they did so persistently thereafter, reaching the pre-1970 level by the early 1990s.

The fourfold increase in the price of oil during 1973 and 1974 transformed the outlook for coal, and this transformation affected both the price of coal and the relationship between coal prices and labor productivity. The effect upon coal prices was the most obvious and immediate, especially in Appalachia, where 65 percent of national Btu output from coal was then produced. The extraordinary increase in Appalachian coal prices in 1974 resulted from the combined effects of rapidly increasing oil prices following the late 1973 Arab Oil Embargo, increasing curtailments of natural gas deliveries, and the impending and actual strike by the United Mine Workers of America (UMWA) in late 1974 (U.S. Executive Office of the President 1976). The effects on output price showed up first and most strongly in Appalachia because it was the most well-developed coal-producing region, and spot and short-term contracts were far more prevalent there than elsewhere in the country (Joskow 1987). The UMWA strike passed quickly enough, but the high oil prices and continuing natural gas curtailments remained and were joined by official federal government policy to encourage domestic production of energy, epitomized by Project Independence (U.S. Federal Energy Administration 1974).

The transformed outlook created a surge of investment in coal and a very noticeable increase in the proportions of other factors of production to labor. Labor input rose sharply during the 1970s. Peak employment occurred in 1979 with 405 million employee hours, 58 percent above the 1972 level, corresponding with a 33 percent increase in output. Thereafter, output continued to increase, by another 33 percent by 1995, but labor input fell by 55 percent from the 1979 peak to 28 percent below its 1972 level. Part of this reduction is explained by the shift of production to higher labor productivity regions, notably the PRB, but trade journals and industry lore leave little doubt that a major response of operators, when faced with disappointing output prices in the 1980s, was to reduce labor input.[18]

---

18. For most of the eleven mining groups, labor input peaked in 1978–80. Labor input continued to rise only for the Interior and Western longwall groups, which enjoyed phenomenal rates of increase in output (11 percent and 15 percent per annum, respectively, to 1995) from very small 1979 levels.

The investment surge in the 1970s was not limited to labor, and the increases in other factors of production affected labor productivity. Detailed data on other factors of production are not available at the mine level, but aggregate input statistics are available at the industry level, and their testimony is eloquent. The comparison of the near panic year of 1974 with the preceding year is indicative of what characterized the mid and late 1970s. Quantities of input increased by 23 percent for labor, 85 percent for materials, 117 percent for energy, and 216 percent for capital services, whereas output increased in this strike-constrained year by only 1.9 percent.[19] Observed labor productivity declined by 17 percent, but the more important effect, from the standpoint of the relation between prices and labor productivity, was the increase in the ratios of capital to labor, energy to labor, and materials to labor. For the same output-labor price ratio, labor productivity shifted upward as a result of the even greater increases of other input quantities, all fueled by the stunning transformation in the outlook for coal after 1973.

The dramatic changes in output price and in factor proportions associated with the events of the mid-1970s and the transformation of the outlook for coal are the justification for the dummy variable that is introduced in equation (5) as a means of differentiating various time related influences on labor productivity. A curious result obtains, however. Although the coefficients for this variable are significant for nearly all the relevant mining groups, the sign is consistently different for the underground and surface mined coal groups. The negative coefficient for underground mining is what would have been expected: When output and labor input prices are held constant, the post-1973 world brought enhanced labor productivity reflecting the changes in the ratios of capital (and other inputs) to labor. In contrast, the positive coefficient for surface mining indicates lower labor productivity in the post-1973 world despite the increased proportions of other inputs to labor.

The explanation for this seeming paradox lies in the sequencing of regulatory requirements imposed upon the coal industry during the 1970s. The first major piece of regulatory legislation was the Mine Safety and Health Act, passed by Congress in 1969. The productivity-depressing effects of this legislation fell primarily on underground mining, and those requirements had been largely internalized by the mid-1970s (Baker, 1981). Surface mining regulations were imposed later. The defining legislation was the federal Surface Mining Control and Reclamation Act (SMCRA), which was enacted in 1977. Some states had imposed comparable requirements earlier, but widespread implementation of SMCRA requirements did not occur until the late 1970s. Because the MSHA data begin in 1972,

---

19. This comparison is based on aggregate industry data updated through 1991 that was provided by Dale Jorgenson and Kevin Stiroh, as reported in the appendices to Ellerman and Berndt (1996). See also note 4.

much of the productivity-depressing effect of the regulation of underground mining is already incorporated in the base year, whereas the full productivity-depressing effect of SMCRA on surface mining in later years is reflected in the indexes.

After 1973, the outlook was bright for coal, however mined, but surface mined coal had to contend with regulatory costs that underground mining had already internalized by 1973. The effect was to increase inputs and thereby to reduce surface mining productivity offsetting what otherwise would have been an increase in labor productivity due to the changed factor proportions, as observed in underground mining. The statistical result is that the sign of the 1972–73 dummy is reversed for surface mining, indicating higher labor productivity in these early years than in later ones, when labor input and output prices are held constant.

The later and staggered implementation of SMCRA implies that a dummy for the years 1972 and 1973 would not be a particularly good indicator for this effect. In fact, extending the 1972–73 dummy to include some later years for the surface mining regions greatly improves the fit of equation (5) as well as the precision of the estimated coefficients. For instance, expanding the 1972–73 dummy for the PRB to include 1974 and 1975 improves the fit from 0.69 to 0.95, as seen from the PRB entry in table 9.7. Every surface mining region exhibits a similar partition of data points, although the year that determines the shift differs from one group to another. Table 9.7 provides the reestimated coefficients for the auxiliary regression, corresponding to table 9.5 above, for the surface mining groups when the dummy is varied so that it corresponds to the year in which the shift of regime is observed.

For all surface mining groups, the fit is improved—significantly so for the Interior, PRB, and other Western surface mining groups. The effect of implementing this dummy for presumed SMCRA effects is to make the output price elasticities negative and statistically significant for four of the five regions instead of only two, and to change the Appalachian Surface mining coefficient from being significant and positive to being insignificant. The SMCRA dummy is highly significant and positive for all groups except Lignite. We have no explanation for the unexpected sign for the Lignite group, other than the usual note that the number of mines is small (see table 9.6) and the coal very different.

For some of the mining groups, prices and the dummy variable so completely account for time effects in the primary panel data regression that the price effect indexes (equation [9]) predict the values for the yearly time dummies. The resulting price effect indexes are plotted in figure 9.5. The index for Western longwall mining is erratic, but all the indexes display the same pattern that can be observed in the time dummies from the primary panel data regression, namely, decline and recovery, with differing rates of decline and recovery by mining technique.

Residual time effects are what remain of the undifferentiated time effects

Table 9.7 Auxiliary Regression with Alternative Surface Mining Regulation Dummies

Mining Group	Time Period of Dummy	Log Price Effect	Log Wage Effect	Dummy Effect	Adjusted R^2	p-value of Test of $\varepsilon_P = \varepsilon_W$
Appalachia surface	1972–74	0.051 (1.5)	0.035 (0.2)	0.351 (13.1)	0.886	0.6172
Interior surface	1972–77	−0.310 (−5.7)	0.153 (0.7)	0.250 (11.5)	0.919	0.4227
Western surface	1972–76	−0.605 (−6.1)	0.732 (2.2)	0.425 (12.8)	0.906	0.6464
Lignite	1972–77	−0.879 (−8.8)	0.084 (0.4)	−0.159 (−3.2)	0.918	0.0002
Powder River Basin	1972–75	−0.454 (−11.0)	0.379 (1.6)	0.320 (12.4)	0.947	0.7249

Note: t-statistics in parentheses.
[a]Except Powder River Basin and Lignite.

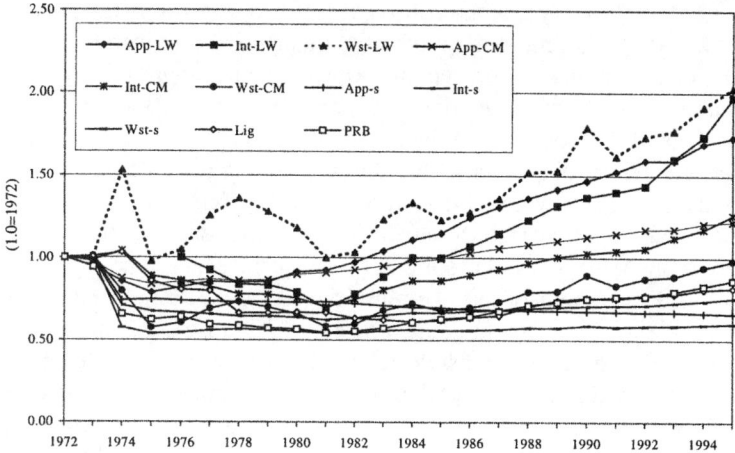

Fig. 9.5 Price effect indexes

after accounting for the influence of changing output price and the anomalous early years (equation [10]). The most remarkable feature of the residual time indexes is the absence of a strong trend for any subaggregate. There are some large variations, particularly by Western longwall-mining and four surface-mining groups in the 1970s, but for the most part the residual time effects appear to be true, trendless residuals. As a result, the auxiliary regression in tables 9.5 and 9.7 indicate that the distinctive pattern of declining productivity in the 1970s and rapid recovery thereafter is largely explained by the effects of the extraordinary changes in output price that were experienced from 1972 through 1995.

There is also a clear difference in the time trend by technique. The auxiliary regressions in tables 9.5 and 9.7 suggest that the difference is attributable to differing abilities to respond to changes in output price. Whether it is Appalachia, the Interior, or the West, the ordering of elasticities is always largest for longwall mining, next for continuous mining, and least for surface mining. Such a difference is possible, but it must also be recognized that differences in the underlying rates of technical improvement over time would tend to be attributed to price in the auxiliary regressions. The crude categorical variable we use to separate the pre-1974 and pre-SMCRA years is correlated with the years when output prices were rising, so that what might otherwise remain as a residual time effect is confounded with the price effect. It would not be surprising to observe such effects, since longwall mining is a newer technology than continuous mining, and has been increasing its share of production in all parts of the country. In contrast, continuous and surface mining are more conventional, "mature" technologies for which there may not be as much potential for improvement.

Still, even allowing for a greater degree of learning with the newer technology, surface mining remains a distinct laggard. Moreover, the Appalachian surface mining group remains a prominent exception to the generally significant negative relation between labor productivity and output price. One explanation, which has found confirmation in discussions with industry participants, is depletion. Surface mining reserves are inherently limited from below by underground reserves. The depth at which it is more economical to burrow into the earth to extract the coal than to remove the overburden determines the split between surface and underground reserves and the extent of surface mining reserves. Although underground mining reserves are also limited from below because costs increase with depth, they are at least expansible below, as advances in mining technology reduce costs and make greater depths more economically accessible. Such a depletion effect would be most likely to occur in Appalachia, and it could account for the failure of Appalachian surface mining to exhibit any price elasticity. For this mining group, for which prices peaked early, the productivity-depressing effects of depletion at individual mines may be offsetting the productivity-enhancing responses to lower output prices that operators would otherwise be making.

In the end, two features of the productivity time trends are clear. The sharp increase and subsequent decline in coal price over the years 1972–95 has significantly influenced coal-mining labor productivity. This factor appears to explain most of the reduction in observed productivity during the 1970s, along with the effects of surface-mining regulations during the latter half of the decade. There is secondly a marked tendency for underground mines, especially longwall mines, to experience more improvement in labor productivity over time than surface mines.

9.5.5 Aggregating the Sources of Productivity Change into a National Aggregate

The five separate productivity effects—scale, fixed, price, residual time, and microheterogeneity—can be aggregated in two ways. For any subaggregate, the five indexes can be multiplied, as in equation (14), to provide a predicted productivity index for that mining group. For most of the mining groups, the predicted productivity index is effectively indistinguishable from the observed aggregate indexes, as indicated in table 9.8, which gives the R^2 from a regression of the observed aggregate labor productivity on the reconstructed aggregate indices for the eleven subaggregates.

Three surface mining groups—Interior, Lignite, and PRB—have R^2's less than 0.95. These discrepancies, which are still not large (except for Lignite), reflect the error in the approximation used to split the last term of equation (8) into three separate indexes.

A second aggregation of the indexes can be made across mining groups to create national indexes for each source of productivity change. Here,

Table 9.8 For for Predicted Aggregate Productivity with Observed Aggregate Productivity

	Longwall	Continuous	Surface
Appalachian	0.998	0.995	0.981
Interior	0.999	0.991	0.872
Western	0.990	0.952	0.958
Lignite	n.a.	n.a.	0.758
Powder River Basin	n.a.	n.a.	0.908

Note: n.a. = not applicable.

Table 9.9 Sources of Coal Mining Labor Productivity Growth (percent annual rates of change)

	1972–78	1978–95	1972–95
Observed	−7.00	+5.24	+2.05
Predicted	−7.10	+5.44	+2.17
Scale effect	−2.06	+1.62	+0.66
Fixed effect	+1.68	+1.74	+1.73
Price effect	−4.72	+1.70	+0.03
Residual time effect	−1.00	+0.08	−0.20
Microheterogeneity	−0.99	+0.30	−0.04

the index for each subaggregate is weighted by its share of national output, and the resulting national indexes for each source of productivity change are then multiplied to form a national aggregate index of coal-mining labor productivity.

The observed change in national aggregate labor productivity for coal mining can be decomposed almost exactly into the sources of productivity change identified by this analysis. Table 9.9 shows annual rates of growth for the indexes for the periods of falling and rising productivity and for the entire period 1972–95.

During the 1970s, nearly everything seemed to conspire to reduce labor productivity, but the largest effect was attributable to the rising price of coal. The higher marginal revenue product of labor justified applying more labor to the task, and both statistics and anecdotes suggest that the first response of coal-mine operators was almost literally to throw labor (and other inputs) at the coal face. The inevitable result was lower productivity. The only phenomenon countering these productivity-depressing trends was the persistent improvement embodied in each successive vintage of new mines, as indicated by the fixed effect index. By the end of the 1970s, this source of productivity improvement was 15 percent above the 1972 level, but even this was more than overwhelmed by the combined effect of the other negative factors.

As seen in table 9.9 the period of rising labor productivity during the

1980s and 1990s is largely explained by three phenomena that contribute about equally. New mines (fixed effect) continued to have higher productivity, as they did during the 1970s; but the contributions from scale and price effects are what explain the more rapid observed increase in labor productivity since 1980. In the case of the price effects, the explanation is opposite in sign to what occurred during the 1970s. Also, during the 1980s and 1990s, continuing mines in all mining groups, particularly those in the West and those using longwalls, were able to increase output steadily with concomitant improvements in labor productivity.

9.5.6 What Is the Rate of Advance of the Technological Frontier?

Not far beneath the surface of most productivity research lies a desire to identify and quantify the rate of technological change, and this inquiry is no exception. For the U.S. coal industry, the question is especially intriguing because aggregate statistics suggest a period of significant technical regress in the 1970s. Properly defined as the technical know-how of producing coal, such regress seems implausible. Our analysis suggests that the observed reduction in labor productivity is largely explained by the unprecedented increase in the real price of coal during the mid-1970s and, to a lesser extent, by the internalization of regulatory requirements. Even though these factors were reducing observed labor productivity, the technical capability to produce coal was improving.

The national fixed effect index in table 9.9 would appear to be a likely candidate as a measure of the rate of underlying technical change, because of its very steady 1.7 percent rate of increase from 1972 to 1995. Yet, this index has its own problems. It is just the aggregation over the eleven subaggregates, and the component subindexes are not increasing for all of the mining groups, including some that exhibit the greatest improvement in labor productivity. Interestingly, mining groups that exhibit little or no growth in the fixed effects index invariably have a steadily increasing scale effects index. One index or the other contributes most of the increase in productivity over the whole period, and whichever one it is, the other contributes little. Moreover, the index that is more or less steadily rising appears to be related to average mine life and mining technique. Table 9.10 shows the annual rates of change for these two indexes from 1972 through 1995, and for the two combined, as well as the average mine life for each mining subaggregate.

The eleven subaggregates are listed in descending order of average mine life, and there is a definite tendency for one effect or the other to dominate, as indicated by the bold-faced numbers, depending on average mine life and mining technique. The scale effect tends to be the main driver of productivity improvement for subaggregates with longer mine lives, whereas the fixed effect is the main driver for subaggregates with shorter mine lives. Also, scale effects are more important for large western surface mines and

Table 9.10 Relation of Average Mine Life to Scale and Fixed Effects Indexes

		Average Annual Growth Rate, 1972–1995		
	Average Mine Life	Scale Effects	Fixed Effects	Combined
Powder River Basin	15.00	+2.77	+0.46	+3.23
Lignite	12.65	+3.43	−2.37	+1.06
Appalachian longwall	10.96	+2.21	−0.09	+2.12
Western surface	8.99	+0.77	+0.09	+0.86
Western longwall	7.72	+2.97	+0.60	+3.57
Interior longwall	7.57	+1.00	−0.55	+0.45
Interior continuous	7.49	+0.46	+1.61	+2.07
Western continuous	7.00	+0.46	+3.15	+3.61
Appalachian continuous	4.57	−0.30	+3.17	+2.87
Interior surface	4.14	−0.72	+2.39	+1.67
Appalachian surface	4.12	+0.87	+2.16	+3.02
National total	n.a.	+0.66	+1.73	+2.38

Note: n.a. = not applicable.

for longwall mining regardless of geographic region, whereas fixed effects are more important for continuous mining in all regions and for surface mining in the East.

The appearance of an underlying rate of technical change in one or the other index can be explained. Subaggregates with average mine lives of four years experience a great deal of entry and exit over a twenty-three-year period, and such rapid turnover creates ample opportunity to embody new technology in the many new mines. Moreover, with a short expected life, the emphasis must be on achieving the design output level early and maintaining it. The opposite circumstance holds for subaggregates with very long mine lives, such as the PRB, where little entry or exit occurs and there is concomitantly less opportunity to introduce technical improvements by this route. Nevertheless, operators would not likely forego incorporating technical advances into current operations. These advances could be expected to reduce cost, improve the competitive position of mines making the improvement, and lead to an expansion of output. Such a pattern of incorporating technical change would tend both to show up as a scale effect and to weaken any fixed effect. In this regard, it is worth noting that although most mining groups exhibit positive productivity-output elasticities, the only groups with significantly rising scale effect indexes are those with longer-lived mines.

Mining technique also seems to correlate with the predominance of the scale or fixed effect index, as seen most clearly for the mining groups with average mine lives of about seven years. Scale effects are more important for longwall mining, and fixed effects are more important for continuous mining. This distinction picks up a recurrent story in the industry and reflects the greater lumpiness of longwall mining equipment. It is often reported that longwall cutting machines's ability to separate coal from the face often exceeds the ability of the conveyor systems to deliver the coal to the surface. Consequently, installation of a new longwall machine is often followed by a process of de-bottlenecking, which increases production and improves productivity. In a sense, the full technological potential is embodied in the new mine, but the manner by which that potential is ultimately exploited causes it to show up in our regressions as a scale effect rather than as a fixed effect. In contrast, continuous miners are more divisible with respect to cutting capability at the coal face, and less prone to oversizing with respect to the mine's delivery capabilities.

The tendency for the appearance of a continuing rate of technological advance to show up in either the scale or fixed effect index suggests that the combination of these two indexes at the regional and national level would provide an appropriate statistic for the rate of technological change. Mines do not have uniform lives within the mining groups. Mining groups with short average mine lives have long-lived mines in which technological improvements would appear as scale effects, just as groups with long average mine lives have some mines with short lives, for which technological advances would appear in the fixed effect coefficient. Because these exceptions carry less weight within the group, the effect would be weak, as is manifest in the mining group index. From this point of view, combining the two to make a single index of technological change would capture the full effect within a particular mining group. At the same time, neither the scale nor the fixed effect index reflects only the advance of the technological frontier. As we have had occasion to note, other effects are also reflected, such as those of overcapacity, geology, and the increasing number of nonunion mines.

We have computed these "technological change" indexes for the eleven subaggregates and then aggregated them to form a national index of technological advance. As seen in figure 9.6 the combined technical change index is not entirely satisfactory in conforming to our prior expectation of steady technological advance. The national index is close to being monotonically rising, but from 1972 through 1978 it plateaus. The cause of this plateau can be determined from the highly detailed data from which this index is built. Table 9.11 provides the contributions of the mining groups to the scale, fixed effect, and combined technical change indexes, as well as some explanatory statistics.

From a purely mathematical standpoint, the plateau in the national technological change index between 1972 and 1978 is caused by the boldfaced scale contributions, which sum to -0.1465. If these effects are removed, the combined national index would be $+0.1237$, which would yield an average annual rate of advance of about 2 percent. The underlying

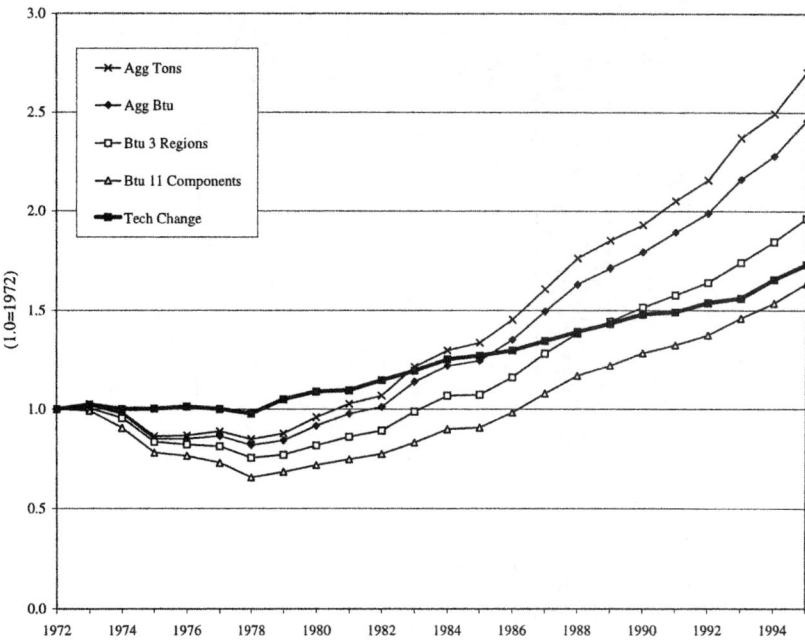

Fig. 9.6   Index of technological advance compared to aggregate measures of U.S. coal labor productivity

cause of these negative scale contributions is the large increase in number of mines between 1972 and 1978 without a commensurate increase in production. In 1978 the number of mines peaked at 5,209, compared with 2,883 in 1972. Not only did aggregate demand increase less than would have been required to match this investment, but for many subaggregates, production declined substantially. As a result, output per mine and labor productivity declined for all subaggregates except the large western surface mines. When aggregated to the national level, these transitory effects of overinvestment in coal-mining capacity mask the underlying rate of technological change.

This surge of investment in new mines is the long-run response to sharply higher coal prices in the mid-1970s, in a manner analogous to the short-run response discussed under section 5.4. New mines could be expected to embody new technology and to cause the fixed effect index to rise, and for all the major mining groups in the 1970s, the fixed effect contributions are positive.[20] Yet, if investment exceeds the actual growth in demand, output per mine will be less and, with positive productivity-

---

20. The numbers of mines in 1978 for the Interior Longwall, Western Longwall, Lignite, and PRB mining groups in 1978 were two, five, eighteen, and thirteen, respectively.

Table 9.11 Contributions from Scale and Fixed Effects, 1972–78

	Scale Contribution	Fixed Contribution	Combined Contribution	Ratio of Number of Mines (1978/1972)	Ratio of Total Output (1978/1972)
Appalachian longwall	−.0110	+.0012	−.0098	1.63	1.01
Interior longwall	−.0005	−.0002	−.0007	2.00	1.21
Western longwall	−.0007	−.0009	−.0016	2.50	1.60
Appalachian continuous	−.0673	+.0420	−.0253	1.55	0.71
Interior continuous	−.0126	+.0040	−.0086	1.12	0.81
Western continuous	−.0004	+.0046	+.0042	1.23	1.71
Appalachian surface	−.0153	+.0275	−.0122	2.07	1.59
Interior surface	−.0387	+.0269	−.0118	2.62	0.81
Western surface extraction	+.0033	+.0050	+.0083	2.15	2.72
Lignite	+.0101	−.0092	+.0009	1.29	3.29
Powder River Basin	+.0098	−.0003	+.0095	2.60	5.89
National total	−.1234	+.1006	−.0228	1.81	1.13

[a]Except Powder River Basin and Lignite.

output elasticities, productivity will decline and be reflected in the scale effects indexes.

An illustrative comparison can be made between Appalachian and Interior surface mining in table 9.10. Both experienced a doubling in their number of mines, and the fixed effect contributions to productivity were positive and of approximately equal magnitude. For both, the investment in new mines exceeded actual demand, which led to negative scale effect contributions. However, the disproportion between new mines and the actual increase of demand was much less for Appalachian surface mining than for Interior surface mining, because demand increased by 60 percent for the former, whereas it declined by 20 percent for the latter. As a result, the net balance between scale and fixed effects was positive for Appalachian surface mines, but negative for Interior surface mines.

Like the fixed effects index, the scale effects index reflects influences other than the underlying advance of the technological frontier. In the late 1970s, for instance, it appears to have been depressed by the effects of overinvestment and resulting overcapacity in the coal fields. Nevertheless, this index comes closer to reflecting the underlying rate of technical change than any other that arises out of our analysis. Neither the 1972–78 period nor the 1978–95 epoch is appropriate for gauging this underlying rate because of the interaction between overcapacity and scale effects, namely, to depress the technical change index in the former period and accelerate it in the latter. The entire 1972–95 period offers a better measure because it spans this period of significant distortion in production relationships.

As is shown in table 9.10, the rates for the subaggregates vary from a high of 3.6 percent for Western longwall mining to a low of 0.5 percent for Interior longwall mining. This is a wide range, particularly for the same mining technique, but the small numbers for these two mining groups make the potential contribution of a single or a few idiosyncratic mines especially problematic. Greater confidence may be placed in mining groups for which larger numbers obtain—Appalachian and Interior surface mining, and Appalachian continuous mining—which indicate an underlying rate between 1.7 percent and 3.0 percent per annum.

9.6 Concluding Remarks

Within the last several decades, significant theoretical and empirical developments have occurred in modeling, measuring, and interpreting relationships among productivity growth, embodied and disembodied technological progress, scale economies, and capacity utilization. Our paper builds on this growing literature and begins to exploit a very rich, large microdatabase containing thousands of individual coal mines' annual observations, and a quarter-century–long time series domain, as well.

The MSHA data set is as rich as any database on production at the microlevel for any industry of which we are aware. Still, information on mine-specific capital investments; labor force characteristics (e.g., age, experience, and union status); utilization of energy inputs, materials, and auxiliary services; and geological and regulatory environments, is lacking. This limitation necessitated our focus in this research on variations among mines over time in labor productivity, defined as Btu-adjusted coal output per hour of labor input.

Our initial analysis of this extraordinary data set has yielded numerous insights that would not have been possible with highly aggregated data. For example, scale effects tend to be the principal force increasing productivity in areas where mines with longer lives predominate, while fixed effects appear to be more important for subaggregates with shorter lives. For long-lived mines, such as longwalls in all regions and western surface mines (including Lignite and the PRB), increased output levels and rising productivity may be associated with unobserved later investment and the removal of logistical bottlenecks. The observed increase in labor productivity would appear to be the result of learning and disembodied improvements, but may in fact reflect unobserved embodiment or the delayed realization of initially embodied technical advances. By contrast, for those subaggregates dominated by short-lived mines, such as continuous mining in all regions and eastern surface mines, the rapid turnover due to entry and exit necessitates rapid exploitation from new technologies—achieving optimal capacity quickly and maintaining it. For short-lived mines, the embodiment of new vintage technologies apparently manifests itself as growth over time in the fixed effects index.

These two distinct microeconomic forces—scale and fixed effects—can be combined, yielding an aggregate time series with persistent positive labor productivity growth for all years except for a no-growth epoch from 1972–78. The micronature of the data set allows us to explain this pattern, as well. As coal output prices increased more rapidly than wages between 1972 and 1978, companies opened mines that were not only smaller, but also apparently geologically inferior, for labor productivity at these marginal mines was clearly much lower than for continuing mines. Not surprisingly, these mines closed within several years, as real coal output prices fell, thereby bringing about a price-induced increase in industry-level labor productivity. Although this price effect explanation is intuitively plausible based on economic theory, the microlevel data uniquely permit us to assess empirically and confirm this prediction. More generally, the productivity effects of significant changes in the relation between output and labor input prices over this time period explain most of what appeared to be a period of technical regress in the 1970s and subsequent high rates of productivity improvement.

After identifying and accounting for these scale, fixed, and price effects, we are left with residuals that exhibit considerable variation, but which revert to zero. In brief, these microdata have enabled us to decompose the productivity residual into distinct and more specific components. In this way, not only does our micro analysis complement aggregate industry studies, but it provides considerable unique insight into the root causes of aggregate growth.

References

Baker, Joe G. 1981. Sources of deep coal mine productivity change, 1962–1975. *Energy Journal* 2 (2): 95–106.
Berndt, Ernst R., and A. Denny Ellerman. 1996. Investment, productivity and capacity in U.S. coal mining: Macro vs. micro perspectives. Unpublished Working Draft available from the authors.
Berndt, Ernst R., A. Denny Ellerman, Susanne Schennech, and Thomas M. Stoker. 1999. Panel data analysis of U.S. coal mine productivity. MIT Center for Energy and Environmental Policy Research, Working Paper no. MIT-CEEPR WP-2000-004, March.
Coal age. Various years. U.S. longwall census. Chicago: Intertec.
Coal markets. Various issues. Washington, D.C.: Fieldston.
Ellerman, A. Denny, Thomas M. Stoker, and Ernst R. Berndt. 1998. Sources of productivity growth in the American coal industry. MIT Center for Energy and Environmental Policy Research, Working Paper no. MIT-CEEPR WP 98-004, March.
Green, P. J., and B. W. Silverman. 1994. *Nonparametric regression and generalized linear models: A roughness penalty approach.* London: Chapman and Hall.
Jorgenson, Dale W. 1990. Productivity and economic growth. In *Fifty years of economic measurement: The Jubilee of the Conference on Research in Income and Wealth,* ed. Ernst R. Berndt and Jack E. Triplett, 19–118. Studies in Income and Wealth, vol. 54. Chicago: University of Chicago Press. Reprinted in Jorgenson, Dale W. 1995. *Productivity: International comparisons of economic growth,* vol. 2, 1–98. Cambridge: MIT Press.
Jorgenson, Dale W., Frank M. Gollop, and Barbara M. Fraumeni. 1987. *Productivity and U.S. economic growth.* Cambridge: Harvard University Press.
Joskow, Paul M. 1987. Contract duration and relationship-specific investments: Empirical evidence from coal markets." *American Economic Review* 77:168–85.
Keystone coal industry manual. 1996. Chicago: Intertec.
U.S. Department of Energy, Energy Information Administration. Various years, 1993–95. *Coal industry annual* (published as *Coal production* prior to 1993). Washington, D.C.
———. 1995. *Longwall mining* (DOE/EIA-TR-0588) March.
U.S. Department of Interior, Bureau of Mines. Various years, to 1976. *Minerals yearbook.* Washington, D.C.
U.S. Department of Labor, Bureau of Labor Statistics. 1996. *Employment, hours and earnings, United States.* Washington, D.C.
U.S. Department of Labor, Mine Safety and Health Administration. *Part 50 coal mining address/employment and accident/injury files.* Division of Mining Information Systems, Denver, Co.

U.S. Executive Office of the President. 1976. *A study of coal prices.* Washington D.C.: Council on Wage and Price Stability, March.
U.S. Federal Energy Administration. 1974. Project Independence Report. Washington, D.C.

Comment   Larry Rosenblum

The authors should be commended for digging below the surface of aggregate industry data to examine trends in coal mining. Using mine-level data, they discern four trends: Labor productivity is positively influenced by scale, and mine size more than doubled (U.S. Department of Energy 1993 shows that average mine size triples over this period); newer vintages of mines are more productive than older vintages, ceteris paribus; the Powder River Basin is much more productive than other regions, and coal production there increased enormously; and the rapid rise in coal prices allowed less productive, smaller mines to enter or remain in the 1970s, and the coal price collapse of the early 1980s forced many of these mines to exit the industry. The result of these trends was that labor productivity declined sharply in the 1970s and rose after 1979.

These conclusions are quite plausible, and reaching them with a data set that has coal production and hours data is quite remarkable. One of the surprising results of the paper is the large scale effects, on the order of 40 percent. The authors acknowledge that the scale effects should not be interpreted as a measure of returns to scale because other inputs, most notably capital, are omitted. This poses the question of how to interpret the scale effect. Because the model is a reduced form, it can be instructive to compare this model to a structural model so that we can interpret the parameters. For simplicity, we assume production for mine i in period t follows a Cobb-Douglas form in which output Q is produced by capital K and labor L, and b and c are output elasticities. (The other symbols in the following equation follow the authors' notation.) Labor productivity can be written as

$$\begin{aligned}
\ln(Q_{it}/L_{it}) = &\ (2 - b - c)\alpha_i & \text{(Fixed Effect)} \\
&+ (2 - b - c)\tau_t & \text{(Time Effect)} \\
&+ (b + c - 1)\ln Q_{it} & \text{(Scale Effect)} \\
&+ b(2 - b - c)\ln K_{it} - (1 - c(2 - b - c))\ln L_{it}.
\end{aligned}$$

Larry Rosenblum is a researcher with the Productivity and Technology Office of the U.S. Bureau of Labor Statistics.

It is clear that the production function yields a model that is empirically identical to the reduced form except for the last term. This last term is simply some variation on the capital intensity of the mine. As long as capital intensity can be completely characterized by a mean and a common trend, the last term can be subsumed into the fixed and time effects. Without loss of generality, the last term can be written as some function $g^{it}(K_{it}, L_{it})$. There is a mine specific mean $g^i(K_i, L_i)$ and a common time trend over all mines $g^t(K_t, L_t)$. Adding the mean to the fixed effects and the common trend to the time effects, and subtracting these terms from the function g^{it}, the equation becomes

$$
\begin{aligned}
\ln(Q_{it}/L_{it}) = &\ (2 - b - c)\alpha_i + g^i(K_i, L_i) && \text{(Fixed Effect)} \\
& + (2 - b - c)\tau_i + g^t(K_t, L_t) && \text{(Time Effect)} \\
& + (b + c - 1)\ln Q_{it} && \text{(Scale Effect)} \\
& + g^{it}(K_{it}, L_{it}) - g^i(K_i, L_i) - g^t(K_t, L_t)
\end{aligned}
$$

The final term will be zero as long as the time and fixed effects completely describe g^{it}. However, if capital intensity cannot be completely characterized by a mean and a trend, the final term is not zero and may be correlated with other terms, leading to potential biases in the estimates. Of principle concern is the likelihood that output and capital intensity may be positively correlated. This is equivalent to wondering if larger mines are more capital intensive. By any measure, returns to scale of 40 percent are quite large and impart a large cost advantage to large producers, so the possibility that the scale effects are overestimated must be considered, and the authors should investigate this more thoroughly in their paper. However, coal mines are not like other producers because the scope of production is circumscribed by the size of the coal field. As a result, mining is an industry where economies of scale might exist without the usual industry dynamics. Instead, large mines should enjoy high rents instead of increasing market share, and this can be empirically tested.

Although there is no definitive test for the correlation of output and capital intensity with this data set because capital data are unavailable, examining the scale effects in more detail might provide reassurance that such scale effects exist. If scale effects exist, we should expect that small mines are more likely to exit than are large mines of the same vintage, ceteris paribus. We might also expect that across regions, but within a type of mine, scale economies should be approximately equal. Similarly, economies of scale are not likely to vary significantly across time unless new technologies alter the optimal scale of operation. Splitting the sample in half across time should produce similar estimates in each time period, and both should be similar to the original estimates. Finally, the model could be estimated imposing constant returns to scale to see if many of the plausible inferences about entry and exit and time effects are obtained. If not, this further strengthens the likelihood of increasing returns to scale.

Regardless of this potential omitted variable bias, we need to take care in interpreting scale effects. Because scale effects include both returns to scale and the effect of omitted inputs such as capital services, the data do not allow the authors to compare the importance of pure scale effects to other determinants of labor productivity. If larger mines are much more capital intensive, the scale effects do not suggest a course of action for improving productivity in coal mining. That is, the presence of returns to scale suggests that (labor or multifactor) productivity will increase as long as new mines are larger than the average existing mine. If the scale effect largely reflects differing capital intensities, then multifactor productivity will not be improved by altering average mine size.

The authors estimate labor productivity effects in two stages. In the first, labor productivity depends on scale effects, aggregate time effects, and fixed effects. In the second stage, time effects are divided into price effects, residual time effects, and microheterogeneity effects. The authors use this two-stage technique so that each effect can be identified and so that no bias arises from entering price and wage data into the first equation.

This is a wise strategy because wage and especially coal price data cannot be observed for each mine. Instead, a state average price is used for coal and a national price for labor. As a result, price effects and microheterogeneity may overlap in their effect. That is, price trends reflect the effect of changing prices on the time effect of mine labor productivity, whereas microheterogeneity reflects unobserved changes in the composition of mines over time, including differences in the prices received for their coal and paid to their workers. It is certainly plausible that relative coal prices are nearly constant across mines within a region, but as table 9C.1 illustrates, this is unlikely because coal prices are often determined by long-term contracts. Unless these contracts expire at the same time, relative coal prices are bound to vary across mines within a region. Again, the aggregate price trend effect is not mismeasured, but the disaggregation is not as clear cut as the analysis implies.

Table 9C.1 shows both the open market and contract price for coal for selected states. In some states the prices differ dramatically. Furthermore, contracts are often for as much as twenty years, and in 1993 almost half of all coal was sold under contract. This means that the contract price may bear little relationship to the marginal cost of producing coal and that these prices may well include rents to the mine or the contract holder, depending on the price of coal. When aggregating coal production to create regional or national statistics, the authors use superlative indexes that employ value share weights. These weights are appropriate as long as price reflects the marginal cost of production, but if coal prices have been fixed years before production takes place, value share weights may not accu-

Table 9C.1   Average Mine Coal Price by Area, 1994

Area	Open Market	Captive Market
Illinois	22.28	22.44
Kentucky	24.90	23.55
Ohio	23.68	52.54
Pennsylvania	26.38	19.86
West Virginia	26.43	32.35
Wyoming	6.37	12.77
Appalachia	26.98	35.11
Interior	22.05	11.88
Western	10.23	14.16

Source: U.S. Department of Energy (1994a).

rately reflect marginal costs. As the authors show in table 9.1, the stylized facts of a productivity slowdown followed by a rebound can be seen in four very different productivity measures. However, the preferred measure (eleven-region weighted labor productivity) shows the greatest productivity slowdown followed by the weakest rebound. Although the contract prices do not affect the parameter estimates derived from microdata in the first stage of the model, the growth accounting exercise depends on the choice of the aggregate measure of labor productivity, which in turn depends on the index formula used to aggregate individual mines.

Next, the authors might want to consider a couple of tests to strengthen their findings. First, mine output is included in the sample provided there is any output in a given year. However, labor strife has been common in coal mining, especially in 1981. Furthermore, a strike makes a mine appear to be smaller than its true size. If strikes curtail labor productivity, scale effects will appear greater than if dummy variables are used to control for strike periods or the production is adjusted to reflect a full year of production. Similarly, the authors use a dummy variable for 1972 and 1973 to control for the sharp price rise of coal, but no similar dummy when prices collapse. The authors might demonstrate that the scale, time, and fixed effects remain when either corresponding dummy variables are added or the sample is limited to 1974–95.

Finally, I have one small quibble. The authors divide the analysis into two regimes, 1972–78 and 1979–95, presumably because a variety of labor productivity measures in figure 9.5 begin their rebound in 1979. However, the regime of high energy prices lasted until 1986, and coal prices peaked in 1984 (U.S. Department of Energy 1994a, table 9.12). Price effects are the largest source of declining labor productivity prior to 1979. If price effects are dominant and strongly influence mine size, then a later date might be more insightful for the analysis.

Despite these qualifications, the basic conclusions of the paper provide a coherent explanation of labor productivity trends in coal mining. A jump in the price of coal after 1973 not only allowed small mines to remain in the industry but also encouraged small mines to enter. Because small mines have lower labor productivity than do bigger mines, labor productivity declined throughout the 1970s even though entering mines had larger fixed effects (presumably reflecting greater efficiency) than did existing mines. The price collapse of the 1980s unwound the entry of relatively inefficient mines as mines became larger and entering mines continued to have greater labor productivity than did existing mines, ceteris paribus. The result was a productivity rebound.

References

U.S. Department of Energy, Energy Information Agency. 1993. *The changing structure of the US coal industry: An update.* Washington, D.C.: GPO.

U.S. Department of Energy, Energy Information Agency. 1994a. *Coal industry annual.* Washington, D.C.: GPO.

———. 1994b. *Historical energy review 1973–92.* Washington, D.C.: GPO.

10
Service Sector Productivity Comparisons: Lessons for Measurement

Martin Neil Baily and Eric Zitzewitz

10.1 Introduction

Output per hour in the nonfarm business sector grew at only 1.4 percent per year in 1973–95, with the weakness apparently concentrated in the service sector. Stagnant productivity in services seemed to belie the rapid adoption of information technology in this sector and the rapid pace of change in many service industries.

This puzzle, together with the parallel concern about measuring the cost of living, fueled efforts to improve price and hence productivity measurement. The measurement improvements that have been instituted at the Bureau of Economic Analysis (BEA) and the Bureau of Labor Statistics (BLS) resulted in an upward revision of 0.3 percentage in the rate of output per hour growth in the nonfarm business sector (from 1.1 to 1.4 percent). Moreover, starting in 1996 overall labor productivity growth accelerated sharply to around 3 percent per year, with the acceleration occurring in both service-producing industries and goods-producing industries (see the disussion in Council of Economic Advisers 2001).

There remain questions, however, about how well service sector output is being measured, and these questions apply to services sold both for final use and for intermediate use. Measurement errors in the former affect estimates of both industry level and overall output and productivity, whereas errors in the latter affect only our understanding of productivity by industry. Despite the overall improvement in service sector

---

Martin Neil Baily is a Senior Fellow at the Institute for International Economics. Eric Zitzewitz is a graduate student at the Massachusetts Institute of Technology. They were, respectively, principal and economics analyst at the McKinsey Global Institute.

The authors would like to thank Robert J. Gordon and other participants in the conference.

productivity growth, data anomalies remain, including sectors where reported productivity is declining.[1]

Starting with an international comparison of service sector productivity published in 1992, there have been a series of projects initiated by the McKinsey Global Institute and carried out in collaboration with McKinsey & Company offices worldwide and a number of academic economists.[2] Although the emphasis of these projects has been to measure and explain productivity by industry by country for a range of service sector and goods-producing industries, another important concern has been with employment creation and the extent to which productivity increases will cause or alleviate unemployment.

The purpose of this paper is to ask whether the results of these international comparisons cast any light on the problem of service sector output measurement. To do this, we present case studies of five service industries: retail banking, public transport, telecom, retailing, and airlines. We describe how we have measured output and what we believe are the main explanations for the resulting cross-country productivity differences. To make one point clear at the outset, these studies have not generally developed new output measures. The basic output measures in the five cases are the BLS index of retail banking output; vehicle kilometers in public transport; access lines and call minutes in telecom; value added in retailing; and revenue passenger kilometers (RPK) for airlines. In selecting output measures, the goal has been to find metrics that are intuitive and understandable to noneconomists, and business consultants in particular, and that are at least acceptable to economists. Where possible, we have had a strong preference for physical output measures in goods-producing sectors, such as liters of beer. We also have used similar tangible output measures for services, such as call minutes of telecom services used.

Where our efforts may help improve the measurement process is by providing an understanding of how these industries have evolved (because the cross section allows us to see industries at different stages of evolution); how innovations have been used to generate customer value; and what has caused the productivity differences.

In industries where the share of purchased inputs in output is large and may differ significantly across countries, we have used value added as the output measure, and this applies to the retail case we describe later. Value

---

1. There is concern that efforts to improve measurement may be biased because most researchers are looking for reasons that output and productivity are understated, whereas in practice it is possible that quality has deteriorated in some service industries. We are aware of this problem, but in general we find that successful service sector innovations must drive out existing providers, so the presumption is that industry evolution is generating consumer surplus as people choose the new combination of price and service quality.

2. See the reference list for the specific citations. The number of people working on these projects is too numerous to mention each individually. Bill Lewis, the director of the McKinsey Global Institute, has supervised all of the projects.

added is not the favored output measure among productivity economists, who prefer to use a production function with gross value of production as the output and materials as one of the factor inputs. The McKinsey analyses do use the production function as the central conceptual framework for explaining productivity differences at the production process level, but we do not estimate formal production functions. The concept of value added is intuitive to business consultants whose own work is often based on the value chain concept. Where possible we try to carry out a double deflation estimate of value added, using purchasing power parity (PPP) for inputs as well as outputs. That is often hard to do, and the estimates are subject to error.

10.1.1 Quality

Because our analyses have largely been of cross-sectional comparisons at a point in time, we have been able to avoid the problem of changing quality over time. Where, based on industry knowledge, we find significant quality differences across countries in a given year, we try to control for those differences. For example, in autos, we had access to conjoint studies carried out in the United States and Europe that estimated the quality premiums of Japanese and European nameplates over U.S. nameplates.[3] In services, a recent example of quality adjustment for telecom service in Brazil had to account for the difficulties of noisy connections as well as the inability to place a call. In this case we estimated the investment in equipment that Brazil would have to make to bring its service quality up to the U.S. level, and we effectively reduced capital productivity and hence TFP to reflect this adjustment. A purer alternative would have been to estimate the price adjustment that would have made consumers indifferent to the different service levels (the conjoint approach). We did not have the data to do this. Moreover, the answers would likely have been very different for the United States and Brazil.

The quality adjustment is not always done in an unbiased way—for example, suppose we find that Country A has productivity that is twice as high as Country B using a raw output number, and that service quality is somewhat higher in Country A. Lacking a quantitative adjustment that can be made with reasonable resource cost, we may decide to ignore the quality difference on the grounds that it will not change the overall analysis of the causes of the productivity differences much.

10.1.2 Interaction between Measurement and Causality

A basic tenet of scientific research is that data collection should be independent of the hypothesis being tested by the data. A double-blind clinical

---

3. This approach is similar to the hedonic approach pioneered by Griliches.

trial of a new drug is a standard example. Economists try to follow the same rules by using standard government data or by collecting data in an objective or arms-length manner. Though sensitive to the demands of rigorous hypothesis testing, the McKinsey studies have not operated in the same way. We are not generally testing some aspect of economic theory. Instead, we are trying to provide our best estimate of both the *magnitudes* of the productivity differences among industries in different countries and the *explanations* for those differences at the production process level. When a McKinsey team working on one of the case studies reports to us that there is a productivity gap of, say, 40 percent between the U.S. and another country, we do not accept that figure until the team has made plant visits and has talked to experts in the industry and found supporting data to explain at the operational level why the productivity gap occurs. What is different about the check-clearing process, for example, that can account for a large labor productivity difference across countries.[4] Sometimes, in that process, we discover that substantial adjustments must be made to the productivity numbers. For example, we may find that the scopes of the industries are different in the countries, or that some workers employed by one industry actually work in another industry.

The drawback with this approach is that our analysis of causality at the production process level is not true hypothesis testing. The advantage is that we believe it provides much greater reliability. Subsequently, we do attempt to test hypotheses at a different level. Having determined the productivity gaps and the reasons at the production process (or production function) level, we then ask the higher-level question of why companies operate differently in the different countries.

The paper goes through each of the case studies in turn, attempting to draw out the lessons for measurement. We conclude with a review of the findings.

10.2 Retail Banking

Retail banking has undergone rapid changes in its competitive and regulatory environment since the early 1980s, and the fact that these changes have varied in speed and intensity across countries makes it an interesting industry in which to study their effects. In the United States, the deregulation of interest rates and money market checking accounts in the early 1980s increased competitive pressure on retail banks. The increased pressure together with an increasing application of IT coincided with an acceleration in labor productivity growth (as measured by the BLS, fig. 10.1).

---

4. Because our focus is on productivity comparisons, our method does not generally identify ways in which best practice could improve. Our use of the term *best practice* does not imply that we think such improvement is impossible.

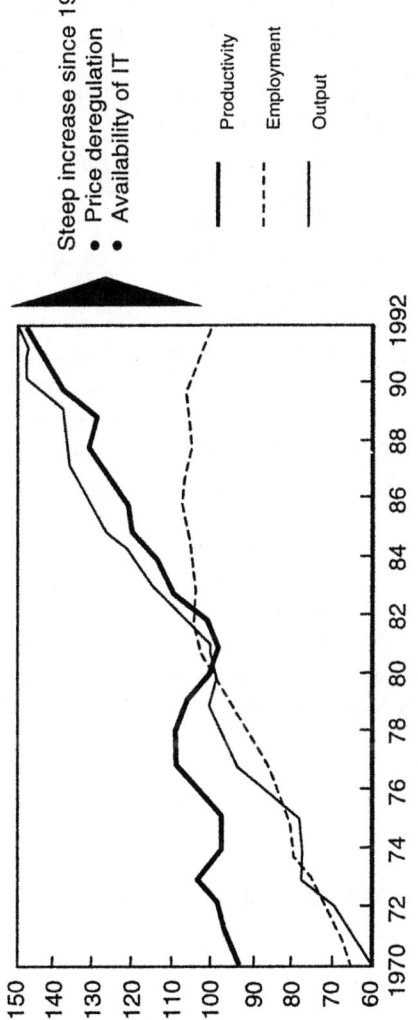

Fig. 10.1 Labor productivity, output, and employment: U.S. commercial banks (Index: 1980 = 100)

Note: Includes both traditional products and mortgages, FTEs
Source: Output and productivity data provided by the Bureau of Labor Statistics

In the late 1980s and early 1990s, competition and IT use were further increased by the emergence of specialized processing and mortgage/consumer loan companies, the liberalization of interstate banking, and the emergence of a market for corporate control.

Outside the United States, the retail banking industry is typically more concentrated, and the increase in competitive intensity in retail banking has been less dramatic. In most countries, lower competitive intensity has been accompanied by lower productivity, but the Netherlands has achieved the highest productivity of the countries we have studied with highly concentrated sectors. High concentration may have contributed to high productivity by aiding in the development of an electronic payments system and by reducing the pressure for expanding the branch network.

10.2.1 Productivity Measurement

The recent changes and cross-country differences in the banking industry complicate productivity measurement. The traditional banking products included in the BLS output index (numbers of transactions and deposit and loan accounts) are easier to capture in physical measures than are the newer products into which retail banks are expanding. Recent changes in technology have also increased the cross-country and time series differences in the convenience with which banking products are offered.

Measuring Output

We measure the overall output of traditional banking products using a methodology similar to that of the BLS. We use our banking practice knowledge to divide the employment[5] involved in producing traditional retail banking products into three functions: processing payment transactions, maintaining deposit accounts, and lending. We then construct functional productivity indexes and an aggregate productivity, which is the average of the functional productivity measures weighted by employment.

This yields the same results as weighting outputs by the labor required to produce them.[6] This is the same procedure we use in the other service industries with multiple outputs: airlines (RPK and passengers moved) and telecom (access lines and call minutes). Using labor requirements as weights is necessary because these outputs are usually not separately

---

5. Ideally we would use total factor input in measuring productivity, but measures of the physical capital involved in producing retail banking services (as distinct from the other assets of a bank) are very difficult to construct and make consistent across countries.

6. To see this, consider the following expression for countries A and B and products C and D: $(Q_C^A/L_C^A)/(Q_C^B/L_C^B)*[L_C^A/(L_C^A + L_D^A)] + (Q_D^A/L_D^A)/(Q_D^B/L_D^B)*[L_D^A/(L_C^A + L_D^A)]$, which is the average of the two product-level productivity ratios, weighted by the labor share of the products in country A. This is equivalent to $[Q_C^A*(L_C^B/Q_C^B) + Q_D^A*(L_D^B/Q_D^B)]/(L_C^A + L_D^A)$, where the products of country A are weighted using the unit labor requirements in country B.

priced in a way that reflects their true cost. Just as airline passengers do not pay separate per flight and mileage charges, banking customers pay for their deposit accounts in the form of an interest margin and usually receive their transactions for free.

Defining Output: Volume versus Value, Stock versus Flow

In following the BLS output measurement methodology, we have made two important decisions about measuring output in banking that are worth reviewing. We measure the number, not the value, of transactions and accounts under the assumption that both the customer value and bank input requirements are more constant per transaction/account than per dollar value. This is obviously not completely true for any product, especially for lending, where large loans typically are reviewed more carefully and provide a greater service to the borrower than do smaller loans. We compensate partially for this problem by weighting loan and deposit accounts by the cost factors estimated in the functional cost analysis, thus capturing the fact that maintaining an average mortgage requires more work than does maintaining an average credit card account, but not the fact that high-value mortgages can require more work than smaller ones.

Another decision we made is to measure the stock of deposit and loan accounts outstanding, rather than the flow of new accounts. Because the turnover of accounts is more rapid in the United States than in other countries and has become more rapid over time, this decision may understate both the level and growth in U.S. productivity. Failing to capture the higher account turnover is more justified in some cases than in others. Some mortgage refinancing is probably not positive net economic output but can be viewed as a particularly inefficient way of adjusting a fixed interest rate to market conditions. At the same time, some of the shorter average life of mortgages in the U.S. is caused by higher mobility; the accommodation of this mobility by the mortgage industry through a higher loan turnover ratio probably does reflect additional output. Thus far, we have only addressed this issue by adjusting downward the numbers of deposit accounts in countries that have a high share of unused dormant accounts.[7]

Unresolved Issues: New Products and Convenience

In response to the increasing offering of nontraditional banking products by retail banks, we attempted in a couple of projects to include physical measures of these products, such as the number of equity transactions or mutual fund accounts. We abandoned these measures mainly because

---

7. This adjustment was originally motivated by the fact that in Sweden customers average eight deposit accounts per capita (compared with 1.5 in the United States), mainly because Swedish banks do not attempt to discourage low/zero-balance dormant accounts.

they produced implausibly low productivity levels for the U.S. securities industry. About half a million people work in the U.S. securities industry, most of whom are involved in functions other than the processing of transactions and the maintenance of mutual funds. These functions are present to a much greater degree in core financial markets like the United States and United Kingdom than in peripheral markets, but we have not found a methodology for adjusting either the output or input figures to reflect this difference. Other nontraditional banking products (such as insurance) present similar problems.

Capturing differences in the convenience with which banking services are provided is another unresolved issue in these productivity comparisons. The increasing penetration of ATMs, PC banking, and other delivery channels has obviously increased convenience greatly over time. Fortunately for our cross-country productivity measures, these changes have occurred at a roughly similar pace throughout the advanced countries, and our banking practice judged the level of convenience offered in transaction and deposit products to be roughly similar across countries.

Important differences in convenience do exist in lending, however. Information technology has allowed lenders to centralize lending decisions, improving the quality and timeliness of the decisions. Mortgage and other loan decisions are now made in minutes rather than days, and better information has allowed lenders to extend credit to more risky borrowers than in the past. This technology was initially developed in the United States by specialized lenders such as Countrywide Credit, whose growth helped encourage its adoption by the rest of the U.S. industry. Outside of the United Kingdom, this technology has penetrated other countries more slowly, and thus the convenience associated with rapid lending decisions (i.e., greater availability of credit) is greater in the United States. We have not yet developed a good methodology for capturing this extra convenience.

10.2.2 Productivity Results

Overall we find the Netherlands to have the highest productivity of the countries studied, with the United States and France tied for second (table 10.1). The Netherlands leads the United States in all three functions, but especially in processing payments. The Dutch advantage comes from the combination of a more efficient electronic payments system and an efficient branch network (table 10.2).

After adjusting for these two factors, the United States actually uses its labor more efficiently, in part due to more centralization of processing and use of part-time labor in the branches.

Electronic Payments

The development of the electronic payments system in the Netherlands was led by the Postbank. When the Postbank introduced its electronic

Table 10.1   Labor Productivity in Retail Banking, 1995 (Index: U.S. = 100)

Country	Productivity	Country	Productivity
Netherlands	148	Australia (1994)	60
United States	100	Brazil	40
France	100	Colombia (1992)	30
Germany	85	Mexico (1992)	28
Sweden (1993)	80	Venezuela (1992)	25
Korea	71	Argentina	19
United Kingdom (1989)	64		

payments system, the other banks fought back by launching a joint alternative electronic payment system of their own. Their collaborative effort facilitated the development of standardized payment specifications that are essential for efficient electronic payment systems. In the Dutch case, the banks' joint efforts led to the establishment of a unique IT format adjusted for small payment transactions, a nationwide account numbering system, and convenient payment vehicles such as electronic debit cards. The end result has been widespread acceptance of electronic payments, with high levels of efficiency and customer convenience in payments. Other countries such as Germany and France also have Dutch-style electronic payments systems, but these countries have lost this advantage through dense branch networks (Germany) and inefficient labor utilization.

The United States has had difficulty setting up shared electronic payments systems for two key reasons. First, the highly fragmented nature of the U.S. retail banking industry, as well as state laws that have limited the interstate activities of banks, have impeded the development of common standards for IT and account numbering. Second, customers have been reluctant to switch to electronic payments; Americans continue to rely on checks for 70 percent of all transactions, perceiving them as safer and better suited to record keeping than other payment vehicles. However, in the countries that have recently started shifting over to electronic payments, such as the United Kingdom and New Zealand, customers have been given a small incentive to shift and have responded to that incentive. We believe there is a substantial unexploited opportunity for the United States to raise banking productivity and, once the transition has been made, to increase customer convenience.

Branching

The consolidation of the branch network in the Netherlands is helped by that country's high population density and concentration. The density of the Netherlands allows the banking industry to have 2.5 and 6 times more branches per square kilometer of residential area than France or the United States, respectively, despite having 45 percent and 30 percent fewer branches per capita. The Dutch banks have not squandered this natural

Table 10.2   Drivers of Productivity in Payment Services (Index: U.S. = 100)

	Netherlands	France	Germany	United States	Cause of High Performance
Share of electronic payments	175	154	182	100	Joint standard setting
Branches per capita	119	93	79	100	High population density
Average labor utilization	74	56	54	100	Labor Organization
Overall payments productivity	154	80	78	100	

Source: McKinsey Global Institute and the Max Geldens Foundations for Societal Renewal 1997.

advantage (as the German and Korean banks have) by overexpanding their branch network, in part because the high levels of concentration reduces the pressure to compete through branch proliferation. The absence of regulations or understandings on pricing has also reduced the incentive to focus on competing through branching.

Labor Organization

The U.S. industry has been most successful relative to other countries in organizing its labor efficiently. The U.S. industry makes much greater use of part-time labor to staff efficiently for daily and monthly activity peaks in the branches. Using part-time labor is more difficult outside the United States because of collective bargaining agreements or semivoluntary adherence to traditional labor practices. Greater penetration of IT in the United States also allows the lending decision making, transaction processing, and account maintenance functions to be centralized.

10.2.3 Lessons from the Banking Case

Two main implications for measuring productivity growth and levels can be drawn from the banking case. The first is that there have been significant increases in the efficiency of banks associated with the increased penetration of IT. Our industry practice views the pace of change as being at least as rapid as in manufacturing industries. At present the BEA effectively assumes away labor productivity growth in all financial services (changes in real output over time are set equal to changes in full-time equivalent persons engaged in the sector). They could certainly improve on that for retail banking by making use of the BLS banking productivity estimates (which show productivity growth of 4.5 percent per year since deregulation in 1982). The second implication is that even the BLS estimates may be missing changes in the true output of the sector. Some of the increase in the turnover of accounts in the United States probably represents increased true economic output; both the BLS and our measure of output miss this increase. More importantly, the increased convenience and availability of lending is not captured in these estimates.

10.3 Telecom

Our telecom case studies have all focused on the traditional, fixed-line residential and commercial services, which still account for about 80 percent of telecom revenues. Data for mobile phones are included in the analysis, raising the coverage of the case study to roughly 90 percent of revenue, but the overall results are still dominated by the fixed line business.

The telecom industry essentially provides two outputs. The first is access lines, which provide access to the telephone network and the option of making and receiving calls, and the second is the actual call minutes themselves. These two outputs are priced and consumed at very different relative levels across countries, and this complicates attempts to measure productivity. For example, in Brazil the supply of access lines was restricted by high import tariffs on capital goods and the government's diversion of telecom earnings to finance budget deficits. As a result, access lines per capita are very low given income levels (the black market rate for a line has reached $5,000), but use of these lines is very high. In other countries, such as Japan and Germany, access lines are easily available and monthly fees are low, but calls are expensive and use is low. Aggregating the two telecom outputs into a common productivity measure is one of the major challenges of the case.

10.3.1 Productivity Measurement

Telecom is one of the three case industries with multiple physical outputs where the outputs are not separately priced in a way that reflects their true cost or value to the customer. As in the other industries, we attempted to aggregate the outputs using weights based on the inputs required to produce them. Unlike banking, data for telecom is available for both labor and capital input. Labor input in telecom is used primarily to maintain and install access lines; only about 15 percent of the labor is used in activities where labor requirements are determined by call traffic. Capital, however, is mainly the switching equipment and lines that are used to provide call minutes.

As in banking, we constructed our labor, capital, and TFP measures by weighting outputs according to their input requirements. Labor productivity was measured as a weighted average of access lines maintained and call minutes per hour worked, and capital productivity was measured as call minutes per unit of network capital services.[8] Labor and capital productivity were then averaged to form TFP, using weights based on the labor and capital shares in value added. The advantage of this procedure is that it produces both an acceptable overall measure of productivity as well as component labor and capital productivity measures that are meaningful to our industry audience.

Capital services are constructed using a perpetual inventory method with sudden death depreciation. Capital is divided into four categories (switching equipment, cable/wire, land and buildings, and general purpose) and assigned service lives based on asset lives given by the Federal Communications Commission (FCC) to the Regional Bell Operating Companies. Capital expenditures are converted into U.S. dollars using PPPs

---

8. The capital involved in maintaining the network was impossible to separate from the network capital but is a relatively small share of overall capital. Because the network maintenance–related capital was included as providing call minutes, we may have slightly underweighted access lines relative to call minutes in constructing our output measure.

for structures, equipment, and telecom equipment. That capital goods tariffs caused access lines to cost $2,700 in Brazil instead of $2,300 does not lower Brazilian capital productivity as measured. But Deutsche Telekom specifications, which raised capital requirements 20 percent by calling for main wires to be "tank proof" (i.e., able to survive being run over by a tank) even when they are placed underground and requiring the use of underground as opposed to aerial cables, do reduce German capital productivity as measured. Capital productivity is also adjusted for service quality. In Brazil, where service quality is lower due to the use of mechanical and analog instead of digital switches and to lower switching capacity per access line, we estimate the capital that would be required to upgrade Brazilian service to U.S. standards (about 5 percent more capital per line) and lower Brazilian capital productivity by this amount.

The main issue with using input requirements as a method for valuing output is that they may not reflect the value of the output to the consumer. The high black market price for access lines in Brazil suggests that adding one million lines in Brazil would be more valuable than adding one million lines in the United States. Likewise, a German consumer who is paying four cents per minute for a local call is probably getting more value from his or her average call minute than is the American with free local calling whose teenagers gossip for hours to their friends.

To give one check of whether calls in the United States are of lower value than calls in other countries, we looked at data on average call length. We found that the average call length in the United States is about the same as in Europe. Gossiping teens do not explain the usage differences. Moreover, one point of view is that there are externalities associated with telecom usage, where it drives productivity improvements elsewhere in the economy. Another check of the results was carried out by the McKinsey team in the United Kingdom, where a study was being carried out as this paper was written. The team examined the share of telecom revenues accounted for by payments for the access line and payments that are determined by call-minutes. Data were collected for the United States, United Kingdom, Germany, France and Sweden. As expected, the United States has the largest share of revenues from access line charges (35 percent), but the other countries' shares are not all that different. The lowest is France, at 20 percent, where local calls are very expensive. The others are Sweden 34 percent, United Kingdom 27 percent, and Germany 26 percent. Using the average revenue share of 28 percent to weight lines and minutes gave productivity results that were pretty much the same as the ones reported here.

The countries in which we have studied telecom productivity can be roughly divided into three groups (table 10.3). The United States is the only country studied that had both high labor and capital productivity, which mainly reflect high access lines per employee and high network utili-

Table 10.3   Productivity in Telecom (Index to U.S. = 100, 1995)

	United States	Germany	Korea	Japan	Argentina	Brazil
Total factor productivity	100	42	66	49	56	64
Labor productivity	100	51	82	74	70	45
Access lines per FTE	100	83	88	80	75	46
Call minutes per FTE	100	39	57	33	36	39
Capital productivity	100	38	58	40	51	75
Access lines per dollar of capital services	100	61	65	42	48	86
Call minutes per line	100	48	112	106	90	109
Call minutes per capita	100	37	40	30	14	12
Access lines per capita	100	79	62	71	28	14

Source: McKinsey Global Institute (1998a, b).

zation, respectively. The United States had thus efficiently (relative to other countries, at least) built and maintained a large network and achieved high usage of that network. Most of the other countries studied have achieved fairly high labor productivity but low network utilization. Brazil, on the other hand, had low labor productivity, which resulted in an insufficient supply of access lines and thus high network usage. Before privatization Argentina actually suffered from both low labor and low capital productivity, although labor productivity has recently improved.

Labor Productivity

Cross-country differences in labor productivity are due to differences in the adoption of advanced technology such as digital switching and to differences in the pressure to rationalize employment in order to take advantage of the new technology. In Brazil less than 50 percent of access lines are digitally switched, compared with over 80 percent in the Organization for Economic Cooperation and Development (OECD) countries. Digitally switched lines require one-fifth as much maintenance technician time as analog lines to maintain, and Brazilian regional telecoms with higher digitalization had lower cash (non capital, i.e., mainly labor) operating costs. In addition, less IT is used in Brazil in directory assistance and customer service, which also leads to lower labor productivity.

New technology is important in enabling higher labor productivity, but in countries that have adopted digital switching and other modern technologies, labor requirements per line have declined rapidly. In the United States, for example, access lines per employee have grown at 7 percent per year since 1980. In most cases this potential productivity growth is more rapid than the growth in demand for access lines, and telecoms therefore have to reduce employment in order to capture the full benefit of the new technology. In general, we have found that private telecoms facing at least limited competition have been more likely than state-owned telecoms to make these reductions. For example, the one private regional telecom in Brazil has labor productivity that is 30 percent above average despite an only average level of digitalization.

Capital Productivity

The most important factors explaining differences in network usage and thus capital productivity are pricing and the availability and marketing of demand-enhancing call completion services. The marginal pricing of local, long-distance, and international calls is much lower in the United States than in Germany, Japan, and Korea, and demand for calls per capita is much higher. Most U.S. customers pay a higher monthly fee and receive free local calls, whereas most other countries do not offer free local calls as an option. In addition, services that increase call origination and termination are more available and more aggressively marketed in the United

States. Business call centers, voice mail, call waiting, and call forwarding have much higher penetration in the United States than in other countries, and the U.S. telecoms do not tax answering machines as Deutsche Telekom does. Telecoms in the United States have historically expended much more effort and money marketing telecom services, whereas in other countries there has been less focus on stimulating demand. In Germany advertising has even carried the opposite message: Several decades ago Deutsche Telekom ran advertisements advising consumers to "Fasse Dich kurz"—keep it brief.

10.3.2 Lessons from the Telecom Case

The differences in the pricing and availability of telecom outputs across countries provides evidence of how large the consumer surplus associated with telecom services can be. Even when the rights to an access line were trading at $5,000 in Brazil, there were seven lines per hundred population, and almost all consumers could have sold their line on the black market since the rights to a phone line were transferable. Thus roughly 7 percent of the population valued a phone line at over $5,000 in a country with 22 percent of U.S. GDP per capita. This suggests that the consumer surplus generated by the access lines that are available in the United States is significantly larger than the cost of building and maintaining the lines. Likewise, demand for local calls appears fairly inelastic above one to two cents per minute; even though the price of local calls is 5 cents per minute, U.K. consumers still demand over 1,300 minutes per capita. This suggests that the consumer surplus from call minutes is also large.

We have not even begun to attempt to measure this consumer surplus, although others have (e.g., Hausman 1997). The evidence in our case studies on pricing and demand across countries, however, suggests that understanding consumer surplus is important to understanding both telecom's final output and its contribution to the output of other sectors.

10.4 Retailing

In a series of studies, McKinsey Global Institute has examined cross-country comparisons of productivity and employment for general merchandise retailing, food retailing, and a combination of both. In this paper we will draw on the work that was done in the Netherlands, which covered all retailing. It is not ideal to combine food and nonfood, although given the presence of hypermarkets in Europe, it can be difficult to separate the two.

The importance of the retail sector to the national economy is often underestimated. Yet, it accounts for 5 to 6 percent of GDP and 7 to 11 percent of employment in the United States and Europe. It is particularly important in creating jobs for groups with high unemployment levels, employing relatively large numbers of women, young people, and people with little education. The sector is also a major provider of part-time work.

Because of this, our studies of retailing have often focused on employment. The existence of very high minimum wages in Europe (effectively about $8 an hour in France, given payroll taxes), together with zoning restrictions that inhibit the development of high service retailing formats—notably shopping malls with department store anchors and specialty chains—has adversely affected the creation of low-skill jobs.

10.4.1 Productivity Measurement

Format Evolution

Retail has undergone a major structural shift in the late twentieth century, as traditional stores have been partially replaced, first by department stores and then by specialized chains, mass merchandisers, and mail order. In order to understand the effects of this structural shift on productivity and employment in the sector, we have segmented the industry into six different store formats: (a) mass merchandisers, such as Safeway or Wal-Mart; (b) out-of-town specialized chains, such as IKEA and Home Depot; (c) in-town specialized chains, such as The Gap, Benetton, and The Body Shop; (d) department stores, such as Saks, Bloomingdales, and Nordstrom; (e) mail-order companies, such as Lands' End; and (f) traditional stores, such as bakeries and small hardware stores. E-commerce dealing was not significant at the time of the study.

These different store formats offer different value propositions to their customers. Mass merchandisers and, to a lesser extent, out-of-town specialty chains and mail order compete mainly by offering low prices (table 10.4).

In-town specialty chains and department stores compete more by offering high service levels, for example in the form of a targeted selection of merchandise. The traditional stores that remain survive by offering high service, usually in the form of convenient locations. In general, mass merchandisers and specialty chains are more productive than the other store types, and in both the United States and Europe the industry is shifting toward these formats.

Measuring Retail Service

The coexistence of in-town specialty chains with mass merchandisers despite value added to sales ratios that are over twice as high can only be explained if these specialty chains are providing extra service that customers value.[9] Given that the level of service provided by retailers can differ

---

9. Part of the difference in the gross margin-to-sales ratio can be explained by the fact that mass merchandisers specialize in fast-moving, lower margin goods, but there are also significant cross-format differences in prices for the same categories or even the same items. One can usually find items more cheaply at mass merchandisers like Wal-Mart, but many prefer a shorter drive and the greater availability of informed sales personnel in specialty chains.

Table 10.4 Productivity, Throughput and Service Level of Retail Formats (Index: Mass merchandisers = 100)

	Mass Merchandisers	Out-of-Town Specialty Chains	In-Town Specialty Chains	Department Stores	Mail-Order	Traditional Stores
Gross margin per hours worked	100	100	80	90	80	60
Sales per hour worked	100	70	35	55	70	25
Gross margin per sales	100	140	230	160	110	240

Note: Index is based on U.S. data. Traditional stores attain high margins partly by locating in areas underserved by more advanced formats.
Source: McKinsey Global Institute and the Max Geldens Foundations for Societal Renewal (1997).

so much, we rejected a simple throughput measure of retailing output. In principle, what we would like to measure is the value added[10] of retailers at some set of international prices. But this is complicated. Retail prices are available for food and general merchandise goods from the OECD and International Comparisons Project (ICP) PPP projects, but these retail prices are not usually collected in comparable formats (in part because comparable formats do not always exist), and wholesale prices are harder to obtain. As a result, double-deflated PPPs that truly reflect the cost (in terms of the gross margin a consumer must pay) of retailing service are essentially impossible to construct.

Because the ideal measure was not feasible, we considered two alternatives.[11] The first was to use the PPP for consumption as a measure of the "opportunity cost" of consuming retail service vis-à-vis other consumer goods and services. The rationale for using the consumption goods PPP is that the general price level of all consumption goods should give one at least an unbiased estimate of the price level of a specific consumption good, retail service. The problem with this method was revealed when we studied countries with very high relative retail wages (at PPP), such as France and Sweden. High retail wages increase our measured labor productivity for two reasons. The first is that high wages encourage retailers to forego providing marginal services, such as grocery bagging.[12] By eliminating jobs with low marginal labor productivity, average labor productivity should rise; this effect we would like to capture in our measure. Unfortunately, high relative retail wages also force up the relative price of retail service, which causes our measure to overstate retail productivity. Because we cannot construct a retailing service PPP, we cannot correct for this effect.

The retailing study made in the Netherlands attempted to overcome this problem by using, essentially, a same-format PPP. It is based on the assumption that the absolute productivity level of out-of-town specialized chains is similar in the Netherlands and the United States, because the retail concept applied in this format is very similar in the two countries. This assumption implies that the service and efficiency levels (value added per good and the number of goods sold per hour) are comparable, as is productivity. We used the absolute productivity level of out-of-town spe-

---

10. For retail, gross margin and value added are essentially equal. In the exposition of the methodology, we use the terms interchangeably in order to get concepts across more easily. In calculating our results, we mainly used data on gross margin because it is more widely available.

11. Actually, the Dutch team also used a third method that we are not reporting that adjusts for format mix only. See McKinsey Global Institute and the Max Geldens Foundations for Societal Renewal (1997).

12. One might have expected retailers to respond to high wages by substituting capital for labor, but because structures and rent (the main component of capital in retailing) are also more expensive in Europe, the main difference is the absence of marginal services in Europe.

cialized chains as a bridge and combined it with relative format productivities within each country (captured by relative values added per hour for the different formats within each country) to calculate absolute format productivities. We calculated retail sector productivity in each country by weighting the absolute format productivity with the share in retail employment of each format. This method actually calculates relative productivities rather than retail outputs, but there is an implied relative output figure computed by multiplying retail sector productivity by the number of hours worked. The implicit assumption is that when a U.S. Toys "R" Us employs more workers than a European Toys "R" Us to generate the same quantity of sales, it is producing 30 percent more retailing service. Toys "R" Us does provide more service in the United States; its opening hours are longer; and check out lines shorter. However, it may be an overestimate to say that extra employees translate into extra service one for one.

Unfortunately, the data were only available to apply this method to the U.S. comparison with the Netherlands. This approach suggests a higher relative productivity in the United States than does the regular PPP comparison. It may go too far and overstate the value of customer service in the United States, but it does provide a new estimate of the quantitative impact of the service component.

10.4.2 Productivity Results

The productivity results using the OECD PPPs indicate that retailing productivity is pretty much the same among the European countries and the United States. Using OECD PPPs, the productivity at the U.K., U.S., France, and German industries is 108, 105, 101, and 101, respectively, with the Netherlands indexed to 100. This similarity reflects two offsetting forces. The United States has fewer low productivity traditional or mom-and-pop stores (fig. 10.2). Its low relative wages in retail allow for more marginal services to be provided and may lower the relative price of retail service, causing our value added at consumption PPP to underestimate U.S. productivity.

The result of the United States–Netherlands comparison using the format bridge approach raises U.S. relative productivity by about 15 percent. This could be an overstatement of the difference. As we noted earlier, comparable formats tend to have higher staffing levels in the United States, and the bridge assumption implicitly says that the additional staff have the same average productivity as the intramarginal employees. That likely overstates their productivity, and the true U.S. productivity figure is probably between these two estimates.

Although productivity levels are fairly similar in the United States and Europe, U.S. retailing output and employment are 50 to 80 percent higher. Higher output is only partly due to 20 to 40 percent higher U.S. consumption of retailed goods. The U.S. format mix is shifted toward more service-

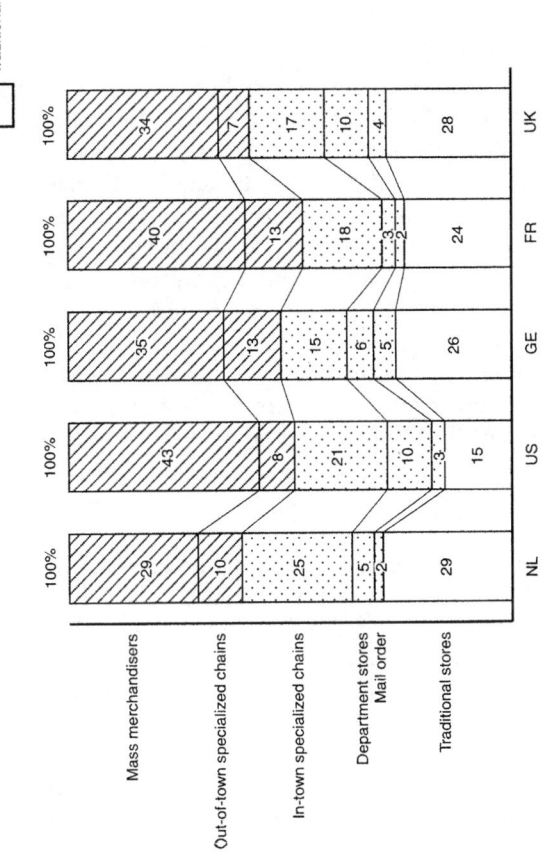

Fig. 10.2 International comparison of market shares of retail formats, 1994 (percent of total sales)

Source: McKinsey Global Institute and the Max Geldens Foundation for Societal Renewal 1997

intensive formats such as in-town specialty chains, and U.S. stores provide more service in a given format—in the form of longer opening hours, more sales assistance, shorter checkout lines, and so on. The less output and employment-intensive European format mix is partly due to zoning laws that prevent the development of shopping centers where in-town specialty chains can be successful. The lower employment and service levels within given formats is mainly due to high minimum wages and social costs, which cut off the lower edge of the employment distribution. This results in fewer open checkouts, no queue busters, shorter opening hours, less cleaning of the stores, fewer customer representatives, and no bag packers.

10.4.3 Lessons from the Retailing Case

The McKinsey retail practice told us back when the original service sector study was carried out some years ago that this industry in the U.S. is highly competitive and innovative. Aggregate data that suggested weak productivity growth in retailing seemed implausible to them and suggested that the data may be missing the shift in U.S. retailing employment toward specialty and higher service retailing formats where throughput per employee is low. The most obvious sign of this is the rapid growth of shopping malls. Ever since, we have been trying to capture the productivity differences that occur in cross-country comparisons because of the very different evolutions of retailing in the United States and other countries.

We believe that the format bridge approach is an appealing way to approach the problem. The PPPs are based on efforts to compare like goods to like goods. We have tried to compare like retailing service to like retailing service. As long as these bridges are competing in a major way in markets in the different countries, they can provide a PPP equivalent.

The lesson for the measurement of output and productivity over time in the United States is not a new one. Retailing is a service industry, not just a conveyor belt to bring the goods to customers. Fueled by the availability of cheap land and low wage labor, and facilitated by format evolution and information technology, the United States has sharply increased its consumption of this retailing service. Parts of the retailing sector have sought competitive advantage through low prices or convenience, whereas other parts offer specialized inventories, advice and luxurious surroundings. We are not aware that current price and output measures attempt to capture the way in which the quality of retailing service has changed over time. The productivity measure from the McKinsey Netherlands team was just a start, but it suggested that the impact of service quality differences may be quantitatively significant.

10.5 Public Transportation

Almost all of the McKinsey industry case studies have been of industries in the market portion of the economy—that is, where market-based transactions and pricing typically prevail.[13] This was mainly by design; productivity comparisons are much more difficult where there is not a market valuation of output, and McKinsey's experience has traditionally been in the market economy. Recently, however, our European consulting practice has been developing more expertise in nontraditional areas like the provision of public services. Given the privatization and reform of public services that have taken place in Europe in recent years, our Netherlands office felt that these services might represent an important area of improvement potential for the Dutch economy. We selected public transportation as an industry in which output was relatively straightforward to measure yet had also been historically sheltered from market forces in the Netherlands.

10.5.1 Productivity Measurement

In the telecom case we defined output as including both the use of telecom services (call minutes) and the creation of the option to use telecom services (access lines). Public transportation is another industry in which the provision of an option to use services is an important component of output. Two half-full buses running a route every thirty minutes represent more output than a full bus running a route every hour. Even though the same number of people travel, those that traveled had more choices about when to travel, and thus experience a higher degree of convenience. This higher convenience is similar to that associated with having phone lines in every apartment (rather than a common phone in the hallway), more frequent flight connections due to a hub-and-spoke system, faster turn around times on a mortgage, or a conveniently located retail shop with exactly the fashions you want to buy.

Assigning a value to more convenient service is at least as difficult in public transportation as it is in other services. In retail, one can observe the margins paid in discounters and more focused specialty retailers that compete for the same customers and attribute the difference in margin to the extra value offered by the specialty store. But in public transportation more convenient and less convenient systems do not compete directly, and even when they do, fares are usually not as "market-determined" as are margins in retail.

As in the other industries (telecom, banking, and airlines) in which we have had difficulty deriving a market valuation of convenience, in public transportation we approached this issue from the input requirement side. In public transportation, labor input requirements are most directly deter-

---

13. All told, the McKinsey Global Institute has studied eight service industries (airlines, banking, film/TV/video, public transportation, restaurants, retail, software, and telecom) and twelve goods-producing industries (auto, auto parts, beer, computer hardware, construction, consumer electronics, furniture, metal working, processed food, semiconductors, soap and detergents, and steel). We have conducted country studies of Australia, Brazil, France, Germany, Japan, Korea, the Netherlands, and Sweden.

mined by the vehicle kilometers of service offered, not the passenger kilometers consumed. We collected data separately for four different modes of passenger transportation (long distance train, metro/subways, trams, and buses) in order to test for possible mix effects.

A difficulty in comparing productivity across countries is that city size and structure can influence the viability and efficiency of public transportation. In order to ensure that these differences were not driving the results, we compared five cities with similar populations, sizes of bus/tram/metro networks, and roughly similar population densities: Amsterdam, Rotterdam, Stuttgart, Zurich, and Stockholm. The city results broadly confirmed the results we obtained at the country level.

10.5.2 Productivity Results

Sweden had the highest productivity at the country level, and Stockholm had by far the highest productivity in our city comparison (table 10.5). The Netherlands placed fifth out of seven in our country comparison, ahead of only France and Germany, whereas Rotterdam and Amsterdam were third and fifth out of five in the city comparison. The Swedish productivity advantage was so large that despite higher service frequencies and lower usage, passenger kilometers per hour worked were also higher in Sweden (table 10.6).

Why was Sweden more productive? Two possibilities were that Sweden had a more productive mix of modes or that Sweden was obtaining higher labor productivity at the expense of low capital productivity. But Sweden had significantly higher productivity in both long-distance trains and in buses/trams/metros, and the productivity differences across buses/trams/metros were insignificant. Annual loaded hours per vehicle were roughly the same in Sweden and the Netherlands (18 percent higher and 13 percent lower in trains and buses/trams/metros in Sweden, respectively), suggesting that capital-labor substitution did not account for the differences.

The most important reason that labor productivity was higher in Sweden was simply that labor was more efficiently utilized. Driver, maintenance, and overhead labor were 30 to 50 percent lower per vehicle-hour in Stockholm than in Amsterdam or Rotterdam. In Amsterdam only 35 percent of paid driver time is actually spent driving, compared with 59 percent in Stockholm. In addition, average driving speeds are higher in Stockholm due to lower levels of congestion and higher penetration of high-speed rail.

Part of the difference in labor utilization is due to work rules. Work rules in public transportation are designed to provide security and protection for employees and passengers; but if applied too rigidly, these rules can have the side effect of lowering productivity. For example, in the Netherlands drivers are permitted a fifteen-minute break every four hours of driving to reduce fatigue and improve safety. When buses operate on hourly

Table 10.5 International and City Comparison of Economic Performance in the Public Transportation Sector, 1995 (Index: NL = 100; and AM = 100)

	Netherlands	France	Germany	Switzerland	United Kingdom	Japan	Sweden
Output	100	79	97	193	169	135	215
Labor productivity	100	61	87	113	125	144	188
Employment	100	131	111	171	136	93	115

	Amsterdam	Rotterdam	Stuttgart	Zurich	Stockholm
Output	100	148	103	367	347
Labor productivity	100	169	152	243	415
Employment	100	87	68	151	84

Source: McKinsey Global Institute and the Max Geldens Foundations for Societal Renewal (1997).

Table 10.6 Alternative Productivity Comparisons between Country and City, 1995 (Index: NL = 100; and AM = 100)

	Country Comparison		City Comparison		
	Netherlands	Sweden	Amsterdam	Rotterdam	Stockholm
Demand productivity					
Passenger kilometers per hour worked	100	130	100	100	261
Supply productivity					
Vehicle kilometers per hour worked	100	188	100	169	415
Vehicle utilization					
Passengers per vehicle	100	69	100	59	63

Source: McKinsey Global Institute and the Max Geldens Foundations for Societal Renewal (1997).

schedules, however, tight adherence to this rule can reduce labor usage significantly because the actual running time of the route can only be forty-five minutes. Otherwise, the fifteen-minute break every four hours would throw off the entire schedule. Allowing one five-minute break every hour would both provide more break time and increase productivity. In addition to this rule, Dutch public transportation is also subject to numerous other rules, mandating, for example, a five-minute boarding/mounting time, a twenty-minute turn-out time, a four-minute walking time after breaks, a second paid break after seven hours of accumulated working time, and in some locations (including Amsterdam) a fifteen- to twenty-minute end-of-the-line break. In Sweden, unions have allowed work rule revisions that enhance productivity in exchange for higher pay, and drivers have an incentive to contribute to higher utilization due to performance-based wages.

The emphasis on productivity in Sweden can be traced partly to increased market competition. Since 1989, local and regional bus, tram, and metro services have been exposed to competition through competitive bidding for three- to five-year concessions for parts of local/regional networks. The essential feature of this system is that local governments first decide on the service frequency desired, and then the operators compete on the cost to fulfill these service requirements. To minimize entry barriers in the operation of services, the local authorities have split the incumbent public transportation companies into two parts: One, which remains closely related to local government, is responsible for planning and designing the network, owns the rolling stock, and runs the bidding process for specific concessions. The other part of the incumbent companies was split into operational companies that compete for the concessions. Around 70 percent of bus, tram, and metro services are now managed this way in Sweden. Similar bidding systems have been put in place in other high productivity countries: the United Kingdom and Japan. Labor utilization and productivity have increased more rapidly in countries in which market competition has been introduced, and service frequencies have generally increased, not decreased as might have been feared. From 1980 to 1995, productivity increased 71 and 45 percent in the United Kingdom and Sweden, both of which introduced market competition, but increased only 20 and 12 percent in the Netherlands and France, which did not.

10.5.3 Lessons from the Public Transport Case

Public transport provides another example of a service industry that produces outputs that are difficult to value at market prices. In this industry, as in banking, telecom, and airlines, productivity measures can be developed by assuming that the economic value of a standardized output is related to the input required to produce it. What we learn from our public transportation case (and from banking, telecom, and airlines) is that meaningful measures of cross-country output and productivity can be developed using relatively simple methodologies; that is, they result in measures of productivity that are consistent with what detailed knowledge of the production processes in the industry would lead one to expect.

10.6 Airlines

The airline industry is only a small part of the economy, but it is one that is studied intensively. It is an industry that provides some useful lessons about the effects of regulation and government ownership and the impact of changes in the quality of service. In particular, customer value in this industry is driven heavily by the ability of airlines to provide frequent service between any two destinations. In the United States this has meant that once the industry was deregulated, the major airlines soon found it essential to their competitive positions to develop the hub-and-spoke system.[14] This system results in some obvious congestion costs. As multiple flights arrive together at a hub, passengers find a congested terminal; ground personnel have to service the planes all at the same time; and air traffic controllers face take-off and landing delays. The European industry has only recently been deregulated, and indeed is still not fully competitive, so it has been slower to develop hub and spoke. But the same forces are now driving that industry also.

10.6.1 Productivity Measurement

The main international productivity comparison was between a sample of nine U.S. airlines (America West [HP], American Airlines [AA], Continental [CO], Delta [DL], Northwest [NW], Southwest [SW], Trans World [TW], United [UA], and US Airways [US]), and eight European airlines (Air France [AF], Alitalia [AZ], British Airways [BA], Iberia [IB], KLM [KL], Lufthansa [LH], SAS [Scandinavian; SK], and Swissair [SR]). As part of our studies of Brazil and Korea, we have also looked at productivity in the airlines of these two countries (Varig, VASP, Transbrasil, TAM, and Rio Sul [a subsidiary of Varig] for Brazil; and Korean Air and Asiana for Korea). We will discuss briefly the productivity findings for these industries also and how they differ from the United States and Europe.

We have estimated both labor and capital productivity, allowing an estimate of total factor productivity for the industries. For capital productivity we consider only the capital services from airplanes. The main reason for excluding IT and ground equipment is the difficulty in obtaining reliable numbers. Also, IT and ground equipment amount to only a small fraction

---

14. Even prior to deregulation there were elements of a hub-and-spoke system, as busy airports such as Atlanta or Chicago were frequently points of plane changes. However, regulation prevented the full development of the system with multiple hubs and complete spokes.

of the total physical capital stock of an airline (approximately 25 percent). We estimate the current market value of all the planes of the carriers included in this study and depreciate it over the remaining lifetime of the plane (maximum lifetime = 25 years). Leased aircraft are treated the same as purchased aircraft. The physical output for capital productivity is revenue passenger kilometers (RPK).

For labor productivity we followed a business activity approach that is natural for business consultants and is quite revealing in terms of diagnosing the reasons for the productivity differences, but that is not a standard approach among economists. Each functional group of employees was assigned an output measure reflecting the particular tasks they were engaged in, and the productivities of each employee group were weighted by labor shares, as in banking and telecom. For cabin attendants we used RPK; for ground handling and ticketing we used number of passengers flown; and for pilots and maintenance we used hours flown. Because the two products of "getting onto the plane" and "being flown X kilometers from point A to point B" are not separately priced, this approach (which is equivalent to weighting the functional outputs with unit labor requirements) provides an automatic adjustment for differences in stage length. In this way it is better than the traditional method of using only RPK, because this approach captures the fact that three 1,000-mile flights are typically priced higher, require more input, and provide more customer value than one 3,000-mile flight. We did check our results, however, using an overall measure of RPK per employee; and because average stage lengths are not very different across the countries we studied,[15] we obtained roughly similar results.

The labor productivity numbers are adjusted for differences in degree of third-party outsourcing of ground handling, ticket sales, and maintenance among the comparison countries. We also excluded cargo-only employers to be consistent with our output measures. The data used throughout this case study are drawn from international aviation databases and reports, including statistics provided by the International Air Transport Association (IATA) and the U.S. Department of Transportation (DOT). The information for Brazil was also obtained from the Departamento de Aviacao Civil (DAC).

10.6.2 Productivity Results

Table 10.7 shows the labor, capital, and TFP results for Europe, Brazil, and Korea, with the United States indexed to 100 for 1995. We found that the European airlines operated with about two-thirds the labor productiv-

---

15. Average stage lengths are much longer for airlines like Qantas and Singapore Airlines. This is one reason why studies that use only RPK as an output measure can yield misleadingly high relative productivity for these airlines.

Table 10.7   Airline Productivity, 1995 (U.S. = 100)

	TFP[a]	Labor Productivity	Capital Productivity
United States	100	100	100
Europe	75	66	92
Brazil	61	47	79
Korea		100	

Source: McKinsey Global Institute (1998a).
[a]TFP = (Labor Productivity)$^{0.5}$ × (capital productivity)$^{0.5}$

ity of the United States; Brazil had productivity less than half; but Korea had the same level of productivity as the United States. When MGI compared the United States to Europe in an earlier study, we found that European labor productivity was 79 percent of the U.S. amount. Moreover, the earlier study estimated productivity on a per-employee basis without adjustments for the differences in hours worked per full-time employee—an adjustment that would have raised European productivity. Although the sample of airlines was somewhat different in the earlier study, these figures suggest that Europe has fallen further behind the United States in the six-year interval after 1989.

The gaps in capital productivity, reflecting differences in RPK per plane, were much smaller, with the United States and Europe being essentially the same, and Brazil at almost 80 percent of the United States figure. Data on the stock of planes in Korea was not available. The European airlines are able to maintain about the same aircraft utilization as the U.S. airlines. The load factors are lower in Brazil. The TFP figures give equal weight to labor and capital, reflecting a rough estimate of the income shares in value added.

Figure 10.3 shows the breakdown of the labor productivity figure into the performance of the different groups of workers.

The most striking differences in operations occur in the ground personnel, including handling, maintenance, ticketing, sales and promotion, and other. As in the prior study, we found substantial overstaffing in these activities, reflecting the legacy of state-owned companies, inflexible workrules that reduce multitasking, and weak competitive pressure for cost reduction.[16] The airlines in Brazil have many of the characteristics of the European airlines, only more so. Varig was state owned until fairly recently and is now employee owned. It has received substantial tax breaks to maintain solvency. Aggressive competitors such as TAM are entering the domestic market, but slots and route allocations are controlled by the Air

---

16. British Airways, the European carrier that has been privatized and that competes against U.S. carriers, has productivity comparable to the U.S. airlines.

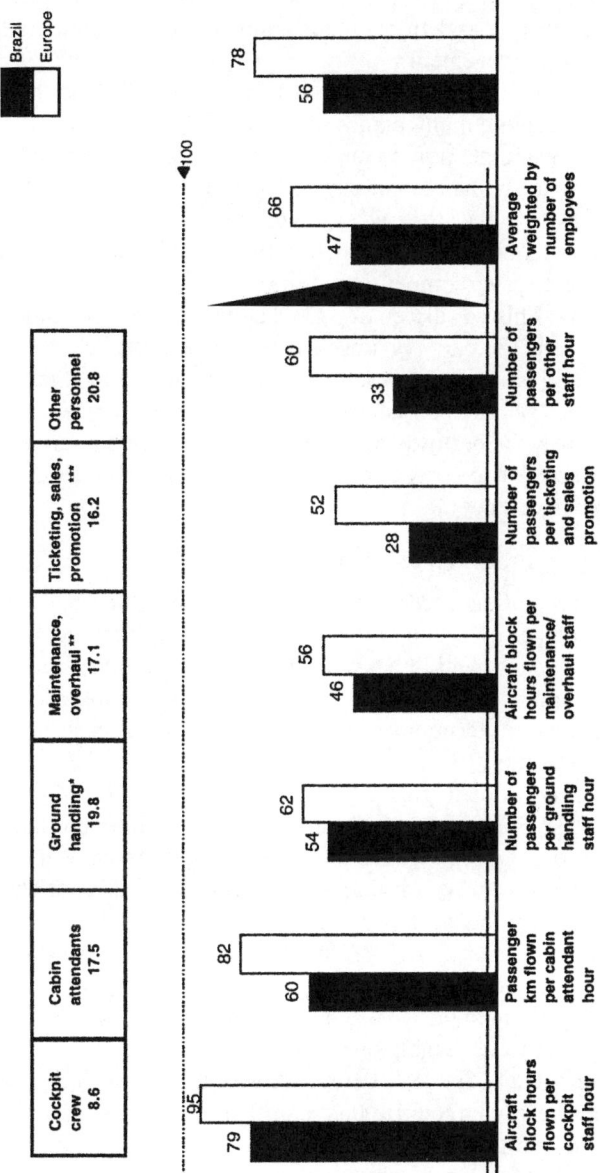

Fig. 10.3 Labor productivity levels in the airline industry, 1995 (U.S. productivity = 100)
Source: McKinsey Global Institute (1998a)
* Adjusted for 10% higher outsourcing to third parties for Brazil
** Adjusted for different degree of third party outsourcing
*** Adjusted for different percentage of tickets sold through airlines directly

Force. Brazil also suffers from IT inefficiencies. Importation of IT was prohibited for many years and remains costly. The Brazilian airlines in 1995 were behind Europe and the United States in using computers for scheduling and load management.

The differences in maintenance productivity reflect in part the impact of standardization. Having many planes of the same type (Southwest has all 737s) gives an advantage in maintenance. The U.S. airlines are able to reap economies of scale in maintenance, whereas Brazil has too few planes and too many types of planes for efficient operation.

We obtained less detailed information about Korea. Unlike many cases in Korea there is fierce price competition in the industry even though there are only two players. This has driven down ticket prices (average domestic air fares in 1995 were 13 cents per km in the United States, 19 cents in Brazil, and 8 cents in Korea) and promoted cost reduction and efficiency, at least in labor use. We have consistently found that intense price competition in an industry is the best way to force high productivity, but it is not always true that having two competing companies is sufficient, as apparently it is for Korean airlines.

10.6.3 The Impact of the Hub-and-Spoke System

Shortly after deregulation freed managers to restructure their networks, the U.S. industry moved to a hub-and-spoke network. By the mid-1980s, the hub-and-spoke system had already revolutionized the U.S. airline industry; and at the end of the decade, U.S. airlines operated about 30 hubs that, in terms of flight pattern and frequency, produce a different output than do nonhub airports.

The hub technology is distinguished from the operation of a large airport or homebase like Frankfurt or London-Heathrow by the coordination of the incoming and outgoing flights and the resulting flight pattern. Several times during the day, waves of flights come in and leave again about 60 to 90 minutes later. In between passengers from any arriving flight can transit to a connecting flight. In 1989 for instance, Northwest's hub in Minneapolis/St. Paul had about eight waves or banks per day with the biggest departure peaks at about 9:00 A.M., 1:00 P.M., and 6:00 P.M. to 7:00 P.M. The arrival peaks were roughly one hour earlier.

The transition created by the 1978 deregulation of the U.S. airline industry has sometimes been characterized as a shift from a linear system of direct nonstop and one-stop flights to a hub-and-spoke system involving connections at a set of central points where passengers are exchanged among flights. This is misleading because the frequency of passengers making connections barely changed, from 28 percent in 1978 to 32 percent in 1993 (Morrison and Winston 1995). Instead, what happened was that major carriers that had previously established hub operations serving a restricted set of spokes were allowed to increase the number of spokes served from large hubs like Chicago and Atlanta greatly, whereas other carriers (some previously small regional airlines) established competing hubs that came to be dominated by a single carrier, sometimes as the result of a merger between two carriers previously serving the same hub. As the largest carrier in each hub city expanded into all the feasible spoke cities, competing airlines that previously had possessed protected rights on those routes were forced to abandon them. The result was the virtual elimination of interline connections, which in 1978 had represented 14 percent of all passengers and half of all connections. The remaining two-thirds of passengers who did not make connections in 1993 were served, as in 1978, by an abundance of nonstop flights on busy city-pair markets, both short-haul and transcontinental, and by nonstop flights on many new routes to spokes from the several new hubs.

The transformation of the U.S. airline industry to the hub-and-spoke system was driven by demand and revenues, rather than by cost. Given the traffic dispersion in the United States and given customers' desires for frequency between origination and destination cities, the hub-and-spoke technology is the only economical way to offer fast and frequent air transportation at times convenient to most of the travelers. Consequently, the carrier that could offer an advanced hub-and-spoke network could attract more customers and gain a competitive advantage over its competitors.

Whereas the hub-and-spoke system has increased service quality and variety for most of the customers (particularly higher frequency of flights), we think that this innovation has generally had a negative impact on measured labor and capital productivity, given that we are not able to measure the added customer value as an output. The productivity price for the hub-and-spoke technology is extremely peak-driven operations at the hub, with unfavorable implications for labor and capital utilization. This means that our physical output measures are missing an important qualitative aspect of the U.S. airline industry—namely the overall network performance, or the ability to provide frequent services to hundreds of destinations in a reasonable time. To the benefit of the consumer, this output quality is provided at the expense of higher factor inputs, without being captured in our productivity measure.

10.6.4 Lessons from the Airline Study

The main implication for productivity measurement from our case study is that improvements in the quality of service should be considered in a correct measure of output for this industry. Airlines advertise the quality of their food and the friendliness of their personnel (arguably attributes of service that have deteriorated since deregulation), but it is MGI's conclusion from working with many airlines around the world that frequency and reliability of service are the key factors in service quality, particularly among business travelers. This means that the industry developed a major innovation in the 1980s in the hub-and-spoke system after deregulation, the benefits of which were not captured in productivity measures. Quantitative estimates of the productivity penalty associated with hub-and-spoke or of the increased customer value from increased service would have been valuable. Since the development of this system has been the principal structural change occurring in this industry since 1980, it is likely that its impact on true productivity has been substantial.

This conclusion bears on the debate about the impact of IT. As we have seen from the experience of Brazil, operating a point-to-point airline with inadequate IT exacts a productivity penalty. Operating a hub-and-spoke system without IT would be impossible. The share of IT hardware in the total capital stock of the industry is small. The impact of the technological change facilitated by IT has been large.

10.7 Summary and Conclusions

The first step in correctly measuring the output of an industry is to understand that industry: how it is changing and how this change is being driven by consumer demand. Although we have used relatively simple measures of output in the service industries we have studied, we have generally been able to satisfy ourselves that the resulting productivity comparisons make sense in terms of what is going on at the production process level and how the industries are evolving.

In banking, we found that an index of output, based on the three main functions of retail banks, performed pretty well as an indicator of relative performance. An important lesson from this work is that shifting to electronic funds transfers has a very large impact on productivity. In general, MGI has found that increased competition improves productivity, but banking in the Netherlands provides one example where a relatively concentrated industry was able to make the shift in technology more easily. Hopefully, government coordination through Federal Reserve actions will accomplish the same goal in the United States while maintaining competitive intensity.

Despite the useful lesson from the simple output measure in banking, the case illustrates the limitations of our measurement. An important change in the mortgage industry has been the introduction of streamlined processes and computerized credit assessments. This has reduced the intermediation margin and speeded up the approval of loans. Neither of these changes in cost or in quality is captured in our output measure or in others that we know of. Further, the growth of the securities industry has been very rapid. Much of the activity consists of selling services and giving investment advice, and the intrinsic value of both activities is hard to value. An additional issue has arisen when we have extended our analysis to countries such as Korea, whose banking system allocated loans without adequate concern for the returns and found itself with a seriously bad debt problem even prior to the current crisis. Measuring banking output on the wholesale side would pose new challenges.

The banking case gave clear evidence of the importance of IT on productivity. ATMs, check processing equipment, use of terminals to access information, call centers, loan processing, and of course electronic funds transfers are all important in this industry.

Looking forward, we anticipate substantial changes in the retail banking industry. It is possible that the main functions currently carried out by banks will migrate to other institutions. To an extent this has already happened, as specialized lending institutions have taken over large parts of the credit card and mortgage markets. Retailers already provide ATMs, credit cards, and cash-back services and may expand to offer most or all of the current services provided by banks. Unless measurement approaches evolve with the industry, errors may worsen in the future.

In telecom there are three main attributes of service in developed countries: the access line, the call minutes, and the mobility of the call. We were able to capture two of these. Clearly, as Hausman (1997) has shown, it would be possible to capture the value of the third element. We have ourselves explored a hedonic or conjoint approach to the problem in which we would be able to price mobility, given the alternate pricing schemes in effect in different countries, but we did not complete the task. In the developing country context, problems such as noise on the line, lack of call completion, and cutoffs become important elements in service quality. They remind us that over the long term, service quality has greatly increased in the United States.

Going forward, we expect that new technology will allow major improvements in service variety and quality. High-speed data transmission will allow new services to be provided. It is likely that phone service with picture as well as sound will improve in quality and become more common. The phone companies will soon allow people to have a single number and have calls that track the location of the person. (Hopefully one will be able to switch such services off as well as on.)

Information technology, notably digital switching, bill processing, and cellular service, has been important to productivity in this industry. It will be central to the changes in service going forward.

Retail has been the industry where measurement has been most difficult for our studies to resolve satisfactorily. This is one of the largest industries in the United States. It has changed dramatically over time, and employment has grown. It is a sector where consumers clearly value its output. The evolution of retailing formats from traditional stores to discounters, category killers, and high-service specialty stores has transformed the industry; indeed, it has transformed the cities and suburbs. Given the difficulties we have experienced in our cross-country comparisons, we are in no position to preach to the statistical agencies about how to solve the measurement problem. However, we know there is a problem that needs to be solved.

The continuing trend in the industry is that discounters invade the product and service lines that are started by innovations among the specialty players. This lowers prices to consumers and passes back to them the benefits of innovation, a process familiar in all industries. Without new measurement methods, however, productivity growth will continue to be understated.

Information technology has played an important role in this industry in allowing retailers to eliminate the wholesale function and work directly with manufacturers. IT speeds checkout and tracks inventory. It allows companies to track demand and focus on the items consumers want.

Adequate tracking and benchmarking of public services can provide a spur to improved performance in the public sector. The Netherlands study made benchmark comparisons of public transportation services productivity, revealing the very high price paid by riders in Amsterdam for the work rules and restrictions in place in that city. Given the size and importance of the public sector, such benchmarking studies have tremendous potential importance.

Recent improvements in BLS tracking of discount fares have improved the measurement of prices and hence real output in the airline industry. Now that the hub-and-spoke system is firmly in place, changes in service frequency and reliability may or may not be major factors in service quality change going forward. In order to understand the historical development of productivity in the industry, however, it would be essential to factor in the effect of this innovation.

This industry has been adjusting to the impact of deregulation over the past several years. New entry has changed the competitive intensity and forced major restructuring. That process continues and it may or may not induce new innovations in service quality going forward.

Information technology was an important element in overall productivity for the industry. It allows for more efficient use of resources and means that companies can operate with the increased complexity of hub and spoke.

10.7.1 Common Themes

For the purposes of international comparisons, we have concluded that simple physical output measures work surprisingly well. These output measures can be related to the inputs used in their delivery, as we saw in banking, telecom, and airlines. We can make adjustments to the basic measures for quality differences, or we can ignore those that do not seem to make a substantive difference to the overall conclusions we reach about the causes of productivity differences. The one case where a simple physical measure was inadequate—retailing—is the case that was hard to solve any other way.

Analyses of these case study industries suggest that the simple output measures will be much less adequate for productivity growth over time. The knowledge that MGI can offer in this area is to point to the most important drivers of industry change. If the data collection techniques in use are not capturing the impact of industry evolution, then they are likely to be substantially in error. We have seen plenty of evidence of the importance of quality change and convenience.

A possible general approach to improving the measurement of these convenience and quality changes is to measure and value convenience-related customer time savings and to use hedonics to estimate market valuations of service quality differences where possible. Developing exact procedures will obviously require further study, but our cross-country findings suggest that quality and convenience are potentially very important sources of error.

All of the cases, with the possible exception of public transportation, showed that IT was a vital component of the industry business systems. Based on what we learned of these industries, the value of computer hardware was only a small component of total capital and, on a growth accounting basis, IT would make only a small contribution to labor productivity. Nevertheless, we found that the current business systems in these industries would be impossible without IT. A substantial increment to productivity is associated with its use. Brazil, which had specific regulations about IT purchases, and had productivity limited by inadequate IT in airlines and banks illustrates this point.

References

Council of Economic Advisers. 2001. *Economic report of the president.* Washington, D.C.: GPO.

Hausman, Jerry A. 1997. Valuing the effect of regulation on new services in telecommunications. *Brookings Papers on Economic Activity: Microeconomics, 1997,* 1–54.

McKinsey Global Institute and the Max Geldens Foundations for Societal Renewal. 1997. *Boosting Dutch economic performance.* Amsterdam: McKinsey & Co.

McKinsey Global Institute. 1998a. *Productivity—The key to an accelerated development path for Brazil.* Washington, D.C.: McKinsey & Company.

McKinsey Global Institute. 1998b. *Driving productivity and growth in the U.K. economy.* Washington, D.C.: McKinsey & Company.

Morrison, Steven, and Clifford Winston. 1995. *The evolution of the airline industry.* Washington, D.C.: Brookings Institution.

Comment   Robert J. Gordon

The Baily-Zitzewitz paper continues the tradition of the McKinsey Global Institute in displaying admirable creativity and imagination to overcome seemingly intractable obstacles to making valid cross-country comparisons of levels of productivity. We emerge from the analysis with both new measures of the extent of productivity differences across countries in five industries and considerable understanding of the underlying sources of these differences. In this comment I begin by extracting from the paper some of the most interesting generalizations about the sources of cross-country productivity differences and subsequently discuss what we learn (and do not learn) about the "lessons for measurement" previewed in the paper's title. In the final section of this comment I offer a few thoughts about the treatment of airlines. To preview what comes later, my main quibble about the paper is that the lessons for measurement are directed more at the consulting community than at the practitioners of productivity measurement in national statistical offices; we learn less than one might hope about how some of the insights from the industry studies can be applied to the measurement of the time series evolution of productivity, either at the level of these five industries or for the economy as a whole.

Generalizations about the Sources of High Productivity

Perhaps the most striking of the paper's conclusions is that there is no single national model for achieving the highest productivity in every industry. Unlike the earlier McKinsey Global Institute study of the service sector (1992), in which the United States seemed to emerge as the clear leader in most industries, here the leadership role is shared, with the U.S. clearly ahead only in telecom and airlines, the Netherlands in banking, Sweden in public transport, and an ambiguous verdict in retailing (subsequently we return to the measurement issues specific to retailing). Another common theme that runs through the Baily-Zitzewitz paper is American exceptionalism, which has mixed implications for productivity, from backwardness about electronic payments in the banking industry; to admirably high usage of telephone lines; to a retailing system driven by low-cost land and lenient land-use laws; to public transit that is so nonexistent that it is not worthy of study in the paper; to a set of large airlines benefitting from economies of scale that in part reflect national geography, dispersed families, a common language, and lenient regulation of mergers.

Implicit in the paper's case studies is the generalization that government policy is capable of both harm and good. Some of the harm is created by

---

Robert J. Gordon is the Stanley G. Harris Professor in the Social Sciences at Northwestern University, a research associate of the National Bureau of Economic Research, and a research fellow of the Center for Economic Policy Research.

that age-old enemy of efficiency, namely high tariffs, evident in the paper's emphasis on the distorted prices of imported capital goods that hinder the development of the Brazilian telecom industry. Work rules in public transportation are another government-imposed source of inefficiency, as in the example of inefficient Dutch public transport contrasted with Sweden's. Shop closing hours and zoning restrictions are among the regulations cited by Baily and Zitzewitz to explain the more advanced development of mass-merchandising retail formats in the United States compared with Europe. Labor market regulations restricting the development of part-time employment interact with shop closing hours to reduce the convenience (and consumer surplus) enjoyed by European consumers compared to their American counterparts.

However, there are important measurement and policy issues that are implicit in the discussion of retailing but that never rise to the surface in the Baily-Zitzewitz presentation. Mass merchandisers achieve higher gross margins and sales per employee than do older formats and help the United States achieve its productivity advantage in retailing, but this has been achieved by a systematic and controversial set of U.S. government policies that has encouraged the development of metropolitan areas that by European standards have very low population densities. The most important policies that have steered the United States resolutely toward low density and high dispersal are the massive investment in interstate highways, which in most metropolitan areas have no tolls or user charges; the starvation of investment in public transport; the tax deductibility of mortgage interest payments, which encourages overinvestment in houses and large lots; and the dispersed governmental system, which permits local zoning regulations that restrict the minimum lot size in many suburban jurisdictions. Low density imposes numerous costs on American society that are hidden in standard productivity measures, including excessive investment in automobiles and highways that consume resources to an extent that is unnecessary in European cities, and the time and aggravation costs of suburban road congestion and long travel times from home to work. Thus the criticism of European zoning regulations for inhibiting the development of modern retailing formats implicit in the Baily-Zitzewitz paper must be set against the costs of low-density suburban development, which remain unmeasured either by the authors or in official measures of productivity.

The contrast between the European system and American system has increasingly attracted the interest of academic economists in recent years (see, for example, Gordon 1997). Low minimum wages and a relatively light burden of social security taxes in the United States greatly boost the wage for the marginal unskilled American employee, especially in the retail sector, and lead to rapid growth of employment in types of jobs that scarcely exist in some European countries, particularly grocery baggers (mentioned by Baily and Zitzewitz), buspeople in restaurants, parking lot cashiers, and valet parking attendants. Thus in the U.S. retail sector two opposing forces affect productivity in retailing compared with Europe: The low-density suburbs and lax regulations on land use encourage the rapid development of mass merchandising and out-of-town specialty formats, boosting the level of productivity, whereas the heavy use of unskilled low-wage workers for grocery bagging and other tasks reduces productivity (while creating unmeasured increases in consumer convenience).

Far from causing universal harm to productivity, government policies can actually be the source of good. The much more advanced use of electronic transfers by the European banking system, and the quaint backwardness of the U.S. banking system, is traced by the authors partly to the role of the Netherlands Postbank in taking the lead in electronic payments and forcing privately owned banks to follow. Also important in explaining U.S. backwardness is the set of government regulations that until recently prevented interstate banking and created an inefficient system of thousands of unit banks. Even to this day, a wire transfer into or out of my own personal bank account is a rare event, almost always involving a payment coming from a European source, and the instructions for making a wire transfer to my account are so complex that seven lines of text are required.[1] Another lesson for policymakers, especially in the U.S. Department of Justice, is that in some cases a high level of concentration encourages efficiency by reducing administrative overhead and encouraging innovation, whereas low level of concentration can lead to inefficiency. Although primarily implied by the Baily-Zitzewitz study of banking, this conclusion is true for the European airline industry, where fleet sizes of particular aircraft types are too small to benefit from economies of scale in aircraft maintenance.

Measurement Issues

The Baily-Zitzewitz paper grapples imaginatively with the issue of measuring output in industries with multiple unpriced outputs, such as banking and telecom. They combine volume measures of such functions as telephone access lines and call units, or in the case of banking, processing

1. The reluctance of U.S. businesses to use electronic transfers extends far beyond the banking system itself. No credit card or other national merchant that sends me bills includes codes on the bill for electronic payment. For years I used an electronic bill-paying system run by Fidelity Investments, which allowed me to avoid writing checks but which required Fidelity to print computer-written checks and physically mail them to merchants. I abandoned this system because the mailing addresses and postal box numbers of the merchants changed so rapidly that keeping Fidelity informed of the changes became a headache compared to the old-fashioned method of sticking a check in a window envelope with a pre-printed payment stub. Further, at least half my checks are written in idiosyncratic transactions that would not be worth setting up merchant numbers and account numbers for simple one-time payments to local merchants or workmen (all of whom would have electronic account numbers printed on their invoices if located in the Netherlands).

payment transactions, maintaining deposit accounts, and lending. Weights to combine the separate types of outputs are based on estimates of labor requirements rather than on costs or revenue shares, and the authors appeal to lack of data rather than theoretical purity to justify their choice. In some industries, especially airlines, there is enough data to run a regression to separate the per-passenger part of the fare from the mileage component, but the drastic change in the weight of these components after U.S. deregulation (with the per-passenger charge rising to reflect cost and the per-mile component declining substantially) reminds us that revenue weights in some industries and eras may be a reflection of regulations more than the basic economics of the industry.

We can assess the methodology in the Baily-Zitzewitz paper both within its own context, providing a consultant's expertise on the sources of productivity differences across countries, and on the more ambitious goal set forth in the paper's introduction, "to ask whether the results of these international comparisons cast any light on the problem of service sector output measurement." I have few objections to the case studies themselves. A purist might object that adjustments are introduced in an ad hoc way, as in the 5 percent adjustment for the lower quality of telecom service in Brazil. Symmetry would require a substantial adjustment to the productivity of European airlines for the higher labor requirements of ground handling caused by the costly necessity of separating domestic and international operations, and for additional expenses of remote ticket offices required by different languages and the more complex ticketing requirements of international tickets. I find adjustments in some industries and not others and wonder whether the results would be affected much (if at all) if the adjustments were equally thoroughgoing in each industry.

The paper is less successful in its broader ambition of providing lessons for the measurement of productivity in the services sector at the level of national statistical agencies. The central problem is that the basic mission of statistical agencies is to measure the level of labor productivity and multifactor productivity for their own economy over a time span consisting of many years and decades. Yet the paper never delves into the implications of its own analysis for the growth rate of productivity over time. For instance, the authors state that "even the BLS [U.S. Bureau of Labor Statistics] estimates may be missing changes in the true output of the sector," yet no attempt is made to substitute the authors' methodology in banking for that of the BLS or to measure the difference made by the two methodologies over, say, the last decade.

The authors' lack of interest in time series issues extends even to their unwillingness to use past evidence gathered in McKinsey (1992) to measure changes over time in the industries that both studies looked at: namely, banking, telecom, retailing, and airlines. The authors missed the opportunity to take their current weights and their measures of outputs and inputs applied equally to the data used in the 1992 study and the current study, and to calculate annualized growth rates in productivity for the years between the two sets of data, and then to have compared and analyzed differences in these growth rates from those computed in official data for the same industries, for example, by the BLS and similar sources for other countries. For instance, how rapidly would their measure of telecom productivity of access lines and call units increase compared to the current BLS estimate that output per hour in the U.S. telecom industry grew at a rate of 5.4 percent per annum and the U.S. commercial banking industry at a rate of 3.1 percent per annum over the time interval 1987–96?

Another measurement issue closely related to the Baily-Zitzewitz analysis of retailing emerges in the Boskin commission report on the U.S. Consumer Price Index (CPI), the so-called output substitution bias. There are two extreme views regarding the difference in retail prices across retailing formats. At one extreme, the official view of the CPI is that any difference in price between, say, a ma-and-pa neighborhood drug store and Wal-Mart is entirely reflected in a difference in service. If the arrival of a new Wal-Mart in town causes the price of toothpaste to drop from $2.59 at the old-format store to $1.49 at the Wal-Mart, the entire price difference of $1.10 must be due to the superior service and location of the old-format store. This is implicitly the view of Baily and Zitzewitz, who state, "We believe that the format bridge approach is an appealing way to approach the problem.... We have tried to compare like retailing service to like retailing service."

At the opposite extreme is the view that the entire price decline of $1.10 in this example represents a price decline, with no difference in quality, and that the CPI is biased upward for ignoring this decline in price and attributing the entire difference in price to a difference in service quality. The Boskin Commission report seemed to adopt this position, although when pressed, most commission members including myself would assume that the truth lies somewhere between the two positions rather at the lower extreme of ignoring any difference in service quality.

Here, however, I would like to differ with both the CPI and the Baily-Zitzewitz paper. There are three persuasive reasons to believe that consumers view most of the price reduction available "when Wal-Mart comes to town" as a true reduction in price rather than as a reduction in service quality. By far the most important reason is that consumers have been voting with their feet and their autos, flocking to Wal-Mart. The market share of discount department stores rose from 44 percent to 68 percent between 1988 and 1998 as consumers chased the lower prices. If lower prices had been completely offset by lower service quality, there would have been no shift in market shares. Second, there is no difference in service quality between the newer-format mass merchandise discount stores (Wal-Mart, Target, Kmart) and the older-format department stores that cater to the same customers (Sears and Montgomery Ward). All these stores rely on self-service, so there is no reduction in service quality when a customer shifts from old format to new format. The basic reason that the new-format stores charge lower prices is that they are more efficient, with innovative electronic inventory management systems pioneered by Wal-Mart and Target stores. Faced with this competition and fleeing customers, Montgomery Ward and Woolworths went bankrupt, further evidence that their price differential was not supported by superior service. Third, new-format stores may actually provide *superior* service. A front-page article in the *Wall Street Journal* (24 November 1999) traced part of the customer preference for Wal-Mart compared with Sears to the availability of shopping carts at the former but not the latter, and the ability to do all checking out on a single stop at exit checkout aisles in the new-format stores, instead of at separate islands in each department. This is reminiscent of the process by which grocery supermarkets made individual butcher and produce shops obsolete by combining lower prices with single rather than multiple checkouts.

When discussing upward bias in indexes of consumer prices, by far the most elusive area is the consumers' surplus provided by new products. At one point Baily and Zitzewitz allude to several ingredients that would help in the construction of a measure of the consumers' surplus provided by telephone communication, including the fact that rights to an access line in Brazil were trading at \$5,000 in a country with only 22 percent of the value of U.S. real GDP per capita, and that U.K. customers demand over 1,300 annual minutes per capita at a price of 5 cents per minute, indicating that U.S. customers enjoying free local calls are enjoying a substantial consumers' surplus. The frustrated reader vainly hopes that the authors will work out these implicit calculations and express them as a ratio to total consumption or real GDP, but the reader receives no help from the authors and wonders whether 1,300 annual minutes × \$0.05 (i.e., a mere \$65) actually warrants the adjective "large." Also, we do not learn whether the total cost of phone calls in the United States is less, or whether there is just a redistribution between light and heavy users implied by a higher access charge and lower unit cost in the United States as contrasted with the United Kingdom.[2]

The Airline Industry

Because airline management is my particular area of industry expertise, I will conclude with a few comments on the paper's treatment of airlines. The current paper is more sophisticated than the related study of airlines

---

2. Also, the presumption that local calls are typically free in the U.S. may be an obsolete observation. Local phone service in the United States has become inordinately confusing, with multiple telephone bills for the same phone line; and on inspection of my phone bill for October 1999, I discovered that for my main home phone line I had no free call privileges but instead was charged at a rate that averaged \$0.0338 per minute, hardly different from the author's quoted rate for the United Kingdom several years ago.

in the McKinsey (1992) volume but still requires a few comments and corrections.[3] The authors distinguish the U.S. hub technology, which they agree started before deregulation in 1978 but further developed (by opening new hubs and filling in missing spokes in old hubs) by the mid-1980s, from a "large airport like Frankfurt or London-Heathrow." They seem to imply that the major home bases of the large European airlines are something different than the hub-and-spoke system operated by the U.S. airlines. The only sense in which their comment is correct is that London-Heathrow is so constrained by slot limitations that of necessity arrivals and departures are spread evenly over the day and do not exhibit the peaking of scheduled banks of flights characteristic of U.S. hubs, which (other than Chicago O'Hare) are not subject to slot controls. But the other large European airports were operating hub-and-spoke systems by the early 1970s that were much more developed in the United States simply because by definition each large European airline had landing rights between its home base and each outlying spoke, whether in Europe, the United States, Asia, Africa, or Latin America. Because the only two U.S. airlines offering substantial service to Europe at that time (TWA and PanAm) funneled their passengers through New York's Kennedy airport, for many residents of U.S. cities like Chicago or San Francisco, the best and fastest way to get to most cities in Europe was to fly on a foreign airline to its hub, whether London, Amsterdam, Frankfurt, Zurich, or Paris, and continue on that same airline to the spoke city (Lisbon, Rome, etc). Today Amsterdam, Frankfurt, and Paris De Gaulle are large hubs with all the characteristics of the major U.S. airports that Baily and Zitzewitz describe, with banks or waves of flights arriving periodically, and idle periods in between. Amsterdam and De Gaulle each have six banks of flights daily, fewer than O'Hare, Atlanta, Minneapolis, and other large U.S. hubs; and the peaking of flight operations is evident in Amsterdam between 8:30 A.M. and 10:30 A.M., when seventy-five jets depart, or in Frankfurt from 12:30 P.M. to 2:00 P.M., when a like number of jet departures occur.

There is no argument with the authors' conclusion that the development of U.S. hubs was driven by demand and revenues and is doubtless cost-inefficient by peaking baggage sorting and other ground operations and leaving idle periods between. The cost inefficiency is particularly evident at smaller hubs like Northwest Airlines' operation at Memphis, with just three banks per day; and so costly are small hubs with infrequent banks that American Airlines closed down three of them (San Jose, Nashville, and Raleigh-Durham) in the early 1990s. My quibble is that this does not represent a difference between the United States and Europe, either for

---

3. I was a discussant of the published article drawn from the Baily (1992) study. The discussion of airlines in the current study adopts many of the suggestions made in my earlier comment, particularly about the nature of the transition of the U.S. route structure after deregulation.

the larger European hubs discussed here or the smaller hubs like Brussels, Zurich, Copenhagen, and Milan.

The major omission in the airline case study is the failure to recognize that at least some of the higher labor requirements of European airlines are due to the inherently more international nature of their operations. The typical European airline has a far greater percentage of its flights that cross borders to another country than does the typical U.S. airline and thus faces physical barriers within airports that require duplicate staff for domestic and international flights. The Schengen agreement that has lifted passport controls among many European countries has, if anything, made the situation more complex and labor intensive. The Frankfurt airport was required to build a whole new set of third-floor lounges so that it could service the same gates from a second-floor lounge if extra-Schengen and a third-floor lounge if intra-Schengen; and passengers are frequently required to travel by bus to aircrafts that are parked at jetways and could have been reached by foot through the regular concourses but for the rules that require bypassing passport control stations. The extra control personnel and bus drivers may in some cases be on the payroll of the airlines and others on the payroll of airports, but they doubtless account for some of the European airlines' inefficient labor use.

Finally, part of the European airlines' inefficiency is due to differences in language across the continent. On one visit I found that Lufthansa had two people working in Florence, Italy, in a ticket office servicing one flight per day. Not surprisingly, Baily and Zitzewitz show that Europe's worst functional productivity ratio is in ticket and sales personnel. Why doesn't United Airlines, which serves places like Burlington, Vermont, with two or three flights per day, have a ticket sales office in those cities? Most of the difference must be due to language. German travelers in far-off Florence want the security blanket of a Lufthansa office where they can speak German if they want to change their plans or reconfirm their reservations. Airlines in the United States do all this with monolingual continent-wide toll-free numbers.

These observations do not imply that the paper made mistakes in its analysis of airlines, but rather that it omitted some of the sources of the U.S. productivity advantage. Just as it is a time-honored principle of economics that tariffs breed inefficiency, so too it is a time-honored source of the century-long American productivity advantage that numerous industries, especially in transportation, benefit from the economies of scale implicit in a continent-wide zone free of barriers to the movement of people or goods and able to communicate in a common language. Perhaps the greatest surprise suggested by the current paper is that Americans remain so steadfastly backward in writing checks instead of carrying out their financial transactions electronically. The second greatest surprise, not discussed explicitly in the paper, is that Europe has raced far ahead of the

United States in mobile phone technology and usage by agreeing to a single standard, instead of the four competing standards in the U.S. cellular phone industry. Sometimes, it makes sense for the government to impose industry concentration and uniformity.

References

Baily, Martin Neil. 1993. Competition, regulation, and efficiency in service industries. *Brookings Papers on Economic Activity, Microeconomics:* 71–130.
Gordon, Robert J. 1997. Is there a tradeoff between unemployment and productivity growth? In *Unemployment policy: Government options for the labour market,* ed. D. Snower and G. de la Dehesa, 433–63. Cambridge: Cambridge University Press.
McKinsey Global Institute. 1992. *Service sector productivity.* Washington, D.C.: McKinsey & Co.

11   Different Approaches to International Comparison of Total Factor Productivity

Nazrul Islam

11.1 Introduction

Neoclassical economic theory has generally emphasized difference across countries in factor endowments and has devoted less attention to the possibility and actuality of difference in productivity and technology. However, empirical researchers have noticed that countries persistently differ in terms of productivity too. For a long time, international differences in total factor productivity (TFP) were studied following the time-series growth accounting approach. This methodology has reached a high level of sophistication thanks to efforts by such researchers as Kendrick, Denison, Jorgenson, and others. However, because of data constraints mainly, the application of this methodology has until recently remained limited to small samples of developed countries. Yet, from the point of view of technological diffusion and TFP-convergence, the extent and evolution of TFP difference in wider samples of countries are of particular interest. This has given rise to two new approaches to international TFP comparison. These are: (1) the cross-section growth accounting approach suggested by Hall and Jones (1996), and (2) the panel regression approach presented in Islam (1995). In this paper, we provide a comparison of methodologies of these three approaches and of results that have been presented on their basis.

The time series growth accounting approach has been implemented in

---

Nazrul Islam is assistant professor of economics at Emory University.

I would like to thank Chad Jones, the designated discussant of this paper at CRIW, for his detailed comments. Also helpful were comments by Susanto Basu, Charles Hulten, Boyan Jovanovic, Ishaq Nadiri, and other participants of the conference and the earlier NBER seminar. Thanks are also due to Dale Jorgenson for his encouragement to my work on this paper. All remaining shortcomings and errors are mine.

two forms, namely the *absolute form* and the *relative form*. The main limitation of the absolute form is that it can give TFP comparison only in terms of TFP growth rates and not in terms of TFP levels. The relative form of the time series approach overcomes this limitation. It produces TFP levels and growth rates for all years of a sample period. The more sophisticated form of time series approach, as of Jorgenson and his associates, distinguishes growth in both quality and quantity of inputs. This requires disaggregated data on different types of capital and labor and their compensation. It is difficult to find this type of data for wider samples of countries. Hence, it is likely that the application of the sophisticated version of the time series approach will remain limited to only the developed countries for some time to come.

Both the cross-section growth accounting approach and the panel regression approach have their methodological strengths and weaknesses. The advantages of the cross-section growth accounting approach are that it does not impose a specific form on the aggregate production function and does not require econometric estimation of the parameters. It also allows factor share parameter to vary across countries. However, this approach requires prior ordering of countries and is sensitive to inclusion/exclusion of countries. It also has to rely on some controversial assumptions in order to compute country specific factor shares. The panel regression approach, on the other hand, does not require prior ordering and is not that sensitive to the inclusion/exclusion issue. However, it imposes homogeneity of the share parameter across countries and requires econometric estimation based on specified functional form.

The paper compares the results in two formats. One is for the G-7 countries, and the other is for a wider sample of 96 countries. A comparison of results by Dougherty and Jorgenson (1997) and Wolff (1991) for the G-7 countries show that these agree more with regard to the *initial* TFP-level distribution of the countries than with regard to the *subsequent* TFP distribution. This implies that the two studies differ with regard of the TFP *growth* experienced by countries in the sample. These differences arise from the fact that Dougherty and Jorgenson (1997) and Wolff (1991) use different data and very different production functions for growth accounting, although both these works represent the relative form of the time-series growth accounting approach.

The comparison for 96 countries is between relative TFP level indices produced by Hall and Jones (1996) on the one hand and by Islam (1995) on the other. This comparison shows that there is more agreement with regard to the bottom end of the distribution than with regard to the top. Hall and Jones index places some rather surprising candidates at the apex of the TFP distribution. Also, the distribution as a whole is more uniform according to the Hall and Jones index than according to the Islam index. The latter yields a more bottom-heavy distribution. These differences can again be attributed to differences in data and methodology. With regard to these two indices, there is also a difference in the focus of measurement. While the Hall and Jones index was for relative productivity levels of 1988, the Islam index pertained to the 1960–85 period as a whole.

Instead of being discouraging, these differences in results can be stimulating for further research. For example, the difference in shape of distributions obtained from the Hall and Jones index and the Islam index helps to pose the question of TFP convergence. This question has already been investigated in the context of small samples of developed countries using time-series growth accounting approach. However, similar analysis is yet to be done for larger samples of countries. Also, before conclusions can be drawn regarding technological diffusion from results regarding the TFP, it is necessary to decompose the TFP into its various components. This is again something that has not yet been attempted for a large cross-section of countries. Both the cross-section growth accounting and the panel regression approach can prove fruitful in undertaking these tasks. In fact, with each year, the length of time series for all countries is getting longer. Hence, it is increasingly becoming feasible to implement even the time series growth accounting approach—if not its sophisticated version then, at least, its cruder versions—for wider samples of countries.

One such recent application has been to the East Asian countries. Young (1992, 1995) and Kim and Lau (1994) apply various forms of the time series growth accounting approach to the East Asian "tiger" economies and find that the TFP growth has very little or no role behind these economies' fast growth. However, subsequent results presented by Collins and Bosworth (1997), Klenow and Rodriguez-Clare (1997), and others show that the role of the TFP growth might not have been that minimal. The results obtained from applications of the cross-section regression methodology have also differed on this issue.

All this shows that there are considerable scope and necessity for further development of the international TFP study. All three approaches that we discuss in this paper can play important role in this regard. Results from one approach can provide useful checks on the results from the other. Moreover, the list of possible approaches is not exhausted by the above three. The *frontier approach* has also been used for international TFP comparison. This approach uses linear programming and has the additional capacity for distinguishing between improved efficiency in using existing technology and advance of the technology itself. However, this approach is also data intensive, and its application has remained limited to developed economies and specific sectors.

The paper is organized as follows. In section 11.2, we provide some broad perspective to the research on international TFP comparison. The methodologies of the three approaches to the TFP comparison are discussed and compared in section 11.3. In section 11.4 we compare the results obtained by use of these different approaches. The issue of decomposition of the TFP is discussed in section 11.5, and in section 11.6, we discuss the issue of TFP convergence. Section 11.7 discusses the controversy regarding the East Asian growth. Section 11.8 contains the concluding remarks.

11.2 Renewed Interest in the TFP Differences across Countries

In recent years, renewed interest is observed in international comparison of total factor productivity (TFP). To the extent that differences in the TFP are related to differences in technology, this indicates a certain departure from the standard neoclassical paradigm. One of the main distinctions between the Ricardian and the neoclassical trade theories concerns assumption regarding technology. While the Ricardian theory allows for long-term technology/productivity differences across countries, the neoclassical trade theory assumes that identical technology is available to all countries, and differences lie only in factor endowment.[1] Similarly, cross-country application of the neoclassical growth theory has generally proceeded on the basis of the assumption of identical production technologies. A central issue around which recent growth discussion has evolved is that of convergence, which is the hypothesis that poorer countries grow faster than richer countries so that the former eventually catch up with the latter. Convergence is an implication that has been ascribed to the neoclassical growth theory (NCGT) because of its property of diminishing returns to capital. However, along the way, the assumption of identical production technology has creeped in. This assumption, often not even recognized, has had considerable influence on the results presented in many prominent recent works on growth.

However, other researchers have not failed to notice that the assumption of identical technologies may not hold. For example, summarizing his results on inter-country comparison of productivity, Dale Jorgenson notes,

> One of the critical assumptions of the Heckscher-Ohlin theory is that technologies are identical across countries. That is a very appealing assumption, since it has been difficult to find a rationale for failures of countries to achieve the same level of technical sophistication. However, data on relative productivity levels for German, Japanese, and U.S. industries . . . reveal that the assumption of identical technologies is un-

---

1. This distinction is not that straightforward, however. The Ricardian trade theory is based on differences in labor productivity, and it did not delve into the causes of these differences. Hence it may be said that, instead of (or in addition to) differences in technology, labor productivity differences in the Ricardian theory arise from differences in factor endowment—in particular, from differences in the quantity and quality of soil. However, the fact remains that technology differences are not ruled out in the Ricardian model as it is done in the standard neoclassical trade model. For a similar discussion of the difference between neoclassical and Ricardian trade theories, see Kenen (1993, p. 46).

tenable. There is not evidence for the emergence of a regime in which the Heckscher-Ohlin assumption of identical technologies would be appropriate. We conclude that the appropriate point of departure for econometric modeling of international competitiveness is a model with perfect competition, constant returns to scale, technologies that are not identical across countries and products of identical industries that are not perfect substitutes (1995b, xxv)

Similarly, Durlauf and Johnson in their analysis of convergence, come to the conclusion that the assumption of identical production technologies may not be appropriate and suggests that "the Solow growth model should be supplemented with a theory of aggregate production differences in order to fully explain international growth patterns" (Durlauf and Johnson 1995, 365).

In the light of the above, interest in cross-country TFP-differences is a welcome development. Of course, the TFP-differences are not identical to technology-differences. There are other factors, besides differences in technology, which contribute to the computed TFP-differences. However, it is certain that technology-difference leads to TFP-difference, and in order to study the former, one has to start from the latter.

The convergence discussion has shown that there are two processes that may lead to convergence: (1) reaching similar levels of capital intensity, and (2) attaining similar levels of technology. Just as capital accumulation in a capital-shallow country can benefit from capital inflows from capital-rich countries, technological progress in a less developed country can benefit from technology-diffusion/transfer from technologically developed countries. Although these two processes are interrelated, it is the first that has received more attention. The standard trade theory devotes considerable attention to the issue of capital (factor) mobility but, because of the assumption of identical technology, says very little about technology diffusion. Similarly, the neoclassical growth theory assumes that technological progress is exogenous and is accessible to all and without any costs. As Solow (1994) explains, this was an abstraction, necessary at that early stage of development of the growth theory. Rise of the new growth theories has been, in part, a response to this abstraction, and this has now brought the issue of generation and diffusion of technology to the forefront of mainstream economics research. Needless to say, current interest in the TFP differences across countries is closely related with recent developments in the growth theory, and international TFP comparison can be an important complement to research on growth theory in general.

11.3 Different Approaches to the TFP Comparison

For a long time, computation of the TFP has been associated with the time series approach to growth accounting. However, two new approaches to international comparison of the TFP have recently emerged. Broadly therefore we now have the following three different approaches:

1. the time series growth accounting approach
2. the cross-section growth accounting approach
3. the panel regression approach

Not every international growth accounting work falls neatly under one or other of the above approaches. There is some overlap. Also, in addition to the above, there is the *frontier approach* to productivity analysis, represented by such works as Färe et al. (1994) and Nishimizu and Page (1982). This approach relies on linear programming and activity analysis and does not impose any parametric production function on the data. The approach can also distinguish between improved efficiency in using existing technology and advance of the technology itself. However, the frontier approach is data intensive, and its application has been limited to developed countries and often to particular sectors of the economy. In this paper, we therefore limit the comparison to the three approaches listed above and leave the extension of the comparison to other approaches to future efforts. We begin by looking briefly at the methodologies of these approaches.

11.3.1 Time Series Approach to International TFP Comparison

By the time series approach to international TFP comparison, we refer to that growth accounting tradition in which the time series of individual countries are analyzed separately, that is, on a country-by-country basis. This, in turn, has taken two forms, namely the *absolute form* and the *relative form*. In the absolute form, the time series data of individual countries are analyzed without relating these to time series data of other countries. In this form, researchers obtain TFP growth rates within individual countries, which are then compared and analyzed. Implementation of the absolute form, therefore, does not require time series data of different countries to be brought to a common denominator. However, by the same token, the absolute form of time series approach can not give comparison of the TFP levels. Instead, the comparison has to be limited to that of the TFP growth rates. The relative form of the time-series approach overcomes this limitation. In this form, data for different countries are brought to a common currency, using either official exchange rates or exchange rates based on purchasing power parity (PPP). These converted data are then analyzed with reference to either a benchmark country or the mean of the sample. The relative form of time series approach can, therefore, give not only the TFP growth rates within each country but also the relative TFP levels of these countries.

Time Series Approach in the Absolute Form

So far as the absolute form of the time series approach is concerned, international TFP comparison is as old as the study of the TFP itself.

The latter goes back to Tinbergen (1959) who extends Douglas's idea of production function to include a time trend representing the level of efficiency. Tinbergen uses this framework to conduct a comparison of TFP growth in France, Germany, the United Kingdom, and the United States for the period of 1870–1910. Solow's (1957) seminal article "Technical Change and Aggregate Production Function" puts growth accounting on firm theoretical foundations and allows (unlike in Tinbergen) the rate of TFP growth to vary from year to year. Initial research that follows Solow's paper focuses on growth accounting for the United States. However, from the confinement of a single country, growth accounting soon spread to samples of countries. Denison (1967) presents a comparison of TFP growth rates among Belgium, Denmark, France, Germany, Italy, the Netherlands, Norway, the United Kingdom, and the United States. Other works of this tradition include Barger (1969), Bergson (1975), Domar et al. (1964), and Kuznets (1971). The sample size of these studies was limited to nine, seven, five, and five, respectively, and all countries included in the samples were the Organization for Economic Cooperation and Development (OECD) members.

Jorgenson raises the TFP computation to a great level of sophistication. He and his associates introduce the use of Divisia and translog indices to growth accounting, integrate income accounting with wealth accounting, and connect growth accounting with multisectoral general equilibrium analysis.[2] Having developed the methodology on the basis of the US data, Jorgenson and his associates proceed to use it for international TFP comparison. In Ezaki and Jorgenson (1973), the methodology is used to analyze economic growth of Japan. In Christensen, Cummings, and Jorgenson (1980), the analysis is extended to a sample of nine countries that includes the United States and its eight major trading partners, namely Canada, France, Germany, Italy, Japan, Korea, the Netherlands, and the United Kingdom.

In its initial phase, growth accounting was mainly focused on the *proportions issue*. This concerns the question of how much of the output growth can be explained by the measured input growth and how much is left to be explained by the TFP growth. Interest in the proportions issue carried over to international TFP comparison as well. In all the studies mentioned above, researchers first show how countries compare with each other in terms of growth rate of output, input, and TFP. They then show how these countries compare among themselves in terms of proportion of output growth that is explained by input growth and by the TFP growth. Since the absolute form of the time series approach readily provides growth rates of input, output, and the TFP, this approach is adequate for investigating the proportions issue.

The studies following the absolute form of time-series growth account-

---

2. See Jorgenson (1995a) for a recent compilation of important papers on this topic.

ing approach were reviewed earlier by Nadiri (1970, 1972). He compiles results from a number of papers, some of which are TFP studies of single countries. Nadiri provides an insightful analysis of differences in TFP growth rates across countries and relates these to corresponding differences in the various input growth rates and other factors. Kravis (1976) presents a similar review. Christensen, Cummings, and Jorgenson (1980) also start their paper with a very useful survey of previous works that employ the absolute form of the time series growth accounting approach.

Time Series Approach in the Relative Form

Jorgenson and Nishimizu (1978) initiate the relative form of the time series approach to international TFP comparison. In this paper, the authors conduct a growth accounting exercise for the US and Japan by considering their data in the relative form. In Christensen, Cummings, and Jorgenson (1981), this method is extended to the same sample of nine countries that were studied earlier in Christensen, Cummings, and Jorgenson (1980). In order to consider data in the relative form, Jorgenson and his associates use the following translog production function:

$$
\begin{aligned}
(1) \quad Y = \exp\Big[& \alpha_0 + \alpha_K \ln K + \alpha_L \ln L + + \alpha_T T + \sum \alpha_C D_C \\
& + \frac{1}{2}\beta_{KK}(\ln K)^2 + \beta_{KL}\ln K \ln L + \beta_{KT}T\ln K + \sum \beta_{KC}D_C \ln K \\
& + \frac{1}{2}\beta_{LL}(\ln L)^2 + \beta_{LT}T\ln L + \sum \beta_{LC}D_C \ln L + \frac{1}{2}\beta_{TT}T^2 \\
& + \frac{1}{2}\sum \beta_{TC}T D_C + \frac{1}{2}\sum \beta_{CC}D_C^2 \Big],
\end{aligned}
$$

where Y is the output, K is the capital input, L is the labor input, T is time, and D_c is a dummy variable for country C. This is the same translog production function that the researchers use earlier for growth accounting in absolute form except that it now includes country dummies. The United States is taken as the reference country, and hence the dummy for the United States is dropped. In this set up, the rate of TFP growth within a country is given by

$$
(2) \quad v_T = \frac{\partial \ln Y}{\partial T} = \alpha_T + \beta_{KT}\ln K + \beta_{LT}\ln L + \beta_{TT}T + \beta_{TC}D_C,
$$

which is approximated by the following translog index of productivity growth:

$$
(3) \quad \bar{v}_T = \ln Y(T) - \ln Y(T-1) - \bar{v}_K[\ln K(T) - \ln K(T-1)] \\
- \bar{v}_L[\ln L(T) - \ln L(T-1)]
$$

where $\bar{v}_K = 1/2[v_K(T) + v_K(T-1)]$, and similarly for $\bar{v}_L$ and $\bar{v}_T$. The novelty of the approach is that this function now allows having an expression for difference in the TFP level among the countries. Thus, the TFP difference between any country C and the United States is expressed as follows:

$$(4) \quad v_C = \frac{\partial \ln Y}{\partial D_C} = \alpha_C + \beta_{KC} \ln K + \beta_{LC} \ln L + \beta_{TC} T + \beta_{CC} D_C.$$

This is approximated by the following translog multilateral index of differences in productivity:

$$(5) \quad \hat{v}_C = \ln Y(C) - \ln Y(US) - \hat{v}_K(C)[\ln K(C) - \ln \overline{K}]$$
$$+ \hat{v}_K(US)[\ln K(US) - \ln \overline{K}] - \hat{v}_L(C)[\ln L(C) - \ln \overline{L}]$$
$$+ \hat{v}_L(US)[\ln L(US) - \ln \overline{L}],$$

where

$$\hat{v}_K(C) = \frac{1}{2}\left[v_K(C) + \frac{1}{2}\sum v_K\right], \quad \hat{v}_L(C) = \frac{1}{2}\left[v_L(C) + \frac{1}{2}\sum v_L\right],$$

and $\ln \overline{K}$ and $\ln \overline{L}$ denote averages of $\ln K$ and $\ln L$ over all countries in the sample. This index is based on Caves, Christensen, and Diewert (1982) and is transitive and base-country invariant. The translog multilateral index of relative output is given by

$$(6) \quad \ln Y(C) - \ln Y(US) = \sum \hat{w}_i(C)[\ln Y_i(C) - \ln \overline{Y_i}]$$
$$- \sum \hat{w}_i(US)[\ln Y_i(US) - \ln \overline{Y_i}],$$

where $\hat{w}_i$, the weight of the ith component in the value of the aggregate output, is given as

$$\hat{w}_i = \frac{1}{2}\left[w_i(C) + \frac{1}{n}\sum w_i\right],$$

and $i = 1 \ldots m$, with m being the dimension of disaggregation. The translog multilateral indexes of relative capital and labor inputs are defined in an analogous manner. This framework allows Christensen, Cummings, and Jorgenson (1981) to conduct TFP comparison in terms of not only the growth rates but also the levels, using the translog indices presented above. The authors use the PPP prices provided by Kravis, Heston, and Summers (1978) to relate time series data of different countries. These PPP prices were available only for 1970. To the extent that the indices computed by Christensen, Cummings, and Jorgenson are tied to the PPP prices of 1970, these indices are not base-year invariant though these are base-country invariant. The indexes of the relative TFP level presented in this study are for 1947–1973, and the coverage for the nine countries was complete from 1960 onwards. Dougherty and Jorgenson (1996, 1997) return to this body of work and present relative TFP level indices for the G-7 countries for the years of 1960–1989.

Wolff (1991) and Dollar and Wolff (1994) also conduct international TFP comparison using the relative form of the time-series growth accounting approach. Wolff's TFP measure is based on the simple equation

$$\text{TFP}_i = \frac{Y_i}{[\alpha_i K_i + (1 - \alpha_i) L_i]}, \tag{7}$$

where Y is output, L is labor measured by hours, and K is aggregate capital stock measured by nonresidential fixed plant and equipment. Wolff (1991) uses Maddison (1982) data which are already converted to the US dollar. This also allows him to take a long historical view. Wolff presents relative TFP indexes for the G-7 countries for the period 1870–1979 with intervals of roughly a decade. The set of TFP indices for the seven countries is complete from 1950 onwards. Dollar and Wolff (1994) concentrate on the manufacturing sector and present relative TFP indices for selected years between 1963 and 1985. Their sample consists of fourteen developed countries, and they use two different databases for their computation.[3]

Time series growth accounting generally requires data over long time periods. Also, in order to implement Jorgenson and his associates' methodology, one needs to distinguish between growth of quality and quantity of inputs. This in turn requires disaggregated data on different types of labor and capital and their respective compensation. This kind of data is available only for a small number of developed countries. Because of these data requirements, the time series growth accounting approach to international TFP comparison has generally remained limited to the G-7 or the OECD member countries. Yet, with regard to the TFP-convergence and technology diffusion, the experience of wider samples of countries is of particular interest. In such global samples, differences in technology and productivity are greater. The knowledge of what is happening to relative levels of labor and total factor productivity in such wider samples of countries should be useful for further development of the growth theory. From this point of view, the cross-section and the panel approaches to the TFP comparison are helpful, because both these approaches can be applied to large samples of countries.

3. The sample includes Australia, Belgium, Canada, Denmark, Finland, France, Germany, Italy, Japan, the Netherlands, Norway, Sweden, the United Kingdom, and the United States. Two databases used are the Dollar-Wolff database and the OECD database.

11.3.2 Cross-section Approach to International TFP Comparison

Cross-section Growth Regressions

While Denison, Jorgenson, and others were perfecting the time-series growth accounting approach in the 1960s, a cross-section approach to growth analysis also emerged. Chenery and his associates played an important role in developing this line of research. These economists were also interested in the proportions issue. In their case, however, the focus is on the proportion of growth that is explained by the neoclassical variables (namely, labor and capital) and the proportion that can be attributed to, what is called, the *structural sources* of growth. The concept of structural sources of growth arose from the observation that many assumptions of the neoclassical growth theory do not hold in developing economies. It was argued that basic, structural departures of developing economies from the neoclassical description create the scope for other, structural sources of growth. (We shall see in section 11.5 that the idea of 'non-neoclassical' sources of growth is not unique with the development economists.) This idea was further developed to formulate the notion of *patterns of development*. Investigation of the proportion issue also became a quest for finding development patterns. In either case, it was required to have long historical data, which unfortunately were not available for developing countries. Note that we are referring to the sixties when many of these countries had just become independent. This prompted development economists to turn to cross-section data in order to compensate for the paucity of time series data. A wide body of literature developed as a result of this line of work, a summary of which can be found in Chenery, Robinson, Sirquin (1985).

The methodology that these development economists pursue is to run cross-section regression with growth rate as the dependent variable and a variety of explanatory variables on the right hand side. Among the latter are the standard neoclassical variables such as the saving and the labor force growth rates. In addition, development economists included variables representing structural sources of growth.[4] Although residuals from these regressions had potentiality with regard to TFP comparison across countries, this was generally not done because the focus was on the proportions-issue.[5]

Cross-section Growth Accounting

The cross-section growth accounting approach to the TFP level comparison has been suggested recently by Hall and Jones (1996, 1997). Their

---

4. Note that these cross-country regressions are actually the precursors of the modern day growth regressions, although this link is not always recognized.
5. As we shall see, growth researchers currently are indeed using residuals from growth regressions to make inferences about productivity.

approach is not based on cross-section regression. Instead, the methodology is similar to the time-series growth accounting approach but now applied along the cross-section dimension. The authors proceed from a production function of the following general form:

(8) $$Y_i = A_i \cdot F(K_i, H_i),$$

where Y is output, K is capital, H is human-capital augmented labor, A is the Hicks-neutral productivity, and i is the country index. H is related to L through the relationship

(9) $$H_i = e^{\phi(S_i)} L_i,$$

where $e^{\phi(S_i)}$ shows the extent by which the efficiency of raw labor gets multiplied because of S years of schooling. Proceeding from equation (8), Hall and Jones arrive, following Solow (1957), at the standard growth accounting equation

(10) $$\Delta \log y_i = \bar{\alpha}_i \Delta \log k_i + (1 - \bar{\alpha}_i) \Delta h_i + \Delta \log A_i.$$

The difference here is that while in Solow, differentiation or differencing proceeds in the direction of time t, Hall and Jones propose to apply the procedure in the cross-sectional direction, that is, in the direction of the subscript i.

This, however, poses a problem. In the usual case of time series growth accounting, there is no ambiguity regarding the direction in which t moves. In the cross-sectional case, however, it depends on the particular way countries are ordered. Hall and Jones order countries on the basis of an index which is a linear combination of the individual country's physical and human capital per unit of labor and its value of α, the share of (physical) capital in income, that is allowed to vary across countries. However, in order to get country specific α, the authors make the assumption that the service price of capital (say, r) is the same across countries. They calibrate r so as to have $\alpha_{USA} = 1/3$. This value of r equals to 13.53 percent. The $\bar{\alpha}_i$ in equation (10) above is the average of α for two adjacent countries, that is, $\bar{\alpha}_i = 0.5(\alpha_i + \alpha_{i-1})$. With regard to $\phi(S)$, Hall and Jones make the assumption that it is piece-wise linear with the value of ϕ being 13.4, 10.1, and 6.8 percent, respectively, for zero to four, four to eight, and eight and more years of schooling. These values are taken mainly from studies by Psacharopoulos (1994) for different regions of the world.

With this arrangement and parameter values, Hall and Jones compute the TFP-level indexes for different countries by summing up the TFP differences over relevant ranges of ordering using the equation

(11) $$\log A_i = \sum_{j=2}^{i} \Delta \log A_j + \log A_1,$$

where A_1 is the TFP value for the base country and is normalized to some arbitrary value. The authors implement this procedure for a very large sample of 133 countries. These TFP indexes are presented in their table 9, and we reproduce them later, in table 11.3.

There are several advantages of the cross-section growth accounting approach. First is that it does not involve imposition of a specific form on the aggregate production function. As the authors emphasize, what is required to arrive at the growth accounting equation (10) is constant returns to scale and differentiability. Second, it allows the factor income share parameters to be different across countries. Third, the approach does not require econometric estimation and hence can avoid the problems associated with such estimation.

However, the cross-section growth accounting approach has some weaknesses too. First, it requires prior ordering of the countries, and the indices may be sensitive to the ordering chosen. Second, equation (11) shows that this index is sensitive to inclusion/exclusion of countries. Third, computation of the country specific values of the factor share parameter is done on the basis of the assumption of a uniform rate of return across countries. Empirical studies however suggest that the hypothesis of uncovered interest rate parity (UIP) does not hold in reality. This contradicts the assumption of a uniform rate of return. Fourth, while theoretically it is good to be able to use capital stock data (instead of just investment rates) and to take account of human capital differences in growth accounting, in reality it is not always an unmixed blessing. Construction of capital stock data through perpetual inventory method cannot avoid using investment rates. In addition, it requires assumptions regarding depreciation profiles and initial levels of capital stocks. Similarly, schooling data across countries have often been found to be unreliable and do not take any note of differences in quality of schooling. Also, estimates regarding returns to schooling for one region may not hold for other regions. Thus, in trying to use capital stock data and to take account of human capital differences in cross-country TFP comparison, it is possible to pick up considerable noise as well as signal. It is difficult to be sure about which of these two predominates. Despite these weaknesses, the cross-section growth accounting approach and the results produced on its basis is a novel addition to the body of knowledge on TFP differences across countries.

In a later paper, Hall and Jones (1999) modify many aspects of their cross-section growth accounting methodology. In particular, they discard the attempt to allow country-specific values of the capital share parameter, α. Instead, they now assume a common value of α and set it to be equal to 1/3. They also now assume the productivity parameter A to be Harrod-neutral instead of being Hicks-neutral. These modifications bring their cross-section methodology closer to the methodology of the panel approach that we discuss next. It appears that the modifications also lead to considerable changes in the results regarding the productivity indexes, and these results now agree more with the results obtained from the panel approach. Unfortunately, Hall and Jones (1999) do not provide the results for the full sample. The comparison in this paper is therefore based on the results presented in their earlier papers.

11.3.3 The Panel Regression Approach to International TFP Comparison

The panel approach to international TFP comparison arose directly from recent attempts to explain the cross-country growth regularities. Proceeding from a Cobb-Douglas aggregate production function $Y_t = K_t^\alpha (A_t L_t)^{1-\alpha}$, where Y is output, K is capital, and L is labor that grows at an exponential rate n, and A is the labor augmenting technology also growing at an exponential rate g, one can derive the following equation for the steady state output per unit of labor[6]:

$$(12) \quad \ln\left[\frac{Y_t}{L_t}\right] = \ln A_0 + gt + \frac{\alpha}{1-\alpha}\ln(s) - \frac{\alpha}{1-\alpha}\ln(n + g + \delta),$$

where s is the fraction of output invested, δ is the rate of depreciation, and t is the length of time required by the economy to reach its steady state starting from the initial period. In the recent growth literature, this equation has been called the *level equation* because the variable on the left-hand side of this equation is in the level form. Many researchers have used this level equation to investigate the determinants of growth.[7] Note that one of the terms on the right hand side of equation (12) is A_0, which is the baseline TFP level of a particular country. Also note that under the assumption that g is common for all countries in the sample, the relative TFP level of any two countries, say i and j, remains unchanged and is equal to the ratio of their initial TFP levels, as we can see below:

$$(13) \quad \frac{A_{it}}{A_{jt}} = \frac{A_{0i} e^{gt}}{A_{0j} e^{gt}} = \frac{A_{0i}}{A_{0j}}.$$

Thus, under the above assumptions, ratios of estimated A_0's can serve as indices of relative TFP levels. The problem, however, lies in estimation of A_0. It is difficult to find variables that can effectively proxy for A_0. It is for this reason that many researchers wanted to ignore the presence of the A_0 term in equation (12) by relegating it to the disturbance term of the

---

6. For details of this derivation, see Mankiw, Romer, and Weil (1992), Mankiw (1995), or Islam (1995).

7. Mankiw, Romer, and Weil (1992) is a famous example. In fact, Hall and Jones (1996) also use level equation for their regression exercises; however, their equation differs from that of Mankiw, Romer, and Weil in terms of the right-hand side variables of interest.

regression equation. This however creates an omitted variable bias problem for the regression results. The panel approach helps to overcome this problem, because under this approach it is possible to control for A_0 indirectly and obtain its estimate.

One problem with the level equation is that it requires the assumption that all countries of the sample are in their steady states, or at least that the departures from steady states are random. This is a questionable assumption. However, a corresponding equation can be derived that can accommodate the transitional behavior. This is given by equation (14):

$$(14) \quad \ln y_{t_2} = (1 - e^{-\lambda\tau})\frac{\alpha}{1-\alpha}\ln(s_{t_1}) - (1 - e^{-\lambda\tau})\frac{\alpha}{1-\alpha}\ln(n_{t_1} + g + \delta)$$
$$+ e^{-\lambda\tau}\ln y_{t_1} + (1 - e^{-\lambda\tau})\ln A_0 + g(t_2 - e^{-\lambda\tau}t_1).$$

In this equation t_1 and t_2 are initial and subsequent points of time, respectively; y is the output per unit of labor, and $\lambda = (n + g + \delta)(1 - \alpha)$ and is known as the rate of convergence, because it measures the speed at which the economy closes the gap between its current and steady state levels of output per unit of labor. As we can see, the term A_0 appears in this equation too, and ignoring it causes the same omitted variable bias problem for this equation, as was the case with the level equation considered earlier. Again, panel data procedures can be applied to overcome this problem by indirectly controlling for variations in A_0. It is then also possible to obtain estimates of A_0.

Islam (1995) implements the panel data approach using both Chamberlain's (1982, 1984) minimum distance estimator (based on the correlated effects model) and the covariance estimator (based on the fixed effects model). The estimated values of A_0 obtained from the procedure provide information to construct indices of relative productivity indexes. The sample consists of 96 countries, which figure in most of the recent empirical studies of growth. These estimates of the relative TFP levels are reproduced later in table 11.3.

Compared with the cross-section growth accounting approach, the panel regression approach has certain advantages. First, it does not require any prior ordering of the countries. Second, the method is less sensitive to inclusion/exclusion of countries. Third, the approach is flexible with regard to use of either the investment rate or the capital stock data and with regard to inclusion of human capital. The fourth advantage is that the results from econometric estimation that this approach relies upon can provide, to an extent, a check on the severity of noise in the data.

However, the approach has some weaknesses too. First, it has to start with a specified form of the aggregate production function. Second, in its applications so far, the approach relies on the homogeneity assumption regarding the factor share parameters. Third, to the extent that the approach relies on econometric estimation, it is subject to the usual pitfalls of such estimation work. One such problem is the potential small sample bias. The theoretical properties of most of the panel estimators are asymptotic in nature and hence are subject to potential small sample bias. It is therefore necessary to be on guard regarding this bias.[8] Another potential econometric problem is endogeneity. Note that equation (14) per se does not have this problem. The right hand-side variables of this equation, namely s_{t_1} and n_{t_1}, are one period into the past compared with the dependent variable y_{t_2}. While the current period's income and growth rate may influence future (and perhaps also current period's) investment and labor force growth rates, these cannot influence saving and fertility behavior of the past. In other words, the right-hand side variables are predetermined and hence cannot create endogeneity. However, a problem of endogeneity may arise via the estimation procedure. Some panel estimators that avoid the endogeneity problem suffer from significant small sample bias. However, through appropriate modification, it is possible to have panel estimator that avoid both small sample bias and the potential endogeneity problem.[9]

11.4 Comparison of Results from Different Approaches

It is clear from the above that there is a basic difference in scope of results obtained from the time series approach on the one hand and the cross-section and the panel regression approaches on the other. This makes comparison of the time series results with results from either the cross-section approach or the panel approach somewhat unsuitable. The paper therefore presents the comparison in two formats. In the first, we compare results for the G-7 countries as presented by Dougherty and Jorgenson (1997, henceforth DJ) and by Wolff (1991, henceforth WO). In the second, we compare the TFP results for a wider sample of ninety-six countries presented by Hall and Jones (1996) and Islam (1995).

11.4.1 Comparison of the TFP Results for the G7 Countries

Both the DJ and the WO indexes are product of application of the relative form of time series approach of growth accounting. However, as noted above, DJ and WO use different data and different production function for growth accounting. These differences show up in the results. Table 11.1 compiles the relative TFP-level indexes presented by DJ and WO in their

---

8. Islam (2000a) provides a Monte Carlo study of the small sample properties of many of the panel estimation procedures used for estimation of the growth convergence equation (14). The results show that the minimum distance procedure and the least squares with dummy variables (LSDV) procedure each have smaller bias than many of the other panel estimators.

9. Islam (2000b) presents a modified minimum distance estimation procedure that avoids the endogeneity problem in estimating the growth convergence equation.

Table 11.1 TFP Comparison for the G7 Countries

	DJ Index of Relative TFP, 1960 (1)	DJ Index of Relative TFP, 1970 (2)	DJ Index of Relative TFP, 1979 (3)	WO Index of Relative TFP, 1960 (4)	WO Index of Relative TFP, 1970 (5)	WO Index of Relative TFP, 1979 (6)
Canada	99.1	110.4	119.7	88.5	103.5	108.9
France	79.4	101.0	117.7	69.0	99.1	115.9
Germany	63.3	82.5	96.1	67.3	89.4	99.1
Italy	65.1	101.0	119.7	57.5	92.0	107.1
Japan	39.0	77.8	84.0	31.9	73.5	89.4
United Kingdom	80.4	94.3	106.0	75.2	92.9	101.8
United States	100.0	109.4	109.0	100.0	113.3	122.1

Notes: The DJ indexes are from Dougherty and Jorgenson (1997, table A3), and the WO indexes are from Wolff (1991, table 1). Dougherty and Jorgenson presented their indexes with a 1985 U.S. TFP level of 100. Wolff's indexes, on the other hand, were based on a 1950 U.S. TFP level of 100. To make the indexes comparable, we have shifted these to a common base of 1960 U.S. TFP of 100.

table A3 and table 1, respectively. Dougherty and Jorgenson (1997) benchmark their indexes to the U.S. TFP level of 1985 as 100, while WO uses the U.S. TFP level of 1950 as the base. In order to make these two sets of indexes more comparable, we shift them to a common base that takes the U.S. TFP level for 1960 as 100. Table 11.1 shows indexes for three particular years, namely 1960, 1970, and 1979. Clearly, these indexes contain both ordinal and cardinal information. Also, because the indexes for all countries and for all years are benchmarked to a single point, the cardinal information contained in these indexes is useful for comparison across both countries and years. It is therefore possible to look at the numbers of table 11.1 from many different angles and observe many different features.

To concentrate on just a few, we present table 11.2. In this table, the ordinal information contained in the indexes is summarized in the form of ranks, and the cardinal aspect of the information is used to get a measure of change in the TFP level over time by taking difference of the indexes. Thus figures in columns 1 and 2 of table 11.2 give the ranking of the countries in 1960 and 1979, respectively, on the basis of the DJ TFP indexes shown in columns 1 and 3 of table 11.1. Figures in column 3 of table 11.2 are obtained by taking the difference of the DJ indexes for 1979 and 1960 for individual countries. The numbers in column 4 of table 11.2 are ranks based on the differences shown in column (3). The numbers in columns 5–8 of table 11.2 are analogously derived based on the corresponding WO figures of table 11.1.

These transformations help us to see more clearly the similarities and dissimilarities in the results from these two studies. First of all, we see that there is a broad agreement with regard to the relative TFP levels of these countries in the initial year of 1960. This agreement is not only in ordinal terms (as can be seen by comparing the numbers of columns 1 and 5 of table 11.2), but also in cardinal term, as can be seen by comparing the numbers of columns 1 and 4 of table 11.1. The main difference seems to arise with regard to the change in the TFP level over time. The TFP ranking of the countries for 1979 produced by the DJ index varies considerably from the ranking produced by the WO index. A comparison of the numbers of columns 2 and 6 of table 11.2 illustrates this. The numbers of columns 3 and 7 of table 11.2 that show the increase of the respective TFP indexes between 1960 and 1979 also demonstrate this aspect of the results. The difference is particularly significant with regard to the United States and Italy. As column 3 of table 11.2 shows, according to the DJ index, Italy seems to have experienced the greatest TFP growth, outstripping Japan by a significant margin. The WO index also attests to Italy's exceptional TFP growth, but does not put Italy ahead of Japan in this respect. The TFP growth proves to be very modest for the United States, according to the DJ index, but not so modest according to the WO index.

This comparison shows that the TFP results may vary even when similar

Table 11.2   TFP Ranking for the G7 Countries

	Rank Based on DJ Index of Relative TFP, 1960 (1)	Rank Based on DJ Index of Relative TFP, 1979 (2)	Increase of DJ-TFP Index, 1960–79 (3)	Rank in Terms of Growth of DJ-TFP Index (4)	Rank Based on WO Index of Relative TFP, 1960 (5)	Rank Based on WO Index of Relative TFP, 1979 (6)	Increase of WO-TFP Index, 1960–79 (7)	Rank in Terms of Growth of WO-TFP Index (8)
Canada	2	1	20.6	6	2	3	20.4	7
France	4	3	38.3	3	4	2	46.9	3
Germany	6	6	32.8	4	5	6	31.9	4
Italy	5	1	54.6	1	6	4	50.0	2
Japan	7	7	45.0	2	7	7	57.5	1
United Kingdom	3	5	25.6	5	3	5	26.6	5
United States	1	4	9.0	7	1	1	22.1	6

Note: The ranks, differences of TFP index, and ranks based on differences all are computed on the basis of the numbers of table 11.1 of this paper.

approach is used. This is because the same approach can be implemented in different ways. To the extent that Dougherty and Jorgenson (1997) and Wolff (1991) were using very different production functions and different data, it is not surprising that the results differ. An interesting question is how much of the difference can be attributed to difference in the data and how much to the difference in the production function used. Answering this question will require further investigation.

11.4.2 Comparison of the TFP results for a Large Sample of Countries

As noted earlier, the Hall and Jones indexes are available for 133 countries. However, their sample includes former socialist countries for which it is not clear whether many of the neoclassical assumptions for growth accounting held true. Their sample also includes many countries for which extraction and export of oil is the dominant economic activity. Although the authors try to correct for this by discounting the GDP of these countries for oil revenues, some issues may still remain. In short, selection of countries may be an issue for Hall and Jones's (1996, hereafter HJ) exercise. This is important because the cross-section growth accounting results are very sensitive to inclusion of countries. In Islam (1995, hereafter IS), as mentioned earlier, the TFP indexes were produced for 96 countries. This is basically the same sample of countries that have widely figured in recent empirical growth studies.[10] In the following, we limit the comparison to this sample of countries.

In one sense, there is an important difference in what is being measured by the HJ and the IS indexes. The HJ indexes are of the relative TFP levels for the particular year of 1988. In contrast, the IS indexes pertain to the relative TFP levels for the entire period of 1960–85. Thus, while the HJ indices are, in a sense, end-of-period indicators of the relative TFP levels, the IS indices represent the relative TFP levels that are in a sense average for the 1960–85 period as a whole. In perusing the comparison below, this important difference must be kept in mind. We shall also try to relate this difference with the difference in observed results.

The basic TFP measures presented in HJ and IS have been compiled in columns 1 and 2 of table 11.3. In addition, the table contains some transformations of these basic measures. The comparison may again be conducted from both the ordinal and the cardinal points of view. Columns 3 and 4 show the ranking of the countries in terms of the HJ and the IS indexes, respectively. The differences in rank are given in column 6. For the cardinal comparison, we need to bring these indices to a common origin and scale. We do this by taking the U.S. TFP level as 100 and expressing the TFP levels of other countries as percentages of the U.S. level. These transformations can be seen in columns 6 and 7 of table 11.3.

---

10. The sample originates with Barro's (1991) pioneering work and continues through Mankiw, Romer, and Weil (1992) and many other subsequent studies.

Table 11.3 TFP Comparison in Large Sample of Countries

	HJ Estimate of Contribution of A (1)	IS Estimate of A(0) (2)	HJ Index Rank (3)	IS Index Rank (4)	Ordinal Difference[a] (5)	HJ-TFP Index (U.S./100) (6)	IS-TFP Index (U.S./100) (7)	Cardinal Difference[b] (8)
Africa								
Algeria	−0.328	6.97	38	53	15	72.04	18.64	53.40
Angola	−1.874	6.63	90	65	−25	15.35	13.27	2.09
Benin	−1.172	6.00	70	81	11	30.97	7.07	23.91
Botswana	−0.991	7.06	63	51	−12	37.12	20.39	16.73
Burundi	−1.888	5.91	91	83	−8	15.14	6.46	8.68
Cameroon	−1.069	6.82	65	60	−5	34.34	16.04	18.29
Central African Republic	−1.762	5.76	85	88	3	17.17	5.56	11.61
Chad	−1.891	5.48	92	94	2	15.09	4.20	10.89
Congo	−0.731	6.53	54	68	14	48.14	12.00	36.14
Egypt	−0.520	6.77	43	62	19	59.45	15.26	44.19
Ethiopia	−2.264	6.10	96	76	−20	10.39	7.81	2.59
Ghana	−1.536	5.72	80	90	10	21.52	5.34	16.18
Ivory Coast	−0.973	6.87	62	58	−4	37.79	16.86	20.93
Kenya	−1.438	6.00	77	80	3	23.74	7.07	16.68
Liberia	−1.297	5.81	72	87	15	27.34	5.84	21.49
Madagascar	−1.820	6.20	87	74	−13	16.20	8.63	7.57
Malawi	−2.039	5.81	95	86	−9	13.02	5.84	7.17
Mali	−1.639	5.76	83	89	6	19.42	5.56	13.86
Mauritania	−1.493	5.57	78	91	13	22.47	4.60	17.87
Mauritius	−0.226	6.97	27	54	27	79.77	18.64	61.13
Morocco	−0.551	7.49	45	37	−8	57.64	31.35	26.29
Mozambique	−1.500	6.53	79	67	−12	22.31	12.00	10.31

(*continued*)

Table 11.3 (continued)

	HJ Estimate of Contribution of A (1)	IS Estimate of $A(0)$ (2)	HJ Index Rank (3)	IS Index Rank (4)	Ordinal Difference[a] (5)	HJ-TFP Index (U.S./100) (6)	IS-TFP Index (U.S./100) (7)	Cardinal Difference[b] (8)
Niger	−1.833	6.10	88	77	−11	15.99	7.81	8.19
Nigeria	−1.401	6.24	74	73	−1	24.64	8.98	15.65
Rwanda	−1.420	5.91	76	84	8	24.17	6.46	17.71
Senegal	−1.153	6.44	69	69	0	31.57	10.97	20.60
Sierra Leone	−1.096	6.05	67	78	11	33.42	7.43	25.99
Somalia	−1.566	5.33	81	96	15	20.89	3.62	17.27
South Africa	−0.439	7.69	42	28	−14	64.47	38.29	26.18
Sudan	−1.116	5.86	68	85	17	32.76	6.14	26.62
Tanzania	−1.922	5.52	93	93	0	14.63	4.37	10.26
Togo	−1.617	6.00	82	82	0	19.85	7.07	12.78
Tunisia	−0.272	7.35	31	41	10	76.19	27.25	48.93
Uganda	−1.818	6.39	86	72	−14	16.24	10.44	5.80
Zaire	−1.871	5.52	89	92	3	15.40	4.37	11.03
Zambia	−1.649	5.48	84	95	11	19.22	4.20	15.02
Zimbabwe	−1.292	6.39	71	71	0	27.47	10.44	17.04
Asia								
Bangladesh	−0.545	6.63	44	63	19	57.98	13.27	44.72
Burma	−1.982	6.20	94	75	−19	13.78	8.63	5.15
Hong Kong	0.086	9.08	5	1	−4	108.98	153.73	−44.75
India	−1.068	6.00	64	74	10	34.37	7.07	27.30
Israel	−0.174	8.17	22	17	−5	84.03	61.88	22.15
Japan	−0.296	8.41	34	10	−24	74.38	78.66	−4.28
Jordan	0.166	7.30	2	44	42	118.06	25.92	92.13
South Korea	−0.410	7.69	40	33	−7	66.37	38.29	28.08
Malaysia	−0.580	7.69	47	31	−16	55.99	38.29	17.70
Nepal	−1.412	6.53	75	66	−9	24.37	12.00	12.36

Pakistan	−0.640	7.01	50	52	2	52.73	19.40	33.33
Philippines	−0.945	6.97	61	55	−6	38.87	18.64	20.23
Singapore	0.027	8.50	7	6	−1	102.74	86.07	16.67
Sri Lanka	−0.733	6.77	55	61	6	48.05	15.26	32.79
Syria	0.228	7.88	1	25	24	125.61	46.30	79.31
Thailand	−0.667	7.25	52	47	−5	51.32	24.66	26.66
Europe								
Austria	−0.043	8.26	14	15	1	95.79	67.71	28.09
Belgium	−0.053	8.41	15	8	−7	94.84	78.66	16.18
Denmark	−0.251	8.36	29	11	−18	77.80	74.83	2.96
Finland	−0.223	7.97	25	23	−2	80.01	50.66	29.35
France	0.029	8.41	6	9	3	102.94	78.66	24.28
Germany	−0.105	8.26	18	14	−4	90.03	67.71	22.33
Greece	−0.298	7.69	35	30	−5	74.23	38.29	35.94
Ireland	−0.261	7.69	30	21	−9	77.03	38.29	38.74
Italy	0.089	8.12	4	19	15	109.31	58.86	50.45
Netherlands	−0.077	8.31	16	12	−4	92.59	71.18	21.41
Norway	−0.249	8.50	28	5	−23	77.96	86.07	−8.11
Portugal	−0.020	7.59	12	34	22	98.02	34.65	63.37
Spain	−0.017	8.41	11	7	−4	98.31	78.66	19.65
Sweden	−0.093	8.31	17	13	−4	91.12	71.18	19.94
Switzerland	−0.136	8.17	20	18	−2	87.28	61.88	25.41
Turkey	−0.287	7.35	33	43	10	75.05	27.25	47.80
United Kingdom	−0.039	8.31	13	4	−9	96.18	71.18	25.00
Americas								
Argentina	−0.315	7.30	37	45	8	72.98	25.92	47.05
Bolivia	−0.757	6.87	56	57	1	46.91	16.86	30.04
Brazil	0.002	7.78	8	26	18	100.20	41.90	58.31
Canada	−0.013	8.69	10	2	−8	98.71	104.08	−5.37
Chile	−0.651	7.16	51	49	−2	52.15	22.54	29.62
Colombia	−0.223	7.40	26	40	14	80.01	28.65	51.36

(*continued*)

Table 11.3 (continued)

	HJ Estimate of Contribution of A (1)	IS Estimate of $A(0)$ (2)	HJ Index Rank (3)	IS Index Rank (4)	Ordinal Difference[a] (5)	HJ-TFP Index (U.S./100) (6)	IS-TFP Index (U.S./100) (7)	Cardinal Difference[b] (8)
Costa Rica	−0.307	7.69	36	27	−9	73.57	38.29	35.28
Dominican Republic	−0.430	7.11	41	50	9	65.05	21.44	43.61
Ecuador	−0.685	7.21	53	48	−5	50.41	23.69	26.72
El Salvador	−0.586	7.25	48	46	−2	55.65	24.66	31.00
Guatemala	−0.192	7.49	24	38	14	82.53	31.35	51.18
Haiti	−1.306	6.48	73	70	−3	27.09	11.42	15.67
Honduras	−0.801	6.58	58	64	6	44.89	12.62	32.27
Jamaica	−0.891	6.87	60	59	−1	41.02	16.86	24.16
Mexico	0.134	7.93	3	24	21	114.34	48.68	65.66
Nicaragua	−0.814	7.45	59	39	−20	44.31	30.12	14.19
Panama	−0.770	7.40	57	42	−15	46.30	28.65	17.65
Paraguay	−0.614	7.54	49	36	−13	54.12	32.96	21.16
Peru	−0.571	7.54	46	35	−11	56.50	32.96	23.54
Trinidad	−0.182	8.17	23	16	−7	83.36	61.88	21.48
Uruguay	−0.363	7.69	39	32	−7	69.56	38.29	31.27
United States	0.000	8.65	9	3	−6	100.00	100.00	00.00
Venezuela	−0.136	8.02	21	22	1	87.28	53.26	34.03
Australia and Other Pacific Countries								
Australia	−0.108	8.12	19	20	1	89.76	58.86	30.90
New Zealand	−0.282	8.12	32	21	−11	75.43	58.86	16.57
Papua New Guinea	−1.071	6.92	66	56	−10	34.27	17.73	16.54

Note: HJ indexes from Hall and Jones (1996); IS indexes from Islam (1995).
[a]HJ Index Rank minus IS Index Rank.
[b]HJ-TFP Index minus IS-TFP Index.

Looking at the numbers on rank, we see that countries that top the list according to the HJ index are Syria, Jordan, Italy, Mexico, and Hong Kong. The top five countries, according to the IS index, are Hong Kong, Canada, the United States, the United Kingdom, and Norway. At the bottom of the list, according to the HJ index, are Ethiopia, Malawi, Burma, Tanzania, and Chad. According to the IS index, the worst-performing countries are Somalia, Zambia, Chad, Tanzania, and Zaire. In general, it seems that there is more agreement regarding the bottom of the list than the top. For some of the countries, such as Senegal, Tanzania, Togo, and Zimbabwe, ranks from the two indexes coincide exactly. For seven other countries, namely Nigeria, Singapore, Austria, Jamaica, Bolivia, Venezuela, and Australia, the ranks differ by only 1. Altogether, difference in rank remains within 5 for thirty-three countries. For another twenty-five countries, the difference lies between 6 and 10. Thus, for more than 60 percent of the countries, the difference in rank remains within 10. However, for thirty countries, the difference in rank ranges between 11 and 20, and for another seven, between 21 and 30. The difference in ranking is particularly high for some of the countries that appear at the top of the HJ list. Thus, for example, for Jordan, the difference in rank is as high as 42. For Syria, this difference is 24. Similarly large differences are obtained for Mexico, Japan, Mauritius, and Angola. One way of formalizing the closeness of various rankings is to compute the rank correlation. The Spearman rank correlation coefficient between the IS and the HJ ranks prove to be 0.9024, and the null hypothesis of independence of these two rankings is overwhelmingly rejected. Similar results are obtained by using the Kendall rank correlation coefficient.

A cardinal comparison leads to similar conclusions: There are more similarities at the bottom of the list than at the top. Thus, for example, the difference between the two indexes remains within 10 percentage points for Angola, Burundi, Ethiopia, Madagascar, Malawi, Myanmar (Burma), Niger, and Uganda. Very large differences, however, are obtained again for such countries as Syria, Jordan, Mexico, and Brazil. According to the HJ index, the TFP levels of these countries are 126, 118, 114, and 100.2 percent of the TFP level of the United States. The corresponding numbers according to the IS index are 46, 26, 49, and 42, respectively. These are widely different numbers. However, for many other countries at the top, such as Japan, Denmark, Norway, and Canada, the difference does not exceed 10 percentage points. For many countries in the middle, the difference is also moderate. Altogether, for 41 countries (i.e., about half the sample), this difference is less than 20 percentage points.

One way of capturing the picture regarding the relative TFP level across countries is to produce the entire distributions. Such distributions are presented in the form of histograms in tables 11.4 and 11.5. The abbreviated names of the countries and the respective indices are also displayed in

Table 11.4   Histogram on the Basis of Hall and Jones Index

10–20	20–30	30–40	40–50	50–60	60–70	70–80	80–90	90–100	100+
ETH (10.4)									
MWI (13.0)									
BUR (13.8)									
TZA (14.6)									
TCD (15.1)	SOM (20.9)			ECU (50.4)		DZA (72.0)			
BDI (15.1)	GHA (21.5)	BEN (31.0)		THA (51.3)		ARG (73.0)			
AGO (15.4)	MOZ (22.3)	SEN (31.6)		CHL (52.1)		CRI (73.6)		DEU (90.0)	USA (100.0)
ZAR (15.4)	MRT (22.5)	SDN (32.8)		PAK (52.7)		GRC (74.2)	FIN (80.0)	SWE (91.1)	BRA (100.2)
NER (16.0)	KEN (23.7)	SLE (33.4)	JAM (41.0)	PRY (54.1)		JPN (74.4)	COL (80.0)	NLD (92.6)	SGP (102.7)
MDG (16.2)	RWA (24.2)	PNG (34.3)	NIC (44.3)	SLV (55.7)		TUR (75.1)	GTM (82.5)	BEL (94.8)	FRA (102.9)
UGA (16.2)	NPL (24.4)	CMR (34.3)	HND (44.9)	MYS (56.0)		NZL (75.4)	TTO (83.4)	AUT (95.8)	HKG (109.0)
CAR (17.2)	NGA (24.6)	IND (34.4)	PAN (46.3)	PER (56.5)	ZAF (64.5)	TUN (76.2)	ISR (84.0)	GBR (96.2)	ITA (109.3)
ZMB (19.2)	HTI (27.1)	BWA (37.1)	BOL (46.9)	MAR (57.6)	DOM (65.1)	IRL (77.0)	CHE (87.3)	PRT (98.0)	MEX (114.3)
MLI (19.4)	LBR (27.3)	CIV (37.8)	LKA (48.0)	BDG (58.0)	KOR (66.4)	DNK (77.8)	VEN (87.3)	ESP (98.3)	JOR (118.1)
TGO (19.9)	ZWE (27.5)	PHL (38.9)	COG (48.1)	EGY (59.5)	URY (69.6)	NOR (78.0)	AUS (89.8)	CAN (98.7)	SYR (125.6)
						MUS (79.8)			

Note: The codes are World Bank abbreviations of the country names. The numbers in parentheses are the relative TFP levels (according to the Hall and Jones 1996 index of the respective countries for 1988, with the TFP level of the United States as 100).

Table 11.5   Histogram on the Basis of Islam Index (percent)

10–20	20–30	30–40	40–50	50–60	60–70	70–80	80–90	90–100	100+
SOM (3.6)									
TCD (4.2)									
ZMB (4.2)									
TZA (4.4)	UGA (10.4)								
ZAR (4.4)	UGA (10.4)								
MRT (4.6)	SEN (11.0)								
GHA (5.3)	HTI (11.4)								
CAR (5.6)	CO (12.0)								
MLI (5.6)	MOZ (12.0)								
LBR (5.8)	NPL (12.0)								
MWI (5.8)	HND (12.6)								
SDN (6.1)	AGO (13.3)	BWA (20.4)	NIC (30.1)						
BDI (6.5)	BDG (13.3)	DOM (21.4)	MAR (31.3)						
RWA (6.5)	EGY (15.3)	CIV (37.8)	GTM (31.4)						
BEN (7.1)	LKA (15.3)	CHL (22.3)	PRY (33.0)						
KEN (7.1)	CMR (16.0)	ECU (23.7)	PER (33.0)						
TGO (7.1)	CIV (16.9)	THA (24.7)	PRT (34.6)						
IND (7.1)	JAM (16.9)	SLV (24.7)	ZAF (38.3)						
SLE (7.4)	BOL (16.9)	JOR (25.9)	KOR (38.3)						
ETH (7.8)	PNG (17.7)	ARG (25.9)	MYS (38.3)		FIN (50.7)	ISR (61.9)			
NER (7.8)	DZA (18.6)	TUN (27.3)	GRC (38.3)		VEN (53.3)	CHE (61.9)			
MDG (8.6)	MUS (18.6)	TUR (27.3)	IRL (38.3)	BRA (41.9)	ITA (58.9)	TTO (61.9)	NLD (71.2)		USA (100.0)
BUR (8.6)	PHL (18.6)	PAN (28.7)	CRI (38.3)	SYR (46.3)	AUS (58.9)	AUT (67.7)	SWE (71.2)		CAN (104.1)
NGA (9.0)	PAK (19.4)	COL (28.7)	URY (38.3)	MEX (48.7)	NZL (58.9)	DEU (67.7)	GBR (71.2)		HKG (153.7)
							DNK (74.8)		
							JPN (78.7)		
							BEL (78.7)		
							FRA (78.7)	SGP (86.1)	
							ESP (78.7)	NOR (86.1)	

Note: The codes are World Bank abbreviations of the country names. The numbers in parentheses are the relative TFP levels (according to the results of Islam 1995), of the respective countries for the 1960–85 period, with the TFP level of the United States as 100.

these histograms. This allows us to see the ordinal and the cardinal positions of the individual countries *within* the respective distributions. We can now visually confirm the observations made earlier. These histograms also help us see the difference in the overall shape of the distributions. It is clear that the distribution according to the IS index is more bottom-heavy than the distribution according to the HJ index.

In interpreting this difference, we first note that the two distributions come from very different methodologies and data. Second, as we have noted, while the HJ indexes can be thought as the end-of-period indexes of the TFP, the IS indexes can be regarded as the average TFP indexes for the period as a whole. Thus the IS indexes may be closer to the initial situation than are the HJ indexes. The fact that the HJ distribution is less bottom-heavy than the IS distribution may therefore indicate that over time more countries have benefited from the technological diffusion process and have been able to move away from their initial low levels of the TFP. More research is required before such a definitive conclusion can be made. However, the above shows how the TFP measures for a broad sample of countries can help us raise and analyze important issues of technological diffusion and convergence. It is to these issues that we now turn.

11.5 TFP Growth and Technological Change

It is widely recognized that the TFP growth may not be synonymous to technological change. Although neoclassical growth model serves as the framework for the TFP computation, and, according to this model, the TFP growth is generally attributed to technical change, the possibility of departures of the actual economy from the neoclassical assumptions has always been a source of concern. In particular, it has been felt that the neoclassical assumptions of perfect factor mobility and equality of marginal product and factor return across sectors are rather stringent. Similar has been the feeling toward the assumption of constant returns to scale in all sectors of the economy. Earlier we noticed how the development economists responded to these departures by proposing the structural sources of growth in addition to the neoclassical ones. However, development economists were not alone in this regard. Initial growth accounting efforts for the U.S. economy (such as Abramovitz 1956 and Solow 1957) showed that growth in labor and capital inputs explained very little of the output growth. The residual obtained was embarrassingly large. This led Denison not to equate the entire residual to technological progress. Instead he resorted to what Solow (1988) describes as the unpacking of the "technological progress in the broadest sense" into the "technological progress in the narrow sense" and several other constituents. Among the latter are, for example, "improved allocation of resources" (which refers to movement of labor from low-productivity agriculture to high-productivity industry) and "economies of scale." According to Denison's (1985) computation, 11 percent of the total U.S. growth (between 1929 and 1982) needs to be imputed to "reallocation," and another 11 percent to "economies of scale."

Jorgenson emphasizes that measured growth of the neoclassical inputs can explain more of output growth than is popularly believed. However, the issue of departure from neoclassical assumptions figures prominently in his works too. He deals extensively with conditions of aggregation and, in particular, shows that existence of the aggregate production function requires that the value-added function and the capital and labor input functions for each sector are identical to corresponding functions at the aggregate level. Identical sectoral production functions in turn imply identical input and output prices. Jorgenson computes input and output growth rates with and without allowing for these price differences and finds that the results differ, particularly for shorter periods. He interprets the resulting differences as contribution to aggregate productivity growth of reallocation of value added, capital input, and labor input among sectors.[11] Jorgenson's computation shows that over relatively shorter periods of time, contribution of reallocation of factors to growth is significant.

But what about the "unpacking of technological progress in the broadest sense" to "technological progress in the narrow sense" in the context of international TFP comparison? This remains yet to be thoroughly done. One work that addresses this issue is Maddison (1987). He works with a conventional (absolute form) time-series growth accounting approach, and his sample includes France, Germany, Holland, Japan, the United Kingdom, and the United States. Apart from the standard neoclassical sources of growth, namely labor and capital, Maddison considers a long list of other possible sources of growth. He refers to these as the "structural effect," the "foreign trade effect," the "economies of scale effect," the "energy effect," the "natural resource effect," the "regulation/crime" effect, and so on. He shows that allowing for these non-neoclassical sources of growth has important influence on international TFP comparison. The relative position of countries change depending on whether or not these non-neoclassical effects are taken into account in computation of the TFP growth. This is because countries differ with regard to the degree of departure from the neoclassical assumptions, and correspondingly with regard to the importance of the non-neoclassical sources of growth in their econ-

---

11. He explained, "For example, if labor input is reallocated from a sector with high wages to a sector with low wages, the rate of aggregate productivity growth increased with no corresponding increase in the rates of sectoral productivity growth. The rate of productivity growth can be represented as a weighted sum of sectoral productivity growth rates and the reallocations of value added and capital and labor inputs" (Jorgenson 1995a, 8).

omy. In his analysis, Maddison considers yet another effect, namely the catch-up effect. Consideration of this effect brings us to the issue of TFP convergence.

11.6 TFP Comparison and the Issue of Convergence

The TFP discussion of the 1960s, 1970s, and early 1980s was dominated by the proportions issue. The convergence issue was not prominent yet.[12] Although the time series studies of international TFP comparison of that period produced results that could be used for convergence analysis, this was generally not done. This is true of works of both the absolute and the relative forms of the time series approach.

The treatment of the catch-up effect in Maddison's (1987) growth accounting was novel. He first computes the convergence rates for individual countries on the basis of labor productivity (with the United States as the reference country), and then multiplies these rates by 0.2 to arrive at a "catch-up bonus" that he thinks the countries enjoyed vis-à-vis the leader (the United States). The factor of 0.2 was a speculation, and by "catch-up bonus" Maddison means the advantage that (technologically) follower countries enjoy vis-à-vis the technologically leading countries.[13] However, as is clear, Maddison's analysis is not a formal examination of the TFP convergence. Also, because Maddison is working with data in absolute form, dynamics of the TFP levels are not explicitly considered. By contrast, the TFP comparison in relative form, as presented by Christensen, Cummings, and Jorgenson (1981), is in fact an analysis of convergence though not couched in the terminology that is now being used. The extension of the time series growth accounting to formal analysis of convergence had to wait until the convergence issue became prominent.

12. For surveys of the recent convergence literature, see Durlauf and Quah (1998), Islam (1996), and Temple (1999).
13. It may be worthwhile to note Maddison's full argumentation for the catch-up bonus: "If the follower countries follow an appropriate policy mix and are not disturbed in the convergence process by war, they should be able to increase productivity at a faster pace than the lead country. They enjoy 'opportunities of backwardness,' which means that over a considerable range of technology, they can emulate the leader and get a given amount of growth with less expenditure on research and development. They can push the rate of capital formation per worker faster without running into diminishing returns, and structural change is rapid. Most of these effects enter into the accounts elsewhere, but when a country mount a successful process of catch up, they are in a 'virtuous circle' situation, which we have assumed will provide an extra efficiency bonus augmenting the yield of factor inputs and other growth components in a way that is not true of the lead country, which is nearer to a 'best practice' situation over a wide range of productive activity" (668–69). What is important in this explanation of the catch-up effect is his observation that "most of these effects enter into accounts elsewhere." Obviously, Maddison is referring to higher rates of capital formation, rapid structural change, etc. It is, however, interesting to delve further into what enters elsewhere and what remains for the catch-up effect to stand for.

We see such an extension in Wolff's work. His analysis, as noted earlier, is similar to that of Christensen, Cummings, and Jorgenson (1980, 1981) in many respects. However, Wolff (1991) proceeds to formalize the findings regarding the TFP convergence. First, he uses several descriptive measures, such as the coefficient of variation of the TFP levels and correlation of the TFP growth rates with the initial levels of TFP to draw conclusions about convergence. Judged by these criteria, Wolff finds significant evidence of TFP catch-up, particularly for the postwar period. Wolff also shows particular interest in possible interaction between the processes of capital deepening and technological diffusion. His hypothesis is that TFP catch-up depends, in part, on capital intensity catch-up. To test this hypothesis, he first switches to variables in relative (to the United States) form, then presents evidence in terms of simple correlation between the TFP growth rate and the capital intensity growth rate. This correlation turns out to be positive. However, in order to check whether any such positive influence remains after controlling for initial difference in the TFP level (from that of the leading country, the United States), he regresses the TFP growth rate on the initial TFP level and capital intensity growth rate. A positive coefficient on the latter variable is taken to be indicative of a positive influence of capital accumulation on TFP catch-up that is over and above the influence that could be predicted simply on the basis of initial TFP level difference. In general, Wolff finds positive coefficients, though not always significant.

Reflecting current interests, Dougherty and Jorgenson (1997) also analyze their growth-accounting results from the viewpoint of the convergence issue. They compute coefficient of variation in per capita output, per capita input, and the TFP across the G7 countries and find that these coefficients have decreased over time for each of these variables. This reflects a process of convergence. Dougherty and Jorgenson extend this analysis to consider the dynamics of capital and labor inputs separately, and distinguish between quality and quantity of these inputs. At this disaggregated level it is found that convergence does not hold for labor, particularly for labor quantity (as measured by hours). However, convergence was true for capital, in terms of both quantity and quality. Dougherty and Jorgenson limit their convergence analysis to graphical treatment and do not run regressions.

Does the TFP convergence hold in wider samples of countries? Since the time series growth-accounting approach has not yet been applied to large sample of countries, this question has not yet been addressed using this approach. But, what about the cross-section growth-accounting or the panel regression approach, both of which work for large sample of countries? These two approaches are relatively new, and so far these have mainly produced TFP indexes for only one time period. Unless similar sets of TFP indexes are produced for several consecutive time periods, the issue of TFP convergence, and hence of technological diffusion, cannot be adequately addressed for large sample of countries.[14]

Dowrick and Nguyen (1989) use a cross-section regression approach to examine TFP convergence in a sample of fifteen OECD countries. Instead of going through a two-stage process, as in WO or DJ, Dowrick and Nguyen want to conduct growth accounting and TFP-convergence testing in the same regression. In doing so, however, they have to assume that the capital-output ratio is the same for all countries of the sample. This assumption allows them to interpret the coefficient on the initial income variable as evidence of TFP convergence. However, the assumption of equal capital-output ratios across countries is somewhat problematic; this is even more true in the context of large samples of countries. A short-cut, single, cross-section regression procedure therefore may not be suitable for TFP convergence analysis.

11.7 Controversy regarding TFP Growth in the East Asian Countries

With each passing year, longer time series are becoming available for developing countries, and this is making application of some versions of the time series growth-accounting procedure possible for these economies too. In fact it is application of this approach to the East Asian economies that has given rise to the recent exciting debate regarding sources of economic growth.[15] It starts with Yuan Tsao Lee's (1990) growth-accounting exercise for Singapore that revealed little evidence of TFP growth. However, Alwyn Young provides the more renowned results in this debate. Young (1992) finds practically no TFP growth for Singapore and less than spectacular TFP growth in Hong Kong. Young (1995) extends the analysis to South Korea and Taiwan and finds limited role of the TFP growth for these countries too. Young (1994) conducts a cross-section regression analysis of growth and uses the residuals to gauge the importance of the TFP growth. The conclusions are similar to those he reached on the basis of time series growth-accounting analysis in Young (1992, 1995). Jong-Il Kim and Lawrence Lau (1994) also reach similar conclusions. Their work is in the tradition of Christensen, Cummings, and Jorgenson (1981) and is an application of the relative form of the time series growth-accounting approach.

Response to the above results has varied. At one extreme are those who have accepted these results, championed them, and have provided various explanations and interpretations for them. Paul Krugman is the most fa-

---

14. See Islam (2000b) for a recent attempt to compute productivity dynamics in a large sample of countries.
15. For a survey of the East Asian TFP debate, see Felipe (1999).

mous name in this regard. Krugman has popularized these conclusions through his influential articles in *Foreign Affairs* (1994) and other periodicals. This has now created a major stir in circles beyond those of economists. In the literature this has been referred to as the "accumulation" view. According to this view, East Asian growth has been mainly due to (factor) accumulation.

However, not everybody agrees with the accumulation view. To begin with, many researchers are reluctant to use the aggregate production function to separate the role of technological progress from that of factor accumulation. There are many sources of this reluctance. One of these goes back to the interaction issue that is emphasized by Moses Abramovitz, Paul David, Richard Nelson, and others (see, e.g., Abramovitz 1956 and 1993, Abramovitz and David 1973, and Nelson 1973, 1981). Proceeding from this issue, Nelson argues for an evolutionary theory of technological progress that emphasizes industry- or firm-level analysis. In studying the East Asian growth, many researchers of this tradition and others have emphasized the role of assimilation of new technology, giving rise to the "assimilation" view of the East Asian growth.[16] However, the assimilation view may not be always in a clear contradiction with the accumulation view because adoption of new technology can occur without accompanying TFP growth. This will happen if the new technology is excessively costly or not efficiently utilized (or both), a point that Krugman (1994) notes.

Since the appearance of the accumulation view, several researchers have published works showing that the role of TFP growth in East Asian economies has not been as small as claimed by accumulationists; this may be called the "revisionist" view. Among works of this view are Collins and Bosworth (1997), Klenow and Rodriguez (1997), and Marti (1996). Both Collins and Bosworth (1997) and Klenow and Rodriguez (1997) use the time series growth-accounting procedure. According to Collins and Bosworth, the TFP growth for Singapore averages to 1.5 percent per year and accounts for 27.8 percent of the output growth for 1960–1994. For more recent periods, the role of the TFP growth is found to be more pronounced. Between 1984 and 1994, according to these authors, the TFP growth averages to 3.1 percent per year and accounts for 51.7 percent of Singapore's output growth. Similarly, Klenow and Rodriguez find that for the 1960–1985 period, the TFP growth in Singapore averages to 3.3 percent per year and accounts for 64.4 percent of that country's output growth. Marti (1996) presents a cross-section growth regression similar to that of Young (1994), but estimated using a more recent version of the

---

16. Among works representing this view are Dahlman and Westphal (1981), Dahlman, Larson, and Westphal (1987), Hobday (1994a,b), Nelson and Pack (1996), Pack and Page (1994), and Page (1994).

Summers-Heston data set. The results prove to be very different. The TFP growth rate for Singapore proves to be 1.49 percent during 1970–1985 compared to 0.1 percent obtained by Young (1994).

The views expressed in these revisionist papers agree in spirit with the TFP results of Hall and Jones and Islam reviewed earlier. According to Hall and Jones, the TFP indexes for Singapore and Hong Kong in 1988 are 103 and 109 percent of the U.S. level, respectively (see tables 11.3 and 11.4.) It is difficult for these economies to attain such high relative TFP levels in 1988 unless they have experienced significant TFP growth during the past years. According to the Islam index, the TFP levels of Singapore and Hong Kong for 1960–1985 are 86.1 and 153.7 percent of the U.S. level, respectively (see tables 11.3 and 11.5). The Islam results agree with one aspect of Young's results, which show that Singapore's TFP performance is significantly worse than that of Hong Kong.[17] However, according to the Islam index, Singapore's relative TFP level is among the top five economies of the world.

The dispute regarding sources of the East Asian growth is yet to be settled. There is clearly some scope of agreement between the assimilation and the revisionist views. The latter concedes an important role to the TFP growth but does not generally inquire into the precise mechanism through which the TFP growth is achieved. The insights obtained from microanalysis are certainly valuable in that regard and can play an important complementary role in our overall understanding of the nature and sources of the East Asian growth.[18]

11.8 Concluding Remarks

This paper compares the methodologies and results of several approaches to the international comparison of TFP. The comparison of results reveals both similarities and dissimilarities. While similarities are heartening, dissimilarities should not prove discouraging. The results compared here were obtained not only from different methodologies but also from different data, different sample, and different time periods. The TFP, by definition, is a complicated social phenomenon. It would rather be surprising if different approaches came out with too similar results. The important thing is to understand why the results differ. This paper tried to enhance this understanding.

In fact, the dissimilarities in results can be a stimulus for further research. In general, the current interest in international TFP comparison is a welcome development. To a certain extent this signifies a departure from

---

17. The same may be said of Hall and Jones results. In their case, however, the difference between TFP levels of Singapore and Hong Kong is not that notable.

18. Wade (1990) presents a very valuable work of this nature.

the erroneous assumption that all countries have identical technologies and differ only in factor proportion. As Lucas (1990) shows, it is difficult to explain international capital flows without recognizing significant productivity differences across countries. Prescott (1998) notes that savings rate differences are not that important—what is all-important is the TFP. Hence he concludes that, " . . . a theory of TFP is needed" (p. 1).

The first step in the development of a theory of TFP has to be better computation and understanding of the TFP differences across countries. The recent extension of the TFP comparison to large samples of countries is a positive development. It is now necessary to go beyond a *static* comparison of levels to an examination of productivity *dynamics* in these large samples. The observed large productivity differences also bring to fore the importance of technological and institutional diffusion, which is now recognized as an important source of convergence. From a policy perspective, it is therefore extremely valuable to know the factors that can accelerate the diffusion process. Study of the TFP dynamics provides the necessary point of departure for the study of technological and institutional diffusion. All the three approaches reviewed in this paper can play important roles in this study.

References

Abramovitz, M. 1956. Resource and output trends in the U.S. since 1870. *American Economic Review* 46 (May): 5–23.
———. 1993. The search for sources of growth: Areas of ignorance, old and new. *Journal of Economic History* 53 (2): 217–43.
Abramovitz, M., and P. David. 1973. Reinterpreting American economic growth: Parables and realities. *American Economic Review* 63 (May): 428–37.
Barger, H. 1969. Growth in developed nations. *Review of Economics and Statistics* 51:143–48.
Barro, R. 1991. Economic growth in a cross-section of countries. *Quarterly Journal of Economics* 106 (2): 407–43.
Bergson, A. 1975. Index numbers and the computation of factor productivity. *Review of Income and Wealth* ser. 21, no. 3 (September): 259–78.
Bernard, A., and C. Jones. 1996. Productivity levels across countries. *Economic Journal* 106:1037–44.
Caves, D. W., L. R. Christensen, and E. W. Diewert. 1982. Multilateral comparison of output, input, and productivity using superlative index numbers. *Economic Journal* 92 (March): 73–86.
Chamberlain, G. 1982. Multivariate regression models for panel data. *Journal of Econometrics* 18:5–46.
———. 1984. Panel data. In *Handbook of econometrics*, ed. Z. Griliches and M. Intrilligator, 1247–1318. Amsterdam: North-Holland.
Chenery, H., S. Robinson, and M. Sirquin. 1985. *Industrialization and growth: A comparative study.* New York: Oxford University Press.

Christensen, L., D. Cummings, and D. Jorgenson. 1980. Economic growth, 1947–1973: An international comparison. In *New developments in productivity measurement and analysis.* Vol. 41 of NBER's *Studies in income and wealth,* ed. J. W. Kendrick and B. Vaccara, 595–698. Chicago: University of Chicago Press.

———. 1981. Relative productive levels, 1947–1973: An international comparison. *European Economic Review* 76:62–74.

Collins, S., and B. P. Bosworth. 1997. Economic growth in East Asia: Accumulation vs. assimilation. *Brookings Papers on Economic Activity,* issue no. 2:135–203.

Dahlman, C., B. Larson, and L. Westphal. 1987. Managing technological development: Lessons from the newly industrializing countries. *World Development* 15 (6): 759–75.

Dahlman, C., and L. Westphal. 1981. The meaning of technological mastery in relation to transfer of technology. *Annals of the American Academy of Political and Social Sciences* 458 (November): 12–26.

Denison, E. F. 1967. *Why growth rates differ.* Washington, D.C.: Brookings Institution.

———. 1985. *Trends in American economic growth, 1929–1982.* Washington, D.C.: Brookings Institution.

Dollar, D., and E. N. Wolff. 1994. Capital intensity and TFP convergence in manufacturing, 1963–1985. In *Convergence of productivity: Cross national studies and historical evidence,* ed. W. J. Baumol, R. R. Nelson, and E. N. Wolff, 197–224. New York: Oxford University Press.

Domar, E., E. M. Scott, B. H. Herrick, P. H. Hohenberg, M. D. Intrilligator, and M. Miyamato. 1964. Economic growth and productivity in the U.S., Canada, U.K., Germany, and Japan in the postwar period. *Review of Economics and Statistics* 46 (1): 33–40.

Dougherty, C., and D. W. Jorgenson. 1996. International comparison of sources of growth. *American Economic Review* 86 (2): 25–29.

———. 1997. There is no silver bullet: Investment and growth in the G7. *National Institute Economic Review* 162:57–74.

Dowrick, S., and D. Nguyen. 1989. OECD comparative economic growth 1950–85: Catch-up and convergence. *American Economic Review* 79:1010–30.

Durlauf, S., and P. Johnson. 1995. Multiple regimes and cross-country growth behavior. *Journal of Applied Econometrics* 10:365–84.

Durlauf, S., and D. Quah. 1998. The new empirics of economic growth. NBER Working Paper no. 6422. Cambridge, Mass.: National Bureau of Economic Research.

Ezaki, M., and D. Jorgenson. 1973. Measurement of macroeconomic performance of Japan, 1951–1968. In *Economic growth: The Japanese experience since the Meiji era,* vol. 1, ed. K. Ohkawa and Y. Hayami, 286–361. Tokyo: Japan Economic Research Center.

Färe, R., S. Grosskopf, M. Norris, and Z. Zhang. 1994. Productivity growth, technical progress, and efficiency change in industrialized countries. *American Economic Review* 84 (1): 66–83.

Felipe, J. 1999. Total factor productivity growth in East Asia: A critical survey. *Journal of Development Studies* 35 (4): 1–41.

Hall, R., and C. Jones. 1996. The productivity of nations. NBER Working Paper no. 5812. Cambridge, Mass.: National Bureau of Economic Research.

———. 1997. Levels of economic activity across countries. *American Economic Review* 87:173–77.

———. 1999. Why do some countries produce so much more per capita output than others? *Quarterly Journal of Economics* 114:83–116.

Hobday, M. 1994a. Export-led technologies in the four dragons: The case of electronics. *Development and Change* 25:333–61.

———. 1994b. Technological learning in Singapore: A test case of leapfrogging. *Journal of Development Studies* 30 (3): 831–58.
Islam, N. 1995. Growth empirics: A panel data approach. *Quarterly Journal of Economics* 110:1127–70.
———. 1996. Convergence: Variations in concepts and empirical results. Unpublished Manuscript.
———. 2000a. Small sample performance of dynamic panel data estimators in estimating the growth-convergence equation. *Advances in Econometrics* 15: 317–39.
———. 2000b. Productivity dynamics in a large sample of countries: A panel study. Manuscript.
Jorgenson, D. 1995a. *Productivity: International comparison of economic growth.* Cambridge: MIT Press.
———. 1995b. *Productivity: Post-war U.S. economic growth.* Cambridge: MIT Press.
Jorgenson, D., and M. Nishimizu. 1978. U.S. and Japanese economic growth, 1952–1974. *Economic Journal* 88:707–26.
Kenen, P. 1993. *International economics.* New York: Prentice Hall.
Kim, J.-I., and L. Lau. 1994. The sources of growth in East Asian newly industrialized countries. *Journal of the Japanese and International Economies* 8:235–71.
Klenow, P. J., and A. Rodriguez-Clare. 1997. The neoclassical revival in growth economics: Has it gone too far? In *NBER Macroeconomics Annual,* ed. B. S. Bernanke and J. Rotemberg, 73–114. Cambridge: MIT Press.
Kravis, I. B. 1976. A survey of international comparisons of productivity. *Economic Journal* 86 (March): 1–44.
Kravis, I. B., A. W. Heston, and R. Summers. 1978. *United Nations International Comparison Project: Phase II: International comparison of real product and purchasing power.* Baltimore: Johns Hopkins University Press.
Krugman, P. 1994. The myth of Asia's miracle. *Foreign Affairs* (November/December): 62–78.
Kuznets, S. 1971. *Economic growth of nations: Total output and production structure.* Cambridge: Harvard University Press.
Lee, Y. T. 1990. An overview of the ASEAN economies. *Singapore Economic Review* 35 (1): 16–37.
Lucas, R. E., Jr. 1990. Why doesn't capital flow from rich to poor countries? *American Economic Review* 80 (2): 92–96.
Maddison, A. 1982. *Phases of capitalist development.* New York: Oxford University Press.
Maddison, A. 1987. Growth and slowdown in advanced capitalist economies: Techniques of quantitative assessment. *Journal of Economic Literature* 25: 649–98.
Mankiw, G. 1995. The growth of nations. *Brookings Papers on Economic Activity,* issue no. 1: 275–325.
Mankiw, G., D. Romer, and D. Weil. 1992. A contribution to the empirics of economic growth. *Quarterly Journal of Economics* 107:407–37.
Marti, C. 1996. Is there an East Asian Miracle? Geneva, Union Bank of Switzerland, Economic Research Working Paper (October).
Nadiri, I. 1970. Some approaches to the theory and measurement of total factor productivity. *Journal of Economic Literature* 8 (2): 1137–77.
———. 1972. International studies of factor inputs and total factor productivity: A brief survey. *Review of Income and Wealth* ser. 18, no. 2: 129–54.
Nelson, R. 1973. Recent exercises in growth accounting: New understanding or dead ends? *American Economic Review* 63 (June): 462–68.
———. 1981. Research on productivity growth and productivity differences: Dead ends and new departures. *Journal of Economic Literature* 29 (September): 1029–64.

Nelson, R., and H. Pack. 1996. The East Asian growth miracle and modern growth theory. Columbia University, Department of Economics, Working Paper.

Nishimizu, M., and J. M. Page Jr. 1982. Total factor productivity growth, technological progress, and technical efficiency change: Dimensions of productivity change in Yugoslavia, 1965–78. *Economic Journal* 92 (December): 920–36.

Pack, H., and J. M. Page. 1994. Reply to Alwyn Young. *Carnegie-Rochester Conference Series on Public Policy* 40:251–57.

Page, J. M. 1994. The East Asian Miracle: Four lessons for development policy. In *NBER Macroeconomics Annual,* ed. S. Fischer and J. Rotemberg, 219–81. Cambridge: MIT Press.

Prescott, E. 1998. Needed: A theory of total factor productivity. *International Economic Review* 39 (3): 525–51.

Psacharopoulos, George. 1994. Returns to investment in education: A global update. *World Development* 22 (9): 1325–43.

Solow, R. 1957. Technical change and the aggregate production function. *Review of Economics and Statistics* 39:312–20.

Solow, R. 1988. Growth theory and after. *American Economic Review* 78:307–17.

Solow, R. 1994. Perspectives on growth theory. *Journal of Economic Perspectives* 8 (1): 45–54.

Temple, J. 1999. New growth evidence. *Journal of Economic Literature* 37 (1): 112–56.

Tinbergen, J. 1959. On the theory of trend movements. In *Jan Tinbergen, selected papers,* trans. H. Wilke, 182–221. Amsterdam: North-Holland. (Originally published as Tinbergen, J. 1942. Zur theorie der langfristigen wirtschaftsentwicklung. *Weltwirtschaftliches Archiv* 55 [1]: 511–49.)

Wade, R. 1990. *Governing the market: Economic theory and the role of government in East Asian industrialization.* Princeton, N.J.: Princeton University Press.

Wolff, E. 1991. Capital formation and productivity convergence over the long term. *American Economic Review* 81:565–79.

Young, A. 1992. A tale of two cities: Factor accumulation and technical change in Hong Kong and Singapore. *NBER Macroeconomics Annual,* 13–54. Cambridge: MIT Press.

Young, A. 1994. Lessons from the NICs: A contrarian view. *European Economic Review* 38:964–73.

Young, A. 1995. The tyranny of numbers: Confronting the statistical realities of the East Asian growth experience. *Quarterly Journal of Economics* 110:641–80.

Comment   Charles I. Jones

This paper provides a nice discussion of the literature on productivity comparisons. My comments on the paper are divided into three parts. I begin narrowly, presenting a closer look at the Islam (1995) and Hall and Jones (1996, 1999) productivity calculations. Next, I try to summarize what I take to be the most important empirical finding of these productiv-

---

Charles I. Jones is assistant professor of economics at Stanford University and a faculty research fellow of the National Bureau of Economic Research.

ity comparisons. Finally, I end by speculating on the reasons for differences in productivity across countries.

First, let me present some narrow remarks on the productivity levels that Islam compares. The Islam productivity levels are computed from a regression with panel data from the fixed country effects. Islam (1995) assumes a Cobb-Douglas functional form for the production function and estimates the parameters of the production function econometrically. The key identifying assumptions in this approach are that the idiosyncratic changes in the productivity level over time are orthogonal to the included "exogenous" variables, including investment rates in physical and human capital.

The Hall and Jones (1996, 1999) productivity levels are calculated in two ways. The first approach, discussed in Islam's paper, is to apply the accounting methods of Solow (1957) across space instead of across time— one can interpret Solow's t as indexing countries instead of years. This approach does not require specifying a functional form for the production function. Rather, one assumes something like constant returns to scale and perfectly competitive factor markets. In addition, one must make assumptions about the ordering of countries (notice that time has a natural order but space does not). In the second approach, emphasized in the published version, Hall and Jones (1999) assumes a Cobb-Douglas functional form for production and obtain the parameter values from existing empirical work or "neoclassical" assumptions. For example, we assume an elasticity with respect to physical capital of one-third and a return to education that is 13.4 percent for the first four years, 10.1 percent for the next four years, and 6.8 percent for additional years beyond the eighth year of education. These returns come from the microestimates reviewed by Psacharopoulos (1994). While the Solow approach is preferable from an intellectual standpoint, it turns out not to produce very different estimates from the Cobb-Douglas approach, at least for reasonable parameter values.

So the difference between the Islam approach and the Hall and Jones approach is one of identifying assumptions. Islam, like Mankiw, Romer, and Weil (1992) before him, uses orthogonality conditions to estimate the shape of the production function. Hall and Jones use neoclassical assumptions about production to get the parameters. Clearly, the two approaches are complementary. We preferred not to use the econometric approach because it seems plausible to us that productivity levels, and changes in the level, are correlated with investment rates in physical and human capital. Indeed, under our assumptions, we show that the correlation between levels is quite strong. A drawback of our approach is that if there are large externalities to physical or human capital accumulation, the neoclassical assumptions will be misleading.

The levels of productivity calculated in these two different ways are plotted in figure 11C.1.

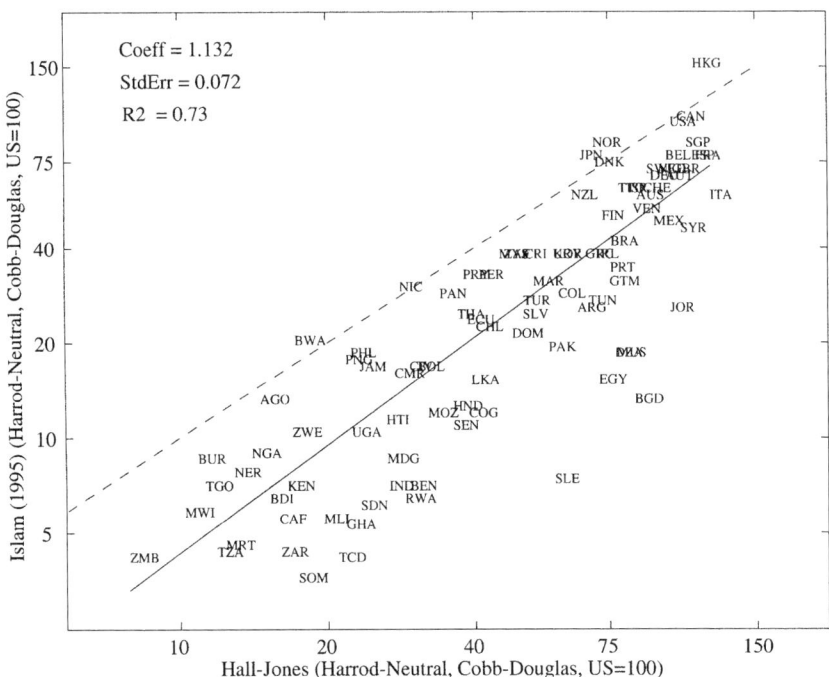

Fig. 11C.1 Productivity levels: Islam and Hall-Jones
Note: The solid line is a regression line; the dashed line is the 45-degree line.

The first thing one sees from this figure is that the productivity levels are fairly similar, at least to a first approximation. The correlation between the two series is 0.85. Of course, there are also some sharp differences for individual countries. The second thing one notices is that the regression line is different from the 45-degree line, mainly due to the intercept. That is, Islam's productivity levels are typically lower than the Hall and Jones productivity levels.

What accounts for the differences? One key difference comes from looking at the shape of the production function implied by Islam's econometric estimates. In particular, led by these estimates, Islam assigns a zero weight to human capital. His econometric specifications with human capital actually suggest a negative coefficient. The weight on physical capital, estimated imposing a zero coefficient on human capital, is about 0.44. To compare our results on a more equal footing, I recalculated the Hall and Jones productivity levels assuming these parameter values. The results are shown in figure 11C.2.

The differences in productivity across countries line up much better in terms of the actual levels, but there is still a fair amount of disagreement

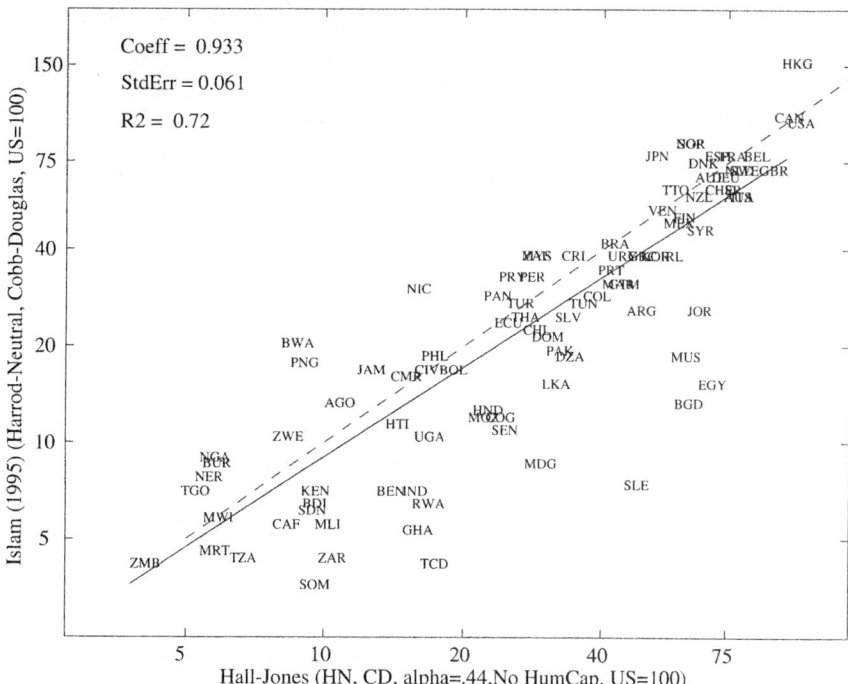

Fig. 11C.2 Productivity levels: Islam and Hall-Jones with Islam's parameters
Note: The solid line is a regression line; the dashed line is the 45-degree line.

for individual countries. This could reflect the fact that Islam's numbers correspond roughly to an average over the 1960 to 1985 period while the Hall and Jones numbers correspond to the year 1988. Or, there could be something else going on. Clearly, however, ignoring human capital is important—any differences in human capital that actually matter for production will show up in Islam's productivity level, largely explaining why he finds lower levels on average. My hunch is that differences in human capital across countries are probably an important contributing factor to differences in output, and that the negative econometric estimates on human capital that Islam and Benhabib and Spiegel (1994) and others find reflect primarily a problem with the econometric approach.

The second comment I would like to make is to provide a summary of what I think is the most important thing we learn from levels accounting. In a paper like this, it is natural to emphasize differences, such as differences in method. Nevertheless, by taking a step back, one can see that many different methods yield the same qualitative answer: Levels accounting finds a large residual.

To put this in perspective and explain how the finding arises, let me introduce some notation. Consider an aggregate production function of the form $Y = K^\alpha(AH)^{1-\alpha}$, where Y is output, K is physical capital, H is human capital, A is productivity (written as labor augmenting or Harrod-neutral), and $0 < \alpha < 1$. Assume that capital is simply foregone consumption, as usual, and assume that human capital per person arises from schooling: $h \equiv H/L = e^{\phi S}$, where $\phi > 0$ is the Mincerian return to schooling and S is years of schooling. In a framework like this, one can decompose output per worker, $y \equiv Y/L$ into the product of three terms:

$$y = \left(\frac{K}{Y}\right)^{\alpha/1-\alpha} hA.$$

That is, output per worker is the product of a capital intensity term, a human capital term, and a productivity term.

We can apply this equation across countries at a point in time to conduct a levels accounting exercise, assuming neoclassical values for α and ϕ, as discussed above. A useful summary of this accounting, taken from Hall and Jones (1999), is found by considering the ratios of the terms in the above equation for the five richest and five poorest countries. The ratio of output per worker in the five richest countries to the five poorest countries is a factor of 31.7. A relatively small portion of this difference is due to differences in capital intensity and human capital, factors of 1.8 and 2.2, respectively. Differences in productivity between these countries are far more important, contributing a factor of 8.3 to the difference in output per worker. (Notice that $31.7 \approx 1.8 \times 2.2 \times 8.3$.)

The intuition for this result is also fairly easy to see. In a standard neoclassical model, the capital-output ratio is proportional to the investment rate in steady state. Differences in investment rates between the rich countries and poor countries are fairly small; for this sample the average difference is about a factor of 3. With $\alpha = 1/3$, it is the square root of this difference that matters, which is why capital intensity accounts for only about a factor of 1.8. A similar calculation applies to human capital. The rich countries have about eight more years of schooling on average than the poor countries. With a return to education of about 10 percent per year, this can explain a difference of 0.8 in logs, and the exponential of 0.8 is about 2.2. Differences in investment rates and educational attainment are fairly small across countries, particularly when "multiplied" by neoclassical parameter values. Therefore, the residual (productivity) is left to explain the bulk of differences in output per worker across countries.

My third and final comment, then, concerns the economic factors that can explain the differences in these residuals across countries. I can think of three possible explanations. One explanation is other inputs that are not included in the analysis. For example, differences in the experience of the labor force, the quality of education, or the quality of capital (e.g., vintage effects) could explain the differences. Klenow and Rodriguez-Clare (1997) and Sinclair (1998) have looked into these explanations and find that differences in productivity are still substantial even after these effects are taken into account. Another explanation is that differences in productivity reflect true differences in technologies across countries. This seems plausible, but begs the question of why countries do not use the latest new ideas. The answer may be quite similar to the answer to the question of why some countries have so much lower capital intensity and educational attainment than others. A final possible explanation is differences in the utilization of resources. In part, this is simply a measurement story, but it could have deeper roots. For example, in a simple farmer and thief model, some of the farmer's education and labor effort could go to protecting his output rather than to producing output, and some capital could be used as fences rather than as tractors. Hall and I explore these explanations in greater detail.

According to the results of several approaches, differences in productivity levels across countries are substantial. If we are to understand why some countries are so much richer than others, then it seems likely that we will require an explanation for why some countries get so much more out of their inputs. To paraphrase the title of a recent paper by Prescott (1997), we will need a theory of productivity differences.

References

Benhabib, Jess, and Mark M. Spiegel. 1994. The role of human capital in economic development: Evidence from aggregate cross-country data. *Journal of Monetary Economics* 34:143–73.

Hall, Robert E., and Charles I. Jones. 1996. The productivity of nations. NBER Working Paper no. 5812. Cambridge, Mass.: National Bureau of Economic Research (November).

———. 1999. Why do some countries produce so much more output per worker than others? *Quarterly Journal of Economics* 114 (February): 83–116.

Islam, Nazrul. 1995. Growth empirics: A panel data approach. *Quarterly Journal of Economics* 110 (November): 1127–70.

Klenow, Peter, and Andres Rodriguez-Clare. 1997. The neoclassical revival in growth economics: Has it gone too far? In *NBER Macroeconomics Annual*, ed. Ben S. Bernanke and Julio J. Rotemberg, 73–114. Cambridge: MIT Press.

Mankiw, N. Gregory, David Romer, and David Weil. 1992. A contribution to the empirics of economic growth. *Quarterly Journal of Economics* 107 (2): 407–38.

Prescott, Edward C. 1997. Needed: A theory of total factor productivity. Federal Reserve Bank of Minneapolis, Staff Report no. 242.

Psacharopoulos, George. 1994. Returns to investment in education: A global update. *World Development* 22 (9): 1325–43.

Sinclair, Robert D. 1998. Accounting for embodied technical change and the quality of human capital: A new look at cross-country productivity levels. Stanford University, Department of Economics, Mimeograph.

Solow, Robert M. 1957. Technical change and the aggregate production function. *Review of Economics and Statistics* 39 (3): 312–20.

12 Whatever Happened to Productivity Growth?

Dale W. Jorgenson and Eric Yip

12.1 Introduction

In this paper we present international comparisons of patterns of economic growth among the G7 countries over the period 1960–95. Between 1960 and 1973 productivity growth accounted for more than half of growth in output per capita for France, Germany, Italy, Japan, and the United Kingdom and somewhat less than half of output growth in Canada and the United States. The relative importance of productivity declined substantially after 1973, accounting for a predominant share of growth between 1973 and 1989 only for France.

Since 1989 productivity growth has almost disappeared as a source of economic growth in the G7 countries. Between 1989 and 1995 productivity growth was negative for five of the G7 countries, with positive growth only for Japan and the United States. The level of productivity for Canada in 1995 fell almost to the level first achieved in 1973, and declines in Italy and the United Kingdom brought productivity down to the levels of 1974 and 1978, respectively. Since 1989 input per capita has grown more slowly than the average for the period 1960–89, except for Germany.

The United States has retained its lead in output per capita throughout the period 1960–95. The United States has also led the G7 countries in input per capita, while relinquishing its lead in productivity to France. However, the United States has lagged behind Canada, France, Germany,

---

Dale W. Jorgenson is the Frederic E. Abbe Professor of Economics at Harvard University. Eric Yip is a consultant at McKinsey and Company.

We gratefully acknowledge financial support by the Program on Technology and Economic Policy of Harvard University. Responsibility for any remaining deficiencies rests solely with the authors.

Italy, and Japan in the growth of output per capita, surpassing only the United Kingdom. Except for Germany and the United Kingdom, the United States has lagged behind all the G7 countries in growth in input per capita, and U.S. productivity growth has exceeded only that of Canada and the United Kingdom.

Japan exhibited considerably higher growth rates in output per capita and productivity than the other G7 countries from 1960 to 1995, but most of these gains took place before 1973. Japan's productivity level, along with the levels of Germany and Italy, remain among the lowest in the G7. Japan's performance in output per capita owes more to high input per capita than to high productivity. The growth of Japanese input per capita greatly exceeded that for other G7 countries, especially prior to 1973.

During the period 1960–95, economic performance among the G7 countries became more uniform. The dispersion of levels of output per capita fell sharply before 1970 and has declined modestly since then. The dispersion in productivity levels also fell before 1970 and has remained within a narrow range. The dispersion of levels of input per capita has been stable throughout the period 1960–95. However, the relative positions of the G7 countries have been altered considerably with the dramatic rise of Japan and the gradual decline of the United Kingdom.

We can rationalize the important changes in economic performance that have taken place among the G7 countries on the basis of the neoclassical theory of economic growth, extended to incorporate persistent differences among countries. Productivity growth is exogenous, whereas investment is endogenous to the theory. Obviously, the relative importance of exogenous productivity growth has been greatly reduced, and a more prominent role must be assigned to endogenous investment in tangible assets and human capital.

In section 12.2 we describe the methodology for allocating the sources of economic growth between investment and productivity. We introduce constant quality indexes of capital and labor inputs that incorporate the impacts of investments in tangible assets and human capital. The constant quality index of labor input combines different types of hours worked by means of relative wage rates. The constant quality index of capital input weights different types of capital stocks by rental rates, rather than the asset prices used for weighting capital stocks.

Differences in wage rates for different types of labor inputs reflect investments in human capital through education and training, so that a constant quality index of labor input is the channel for the impact of these investments on economic performance. The constant quality index of capital input includes a perpetual inventory of investments in tangible assets. The index also incorporates differences in rental prices that capture the differential impacts of these investments.

In section 12.3 we analyze the role of investment and productivity as sources of growth in the G7 countries over the period 1960–95. We subdivide this period at 1973 to identify changes in performance after the first oil crisis. We employ 1989 as another dividing point to focus on the most recent experience. We decompose growth of output per capita for each country between growth of productivity and growth of input per capita. Finally, we decompose the growth of input per capita into components associated with investments in tangible assets and human capital.

International comparisons reveal important similarities among the G7 countries. Investments in tangible assets and human capital now account for the overwhelming proportion of economic growth in the G7 countries and also explain the predominant share of international differences in output per capita. Heterogeneity in capital and labor inputs and changes in the composition of these inputs over time are essential for identifying persistent international differences and for accounting for growth.

In section 12.4 we test the important implication of the neoclassical theory of growth that relative levels of output and input per capita must converge over time. For this purpose we employ the coefficient of variation to measure convergence of levels of output per capita, input per capita, and productivity among the G7 countries over the period 1960–95. As before, we divide the period at 1973 and 1989. We also analyze the convergence of capital and labor inputs per capita implied by the theory.

In section 12.5 we summarize the conclusions of our study and outline alternative approaches to endogenous growth through broadening the concept of investment. The mechanism for endogenous accumulation of tangible assets captured in Solow's (1956) version of the neoclassical theory provides the most appropriate point of departure. Investments in human capital, especially investment in education, can now be incorporated into the theory. When measures of the output of R&D activities become available, investment in intellectual capital can be made endogenous.

12.2 Investment and Productivity

Ongoing debates over the relative importance of investment and productivity in economic growth coincide with disputes about the appropriate role for the public sector. Productivity can be identified with spillovers of benefits that fail to provide incentives for actors within the private sector. Advocates of a larger role for the public sector hold the position that these spillovers can be guided into appropriate channels by an all-wise and beneficent government. By contrast proponents of a smaller government search for methods of decentralizing investment decisions among participants in the private sector.

Profound differences in policy implications militate against any simple resolution of the debate on the relative importance of investment and productivity. Proponents of income redistribution will not lightly abandon the search for a silver bullet that will generate economic growth without the necessity of providing incentives for investment. Advocates of growth strategies based on capital formation will not readily give credence to claims of spillovers to beneficiaries who are difficult or impossible to identify.

To avoid the semantic confusion that pervades popular discussions of economic growth, it is essential to be precise in defining investment. Investment is the commitment of current resources in the expectation of future returns and can take a multiplicity of forms. The distinctive feature of investment as a source of economic growth is that the returns can be internalized by the investor. The most straightforward application of this definition is to investment in tangible assets that creates property rights, including rights to the incomes that accrue to the owners of the assets.

The mechanism by which tangible investments are translated into economic growth is well understood. For example, an investor in a new industrial facility adds to the supply of these facilities and generates a stream of property income. Investment and income are linked through markets for capital assets and their services. The increase in capital input contributes to output growth in proportion to the marginal product of capital. The stream of property income can be divided between capital input and its marginal product. Identifying this marginal product with the rental price of capital provides the basis for a constant quality index of capital input.

The seminal contributions of Becker (1993), Machlup (1962), Mincer (1974), and Schultz (1961) have given concrete meaning to a notion of wealth including investments that do not create property rights. For example, a student enrolled in school or a worker participating in a training program can be viewed as an investor. Although these investments do not create assets that can be bought or sold, the returns to higher educational qualifications or better skills in the workplace can be internalized by the investor.

An individual who completes a course of education or training adds to the supply of people with higher qualifications or skills. The resulting stream of labor income can be divided between labor input and its marginal product. The increase in labor contributes to output growth in proportion to the marginal product. Identifying this marginal product with the wage rate provides the basis for a constant quality index of labor input. Although there are no asset markets for human capital, investments in human and nonhuman capital have in common that returns to these investments can be internalized.

The defining characteristic of productivity as a source of economic growth is that the incomes generated by higher productivity are external to the economic activities that generate growth. Publicly supported R&D programs are a leading illustration of activities that stimulate productivity growth. These programs can be conducted by government laboratories or financed by public subsidies to private laboratories. The resulting benefits are external to the economic units conducting R&D. These benefits must be carefully distinguished from the private benefits of R&D that can be internalized through the creation of intellectual property rights.[1]

The allocation of sources of economic growth between investment and productivity is critical for assessing the explanatory power of growth theory. Only substitution between capital and labor inputs resulting from investment in tangible assets is endogenous in Solow's (1956) neoclassical theory of growth. However, substitution among different types of labor inputs is the consequence of investment in human capital, whereas investment in tangible assets induces substitution among different types of capital inputs. Neither form of substitution is incorporated into Solow's (1957) model of production.

The distinction between substitution and technical change emphasized by Solow (1957) parallels the distinction between investment and productivity as sources of economic growth. However, Solow's definition of investment, like that of Kuznets (1971), was limited to tangible assets. Both specifically excluded investments in human capital by relying on increases in undifferentiated hours of work as a measure of the contribution of labor input.

The contribution of investment in tangible assets to economic growth is proportional to the rental price of capital, which reflects the marginal product of capital. By contrast the asset price of capital reflects the present value of the income from a capital asset over its entire lifetime. Both Kuznets (1971) and Solow (1970) identified the contributions of tangible assets to growth with increases in the stock of capital, weighted by asset prices. By failing to employ the marginal products of tangible assets as weights, Kuznets and Solow misallocated the sources of economic growth between investment in tangible assets and productivity.[2]

Investment can be made endogenous within a neoclassical growth model, whereas productivity growth is exogenous. If productivity greatly predominates among sources of growth, as indicated by Kuznets (1971) and Solow (1970), most of growth is determined exogenously. Reliance on the Solow residual as an explanatory factor is a powerful indictment of the limitations of the neoclassical framework. This viewpoint was expressed by Abramovitz (1956), who famously characterized the Solow residual as a measure of our ignorance.

Jorgenson and Griliches (1967) introduced constant quality indexes of capital and labor inputs and a constant quality measure of investment

---

1. Griliches (1992, 1995) has provided detailed surveys of spillovers from R&D investment. Griliches (1992) gives a list of survey papers on spillovers.
2. The measurement conventions of Kuznets and Solow remain in common use. See, for example, Hall and Jones (1999) and the references given by Jorgenson (1990).

goods output in allocating the sources of growth between investment and productivity. This greatly broadened the concept of substitution employed by Solow (1957) and altered, irrevocably, the allocation of economic growth between investment and productivity. They showed that 85 percent of U.S. economic growth could be attributed to investment, whereas productivity accounted for only 15 percent (Jorgenson and Griliches 1967, table IX, p. 272).

The measure of labor input employed by Jorgenson and Griliches combined different types of hours worked, weighted by wage rates, into a constant quality index of labor input, using methodology that Griliches (1960) had developed for U.S. agriculture.[3] Their constant quality index of capital input combined different types of capital inputs by means of rental rates, rather than the asset prices appropriate for measuring capital stock. This model of capital as a factor of production was introduced by Jorgenson (1963) and made possible the incorporation of differences in capital consumption and the tax treatment of different types of capital income.[4]

Jorgenson and Griliches identified technology with a production possibility frontier. This extended the aggregate production function—introduced by Douglas (1948) and developed by Tinbergen (1959) and Solow (1957)—to include two outputs, investment and consumption goods. Jorgenson (1966) showed that economic growth could be interpreted, equivalently as embodied in investment in the sense of Solow (1960) or disembodied in productivity growth. Jorgenson and Griliches removed this indeterminacy by introducing constant quality price indexes for investment goods.

Greenwood, Hercowitz, and Krusell (1997) have recently revived Solow's (1960) concept of embodied technical change. Greenwood, Hercowitz, and Krusell have applied the constant quality indexes for producers' durable equipment constructed by Gordon (1990) to capital input, but not to the output of investment goods, as Gordon did. Within the framework presented by Jorgenson (1966) both the output of investment goods and the input of capital services must be revised in order to hold the quality of investment goods constant. This approach has been employed by Jorgenson and Stiroh (1995, 1999) in assessing the impact of investment in information technology. For this purpose they employ constant quality price indexes for computers and related equipment from the U.S. National Income and Product Accounts.

---

3. Constant quality indexes of labor input are discussed in detail by Jorgenson, Gollop, and Fraumeni (1987), Chapters 3 and 8, pp. 69–108 and 261–300; Bureau of Labor Statistics (BLS; 1993); and Ho and Jorgenson (1999).

4. Detailed surveys of empirical research on the measurement of capital input are given by Jorgenson (1996) and Triplett (1996). BLS (1983) compiled a constant quality index of capital input for its official estimates of productivity, renamed multifactor productivity. BLS retained hours worked as a measure of labor input until 11 July 1994, when it released a new multifactor productivity measure incorporating a constant quality index of labor input.

Christensen and Jorgenson (1969, 1970) imbedded the measurement of productivity in a complete system of U.S. national accounts. They provided a much more detailed model of capital input based on the framework for the taxation of corporate capital income developed by Hall and Jorgenson (1967, 1969, 1971). Christensen and Jorgenson extended this framework to include noncorporate and household capital incomes. This captured the impact of differences in returns to different types of capital inputs more fully.

Christensen and Jorgenson identified the production account with a production possibility frontier describing technology and the income and expenditure account with a social welfare function describing consumer preferences. Following Kuznets (1961), they divided the *uses* of economic growth between consumption and saving. They linked saving to the wealth account through capital accumulation equations for each type of asset. Prices for different vintages of assets were linked to rental prices of capital inputs through a parallel set of capital asset pricing equations.

In 1973 Christensen and Jorgenson constructed internally consistent income, product, and wealth accounts. Separate product and income accounts are integral parts of both the U.S. National Income and Product Accounts[5] and the United Nations' (1968) *System of National Accounts* designed by Stone.[6] However, neither system included wealth accounts consistent with the income and product accounts.

Christensen and Jorgenson constructed income, product, and wealth accounts, paralleling the U.S. National Income and Product Accounts for the period 1929–69. They also implemented a vintage accounting system for the United States on an annual basis. The complete system of vintage accounts gave stocks of assets of each vintage and their prices. The stocks were cumulated to obtain asset quantities, providing the perpetual inventory of assets employed by Goldsmith (1955–56, 1962).

The key innovation was the use of asset pricing equations to link the prices used in evaluating capital stocks and the rental prices employed in the constant quality index of capital input.[7] In a prescient paper on the measurement of welfare, Samuelson (1961) had suggested that a link between asset and rental prices was essential for the integration of income

---

5. See Bureau of Economic Analysis (BEA; 1995).

6. The United Nations System of National Accounts (SNA) is summarized by Stone (1992) in his Nobel Prize address. The SNA has been revised by the Inter-Secretariat Working Group on National Accounts (1993).

7. Constant quality price indexes for investment goods of different ages or vintages were developed by Hall (1971). This made it possible for Hulten and Wykoff (1982) to estimate relative efficiencies by age for all types of tangible assets, putting the measurement of capital consumption required for constant quality index of capital input onto a firm empirical foundation. The BEA (1995) has adopted this approach in the latest benchmark revision of the U.S. National Income and Product Accounts, following methodology described by Fraumeni (1997).

Table 12.1   Disaggregation of Capital by Asset Characteristics

Asset Type	Ownership Sector
1. Equipment 2. Nonresidential structures 3. Residential structures 4. Nonfarm inventories 5. Farm inventories 6. Consumer durables 7. Residential land 8. Nonresidential land	1. Corporations and government 2. Unincorporated businesses 3. Households and nonprofit institutions 4. General government

and wealth accounting.[8] The vintage system of accounts employed the specific form of this relationship developed by Jorgenson (1967).

Christensen, Cummings, and Jorgenson (1980) presented annual estimates of sources of economic growth for the United States and its major trading partners for the period 1960–1973. These estimates included constant quality indexes of capital and labor input for each country. Christensen, Cummings, and Jorgenson (1981) gave relative levels of output, input, and productivity for these same countries for the period 1960–1973, also based on constant quality indexes. Our first objective in this paper is to extend these estimates to 1995 for the G7 countries.[9] We have chosen GDP as a measure of output. We include imputations for the services of consumers' durables as well as land, buildings, and equipment owned by nonprofit institutions in order to preserve comparability in the treatment of income from different types of capital.

Our constant quality index of capital input is based on a disaggregation of the capital stock among the categories given in table 12.1, classified by asset type and ownership in order to reflect differences in capital consumption and tax treatment among assets. We derive estimates of capital stock and property income for each type of capital input from national accounting data. Similarly, our constant quality index of labor input is based on a disaggregation of the work force among the categories presented in table 12.2, classified by sex, educational attainment, and employment status. For each country we derive estimates of hours worked and labor compensation for each type of labor input from labor force surveys.

12.3 Sources of Growth

In table 12.3 we present output per capita annually for the G7 countries over the period 1960–95, expressed relative to the United States in 1985.

---

8. See Samuelson (1961), especially p. 309.
9. Dougherty and Jorgenson (1996, 1997) have updated the estimates of Christensen, Cummings, and Jorgenson (1980, 1981) through 1989.

Table 12.2 **Disaggregation of Labor by Demographic Characteristics**

Sex:
Educational Attainment:
1. One to eight years grade school
2. One to three years secondary school
3. Completed secondary school
4. One to three years college
5. Four or more years of college

Employment Status:
1. Business sector employee
2. Self-employed or unpaid family worker
3. General government employee

Table 12.3 **Levels of Output and Input per Capita and Productivity (U.S. = 100.0 in 1985)**

	United States	Canada	United Kingdom	France	Germany	Italy	Japan
			Output per Capita				
1960	55.6	43.1	37.5	29.2	32.9	22.7	17.3
1973	80.9	65.4	53.6	50.9	53.6	41.4	54.0
1989	109.7	96.7	70.8	70.6	75.6	63.7	83.3
1995	116.3	94.6	72.6	74.6	83.5	69.2	92.8
			Input per Capita				
1960	70.2	55.6	53.0	42.5	61.7	44.8	50.1
1973	85.6	69.4	60.1	56.3	72.5	49.7	68.6
1989	108.0	98.8	71.7	63.3	88.5	73.2	96.7
1995	112.5	100.1	77.5	68.7	98.5	80.1	106.7
			Productivity				
1960	79.2	77.5	70.9	68.8	53.4	50.7	34.5
1973	94.5	94.3	89.1	90.5	73.9	83.3	78.7
1989	101.6	97.9	98.8	111.5	85.4	87.0	86.1
1995	103.4	94.5	93.7	108.6	84.8	86.5	87.0

For completeness we present output and population separately in tables 12.4 and tables 12.5. We use 1985 purchasing power parities (PPPs) from the OECD (1987) to convert quantities of output per capita from domestic currencies for each country into U.S. dollars. The United States was the leader in per capita output throughout the period, and Canada ranked second for most of the period. Among the remaining five countries the United Kingdom started at the top and Japan at the bottom; by 1995 these roles were interchanged with Japan overtaking all four European countries and the United Kingdom lagging behind France and Germany.

In table 12.3 we present input per capita annually for the G7 countries over the period 1960–95, relative to U.S. input per capita in 1985. We express quantities of input per capita in U.S. dollars, using PPPs constructed

Table 12.4 Growth Rate and Level in Output

	United States	Canada	United Kingdom	France	Germany	Italy	Japan
			Growth Rate (percentage)				
1960–73	4.11	4.99	3.28	5.28	4.60	5.29	9.95
1973–89	2.94	4.79	1.40	2.97	2.67	4.36	3.79
1973–95	2.83	2.98	2.15	2.28	1.85	2.18	3.31
1989–95	2.00	0.94	0.78	1.49	2.45	1.32	2.14
1960–89	3.43	4.26	2.50	3.77	3.25	4.03	6.39
1960–95	3.18	3.69	2.21	3.38	3.12	3.56	5.66
			Level (billions of 1985 U.S. dollars)				
1960	1,826	140	357	243	332	207	292
1973	3,115	268	547	482	603	412	1,066
1989	4,930	481	738	724	852	666	1,863
1995	5,560	509	773	791	987	721	2,118
			Level (U.S. = 100.0 in 1985)				
1960	42.1	3.2	8.2	5.6	7.7	4.8	6.7
1973	71.9	6.2	12.6	11.1	13.9	9.5	24.6
1989	113.8	11.1	17.0	16.7	19.7	15.4	43.0
1995	128.3	11.7	17.8	18.3	22.8	16.6	48.9

Table 12.5 Growth Rate and Level in Population

	United States	Canada	United Kingdom	France	Germany	Italy	Japan
			Growth Rate (percentage)				
1960–73	1.22	1.79	0.54	1.01	0.86	0.67	1.18
1973–89	1.00	1.22	0.01	0.47	−0.17	0.45	1.07
1973–95	0.94	1.20	0.20	0.51	0.11	0.22	0.61
1989–95	1.03	1.31	0.36	0.57	0.79	−0.07	0.33
1960–89	1.08	1.47	0.31	0.73	0.39	0.47	0.96
1960–95	1.07	1.44	0.32	0.70	0.46	0.38	0.85
			Level				
1960	180.8	17.9	52.4	45.7	55.4	50.2	93.3
1973	211.9	22.6	56.2	52.1	62.0	54.8	108.7
1989	247.3	27.4	57.4	56.4	62.1	57.5	123.1
1995	263.2	29.6	58.6	58.4	65.1	57.3	125.6
			Level (U.S. = 100.0 in 1985)				
1960	75.8	7.5	22.0	19.2	23.2	21.1	39.1
1973	88.9	9.5	23.6	21.9	26.0	23.0	45.6
1989	100.0	10.9	23.8	23.2	25.6	24.0	50.6
1995	110.4	12.4	24.6	24.5	27.3	24.0	52.7

for this study.[10] The United States was the leader in per capita input as well as output throughout the period. Germany started in second place but lost its position to Canada in 1975 and Japan in 1976. In 1995 Japan ranked next to the United States in input per capita with Canada third. France started at the bottom of the ranking and remained there for most of the period. Canada, France, Italy, and Japan grew relative to the United States, whereas Germany and the United Kingdom declined.

In table 12.3 we present productivity levels annually for the G7 countries over the period 1960–95, where productivity is defined as the ratio of output to input. In 1960 the United States was the productivity leader with Canada closely behind. In 1970 Canada became the first country to overtake the United States, remaining slightly above the U.S. level for most of the period ending in 1984. France surpassed the U.S. in 1979 and became the international productivity leader after 1980. The United Kingdom overtook Canada and nearly overtook the United States in 1987, but fell behind both countries in 1990. Japan surpassed Germany in 1970 and Italy in 1990, and Italy overtook Germany in 1963 and maintained its lead during most of the period ending in 1995.

We summarize growth in output and input per capita and productivity for the G7 countries in table 12.6. (For completeness we present growth rates of output and population separately in tables 12.4 and 12.5.) We present annual average growth rates for the period 1960–95 and the subperiods 1960–73, 1973–89, and 1989–95. Japan was the leader in output growth for the period as a whole and before 1973. The United Kingdom grew more slowly than the remaining six countries during the period as a whole and after 1960. Output growth slowed in all the G7 countries after 1989, and Canada's growth rate was negative. Differences in growth rates among the G7 countries declined substantially after 1973.

Japan also led the G7 in growth of input per capita for the period 1960–95 and before 1973. Italy was the leader during the subperiod 1973–89, and Germany led during 1989–95. There is little evidence of a slowdown in input growth after 1973; differences among input growth rates are much less than among output growth rates. Japan led the G7 in productivity growth for the period as a whole and before 1973, whereas France was the leader from 1973 to 1989. All the G7 countries—with the exception of Japan and the United States—experienced negative productivity growth after 1989. The United States had a slightly higher productivity growth rate than Japan during this period. In table 12.3 we present levels of output and input per capita and productivity relative to the U.S. level in 1985.

Our constant quality index of capital input weights capital stocks for each of the categories given in table 12.1 by rental prices, defined as property compensation per unit of capital. By contrast, an index of capital

---

10. Our methodology is described in detail by Dougherty (1992).

Table 12.6   Growth in Output and Input per Capita and Productivity (percentage)

	United States	Canada	United Kingdom	France	Germany	Italy	Japan
			Output per Capita				
1960–73	2.89	3.20	2.74	4.26	3.74	4.62	8.77
1973–89	1.90	2.45	1.75	2.04	2.15	2.69	2.71
1973–95	1.65	1.68	1.38	1.74	2.02	2.34	2.46
1989–95	0.97	−0.37	0.42	0.92	1.66	1.40	1.81
1960–89	2.34	2.79	2.19	3.04	2.86	3.56	5.43
1960–95	2.11	2.24	1.89	2.68	2.66	3.19	4.81
			Input per Capita				
1960–73	1.53	1.70	0.98	2.15	1.24	0.79	2.42
1973–89	1.45	2.21	1.10	0.74	1.25	2.42	2.15
1973–95	1.24	1.67	1.15	0.91	1.39	2.17	2.01
1989–95	0.68	0.21	1.30	1.37	1.78	1.49	1.63
1960–89	1.49	1.98	1.04	1.37	1.25	1.69	2.27
1960–95	1.35	1.68	1.09	1.37	1.34	1.66	2.16
			Productivity				
1960–73	1.36	1.51	1.76	2.11	2.50	3.82	6.35
1973–89	0.45	0.23	0.65	1.31	0.90	0.27	0.56
1973–95	0.41	0.01	0.23	0.83	0.62	0.17	0.45
1989–95	0.29	−0.59	−0.88	−0.45	−0.11	−0.10	0.18
1960–89	0.86	0.80	1.15	1.67	1.62	1.86	3.16
1960–95	0.76	0.57	0.80	1.30	1.32	1.53	2.65

stock weights different types of capital by asset prices rather than by the rental prices appropriate for capital input. The ratio of capital input to capital stock measures the average quality of a unit of capital, as reflected in its marginal product. This enables us to assess the magnitude of differences between the constant quality index of capital input and the unweighted index of capital stock employed by Kuznets (1971) and Solow (1970).

In table 12.7 we present capital input per capita annually for the G7 countries over the period 1960–95, expressed relative to the United States in 1985. The United States was the leader in capital input per capita through 1991, when Canada overtook the United States and emerged as the international leader. All countries grew substantially relative to the United States, but only Canada surpassed the U.S. level. Germany led the remaining five countries throughout the period, and the United Kingdom was the laggard among these countries, except for the period 1962–73, when Japan ranked lower.

The picture for capital stock per capita has some similarities to capital input, but there are important differences. The United States led throughout the period in capital stock, whereas Canada overtook the United

Table 12.7 Levels of Capital Input and Capital Stock per Capita and Capital Quality (U.S. = 100.0 in 1985)

	United States	Canada	United Kingdom	France	Germany	Italy	Japan
			Capital Input per Capita				
1960	58.5	41.7	21.0	24.0	26.0	17.1	21.6
1973	79.0	61.9	32.4	46.8	56.6	38.4	31.6
1989	109.4	106.7	52.6	76.4	91.9	80.7	56.4
1995	114.3	119.2	60.4	87.1	108.5	97.3	68.3
			Capital Stock per Capita				
1960	68.2	43.3	18.8	18.8	20.1	19.6	17.3
1973	85.8	60.3	28.0	38.1	41.3	37.5	25.4
1989	105.3	93.3	42.9	63.4	62.9	65.9	47.8
1995	109.4	98.5	48.2	71.8	74.9	79.6	58.7
			Capital Quality				
1960	85.8	96.3	111.8	127.2	129.1	87.6	124.7
1973	92.1	102.7	116.1	122.8	137.1	102.2	124.1
1989	103.9	114.3	122.7	120.6	146.1	122.5	118.0
1995	104.5	121.0	125.2	121.3	144.8	122.2	116.3

States in capital input. France, Germany, and Italy had similar stock levels throughout the period with Italy leading this group of three countries in 1995. Similarly, Japan and the United Kingdom had similar levels throughout the period; Japan ranked last until 1976 but surpassed the United Kingdom in that year. Capital stock levels do not accurately reflect the substitutions among capital inputs that accompany investments in tangible assets.

Capital quality is the ratio of capital input to capital stock. The behavior of capital quality highlights the differences between the constant quality index of capital input and capital stock. Germany was the international leader in capital quality throughout most of the period 1960–95, and the United States ranked at the bottom. There are important changes in capital quality over time and persistent differences among countries. Heterogeneity of capital input within each country and between countries must be taken into account in international comparisons of economic performance.

We summarize growth in capital input and capital stock per capita and capita quality for the G7 countries in table 12.8. Italy was the international leader in capital input growth, and the United States was the laggard for the period 1960–95. There was a modest slowdown in capital input growth after 1973 and again after 1989 as well as similar slowdowns in capital stock growth. Italy was the leader in capital quality growth, and Japan was the laggard. In table 12.7 we present levels of capital input and capital stock per capita and capital quality relative to the United States in 1985.

Our constant quality index of labor input weights hours worked for each

Table 12.8   Growth in Capital Input and Capital Stock per Capita and Capital Quality (percentage)

	United States	Canada	United Kingdom	France	Germany	Italy	Japan
			Capital Input per Capita				
1960–73	2.32	3.03	3.34	5.15	6.00	6.20	2.93
1973–89	2.03	3.40	3.02	3.06	3.02	4.65	3.63
1973–95	1.68	2.98	2.82	2.82	2.95	4.23	3.51
1989–95	0.74	1.85	2.29	2.19	2.77	3.12	3.18
1960–89	2.16	3.24	3.17	4.00	4.36	5.34	3.32
1960–95	1.92	3.00	3.02	3.69	4.09	4.96	3.29
			Capital Stock per Capita				
1960–73	1.77	2.54	3.06	5.42	5.54	5.01	2.97
1973–89	1.28	2.73	2.68	3.17	2.63	3.52	3.94
1973–95	1.11	2.23	2.48	2.88	2.71	3.42	3.80
1989–95	0.64	0.91	1.94	2.08	2.92	3.15	3.42
1960–89	1.50	2.65	2.85	4.18	3.93	4.18	3.51
1960–95	1.35	2.35	2.69	3.82	3.76	4.01	3.49
			Capital Quality				
1960–73	0.55	0.49	0.29	−0.27	0.46	1.19	−0.04
1973–89	0.75	0.67	0.35	−0.11	0.40	1.13	−0.32
1973–95	0.57	0.75	0.35	−0.05	0.25	0.81	−0.30
1989–95	0.09	0.95	0.34	0.10	−0.15	−0.03	−0.24
1960–89	0.66	0.59	0.32	−0.18	0.43	1.16	−0.19
1960–95	0.56	0.65	0.32	−0.14	0.33	0.95	−0.20

of the categories given in table 12.2 by wage rates defined in terms of labor compensation per hour. An index of hours worked adds together different types of hours without taking quality differences into account. The ratio of labor input to hours worked measures the average quality of an hour of labor, as reflected in its marginal product. This enables us to assess the magnitude of differences between the constant quality index of labor input and the unweighted index of hours worked employed by Kuznets (1971) and Solow (1970).

In table 12.9 we present labor input per capita annually for the G7 countries for the period 1960–95, relative to the United States in 1985. The United Kingdom led until 1962 but was overtaken by Japan in that year. The United States surpassed the United Kingdom in 1977, but the two countries grew in parallel through 1995 with the United States maintaining a slight lead over most of the period. France ranked at the bottom of the G7 for most of the period but led Italy from 1965 to 1979. Japan remained the international leader through 1995 with levels of labor input more than one-third of the United States and the United Kingdom and more than double that of France.

The picture for hours worked per capita has some similarities to labor

Table 12.9 Levels of Labor Input and Hours Worked per Capita and Labor Quality (U.S. = 100.0 in 1985)

	United States	Canada	United Kingdom	France	Germany	Italy	Japan
			Labor Input per Capita				
1960	77.8	69.0	95.5	60.5	98.6	66.6	91.2
1973	89.1	75.4	89.8	63.0	84.3	56.6	117.7
1989	107.0	93.0	89.3	55.2	86.1	68.7	141.0
1995	111.1	87.5	93.7	57.5	90.8	70.2	146.2
			Hours Worked per Capita				
1960	91.1	80.4	110.2	105.0	120.4	89.2	134.4
1973	95.5	83.7	96.6	97.4	98.7	74.6	145.3
1989	104.5	93.4	92.7	77.8	93.5	85.5	150.2
1995	105.3	84.3	92.6	74.2	95.4	84.2	152.1
			Labor Quality				
1960	85.4	85.8	86.7	57.7	81.9	74.7	67.9
1973	93.3	90.1	92.9	64.7	85.4	75.9	81.0
1989	102.4	99.6	96.4	71.0	92.0	80.3	93.9
1995	105.5	103.8	101.3	77.5	95.2	83.4	96.1

input, but there are important differences. Japan was the international leader in hours worked per capita throughout the period, and Germany led the four European countries for most of the period. The United States overtook France in 1975 and Germany and the United Kingdom in 1977. At the beginning of the period Canada ranked last but lost this position to Italy in 1965. Italy was the laggard in hours worked until 1983, when France fell to the bottom of the G7, remaining there through 1995. Hours worked do not accurately reflect the substitutions among labor inputs that accompany investments in human capital.

Labor quality is the ratio of the constant quality index of labor input to the unweighted index of hours worked. The behavior of labor quality highlights the differences between labor input and hours worked. Canada, the United States, and the United Kingdom were the leaders in labor quality; labor quality in these three countries grew in parallel through 1995. France was the laggard among G7 countries in labor quality throughout most of the period 1960–95. There are important changes in labor quality over time and persistent differences among countries. Heterogeneity within each country and between countries must be taken into account in international comparisons of economic growth.

We summarize growth in labor input and hours worked per capita and labor quality in table 12.10. Japan led the G7 countries in labor input growth for the period 1960–95 and before 1973. Canada was the international leader during the subperiod 1973–89, and Germany was the leader after 1989. The United States led growth in hours worked for the period as a whole and after 1989, and Japan was the leader before 1973, and Italy

Table 12.10 Growth in Labor Input and Hours Worked per Capita and Labor Quality (percentage)

	United States	Canada	United Kingdom	France	Germany	Italy	Japan
			Labor Input per Capita				
1960–73	1.05	0.69	−0.48	0.31	−1.20	−1.25	1.96
1973–89	1.14	1.31	−0.03	−0.82	0.13	1.21	1.13
1973–95	1.00	0.68	0.20	−0.41	0.34	0.97	0.98
1989–95	0.64	−1.01	0.80	0.68	0.90	0.34	0.60
1960–89	1.10	1.03	−0.23	−0.32	−0.47	0.11	1.50
1960–95	1.02	0.68	−0.05	−0.14	−0.23	0.15	1.35
			Hours Worked per Capita				
1960–73	0.37	0.31	−1.01	−0.57	−1.53	−1.38	0.60
1973–89	0.56	0.69	−0.26	−1.41	−0.34	0.86	0.21
1973–95	0.44	0.03	−0.20	−1.24	−0.16	0.55	0.21
1989–95	0.13	−1.70	−0.02	−0.79	0.34	−0.27	0.21
1960–89	0.47	0.52	−0.60	−1.03	−0.87	−0.15	0.38
1960–95	0.42	0.14	−0.50	−0.99	−0.67	−0.17	0.35
			Labor Quality				
1960–73	0.68	0.38	0.53	0.88	0.32	0.13	1.36
1973–89	0.58	0.62	0.23	0.58	0.47	0.35	0.92
1973–95	0.56	0.64	0.39	0.83	0.50	0.42	0.78
1989–95	0.50	0.70	0.82	1.47	0.56	0.62	0.39
1960–89	0.62	0.51	0.37	0.72	0.40	0.25	1.12
1960–95	0.60	0.55	0.44	0.85	0.43	0.31	0.99

led between 1973 to 1989. Growth was positive throughout the period for Japan and the United States, mostly negative for the four European countries, and alternately positive and negative for Canada. Growth in labor quality was positive for all seven countries with a modest decline after 1973 and a revival after 1989. In table 12.9 we present labor input and hours worked per capita and labor quality relative to the U.S. in 1985.

Using data from table 12.6, we can assess the relative importance of investment and productivity in per capita growth for the G7 countries. For Canada, the United Kingdom, and the United States, investments in tangible assets and human capital greatly predominated as sources of growth over the period 1960–95. We can attribute slightly more than half of Japanese growth to productivity, whereas proportions for the four European countries—France, Germany, Italy, and the United Kingdom—are slightly less than half. After 1973 growth in output and productivity declined for all seven countries; however, growth in input has not declined, so the relative importance of productivity has sharply diminished.

Similarly, using data from table 12.8 we can combine estimates of growth in capital input, capital stock, and capital quality to assess the importance of changes in quality. Capital input growth is positive for all countries for the period 1960–95 and all three subperiods. Capital quality growth is positive for the period as a whole for all G7 countries, except France and Japan. Although capital stock greatly predominates in capital input growth, capital quality is quantitatively significant, so that the heterogeneity of capital must be taken into account in assessing the role of investment in tangible assets.

Finally, using data from table 12.10 we can combine estimates of growth in labor input, hours worked, and labor quality to assess the importance of hours and quality. Labor input growth is negative for the period 1960–95 in France, Germany, and the United Kingdom and is slightly positive for Italy. Growth in hours worked is mostly negative for all four countries throughout the period. However, growth in labor quality has helped to offset the decline in hours worked in Europe. For Canada, Japan, and the United States, labor quality predominates in the growth of labor input, so that the heterogeneity of labor input is essential in assessing the role of investment in human capital.

12.4 Convergence

The objective of modeling economic growth is to explain the *sources* and *uses* of growth endogenously. National income is the starting point for assessments of the uses of growth through consumption and saving. The concept of a measure of economic welfare, introduced by Nordhaus and Tobin (1972), is the key to augmenting national income to broaden the concepts of consumption and saving. Similarly, GDP is the starting point for attributing the sources of economic growth to growth in productivity and investments in tangible assets and human capital.

Denison (1967) compared differences in growth rates for national income per person employed for the period 1950–62 with differences of levels in 1960 for eight European countries and the United States. However, he overlooked the separate roles for a production account with the national product and inputs of capital and labor services and an income and expenditure account with national income, consumption, and saving. From an economic point of view this ignored the distinction between the sources and uses of economic growth.

Denison compared differences in both growth rates and levels of national income per person employed. The eight European countries as a whole were characterized by more rapid growth and a lower level of national income per capita. Although this association was not monotonic for comparisons between individual countries and the United States, Denison concluded that[11]

---

11. See Denison (1967), especially Chapter 21, "The Sources of Growth and the Contrast between Europe and the United States," pp. 296–348.

Aside from short-term aberrations Europe should be able to report higher growth rates, at least in national income per person employed, for a long time. Americans should expect this and not be disturbed by it.

Kuznets (1971) provided elaborate comparisons of growth rates for the fourteen countries included in his study. Unlike Denison (1967), he did not provide level comparisons. Maddison (1982) filled this gap by comparing levels of national product for sixteen countries[12] on the basis of estimates of PPPs by Kravis, Heston, and Summers (1978).[13] These estimates have been updated by successive versions of the Penn World Table and made it possible to reconsider the issue of convergence of output per capita raised by Denison (1967).[14]

Abramovitz (1986) was the first to take up the challenge of analyzing convergence of output per capita among Maddison's sixteen countries. He found that convergence appeared to characterize output levels in the postwar period, but not the period before 1914 and the interwar period. Baumol (1986) formalized these results by running a regression of growth rate of GDP per hour worked over the period 1870–1979 on the 1870 level of GDP per hour worked.[15] A negative regression coefficient is evidence for beta-convergence of GDP levels.

In a notable paper titled "Crazy Explanations for the Productivity Slowdown," Romer (1987) derived a version of the growth regression from Solow's (1970) growth model with a Cobb-Douglas production function. Romer also extended the data set for growth regressions from Maddison's (1982) group of sixteen advanced countries to the 115 countries included in Penn World Table (Mark 3), presented by Summers and Heston (1984). Romer's key finding was that an indirect estimate of the Cobb-Douglas elasticity of output with respect to capital was close to three-quarters. The share of capital in output implied by Solow's model was less than half as great on average.[16]

---

12. Maddison added Austria and Finland to Kuznets' list and presented growth rates covering periods beginning as early as 1820 and extending through 1979. Maddison (1991, 1995) has extended these estimates through 1992.

13. For details see Maddison (1982, 159–168). Purchasing power parities were first measured for industrialized countries by Gilbert and Kravis (1954) and Gilbert (1958).

14. A complete list through Mark 5 is given by Summers and Heston (1991), while the results of Mark 6 are summarized by the World Bank (1994) in the *World Development Report 1993*.

15. This growth regression has spawned a vast literature, summarized by Levine and Renelt (1992); Baumol (1994); and Barro and Sala-i-Martin (1994). Much of this literature has been based on successive versions of the Penn World Table.

16. Unfortunately, this Mark 3 data set did not include capital input. Romer's empirical finding has spawned a substantial theoretical literature, summarized at an early stage by Lucas (1988) and, more recently, by Grossman and Helpman (1991, 1994); Romer (1994); Barro and Sala-i-Martin (1994); and Aghion and Howitt (1998). Romer's own important contributions to this literature have focused on increasing returns to scale, as in Romer (1986), and spillovers from technological change, as in Romer (1990).

Mankiw, Romer, and Weil (1992) undertook a defense of the neoclassical framework of Kuznets (1971) and Solow (1970). The empirical portion of their study is based on data for ninety-eight countries from the Penn World Table (Mark 4), presented by Summers and Heston (1988). Like Romer (1987), Mankiw, Romer, and Weil derived a growth equation from the Solow (1970) model; however, they also augmented this model by allowing for investment in human capital.

The results of Mankiw, Romer, and Weil (1992) provided empirical support for the augmented Solow model. There was clear evidence of the convergence predicted by the model, where convergence was conditional on the ratio of investment to GDP and the rate of population growth; both are determinants of steady state output. In addition, the estimated Cobb-Douglas elasticity of output with respect to capital coincided with the share of capital in the value of output. However, the rate of convergence of output per capita was too slow to be consistent with the 1970 version of the Solow model.

Islam (1995) exploited an important feature of the Summers-Heston (1988) data overlooked in previous empirical studies, namely, benchmark comparisons of levels of the national product at five year intervals, beginning in 1960 and ending in 1985. Using econometric methods for panel data, Islam tested an assumption maintained in growth regressions, such as those of Mankiw, Romer, and Weil. Their study, like that of Romer (1987), assumed identical technologies for all countries included in the Summers-Heston data sets.

Substantial differences in levels of productivity among countries have been documented by Denison (1967); Christensen, Cummings, and Jorgenson (1981); and earlier in section 12.2. By introducing panel data techniques, Islam (1995) was able to allow for these differences. He corroborated the finding of Mankiw, Romer, and Weil (1992) that the elasticity of output with respect to capital input coincided with the share of capital in the value of output.

In addition, Islam (1995) found that the rate of convergence of output per capita among countries in the Summers-Heston (1988) data set was precisely that required to substantiate the unaugmented version of the Solow (1970). In short, "crazy explanations" for the productivity slowdown, like those propounded by Romer (1987, 1994), are not required. Moreover, the model did not require augmentation, as suggested by Mankiw, Romer, and Weil (1992). However, differences in productivity among these countries must be taken into account in modeling differences in growth rates.

The conclusion from Islam's (1995) research is that the Solow model is the appropriate point of departure for modeling the accumulation of tangible assets. For this purpose it is unnecessary to endogenize investment in human capital as well. The rationale for this key empirical finding is that the transition path to balanced growth equilibrium requires decades after changes in policies that affect investment in tangible assets, such as tax policies. By contrast, the transition after changes in policies affecting investment in human capital requires as much as a century.

In figure 12.1 we present coefficients of variation for levels of output and input per capita and productivity for the G7 countries annually for the period 1960–95. The coefficients for output decline by almost a factor of two between 1960 and 1974 but then remain stable throughout the rest of the period. Coefficients for productivity decline by more than a factor of two between 1960 and 1970 and then stabilize. Coefficients for input per capita are nearly unchanged throughout the period. This is evidence

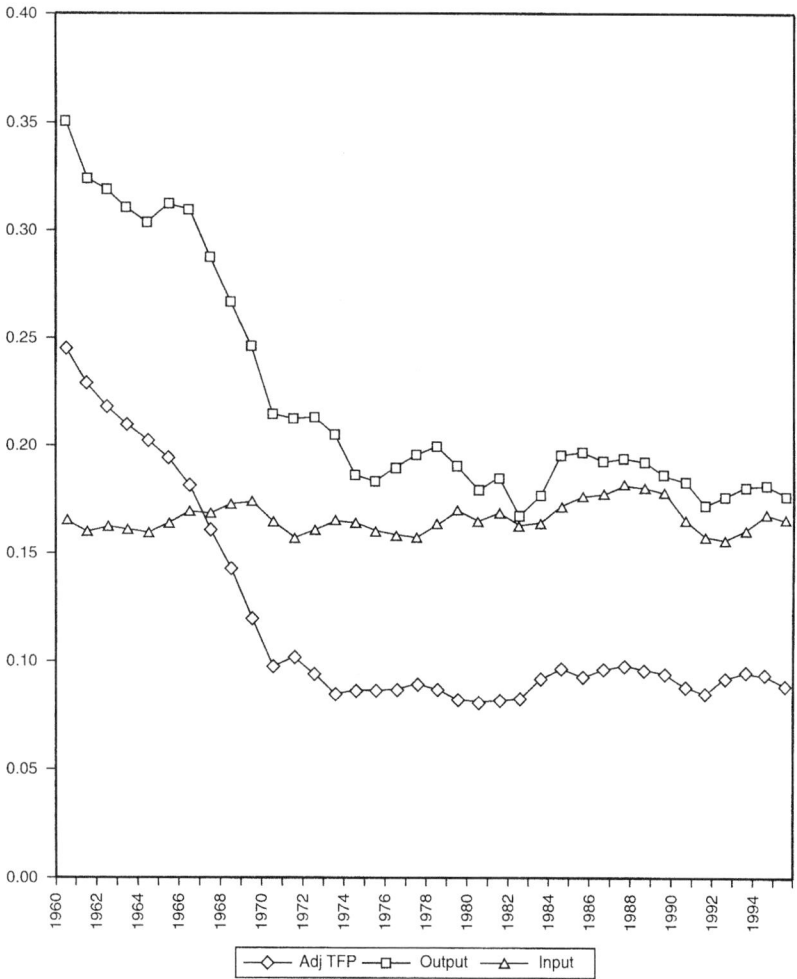

Fig. 12.1   Convergence of output and input per capita and productivity

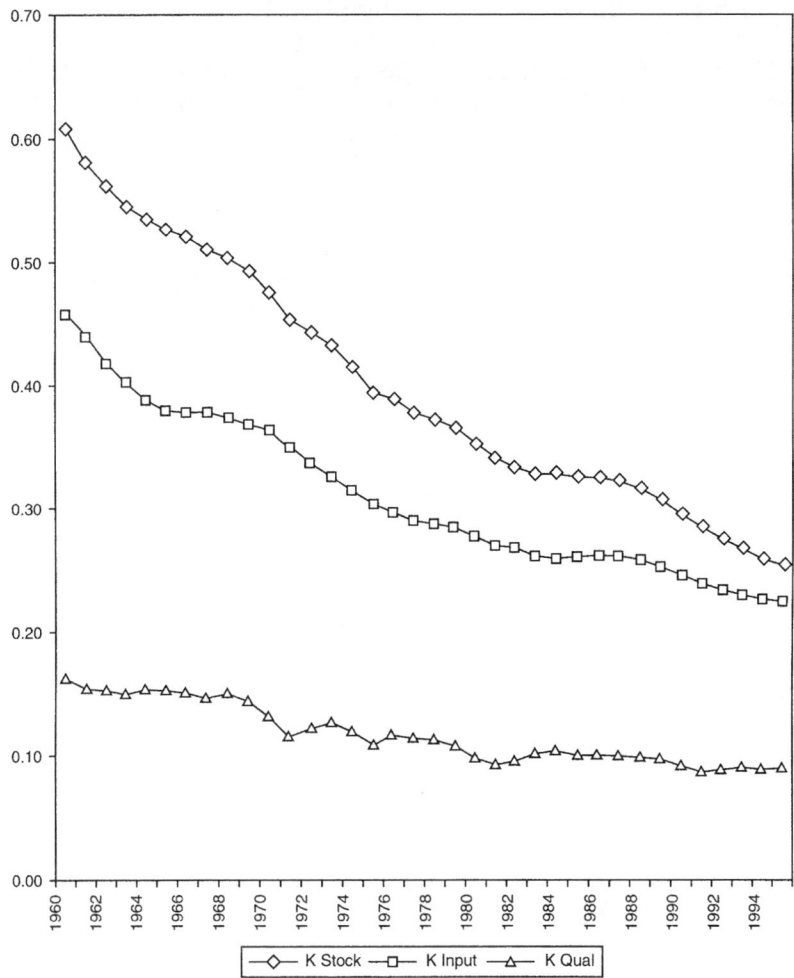

Fig. 12.2 Convergence of capital input, capital stock per capita, and capital quality

for the sigma-convergence of output and input per capita and productivity implied by Solow's neoclassical theory of growth, allowing for differences in productivity of the type identified by Islam.

Figure 12.2 presents coefficients of variation for levels of capital input and capital stock per capita and capital quality for the G7 countries. The coefficients for capital input decline gradually throughout the period. Coefficients for capital stock are slightly larger than those for capital input but behave in a similar manner. Coefficients for capital quality are stable until 1968 and then decline to a slightly lower level after 1971. This is also evidence of the sigma-convergence implied by Solow's growth model with persistent differences in levels of capital quality among countries.

Finally, coefficients of variation for levels of labor input and hours worked per capita and labor quality for the G7 are given in figure 12.3. The coefficients for labor input rise gradually. The coefficients for hours worked rise gradually until 1973 and then stabilize for most of the period. The coefficients for labor quality gradually decline. Again, this is evidence for sigma-convergence with persistent international differences in labor quality.

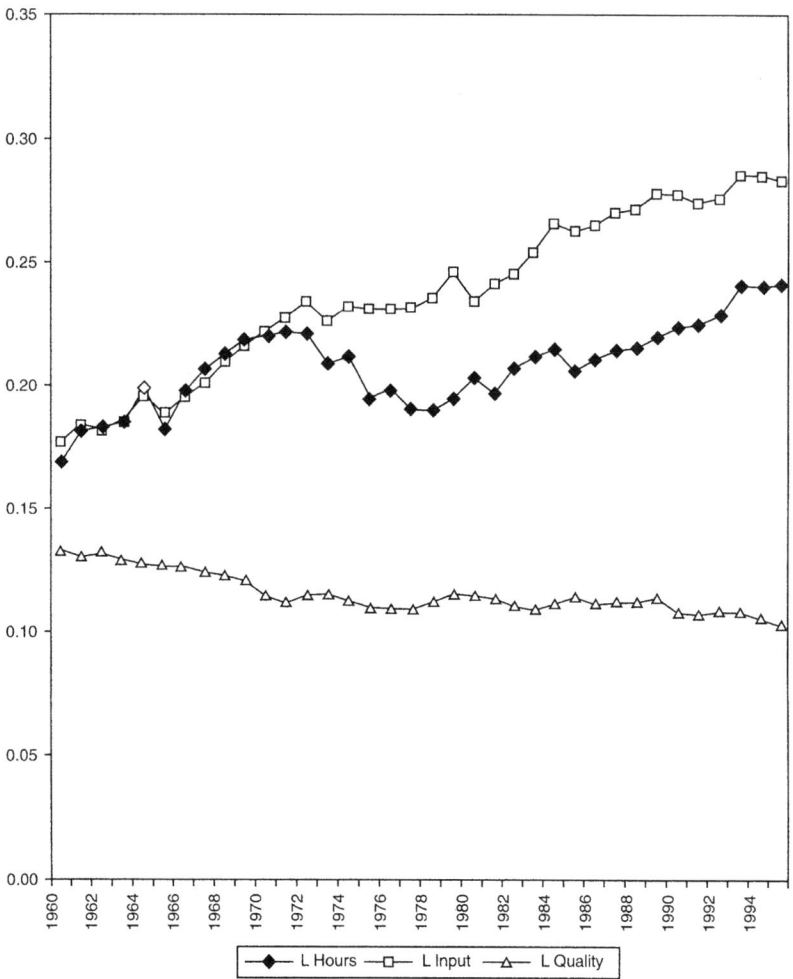

Fig. 12.3 Convergence of labor input, hours worked per capita, and labor quality

The evidence of sigma-convergence among the G7 countries presented in figures 12.1, 12.2, and 12.3 is consistent with a new version of the neoclassical growth model, characterized by persistent but stable international differences in productivity, capital quality, labor quality, and hours worked per capita. Islam showed that a simpler version of the model with constant differences in productivity among countries successfully rationalizes differences in growth of per capita output among a much broader group of countries over the period 1960–85.

12.5 Endogenizing Growth

Investment is endogenous in a neoclassical growth model, whereas productivity is exogenous. Solow's (1957) definition of investment was limited to tangible assets. In order to increase the explanatory power of growth theory, it is necessary to broaden the concept of investment to include human capital. The mechanism by which investments in education and training are translated into economic growth is well understood. An increase in the supply of more highly educated or trained individuals generates a stream of labor income that represents a return to investment in human capital that can be internalized by the investor.

Constant quality indexes of labor input are an essential prerequisite for incorporating human capital into an empirical model of economic growth. The marginal products of workers with different levels of education and training are used to weight the corresponding hours of work. Jorgenson and Fraumeni (1989) have broadened the vintage accounting system developed by Christensen and Jorgenson (1973) to include investments in human capital. The essential idea is to treat individual members of the U.S. population as human assets with asset prices given by their lifetime labor incomes. Jorgenson and Fraumeni have implemented the vintage accounting system for both human and nonhuman capital for the United States on an annual basis for the period 1948–84.

In a vintage accounting system for human capital, wage rates correspond to marginal products and can be observed directly from the labor market. Lifetime labor incomes play the role of asset prices in accounting for human wealth. These incomes are derived by applying asset pricing equations to future wage rates, discounting them back to the present. Asset prices for tangible assets can be observed directly in markets for investment goods; asset pricing equations are used to derive rental prices for capital services. These rental prices are the marginal products of tangible capital assets.

Jorgenson and Fraumeni (1992b) have developed a measure of the output of the U.S. education sector. Although education is a service industry, its output is investment in human capital. Investment in education can be measured from the impact of increases in educational attainment on lifetime incomes of individuals enrolled in school. Investment in education, measured in this way, is similar in magnitude to the value of working time for all individuals in the labor force.

Second, Jorgenson and Fraumeni (1992a) have measured the inputs of the education sector, beginning with the purchased inputs by educational institutions. Most of the value of the output of educational institutions accrues to students through increases in their lifetime incomes. Student time is the most important input into the educational process. Given the outlays of educational institutions and the value of student time, the growth of the education sector can be allocated to its sources.

An alternative approach, employed by Schultz (1961), Machlup (1962), Nordhaus and Tobin (1972), and many others, is to apply Goldsmith's (1955–56) perpetual inventory method to private and public expenditures on educational services. Unfortunately, the approach has foundered on the absence of a satisfactory measure of the output of the educational sector and the lack of an obvious rationale for capital consumption.[17]

Given vintage accounts for human and nonhuman capital, Jorgenson and Fraumeni (1989) constructed a system of income, product, and wealth accounts, paralleling the system Jorgenson had developed with Christensen. In these accounts the value of human wealth was more than ten times the value of nonhuman wealth, whereas investment in human capital was five times investment in tangible assets. Full investment in the U.S. economy is defined as the sum of these two types of investment. Similarly, the value of nonmarket labor activities is added to personal consumption expenditures to obtain full consumption. The product measure included these new measures of investment and consumption.

Because the complete accounting system included a production account with full measures of capital and labor inputs,[18] Jorgenson and Fraumeni were able to generate a new set of accounts for the *sources* of U.S. economic growth. The system also included an income and expenditure account with income from labor services in both market and nonmarket activities and an allocation of full income between consumption and saving. This provided the basis for the *uses* of U.S. economic growth and a new measure of economic welfare. The system was completed by a wealth account containing both human wealth and tangible assets.

Jorgenson and Fraumeni aggregated the growth of education and noneducation sectors of the U.S. economy to obtain a new measure of U.S. economic growth. Combining this with measures of input growth, they obtained a new set of accounts for the sources of growth. Productivity contributes almost nothing to the growth of the education sector and only a modest proportion to output growth for the economy as a whole, so that productivity accounts for only 17 percent of growth.

17. For more detailed discussion, see Jorgenson and Fraumeni (1989).
18. Our terminology follows that of Becker's (1965, 1993) theory of time allocation.

The introduction of endogenous investment in education increases the explanatory power of the theory of economic growth to 83 percent. However, it is important to emphasize that growth is measured differently. The traditional framework for economic measurement of Kuznets (1971) and Solow (1970) excludes nonmarket activities, such as those that characterize the major portion of investment in education. The intuition is familiar to any teacher, including teachers of economics: What the students do is far more important than what the teachers do, even if the subject matter is the theory of economic growth.

A third approximation to the theory of economic growth results from incorporating all forms of investment in human capital, including education, child rearing, and addition of new members to the population. Fertility could be made endogenous by using the approach of Barro and Becker (1988) and Becker and Barro (1988). Child rearing could be made endogenous by modeling the household as a producing sector along the lines of the model of the educational sector just outlined. The results presented by Jorgenson and Fraumeni (1989) show that this would endogenize 86 percent of U.S. economic growth. This is a significant, but not overwhelming, gain in explanatory power.

In principle, investment in new technology could be made endogenous within a neoclassical growth model by extending the concept of investment to encompass intellectual capital. For example, the Bureau of Economic Analysis (BEA; 1994) has provided a satellite system of accounts for research and development, based on Goldsmith's (1955–56) perpetual inventory method, applied to private and public expenditures. Unfortunately, this is subject to the same limitations as is the approach to human capital of Schultz (1961) and Machlup (1962). The BEA satellite system has foundered on the absence of a satisfactory measure of the output of R&D and the lack of an appropriate rationale for capital consumption.

The standard model for investment in new technology, formulated by Griliches (1973), is based on a production function incorporating inputs of services from intellectual capital accumulated through R&D investment. Intellectual capital is treated as a factor of production in precisely the same way as are tangible assets in section 12.2. Hall (1993) has developed the implications of this model for the pricing of the services of intellectual capital input and the evaluation of intellectual capital assets.

The model of capital as a factor of production first propounded by Jorgenson (1963) has been successfully applied to tangible assets and human capital. However, implementation for intellectual capital would require a system of vintage accounts including not only accumulation equations for stocks of accumulated R&D but also asset pricing equations. These equations are essential for separating the revaluation of intellectual property due to price changes over time from depreciation of this property due to aging. This is required for measuring the quantity of intellectual capital input and its marginal product.

The disappearance of productivity growth in the G7 countries documented in this paper is a serious challenge for theories of growth based on externalities, like those of Lucas (1988) and Romer (1986, 1990). These theories rest on spillovers of benefits that appear as productivity growth within a classification of the sources of economic growth. Externalities have become relatively less important during the period of our study. This has increased, not reduced, the explanatory power of the new version of the neoclassical theory of economic growth that we have outlined.

At this point the identification of the externalities that have contributed to past economic growth in the G7 countries is only a matter for speculation. However, a broader concept of investment is urgently required as a guide for a forward-looking growth strategy. Government policies for channeling externalities must be replaced by assignments of property rights and the design of appropriate price systems for decentralizing investment decisions among participants in the private sector. This strategy will require careful attention to the incentives facing investors in tangible assets, human capital, and intellectual property.

Appendix
Data Sources

Canada

Data on nominal and real Canadian GDP, general government output, and subsidies are available in the National Income and Expenditure Accounts (NIEA) from Statistics Canada. Labor hours and employment are available from a number of sources, including the Census, Labor Force Survey, the Input-Output Division, and the Labor Force Historical Review. The labor compensation shares by sex and educational attainment are calculated by using data of wage and salary income per employed person for Census years; non-Census years estimates are obtained by interpolation. Capital stock data are available in the NIEA and the Financial Flows Section of National Balance Sheet Accounts.

France

Data on nominal and real GDP, general government output, indirect taxes, and subsidies are available in De Compte Nationaux, Le Mouvement Economique en France (for 1949–79), and Compte et Indicateurs Economiques 1996, published by Institut National de la Statistique et des Etudes Economiques (INSEE). Data on employment by sex and educational attainment level are available in the annual Enquete de l'Emploi and Population Active, Emploi et Chomage Depuis 30 Ans, both published by

INSEE. Data on average workweeks and weekly hours worked by sex and employment status are again available in Eurostats Labour Force Sample Survey for earlier years, and upon special request from Eurostats for 1985 onwards. French Economic Growth by Carre, Dubois, and Malinvaud provides data on annual hours worked in the 1960s. As for labor compensation shares, the French Survey of Employment, the Enquete sur la Formation et la Qualification Professionnelle, De Compte Nationaux, Le Mouvement Economique en France contains data on wages and salaries for various categories. French capital stock data can be obtained from INSEE publication Comptes de Patrimoine, De Compte Nationaux, Comptes et Indicateurs Economiques and the OECD National Accounts, volume 2. Consumer durable expenditure can be obtained in a separate account, the INSEE publication La Consommation des Menages.

Germany

Data on nominal and real GDP, general government output, indirect taxes, and subsidies are available in the Volkswirtschaftliche Gesamtrechnungen (VGR) and Statistisches Jahrbuch. Employment data can be obtained from VGR, Beruf Aubildung und Arbeitsbedingungen (for some recent years), Wirtschaft und Statistik, and Stand und Entwicklung der Erwerbstatigkeit, which contains the annual results of the German Microcensus, a household survey similar to the U.S. Current Population Survey. Labor income data are available through the Luxembourg Income Study (LIS). Most capital stock series can be found in VGR, whereas consumer durable expenditure on various categories are obtained in Einkommens und Verbrauchsstichprobe and the Laufende Wirtschaftsrechnungen.

Italy

Data on nominal and real GDP, general government output, indirect taxes, and subsidies are available in the Annuario di Contabilita Nazionale and the Conti Economici Nazionali. Employment data are available in Statistiche del Lavoro and the Rilevazione delle Forze di Lavoro. Labor hours can also be found in the Rilevazione di Lavoro, which provides data as well as from the Eurostats. The census publication Censimenti contains employment and hours data in five categories for the years 1961, 1971, 1981 and 1991. Labor compensation data are again obtained from the LIS. Capital stock data are available through the Italian business association, Confindustria, in a study carried out by Alberto Heimler; Gennaro Zezza of the Centro Studi Confindustria supplied estimates of total business inventories in 1985 prices.

Japan

Data on nominal and real GDP, general government output, indirect taxes, and subsidies are available from the National Economic Accounts, published by the Economic Planning Agency. The sources of data for the number of workers and employees are the Population Census of Japan, Report on the Labor Force Survey, and the Basic Survey on Wage Structures. Masahiro Kuroda of Keio University supplied the capital stock data.

United Kingdom

Data on nominal and real GDP, general government output, indirect taxes, and subsidies are available in the Blue Book published by the Central Statistical Office (CSO). Employment by sex and employment status are available in the Employment Gazette, Historical Supplement No. 2, and Employment and Earning, published by the U.K. Department of Employment, and by special request from Quantime, a subsidiary of SPSS. Data on total general government employment are available in Economic Trends, published by CSO. Data on average workweeks and weekly hours worked by sex and employment status are available in Eurostats Labour Force Sample Survey for earlier years and upon special request from Eurostats for 1985 onwards. General Household Survey provides data in labor income that can be used in calculating labor shares. Capital stock data are available in the Blue Book with the exception of data on land, which is taken from Annual Abstract of Statistics and Inland Revenue Statistics.

United States

Data on nominal and real GDP, general government output, indirect taxes, and subsidies are available in the U.S. National Income and Product Accounts, published by the Bureau of Economic Analysis. Labor hours and employment are available from the Census of Population and the Current Population Survey, published by the Bureau of the Census. The labor compensation shares by sex and educational attainment are calculated by adding estimates of fringe benefits to data on wage and salary income per employed person from the Census. Capital stock data are available from the Capital Stock Study of the Bureau of Economic Analysis and the National Balance Sheet, published by the Board of Governors of the Federal Reserve System. Further details are given by Jorgenson (1990).

Other Data Sources

Data on investment tax credits and average marginal corporate tax rates for Canada, the United Kingdom, France, Germany, and Italy are available in the data set supplied by Julian Alworth. The Institute for Fiscal Studies also provides estimates of statutory rates, and net present value of allowances for buildings and producer durable equipment for 1979 to 1994 in their recent publication Taxing Profits in a Changing World. The OECD publication Labour Force Statistics contains data on population from 1976 to 1996. Dougherty (1992) provides further details.

References

Abramovitz, Moses. 1956. Resources and output trends in the United States since 1870. *American Economic Review* 46 (2): 5–23.
———. 1986. Catching up, forging ahead, and falling behind. *Journal of Economic History* 46 (2): 385–406.
Aghion, Philippe, and Peter Howitt. 1998. *Endogenous growth theory.* Cambridge: MIT Press.
Barro, Robert J., and Gary S. Becker. 1988. Fertility choice in a model of economic growth. *Econometrica* 7 (2): 481–502.
Barro, Robert J., and Xavier Sala-i-Martin. 1994. *Economic growth.* New York: McGraw-Hill.
Baumol, William J. 1986. Productivity growth, convergence, and welfare. *American Economic Review* 76 (5): 1072–85.
———. 1994. Multivariate growth patterns: Contagion and common forces as possible sources of convergence. In *Convergence of productivity,* ed. William J. Baumol, Richard R. Nelson, and Edward N. Wolff, 62–85. New York: Oxford University Press.
Becker, Gary S. 1965. A theory of the allocation of time. *Economic Journal* 75 (296): 493–517.
———. 1993. *Human capital.* 3rd ed. Chicago: University of Chicago Press.
Becker, Gary S., and Robert J. Barro. 1988. A reformulation of the economic theory of fertility. *Quarterly Journal of Economics* 103 (1): 1–25.
Bureau of Economic Analysis (BEA). 1994. A satellite account for research and development. *Survey of Current Business* 74 (11): 37–71.
———. 1995. Preview of the comprehensive revision of the National Income and Product Accounts: Recognition of government investment and incorporation of a new methodology for calculating depreciation. *Survey of Current Business* 75 (9): 33–41.
Bureau of Labor Statistics (BLS). 1983. *Trends in multifactor productivity.* Bulletin no. 2178. Washington, D.C.: U.S. Department of Labor.
———. 1993. *Labor composition and U.S. productivity growth, 1948–90.* Bulletin no. 2426. Washington, D.C.: U.S. Department of Labor.
Christensen, Laurits R., Dianne Cummings, and Dale W. Jorgenson. 1980. Economic growth, 1947–1973: An international comparison. In *New developments in productivity measurement and analysis,* ed. J. W. Kendrick and B. Vaccara, 595–698.
———. 1981. Relative productivity levels, 1947–1973. *European Economic Review* 16 (1): 61–94.
Christensen, Laurits R., and Dale W. Jorgenson. 1969. The measurement of U.S. real capital input, 1929–1967. *Review of Income and Wealth* ser. 15, no. 4 (December): 293–320.
———. 1970. U.S. real product and real factor input, 1929–1967. *Review of Income and Wealth* ser. 16, no. 1 (March): 19–50.
———. 1973. Measuring economic performance in the private sector. In *The measurement of economic and social performance,* ed. M. Moss, 233–338. New York: Columbia Press.
Denison, Edward F. 1967. *Why growth rates differ.* Washington, D.C.: Brookings Institution.
Dougherty, Chrys. 1992. *A comparison of productivity and economic growth in the G-7 Countries.* Ph.D. dissertation. Harvard University, Department of Economics.

Dougherty, Chrys, and Dale W. Jorgenson. 1996. International comparisons of the sources of economic growth. *American Economic Review* 86 (2): 25–29.

———. 1997. There is no silver bullet: Investment and growth in the G7. *National Institute Economic Review* 162 (October): 57–74.

Douglas, Paul H. 1948. Are there laws of production? *American Economic Review* 38 (1): 1–41.

Fraumeni, Barbara M. 1997. The measurement of depreciation in the U.S. National Income and Wealth Accounts. *Survey of Current Business*. Vol. 77 (7) 7–23.

Gilbert, Milton, and Irving B. Kravis. 1954. *An international comparison of national products and the purchasing power of currencies.* Paris: Organization for European Economic Cooperation.

Goldsmith, Raymond. 1955–56. *A Study of Saving in the United States,* 3 vols. Princeton: Princeton University Press.

———. 1962. *The national wealth of the United States in the postwar period.* New York: National Bureau of Economic Research.

Gordon, Robert J. 1990. *The measurement of durable goods prices.* Chicago: University of Chicago Press.

Greenwood, Jeremy, Zvi Hercowitz, and Per Krusell. 1997. Long-run implications of investment-specific technological change. *American Economic Review* 87 (3): 341–62.

Griliches, Zvi. 1960. Measuring inputs in agriculture: A critical survey. *Journal of Farm Economics* 40 (5): 1398–1427.

———. 1973. Research expenditures and growth accounting. In *Science and technology in economic growth,* ed. B. Williams, 59–95. London: Macmillan.

———. 1992. The search for R&D spillovers. *Scandinavian Journal of Economics* 94 (supplement): 29–47.

———. 1995. R&D and productivity: Econometric results and measurement issues. In *Handbook of the economics of innovation and technological change,* ed. P. Stoneman, 52–89. Oxford: Basil Blackwell.

Grossman, Gene M., and Elhanan Helpman. 1991. *Innovation and growth.* Cambridge: MIT Press.

———. 1994. Endogenous innovation in the theory of growth. *Journal of Economic Perspectives* 8 (1): 23–44.

Hall, Bronwyn H. 1993. Industrial research in the 1980s: Did the rate of return fall? *Brookings Papers on Economic Activity, Microeconomics:* (2): 289–331.

Hall, Robert E. 1971. The measurement of quality change from vintage price data. In *Price indexes and quality change,* ed. Z. Griliches, 240–71. Cambridge: Harvard University Press.

Hall, Robert E., and Charles I. Jones. 1999. Why do some countries produce so much more output per worker than others? *Quarterly Journal of Economics* 114 (1): 83–116.

Hall, Robert E., and Dale W. Jorgenson. 1967. Tax policy and investment behavior. *American Economic Review* 57 (3): 391–414.

———. 1969. Tax policy and investment behavior: Reply and further results. *American Economic Review* 59 (3): 388–401.

———. 1971. Applications of the theory of optimal capital accumulation. In *Tax incentives and capital spending,* ed. G. Fromm, 9–60. Amsterdam: North-Holland.

Ho, Mun S., and Dale W. Jorgenson. 1999. *The quality of the U.S. work force, 1948–95.* Harvard University, Department of Economics. Manuscript.

Hulten, Charles R., and Frank C. Wykoff. 1982. The measurement of economic depreciation. *Depreciation, inflation and the taxation of income from capital,* ed. C. R. Hulten, 81–125. Washington, D.C.: Urban Institute Press.

Inter-Secretariat Working Group on National Accounts. 1993. In *System of National Accounts 1993,* 379–406. New York: United Nations.

Islam, Nazrul. 1995. Growth empirics. *Quarterly Journal of Economics* 110 (4): 1127–70.

Jorgenson, Dale W. 1963. Capital theory and investment behavior. *American Economic Review* 53 (2): 247–59.

———. 1966. The embodiment hypothesis. *Journal of Political Economy* 74 (1): 1–17.

———. 1967. The theory of investment behavior. In *Determinants of investment behavior,* ed. R. Ferber, 247–59. New York: Columbia University Press.

———. 1990. Productivity and economic growth. In *Fifty years of economic measurement,* ed. E. R. Berndt and J. Triplett, 19–118. Chicago: University of Chicago Press.

———. 1996. Empirical studies of depreciation. *Economic Inquiry* 34 (1): 24–42.

Jorgenson, Dale W., and Barbara M. Fraumeni. 1989. The accumulation of human and nonhuman capital, 1948–1984. In *The measurement of saving, investment, and wealth,* ed. R. E. Lipsey and H. S. Tice, 227–82. Chicago: University of Chicago Press.

———. 1992a. Investment in education and U.S. economic growth. *Scandinavian Journal of Economics* 94 (supplement): 51–70.

———. 1992b. The output of the education sector. In *Output measurement in the services sector,* ed. Z. Griliches, 303–38. Chicago: University of Chicago Press.

Jorgenson, Dale W., Frank M. Gollop, and Barbara M. Fraumeni. 1987. *Productivity and U.S. economic growth.* Cambridge: Harvard University Press.

Jorgenson, Dale W., and Kevin J. Stiroh. 1995. Computers and growth. *Economics of Innovation and New Technology* 3 (3–4): 295–316.

———. 1999. Information technology and growth. *American Economic Review* 89 (2): 109–15.

Jorgenson, Dale W., and Zvi Griliches. 1967. The explanation of productivity change. *Review of Economic Studies* 34 (99): 249–80.

Kravis, Irving B., Alan Heston, and Robert Summers. 1978. *International comparisons of real product and purchasing power.* Baltimore: Johns Hopkins University Press.

Kuznets, Simon. 1961. *Capital in the American economy.* Princeton: Princeton University Press.

———. 1971. *Economic growth of nations.* Cambridge: Harvard University Press.

Levine, Ross, and David Renelt. 1992. A sensitivity analysis of cross-country regressions. *American Economic Review* 82 (4): 942–63.

Lucas, Robert E. 1988. On the mechanics of economic development. *Journal of Monetary Economics* 22 (1): 2–42.

Machlup, Fritz. 1962. *The production and distribution of knowledge in the United States.* Princeton: Princeton University Press.

Maddison, Angus. 1982. *Phases of capitalist development.* Oxford: Oxford University Press.

———. 1991. *Dynamic forces in capitalist development.* Oxford: Oxford University Press.

———. 1995. *Monitoring the world economy.* Paris: Organization for Economic Cooperation and Development.

Mankiw, N. Gregory, David Romer, and David Weil. 1992. A contribution to the empirics of economic growth. *Quarterly Journal of Economics* 107 (2): 407–37.

Mincer, Jacob. 1974. *Schooling, experience, and earnings.* New York: Columbia University Press.
Nordhaus, William D., and James Tobin. 1972. Is growth obsolete? In *The measurement of economic and social performance,* ed. M. Moss, 509–32. New York: Columbia University Press.
Romer, Paul. 1986. Increasing returns and long-run growth. *Journal of Political Economy* 94 (5): 1002–37.
———. 1987. Crazy explanations for the productivity slowdown. In *NBER macroeconomics annual,* ed. Stanley Fischer, 163–201. Cambridge: MIT Press.
———. 1990. Endogenous technological change. *Journal of Political Economy* 98 (5, pt. 2): S71–S102.
———. 1994. The origins of endogenous growth. *Journal of Economic Perspectives* 8 (1): 3–20.
Samuelson, Paul A. 1961. The evaluation of "social income": Capital formation and wealth. In *The theory of capital,* ed. F. A. Lutz and D. C. Hague, 32–57. London: Macmillan.
Schultz, Theodore W. 1961. Investment in human capital. *American Economic Review* 51 (1): 1–17.
Solow, Robert M. 1956. A contribution to the theory of economic growth. *Quarterly Journal of Economics* 70 (1): 65–94.
———. 1957. Technical change and the aggregate production function. *Review of Economics and Statistics* 39 (3): 312–20.
———. 1960. Investment and technical progress. In *Mathematical methods in the social sciences,* ed. K. J. Arrow, S. Karlin, and P. Suppes, 89–104. Stanford: Stanford University Press.
———. 1970. *Growth theory: An exposition.* New York: Oxford University Press.
———. 1992. *Growth theory.* 2nd ed. New York: Oxford University Press.
Stone, Richard. 1992. The accounts of society. In *Nobel lectures: Economic sciences, 1981–1990,* ed. K. G. Maler, 115–39. River Edge, N.J.: World Scientific.
Summers, Robert, and Alan Heston. 1984. Improved international comparisons of real product and its composition: 1950–1980. *Review of Income and Wealth* ser. 30, no. 1 (March): 1–25.
———. 1988. A new set of international comparisons of real product and price levels: Estimates for 130 countries, 1950–1985. *Review of Income and Wealth* ser. 34, no. 1 (March): 19–26.
———. 1991. The Penn World Table (Mark 5): An expanded set of international comparisons, 1950–1988. *Quarterly Journal of Economics* 106 (2): 327–68.
Tinbergen, Jan. 1959. On the theory of trend movements. In *Jan Tinbergen, selected papers,* trans. Hans Wilke, 182–221. Amsterdam: North-Holland. (Originally published as Tinbergen, Jan. 1942.) Zur theorie der langfristigen wirtschaftsentwicklung. *Weltwirtschaftliches Archiv* 55 [1]: 511–49.
Triplett, Jack. 1996. Measuring the capital stock: A review of concepts and data needs. *Economic Inquiry* 34 (1): 36–40.
United Nations (UN). 1968. *A system of national accounts.* New York: UN.
World Bank. 1994. *World development report 1993.* Washington, D.C.: World Bank.

13

Productivity of the U.S. Agricultural Sector: The Case of Undesirable Outputs

V. Eldon Ball, Rolf Färe, Shawna Grosskopf, and Richard Nehring

13.1 Introduction

The purpose of this paper is two-fold: (a) to show how to model the joint production of desirable (marketed) and undesirable (nonmarketed, or "bad") outputs in a way that is useful for productivity analysis, and (b) to apply that model to data on the U.S. agricultural sector using activity analysis techniques.

To put our work in perspective with the productivity literature, we note that we follow Solow (1957) in the sense that we are modeling a production technology in order to identify productivity growth and technical change. Our approach differs significantly from Solow's in several ways. Instead of a single output, we include a vector of good outputs as well as a vector of undesirable outputs in our model. Thus, instead of a single output production function, we use distance functions as our representation of technology. These allow us to model joint production of goods and bads. Instead of specifying a parametric form of the technology, we use activity analysis

---

V. Eldon Ball is leader, agricultural productivity program, Economic Research Service, U.S. Department of Agriculture. Rolf Färe is professor of economics and agricultural economics and resource economics at Oregon State University. Shawna Grosskopf is professor of economics at Oregon State University. Richard Nehring is agricultural economist, Economic Research Service, U.S. Department of Agriculture.

The second and third authors' work was supported by Cooperative Agreement A-ERS-43-3AEM-2-80056 with the Environmental Research Service, U.S. Department of Agriculture and USEPA-CR823009-01-0 with the U.S. Environmental Protection Agency. The results and recommendations are those of the authors and not necessarily those of the supporting agencies. We would like to thank Mary Ahearn, Robin Sickles, Bill Weber, and the editors for their comments. Please direct correspondence to Shawna Grosskopf.

to construct a nonparametric representation of technology that also allows us to identify the production frontier. That, in turn, permits us explicitly to identify deviations from frontier performance and shifts in the frontier itself. Following Caves, Christensen, and Diewert (1982) we employ a discrete approach rather than the differential approach used by Solow. Finally, our approach does not require information on input and output prices or shares, which are used to aggregate inputs and outputs in the growth accounting/Solow approaches. Clearly, that is particularly useful in the case in which one wishes to include joint production of desirable and undesirable outputs, since the latter are typically nonmarketed.

The paper begins with a discussion of how we model the joint production of desirable and undesirable outputs both conceptually and empirically. Next we turn to a discussion of the Malmquist productivity index and how it may be computed. Since the Malmquist productivity index is defined in terms of output distance functions, it seeks the greatest feasible expansion of all outputs, both good and bad. Since the expansion of bad outputs may be undesirable (due to regulations, for example), we turn to a modified version of that index, which we refer to as the Malmquist-Luenberger productivity index in section 13.4. This index allows for contractions of undesirable outputs and expansions of "good," or desirable, outputs.

We apply our methods to a panel of state-level data recently made available by the U.S. Department of Agriculture's Economic Research Service (ERS). This data set includes variables that proxy effects of pesticides and fertilizer on groundwater and surface-water quality for the 1972–93 time frame. Although we consider our results to be preliminary, we find—as expected—that measured productivity differs when undesirable outputs are accounted for.[1] Our preferred model—the Malmquist-Luenberger index—generally reports higher productivity growth for states with declining trends in water contamination resulting from the use of pesticides and chemical fertilizers.

13.2 Modeling Technologies with Good and Bad Outputs

The production of desirable outputs is often accompanied by the simultaneous or joint production of undesirable outputs. Examples include the paper and pulp industry, electricity generation, and agriculture, among many others.

If we wish to measure productivity when both desirable and undesirable outputs are produced, we should obviously account explicitly for their

---

1. At the moment we cannot say whether the differences we observe are significant. Future research plans include application of bootstrapping methods to allow us to pursue such hypothesis testing.

joint production. If we denote desirable outputs by $y \in \Re_+^M$, undesirable outputs by $b \in \Re_+^I$, and inputs by $x \in \Re_+^N$, then the technology may be written as

(1) $\qquad T = [(x, y, b): x \text{ can produce } (y, b)]$.

The technology consists of all feasible input and output quantities; that is, it consists of all desirable and undesirable outputs that can be produced by the given input vectors.

To model the joint production of the good and bad outputs, it is convenient to model the technology in terms of the output sets, that is,

(2) $\qquad P(x) = [(y, b):(x, y, b) \in T]$.

Clearly, T can be recovered from $P(x)$ as

(3) $\qquad T = [(x, y, b):(y, b) \in P(x), x \in \Re_+^M]$.

Thus the technology is equivalently represented by either its output sets $P(x)$, $x \in \Re_+^N$ or its technology set T.

For the case in which a single desirable output is produced, the technology is often modeled by means of a production function $F(x)$. This function is defined on the output set $P(x)$ as

(4) $\qquad F(x) = \max[y: y \in P(x)]$.

As before, the output sets and hence the technology may also be recovered from this representation of technology, namely as

(5) $\qquad P(x) = [y: F(x) \geq y]$.

We model the idea that reduction of bad outputs is costly by imposing what we call "weak disposability of outputs," that is,

(6) $\qquad (y, b) \in P(x) \text{ and } 0 \leq \theta \leq 1 \text{ imply } (\theta y, \theta b) \in P(x).$[2]

In words, this states that reduction of undesirable outputs is feasible only if good outputs are also reduced, given fixed input levels. Hence it may be infeasible to reduce the undesirable outputs only, that is, if (y, b) is feasible and $b' < b$ then it may be impossible to produce (y, b') using x, that is, $(y, b) \in P(x)$ and $(y, b') \notin P(x)$. Clearly, if undesirable outputs could be disposed of costlessly (freely), then this problem would not arise.

With respect to the good outputs, we assume that they are freely or strongly disposable, that is,

(7) $\qquad$ if $(y, b) \in P(x)$ and $y' \leq y$ imply $(y', b) \in P(x)$.

---

2. Shephard (1970) introduced the notion of weak disposability of outputs.

The reason for distinguishing between desirable and undesirable outputs in terms of their disposability is that the former typically have a positive price, whereas the latter are typically not marketed and, therefore, do not have readily observable prices.

The notion that desirable and undesirable outputs are jointly produced is modeled by what Shephard and Färe (1974) call "null-jointness." In words this means that if no bad outputs are produced, then there can be no production of good outputs. Alternatively, if one wishes to produce some good outputs then there will be undesirable byproducts of production. More formally, we have

(8) $\quad\quad\quad (y,b) \in P(x)$ and $b = 0$ then $y = 0$,

that is, if (y, b) is a feasible output vector consisting of desirable outputs y and undesirable outputs b, then if no undesirable outputs are produced ($b = 0$) then by null-jointness, production of positive desirable outputs is not feasible, so $y = 0$.

In order to develop a framework for the empirical measurement of productivity with good and bad outputs, we need to formulate an explicit reference technology. Here we assume that at each time period $t = 1, \ldots, \bar{t}$ there are $k = 1, \ldots, K$ observations of inputs and outputs,

(9) $\quad\quad\quad (x^{t,k}, y^{t,k}, b^{t,k}), \quad k = 1, \ldots, K, \quad t = 1, \ldots, \bar{t}.$

Following Färe, Grosskopf, and Lovell (1994) we define the output sets from the data as an activity analysis or data envelopment analysis (DEA) model,[3] namely

(10) $\quad P^t(x^t) = [(y^t, b^t) : \sum_{k=1}^{K} z_k^t y_{km}^t \geq y_m^t, \quad m = 1, \ldots, M,$

$$\sum_{k=1}^{K} z_k^t b_{ki}^t = b_i^t, \quad i = 1, \ldots, I,$$

$$\sum_{k=1}^{K} z_k^t x_{kn}^t \leq x_n^t, \quad n = 1, \ldots, N$$

$$z_k^t \geq 0, \quad k = 1, \ldots, K],$$

where z_k^t are the intensity variables, which serve to form the technology from convex combinations of the data.

To illustrate the model in equation (10), we assume that there are two firms $k = 1, 2$ producing one desirable and one undesirable output with the data in table 13.1.

The data in table 13.1 and the corresponding output set are illustrated in figure 13.1. The two observations are labeled $k = 1$ and $k = 2$ in the figure. Each uses one unit of input to produce their good and bad outputs.

---

3. Charnes, Cooper, and Rhodes (1978) first coined the terminology "DEA."

Table 13.1   Hypothetical Data Set

Observation (k)	Good (y)	Bad (b)	Input (x)
1	1	(1/2)	1
2	2	2	1

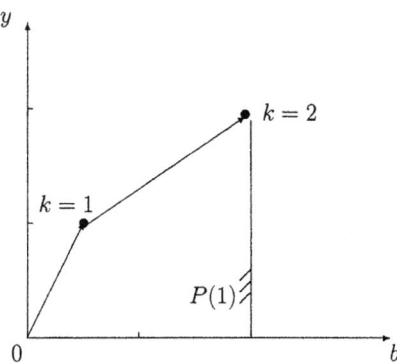

Fig. 13.1 Output set with weak disposability and null-jointness of bads

The output set $P(1)$ is constructed from these two observations such that outputs are weakly disposable and the good output y is strongly disposable. Moreover, the figure shows that if $b = 0$ then $y = 0$; thus the two outputs are jointly produced or null-joint in the terminology of Shephard and Färe.

In general one can show that equation (10) satisfies equations (6) and (7) in addition to satisfying constant returns to scale, that is,

(11) $\qquad P(\lambda x) = \lambda P(x), \quad \lambda > 0.$

In words, constant returns to scale means that proportional scaling of the input vector x yields proportional scaling of the output set $P(x)$.

Moreover, one can also show that inputs are strongly disposable in the following sense:

(12) $\qquad P(x') \subseteq P(x) \text{ for } x \geq x'.$

For the good and bad outputs to satisfy null-jointness at each period t, we need to assume that the bad outputs satisfy the following two conditions:

$$\sum_{k=1}^{K} b_{ki}^t > 0, \quad i = 1, \ldots, I,$$

$$\sum_{i=1}^{I} b_{ki}^t > 0, \quad k = 1, \ldots, K.$$

The first inequality says that each bad is produced by at least one firm. The second states that each firm produces at least one bad. Now, referring back to the activity analysis formulation of technology in equation (10), suppose that the right-hand side of the constraints on the bad outputs are such that $b_i^t = 0, i = 1, \ldots, I$. If we have null-jointness that means that we should also have $y_m^t = 0, m = 1, \ldots, M$. The inequalities above guarantee that this is so, since together they require that each intensity variable is multiplied by at least one nonzero value of b_{ki}^t. Thus the only way to have $\sum_{k=1}^{K} z_k^t b_{km}^t = 0$ when these constraints hold is to have $z_k^t = 0$ for all k, which would imply that $y_m^t = 0, m = 1, \ldots, M$ as required for null-jointness of y and b.[4]

Next we show that the model in equation (10) has the property that decreases in the production of bads require that inputs be increased. We demonstrate this property using the data in table 13.1. Based on our data, if we wish to produce $(y, b) = (2, 2)$, then we must employ one unit of input. Now if we wish to produce $(y, b) = (2, 1)$; that is, if we wish to reduce the bad output by one unit, then we must increase our input usage to $x = 2$.[5] This shows that resources may be required to "clean up" the bad outputs. For additional properties of the production model in equation (10), see Färe and Grosskopf (1996).

13.3 The Malmquist Productivity Index

In this section we discuss the Malmquist productivity index as proposed by Färe et al. (1989). Their index is based on Shephard's output distance function and is the geometric mean of two of the Malmquist indexes introduced by Caves, Christensen, and Diewert (1982).

The output distance function, introduced into economics by Shephard (1970), is given by

(13) $$D_o(x, y, b) = \inf[\theta : (y/\theta, b/\theta) \in P(x)]$$
$$= \inf[\theta : (x, y/\theta, b/\theta) \in T]$$

where the last equality holds, since $(x, y, b) \in T$ if and only if $(y, b) \in P(x)$; see equations (2) and (3). The output distance function is the largest feasible expansion of the output vector (y, b), and it has the property of being a complete representation of the technology, that is,

(14) $$D_o(x, y, b) \leq 1 \quad \text{if and only if} \quad (y, b) \in P(x).$$

---

4. Note that it is the strict equality on the bad output constraints that drives this result; thus null-jointness and weak disposability are intimately related in the activity analysis model.

5. Scaling observation $k = 1$ by a factor of 2 yields the desired result.

Thus the output distance function assigns a value to the input-output vector (x, y, b) of less than or equal to 1 for feasible input-output vectors only.

As a representation of the technology, the distance function inherits the properties assumed for the technology; see Färe (1988) or Shephard (1970) for details. In addition to the inherited properties it is homogeneous of degree $+1$ in good and bad outputs (y, b).

In the simple case in which a single (good) output is produced, there is the following direct relationship between the production function $F(x)$ and the output distance function $D_o(x, y)$.

$$(15) \qquad D_o(x, y) = \frac{y}{F(x)}$$

To see this we note that since $D_o(x, y)$ is a complete representation of the technology, we have

$$(16) \qquad P(x) = [y : D_o(x, y) \leq 1].$$

Now, if we apply the definition of a production function to equation (16) and use the fact that $D_o(x, y)$ is homogeneous of degree $+1$ in outputs, we have

$$(17) \qquad F(x) = \max[y : y \in P(x)] = \max[y : D_o(x, y) \leq 1]$$
$$= \max[y : y \cdot D_o(x, 1) \leq 1]$$
$$= \frac{1}{D_o(x, 1)}.$$

Now $D_o(x, 1) \cdot y = D_o(x, y) = y/[F(x)]$.

Färe, Grosskopf, Lindgren, and Roos (1989, hereafter FGLR) define the Malmquist productivity indexes for adjacent periods as

$$(18) \qquad M_t^{t+1} = \left[\frac{D_o^{t+1}(x^{t+1}, y^{t+1}, b^{t+1})}{D_o^{t+1}(x^t, y^t, b^t)} \frac{D_o^t(x^{t+1}, y^{t+1}, b^{t+1})}{D_o^t(x^t, y^t, b^t)} \right]^{1/2}.$$

This index is the geometric mean of the two output-oriented Malmquist indexes introduced by Caves, Christensen, and Diewert (1982), namely

$$(19) \qquad \frac{D_o^{t+1}(x^{t+1}, y^{t+1}, b^{t+1})}{D_o^{t+1}(x^t, y^t, b^t)} \quad \text{and} \quad \frac{D_o^t(x^{t+1}, y^{t+1}, b^{t+1})}{D_o^t(x^t, y^t, b^t)}.$$

It is of interest to compare the FGLR formulation with Robert Solow's (1957) index, noting of course that the Malmquist indexes are all in discrete time.

Solow assumes that the technology can be represented by an aggregate production function

$$(20) \quad y^t = F(x^t, t) = A(t)(x_1^t)^{\alpha(t)}(x_2^t)^{1-\alpha(t)},$$

where the residual $A(t)$ captures technical change and $\alpha(t)$ is input x_1's output share in period t. Here, we simplify by setting $\alpha(t) = \alpha$ for all t. Then, using the equivalences derived above between production functions and distance functions in the scalar output case, we can insert Solow's production function into the Malmquist index in equation (18), which yields

$$(21) \quad M_t^{t+1} = \left\{ \frac{[A(t+1)(x_1^t)^\alpha(x_2^t)^{1-\alpha}]/y^t}{[A(t+1)(x_1^{t+1})^\alpha(x_2^{t+1})^{1-\alpha}]/y^{t+1}} \frac{[A(t)(x_1^t)^\alpha(x_2^t)^{1-\alpha}]/y^t}{[A(t)(x_1^{t+1})^\alpha(x_2^{t+1})^{1-\alpha}]/y^{t+1}} \right\}^{1/2}$$

$$= \frac{[(x_1^t)^\alpha(x_2^t)^{1-\alpha}]/y^t}{[(x_1^{t+1})^\alpha(x_2^{t+1})^{1-\alpha}]/y^{t+1}} = \frac{A(t+1)}{A(t)}.$$

This shows that the Malmquist index proposed by FGLR is the discrete analog of the Solow residual where $\alpha(t) = \alpha$.

FGLR also show that their Malmquist index decomposes into two component measures, one accounting for efficiency change (MEFFCH_t^{t+1}) and one measuring technical change (MTECH_t^{t+1}). These are

$$(22) \quad \text{MEFFCH}_t^{t+1} = \frac{D_o^{t+1}(x^{t+1}, y^{t+1}, b^{t+1})}{D_o^t(x^t, y^t, b^t)}$$

and

$$(23) \quad \text{MTECH}_t^{t+1} = \left[\frac{D_o^t(x^{t+1}, y^{t+1}, b^{t+1})}{D_o^{t+1}(x^{t+1}, y^{t+1}, b^{t+1})} \frac{D_o^t(x^t, y^t, b^t)}{D_o^{t+1}(x^t, y^t, b^t)} \right]^{1/2}$$

where

$$(24) \quad M_t^{t+1} = \text{MEFFCH}_t^{t+1} \cdot \text{MTECH}_t^{t+1}.$$

In the Solow formulation we would have

$$(25) \quad \text{MEFFCH}_t^{t+1} = 1$$

and

$$(26) \quad \text{MTECH}_t^{t+1} = \frac{A(t+1)}{A(t)},$$

implying that there is no efficiency change in the Solow formulation (production is implicitly assumed to be technically efficient) and therefore productivity change is due solely to technical change.

To illustrate the Malmquist index we simplify our model and assume that one input x is used to produce one output y.

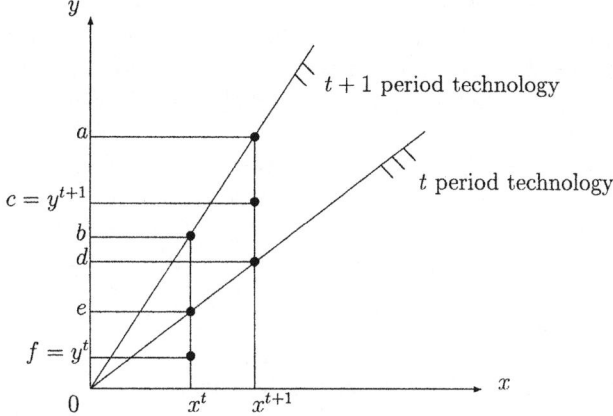

Fig. 13.2 Output-oriented Malmquist productivity index

Two technologies T^t and T^{T+1} are included in figure 13.2 along, with two observations, (x^t, y^t) and (x^{t+1}, y^{t+1}). Notice that these observations are not technically efficient; rather, production occurs "below" the boundary of the associated total product set in both periods. The Malmquist index as measured along the y-axis equals

$$(27) \quad M_t^{t+1} = \left(\frac{0c/0a}{0f/0b} \frac{0c/0d}{0f/0e} \right)^{1/2}.$$

Under constant returns to scale (as in our figure), this is equivalent to the ratio of the average products in the two periods, which has clearly increased over time. Thus the overall index will be greater than one indicating an improvement in productivity between period t and $t+1$.

One of the nice features of the Malmquist index is the fact that we can identify the two component measures defined above (see equations [22] and [23]), which allows us to identify sources of productivity change over time. In our figure, the efficiency change component is

$$(28) \quad \text{MEFFCH}_t^{t+1} = \left(\frac{0c}{0a} \frac{0e}{0f} \right),$$

and the technical change component is

$$(29) \quad \text{MTECH}_t^{t+1} = \left(\frac{0a}{0d} \frac{0b}{0e} \right)^{1/2}.$$

The efficiency change term MEFFCH_t^{t+1} tells us whether an observation is getting closer or farther from the frontier over time; that is, it tells us whether an observation is catching up to the frontier. In our example, the observation is actually falling farther behind the frontier over time; that is, it was closer to the frontier in period t than in period $t + 1$. Thus the value of this term would be less than 1, indicating a decline in technical efficiency over time.

On the other hand, our figure illustrates that technical progress has occurred between t and $t + 1$. This is captured in our technical change component MTECH_t^{t+1}, which is greater than 1 for our observation. MTECH_t^{t+1} tells us how much the frontier has shifted over time evaluated at the observed inputs in periods t and $t + 1$ (the index takes the geometric mean of the shifts in the frontier at these two input levels).

In our example there has been a decline in efficiency over time, but an improvement in terms of technical change. The product of these two yields the overall productivity change, which in this example is greater than 1, signalling an overall improvement in productivity. This means that technical change accounted for the observed improvement in productivity in this case.

To calculate the productivity index and its component measures we estimate the component distance functions using linear programming techniques. These are discussed in some detail in Färe, Grosskopf, Norris, et al. (1994) for the interested reader.

13.4 The Malmquist-Luenberger Productivity Index

We now turn to the Malmquist-Luenberger productivity index, which—unlike the Malmquist index described earlier that treats all outputs the same—allows us to credit observations for increases in good outputs yet "debit" them for increases in undesirable outputs. This index was introduced by Chung (1996) and Chung, Färe, and Grosskopf (1997), and it is based on the output-oriented directional distance function. This distance function differs from the Shephard output distance function in that it does not necessarily change outputs (y, b) proportionally, but rather changes them in a preassigned direction. This new distance function is a special case of the directional technology distance function (see Chambers, Chung, and Färe 1998, where the latter is essentially the shortage function due to Luenberger; see, e.g., Luenberger 1992, 1995).

Consider a direction vector $(g_y, -g_b) \neq 0$, where $g_y \in \Re_+^M$. Then the output-oriented directional distance function is defined as

(30) $\quad \mathbf{D}_o(x, y, b; g_y, -g_b) = \sup[\beta : (y + \beta g_y, b - \beta g_b) \in P(x)].$

This function is defined by adding the direction vector to the observed vector and scaling that point by simultaneously increasing good outputs and decreasing bad outputs. Figure 13.3 illustrates.

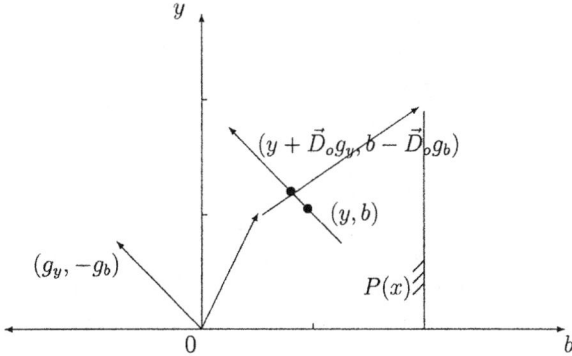

Fig. 13.3 Output-oriented directional distance function

In this figure the output set is denoted by $P(x)$ and the output vector (y, b) is an element of that set. The direction vector is $(g_y, -g_b)$ and the distance function expands the output vector as much as is feasible along the direction vector. It ends up at $(y + \vec{D}_o g_y, b - \vec{D}_o g_b)$, where $\vec{D}_o = \vec{D}_o(x, y, b; g_y, -g_b)$.

In order to see the relation between the directional and the Shephard output distance functions, suppose we change the direction slightly (eliminate the negative sign on the bad outputs) and choose $g_y = y$ and $g_b = b$, then

(31) $\quad \vec{D}_o(x, y, b; y, b) = \sup[\beta : (y + \beta y, b + \beta b) \in P(x)]$

$\qquad = \sup\{\beta : [y(1 + \beta), b(1 + \beta) \in P(x)]\}$

$\qquad = \sup\{1 - 1 + \beta : [y(1 + \beta), b(1 + \beta) \in P(x)]\}$

$\qquad = -1 + \sup\{(1 + \beta) : [y(1 + \beta), b(1 + \beta) \in P(x)]\}$

$\qquad = \dfrac{1}{D_o(x, y, b) - 1}.$

Thus, if we choose the directions $g_y = y$ and $g_b = b$, we find that the directional distance function is essentially Shephard's output distance function. In our figure, the observed point would be projected to the frontier in this case by scaling to the Northeast in our figure, seeking the largest feasible increase in both good *and* bad outputs. This would mean that observations with relatively more bads, ceteris paribus, would be deemed more efficient, which is inconsistent with the notion that the bads are undesirable. If we ignore the undesirable outputs and scale only on the good outputs (as in the traditional output distance function and Malmquist index), we would go due North to the frontier. To sum up,

$$(32) \quad \mathbf{D}_o(x, y, b; y, b) = \left[\frac{1}{D_o(x, y, b)}\right] - 1.$$

or

$$(33) \quad D_o(x, y, b) = \frac{1}{1 + \mathbf{D}_o(x, y, b; y, b)}.$$

The Malmquist-Luenberger index used here is defined by choosing the direction as the observed vector of good and bad outputs $(y, -b)$ and making use of the Malmquist index in equation (18) and the idea of equation (33).

$$(34) \quad \mathrm{ML}_t^{t+1} = \left[\frac{1 + \mathbf{D}_o^t(x^t, y^t, b^t; y^t, -b^t)}{1 + \mathbf{D}_o^t(x^{t+1}, y^{t+1}, b^{t+1}; y^{t+1}, -b^{t+1})}\right.$$
$$\left. \cdot \frac{1 + \mathbf{D}_o^{t+1}(x^t, y^t, b^t; y^t, -b^t)}{1 + \mathbf{D}_o^{t+1}(x^{t+1}, y^{t+1}, b^{t+1}; y^{t+1}, -b^{t+1})}\right]^{1/2}.$$

The definition is such that if the direction had been (y, b) instead of $(y, -b)$, it would coincide with the Malmquist index in equation (18). As in that case, improvements in productivity are signalled by values of the index greater than unity.

Like the Malmquist index, the Malmquist-Luenberger index can be decomposed into components, namely an efficiency change and a technical change component,[6]

$$(35) \quad \mathrm{MLEFFCH}_t^{t+1} = \frac{1 + \mathbf{D}_o^t(x^t, y^t, b^t; y^t, -b^t)}{1 + \mathbf{D}_o^{t+1}(x^{t+1}, y^{t+1}, b^{t+1}; y^{t+1}, -b^{t+1})}$$

$$(36) \quad \mathrm{MLTC}_t^{t+1} = \left[\frac{1 + \mathbf{D}_o^{t+1}(x^t, y^t, b^t; y^t, -b^t)}{1 + \mathbf{D}_o^t(x^t, y^t, b^t; y^t, -b^t)}\right.$$
$$\left. \cdot \frac{1 + \mathbf{D}_o^{t+1}(x^{t+1}, y^{t+1}, b^{t+1}; y^{t+1}, -b^{t+1})}{1 + \mathbf{D}_o^t(x^{t+1}, y^{t+1}, b^{t+1}; y^{t+1}, -b^{t+1})}\right]^{1/2}.$$

As for the Malmquist index, the product of these two components equals the Malmquist-Luenberger index ML_t^{t+1} and the components have similar interpretations. Values greater than 1 indicate improvements, and values less than 1 indicate declines in performance.

The directional distance functions, like the Shephard distance functions,

---

6. One may further decompose both of these components, analogous to the Malmquist index decomposition developed in Färe, Grosskopf, and Lovell (1994) or Färe, Grosskopf, Norris, et al. (1994).

can be estimated as solutions to linear programming problems. As an example, let us consider the $(k', t + 1)$ observation of data relative to the period t reference technology, that is,

(37) $\quad \mathbf{D}_o^t(x^{t+1,k'}, y^{t+1,k'}, b^{t+1,k'}; y^{t+1,k'}, -b^{t+1,k'}) = \max \beta$

subject to

$$\sum_{k=1}^{K} z_k^t y_{km}^t \geq (1 + \beta) y_{k'm}^{t+1}, \quad m = 1, \ldots, M,$$

$$\sum_{k=1}^{K} z_k^t b_{ki}^t = (1 - \beta) b_{k'i}^{t+1}, \quad i = 1, \ldots, I,$$

$$\sum_{k=1}^{K} z_k^t x_{kn}^t \leq x_{k'n}^{t+1}, \quad n = 1, \ldots, N$$

$$z_k^t \geq 0, \quad k = 1, \ldots, K.$$

Our empirical illustration includes computations of both the Malmquist (goods only) and Malmquist-Luenberger productivity indexes. One may also compute what we call a Luenberger productivity indicator, which is also based on the directional distance functions described above. This index has an additive rather than multiplicative structure and is described briefly in appendix A.

Next, we turn to our empirical illustration.

13.5 Empirical Illustration: The Case of U.S. Agriculture

In this section we provide an empirical illustration of the measurement of productivity in the presence of undesirable outputs using a unique data set developed by the U.S. Department of Agriculture's (USDA's) Economic Research Service (ERS), in cooperation with the USDA's Natural Resources Conservation Service (NRCS). As part of our illustration, and paralleling the discussion of the theoretical models, we include results for: (a) productivity based on goods alone, using the Malmquist productivity index, and (b) productivity including both goods and bads using the Malmquist-Luenberger index (our preferred model). Before turning to these results, we first turn to a discussion of the data.

The data used to construct our productivity indexes based on desirable outputs and inputs alone are described in Ball et al. (1999). The inputs include services of capital, land, labor, and intermediate goods. The desirable outputs are crops and livestock. The data are available for forty-eight states over the period 1960–93 and are used to construct a state-by-year panel.

As a first step, we construct longitudinal indexes of outputs and inputs. An index of relative real output (alternatively, real input) between two states is obtained by dividing the nominal output (input) value ratio for the two states by the corresponding output (input) price index. We construct multilateral price indexes using a method proposed independently by Elteto and Köves (1964) and Szulc (1964) (henceforth EKS). The "EKS" index is based on the idea that the most appropriate index to use in a comparison between two states is the Fisher index, which is expressed as the geometric mean of the Laspeyres and Paasche indexes.

When the number (K) of states exceeds two (i.e., $K > 2$), the application of the Fisher index number procedure to the $[K(K-1)]/2$ possible pairs of states yields a matrix of bilateral price indexes that does not satisfy Fisher's circularity test. The problem is to obtain results that satisfy the circularity test and that deviate the least from the bilateral Fisher indexes.

If P_{EKS}^{ij} and P_F^{ij} represent the EKS and Fisher indexes between states i and j, the EKS index is formed by minimizing the following distance criterion:

$$\Delta = \sum_{i=1}^{K}\sum_{j=1}^{K}[\ln P_{EKS}^{ij} - \ln P_F^{ij}(p^j, p^i, y^j, y^i)]^2$$

From the first-order conditions for a minimum, it can be shown that the multilateral index with the minimum distance is given by

$$(38) \quad P_{EKS}^{ij} = \left[\prod_{k=1}^{K}\frac{P_F(p^j, p^i, y^j, y^i)}{P_F(p^i, p^k, y^i, y^k)}\right]^{1/K}.$$

The EKS index between states i and j is, therefore, a geometric mean of K (the number of states) ratios of bilateral Fisher indexes. The multilateral EKS indexes defined by equation (38) satisfy transitivity while minimizing the deviations from the bilateral Fisher indexes.

Comparisons of levels of capital, land, labor, and intermediate inputs require relative input prices. Relative price levels of capital inputs among states are obtained via relative investment-goods prices, taking into account the flow of capital services per unit of capital stock.

Differences in the relative efficiency of land prevents the direct comparison of observed prices. We construct price indexes for land based on an application of the hedonic regression technique. This approach assumes that the price of a good is a function of its characteristics, and it estimates the imputed prices of such characteristics by regressing the prices of goods on their differing quantities of their characteristics.

For our cross-section of states, we estimate the following equation by ordinary least squares (OLS):

$$(39) \quad \ln w_k^j = \sum_{k=1}^{K}\delta_k D_k + \sum_{m=1}^{M}\beta_m x_{km}^j + \varepsilon_{kj}, \quad k = 1,\ldots, K,$$

where w_k^j is the price of the jth parcel of land in state k, x_{km}^j is the mth characteristic of the jth parcel of land in state k, and D_k is a dummy variable equal to unity for the corresponding state and zero otherwise. When the log of price is related to linear-state dummy variables as above, a hedonic price index can be calculated from the antilogs of the δ_k coefficients.

In constructing indexes of relative labor input, we assume that the relative efficiency of an hour worked is the same for a given type of labor in all forty-eight states. Hours worked and average hourly compensation are cross-classified by sex, age, education, and employment class (employee versus self-employed and unpaid family workers). Since average hourly compensation data are not available for self-employed and unpaid family workers, each self-employed worker is imputed the mean wage of hired workers with the same demographic characteristics.

Finally, all our calculations are base-state invariant, but they are not base-year invariant. We use 1987 as the base year for all our time series indexes. The reason for this is that the detailed price comparisons are carried out only for 1987, which means that we construct price indexes for the remaining years by chain linking them to 1987. Thus we have a "true" panel of data with both time and spatial consistency and comparability.

The data for the undesirable outputs were constructed in collaboration with ERS, EPA, and NCRS; details are included in appendix B and are based on Kellogg, Nehring, and Grube (1999), Kellogg and Nehring (1997), and Kellogg, Nehring, Grube, Plotkin, et al. (1999). These undesirable outputs were intended to capture the effects of the agricultural use of chemical pesticides and fertilizers on groundwater and surface water quality. There are essentially two sets of undesirable outputs. The first set includes separate indexes of nitrogen and pesticide leaching into groundwater and runoff into surface water. This first set of undesirable outputs does not attempt to adjust for toxicity or risks from exposure. To summarize, the first set of undesirable outputs includes the following:

nitrogen leaching (from fertilizer)
nitrogen runoff (from fertilizer)
pesticide leaching
pesticide runoff

In contrast, the second set of indexes of undesirable outputs does explicitly account for toxicity and, hence, environmental risk. However, these risk-adjusted indexes are available only for pesticides. In this case we have risk-adjusted indexes for both pesticide runoff and leaching. We also have two types of risk: that associated with exposure to humans and that associated with exposure to fish. To sum up, we have the following for the risk-adjusted case:

human risk–adjusted effect of pesticide leaching
human risk–adjusted effect of pesticide runoff

fish risk–adjusted effect of pesticide leaching
fish risk–adjusted effect of pesticide runoff

As with the data on good output and input quantities, we normalize on 1987.

In our empirical illustration we begin by computing Malmquist productivity and its components based solely on the data on good outputs and inputs. This provides us with a benchmark for the traditional approach that does not explicitly account for byproducts of agricultural production. Next we compute Malmquist-Luenberger productivity indexes with a number of alternative good and bad specifications.

As a reference point, we first compute productivity with the Malmquist index for the traditional model in which only good outputs are included. Table 13.2 includes a summary of average annual productivity changes for this model for each of the forty-eight states in our sample, including the extended decomposition of productivity into technical change, efficiency change, and change in scale efficiency (as in Färe, Grosskopf, Norris, et al. 1994). Recalling that values above 1 signal improvements and those below 1 declines in performance,[7] these results suggest that there has been widespread improvement in productivity in the agricultural sector, due largely to technical change. Another noteworthy feature is the high level of technical efficiency across the board.

Turning now to the analysis of productivity in which we explicitly account for potential detrimental effects of pesticide and fertilizer use, we begin with a brief overview of the trends in production of undesirable outputs. Table 13.3 displays average annual growth rates in the non–risk adjusted measures of undesirable outputs by state. The first two columns proxy the effects of excess pesticides and nitrogen fertilizers on ground water quality; the second two proxy their effects on surface water quality. The average annual increase for all the states in our sample is on the order of 1.5 percent in groundwater contamination and between 2.7 and 3.7 percent in surface water contamination. A quick glance at the individual state averages reveals considerable variation. One interesting pattern we observe is that if we average over the major corn-producing states (Illinois, Indiana, Iowa, Michigan, Minnesota, Missouri, Nebraska, Ohio, Wisconsin, and South Dakota) they have average increases above the national average in pesticide runoff and leaching, particularly in the earlier part of our time period 1972–81. In the later part of the period 1981–93, growth rates declined but were still positive. In contrast, if we average across the large cotton-producing states (Alabama, Arizona, Arkansas, California, Georgia, Louisiana, Mississippi, North Carolina, Tennessee, and Texas) we observe below-average pesticide runoff and leaching, with a decline in leaching and increase in runoff from the earlier part of the period to the later

---

7. Subtracting 1 from the value in the table gives the average annual percentage increase or decrease in the associated index.

Table 13.2   Traditional Malmquist Model: No Bads

	MALMQ	EFFCHG	TECHCH	SCALECH	VRSEFFCH
Alabama	1.0097	1.0011	1.0086	1.0001	1.0010
Arizona	1.0090	0.9986	1.0104	1.0000	0.9986
Arkansas	1.0330	1.0069	1.0260	0.9914	1.0157
California	1.0200	1.0000	1.0200	1.0000	1.0000
Colorado	1.0119	0.9901	1.0220	0.9901	1.0000
Connecticut	1.0227	1.0000	1.0227	1.0000	1.0000
Delaware	1.0406	1.0000	1.0406	1.0000	1.0000
Florida	1.0234	1.0000	1.0234	1.0000	1.0000
Georgia	1.0234	0.9997	1.0237	0.9983	1.0014
Idaho	1.0240	0.9974	1.0267	0.9997	0.9977
Illinois	1.0281	1.0000	1.0281	1.0000	1.0000
Iowa	1.0043	0.9776	1.0273	0.9776	1.0000
Indiana	1.0223	0.9932	1.0293	0.9997	0.9935
Kansas	1.0164	0.9865	1.0302	0.9927	0.9938
Kentucky	1.0059	0.9988	1.0072	1.0016	0.9971
Louisiana	1.0161	0.9902	1.0262	0.9999	0.9903
Maine	1.0037	0.9873	1.0166	1.0000	0.9873
Maryland	1.0063	0.9925	1.0140	1.0012	0.9913
Massachusetts	1.0180	1.0000	1.0180	1.0000	1.0000
Michigan	1.0091	0.9934	1.0158	1.0020	0.9914
Minnesota	1.0031	0.9799	1.0237	0.9857	0.9940
Mississippi	1.0233	0.9959	1.0275	0.9965	0.9994
Missouri	0.9950	0.9870	1.0081	0.9996	0.9874
Montana	1.0085	0.9955	1.0130	1.0037	0.9918
North Carolina	1.0354	1.0047	1.0305	1.0035	1.0012
North Dakota	1.0132	0.9876	1.0259	1.0003	0.9873
Nebraska	1.0244	0.9960	1.0285	0.9940	1.0020
New Hampshire	1.0137	1.0045	1.0092	1.0045	1.0000
New Jersey	1.0102	1.0049	1.0052	0.9995	1.0054
New Mexico	1.0072	0.9998	1.0075	0.9998	1.0000
Nevada	0.9992	0.9903	1.0090	1.0000	0.9903
New York	1.0134	0.9979	1.0155	1.0002	0.9978
Ohio	1.0039	0.9955	1.0085	1.0012	0.9943
Oklahoma	0.9953	0.9904	1.0049	1.0018	0.9886
Oregon	1.0058	0.9990	1.0068	1.0000	0.9990
Pennsylvania	1.0056	0.9962	1.0094	1.0016	0.9946
Rhode Island	1.0112	1.0019	1.0093	1.0019	1.0000
South Carolina	1.0115	0.9980	1.0135	1.0002	0.9977
South Dakota	1.0094	0.9850	1.0248	1.0015	0.9835
Tennessee	1.0093	0.9998	1.0095	1.0020	0.9977
Texas	1.0128	0.9998	1.0130	0.9998	1.0000
Utah	1.0095	0.9989	1.0107	1.0022	0.9967
Vermont	1.0125	1.0000	1.0125	1.0000	1.0000
Virginia	1.0090	0.9969	1.0121	1.0011	0.9958
Washington	1.0330	1.0000	1.0330	1.0000	1.0000
West Virginia	1.0035	0.9927	1.0109	0.9991	0.9936
Wisconsin	1.0116	0.9923	1.0195	0.9923	1.0000
Wyoming	1.0112	0.9964	1.0149	1.0031	0.9933
Grand mean	1.0135	0.9958	1.0177	0.9989	0.9969

Notes: Average annual productivity change (geometric mean) 1972–1993. MALMQ = Malmquist. EFFCHG = efficiency change. TECHCH = technology change. SCALECH = scale efficiency change. VRSEFFCH = change in efficiency under variable returns to scale (VRS).

Table 13.3   Growth Rates of Undesirable Outputs, 1972–93

	Pesticide Leaching	Nitrogen Leaching	Pesticide Runoff	Nitrogen Runoff
U.S. Growth	1.457975	1.605701	2.720772	3.742445
Alabama	−0.66178	−1.86044	0.158949	0.347739
Arizona	−4.30669	0.916722	2.436606	3.300701
Arkansas	−1.06582	5.730058	1.126583	6.048018
California	−4.17287	−0.31007	3.456654	2.886361
Colorado	3.345479	−0.20643	4.996925	2.71688
Delaware	3.359957	2.147653	4.197571	3.300701
Florida	−1.54628	−3.3083	1.398584	0.41434
Georgia	−2.71806	−1.90331	−0.49902	0.224131
Idaho	7.377519	1.75107	7.314736	n.a.
Illinois	4.4356	1.660584	4.313539	1.903807
Indiana	4.456804	−1.12226	4.548081	−0.56724
Iowa	3.499369	5.640201	3.94283	6.778445
Kansas	4.754962	2.30858	4.968092	4.028983
Kentucky	7.069839	−0.36536	9.034774	2.624652
Louisiana	1.125453	3.579004	3.035036	5.306479
Maryland	3.78025	1.948008	4.713547	2.739829
Michigan	4.618252	2.493359	5.89248	4.306935
Minnesota	3.862868	5.672146	4.832284	7.276444
Mississippi	−1.76854	0.856069	0.372424	1.971661
Missouri	0.825782	1.66205	3.510189	2.838578
Montana	6.271978	7.162273	8.527898	n.a.
Nebraska	4.784035	2.174189	4.648753	2.708397
Nevada	−12.214	n.a.	n.a.	n.a.
New Jersey	0.030331	0.988759	2.943945	3.300701
New Mexico	−1.55457	0.61349	3.799125	6.601402
New York	4.419186	−0.05891	8.909959	4.034752
North Carolina	0.228167	0.009149	0.402215	1.539176
North Dakota	6.379878	22.63614	6.55775	23.59918
Ohio	4.738903	4.12331	4.840595	5.412055
Oklahoma	1.091972	4.995701	2.390846	5.991969
Oregon	5.804647	−2.97216	5.881847	n.a.
Pennsylvania	3.816409	0.367492	6.010053	2.271067
South Carolina	−4.32401	0.989152	−4.94202	1.698452
South Dakota	3.79704	10.19079	5.526619	12.30475
Tennessee	1.808472	0.930429	2.213043	3.36549
Texas	1.983041	2.23293	1.440772	3.657867
Utah	3.129082	−1.12566	4.249905	n.a.
Virginia	1.680214	1.396692	4.965877	4.72977
Washington	6.299346	−3.54085	8.745588	n.a.
West Virginia	1.343964	0.272183	4.896003	3.300701
Wisconsin	3.943217	3.907079	5.88467	7.66399
Wyoming	3.195111	0.207072	6.247087	n.a.
Corn states				
1972–81	5.94335	7.54430	6.52824	7.34857
1981–93	3.38477	−1.88265	3.70539	1.22602
1972–93	3.99776	2.42642	4.38584	3.67482

Table 13.3 (continued)

	Pesticide Leaching	Nitrogen Leaching	Pesticide Runoff	Nitrogen Runoff
Cotton states				
1972–81	1.19993	4.48643	1.21995	4.11132
1981–93	−3.47005	−1.99648	1.67742	3.67881
1972–93	−0.97291	1.06712	1.24173	3.33962

Note: Pesticide data are in acre treatment terms. n.a. = not available.

part. Corn states have higher growth rates of nitrogen leaching and runoff than cotton states as well for the full time period, but this is due to very fast growth in the earlier years and dramatic relative declines (and reductions in nitrogen leaching) in the later part of the time period.

When we turn to the human risk– and fish risk–adjusted measures of pesticide leaching and runoff that are summarized in table 13.4, the patterns over the time period are even more dramatic, reflecting the changes in chemical use over our time period (which are accounted for in our risk adjustment).[8] Here we see average reductions in groundwater contamination of almost 3 percent and surface water contamination of almost 5 percent when adjusted for risk to humans. When adjusted for risk to the fish population, we observe a decrease of more than 4 percent in groundwater contamination and a 5 percent *increase* in surface water contamination. Again, a glance at the state-by-state results reveals very wide variation.

Although the non–risk adjusted patterns are more clear-cut, we do see differences when we compare corn- and cotton-producing states: On average, corn-producing states show declines in fish risk–adjusted effects of pesticides, whereas, on average, the major cotton-producing states show increases over the entire time period, although both cotton and corn states show declines in the later years compared to the earlier years. In terms of the human risk–adjusted trends, both cotton and corn states showed increases in all but human risk–adjusted runoff over the earlier part of our period (1972–81), but have reduced both leaching and runoff over the later part (1981–93) of our time period. Recall that on average the major corn- and cotton-producing states exhibited positive (but falling) growth in non–risk adjusted leaching and runoff, with rates for corn-producing states exceeding those of cotton-producing states on average. In contrast, based on patterns for risk adjusted water pollution, corn-producing states have reduced their pesticide damages, especially relative to cotton-producing states. Thus, other things being equal, we would expect that the Malmquist-Luenberger model would signal lower productivity growth, es-

---

8. If there is strong variation from year to year, then these patterns may be obscured when we are looking at average annual changes, as we do here.

Table 13.4 **Growth Rates: Human– and Fish–Risk Adjusted Leaching and Runoff, Average Annual Growth Rates 1972–93**

	Human Risk		Fish Risk	
	Leaching	Runoff	Leaching	Runoff
Alabama	−5.08470	−1.06678	−0.20990	6.09136
Arizona	n.a.	−10.83268	n.a.	17.80097
Arkansas	−1.27859	3.40360	−4.09960	5.20793
California	3.24825	5.80737	−3.73905	17.19049
Colorado	−1.16701	−12.73851	−6.14268	−4.54310
Delaware	−2.05306	−6.86531	10.87384	−4.47528
Florida	−10.59873	−19.54001	−0.02943	7.87374
Georgia	−4.99913	−13.72472	3.41988	1.54338
Idaho	−9.78556	−13.78041	n.a.	−20.54799
Illinois	−1.20208	−5.39991	−16.98420	−4.12020
Indiana	−1.65013	−8.41646	8.37802	−3.38601
Iowa	−4.93930	−4.57139	−16.34977	−3.18199
Kansas	0.91712	−3.86589	−1.49433	1.23912
Kentucky	2.06691	1.34536	1.03638	1.61903
Louisiana	−1.17057	4.74926	−1.64338	11.82326
Maryland	−2.65318	−4.94753	1.17823	−0.06571
Michigan	−1.69295	−1.93151	−14.94175	0.38559
Minnesota	−7.97353	−1.74013	−21.99322	−0.44378
Mississippi	−4.89603	1.58262	8.43648	14.43836
Missouri	−1.80773	−11.42821	2.65703	−1.57733
Montana	3.42449	−3.64715	n.a.	−1.90672
Nebraska	−0.55471	−3.09422	−16.65064	2.17545
Nevada	n.a.	n.a.	n.a.	n.a.
New Jersey	−6.35944	9.83772	1.23985	−0.49122
New Mexico	−4.70814	−8.79969	−9.30233	−6.00275
New York	−4.35752	−0.85828	−4.13647	2.71222
North Carolina	−4.08713	−12.08633	4.46486	−0.34217
North Dakota	−12.60767	−4.53576	n.a.	3.42076
Ohio	−1.28696	−8.31534	−20.45495	−0.17986
Oklahoma	−5.13906	−6.80717	3.45326	−0.42510
Oregon	0.83694	4.42137	8.11467	−2.70753
Pennsylvania	−4.09475	2.86996	−6.62414	3.64236
South Carolina	−3.60931	−8.14836	1.32843	−0.42646
South Dakota	−12.84851	−3.35518	−24.51314	−3.90894
Tennessee	−2.32381	0.83153	1.89718	8.54155
Texas	−0.98647	−5.75428	−0.31741	4.98538
Utah	n.a.	−29.62295	n.a.	−40.13550
Virginia	−2.62515	−11.10284	8.18294	3.49778
Washington	−4.96490	−2.82736	−22.56023	−8.96142
West Virginia	−5.01294	−8.97672	n.a.	−6.41974
Wisconsin	−7.56621	−0.85298	−14.81612	1.11831
Wyoming	−8.16177	−11.15268	n.a.	−14.15974
United States	−2.69915	−4.83464	−4.29376	5.17032
Corn states				
1972–81	4.31171	−3.89088	3.69083	4.20984
1981–93	−7.78590	−6.16768	−26.36327	−6.55263
1972–93	−2.60121	−5.19191	−13.48294	−1.94014

Table 13.4 (continued)

	Human Risk		Fish Risk	
	Leaching	Runoff	Leaching	Runoff
Cotton states				
1972–81	1.77296	−2.60857	13.20231	9.02206
1981–93	−6.89547	−3.13453	−9.02549	8.98561
1972–93	−3.18043	−2.90912	0.50071	9.00123

Note: n.a. = not available.

pecially in the earlier years (relative to productivity without the undesirable outputs), in corn-producing states when we include indexes of pesticide runoff and leaching that are not adjusted for risk; and productivity improvements (relative to the goods-only case) when we include indexes of pesticide runoff and leaching that are adjusted for human and fish risk.

We include our disaggregated results in appendix C.[9] Here we focus on selected states and begin with our results using non–risk adjusted measures of water contamination; see table 13.5. We display annual average productivity growth rates in our data for two subperiods: 1972–81 and 1981–93. These were chosen to capture the observed trends in our measures of water contamination. The first two columns of data summarize the Malmquist productivity growth for the case in which we ignore bads; that is, we include only marketable agricultural outputs in our model. Generally, productivity increases on average between the two time periods. If we include the undesirable outputs in our model and penalize states for increases in water contamination (see the columns labeled "Malmquist-Luenberg"), the average growth rates are typically different, as expected.

To get a sense of whether the difference accords with intuition, we include in the last two columns an indicator of whether water contamination increased or decreased between the two time periods. For example, if we look at the pattern for Colorado under heading A, we see that productivity increased between the two time periods when we look at goods only. When we include nitrogen leaching and runoff, the productivity growth in each period is lower; that is, there is a positive gap between the goods-only index and the good and bad index (Malmquist-Luenberger), and that gap increases over time, which is consistent with the observed increase in this

---

9. We note that for the individual states, we encountered cases in which there were no solutions to what we call the "mixed period problems," that is, those in which data in one period are compared to the frontier in a different period. This occurred in both the standard Malmquist case and the Malmquist-Luenberger case. The number of such instances is recorded under the 0's columns in the appendix tables. We conjecture that data smoothing would reduce the incidence of nonsolutions, since we encountered very few problems when we constructed averages over the major cotton- and corn-producing states. We also suspect that the "bads" data—which are not generated in the same way as the rest of the data set—may not be consistent with the production theoretic model that underlies our analysis.

Table 13.5 Average Change in Productivity in Selected States: 1972–81 versus 1981–93

	Malmquist (goods only)		Malmquist-Luenberger (goods and bads)			Gap			Water Contamination	
	1972–81 (a)	1981–93 (b)	1972–81 (c)	1981–93 (d)	1972–81 (e)	1981–93 (f)	Change (g)		Up	Down
A. Nitrogen Leaching and Runoff										
Colorado	0.9909	1.0393	0.9881	1.0340	0.0028	0.0053	0.0025		x	
Maryland	1.0008	1.0062	1.0019	1.0140	−0.0011	−0.00781	−0.0066			x
Michigan	1.0045	1.0162	0.9930	1.0021	0.0115	−0.0059	−0.0174			x
Nebraska	1.0144	1.0410	1.0343	1.0439	−0.0199	−0.0029	0.0170		x	
New York	1.0154	1.0182	1.0027	0.9945	0.0127	0.0237	0.0110		x	
Ohio	0.9993	1.0151	1.0159	1.0297	−0.0165	−0.0145	0.0020		x	
Pennsylvania	1.0071	1.0066	1.0076	1.0100	−0.0005	−0.0033	−0.0029			x
Texas	1.0146	1.0147	1.0166	1.0288	−0.0019	−0.0141	−0.0121			x
Wisconsin	1.0075	1.0171	0.9873	1.0507	0.0202	−0.0335	−0.0537			x
B. Pesticide Leaching and Runoff										
Colorado	0.9909	1.0393	0.9851	1.0415	0.0058	−0.0022	−0.0081			x
Maryland	1.0009	1.0062	1.0026	1.0108	−0.0019	−0.0046	−0.0028			x
Michigan	1.0045	1.0162	0.9956	1.0163	0.0088	−0.0001	−0.0089			x
Nebraska	1.0160	1.0355	1.0127	1.0335	0.0033	0.0020	−0.0013			x
New York	1.0154	1.0182	1.0030	1.0020	0.0124	0.0162	0.0039		x	
Ohio	0.9993	1.0151	0.9947	1.0157	0.0046	−0.0006	−0.0051			x
Pennsylvania	1.0071	1.0066	1.0084	1.0084	−0.0013	−0.0018	−0.0005			x
Texas	1.0146	1.0147	1.0046	1.0274	0.0100	−0.0126	−0.0226			x
Wisconsin	1.0075	1.0171	1.0004	1.0099	0.0071	0.0072	0.0001		x	

Note: Values in column e = a − c; in column f, b − d; in column g, f − e.

type of pollution in Colorado over the two time periods. Generally, we would expect to see a positive value in the gap-change column when pollution increases, and a negative gap change when pollution declines.

The data under heading B confirm this pattern for our other non–risk adjusted measures of pollution: pesticide leaching and runoff. For example, the decline in this measure of pollution for Colorado results in a higher measured average growth in productivity in the 1981–93 period using the Malmquist-Luenberger index (which accounts for bads) than in the simple Malmquist measure (which includes only good outputs).

Table 13.6 includes a sample of our results when we use the risk adjusted measures of pollution. We note that, on average, trends in these adjusted measures of pollution—with the exception of fish risk–adjusted runoff—decline over the 1972–93 time period.[10] Thus we would expect to see Malmquist-Luenberger indexes (that adjust for pollution) that are higher than their unadjusted counterparts, particularly in the 1981–93 period for states that realize declines in these types of pollution. Comparing the growth rates in the second and fourth columns (or the difference in column f) confirms this result for both the case of fish risk– and human risk–adjusted measures of pollution.

As an even more general summary of these results, we calculate productivity growth for average cotton- and corn-growing states; the results are displayed in table 13.7. By partitioning the time period into the two subperiods 1972–81 and 1981–93, we see a pattern of falling pollution for all but the fish risk–adjusted measure of pollution in the cotton states. As expected, this yields average productivity growth in the latter period that is higher when we account for both goods and bads (Malmquist-Luenberger in 1981–93 column), than when we ignore them (Malmquist 1981–93 column).

Thus, for many states, we find that if we account for risk adjusted water contamination caused by the use of agricultural chemicals, agricultural productivity growth—especially in the latter part of the time period studied here—is higher than the traditional growth measures that ignore these byproducts. This is consistent with the general pattern of falling human– and fish risk–adjusted runoff and human risk–adjusted measures of leaching we observe in the raw data.

---

10. For example, we can trace the dramatic shifts in the use and composition of pesticides over the period between 1960 and 1993, which involved a major increase in the use of herbicides relative to insecticides and the substitution of more environmentally benign pesticides for highly toxic pesticides. In the early 1960s, concern about the environmental consequences was minimal. Rising concern in the mid-1960s ultimately resulted in the EPA ban on the agricultural use of many chemicals in the 1970s and 1980s, including DDT (1972) and toxaphene (1983), which had been widely used in cotton production. The banning of aldrin, chlordane, and heptachlor had similar effects for corn producers. Nevertheless, there are major corn herbicides, such as atrazine, that have not been banned, and that constitute major components of our indexes of pesticide pollution, especially for corn-producing states.

Table 13.6 Average Change in Productivity in Selected States: 1972–81 versus 1981–93

	Malmquist (goods only)		Malmquist-Luenberger (goods and bads)		Gap		Change	Water Contamination	
	1972–81 (a)	1981–93 (b)	1972–81 (c)	1981–93 (d)	1972–81 (e)	1981–93 (f)	(g)	Up	Down
			A. Fish Risk–Adjusted Leaching and Runoff						
Indiana	1.0269	1.0432	0.9929	1.0528	0.0340	−0.0096	−0.0436		x
Illinois	1.0381	1.0682	1.0395	1.0728	−0.0014	−0.0045	−0.0031		x
Missouri	0.9967	0.9815	0.9854	0.9853	0.0113	−0.0037	−0.0150		x
Ohio	0.9993	1.0151	0.9927	1.0302	0.0066	−0.0151	−0.0217		x
Wisconsin	1.0075	1.0171	1.0097	1.0143	−0.0022	0.0028	0.0050	x	
			B. Human Risk–Adjusted Leaching and Runoff						
Arkansas	1.0360	1.0329	1.0515	1.0251	−0.0154	0.0078	0.0232	x	
Louisiana	1.0184	1.0218	1.0295	0.9827	−0.0111	0.0391	0.0502	x	
Nebraska	1.0160	1.0355	1.0156	1.0719	0.0003	−0.03632	−0.0366		x
Ohio	0.9993	1.0151	0.9832	1.0247	0.0162	−0.0096	−0.0257		x
Texas	1.0146	1.0147	1.0065	1.0206	0.0081	−0.0059	−0.0140		x

Table 13.7   Average Change in Productivity in Hypothetical Corn and Cotton States: 1972–81 versus 1981–93

	Malmquist (goods only)		Malmquist-Luenberger (goods and bads)		Gap			Water Contamination	
	1972–81 (a)	1981–93 (b)	1972–81 (c)	1981–93 (d)	1972–81 (e)	1981–93 (f)	Change (g)	Up	Down
Corn state									
Nitrogen	0.9967	0.9870	1.0061	0.9990	−0.0094	−0.0129	−0.0026		x
Pesticides	0.9967	0.9870	0.9986	1.1018	−0.0019	−0.0237	−0.0219		x
Human risk	0.9967	0.9870	0.9930	1.0046	0.0037	−0.0175	−0.0212		x
Fish risk	0.9967	0.9870	1.0060	1.0252	−0.0093	−0.0382	−0.0289		x
Cotton state									
Nitrogen	0.9919	0.9874	1.0126	1.0205	−0.0206	−0.0331	−0.0125		x
Pesticides	0.9919	0.9874	1.0108	1.0159	−0.0188	−0.0285	−0.0096		x
Human risk	0.9919	0.9874	1.0124	1.0131	−0.0205	−0.0257	−0.0052		x
Fish risk	0.9919	0.9874	1.0262	1.0252	−0.0343	−0.0336	0.0007	x	

Notes: Hypothetical corn state is averaged over Illinois, Indiana, Iowa, Michigan, Minnesota, Missouri, Nebraska, Ohio, Wisconsin, and South Dakota. Hypothetical cotton state is averaged over Alabama, Arizona, Arkansas, California, Georgia, Louisiana, Mississippi, North Carolina, Tennessee, and Texas.

13.6 Summary

In this paper we provide an overview of some approaches to modeling and measuring productivity in the presence of joint production of desirable and undesirable outputs. These have in common an axiomatic production theoretic framework, in which joint production is explicitly modeled using the notion of null-jointness proposed by Shephard and Färe; and weak disposability of outputs is imposed to model the fact that reduction of bad outputs may be costly.

In measuring productivity in the presence of undesirable outputs, traditional growth-accounting and index number approaches face the problem that prices of the undesirable outputs typically do not exist, since such outputs are generally not marketed. An alternative that does not require price information is the Malmquist productivity index, which is based on ratios of Shephard-type distance functions. These do not require information on prices, which suggests that they would be an appropriate methodological tool. Although an improvement over ignoring undesirable outputs, the Malmquist index computed with bads may not have well-defined solutions, and it effectively registers increases in the bads (as in the goods), ceteris paribus, as improvements in productivity.

In order to address these problems we introduce an alternative productivity index based on a generalization of the Shephard distance functions, namely, what we call directional distance functions. Not only are these distance functions generally computable in the presence of undesirable outputs, but they also allow us to credit firms for *reductions* in undesirable outputs while crediting them for *increases* in good outputs. The Malmquist-Luenberger index is constructed from directional distance functions but maintains the Malmquist multiplicative structure, allowing us to compare our results with the traditional Malmquist productivity index, which credits only for increases in good outputs. Although not included here, the Luenberger productivity indicator is another model that is based on directional distance functions but that has an additive structure.[11] All of these productivity indexes are computable using linear programming techniques very similar to traditional data envelopment analysis. Further attention should be paid, however, to dealing with mixed period problems with no solutions, perhaps through data-smoothing techniques.

We apply our methods to state level data recently made available by ERS, which include variables that proxy effects of pesticides and nitrates (found in fertilizers) on groundwater and surface water. As expected, we

---

11. The directional distance function, of course, combines both additive and multiplicative features. The additivity, and ability simultaneously to adjust inputs and outputs, while not exploited here, may be used to establish the duality of the directional distance function (which scales on outputs and inputs) to profits. See Chambers, Chung, and Färe (1998).

find that measured productivity differs when we account for bads—declines in water contamination were associated with improvements in the Malmquist-Luenberger index as expected, ceteris paribus. Future research plans include pursuit of hypothesis testing, using (for example) bootstrapping techniques.

Another potentially fruitful avenue of research in this area would be to compute the shadow prices of the undesirable outputs to provide a benchmark for the opportunity cost of reducing undesirable outputs from the production side, as proposed by Färe and Grosskopf (1998). We would also like to generalize our production model better to model the roles of the environment and of consumers who evaluate the risks imposed by changes in the quality of groundwater and surface water. Along these lines, Färe and Grosskopf also proposed development of a network model to include the interaction of the environment with bads and consumers; this could be employed to provide a benchmark for computing shadow prices that reflect consumer evaluation of reductions in agricultural by-products.

Appendix A
The Luenberger Productivity Indicator

Both productivity indexes discussed in sections 13.3 and 13.4 are multiplicative in nature. Here we introduce a productivity measure, which is additive. We follow W. E. Diewert (1993) and refer to the additive measure as an indicator. The indicator introduced here is an output-oriented version of the Luenberger productivity indicator introduced by Chambers (1996). It is based on the output-oriented directional distance function discussed in section 13.4 above. We define the index as

(38) $\quad L_t^{t+1} = 1/2[\mathbf{D}_o^{t+1}(x^t, y^t, b^t; y^t, -b^t) - \mathbf{D}_o^{t+1}(x^{t+1}, y^{t+1}, b^{t+1}; y^{t+1}, -b^{t+1})$
$\quad\quad + \mathbf{D}_o^t(x^t, y^t, b^t; y^t, -b^t) - \mathbf{D}_o^t(x^{t+1}, y^{t+1}, b^{t+1}; y^{t+1}, -b^{t+1})].$

As we did in section 13.4, we take the direction $(g_y, -g_b)$ to be the observed values of the good y and bad b outputs. Following the idea of Chambers, Färe, and Grosskopf (1996), the Luenberger index can be additively decomposed into an efficiency change and a technical change component,

(39) $\quad\quad\quad \text{LEFFCH}_t^{t+1} = \mathbf{D}_o^t(x^t, y^t, b^t; y^t, -b^t)$
$\quad\quad\quad\quad\quad - \mathbf{D}_o^{t+1}(x^{t+1}, y^{t+1}, b^{t+1}; y^{t+1}, -b^{t+1})$

and

(40) $\text{LTECH}_t^{t+1} = \frac{1}{2}[(\mathbf{D}_o^{t+1}(x^{t+1}, y^{t+1}, b^{t+1}; y^{t+1}, -b^{t+1})$
$- \mathbf{D}_o^t(x^{t+1}, y^{t+1}, b^{t+1}; y^{t+1}, -b^{t+1})$
$+ \mathbf{D}_o^{t+1}(x^t, y^t, b^t; y^t, -b^t) - \mathbf{D}_o^t(x^t, y^t, b^t; y^t, -b^t)]$,

respectively. The sum of these two components equals the Luenberger index. This index can be computed using the same programming problems described in the discussion of the Malmquist-Luenberger index.

In passing we note that one may also define a Luenberger productivity indicator based on a directional distance function, which, in addition to scaling on good outputs, also scales on the input vector. This feature implies that one cannot transform it into multiplicative form as we have done with the Malmquist-Luenberger index. It has the advantage, however, of being dual to the profit function, which implies that it is a natural component of profit efficiency. This type of Luenberger productivity indicator was employed by Chambers, Färe, and Grosskopf (1996).

Appendix B
Environmental Indicators of Nitrogen and Pesticide Leaching and Runoff from Farm Fields

Indicators of groundwater and surface water contamination from chemicals used in agricultural production, and trends over regions and over time in factors that are known to be important determinants of chemical leaching and runoff, have been used to calculate indexes for environmental contamination. The determinants include the intrinsic leaching potential of soils; cropping patterns; chemical use; chemical toxicity; and annual rainfall and its relationship to surface runoff and to percolation through the soil. Consequently, the indexes of undesirable outputs that have been estimated represent changes over time and over regions (states) in the potential for agricultural contamination of water resources. The changes are assumed to be useful proxies for actual contamination.

Eight indexes of undesirable outputs have been compiled for the 1972–93 period, and can be matched with recently completed series of conventional inputs and outputs to create a 21×48 panel of inputs and both desirable marketed and undesirable unmarketed outputs of agricultural production activities in the United States. The eight indexes include four that are not adjusted for risk of exposure to toxic chemicals, and four that include a risk adjustment. The four undesirable outputs that have been

This appendix was written by Richard Nehring (ERS) and Robert Kellogg (NRCS) based on several working papers, including those cited in the bibliography.

compiled with adjustments for environmental weights relating to weather and soil/chemical characteristics, but not adjusting for risk, are

1. nitrates in groundwater, measured as adjusted pounds of excess nitrogen,
2. nitrates in surface water, measured as adjusted pounds of excess nitrogen,
3. pesticides in groundwater, measured as adjusted acre treatments of pesticides, and
4. pesticides in surface water, measured as adjusted acre treatments of pesticides.

The new indexing approaches incorporate the diversity of soil and climatic conditions across the United States into base-year environmental weights by estimating intrinsic vulnerability factors for each of the 3,041 counties in the United States. These environmental weights are converted to indexes of pesticide contamination using county-level crop production statistics and the best available pesticide use estimates by crop and by region. Indexes of nitrate contamination are constructed by multiplying county-level estimates of excess nitrogen from crop production by the county-level environmental weights. The non–risk adjusted pesticide leaching index was derived by adapting the field-level screening procedure used by USDA's National Resource Conservation Service (NRCS) to help farmers evaluate the potential for pesticide loss from a field, and extending the procedure to the national level. All indexes represent chemical loss at the edge of the field for runoff and at the bottom of the root zone for leaching.

The four undesirable outputs that have been compiled with adjustments for environmental weights relating to climate and soil/chemical characteristics, including risk, are

1. pesticides in groundwater, measured as adjusted pounds of pesticide based on chronic human exposure in drinking water;
2. pesticides in groundwater, measured as adjusted pounds of pesticide based on chronic safe levels for fish;
3. pesticides in surface water, measured as adjusted pounds of pesticide based on chronic human exposure in drinking water; and
4. pesticides in surface water, measured as adjusted pounds of pesticide based on chronic safe levels for fish.

The pesticide and nitrogen indexes reflect land-use soil characteristics of about 160,000 sample points for 1982 and 1992 and are based on USDA's 1992 National Resources Inventory (NRI). The NRI was used to determine the percent composition of soil types in each resource subregion by crop. The percent composition for 1982 was applied to 1972–86, and the percent composition for 1992 was applied to 1987–93.

Estimates of the eight undesirable indicators are based on major crop production that accounts for the bulk of chemical use in most states analyzed. For pesticide indexes adjusted for risk we used county data on acres planted for seven crops—barley, corn, cotton, rice, sorghum, soybeans and wheat. For nitrogen indexes and pesticide indexes not adjusted for risk, we used county data on acres planted and yields for the same seven crops. County data on acres planted and yields are available from the National Agriculture Statistics Service (NASS) for 1972 to the present.

The pesticide-use time series was derived from two sources, USDA and Doane's. The Doane Pesticide Profile Study provided a database of application rates and percent acres treated by chemical, crop, and year for 1987–93 for the United States as a whole and broken down into seven agricultural production regions. For 1972–86, the Doane pesticide use data and NASS chemical use surveys for selected years were used to generate similar estimates. A total of approximately 200 pesticides was included with somewhat greater coverage in more recent years (i.e., 1986–93 compared to 1972–86), and with greater coverage in the acre treatment formulation than in the risk adjusted index. Pesticide use parameters for all years are made for each of seven Doane reporting regions. Application rates and estimates of percent of acres treated for each chemical used in these seven regions were imputed to the 2,200 resource polygons for each crop.

State-level nitrogen fertilizer application rates were obtained from NASS and ERS survey data on commercial fertilizer applications. Annual data were available for ten major corn states, six major cotton states, and sixteen major wheat states. For other states, application rates were estimated based on other survey data rates used in neighboring states. All nitrogen application rates used represent average rates for the state. Excess nitrogen is defined as the difference between the amount of nitrogen applied from all sources (chemical fertilizers plus soybean and legume credits) and the amount of nitrogen removed in the crop production process (see Kellogg, Maizell, and Goss 1992). During 1972–93, residual nitrogen from barley, corn, cotton, rice, sorghum, soybeans, and wheat accounted for the bulk of residual nitrogen in most of the states analyzed.

In addition to the soil and chemical environmental weights as previously described, the risk adjusted pesticide indicators involve estimation of environmental risk. Environmental risk was estimated using threshold exceedence units (TEUs). Threshold concentrations used for each chemical correspond to the maximum safe level for human chronic exposure in drinking water. Where available, water quality standards were used. For other pesticides, estimates of the maximum safe level were made from published toxicity data. For each chemical used on each crop and soil type in each resource substate area, the per-acre pesticide loss concentration was calculated and then divided by the threshold concentration. Where the threshold concentration was exceeded, the ratio was multiplied by the acres treated to obtain estimates of TEUs. TEUs per substate area were obtained by summing TEUs over chemicals, crops, soil type, and resource polygons in each substate area. TEUs per state were obtained by converting substate estimates to state estimates using conversion factors derived from the National Resource Inventory. This procedure was repeated for each year in the time series to produce a spatial-temporal environmental indicator. Separate indicators were constructed for pesticides in leachate and pesticides dissolved in runoff. Irrigated acres were included in the total acres, but were not treated differently than nonirrigated acres with respect to the potential for pesticide loss. The fish-related indicators were calculated using threshold concentrations based on chronic "safe" levels for fish.

Other measures of outputs and inputs needed to estimate TFP growth are calculated only as state aggregates, so the eight undesirable outputs need to be aggregated to the state level. Since changes in fertilizer and pesticide use, environmental loadings from these chemicals, and computed environmental weight vary dramatically by state and county, this aggregation is the important last step in the index construction, making possible an accounting of the geographic diversity of the potential for water contamination. Some summary information by state is displayed in table 13B.1.

Table 13B.1 Pesticide Leaching and Runoff Scores as Percent of U.S. Total, 1984 versus 1993

	Leaching Score		Runoff Score	
	1984	1993	1984	1993
Colorado	1.06	1.07	0.26	0.28
Illinois	7.48	9.36	11.63	10.04
Indiana	5.87	7.37	5.79	5.40
Kansas	2.48	4.19	3.83	4.51
Kentucky	2.68	2.71	1.54	1.59
Maryland	1.30	1.17	0.38	0.29
Michigan	3.09	3.32	0.94	0.96
Minnesota	2.48	2.83	4.22	4.05
Montana	0.30	0.41	0.23	0.40
Nebraska	6.03	8.79	3.30	3.19
New York	1.14	1.07	0.22	0.38
Pennsylvania	2.06	1.81	0.85	0.80
South Dakota	0.81	1.13	1.28	1.58
Texas	1.52	2.18	3.15	3.93
Virginia	2.05	1.26	0.33	0.24
West Virginia	0.07	0.05	0.02	0.02
Wisconsin	2.65	2.79	0.88	1.04
Subtotal	43.07	51.51	38.85	38.70
Major corn states	38.17	46.98	47.12	43.57
Major cotton states	38.37	31.44	42.22	45.01
Other states	23.46	21.58	10.66	11.42
Total	100.99	100.00	100.00	100.00

Appendix C
State-Specific Results

	Average Annual Change in Productivity, 1972–93							
	Malmquist (goods)	Pesticides				Nitrates		
		Malmquist	0's	Malmquist-Luenberg	0's	Malmquist	0's	Malmquist-Luenberg	0's
Alabama	1.0097	0.9985		n.s.		1.0021		1.0187	15
Arizona	1.0090	0.9292	3	0.9509	20	0.9731	15	n.s.	
Arkansas	1.0033	0.9403	14	n.s.		1.0621		n.s.	
California	1.0200	1.0366	7	1.0172		1.1040	14	1.0620	15
Colorado	1.0119	1.0028		1.0075		1.0112	2	1.0051	
Delaware	1.0406	1.0322		n.s.		1.0062		n.s.	
Florida	1.0234	0.9690		0.9811	18	1.0223		1.0055	16
Georgia	1.0234	0.9838		n.s.		1.0054		n.s.	
Idaho	1.0240	1.0173		1.0203	6	1.1215	19	1.0508	15
Illinois	1.0281	1.0284		1.0289	4	1.0491		n.s.	
Indiana	1.0223	1.0201		1.0242	2	1.0139		1.0043	15
Iowa	1.0043	0.9997		1.0051		1.0070		1.0600	17
Kansas	1.0164	1.0190		1.0143		1.0323		1.0182	10
Kentucky	1.0059	1.0074		1.0040		1.0078		1.0016	5
Louisiana	1.0161	1.0089	11	n.s.		1.0221		1.0001	9
Maryland	1.0063	1.0081		1.0004		1.0058		1.0016	

Michigan	1.0091	1.0067		1.0051	1.0059		1.0070	
Minnesota	1.0031	0.9965		0.9982	1.0175	7	0.7967	20
Mississippi	1.0233	1.0201	11	n.s.	1.0276		n.s.	
Missouri	0.9950	1.0002		1.0020	1.0185		1.0010	8
Montana	1.0085	0.9920		1.0079	1.1133	17	0.9528	
Nebraska	1.0244	1.0266		1.0221	1.0350		1.0456	3
Nevada	0.9992	n.s.		n.s.	n.s.		1.0325	5
New Jersey	1.0102	1.0012		1.0164	1.0034	2	1.0017	
New Mexico	1.0072	0.9984	6	0.9829	1.0261	3	1.0034	
New York	1.0134	0.9982		0.9995	0.9990		0.9941	1
North Carolina	1.0354	1.0362		1.0435	1.0326		n.s.	
North Dakota	1.0263	1.0108	8	0.9971	0.9467	17	0.9981	7
Ohio	1.0039	1.0057		1.0041	1.0147		1.0137	3
Oklahoma	0.9953	0.9793		0.9974	1.0074	11	n.s.	
Oregon	1.0058	n.s.		0.9959	n.s.		n.s.	
Pennsylvania	1.0056	1.0084		1.0069	1.0020	1	1.0007	
South Carolina	1.0115	0.9800		n.s.	1.0016		n.s.	
South Dakota	1.0094	0.9895		0.9972	0.7654	19	0.9249	13
Tennessee	1.0093	1.0066	5	1.0270	1.0088		1.0199	5
Texas	1.0127	1.0268	1	1.0157	1.0139		1.0179	2
Utah	1.0095	n.s.		1.0129	1.0424	16	1.0028	16
Virginia	1.0090	1.0050		1.0079	1.0055		1.0100	10
Washington	1.0030	n.s.		n.s.	n.s.		n.s.	
West Virginia	1.0035	1.0169	1	1.0135	0.9999		1.0048	
Wisconsin	1.0116	0.9925		1.0053	0.8611	11	1.0112	
Wyoming	1.0112	0.9593		0.9961	0.9914	15	1.0063	1

(*continued*)

Appendix C. (continued)

	Malmquist (goods)	Human Risk–Adjusted			Fish Risk–Adjusted		
		Malmquist	0's	Malmquist-Luenberg	0's	Malmquist	0's	Malmquist-Luenberg	0's

	Malmquist (goods)	Malmquist	0's	Malmquist-Luenberg	0's	Malmquist	0's	Malmquist-Luenberg	0's
Alabama	1.0097	1.0139	1	1.0136	3	n.s.		n.s.	17
Arizona	1.0090	n.s.		1.0183	1	n.s.		1.0263	20
Arkansas	1.0033	1.0294		1.0340	4	1.1319		1.0401	20
California	1.0200	0.9561	11	1.0010	5	1.2457	2	1.0156	1
Colorado	1.0119	1.0297		1.0172		1.0343		1.1309	0
Delaware	1.0406	1.0868	5	1.0001	15	1.0374	3	1.0963	18
Florida	1.0234	n.s.		n.s.		1.1310	4	1.0488	15
Georgia	1.0234	1.1407	4	n.s.		0.9555		n.s.	
Idaho	1.0240	n.s.		1.0389		n.s.		0.9961	9
Illinois	1.0281	0.9959		n.s.		1.0585		1.0687	2
Indiana	1.0223	0.9981		1.0218	5	1.0382	2	1.0202	2
Iowa	1.0043	0.9592		n.s.		1.0651		1.0687	16
Kansas	1.0164	1.0263		1.0166		1.0348		1.0194	15
Kentucky	1.0059	1.0047		1.0016		1.0112		0.9967	1
Louisiana	1.0161	1.0181		0.9983	3	1.1414		1.0185	16
Maryland	1.0063	1.0055	1	1.0168		1.0282	4	0.9778	13
Michigan	1.0091	0.9836		1.0137	5	1.0147		1.0278	2
Minnesota	1.0031	0.9697		n.s.		1.0420		1.0246	5

Mississippi	1.0233		1.0283	2	1.1493		n.s.	
Missouri	0.9950		0.9849	4	1.0552		0.9937	2
Montana	1.0085		1.0015		n.s.		0.9736	8
Nebraska	1.0244		1.0445	6	1.1066		1.0541	13
Nevada	0.9992		n.s.		n.s.		1.0068	7
New Jersey	1.0102	1	1.0081	2	0.5782	15	0.9508	17
New Mexico	1.0072		1.0193		1.1456	3	1.0248	
New York	1.0134		1.0079		0.9129	1	1.0144	
North Carolina	1.0354	1	1.0307	3	0.9680		1.0336	2
North Dakota	1.0263	15	1.0513	3	1.1250		1.0263	8
Ohio	1.0039		0.9978	2	1.0132		1.0101	9
Oklahoma	0.9953		1.0083		1.1751	1	1.0002	1
Oregon	1.0058		1.0093	2	1.0933	19	1.0216	8
Pennsylvania	1.0056		1.0068		.08604	5	0.9811	6
South Carolina	1.0115	2	1.0214	1	0.9473		0.8964	16
South Dakota	1.0094	2	1.0606		1.0189		1.0135	14
Tennessee	1.0093		n.s.		1.0786		1.0165	9
Texas	1.0127		1.0113		1.0424	2	1.0243	15
Utah	1.0095		1.0116		n.s.		0.9767	14
Virginia	1.0090	1	n.s.	1	0.9533		0.9984	20
Washington	1.0030		1.0093	3	1.1747		0.9891	1
West Virginia	1.0035		1.0163		0.9882	2	1.1229	10
Wisconsin	1.0116	1	1.0051	13	1.1167		1.0080	19
Wyoming	1.0112	15	1.0052	2	0.9880	14	1.0078	2
			1.0055					8

Notes: n.s. = no solution. 0's columns contain number of infeasibilities.

References

Ball, V. E., F. M. Gollop, A. Kelley-Hawke, and G. Swinand. 1999. Patterns of State productivity growth in the U.S. farm sector: Linking state and aggregate models. *American Journal of Agricultural Economics* 81:164–79.

Caves, D., L. Christensen, and W. E. Diewert. 1982. The economic theory of index numbers and the measurement of input, output and productivity. *Econometrica* 50 (6): 1393–1414.

Chambers, R. G. 1996. A new look at exact input, output, productivity and technical change measurement. Maryland Agricultural Experimental Station. Mimeograph.

Chambers, R. G., Y. Chung, and R. Färe. 1998. Profit, directional distance functions and Nerlovian efficiency. *Journal of Optimization Theory and Applications* (95): 351–64.

Chambers, R. G., R. Färe, and S. Grosskopf. 1996. Productivity growth in APEC Countries. *Pacific Economic Review* 1 (3): 181–90.

Charnes, A., W. W. Cooper, and E. Rhodes. 1978. Measuring the efficiency of decision making units. *European Journal of Operational Research* 2:429–44.

Chung, Y. 1996. Directional distance functions and undesirable outputs. Ph.D. diss. Southern Illinois University at Carbondale.

Chung, Y., R. Färe, and S. Grosskopf. 1997. Productivity and undesirable outputs: A directional distance function approach. *Journal of Environmental Management* 51:229–40.

Diewert, W. E. 1993. The measurement of productivity: A survey. Canberra, Australia: Swan Consulting.

Eltetö, O., and P. Köves. 1964. On a problem of index number computation relating to international comparison. *Statisztikai Szemle* 42:507–18.

Färe, R. 1988. *Fundamentals of production theory.* Berlin: Springer-Verlag.

Färe, R., and S. Grosskopf. 1996. *Intertemporal production frontiers: With dynamic DEA.* Boston: Kluwer Academic Publishers.

———. 1998. Shadow pricing of good and bad commodities. *American Journal of Agricultural Economics* 80:584–90.

Färe, R., S. Grosskopf, B. Lindgren, and P. Roos. 1989. Productivity developments in Swedish hospitals: A Malmquist output index approach. Southern Illinois University at Carbondale, Department of Economics, Working Paper.

Färe, R., S. Grosskopf, and C. A. K. Lovell. 1994. *Production frontiers.* Cambridge: Cambridge University Press.

Färe, R., S. Grosskopf, M. Norris, and Y. Zhang. 1994. Productivity growth, technical progress and efficiency change in industrialized countries. *American Economic Review* 84:66–83.

Kellogg, R. L., M. Maizel, and D. Goss. 1992. Agricultural chemical use and ground water quality: Where are the potential problem areas? Washington, D.C.: Soil Conservation Service.

Kellogg, R. L., and R. Nehring. 1997. Nitrates in groundwater and nitrates in surface water. Washington, D.C.: Natural Resources Conservation Service and Economic Research Service, Unpublished Data.

Kellogg, R. L., R. Nehring, and A. Grube. 1998. National and regional environmental indicators of pesticide leaching and runoff from farm fields. Unpublished manuscript. See Kellogg homepage at http://www.nhq.nrcs.usda.gov/land/index/publications.html.

Kellogg, R. L., R. Nehring, A. Grube, D. W. Goss, S. Plotkin, and S. Wallace. 1999. Trends in the potential for environmental risk from pesticide loss from farm fields. Poster presented at Soil and Water Conservation Society Conference on The State of North America's Private Land. 19–21 January, Chicago.

Luenberger, D. G. 1992. Benefit functions and duality. *Journal of Mathematical Economics* 21:461–81.

———. 1995. *Microeconomic theory.* Boston: McGraw Hill.

Shephard, R. W. 1970. *Theory of cost and production functions.* Princeton: Princeton University Press.

Shephard, R. W., and R. Färe. 1974. The law of diminishing returns. *Zeitschrift für Nationalökonomie* 34:69–90.

Solow, R. W. 1957. Technical change and the aggregate production function. *Review of Economics and Statistics* 39:312–20.

Szulc, B. 1964. Indices for multiregional comparisons. *Przeglad Statystyczny* 3: 239–54.

Comment   Robin C. Sickles

General Comments

This paper is a new installment in a series of excellent papers by combinations of these authors and their colleagues dealing with the use of Malmquist indexes. Here the Malmquist index is used to decompose productivity growth into technology change and efficiency change (along the lines of Färe et al. 1994) while allowing for the presence of freely nondisposable byproducts—in particular, indexes of leaching and runoff from nitrogen fertilizer and pesticides and indexes of human and fish risk-adjusted effects of such. Ball, Färe, Grosskopf, and Nehring's data set is quite unique and is measured at the state level during the period 1972–93. If the "bads" are excluded, then their analysis suggests widespread productivity growth. When controlling for the effects of positively trending pesticide and fertilizer use, productivity growth falls. The results appeal to intuition and point to an effective tool for productivity index construction when negative externalities are not freely disposable. This work is cutting edge, makes a wonderful stand-alone empirical contribution, and has a modeling framework that can be ported to many other applications. A student and I, for example, are utilizing it in revising China's growth prospects in light of a proper valuation of its environmental pollution as its economy rapidly develops (Jeon and Sickles 2000).

The paper provides, among other things, an answer to the question " ... how do we modify the standard productivity index to reflect the relative value to the producer (consumer) of outputs (services and attributes) when there are no market prices to serve this role?" The empirical

---

Robin C. Sickles is professor of economics and statistics at Rice University.

The author would like to thank R. Färe, S. Grosskopf, and C. A. K. Lovell for their insightful comments and criticisms. The usual caveat applies.

setting for this work is in agriculture, and the authors do a yeoman's job in developing the empirical instruments and theoretical structure to provide answers to this question, as well as to many others. The paper also delivers something else (on which I will focus some of my remarks below), and that something is a way of dealing with the generic problem of the estimation of productivity for service industries and industries in which not only are attributes improperly given positive values, but outputs often are not given negative value. This problem has been explored extensively in the productivity literature, but the authors are quiet on this and the closely related literature on hedonics. A nice starting point is the edited volume by Griliches (1992), which the authors should integrate into their paper.

Clearly, in this type of index number construction, the standard role of statistics and inference is lost; I will address this issue below as well. However, let me point out at this juncture one problem with not having standard errors. Since contiguous states are not independent in agricultural pollution, bootstrapping exercises to attach standard errors to estimates need some form of dependency (Flachaire et al. 2000). This is a relatively new area of research in applied statistics and one that could benefit from a close perusal by the authors. Moreover, the innovation of the directional distance function in this analysis is not clear to me. What is the role of a preassigned direction for changing outputs instead of the proportional changes utilized in the standard Malmquist index?

Pollution produced in the course of agricultural production is called a "negative externality" in economics. Spillovers from publicly produced infrastructures, R&D, and so on have been a topic of serious research interest for some time. Might this literature and the strand promoted in this paper benefit from some cross-fertilization?

If one maintains a constant-returns-to-scale assumption throughout, then the decomposition of the Malmquist index into the technical and efficiency change components is accurate. However, under a variable-returns-to-scale assumption, their Malmquist index remains accurate, but their decomposition may not be completely accurate (Ray and Desli 1997; Grifell-Tatjé and Lovell 1998).

For those of us who question the nonstatistical nature of these indexes, one can link them in a very direct way to more conventional, production-based models and see to what extent it may be robust across methods. I will highlight these links below in a way that hopefully provides comfort to regression-based productivity analysts. Before I do, however, I will try to provide a statistical interpretation to the directional-distance measures that are introduced and analyzed in Ball, Färe, Grosskopf, and Nehring (chapter 13 in this volume; hereafter BFGN), based on a bootstrapping approach recently introduced by Simar and Wilson (2000a, b).

Construction of Stochastic Productive Efficiency Measures Using Programming and Bootstrapping

The Malmquist-Luenberger productivity index used in BFGN is based on the output-oriented directional distance function (Chung, Färe, and Grosskopf 1997). This is different from the Malmquist index, which changes the desirable outputs and undesirable outputs proportionally since one chooses the direction to be $g = (y^t, -b^t)$, more good outputs and less bad outputs. The rationale of this kind of directional choice is that there might be institutional regulations limiting an increase in bad outputs, in particular pollutant emission. To accomplish this the production technology is defined in terms of the output sets, that is, $P(x^t) = (y^t, b^t)|(x^t, y^t, b^t) \in F^t$ and the directional distance function then is defined as $\mathbf{D}_0^t(x^t, y^t, b^t; g) = \sup[\beta|(y^t + \beta g_y, b^t - \beta g_b) \in P(x^t)]$ where g_y and g_b are subvectors for y^t and b^t of the direction vector g.

The Malmquist-Luenberger productivity index is then defined as

$$\mathrm{ML}_0^{t,t+1} = \frac{1 + \mathbf{D}_0^t(x^t, y^t, b^t; y^t, -b^t)}{1 + \mathbf{D}_0^t(x^{t+1}, y^{t+1}, b^{t+1}; y^{t+1}, -b^{t+1})}$$
$$\cdot \frac{1 + \mathbf{D}_0^{t+1}(x^t, y^t, b^t; y^t, -b^t)}{[1 + \mathbf{D}_0^{t+1}(x^{t+1}, y^{t+1}, b^{t+1}; y^{t+1}, -b^{t+1})]^{1/2}},$$

which easily can be decomposed into the product of Malmquist-Luenberger technical change and efficiency change indexes. Solutions based on solving a set of linear programming problems may be infeasible if the direction vector g passing through the output set at $t + 1$ is not producible for technologies existing at time t.

The index numbers outlined above provide us with only point estimates of productivity growth rates and the decompositions into their technical and efficiency components. Clearly there is sampling variability and thus statistical uncertainty about this estimate. In order to address this issue, we begin by assuming a data generating process (DGP) where production units randomly deviate from the underlying true frontier. These random deviations from the contemporaneous frontier at time t, measured by the distance function, are further assumed to result from inefficiency. Using the Simar and Wilson (2000a, b) bootstrapping method, we can provide a statistical interpretation to the Malmquist or Malmquist-Luenberger index.

The following assumptions serve to characterize the DGP.

1. $[(x_i, y_i, b_i), i = 1, \ldots n]$ are independently and identically distributed (i.i.d.) random variables on the convex production set.
2. Outputs y and b possess a density $f(\cdot)$ whose bounded support $D \subseteq R_+^q$ is compact where q is the numbers of outputs.

3. For all (x, y, b), there exist constant $\varepsilon_1 > 0$ and $\varepsilon_2 > 0$ such that $f(\mathbf{D}_0(x, y, b; y, -b)|x, y, b) \geq \varepsilon_1$ for all $\mathbf{D}_0 \in [0, \varepsilon_2]$.
4. For all (x_i, y_i, b_i), $\mathbf{D}_0(x, y, b; y, -b)$ has a conditional probability density function $f(\mathbf{D}_0|x, y, b)$.
5. The distance function $\mathbf{D}_0$ is differentiable in its argument.

Under the those assumptions, $\hat{\mathbf{D}}_0$ is a consistent estimator of $\mathbf{D}_0$, but the rate of convergence is slow. The random sample $\chi = [(x_i, y_i, b_i), i = 1, \ldots, n]$ is obtained by the DGP defined by assumptions 1–4, and bootstrapping involves replicating this DGP. It generates an appropriately large number B of pseudo-samples $\chi^* = [(x_i^*, y_i^*, b_i^*), i = 1, \ldots, B]$ and applies the original estimators to these pseudo-samples. For each bootstrap replication $b = 1, \ldots, B$, we measure the distance from each observation in the original sample χ to the frontiers estimated for either period from the pseudo data in χ^*. This is obtained by solving

$$\hat{\mathbf{D}}_0^{t*}[x^{t+1}(k'), y^{t+1}(k'), b^{t+1}(k'); y^{t+1}(k'), -b^{t+1}(k')] = \max \beta,$$

subject to

$$(1 + \beta)y_m^{t+1}(k') \leq \sum_{k=1}^{K} z^t(k)y_m^{t*}(k) \qquad m = 1, \ldots, M$$

$$\sum_{n=1}^{N} z^t(k)b_n^{t*}(k) = (1 - \beta)b_n^{t+1}(k') \qquad n = 1, \ldots, N$$

$$\sum_{l=1}^{L} z^t(k)x_l^{t*}(k) \leq x_l^{t+1}(k') \qquad l = 1, \ldots, L$$

$$z^t(k) \geq 0 \qquad k = 1, \ldots, K.$$

For two time periods, this yields bootstrap estimates $[\hat{\mathbf{D}}_0^{t*|t}(b), \hat{\mathbf{D}}_0^{t*|t+1}(b), \hat{\mathbf{D}}_0^{t+1*|t}(b), \hat{\mathbf{D}}_0^{t+1*|t+1}(b)]$ for each decision-making unit (DMU). These estimates can then be used to construct bootstrap estimates $\widehat{ML}_0(b)$, $\widehat{MLECH}_0(b)$ and $\widehat{MLTCH}_0(b)$. The bootstrap method introduced by Efron (1979) is based on the idea that if the $\widehat{DGP}$ is a consistent estimator of DGP, the bootstrap distribution of $\sqrt{n}Q[\hat{\mathbf{D}}_0^*(b), \hat{\mathbf{D}}_0]$ given $\hat{\mathbf{D}}_0$ is asymptotically equivalent to the sampling distribution of $\sqrt{n}Q(\hat{\mathbf{D}}_0, \mathbf{D}_0)$ given the true probability distribution $\mathbf{D}_0$ where $Q(\cdot, \cdot)$ is a reasonable function. The confidence interval of the estimator then can be computed by noting that the bootstrap approximates the unknown distribution of $(\widehat{ML}_0^{t,t+1} - ML_0^{t,t+1})$ by the distribution of $[\widehat{ML}_0^{t,t+1}(b) - \widehat{ML}_0^{t,t+1}]$ conditioned on the original data set. Therefore, we can find critical values of the distribution, a_α, b_α by simply sorting the value $[\widehat{ML}_0^{t,t+1}(b) - \widehat{ML}_0^{t,t+1}]$ $b = 1, \ldots, B$ and then find $(\alpha/2)$ percentile and $[100 - (\alpha/2)]$ percentile values. We can also correct finite-sample bias in the original estimators of the indexes using the bootstrap estimates. The bootstrap bias estimate for original estimator $\widehat{ML}_0^{t,t+1}$ is

$$\widehat{bias}_B(\widehat{ML}_0^{t,t+1}) = \frac{1}{B}\sum_{b=1}^{B}\widehat{ML}_0^{t,t+1}(b) - \widehat{ML}_0^{t,t+1}.$$

Therefore, the bias corrected estimate of ML_0^{t+1} is computed as

$$\widehat{\widehat{ML}}_0^{t,t+1} = \widehat{ML}_0^{t,t+1} - \widehat{bias}_B[\widehat{ML}_0^{t,t+1}] = 2\widehat{ML}_0^{t,t+1} - \frac{1}{B}\sum_{b=1}^{B}\widehat{ML}_0^{t,t+1}(b).$$

The variance of bias-corrected estimator will be $4\mathrm{var}(\widehat{ML}_0^{t,t+1})$ as $B \to \infty$. The bias-corrected estimator can have higher mean square error than the original estimator. So, we have to compare $4\mathrm{var}(\widehat{ML}_0^{t,t+1})$, the mean squared error of $\widehat{\widehat{ML}}_0^{t,t+1}$ with the $\mathrm{var}(\widehat{ML}_0^{t,t+1}) + [(\widehat{bias}_B(\widehat{ML}_0^{t,t+1})]^2$, the mean squared error of the original estimator $\widehat{ML}_0^{t,t+1}$. $\mathrm{Var}(\widehat{ML}_0^{t,t+1})$ can be estimated as the sample variance of the bootstrap estimators $[\widehat{ML}_0^{t,t+1}(b)]_{b=1}^{B}$. The bias-corrected estimator will have higher mean squared error if $\mathrm{var}[\widehat{ML}_0^{t,t+1}(b)] > 1/3[\widehat{bias}_B(\widehat{ML}_0^{t,t+1})]^2$. An eleven-step bootstrapping algorithm suggested in Simar and Wilson (2000a, b), which replicates the DGP but which assumes i.i.d. errors recently has been implemented for this model by Jeon and Sickles (2000).

Construction of Productive Efficiency Measures
Using Regression-Based Procedures

The radial measures of technical efficiency the authors consider in this paper are based on the output distance function. The goal of parametric, semiparametric, and fully nonparametric (as well as nonstatistical) linear programming approaches is to identify the distance function and hence relative technical efficiencies. The output distance function is expressed as $D(X, Y) \leq 1$, where Y is the vector of outputs and X is the vector of inputs. The output distance function provides a natural radial measure of technical efficiency that describes the fraction of possible aggregated outputs produced, given chosen inputs. For a J-output, K-input technology, the deterministic distance function can be approximated by $[(\Pi_1^J Y_j^{\gamma_j})/(\Pi_1^K X_k^{\beta k})] \leq 1$ where the coefficients are weights that describe the technology of the firm. When a firm is producing efficiently, the value of the distance function equals 1 and it is not possible to increase the index of total output without either decreasing an output or increasing an input. Random error and firm effects could enter the output distance function in any number of ways. If we shift the output distance function by an exponential function of these terms (in much the way technical change is treated in traditional, single-output production functions), then, following Lovell and colleagues (1994) by multiplying through by the denominator, taking logarithms of outputs and inputs, and imposing the required linear homogeneity of the distance function in outputs, the distance function can be rewritten as

$$-\ln y_J = \sum_{j=1}^{J-1} \ln y^*_{jit} \gamma_j - \sum_{k=1}^{K} \ln x_{kit} \beta_k + \alpha_{it} + \varepsilon_{it},$$

where y_J is the normalizing output, $y^*_{jit} = (y^*_{jit}/y_J)$; and where α_{it} are one-sided (negative in this formulation) efficiency effects, and ε_{it} are random errors. The panel stochastic distance frontier thus can be viewed as a generic panel data model where the effects are interpreted as firm efficiencies and which fits into the class of frontier models developed and extended by Aigner, Lovell, and Schmidt (1977), Meeusen and van den Broeck (1977), Schmidt and Sickles (1984), and Cornwell, Schmidt, and Sickles (1990, hereafter CSS).

Parametric estimation can be carried out by conventional least squares or instrumental variables. Assuming that technological changes diffuse to all firms in the industry, firm-specific efficiencies can be distinguished from technology change, and the total of these, productivity change, can be estimated. Alternative mle estimators that rely on parametric specifications of the composed error are also available.

Semiparametric estimation can also be carried out in several ways. One can utilize a Robinson-type estimator for the mean of the stochastic distance frontier or use kernel-based procedures to model certain dependency structures between the random effects (α_i) and selected regressors, such as the right-hand side y's.

Park, Sickles, and Simar (1998) develop a framework for estimating the sort of model in which we are interested, namely, a panel model in which the stochastic efficiency effects are allowed to be correlated with selected regressors (in particular the y's), thus ensuring the endogenous treatment of multiple outputs in this regression-based distance function specification. Derivation of the semiparametric efficient estimator for the slope coefficients and the corresponding estimator for the boundary function that leads naturally to the construction of a relative efficiency measure in terms of the distance function are found in Park, Sickles, and Simar (1998). In the empirical implementations, one can use the "within" estimator of CSS as the initial consistent estimator and the bootstrap method for selecting the bandwidth in constructing the multivariate kernel-density estimates.

Given the efficient estimator $\hat{\theta}_{N,T}$, α_i are predicted by

$$\hat{\alpha}_i = \overline{S}_i(\hat{\theta}_{N,T}).$$

Under the assumptions of the model above, Park, Sickles, and Simar (1998) prove that as T and $T\sigma^2_{N,T}$ go to infinity:

$$L_P = \left[\sqrt{T}(\hat{\alpha}_i - \alpha_i) \to N(0,\sigma^2)\right].$$

Relative technical inefficiencies of the ith firm with respect to the jth firm can be predicted by $\hat{\alpha}_i - \hat{\alpha}_j$. We are most interested in firm-relative efficiencies with respect to the most efficient firm: $\max_{j=1,\ldots,N}(\hat{\alpha}_j)$.

Although DEA models the technology flexibly, it does not allow for random error. This is a shortcoming that the semiparametric methods overcome while still allowing for flexibility in functional form. Semiparametric estimators based on kernel methods such as Nadaraya-Watson have not been extensively applied in the efficiency literature, especially for multi-output firms. The parametric output distance function can be modified in two ways. First, we can allow efficiencies to be time varying. Second, we can start by making minimal functional form assumptions on the inputs. The distance function can be rewritten as

$$Y_{it} = f(X_{it}) + Y_{it}^* \gamma + \alpha_{it} + \varepsilon_{it}.$$

We can include additional assumptions on the time-varying properties of the technical efficiencies. We apply a specification that is the same as in CSS. Several other authors have allowed efficiencies to change over time. CSS model efficiencies as a quadratic function, while Kumbhakar (1990) models efficiencies as an exponential function of time. Others include Battese and Coelli (1992) and Lee and Schmidt (1993), who allow for other model specifications. Semiparametric estimation proceeds in the following manner. Assuming that the inputs are not correlated with the effects, the conditional expectation for the distance frontier function is

$$E[Y_{it}|X_{it}] = f(X_{it}) + E[Y_{it}^*|X_{it}],$$

where the means of the random effects, α_{it}, are also uncorrelated with the inputs. Subtracting this conditional expectation from the distance function provides us with the model to be estimated,

$$Y_{it} - E[Y_{it}|X_{it}] = Y_{it}^* - E[Y_{it}^*|X_{it}]\gamma + \alpha_{it} + \varepsilon_{it},$$

where

$$f(x_{it}) = E[Y_{it}|X_{it}] - E[Y_{it}^*|X_{it}]\gamma.$$

The model is estimated in two steps. First, the conditional expectations are estimated. To estimate the conditional mean we can use a kernel-based nonparametric regression. Next, the transformed model can be estimated by the CSS estimator. The residuals are then used to estimate the parameters in the time-varying model.

These methods hopefully have demonstrated the isophorphism of regression-based alternatives to the programming-based methods employed by BFGN, and will the provide the productivity researcher with a framework for analysis that gives a more intuitive and familiar look to their methods. I trust that the index number constructions employed by them continue to be adopted and refined by researchers and practitioners in business and in the government.

References

Aigner, D., C. A. K. Lovell, and P. Schmidt. 1977. Formulation and estimation of stochastic frontier production function models. *Journal of Econometrics* 6:21–37.
Battese, G. E., and T. J. Coelli. 1992. Frontier production functions, technical efficiency, and panel data: With application to paddy farmers in India. *Journal of Productivity Analysis* 3 (1/2): 153–69.
Chung, Y. H., R. Färe, and S. Grosskopf. 1997. Productivity and undesirable outputs: A directional distance function approach. *Journal of Environmental Management* 51:229–40.
Cornwell, C., P. Schmidt, and R. C. Sickles. 1990. Production frontiers with cross-sectional and time series variation in efficiency levels. *Journal of Econometrics* 46:185–200.
Efron, B. 1979. Bootstrap methods: Another look at the jackknife. *Annals of Statistics* 7:1–26.
Färe, R., S. Grosskopf, M. Norris, and Y. Zhang. 1994. Productivity growth, technical progress and efficiency change in industrialized countries. *American Economic Review* 84:66–83.
Flachaire, E., A. K. Postert, R. C. Sickles, and L. Simar. 2000. Bootstrapping with dependent heterogeneously distributed data. Rice University. Mimeograph.
Griffel-Tatjé, E., and C. A. K. Lovell. 1998. A generalized Malmquist productivity index. University of Georgia. Mimeograph.
Griliches, Z. 1992. *Output measurement in the service sectors.* Chicago: University of Chicago Press.
Jeon, B. M., and R. C. Sickles. 2000. The role of environmental factors in growth accounting: a nonparametric analysis. Rice University. Mimeograph.
Kumbhakar, S. C. 1990. Production frontiers, panel data, and time-varying technical inefficiency. *Journal of Econometrics* 46:201–12.
Lee, Y. H., and P. Schmidt. 1993. A production frontier model with flexible temporal variation in technical efficiency. In *The measurement of productive efficiency techniques and applications,* ed. H. Fried, C. A. K. Lovell, and S. Schmidt, 237–55. Oxford Academic Press.
Lovell, C. A. K., S. Richardson, P. Travers, and L. Wood. 1994. Resources and functionings: A new view of inequality. In *Models and measurement of welfare and inequity,* ed. W. Eichhorn, 787–807. Heidelberg: Physica-Verlag.
Meeusen, J., and J. van den Broeck. 1977. Efficiency estimation from Cobb-Douglas production functions with composed error. *International Economic Review* 18:435–44.
Park, B., R. C. Sickles, and L. Simar. 1998. Stochastic panel frontiers: A semiparametric approach. *Journal of Econometrics* 84:273–301.
Ray, S. C., and E. Desli. 1997. Productivity growth, technical progress and efficiency change in industrialized countries: A comment. *American Economic Review* 87:1033–39.

Schmidt, P., and R. C. Sickles. 1984. Production frontiers and panel data. *Journal of Business and Economic Statistics* 2:367–74.

Simar, L., and P. Wilson. 1999. Estimating and bootstrapping Malmquist indices. *European Journal of Operational Research* 115:459–71.

———. 2000a. A general methodology for bootstrapping in nonparametric frontier models. *Journal of Applied Statistics* 27:779–8702.

———. 2000b. Testing restrictions in nonparametric efficiency models. *Communications in Statistics: Theory and Methods,* forthcoming.

14

Total Resource Productivity
Accounting for Changing
Environmental Quality

Frank M. Gollop and Gregory P. Swinand

The formal transfer of intellectual dominance from labor productivity to total factor productivity (TFP) celebrated its fortieth anniversary last year. Solow (1957) made clear that measures of efficient resource use should not and need not exclude nonlabor inputs. Many economists took up the challenge and while debate raged over various measurement issues ranging from the treatment of economic depreciation[1] to changing input quality,[2] consensus quickly formed around the superiority of the basic TFP framework. All marketable inputs were to have equal stature in a formal model of productivity measurement.

The prima facie case for further broadening the concept of productivity to include nonmarket resources is equally self-evident. Proper measures of productivity growth are barometers of how well society is allocating its scarce resources. In this context, there is little difference between labor, capital, and material inputs, on the one hand, and air and water resources, on the other. Each is scarce. Consumption of any one entails true opportunity costs. Market failures may generate measurement difficulties, especially with respect to prices, but are not sufficient to justify excluding nonmarket resources from a model of productivity growth. After all, at its most fundamental level, productivity growth is a real, not nominal, concept. The case for expanding TFP to total resource productivity (TRP) is compelling.

What is less self-evident is how to measure TRP. Certainly there are a

---

Frank M. Gollop is professor of economics and director of graduate studies, Department of Economics, Boston College. Gregory P. Swinand is at Indecon Economics Consultants, Indecon House.

1. See Denison (1969, 1972) and Jorgenson and Griliches (1972a, 1972b).
2. See Jorgenson and Griliches (1967), Denison (1979), and Kendrick (1961, 1973).

number of alternatives presented in the literature. Repetto and colleagues (1996) offer an intuition-based generalization of the traditional growth accounting framework. Ball, Färe, Grosskopf, and Nehring (chap. 13, this volume) propose a nonparametric formulation based on activity analysis. There is the temptation to engage in debates about approach (growth accounting, econometrics, or activity analysis) and issues of mathematical formalism, but proper TRP measurement begins from a much more fundamental issue. TRP measurement requires choosing between competing production and welfare-based paradigms, a distinction that is moot for traditional TFP accounting, which considers only outputs and inputs that have well-oiled, perfectly competitive market transactions. Measures of TRP in contrast, cannot ignore jointly produced externalities and market failures. At a minimum, equilibrium conditions (and therefore productivity weights) based on producers' marginal abatement costs are certain to be different from equilibrium conditions based on shadow prices consistent with a model of consumer welfare.

The objective of this paper is to suggest a proper framework for TRP measurement. The paper begins from the premise that TRP measurement is fundamentally a production issue. This follows from the very definition of productivity growth—the changing efficiency with which society transforms its scarce resources into outputs. Traditional productivity measures derived from models of market-based producer behavior have no difficulty satisfying this criterion; neither do properly conceived welfare-based models. The welfare-based model introduced in this paper indeed derives formally from a model of welfare maximization. In this respect, it does depart from the producer perspective common to mainstream productivity work. However, it does not define TRP growth as the net growth in welfare, but as the net growth in social output within the welfare function. It effectively adopts a household-based production approach and thereby is wholly consistent with the evolution of productivity measurement over the past forty years. Viewed in this light, neither the producer nor the welfare-based models introduced later can be judged intellectually superior to the other. They simply are different in two critical respects. First, although the undesirable by-product enters the welfare function directly, how it enters a production-based model is determined by the form of environmental regulation conditioning producer behavior. In short, environmental output may enter differently into producer- and welfare-based models. Second, producers' valuation of the by-product in terms of its marginal abatement cost is likely to differ from society's shadow valuation. In short, the two models originate from different characterizations of economic objectives and models of producer behavior. The producer- and welfare-based models are developed in sections 14.1 and 14.2, respectively. Using data for the U.S. farm sector, TRP measures corresponding to the two models are compared in section 14.3 and contrasted with the conventional TFP measure.

The specific properties of the TRP models are derived and described in detail in the following sections, but before engaging in mathematical formalism, two preliminary observations are in order. First, the TRP models introduced below are derived wholly within the familiar growth accounting paradigm. Models of producer and consumer behavior, equilibrium conditions, and familiar lemmas underlie the models. The ease with which the traditional growth accounting framework can be modified to embrace environmental issues in both traditional producer and now welfare contexts is a testimonial to the resilience of growth accounting. The relative merits of alternative approaches can and should be openly debated, but a subliminal objective of this paper is to demonstrate that our collective excursion into environmental issues need not abandon the growth accounting framework. Second, the reader may have noticed that when this introduction motivates the broadening of standard production theory to accommodate environmental issues, the discussion sometimes references environmental variables in the context of inputs (e.g., air and water resources) and sometimes in the context of production by-products (dirty air and water). This should not be interpreted as ambivalence, but as true indifference. There is a one-to-one mapping between environmental resource consumption and the production of environmental by-products. In terms of production accounts, modeling the consumption of environmental resources as inputs is identical in concept and measure to modeling the environmental consequence as an output. This particular paper characterizes the environmental variable as an output, but the models and their conclusions would be unaffected if it were treated as an input. Neither approach can finesse the pricing problem. The environmental variable, whether modeled as an input or as an output, requires a shadow price, identical except for sign. In the context of environmental variables, environmental outputs are just the negative of environmental inputs. Not surprisingly, symmetry applies.

14.1 A Producer-Based Model

Consider an economy endowed with resources $\underline{X}$ and technology T. The economy produces a conventional output Y and, as a joint-production byproduct, an undesirable output S. Assume that the production of Y is the only source of S.[3] The byproduct S enters the economy's production accounts because of regulatory constraints on S. Producers are held accountable, and therefore S enters the model of producer behavior.

Developing an index of the production sector's aggregate output begins

---

3. Relaxing this assumption would lead to different measures of S entering the economy's production and welfare functions. Only those units of S originating in formal production processes would enter production functions; all S, regardless of source, would enter the welfare function. This complication is unnecessary given the objective of this paper.

by selecting any arbitrary set of nonnegative quantities of outputs Y and S.[4] Given this product set, the economy's aggregate output can be defined as a proportion of quantities of outputs Y and S or, equivalently, as a proportion of conventional output Y holding fixed its environmental quality S/Y. The maximum value of aggregate output (Φ) then can be expressed as a function of Y, its environmental quality S/Y, resources $\underline{X}$, and a time-based technology index T:

(1) $$\Phi = H(Y, S/Y, \underline{X}, T).$$

Though the definition of Φ can accommodate the characterization of S in equation (1) in either ratio (S/Y) or level (S) form, the choice of the ratio form in equation (1) is not the result of mathematical indifference. How S enters the production account is determined by the particular form of regulation. Typically, environmental regulations take the form of rates rather than levels. For example, in the farm sector (the industry selected to illustrate TRP measurement in section 14.3), environmental restrictions for fertilizers and pesticides are posed in terms of application rates per acre planted, not in terms of total tons of pesticides and fertilizers used in U.S. agriculture. Emission standards for automakers are another example. In other industry/pollutant contexts, it may be more appropriate to specify that the byproduct should enter equation (1) as a level, but for present purposes the environmental constraint and therefore the measure of environmental output enters the production account in equation (1) and the resulting model of producer behavior as S/Y. The firm uses resources $\underline{X}$ and technology T to produce two outputs: the marketable output Y and the regulation-mandated output S/Y.

The marginal rates of transformation among the arguments in equation (1) are of note. The function H is increasing in S/Y, $\underline{X}$, and T and decreasing in constant quality output Y. Ceteris paribus, an increase in S/Y (holding Y fixed) frees resources to produce additional aggregate output Φ; an increase in Y consumes resources and therefore reduces aggregate output. There is a positive rate of transformation between Y and S/Y.

The function H exhibits the usual homogeneity properties. H is homogeneous of degree minus one in Y and S because, holding S/Y, $\underline{X}$, and T constant, any proportional increase in Y and S definitionally generates an equal proportional decrease in Φ. In addition, H is assumed to be homogeneous of degree one in $\underline{X}$. As a result, H is homogeneous of degree zero in Y, S, and $\underline{X}$ and exhibits constant returns to scale.

The graphical presentation in figure 14.1 is instructive. Consider an economy producing a single conventional output Y and an undesirable

---

4. At this stage of the analysis, there is no requirement that the selected output levels Y and S be feasible given X and T. The only requirement is that Y and S be nonnegative.

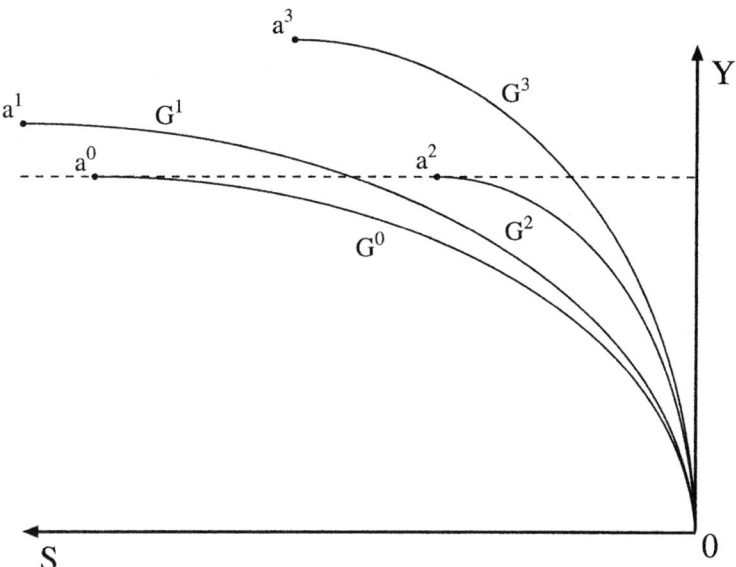

Fig. 14.1 Properties of production possibilities frontiers in conventional (Y) and undesirable (S) outputs

output S. The natural reference point or origin for this analysis is $Y = S = 0$. Because Y is a "good" and S is a "bad," the second quadrant provides the appropriate context. Given $\underline{X}$ and T, the economy can operate efficiently anywhere along its production possibility frontier G^0 defined between the origin and point a^0. Starting G^0 at the origin posits that (a) there is no costless (input free) way to produce Y, and (b) the production of Y is the only relevant source of the by-product S.[5] Production beyond (to the left of) a^0 is economically irrelevant. At point a^0, the economy dedicates all $\underline{X}$ to the production of Y and none to the abatement of S. It follows that production of conventional output Y and by-product S reach their maximums at a^0.

The frontier G^0 has the usual negative slope and smooth curvature indicating that the marginal cost of producing Y and the marginal abatement cost of reducing S are both increasing in their respective arguments. Note, as the economy approaches a^0 along G^0, the marginal abatement cost of S approaches zero.

Increased resource endowments and technical change lead to shifts in the frontier. An increase in $\underline{X}$ leads to frontiers of the form G^1, which, like

---

[5]. Either or both of these conditions could be relaxed without affecting the analysis that follows. Both are maintained for convenience.

G^0, begins at the origin but reaches its maximum at a point a^1 northwest of a^0, implying that, without a change in technology, added production of Y with zero abatement necessarily implies additional S. In the event of technical change, the frontier shifts up, but the frontier's zero abatement boundary depends on the nature of technical change. If technical improvements are embedded solely in the production of Y, the point of maximum possible Y and zero abatement will occur to the left of a^0, as is the case for frontier G^1. If, however, the process of S abatement is the sole source of technical change, then frontier G^0 might shift to take the form represented by G^2, where production of maximum Y (unchanged from G^0) with zero abatement leads to a lower level of S. Technical improvements reflecting efficiency gains in both the production of Y and the abatement of S would lead to frontiers of the form G^3.

Returning to the more general representation H, the task of the producing sector of the economy is to maximize production given the supplies of primary factors of production $\underline{X}$, the sectoral production functions summarized in the technology variable T, market equilibrium conditions for inputs $\underline{X}$ and conventional outputs $\underline{Y}$, and existing societal restrictions (if any) on S/Y. Full compliance is assumed.

Deriving the model of productivity growth for the economy represented by the aggregate production function H begins by setting aggregate output Φ equal to unity. It is important to emphasize that fixing Φ at unity does not imply that output does not or cannot change over time. Given the negative one-to-one relationship between Φ and the scale of conventional output $\underline{Y}$, output growth can be represented either by an increase in Φ or, equivalently, by an identically proportional increase in Y. Fixing Φ at unity does nothing more than force growth to be reflected in the Y variable.

The representation of H now takes the form of the familiar production possibilities frontier:

$$(2) \qquad 1 = H(Y, S/Y, \underline{X}, T)$$

Taking the logarithmic differential of equation (2) with respect to time and solving for $\partial \ln H / \partial T$ yields the following formulation for the production sector's rate of productivity growth (TRP^P):

$$(3) \quad \mathrm{TRP}^P \equiv \frac{\partial \ln H}{\partial T} = -\frac{\partial \ln H}{\partial \ln Y} \frac{d \ln Y}{dT} - \frac{\partial \ln H}{\partial \ln (S/Y)} \left[\frac{d \ln S}{dT} - \frac{d \ln Y}{dT} \right]$$
$$- \sum_i \frac{\partial \ln H}{\partial \ln X_i} \frac{d \ln X_i}{dT}.$$

Necessary conditions for producer equilibrium in a competitive economy transform the logarithmic partials in equation (3) into well-defined variables:

(4)
$$\frac{\partial \ln H}{\partial \ln Y} = -\frac{qY}{P_\Phi \Phi} = -1$$

$$\frac{\partial \ln H}{\partial \ln(S/Y)} = \frac{\rho S}{P_\Phi \Phi} = \frac{\rho S}{qY}$$

$$\frac{\partial \ln H}{\partial \ln X_i} = \frac{w_i X_i}{P_\Phi \Phi} = \frac{w_i X_i}{qY} \quad (i = 1, 2, \ldots, n),$$

where P_Φ is the unit price of aggregate output, q is the unit price of conventional output Y, the w_i represent input prices, and ρ equals the marginal abatement cost of S. It is important to note that the partial derivative in the first line of equation (4) is taken with respect to marketable output Y holding constant its environmental quality content S/Y. This, together with the assumption of a competitive market for Y, permits the necessary condition to be expressed in terms of q, the *observed* market price of Y—a desirable property of a model destined for empirical application. Note also that the value of aggregate output $P_\Phi \Phi$ equals the value of marketable output qY. This follows from the assumption of competitive markets and the definitions of H and Φ. The producers' abatement costs are reflected in both q and P_Φ.

The definition of H and the competitive nature of markets for $\underline{X}$ and Y also guarantee

(5)
$$\sum_i \frac{w_i X_i}{qY} = 1.$$

This follows from the economic characterization of production and competitive markets for Y and $\underline{X}$. First, abatement requires resources $\underline{X}$ so that $\Sigma w_i X_i$ captures the total cost of producing Y as well as abating pollution to the given level S/Y. Second, the competitive market price q reflects the marginal cost of both producing Y and engaging in abatement to the level S/Y. It follows that $qY = \Sigma w_i X_i$ as required by equation (5).

Making the necessary substitutions from equation (4) into equation (3) yields the formula for measuring TRP^P conditioned on a model of producer equilibrium

(6)
$$\text{TRP}^P = \frac{d \ln Y}{dT} + \frac{\rho S}{qY}\left[\frac{d \ln Y}{dT} - \frac{d \ln S}{dT}\right] - \sum_i \frac{w_i X_i}{qY} \cdot \frac{d \ln X_i}{dT}.$$

TRP growth equals the growth in marketable output plus the weighted growth in the product's environmental quality (positive [negative] if $d \ln Y/dT > [<] d \ln S/dT$) less cost-share weighted input growth.

The specification of TRP^P is consistent with the legacy of TFP modeling. The underlying notion of productivity growth is defined wholly from the producers' perspectives. Necessary conditions for producer equilibrium are used to weight all outputs (Y and S/Y) and inputs. As technical change occurs and Y and S/Y grow at different rates, substitution possibilities are evaluated along production possibilities frontiers.

The measure TRP^P has some very nice properties. If, as output grows, either the pollution content per unit of output does not change ($d \ln Y/dT = d \ln S/dT$) or marginal abatement cost is zero ($\rho = 0$), then TRP^P in equation (6) collapses to the traditional TFP form. In the former case, the producer receives credit only for the growth in Y—exactly as in the TFP framework. In the latter instance, although S may be an undesirable by-product of production, society has chosen to impose no binding restriction ($\rho = 0$) on producer behavior. Producers behave rationally and allocate no resources to abatement. (When $\rho = 0$, TRP growth is modeled from peak to peak (at points "a") in figure 14.1.) Productivity growth, viewed from the perspective of the production sector, is properly measured as TFP. However, should society impose a binding regulatory constraint on producers, then, because reducing S/Y is costly in terms of $\underline{X}$ or foregone marketable Y, $\rho > 0$ and the producing sector is induced to consider the S content of its output Y. Consequently, when $\rho > 0$, proper productivity measurement cannot ignore changes in S/Y. Given $\rho > 0$, TRP^P must "grade" producers for changes in environmental quality per unit of output. Ceteris paribus, TRP^P growth $>$ ($<$) TFP growth when the production sector improves (diminishes) the environmental quality of its product. Stated formally, if $\rho > 0$ and $d \ln Y/dT \neq d \ln S/dT$, productivity growth should be measured as a shift in production frontiers defined on both Y and S/Y. Ignoring the nonmarket output term S/Y in equation (6) would lead to a biased measure of producer-based productivity growth.

14.2 A Welfare-Based Model

The notion of productivity growth has stand-alone integrity. It derives from an analysis of the sources of output growth. It equals the weighted growth in output less the weighted growth in inputs. Developing a welfare-based framework for evaluating productivity growth does not challenge this orientation. There is no attempt to replace output growth with welfare growth.

The definition of productivity growth is not at issue. What is at issue is the definition of output and the formulation of the weights in the productivity formula. First, regulatory mandates may be such that the by-product S enters the definition of aggregate output for the production sector differently than it does the societal definition of aggregate output. Second, conventional output, inputs, and the undesirable by-product are weighted differently in the two models. A production-based model relies on relative valuations as defined by marginal rates of transformation along the production possibilities frontier, whereas a welfare-based paradigm is based on marginal rates of substitution defined by the welfare function. Given market failure, marginal rates of transformation and substitution are likely to differ. What is important to emphasize is that the notion of productivity growth as a production concept is not in dispute. The task is to specify aggregate output properly and determine the proper formulation of the value weights for inputs and outputs.

Consider a welfare function U for a representative single-consumer economy

(7) $$U[Y, S, \underline{Z}],$$

where U is a function of marketable output Y, the production by-product S, and a vector of other variables $\underline{Z}$ that may affect welfare. It is assumed that $\partial U/\partial Y > 0$ and $\partial U/\partial S < 0$. Note that S enters equation (7) as a level, not in the form of a ratio. Although producers in the economy's production sector may be conditioned by regulation to denominate environmental output on a per marketable unit basis (S/Y), it is assumed that consumer welfare is affected by overall environmental quality, the aggregate amount of S.

It is further assumed that Y and S are separable from $\underline{Z}$ and that their resulting aggregate defines societal output Ω:

(8) $$U[\Omega(Y, S), \underline{Z}].$$

where $\partial U/\partial \Omega > 0$; $\partial \Omega/\partial Y > 0$, and $\partial \Omega/\partial S < 0$. As a result, the analysis can proceed by evaluating productivity growth through the separable subfunction U^o:

(9) $$U^o[\Omega(Y, S)].$$

Paralleling the above derivation for aggregate output in the production sector, developing a measure of aggregate societal output in terms of its underlying arguments begins by selecting any arbitrary set of nonnegative quantities of Y and S. Given this product set, Ω is defined as a proportion of quantities of marketable output Y and the byproduct S. The maximum value of societal output Ω can then be expressed as a function of Y, overall environmental quality S, resources $\underline{X}$, and the production sector's technology T:

(10) $$\Omega(Y, S) = G(Y, S, \underline{X}, T),$$

where $\partial G/\partial Y < 0$, $\partial G/\partial S > 0$, $\partial G/\partial X_i > 0$, and $\partial G/\partial T > 0$. It follows that

(11) $$U^o[\Omega(Y, S)] = U^o[G(Y, S, \underline{X}, T)].$$

The representative consumer maximizes U^o subject to the usual budget constraint

(12) $$M \equiv qY - \sum w_i X_i,$$

where M is money income. Solving this problem leads to the usual set of necessary conditions for consumer equilibrium:

(13) $$\frac{\partial U^0}{\partial G} \cdot \frac{\partial G}{\partial Y} + \lambda q = 0.$$

$$\frac{\partial U^0}{\partial G} \cdot \frac{\partial G}{\partial S} - \lambda \eta = 0$$

$$\frac{\partial U^0}{\partial G} \cdot \frac{\partial G}{\partial X_i} - \lambda w_i = 0 \quad (i = 1, 2, \ldots, n),$$

where λ is the Lagrange multiplier representing the marginal utility of money income and η is the absolute value of the shadow price of S, the marginal disutility of an additional unit of S.

The objective is to define the welfare-based rate of productivity growth through the societal production function G as valued by society (i.e., through the eyes of a representative consumer). To this end, productivity growth is defined as the rate of growth in aggregate social output (Ω) net of input growth, where all outputs (Y, S) and inputs ($\underline{X}$) are valued by relative prices reflecting the consumer's marginal rates of substitution. This definition of productivity growth is operationalized by setting Ω equal to unity, thereby transforming $G(\cdot)$ in (10) into a social production possibilities frontier and taking the total differential through $U^0[G(Y, S, \underline{X}, T)]$:

(14) $$0 = \frac{\partial U^0}{\partial G} \cdot \frac{dY}{dT} + \frac{\partial U^0}{\partial G} \cdot \frac{\partial G}{\partial S} \cdot \frac{dS}{dT} + \sum_i \frac{\partial U^0}{\partial G} \cdot \frac{dX_i}{dT} + \frac{\partial U^0}{\partial G} \cdot \frac{\partial G}{\partial T}.$$

Substituting equilibrium conditions from equation (13), multiplying all terms by well-chosen "ones," and dividing all terms by the marginal utility of income (λ or its equivalent $\partial U^0/\partial G \cdot \partial G/\partial M$) yields

(15) $$0 = qY \frac{d\ln Y}{dT} - \eta S \frac{d\ln S}{dT} - \sum w_i X_i \frac{d\ln X_i}{dT} + \frac{G \frac{\partial U^0}{\partial G} \cdot \frac{\partial \ln G}{\partial T}}{\frac{\partial U^0}{\partial G} \cdot \frac{\partial G}{\partial M}}.$$

Recognizing that $\partial G/\partial M = 1/P_G$, welfare-based productivity growth (TRP^W) can be derived by dividing all terms in equation (15) by $P_G G$ and solving for the last term in equation (15):

(16) $$\text{TRP}^W \equiv \frac{\partial \ln G}{\partial T} = \frac{qY}{P_G G} \frac{d\ln Y}{dT} - \frac{\eta S}{P_G G} \frac{d\ln S}{dT} - \frac{\sum w_i X_i}{P_G G} \frac{d\ln X}{dT}.$$

Finally, since $qY = M$ and $P_G G = P_\Omega \Omega = (M - \eta S)$,

(17) $$\text{TRP}^W = \left(\frac{M}{M - \eta S}\right)\frac{d\ln Y}{dT} - \left(\frac{\eta S}{M - \eta S}\right)\frac{d\ln S}{dT}$$
$$- \sum\left(\frac{w_i X_i}{M - \eta S}\right)\frac{d\ln X_i}{dT}$$

so that

(18) $$\text{TRP}^W = \left(\frac{M}{M - \eta S}\right)\left[\frac{d\ln Y}{dT} - \frac{\sum w_i X_i}{M}\frac{d\ln X_i}{dT}\right]$$
$$- \left(\frac{\eta S}{M - \eta S}\right)\frac{d\ln S}{dT}$$

and

(19) $$\text{TRP}^W = \left(\frac{M}{M - \eta S}\right)\text{TFP} - \left(\frac{\eta S}{M - \eta S}\right)\frac{d\ln S}{dT}.$$

The welfare-based measure of TRP equals a share-weighted average of the net contribution (net of input growth) of the growth in marketable output from the production sector (i.e., TFP growth) and the growth in the undesirable by-product S. The share weights reflect relative consumer valuations of Y and S.

TRP^W has a number of attractive properties. First, equation (19) makes clear that changes in S have stand-alone importance in the TRP^W formula. The traditional contribution of TFP to TRP^W is augmented (diminished) through reductions in (additions to) S. Assuming $\eta > 0$, any decrease (increase) in S makes a positive (negative) contribution to TRP^W. Second, even if there is no change in S ($d\ln S/dT = 0$), TRP^W does not collapse to TFP growth. This result is guaranteed by the weight on TFP in equation (19), $[M/(M - \eta S)] > 1$. Consider just two examples. First, assume inputs have not changed but conventional output Y has increased while S does not change. Conventional TFP is positive but is a downward-biased measure of true productivity growth because the growth in Y has been achieved without any increase in S. Second, assume that both conventional output and S remain unchanged whereas input requirements have decreased. Once again, TFP is positive but provides a downward-biased measure of TRP^W because the output level of Y has not been maintained at the expense of environmental quality. Third, if reductions in S are of no value to consumers (and, symmetrically, increases in S generate no marginal damage), TRP^W collapses to traditional TFP growth.[6] In this in-

---

6. Equations (17) to (19) suggest that if input growth were zero and the growth rates of Y and S were identical, then the growth rates of TRP^W and conventional TFP would be equal. One should not infer from this, however, that because equal changes in Y and S affect TFP

stance, consumers marginal valuation of S (η) is zero. In this respect, the formula for TRP^W in equation (19) when $\eta = 0$ behaves just as does the formula for TRP^P in equation (6) when $\rho = 0$.

The relationship between TRP^W and TRP^P can be demonstrated by adding and subtracting

$$(20) \qquad \pm \left(\frac{\rho S}{M - \eta S}\right)\left(\frac{d\ln Y}{dT} \frac{d\ln S}{dT}\right)$$

to equation (18), whereby

$$(21) \qquad TRP^W = \left(\frac{M}{M - \eta S}\right) TRP^P - \left(\frac{\rho S}{M - \eta S}\right)\frac{d\ln Y}{dT}$$
$$+ \frac{(\rho - \eta)S}{M - \eta S}\frac{d\ln S}{dT}.$$

The second term on the right-hand side of equation (21) adjusts for the difference in the definitions of the production sector's aggregate output $\Phi(Y, S/Y)$ and aggregate societal output $\Omega(Y, S)$. Ceteris paribus, proportional increases in Y and S reduce the measure of environmental quality in Ω but leaves Φ unaffected. The second term in equation (21) permits the necessary transformation between TRP^W and TRP^P.

The last term in equation (21) is of more interest. This term is nonzero if and only if the marginal abatement cost of $S(\rho)$ does not equal the dollar value of marginal disutility associated with $S(\eta)$. The magnitude of the term reflects the difference between marginal rates of transformation and substitution in H and G, respectively. If $\rho = \eta$, the last term vanishes and the difference between TRP^W and TRP^P reduces to their different characterizations of aggregate output. However, if $\rho \neq \eta$, an additional issue of resource allocation creates a spread between TRP^W and TRP^P. For example, if $\eta > \rho$, then the marginal benefit of further reductions in S exceeds their marginal abatement cost so that those reductions contribute to TRP^W above their expected contributions through TRP^P. The key insight is a simple one. Just as differences in market prices and marginal costs impact the measurement of productivity growth in the face of imperfect product markets,[7] differences between shadow prices and marginal abatement costs have equal relevance in the context of market failure.

---

and TRP^W identically, TRP^W is not a negative function of S. The structure of equation (17) makes clear that, ceteris paribus, welfare is adversely affected by any increase in S. Nonetheless, if Y and S increase at identical rates, TFP growth is an unbiased measure of TRP^W growth. The explanation follows from standard productivity accounting. Placing 100 percent weight on the growth of a single output in a true multiple-output setting introduces no bias if all outputs happen to grow at the same rate. In the scenario set up in this note, if S happens to grow at the same rate as Y, TFP introduces no bias by ignoring S. However, if the growth rates of S and Y differ, TFP growth is a biased measure of TRP^W growth.

7. See Gollop (1987).

14.3 An Application to the U.S. Farm Sector

The objective of this paper is to suggest a proper framework for TRP measurement. To that end, it seems instructive to engage in an empirical exercise to compare and contrast traditional TFP with TRP^P and TRP^W measures. Given changing production practices in agriculture and preliminary data now available on the industry's environmental output, the U.S. farm sector becomes a logical candidate for an application of TRP accounting.

The modern production techniques that have enabled the U.S. farm sector to enjoy high rates of productivity growth necessarily require the use of pesticides, herbicides, and fungicides. The quality of surface water and groundwater sources are clearly affected by the application of these materials. Over time, application practices and chemical types and potency have been modified to mitigate harm to water quality through chemical runoff and leaching while preserving production levels of farm output. Properly designed measures of TRP^P and TRP^W should reflect this history.

Applying the TRP formulas described in sections 14.1 and 14.2 requires (a) price and quantity data on both conventional animal and crop outputs and labor, capital, and material inputs; (b) quantity data on the industry's environmental impact (S); and (c) estimates of both the sector's marginal abatement cost (ρ) and society's valuation of the marginal disutility of water pollution (η). The Environmental Indicators and Resource Accounting Branch of the Economic Research Service at the U.S. Department of Agriculture (USDA) has for some time been engaged in projects to develop data that can support, among other research efforts, models like TRP proposed in this paper. Given the limited illustrative objective of this part of our paper, only a brief overview of the data is provided.

Conventional output and input production accounts for each state in the 1972–93 period are derived from a panel of annual data for individual states. State-specific aggregates of output and labor, capital, and material inputs are formed as Tornqvist indexes over detailed output and input accounts. Hundreds of disaggregated farm product categories, capital asset classes, and material goods go into the construction of the output, capital, and material input indexes, respectively. Each state-specific labor index aggregates over 160 demographically cross-classified labor cohorts. A full description of the underlying data series, sources, and indexing technique is presented in Ball (1985).

The measure of S developed for this paper focuses on pesticides and their effect on ground water. (When completed, the USDA environmental indicator will be a function of both pesticides and fertilizers reaching both surface water and groundwater.) At present, the USDA has developed state- and year-specific pesticide acre-treatment (frequency of application) data adjusted for (a) the leaching potential of different applied chemicals and (b) the leaching vulnerability of soil types measured by water percolation rates for various soils.[8] These acre-treatment data are further adjusted by the authors by using data made available by the USDA. First, acre-treatments are converted to chemical pounds applied using a time series (U.S. average) of chemical pounds applied per acre-treatment. Second, data on rainfall patterns are applied across regions to convert hypothetical percolation rates to actual rates. Finally, in an attempt to model S in toxicity-adjusted units, pounds applied are converted to doses per pound applied using data developed at the USDA by Barnard and colleagues (1997). They define a chronic health risk dose as the quantity of chemical by weight that, if ingested daily over a specified time period, would involve serious health risk to humans. Barnard and colleagues (1997) first compute a dose equivalent for each pesticide, then aggregate over pesticides and states within regions to generate estimates by region of the total change in toxicity and persistence of farm chemicals per pound applied. The state-specific measures of chemical pounds applied just described are adjusted by these regional scalars. The resulting measure of S used in the following illustration represents total pesticide doses generated each year in each state's farm sector.

Application of TRP^P further requires an estimate of the farm sector's marginal abatement cost of improving groundwater quality by one dose. Swinand (1997) estimates a translog cost function together with input cost share equations using the preliminary panel data set described above. Marginal abatement cost (ρ) is estimated to equal \$0.28 per dose. We adopt this estimate.

The model of TRP^W is based on marginal rates of substitution and therefore requires an estimate of the marginal social value (η) of a unit of clean (dose-free) water. Given the definition of the Barnard dose underlying the measure of S, η must correspond to the daily amount of water required for human consumption. Although considerable research exists attempting to estimate η, estimates found in the literature still vary considerably. Two recent survey articles (Boyle, Poe, and Berstrom 1994; Abdalla 1994) discuss various contingent valuation and avoidance cost studies found in the literature and report a wide range in valuation estimates. From both studies, the estimates of an average household's willingness to pay for clean water range from \$56 to \$1,154 per year. Dividing by the average 2.7 persons per household and 365 days per year, these estimates convert to \$0.06 and \$1.17, respectively, per daily allowance of clean (dose-free) water. Limiting attention only to those avoidance cost studies that have been published in peer-reviewed journals, the mean estimate is \$428 and converts to \$0.43 per unit of S, the value for η used in evaluating TRP^W.

TFP and TRP measures are reported in table 14.1 for four subperiods

---

8. See Kellogg, Nehring, and Grube (1998) for a full description.

Table 14.1 An Application of TRP Measurement to the U.S. Farm Sector (average annual rates of growth)

	1972–79	1979–85	1985–89	1989–93
Productivity growth				
TFP	0.0080	0.0274	0.0097	0.0123
TRP^P	0.0075	0.0285	0.0104	0.0129
TRP^W	0.0067	0.0294	0.0109	0.0132
Through TFP growth	0.0083	0.0277	0.0097	0.0123
Through pollution growth	−0.0016	0.0017	0.0011	0.0009
Output growth				
Market output (Y)	0.0239	0.0109	−0.0014	0.0114
Pollution (S)	0.0428	−0.1263	−0.1482	−0.2952
Value shares				
$\rho S/M$	0.0219	0.0099	0.0050	0.0020
$\eta S/(M-\eta S)$	0.0348	0.0155	0.0077	0.0030

spanning 1972–93. The TFP measure ignores the nonmarket by-product S and is derived from the conventional TFP growth accounting formula

$$(22) \quad \text{TFP} \equiv \frac{d\ln Y}{dT} - \sum_i \frac{w_i X_i}{M} \frac{d\ln X_i}{dT}.$$

The TRP^P and TRP^W measures follow directly from equations (6) and (19), respectively.

The source of the numerical differences in table 14.1 between TFP and TRP^P can be identified from a straightforward comparison of the formulas for TFP in equation (22) and TRP^P in equation (6). TFP and TRP^P differ only to the extent that the growth rates of Y and S differ—that is, only to the extent that the conventional product's environmental quality is changing over time. In the 1972–79 period, pollution growth (4.28 percent per year) exceeded conventional output growth (2.39 percent per year), implying that the environmental quality of the farm sector's product was declining during this period. As a result, reported TRP^P < TFP. Beginning with the 1979–85 period, however, the trend reverses. Whereas conventional output increased in two of the post-1979 subperiods and declined only slightly in one, pollution declined at average annual rates of 12.63 percent, 14.82 percent, and 29.52 percent during the 1979–85, 1985–89, and 1989–93 subperiods, respectively. After 1979, the environmental quality of farm sector output increased significantly. As a result, TRP^P > TFP in each period.

The relationship between TFP and TRP^P in table 14.1 depends, as can be seen from equation (6), not only on the sign and magnitude of the relative growth rates of Y and S but also on the production sector's valuation of the pollution externality relative to the total market value of agricultural goods, $\rho S/M$. Because this value share is small in every period, exceeding 0.02 only in the 1972–79 subperiod, the resulting differential between TFP and TRP^P is small even in the post-1979 subperiods, when environmental quality of the farm product improved significantly.

Moreover, as evidenced in the table, the spread between TFP and TRP^P has decreased over time. Given that the annual rate of growth in water pollution in the later 1989–93 period (-29.52 percent) is, in absolute value, nearly seven times its growth rate in the 1972–79 period (4.28 percent), one might expect the resulting spread between TFP and TRP^P to be higher in the later period. The opposite turns out to be the case. The reason is that over the full twenty-one years of the study, water pollution declined at an average 10.6 percent annual rate. Compounded, this implies that pesticide related doses (S) reaching groundwater in 1993 equaled only about 10 percent of doses leached in 1972. Over the same period, the nominal dollar value of agricultural production (M) increased by nearly 135 percent. As a result, the sevenfold higher growth rate in S in the 1989–93 period has a weight that is only one-eleventh of its 1972–79 level. Given dramatic improvements in abatement efforts, the value weight assigned to future improvements definitionally declines.

TRP^W exhibits the same overall relationship with TFP as does TRP^P except that the difference between TFP and TRP^W is larger than the difference between TFP and TRP^P. This follows from (a) $\eta > \rho$ and (b) the differing structures of the weights on the corresponding S terms in equations (6) and (19). Even if $\eta = \rho$, the weight $\eta S/(M - \eta S)$ in equation (19) exceeds $\rho S/M$ in equation (6).

The table 14.1 decomposition of TRP^W into its two source components is informative. As expected, TFP in agriculture makes a positive contribution in every subperiod. This is not the case for the sector's contribution through changing environmental quality as modeled by the second term in equation (19). The sector's growth in pollution in the 1972–79 subperiod decreases TRP^W, whereas reductions in S after 1979 make positive contributions to TRP^W. The switch from the positive 4.28 percent growth in water pollution to the negative 12.63 percent growth rate between 1972–79 and 1979–85 highlights the importance of proper TRP accounting. Ceteris paribus, changes in farming practices added 0.33 percentage points to TRP^W growth between the 1972–79 and 1979–85 periods.

The above results are illustrative only. Not only are the results for the farm sector likely to change when the environmental indicator is fully developed at USDA, but also no attempt should be made to generalize results for the farm sector to other sectors. The magnitudes of the spreads among TFP, TRP^P, or TRP^W are expected to differ greatly across industries. After all, these differentials are functions of many things: the sign and magnitude of the change in S, the magnitudes (both absolute and relative) of η and ρ, and the relative dollar importance of pollution (ηS or ρS) to the market value of conventional output (M). Taking just the latter as an example, Repetto and colleagues (1996) find that the value share of environmental damage to GDP in agriculture (1977–91) ranged from 2 percent to 4 percent, whereas it ranged from 16 percent and 31 percent in electric power (1970–91).[9] In addition, small differences can matter. For example, if instead of the mean value of $0.43 found in the literature, TRP^W had been estimated using $1.17 (the value of η calculated from the maximum marginal social valuation of a unit of clean water found in the literature), average annual TRP^W in table 14.1 would have been 0.35 (instead of 0.13) percentage points below TFP in the 1972–79 period and 0.50 (instead of 0.20) percentage points above TFP in the subsequent 1979–85 subperiod. Assuming $\eta = \$0.43$, changing farm practices with respect to pesticides added 0.33 percentage points to TRP^W growth between the 1972–79 and 1979–85 periods; assuming $\eta = \$1.17$, this contribution increases to 0.85 percentage points.

The sensitivity of TRP^W to estimates of η forms a segue to one final question: How should the BLS, BEA, or any other government agency producing official productivity statistics formally incorporate measures of changing environmental quality into their productivity models? At present, given the substantial variance in estimated shadow prices, one cannot expect any agency to produce an official TRP^W estimate based on a particular value of η, one of the most politically sensitive variables in the environmental policy arena. Without consensus among researchers and policy makers, no agency can be expected to offer the appearance of endorsing a particular measure of η. However, there is an option. A distribution of TRP^W measures can be produced at the industry level based on high and low estimates of η relevant to each industry and found in the referenced literature. That strategy would not only fulfill the agencies' obligations to produce meaningful productivity statistics while responsibly protecting their credibility but, depending on the relative growth rates of the less argumentative Y and S outputs, also provide information on the time intervals and set of industries for which traditional TFP growth measures are upward- or downward-biased measures of TRP^W growth—a result that is independent of the magnitude of η (See equation [17]). The more likely outcome, however, is the politically risk-averse one: Official productivity measurement will continue to focus on conventional inputs and outputs until there is reasonable consensus on an estimate for η. As a result, if one goal of the productivity research community is to have the federal government formally incorporate environmental quality into its official productivity statistics, economists and others interested in environmental issues must narrow the existing variance in shadow price estimates. Careful data measurement and detailed industry analysis are no less important today than they were at the time of Solow's initial article.

9. See Repetto and colleagues (1996), pp. 26–39.

14.4 Concluding Comment

The model of TRP proposed in this paper has a number of desirable properties. First, although it broadens the notion of TFP growth to include nonmarket goods, it preserves the production orientation of productivity accounting. TRP, whether measured as TRP^P or TRP^W, measures productivity growth, not welfare growth. Second, zero growth in pollution is not sufficient to equate TFP with either TRP measure. TRP measures collapse to TFP if and only if producers are unconstrained by society ($\rho = 0$) *and* society derives no marginal disutility from pollution ($\eta = 0$). Third, the TRP formulations provide a natural context for evaluating the impact of regulatory policy on productivity growth. Ceteris paribus, both TRP^P and TRP^W increase in response to regulatory-induced reductions in S, and (note) even if regulation is ineffective ($\rho = 0$), growth in an undesirable by-product S enters the TRP^W formula as long as society derives negative marginal utility from $S(\eta > 0)$. Moreover, the last term in equation (21) permits a quantification of the productivity effect of a regulatory policy that is either too lenient ($\eta > \rho$) or too strict ($\eta < \rho$). As such, TRP measures enhance the role of productivity growth both as a diagnostic tool and as a barometer of the economy's success in allocating and employing its scarce resources.

References

Abdalla, Charles W. 1994. Ground water values from avoidance cost studies: Implications for policy and future research. *American Journal of Agricultural Economics* 76 (December): 1062–67.

Ball, V. Eldon. 1985. Output, input, and productivity measurement in U.S. agriculture, 1948–79. *American Journal of Agricultural Economics* 67 (August): 475–86.

Barnard, Charles H., Stanley G. Daberkow, Merritt Padgitt, Mark E. Smith, and Noel D. Uri. 1997. Alternative measures of pesticide use. *The Science of the Total Environment* 203:229–44.

Boyle, Kevin, Gregory Poe, and John Berstrom. 1994. What do we know about groundwater values? Preliminary implication from and meta analysis of contingent-valuation studies. *American Journal of Agricultural Economics* 76 (December): 1055–61.

Denison, Edward F. 1969. Some major issues in productivity analysis: An examination of estimates by Jorgenson and Griliches. *Survey of Current Business* 49 (5): 1–27.

———. 1972. Final comments. *Survey of Current Business* 52 (5, part 2): 95–110.

———. 1979. *Accounting for slower economic growth: The United States in the 1970s.* Washington, D.C.: Brookings Institution.

Gollop, Frank M. 1987. Modeling aggregate productivity growth: The importance of intersectoral transfer prices and international trade. *Review of Income and Wealth* ser. 33, no. 2 (May): 211–27.

Jorgenson, Dale W., and Zvi Griliches. 1967. The explanation of productivity change. *Review of Economic Studies* 34 (July): 249–83.

———. 1972a. Issues in growth accounting: A reply to Edward F. Denison. *Survey of Current Business,* 52 (5, part 2): 65–94.

———. 1972b. Issues in growth accounting: Final reply. *Survey of Current Business,* 52 (5, part 2): 111.

Kellogg, Robert L., Richard Nehring, and Arthur Grube. 1998. National and regional environmental indicators of pesticide leaching and runoff from farm fields. USDA, Natural Resources Conservation Service, Resource Assessment and Strategic Planning Working Paper.

Kendrick, John. 1961. *Productivity trends in the United States.* Princeton: Princeton University Press.

———. 1973. *Postwar productivity trends in the United States, 1948–1969.* New York: National Bureau of Economic Research.

Repetto, Robert, Dale Rothman, Paul Faeth, and Duncan Austin. 1996. *Has environmental protection really reduced productivity growth?* Baltimore: World Resources Institute.

Solow, Robert M. 1957. Technical change and the aggregate production function. *Review of Economics and Statistics* 39 (August): 312–20.

Swinand, Gregory P. 1997. Modeling and measuring total resource productivity. Working Paper.

Comment   William Pizer

This paper proposes the inclusion of nonmarket resource use in measures of productivity. Much as earlier work argued against labor productivity as a measure of technological change because it excluded changes in capital and materials, the authors rightly argue that the current use of total factor productivity (TFP) excludes changes in the use of valuable, though unmarketed, natural resources.

Consider the following thought experiment: Next year environmental regulations are rolled back to their pre-1970 levels. What would happen? All those resources currently going towards unmeasured (i.e., nonmarketed) environmental improvements would be converted to produce marketable output. Measures of productivity that focused solely on the use of marketed factors and output would register a positive movement. But would technology really have changed? Would welfare really have improved? The authors, myself, and, undoubtedly, many economists would say it has not.

If the general idea of counting nonmarket resources in TFP measures—a total resource productivity (TRP) measure—is not in question, the means of doing so certainly are. This is where the authors have taken an

---

William Pizer is a Fellow in the Quality of the Environment Division at Resources for the Future.

important step forward. While other efforts have focused on ad hoc fixes, or jumped ahead to formal models with very particular assumptions, this paper steps back and looks at the more fundamental question of what TRP should be measuring.

In particular, the authors explore two models that they characterize as production-based and welfare-based. In the production approach, an aggregate production function that includes pollution is used to derive an expression for TRP. Similarly, in the welfare approach, a social welfare function—which aggregates marketed output and pollution into a single consumption good—is used to derive an expression for TRP.

These expressions differ in two important ways: measurement of prices and, given a set of prices, actual definition of TRP. The first of these is fundamentally tied to the welfare/production distinction. However, the latter, I believe, is not.

For a nonmarket good such as pollution abatement, a key question must be the appropriate price to use in valuation. Two prices naturally come to mind—the marginal cost of abatement and the marginal benefit of abatement. The former occurs in a production-based analysis where the current technology, outputs, inputs, and level of pollution control define a marginal cost. In contrast, the latter arises in a welfare-based analysis where preferences and the current level of consumption and pollution define a marginal benefit. In a partial equilibrium framework, we are simply talking about whether to use either supply or demand curves to determine an appropriate price when the quantity is set exogenously (and presumably not where they intersect). In a general equilibrium framework, we are talking about marginal rates of transformation versus marginal rates of substitution. The choice between these two sets of prices boils down to a desire to either measure a true change in production technology or some kind of change in welfare.

A second fundamental question is how TRP ought to be measured once prices are settled upon. In other words, how do we translate changes in output, inputs, and pollution into a meaningful index measure? Based on the following definitions given in the paper (equations [6] and [19]),

TFP growth = (% change in output) − (% change in input)

TRP growth^P = TFP growth + $\frac{\rho S}{qY}$[(% change in Y)

− (% change in S)]

TRP growth^W = $\frac{M}{M - \eta S}$(TFP growth) − $\frac{\eta S}{M - \eta S}$(% change in S)

we can construct the following hypothetical scenarios and discuss their effect on these different measures.

In the above equations, ρ is the marginal cost of abatement, S is the amount of pollution, q is the price of output, Y is the level of output, M is consumer wealth, η is the marginal benefit of abatement, and X is the level of input.

Changes in Alternate Productivity Measures			
Scenario	TFP	TRP^P	TRP^W
X, Y, S rise by 5%	0	0	< 0
Y rises by 5%	5%	> 5%	> 5%
Y, S rise by 5%	5%	5%	5%
X rises by 5%	−5%	−5%	< −5%
X, Y rise by 5%	0	> 0	0

Certain features of TRP measurement are almost axiomatic. If technology—however defined—is not changing, TRP^P should not change. In the current model, for example, the authors assume constant returns to scale production technology in Y, S, and X. Therefore, all those variables rising proportionally does not represent a change in technology.

But what about the welfare-based metric? My intuition would be that if prices are the same, the welfare- and production-based approaches should yield the same answer. The above table indicates that is not the case. Instead, the authors have chosen to use a social production function which, by construction, leads to zero TRP growth as long as pollution is constant and the budget constraint is exactly met. The budget constraint is met as long any increase in conventional output is offset by an equal cost increase in inputs; such as, conventional TFP growth is zero. My question is the following: What does this assumption—that TRP is zero when the budget constraint is met and pollution is constant—have to do with a welfare-based view of TRP?

If, as the authors argue, both measures of TRP, "preserve the production-orientation of productivity accounting," we should be asking ourselves whether TRP is capturing changes in productivity across all production factors including pollution. In this example, an equiproportional increase in output and inputs, holding pollution constant, is clearly an improvement in the productivity of the pollution input, yet TRP^W growth is zero. Consider the analogy with capital: If a proposed TFP index measured no growth when labor and output rose proportionally (e.g., constant labor productivity) *and* capital remained constant, would this be a desirable TFP measure?

In summary, the paper is an excellent treatment of the fundamental issues surrounding the implementation of a resource-based measure of productivity. My main concern is that two important distinctions between the proposed TRP measures have been lumped together as differences between a production- and welfare-based approach. I agree with the authors regarding the distinction in prices. However, the second issue, how we define TRP for a given set of prices, seems inappropriately couched in welfare versus production terms. Based on the authors' modeling, the welfare approach results in a TRP measure with unusual properties. I believe this skirts a more important question: What happens when pollution is more closely tied to an input, such as the use of coal in energy production? Since inputs and outputs are in some sense arbitrary distinctions, a more general version of the question is how much we can bound a TRP measure by simply assuming constant returns to scale in all inputs and outputs. Then, within these bounds, can we identify some TRP measures that are more sensible than others?

Just as the switch to TFP from labor productivity generated considerable research activity and empirical work on its implementation, undoubtedly a switch to TRP will likewise create a wealth of opportunity for additional work. The authors have taken an important step in this direction.

15

A Perspective on What We Know About the Sources of Productivity Growth

Zvi Griliches

In the little time that I have I would like first to remember three people who have died recently and who were important in the development of our topic and also in my life. The most recent to die was Ted Schultz, my teacher and mentor. Ted was the first to make quantitative estimates of the role of R&D and of education in accounting for the "unexplained" growth in output. He opened the way for Gary Becker, myself, and others. Ed Mansfield took technological change seriously and did his own thing, careful studies at the micro level, and he enriched this field immensely. Several years have already passed, but we should also mourn the passing of Ed Denison, one of the pioneers of national accounting and one of the first to parse quantitatively the residual into its components. Even though we often disagreed on particular measurement issues, we all learned a lot from him. They will be missed.

More than 30 years ago, Dale Jorgenson and I looked at data on productivity and saw the challenge in the then unmeasured education and R&D contributions. In our paper we "explained" it all away by correcting for various measurement errors in capital and labor input. By the time Denison corrected some of our overreaching, a significant amount of "unknown" territory was still left to explain.

However, if you look at more recent productivity data, it is possible to claim that we have won! The explanation is now complete. All of the growth is being accounted for by the growth in relevant inputs. Yet, in

---

Zvi Griliches passed away on 4 November 1999. Prior to his death, he had been the Paul M. Warburg Professor of Economics at Harvard University and director of the Productivity and Technical Change program at the National Bureau of Economic Research. He was past president of the Econometric Society and of the American Economic Association and a member of the National Academy of Sciences.

another sense, this "victory" is rather sad. The operation was successful but the patient died. What happened was that the unexplained part disappeared, not that the explained part of the growth increased.

I have three points to make. The first is that the current accounting framework is incomplete. (This is also the message of Dale Jorgenson's paper at this conference.) There are a number of productivity enhancing activities that use resources and maintain and improve our human capital but are not included in our official notions of national output. I have in mind here general education, specific training, health investments, and R&D. There have been notable efforts to calculate the accumulation of national human capital as produced by the education system, from Ted Schultz's early efforts to the more recent extensive contributions by Jorgenson and Barbara Fraumeni. A convincing construction of the nation's health capital is still ahead of us, though initial progress has been made by David Cutler and his coauthors. Estimates of R&D capital have also been produced, but the factual basis for the assumed "depreciation" and "spillover" rates is still rather thin. Yet, as we extend our notion of inputs to include other "capitals," we will also have to extend our notion of output and include the investments in such capital within it. At that point, they will become just like other "produced" inputs within the economic system and will stop being a "source" of growth in multifactor productivity (MFP), in the residual. Unless some of these investments earn social returns that exceed their private costs, they will contribute only to capital deepening, but not to longer term sustained growth in per capita consumption possibilities. For the latter, something must keep the long run rates of return to such investments from falling.

The second point is that longer term productivity growth comes from the discovery of new resources, new methods of doing things, and the exploitation of investment opportunities that such discoveries create. That's what Ted Schultz taught us. He, in turn, built on the ideas of Frank Knight, who was one of the first to claim that new knowledge keeps the long run return to all investment from falling. But new knowledge does not arrive in a steady continuing stream, or as manna from heaven. It does take resources, effort, and serendipity to search, find, and recognize it. It is a badly understood process, with random, but often clustered, outcomes which then create new opportunities for investment and allow the economy to approach a new equilibrium growth rate. Longer term growth in per capita consumption comes from a collection of such traverses, from lurching from one equilibrium to another. But from where do these above average return investment opportunities come? They come from the creation of new knowledge in science, in industrial R&D labs, and from tinkering. They also come from the diffusion of knowledge and technology and from the elimination of various legal and social barriers to efficiency. It is during such traverses to new equilibria that some individuals and the society as a whole earn above average returns on their investments. And it is this area, where Ed Mansfield worked, that is underemphasized in the program of this conference and deserves more attention from us all.

The third point is that in the 1960s, we were struggling with the large unexplained residual. Most of the observed growth was not accounted for by the then-standard input measures. In the last twenty or more years, most of the residual has disappeared. We have had our famous productivity slowdown. Various attempts to explain why measured productivity growth fell, including my own, have not been very successful. Measurement error stories are plausible but seem unlikely to be of great enough magnitude to account for it all. I think that it is time that we turn our searchlights at least partially around from the recent data to the data from the 1950s and 1960s. Are we really sure that we had all that growth in MFP then? If we don't know how to measure productivity growth in the service sectors, and hence we do not even expect substantive growth to show up there, why was measured productivity growing there then but not now? What did the Bureau of Labor Statistics know then that it has forgotten now? Or was the productivity growth real? If so, how and why did it change so much over time?

It is easy to make a long laundry list of desired measurement improvements. The measurement of high-tech output is still in its infancy, though this infant is graying perceptibly. It took twenty years to get us to a reasonable computer price index. It took another ten years to do the same for semiconductors. Large areas still need better measurement, including more mundane industries such as construction. We need a census of capital equipment. Our assumptions about the length of life and economic depreciation rates are based on pitiful scraps of outdated data. The upheavals of the recent decades, the downsizing of companies, the closing of plants, and the outsourcing of many activities must have led to significant abandonments of real capital in the various industries. However, most of it is still on our books, as far as productivity measurement is concerned. We need more data on actual hours worked by people, not just hours paid for, and on machine hours and the changing length of the business workweek. The utilization issue, raised in our original 1967 paper, has not really gone away, as can be seen from the Basu and Fernald paper in this conference. The data situation now is not much better than it was then, either.

The most difficult measurement area concerns the production and dissemination of information and new knowledge. The difficulty comes from the intangible nature of knowledge itself. It spreads without leaving many traces in the sands of the data. How are we to measure and evaluate our investments in science and in economics itself? Almost all of the production of science (as is also the case for other public goods) escapes our current measurement techniques, and it is not even on the agenda of the major statistical agencies. Yet, that is where the future answers to our old questions are likely to come from.

Thus, while I conclude that the glass is still half empty, this should not be taken as reason to despair. Rather, it is a challenge for the next generation of researchers to make progress. There is still a long way to go, but the previous generation has provided them with good shoulders on which to stand.

Contributors

Martin Neil Baily
McKinsey and Company, Inc.
1101 Pennsylvania Avenue
Suite 700
Washington, DC 20004

V. Eldon Ball
Economic Research Service
U.S. Department of Agriculture
1800 M Street, NW Suite 3
Washington, DC 20036-5831

Susanto Basu
Department of Economics
University of Michigan
611 Tappan Street
Ann Arbor, MI 48109-1220

Ernst R. Berndt
Sloan School of Management,
 E52-452
Massachusetts Institute of Technology
50 Memorial Drive
Cambridge, MA 02142

Barry Bosworth
Senior Fellow, Economic Studies
The Brookings Institution
1775 Massachusetts Avenue, NW
Washington, DC 20036-2188

Edwin R. Dean
Department of Economics
The George Washington University
Washington, DC 20052

W. Erwin Diewert
Department of Economics
University of British Columbia
997-1873 East Mall
Vancouver, BC V6T 1Z1
Canada

Denny Ellerman
Sloan School of Management,
 E40-279
Massachusetts Institute of Technology
77 Massachusetts Avenue
Cambridge, MA 02139

Rolf Färe
Department of Economics
Oregon State University
319D Ballard Extension Hall
Corvallis, OR 97331-3612

John Fernald
Research Department, 11th Floor
Federal Reserve Bank of Chicago
230 South LaSalle Street
Chicago, IL 60604

Contributors

Lucia Foster
Center for Economic Studies
Bureau of the Census
4700 Silver Hill Road
Mail Stop 6300
Room 206 Washington Plaza II
Washington, D.C. 20233-6300

Frank M. Gollop
Department of Economics
Boston College
Chestnut Hill, MA 02167

Robert J. Gordon
Department of Economics
Northwestern University
Evanston, IL 60208-2600

Jeremy Greenwood
Department of Economics
Harkness Hall
University of Rochester
Rochester, NY 14627-0156

Shawna Grosskopf
Department of Economics
Oregon State University
309 Ballard Extension Hall
Corvallis, OR 97331-3612

John Haltiwanger
Department of Economics
University of Maryland
College Park, MD 20742

Michael J. Harper
Bureau of Labor Statistics, Room 2140
2 Massachusetts Ave, NE
Washington, DC 20212

Charles R. Hulten
Department of Economics
University of Maryland
Room 3105, Tydings Hall
College Park, MD 20742

Nazrul Islam
Department of Economics
Emory University
Atlanta, GA 30322-2240

Charles I. Jones
Department of Economics
Stanford University
Stanford, CA 94305-6072

Dale W. Jorgenson
Department of Economics
Littauer 122
Harvard University
Cambridge, MA 02138

Boyan Jovanovic
Department of Economics
New York University
269 Mercer Street
New York, NY 10003

C. J. Krizan
Bureau of the Census
Federal Office Building 3
Silver Hill and Suitland Roads
Suitland, MD 20746

M. Ishaq Nadiri
Department of Economics
New York University
269 Mercer Street
New York, NY 10003

Richard Nehring
Economic Research Service
U.S. Department of Agriculture
Room 4088
1800 M Street, NW
Washington, DC 20036-5831

Catherine J. Morrison Paul
Department of Agricultural and
    Resource Economics
3120 Social Sciences and Humanities
    Building
University of California, Davis
Davis, CA 95616

William Pizer
Resources for the Future
1616 P Street, NW
Washington, DC 20036

Ingmar R. Prucha
Department of Economics
Room 3147A, Tydings Hall
University of Maryland
College Park, MD 20742-7211

Mark J. Roberts
Department of Economics
513 Kern Graduate Building
Pennsylvania State University
University Park, PA 16802

Larry Rosenblum
Bureau of Labor Statistics
Room 2140 P5B
2 Massachusetts Avenue, NE
Washington, DC 20212

Robin C. Sickles
Department of Economics
Rice University
6100 South Main Street
Houston, TX 77005-1892

Robert M. Solow
Department of Economics, E52-383B
Massachusetts Institute of Technology
50 Memorial Drive
Cambridge, MA 02139

Thomas M. Stoker
Sloan School of Management,
 E52-455
Massachusetts Institute of Technology
77 Massachusetts Avenue
Cambridge, MA 02139

Gregory P. Swinand
Indecon International Economics
 Consultants
Indecon House
Wellington Quay
Dublin 2
Ireland

Jack E. Triplett
Visiting Fellow, Economic Studies
The Brookings Institution
1775 Massachusetts Avenue, NW
Washington, DC 20036-2188

Eric Yip
McKinsey and Company
75 Park Plaza, 3rd Floor
Boston, MA 02116-3934

Eric Zitzewitz
Department of Economics
Massachusetts Institute of Technology
Cambridge, MA 02139

Author Index

Abbott, Thomas A., 228, 237
Abdalla, Charles W., 600
Abel, A. B., 122n12, 140, 141
Abramovitz, Moses, 6, 9, 17, 181, 492, 497, 513, 526
Adler, Paul, 203
Advisory Commission to Study the Consumer Price Index, 3, 6, 28
Aghion, Philippe, 307, 308, 526n16
Aigner, D., 582
Andrews, William H., Jr., 237
Argotte, Linda, 193
Arrow, K. J., 141, 178, 182, 184, 195, 204–7
Aschauer, David A., 21
Automotive Body Repair News (ABRN), 339
Autor, David, 200
Aw, Bee Yan, 303n1, 310, 311, 314, 332, 334n21, 368
Aylor, Tim, 50

Bahk, Byong-Hyong, 193, 216
Baily, Martin N., 22n13, 39, 263n31, 268n34, 303n1, 309, 310, 311, 312, 314, 315, 318, 319, 321, 323, 326, 356, 364, 462n3
Baker, Joe G., 400
Baldwin, John R., 309, 310n8, 341, 344
Ball, Laurence, 249, 282
Ball, V. Eldon, 66n7, 553, 578, 588, 599
Barger, H., 471
Barnard, Charles H., 600

Barro, Robert J., 25n16, 227n2, 484n10, 526nn15,16, 533
Barsky, Robert, 250n20
Bartel, Ann, 203
Bartelsman, Eric J., 38n26, 267n33, 268n34, 303n1, 308, 309, 310, 311, 312n10, 314, 318, 323, 355
Basu, Susanto, 21, 226n1, 228, 237, 243n12, 247, 253–54, 256, 258n28, 263, 264, 267, 276, 278, 279, 281, 282, 284, 285, 286n43
Battese, G. E., 583
Baumol, William J., 21, 35n24, 526
Baxter, Marianne, 266
Beaudry, Paul, 227n3, 264
Beaulieu, John J., 243n13
Becker, Gary S., 69, 512, 532n18, 533, 609
Benhabib, Jess, 187n5, 203, 266, 505
Bergson, Abram, 471
Berman, Eli, 238n9
Bernard, Andrew B., 309
Berndt, Ernst, 20–21, 22n13, 56, 67, 68, 76, 90, 107n3, 111, 115, 121, 127, 128, 141n34, 147–48, 235, 248, 249, 250–51, 263, 298, 354n28, 381, 385, 386n11, 387, 389, 391n14, 400n19
Bernstein, J. I., 107n3, 119, 122n12, 142, 143, 144n35, 146, 147, 150n38
Berstrom, John, 600
Bils, Mark, 226n1. 250, 254
Binder, M., 136n27, 137

Bischoff, C. W., 122n12, 136n27, 148
Blackman, Sue A. B., 21
Blanchard, Olivier, 267, 308n6
Bonds, Belinda, 50
Boskin, Michael J., 99n4
Bosworth, Barry, 24, 467, 497
Bound, John, 238n9
Boyle, Kevin, 600
Bruno, Michael, 257, 260, 287
Bureau of Economic Analysis (BEA), 515nn5,7, 533
Bureau of Labor Statistics (BLS), 56, 57, 65, 68, 69, 70, 71n15, 72n18, 74, 76, 77, 80, 88, 514n3
Burnside, Craig, 227n4, 243n11, 253, 254, 267, 269, 272

Caballero, Ricardo J., 141, 252, 266–67, 307, 308
Campbell, David, 39, 263n31, 303n1, 309, 310, 311, 312, 315, 319, 321, 356, 364
Campbell, Jeffrey R., 306, 307
Carlton, Dennis W., 250n20
Cas, Alexandra, 23n14
Caselli, Francesco, 200, 201, 203
Cass, David, 23, 31
Caves, Douglas W., 18, 19, 107n3, 108, 110, 308, 367, 473, 542, 546, 547
Chamberlain, G., 479
Chambers, Robert G., 248n18, 254n25, 550, 566n11, 567, 568
Chari, V. V., 194, 211n20, 307n4
Charnes, A., 544n3
Chen, Xiaomin, 303n1, 310, 311, 314, 332, 334n21, 368
Chenery, Hollis, 475
Cho, Jang-Ok, 226n1, 254
Choi, J.-B., 122, 148
Christensen, Laurits, R., 15, 18, 19, 62, 64, 89, 107n3, 108, 110, 120, 127, 129, 367, 471, 472, 473, 494, 495, 496, 515, 527, 531, 542, 546, 547
Chung, Y., 550, 566n11, 579
Clark, Kim, 203
Cobb, Clifford, 4
Coelli, T. J., 583
Cole, Rosanne, 28
Collins, Susan M., 24, 467, 497
Cooley, Thomas F., 226n1, 227, 274, 307n4
Cooper, Russell, 266, 267n33, 307
Cooper, W. W., 544n3
Copeland, Morris A., 6
Cornwell, C., 582

Council of Economic Advisers, 419
Cummings, Diane, 18, 471, 472, 473, 494, 495, 496, 516, 527
Cutler, David, 610

Dahlman, C., 497n16
David, Paul, 193, 194n12, 497
Davis, Steven J., 39, 309, 309, 319, 321, 325, 326, 344, 356, 358
Dean, Edwin, 70, 73n20, 75, 77, 78, 81, 85, 88, 339n25, 344
Debreu, Gerard, 97
Denison, Edward F., 6, 7, 12–15, 17, 22n13, 28, 35n24, 62, 64, 66n8, 69, 70, 79, 88, 173, 184, 465, 471, 492, 493, 525–26, 527, 587nn1,2, 609
Denny, M., 107n3, 112, 115, 119, 121, 122, 127, 128, 134, 139, 147
Denny, Michael, 17
Desli, E., 578
Devereux, Michael, 227n3, 264
Dhrymes, Phoebus, 268n34, 303n1, 309, 310
Dial, Jay, 306
Diamond, Peter A., 266, 267
Diewert, W. Erwin, 11, 15, 18, 19, 22n13, 60, 61, 62, 78, 90, 98, 99n6, 107n3, 108, 109, 112, 114, 120, 122, 125, 127, 129, 239, 248n18, 366–67, 473, 542, 546, 547, 567
Dixit, Avinash, 141
Dollar, D., 474
Domar, Evsey, 29, 33, 36, 37, 60, 77, 78, 257, 264, 471
Doms, Mark, 38n26, 308, 309, 310
Dorsey, Michael, 227n4
Dougherty, Chrys, 466, 474, 480, 482, 484, 495, 516n9, 519n10, 536
Douglas, Paul H., 514
Dowrick, Steven, 21, 496
Dulberger, Ellen, 68n11
Dunne, Tim, 309, 310, 341, 344
Durlauf, S., 469, 494n12
Dwyer, Douglas, 216, 303n1, 309, 310

Easterly, William, 25n16
Eberly, J. C., 141
Eichenbaum, Martin, 227n4, 243n11, 253, 254
Eisner, Robert, 120
Eldridge, Lucy P., 80
Ellerman, Denny, 298, 381, 385, 386n11, 387, 389, 391n14, 400n19

Author Index

Eltetö, O., 554
Epple, Dennis, 193
Epstein, L. G., 122, 133n25, 134, 136n27, 137, 139, 147
Ericson, Richard, 305, 369
Ezaki, M., 471

Färe, R., 19, 470, 544, 546, 547, 550, 552n6, 556, 566n11, 567, 568, 577, 578, 579, 588
Farmer, Robert, 227nn2,3, 266, 282
Federal Reserve Bank of Dallas, 195n13
Feldstein, Martin, 148
Felipe, J., 496n15
Fernald, John, 21, 226n1, 228, 237, 247, 258n28, 263, 267, 276, 278, 279, 281, 282, 284, 285, 286n43
Fisher, Franklin, 11
Flachaire, E., 578
Flug, Karnit, 200
Flux, A. W., 253
Foot, D. K., 148
Foss, Murray, 173
Foster, Lucia, 38n26, 268n34, 277n37
Fox, Kevin J., 22n13, 98
Fraumeni, Barbara M., 21, 68, 69n12, 70, 77n21, 88, 166, 262n29, 268, 270, 272f, 277, 291n44, 380n4, 514n3, 515n7, 531–33, 610
Friedman, Milton, 6
Fuss, Melvyn, 17, 20–21, 107n3, 111, 112, 115, 119, 120n11, 121, 127, 128, 144n35, 235, 248, 250–51, 263

Galeotti, M., 148
Gali, Jordi, 237
Gallant, A. R., 134
Gallman, Robert E., 1n1, 3t
Gilbert, Milton, 526n13
Gilchrist, Simon, 285
Goldberg, Joseph P., 56
Goldin, Claudia, 199, 201
Goldsmith, Raymond, 515, 532, 533
Gollop, Frank M., 21, 69n12, 70, 76, 77, 88, 92, 262n29, 268, 270, 272f, 291n44, 380n4, 514n3, 598n7
Good, D., 141n34
Gordon, Robert J., 22n13, 28, 30, 177, 217, 223, 226n1, 228, 457, 514
Gordon, S., 140n33
Gorman, John A., 66
Gort, Michael, 193–94, 216
Goss, D., 570

Goto, A., 146n36
Gray, Wayne, 355
Green, Edward J., 249
Green, P. J., 387n13
Greenwood, Jeremy, 22n13, 30, 176, 177, 189nn6,7, 194, 204, 307n4, 514
Grifell-Tatjé, E., 578
Griliches, Zvi, 2, 6, 9, 12–15, 17, 18, 20, 22n13, 27, 29n19, 38, 39, 51, 60, 62, 63, 64, 88, 112, 150n38, 174, 182, 195, 200–203, 228, 237, 238n9, 247n17, 253, 266, 267, 303n1, 310, 311, 314, 316, 318, 323, 354n28, 364, 513–14, 533, 578, 587nn1,2
Grosskopf, Shawna, 544, 546, 547, 550, 552n6, 556, 567, 568, 578, 579, 588
Grossman, Gene, 27, 306n3, 526n16
Grube, A., 555, 600n8
Grübler, Arnulf, 194
Gullickson, William, 38, 51, 73n20, 77, 81
Guo, Jang-Ting, 227nn2,3, 282

Haavelmo, Trygve, 243n11
Hall, Alastair, 269n36
Hall, Bronwyn, 39, 533
Hall, E. R., 107n3
Hall, Robert E., 9, 30n20, 62, 63, 90, 142, 226n1, 228, 231, 234, 235, 236, 240, 241, 246, 247, 268, 278, 465, 466, 475–78, 480, 484, 498, 502, 503–6, 513n2, 515
Halstead, Ted, 4
Haltiwanger, John, 38n26, 39, 268n34, 277n37, 303n1, 305, 307, 309, 310, 311, 312, 314, 315n12, 318, 319, 321, 323, 325, 326, 341, 344, 356, 358
Hammour, Mohamad, 307, 308
Hansen, L. P., 134, 136n27, 139
Harper, Michael J., 38, 51, 64–65, 66n7, 67, 73n20, 75, 76, 77, 81, 85, 88, 90
Hausman, Jerry A., 52, 93, 228, 237, 434, 453
Hayashi, Fumio, 140, 141
Heckman, James, 201
Helpman, Elhanan, 27, 306n3, 526n16
Hercowitz, Zvi, 30, 176, 189nn6,7, 200, 514
Herman, Shelby, 68
Heston, Alan, 473, 526, 527
Hicks, John R., 93, 122, 215
Hill, P., 95, 99n6
Ho, Mun S., 514n3
Hobday, M., 497n16

Hopenhayn, Hugo, 194, 211n20, 306, 307n4, 369, 370
Horvath, Michael T. K., 263n31, 278, 282, 285
Howitt, Peter, 307, 308, 526n16
Hulten, Charles, 4, 7n4, 9, 12n7, 13, 21n12, 23n14, 25, 29, 31–33, 35n23, 39, 68, 107n3, 111, 112, 149n37, 176, 189n6, 248, 263n31, 264, 281, 303n1, 309, 310, 311, 312, 315, 318, 319, 321, 356, 364, 515n7

Islam, Nazrul, 465, 466, 479, 480, 484, 494n12, 496n14, 502, 503–5, 527, 531

Jablonski, Mary, 70, 73, 79
Jensen, J. Bradford, 309
Jeon, B. M., 577, 581
Johansen, Leif, 28
John, Andrew, 266
Johnson, P., 469
Johri, Alok, 267n33
Jones, Charles I., 209, 465, 466, 475–78, 480, 484, 498, 502, 503–6, 513n2
Jonscher, Charles, 207
Jorgenson, Dale W., 2, 9, 12–15, 17, 18, 20, 21, 29, 60, 62, 63, 64, 69, 70, 77n21, 78, 88, 89, 90, 112, 119, 120, 127, 129, 141n34, 142, 149, 174, 175, 238n9, 246, 262n29, 268, 269, 270, 272f, 277, 291n44, 374, 380n4, 465, 466, 468–69, 471, 472, 473, 474, 480, 482, 484, 493, 494, 495, 496, 513–14, 515–16, 527, 531–33, 536, 587nn1,2, 609, 610
Joskow, Paul M., 386, 399
Jovanovic, Boyan, 22n13, 176, 177, 183, 193, 194, 195, 196, 202, 211n20, 305, 306n3, 368
Judson, Ruth, 174

Kapur, Sandeep, 195
Katz, Arnold, 68
Katz, Lawrence, 199, 200, 201, 263, 283
Kellogg, R. L., 555, 570, 600n8
Kendrick, John, 6, 62, 354n28, 465, 587n2
Kenen, Peter, 468n1
Kennan, J., 139
Keynes, John Maynard, 56
Kim, Jong-Il, 24, 467, 496
Kimball, Miles S., 227n2, 228, 237, 243n12, 249, 254, 256, 276, 285
Kim, Seongjun, 24

King, Robert G., 227nn2,4, 266
Klarqvist, Virginia, 79
Klenow, P. J., 174, 467, 497, 507
Klepper, Stephen, 193–94
Klette, Tor Jacob, 267
Knight, Frank, 610
Kokkelenberg, Edward C., 33, 35, 91, 122n12, 136n27, 148
Kollintzas, T., 122, 136, 148
Koopmans, T. C., 23, 31
Köves, P., 554
Koyck, L. M., 119
Kravis, Irving B., 471, 473, 526
Kremer, Michael, 308n6
Krizan, C. J., 38n26, 268n34, 277n37
Krueger, Alan, 200
Krugman, Paul, 24, 496–97
Krusell, Per, 30, 176, 182, 185, 189nn6,7, 200, 204, 207–9, 217, 514
Kumbhakar, S. C., 583
Kunze, Kent, 64–65, 70, 73, 78, 79, 339n25, 344
Kuznets, Simon, 471, 513, 515, 520, 522, 526, 527, 533

Lach, Saul, 194, 195, 196
Lahiri, L., 139n30
Lambson, Val E., 305
Larson, B., 497n16
Lau, Lawrence J., 15, 24, 109, 120, 125, 127, 129, 175, 248n18, 467, 496
Lee, Y. H., 583
Lee, Yuan Tsao, 496
Leontief, Wassily, 56
Lépine, N., 146n36
Levine, Ross, 526n15
Lewis, William, 420n2
Lichtenberg, Frank, 203
Lilien, David M., 228
Lindgren, B., 547
Liu, Lili, 303n1, 310, 311, 314
Lochner, Lance, 201
Lovell, C. A. K., 544, 552n6, 578, 581, 582
Lucas, Robert E., 25, 120, 121, 125n16, 180, 282, 306n2, 499, 526n16, 534
Luenberger, D. G., 550
Lyons, Richard K., 252, 266–67

McFadden, Daniel, 120, 127n20
McKinsey Global Institute, 437n11, 443t, 444t, 448t, 449f, 456, 459, 462
MacDonald, Glenn, 195, 211n20, 306n3

Machlup, Fritz, 512, 532, 533
Madan, D. B., 133n25, 136, 137
Maddison, Angus, 22n13, 474, 493–94, 526
Mairesse, Jacques, 39, 247n17
Maizel, M., 570
Malinvaud, E., 122, 126n18
Malmquist, David, 76
Mamuneas, T., 150n38
Mankiw, N. Gregory, 478nn6,7, 484n10, 503, 527
Mansfield, Edwin, 195, 306, 609, 611
Mark, Jerome A., 56, 65
Marschak, Jacob, 237
Marshall, Alfred, 95
Marti, C., 497
Martin, E. M., 6
Mattey, Joseph, 243n13
Meeusen, J., 582
Mincer, Jacob, 69, 512
Moeller, Linda, 72
Mohnen, P., 107n3, 119, 129, 133n25, 144, 146n36, 147
Morrison, Catherine J., 107n3, 111, 115, 121, 127, 127, 129, 141n34, 145, 148, 229, 249
Morrison, Steven, 450
Mortenson, D. T., 120
Moye, William T., 56
Mundlak, Yair, 127n20
Murphy, Kevin J., 306
Musgrave, John C., 63
Mussa, Michael, 140

Nadiri, M. Ishaq, 17, 18, 24, 27, 106, 107n3, 108, 110n6, 115, 116, 117, 118, 119, 122, 123n13, 125, 126–27, 128, 129, 130, 131, 132n24, 133n25, 137, 139, 140, 141n34, 142, 144–45, 146, 148, 150–54, 165, 229, 236, 239, 243n12, 248, 251n21, 298, 472
Nasbeth, Lars, 306
National Academy of Sciences (NAS), 61, 73, 76
Nehring, R., 555, 578, 588, 600n8
Nelson, Richard R., 29, 182, 203–4, 307, 497
Nguyen, D., 496
Nguyen, Duc-Tho, 21
Nishimizu, Mieko, 18, 470, 472
Nordhaus, William, 2–3, 33, 35, 91, 525, 532
Norris, M., 550, 552n6, 556

Norsworthy, J. Randolph, 64–65, 76
Nyarko, Yaw, 193, 211n20

Oliner, Stephen D., 2, 68n11
Olley, G. Steven, 314, 247n17, 303n1, 309, 310, 317, 368
Organisation for Economic Cooperation and Development (OECD), 90, 517
Otto, Phyllis F., 73, 77

Pack, H., 497n16
Page, J. M., Jr., 470, 497n16
Pakes, Ariel, 247n17, 303n1, 305, 306, 309, 310, 314, 317, 368, 369
Parente, Stephen, 183, 184, 185, 194, 204, 209–16
Park, B., 582
Parker, Jonathan A., 250n20
Paul, Catherine J. Morrison, 267n33
Pesaran, M. H., 136n27, 137
Phelan, Christopher, 228, 263n31, 285
Phelps, Edmund, 182
Pindyck, R. S., 139n31, 141, 249
Plotkin, S., 555
Poe, Gregory, 600
Porter, Robert H., 249
Pötscher, B. M., 134
Power, Laura, 307
Prescott, Edward C., 125n16, 226n1, 227, 274, 499, 507
Prucha, Ingmar R., 17, 106, 107n3, 108, 110n6, 115, 116, 117, 118, 119, 122, 123n13, 125, 126–27, 128, 129, 130, 131, 132n24, 133n25, 134, 135, 136, 137, 139, 140, 144–45, 148, 150–54, 165, 229, 236, 239, 243n12, 248, 251n21, 298
Psacharopoulos, George, 476, 503

Quah, D., 494n12

Ramey, Valeria A., 228, 280, 283
Ray, George, 306
Ray, S. C., 578
Rebelo, Sergio, 253
Rees, Albert, 61
Regev, Haim, 303n1, 310, 311, 314, 316, 318, 323, 364
Renelt, David, 526n15
Repetto, Robert, 588, 603
Rhodes, E., 544n3
Richter, Marcel K., 11, 112

Rob, Rafael, 183n2, 195, 211n20, 306n3
Roberts, Kevin, 305
Roberts, Mark J., 303n1, 309n7, 310, 311, 314, 332, 334n21, 341, 355, 368
Robertson, James W., 68
Robinson, S., 475
Rodriguez-Clare, Andres, 174, 467, 497, 507
Rogers, Everett M., 306
Rogerson, Richard, 306
Romeo, Anthony, 195, 527
Romer, David, 249, 282, 478nn6,7, 484n10, 503
Romer, Paul M., 25, 98, 180, 266, 526, 527, 534
Roos, P., 547
Rosen, Sherwin, 119
Rosenblum, Larry, 70, 72n18
Rotemberg, Julio J., 139n31, 227nn2,3, 234n8, 240n10, 249, 259, 266, 280, 289
Rowe, Jonathan, 4
Rudebusch, Glenn D., 269n36
Rustichini, Aldo, 187n5
Rymes, Thomas K., 23n14

Sala-i-Martin, Xavier, 25n16, 526nn15,16
Saloner, Garth, 249
Salter, W. E. G., 28, 215–16
Samuelson, Larry, 309n7, 341
Samuelson, Paul A., 57, 173, 515, 516n8
Sargent, T. J., 136n27, 139
Sato, K., 258
Sbordone, Argia M., 267
Schankerman, M. A., 107n3, 119, 306
Schennech, Susanne, 386n11, 387, 391n14
Schiantarelli, F., 148
Schmidt, P., 139n30, 582, 583
Schmitt-Grohé, Stephanie, 233
Schor, Juliet B., 252n22
Schuh, Scott, 309, 319, 321, 325, 326, 358
Schultz, Theodore W., 512, 532, 533, 609, 610
Schumpeter, Joseph, 304
Schwartz, Mark, 306
Shapiro, Matthew D., 122n12, 139n31, 228, 243n13, 249, 252, 280, 283
Shea, John, 239
Shephard, R. W., 120, 543n2, 544, 546, 547
Sherwood, Mark K., 73n20, 75, 79
Sichel, Daniel E., 2
Sickles, R., 141n34, 577, 581, 582
Siegel, Donald, 145, 267n33, 357n29
Silverman, B. W., 387n13

Simar, L., 578, 579, 581, 582
Sinclair, Robert D., 507
Singleton, K. J., 139
Sirquin, M., 475
Smith, A. M., 90
Smith, Adam, 29, 95
Smith, Phillip, 96
Solon, Gary, 250n20
Solow, Robert, 2, 7, 9–13, 23, 28, 36, 60, 64, 76, 78, 112, 115, 179–82, 183n2, 185–97, 199, 200, 201, 204–17, 222, 228, 231, 234, 235, 236, 279, 469, 471, 492, 511, 513, 514, 520, 522, 526, 527, 531, 533, 541, 547, 587
Spiegel, Mark, 203, 505
Srinivasan, Sylaja, 25, 146n36
Steigerwald, D. G., 140n33
Steigum, E., Jr., 121
Stein, Jeremy, 307n4
Stephenson, J. A., 119
Stigler, George J., 6, 184
Stiroh, Kevin J., 2, 514
Stoker, Thomas M., 298, 385, 386n11, 387, 389, 391n14
Stokey, Nancy, 125n16
Stone, Richard, 515
Strotz, R., 120
Stuart, C., 140n33
Summers, Lawrence H., 263, 283
Summers, Robert, 473, 526, 527
Supina, Dylan, 355
Suzuki, K., 146n36
Sveikauskas, Leo, 74
Swanson, J. A., 107n3, 108, 110
Swinand, Gregory P., 92, 600
Szulc, B., 554

Taber, Christopher, 201
Tannen, Michael, 70
Temple, J., 494n12
Tinbergen, Jan, 7, 471, 514
Tobin, James, 140, 525, 532
Tornqvist, Leo, 60
Treadway, A. B., 120, 121
Trejos, Alberto, 228, 263n31, 285
Triplett, Jack E., 7n4, 28n18, 30, 48, 49n3, 51n5, 56, 68, 354n28, 514n4
Troske, Kenneth, 309, 310
Tybout, James R., 303n1, 310, 311, 314

U.S. Department of Commerce, Bureau of the Census, 3t
U.S. Department of Energy, Energy Infor-

mation Agency, 376n1, 377n2, 385, 414, 417
U.S. Department of Labor
  Bureau of Labor Statistics (BLS), 380
  Mine Safety and Health Administration, 373
U.S. Executive Office of the President, 399
U.S. Federal Energy Administration, 399

Vaccara, Beatrice, 354n28
van den Broeck, J., 582
Varian, Hal, 233n7

Wade, R., 498n18
Wagner, Samuel, 306
Waldorf, William, 65, 70
Wales, T. J., 120, 129
Watkins, G. C., 121, 141n34
Waverman, Leonard, 17, 107n3, 112, 115, 119, 121, 127, 128
Weder, Mark, 228
Weil, D., 478nn6,7, 484n10, 503, 527
Weitzman, Martin L., 31, 32, 305
Wen, Yi, 227n4

Westphal, L., 497n16
White, H., 134
Wilcox, David W., 269n36
Williams, John, 285
Wilson, P., 578, 579, 581
Winston, Clifford, 450
Winter, Sidney G., 307
Wolff, Edward M., 21, 30, 175, 466, 474, 480, 495
Wolman, Alexander, 227n4
Wood, David O., 67, 68, 76, 90, 147–48
Woodford, Michael, 227nn2,3, 234n8, 240n10, 259, 266, 280, 289
World Bank, 526n14
Wykoff, Frank C., 13, 68, 149n37, 515n7

Yatchew, A. J., 133n25, 134, 136n27, 137
Yorukoglu, Mehmet, 194, 204, 307n4
Young, Allan H., 63
Young, Alwyn, 2, 21, 24–25, 467, 496, 497–98
Yun, Kun-Young, 269

Zeckhauser, Richard, 210, 211n18

Subject Index

Agricultural sector, U.S.: comparison of TFP and TRP measures, 59; environmental indicators of nitrogen and pesticide leaching in, 568–75; measurement of productivity with undesirable outputs in, 553–65

Airline industry: comparison of productivity in, 446–52, 456, 461–63; hub-and-spoke system, 450–52, 461–63; labor requirements of, 463

Asian countries. *See* Southeast Asian countries

Auto repair shops, 340–48

Banking industry: information technology in, 422, 424, 426–29, 453, 458; productivity measurement of, 422–29, 456

Baumol stagnation hypothesis, 35n24

Boskin Commission on CPI, 28–29, 48–49, 460

Bureau of Labor Statistics (BLS): improvements in productivity measurement program, 78–79; indexes of hours, 78; output indexes, 78; price indexes, 78; production indexes, 78; productivity measurement by, 55; weighting of indexes, 78–79

Business cycle models: DGE approach to, 226–27; real, 227

Canberra Group on Capital Measurement, 90

Capacity utilization: aggregate, 261–62; changes in, 252–56; differences from production function concept, 228–30; dynamic model of variable, 237–38, 242–46; empirical issues related to, 237–40; first- and second-order approximations, 246–52, 260, 297–98; implications of, 281–82; meaning and measurement of, 242–57; in production function, 19–21

Capital: BLS reformulation of measures of, 66–68; as complement to skilled labor (Griliches), 200–203; concept in endogenous growth theory, 25; entertainment or artistic capital, 95–96; infrastructure capital, 95; knowledge capital, 92–95; old and new, 179–80; quasi-fixity of, 243, 248–49; Solow's 1960 vintage model of, 180–99, 514; user cost of, 119; vintage capital in Solow residual model, 179–80; vintage-specific physical, 194

Capital formation: in neoclassical growth models, 23–24

Capital goods: effect of introduction (1970s), 199; quality of, 174–75; rise of skill in use of, 182–83

Capital-goods sector: Arrow's growth model, 182–84; Krusell's model, 182–83, 185; Parente's model, 182–85

Capital stock: in production function, 19–21

625

Capital utilization: variable, 243
Circular income flow model, 5
Coal industry, U.S.: aggregate statistics for, 374–75; aggregating sources of productivity change in, 404–6; heterogeneity in, 376–77; homogeneous subaggregates in, 377–78; labor productivity, 381–92, 414–18; mining methods and productivity, 376–77; rate of technical change in, 406–11; sources of productivity change, 394–411
Consumer Price Index (CPI), Boskin Commission report, 28–29, 48–49, 460
Consumption-goods sector: Arrow's model, 183; Krusell's model, 183; Parente's model, 183
Convergence: in Dougherty-Jorgenson growth accounting, 495; in Maddison's growth accounting, 494; processes leading to, 468–69; of productivity with input and output per capita, 525–31; theory of TFP growth, 18
Creative destruction: forms of, 307–8; Schumpeter's concept of, 304; theoretical literature on, 308–10

Data envelopment analysis (DEA), 544, 566, 583
Data sources: for analysis of G7 country economic growth, 534–36; for analysis of U.S. agricultural sector productivity, 542, 553, 566; Annual Survey of Manufactures (ASM), 356–57; BLS KLEMS data, 356; for BLS labor composition series, 71–74; Census of Manufactures (CM), 355–57; Census of Service Industries, 348, 357–58; for cross-section approach to growth accounting, 475–78; Doane Pesticide Profile Study, 570; for estimates of technical change, 267–69; for expanded MFP measures, 76–77; for growth accounting using time series, 470–74; Longitudinal Research Database (LRD), 22, 39, 358; in measurement of outputs, inputs, and productivity, 318–19; Mine Safety and Health Administration, 373, 384–85, 400–401, 411–12; National Agricultural Statistics Service (NASS), 570; National Income and Product Accounts (NIPA), 55–57, 515; NBER Productivity Database, 356; for panel regression approach to growth accounting, 478–80; for TRP application to U.S. agricultural sector, 599–600
DEA. *See* Data envelopment analysis (DEA)
Depreciation, 7n4
Diffusion: lag theories of, 193–96
Distance functions: directional technology, 550; output, 542, 546–47, 566; output-oriented directional, 550–53, 566, 568, 578
Divisia index: path independence of, 40; Tornqvist approximation to, 15
Dynamic general equilibrium (DGE): approach to business cycle modeling, 226–28

East Asian countries. *See* Southeast Asian countries
Economic growth: accounts for sources of, 532–33; allocation of investment and productivity for, 513; creative destruction models of, 307–8; effect of factor allocation on, 308–15; externalities in modeling of, 266–67; factors in G7 countries influencing, 511; neoclassical models of, 23–24; new measure of U.S., 532–33; uses of, 515. *See also* Growth accounting; Growth theory, neoclassical
Economy, aggregate: GDP as measure of output in, 231
Education sector: inputs of, 532; investment in human capital as output of, 531–32
Embodiment, of technology in capital, 179–80
Embodiment effect: capital-embodied technical change, 28–30; Solow's concept (1960), 187–99, 514; in technological progress (Solow), 175–77
Embodiment effect (Jorgenson), 175–76
Embodiment model, Solow (1960): adjustments to, 190–99; investment-specific, 187–90, 216–17, 514
Endogenous growth theory: constant marginal product of capital in, 25; production function, 25–26

Factor accumulation concept (Krugman), 497
Factor demand models: advantages of dynamic, 104–5; static, 104; variable factor demand equations, 138–39
Factor demand models, dynamic: applications of, 141; third-generation models of, 121–22

Subject Index 627

Factors of production: land as, 91; markets in circular income flow model, 5; markets in interrelated disequilibrium model, 119–20; in measurement of production, 91–92; optimal allocation, 264–65; reallocation to aggregate production, 304; reallocation in auto repair shops, 340–48; reallocation to economic growth, 493; reallocation on productivity in service sector, 339–50; reallocation in U.S. manufacturing sector, 319–38. *See also* Capital; Inputs; Labor; Outputs
Factor utilization: model of variable, 243. *See also* Capital utilization; Labor
Firms: adjustment cost in theory of, 120–21; variation in capacity utilization, 238
Frontier analysis, 19. *See also* Production possibilities frontier (PPF)
Gross domestic product (GDP): data revisions, ix; as measure of aggregate of output, 231
Growth accounting: based on Solow 1957 residual model, 179–81; catch-up effect (Maddison), 493–94; conventional, 185; cross-section approach, 465–67, 470, 475–78, 495–98; derivation of TRP models from, 589; function of, 6; origins of, 5–7; in Solow's 1960 vintage capital framework, 180–85; times series approach, 465–66, 469–74, 494–95, 497
Growth model (Arrow): learning by doing, 182–83
Growth theory, neoclassical: convergence in, 468; cross-country application of, 468; departures from, 493–94; exogenous technological progress in, 469, 492; human capital, knowledge, and fixed capital in, 531; incorporation of R&D spending in, 17–18; investment endogenous in, 510, 513, 531; new version, 531–34; production function in, 25–26; productivity exogenous in, 510, 513, 531; Solow's version, 511, 513
Growth theory, "old," 23–25
Harrod-Rymes concept: of TFP, 24–25
Hicksian efficiency index, 8–9
Hicksian shift parameter, 7–9
Human capital: alternative ways to measurement of, 94

Industrial revolution: growth path of second, 197–98; growth path of third, 197–99
Information: measurement of dissemination of, 611–12
Information technology (IT): in airline industry, 446–52; in banking industry, 422, 424, 426–29, 453, 458; in public transport, 454; in retail sector, 454; in service sector, 452–55; in telecommunications, 433, 453
Innovation: in capital-embodied technical change, 28; definition of, 92–93; as form of capital accumulation, 25; global and local, 93; introduction of new goods, 27–31; in neoclassical growth models, 25; quality of products with, 27–31
Inputs: aggregate, 260; measurement using Census of Manufactures, 318–38; measurement of intermediate, 87; measurement of labor, 88; measurement in manufacturing sector, 355–60; in public transportation, 441–42; quasi-fixed, 248–49, 251; reallocation of, 303–4, 308–15, 319–38; reproducible capital, 88–90; resource, 91–92
Inventories: National Resource Inventory, 569, 571; Perpetual Inventory Method, 62; for productivity measurement, 90–91
Investment: definition of, 512; in human capital, 512, 531–32; influence of new knowledge on, 610–11; irreversibility effects on, 141; neoclassical theory of, 119; as source of economic growth, 512; Tobin's *q*, 140–41; unmeasured problem of, 184–85
Investment in education: measurement of, 531–32
IT. *See* Information technology (IT)
Knowledge: defining and measuring technological, 173; influence of investment on measurement of dissemination of new, 610–11; measurement of new, 611–12
Knowledge capital: definition of, 92–93; measurement of, 94

Subject Index

Labor: quasi-fixity of, 243, 248–49; variable utilization of, 243, 251
Labor force: complementarity of capital and skilled labor, 200–203; matching workers and machines, 202–3
Labor productivity: in airline industry, 446–50; auto repair industry (1987–95), 340–41; decomposition of, 321–22; de- composition of industry-level, 318; definition of, 86; growth rates of, 321– 27, 365; measurement of, 318–19; re- tail banking comparison, 422–29; in Ricardian trade theory, 468n1; U.S. commercial banks (1970–92), 422–23
Labor productivity, coal mining, 373, 376– 92, 394, 411; decomposition of aggre- gate, 381–83; regression results, 389– 92, 414–16; specification for model, 385–89; in subaggregates of, 383–84
Learning: in adjustments to Solow embodi- ment model, 190–93; from productivity levels accounting, 505; technology- specific spillover effects, 181–82; 196–97; in transitional growth path, 197–99
Learning by doing: Arrow's model, 182–83; in Parente's model of technological progress, 210–11
Longitudinal Research Database (LRD), 22, 39, 358
LRD. *See* Data sources; Longitudinal Re- search Database (LRD)
Luenberger productivity indicator, 566, 567–68
Malmquist-Luenberger productivity index, 542, 550–66
Malmquist productivity index: to analyze U.S. agricultural productivity, 553–65; to decompose productivity growth, 577–78; definition of, 18; output dis- tance functions of, 542, 546, 566; use in frontier analysis, 19
Manufacturing sector: effect of input- output reallocation in, 319–38; exit and entry effects on productivity, 330– 38, 368–70; measuring output and in- put in, 355–60
MFP. *See* Multifactor productivity (MFP)
Mine Safety and Health Act (1969), 374, 384, 400
Mismeasurement: differential, 49; in eco- nomic statistics, 50–53; hypothesis, 48–49

Multifactor productivity (MFP): BLS esti- mates, 21; BLS measures of, 55; decom- position of, 317–18; decomposition of industry-level, 321–22; decomposition of plant- and industry-level, 318, 321–27; growth rates of, 321–27, 365, 365–67; index of plant-level, 318–19; KLEMS measures, 77; as measure of productivity, 86; measurement of, 318–19; as measurement for micro units of, 367; Solow residual, 60
Mutuality principle, 15
National Academy of Sciences (NAS), Panel to Review Productivity Statistics (1979), 61, 76
National Income and Product Accounts (NIPA), 55–57, 184–85, 515
New Growth Theory: challenges to TFP residual, 22; endogenous technical in- novation in, 17
Output distance function, 542, 546–47, 551, 581–82
Output-oriented directional distance func- tion, 550
Outputs: aggregate, 260–62; gross, 86–87; heterogenous plant- and firm-level, 305–8; measurement using Census of Manufactures, 318–38 measurement in manufacturing sector, 355–60; measur- ing and defining banking industry, 424–26, 452–53; with new technology, 203; output substitution bias, 460; in postwar coal industry, 374–76; produc- tion of good and bad, 542–46; in pub- lic transportation, 441–45; reallocation of, 303–4, 308–15, 319–38; in service sector, 452–54; in telecommunications industry, 430–34, 441; using value added as measure of, 420–21
Path dependence: avoidance of, 11–12; conditions for, 12n7; problem of, 11n6
Perpetual inventory method (PIM), 62
Potential Function Theorem, 11–12, 14
PPF. *See* Production possibilities frontier (PPF)
Production: effect of misspecification in pro- cess, 150–55, 157
Production analysis: external and internal effects, 266–67, 300; microfoundations of, 297–301
Production function: in derivation of Solow

Subject Index 629

residual, 11; differences from capacity utilization, 228–30; estimating parameters of, 239–40; firm-level, 232–41; first- and second-order, 246–52, 260, 297–98; first-order approximations of, 246–47, 297–300; measurement of flows in, 19–20; Nadiri-Prucha model, 236; relation to output distance function, 547; second-order approximations, 247–52, 297–300; in Solow-Hall model, 234–36; Solow's, 547–48; in structural approach to technical change, 236–37

Production function, aggregate: across firms, 240–42; tied to productivity (Solow), 7–9

Production possibilities frontier (PPF), 264–65, 280–81, 515, 590–92

Productivity in airline industry, 446–52; in banking industry, 424–29; 461–64; in Census of Manufactures, 318–38; comparison in many countries using two methods, 503–5; concept of depreciation in, 7n4; cross-country differences, 456–58; cyclical behavior of, 225–28; definition of, 85–86; developments in literature of, 57, 60–61; differences in firm- and plant-level, 305–8, 363; differences in levels of, 309–10; efficiency approach to measurement of, 28–29; estimates with revised GDP data, ix; explanations for fluctuations in, 226–27, 272f; five-year changes in industry-level, 327–30; fluctuations in, 226–31; with good and bad outputs, 542–46; growth path (1779–1966), 2–3; index numbers for plant-level, 367–68; microlevel, 367–68; mismeasurement hypothesis, 48–53; in postwar coal industry, 374–76; in public transportation industry, 440–46; in retail sector, 434–40, 453–54; as source of economic growth, 512–13; in telecom industry, 430–34; in U.S. agriculture with undesirable outputs, 553–65; value-added, firm-level residual, 257–60; as welfare, 265f, 279–82. *See also* Labor productivity; Multifactor productivity (MFP)

Productivity, aggregate: decomposition of change in, 364–65; definition of, 364

Productivity analysis: boundaries of, 33–35; conventional approach to, 106–12; Divisia index approach, 103, 112–19; from

tier approach to, 467, 470; normative, 230; recent developments, 23; shift from nonparametric, 21–22; top-down and bottom-up approaches to firms and industries, 35–39

Productivity change: aggregate measures in U.S. coal industry, 378–81; aggregate sources in U.S. coal mining, 404–6; decomposition of aggregate, 364–65

Productivity change, coal mining: aggregating sources of, 404–6; indexes of, 392–94; sources of, 394–411

Productivity growth: alternative decomposition methodologies, 315–18; decomposition in auto repair industry, 340–48; as different from technical change, 10; of output, 365; in process-oriented technical change, 27–28; sensitivity to business cycle and industry sector, 312–14; sources of longer term, 610; welfare-based, 279, 596–98

Productivity growth, aggregate, 261, 271–79, 303; decompositions comparison, 310–11, 314, 364; effect of input-output reallocation in, 303–4, 319–38; 350–55; input and output reallocation contribution to, 310–15; role of entry and exit, 330–38; sensitivity of decomposition results, 312–14

Productivity indexes: Divisia, 15; Malmquist, 18–19, 542, 544, 553–66, 577–78; Malmquist-Luenberger, 542, 550–66; Törnqvist, 15, 60–64, 367

Productivity levels: accounting, 505–7; Malmquist index in comparisons of, 18–19

Productivity slowdown (1960s-70s), 2, 20, 41, 48–50, 181–82, 222

Productivity theory, Jorgenson-Griliches, 13–15, 17

Purchasing power parity (PPP): of International Comparisons Project (ICP), 437–38; in measuring retail sector productivity, 437–40; of OECD, 437–39

Retail sector: cross-country differences in, 456–57; measurement of productivity in, 435–40, 453–54

Service sector: controlling for quality differences in, 421; exit and entry effects on productivity, 348–50, 370–71; growth

630 Subject Index

Service sector (cont.)
and measurement of, 29n19; input-output reallocation effects in, 339–48; MFP estimates, 50–53; productivity changes with factor reallocation, 339–50; role of information technology in, 452–55. *See also* Airline industry; Auto repair shops; Banking industry; Retail sector; Telecommunications; Transportation, public
SNA. *See* System of National Accounts (SNA), United Nations
Solow residual or productivity model, 9–12; advances to reduce, 173–75; aggregate, 272; for aggregate U.S. economy, 226; Berndt-Fuss revisions of, 20–21; conditions for disappearance of, 12–13; continuous-time theory of, 15; to estimate technical change, 234–36; innovations in, 12–15; modified, 230; 1957 paper, 228, 234; nontechnological adjustments to, 276–77, 284; sources of bias in, 9–10; used in real business cycle models, 227; welfare properties of, 280
Southeast Asian countries: analysis using "old" growth theory, 24–25; TFP growth in, 496–98
Statistics Canada, 96
Stigler Committee (1961), 49
Substitution: bias in, 6; concept of (Solow), 514; distinct from technical change, 513
Surface Mining Control and Reclamation Act [SMCRA] (1977), 400–403
System of National Accounts (SNA), United Nations, 88–91

Technical change: aggregate, 107–12, 264–67; association with Hicksian shift parameter, 8–10; bias in, 10; capacity utilization adjustment of, 111–12, 156; capital-embodied models of, 28–30; in coal industry, 406–11; concept of embodied (Solow), 514; dual measures of, 109–11; effect of misspecification on estimates of, 150–55, 157; firm-level estimates of, 269–79; with imperfect competition, 265; measurement of aggregate, 280; measurement using index number approach, 155; methods to estimate, 231–42; in neoclassical growth models, 23–24; process-oriented view of, 27; productivity growth different from, 100; product-oriented, 30–31; relation to TFP growth, 103–4; in U.S. coal industry, 406–11 492–94. *See* Technical change
Technological change. *See* Technical change
Technological progress: adjustment to Solow 1960 model, 190–99; in Arrow's model, 183, 204–7; capital stock growth resulting from, 185; embodiment effect in (Solow), 175–79; investment specific, 180; in Krusell's model, 183, 204, 207–9; mismeasurement of neutral, 218–19; in Parente's model, 183, 204, 209–16; Solow's capital model (1956), 181, 201, 216, 222; Solow's 1960 model of investment-specific, 187–99, 216–17; Solow's 1957 residual model of neutral, 185–87, 189–90, 216. *See also* Capital; Embodiment effect
Technology: adoption of new, 203–4; Domar weighted measure of, 264–66; effect of differences in, 507; flexible function forms for description of, 120; measured by TFP, 226; represented by output distance function, 546–47; second-mover advantages, 195; skill in implementation of new, 182; skills related to specific, 201–2; spillover effects in learning, 196–97
Technology residuals: correlation with data, 273–75; data correlations, 272–73; descriptive statistics of, 271–72
Technology change. *See* Technical change
Telecommunications: productivity measurement in, 429–34, 456–57
TFP. *See* Total factor productivity (TFP)
Threshold exceedence units (TEUs), 570–71
Tornqvist index: chained indexes, 62–64; conditions for exact, 15; weights employed by, 60–61
Total factor productivity (TFP): aggregate measures in coal mining of, 378, 380–84; approaches to international comparisons, 465–66; bias in conventional measure of, 116–19, 155–56; changes in Solow residual measures, 10; definition of, 5; developing theory of, 498–99; differences across countries, 468–99; Harrodian, 24–25; Hicksian, 24–25; measuring technical change, 104;

Subject Index

production function-based models of, 23-27; Solow residual as, 60; for U.S. coal industry (1972-95), 374-75. *See also* Multifactor productivity (MFP)
Total factor productivity (TFP), international: comparison for G7 countries, 480-84; comparison of large sample of countries, 484-92; cross-section growth accounting approach, 465-67, 470; panel regression approach to compare, 465-67, 470, 478-80, 495-96; time series approach to growth accounting, 465-66, 469-74
Total factor productivity (TFP) residual: arguments for and against, 41; balancing welfare and capacity, 31-33; bottom up approach for firms and industries, 38-39; computing, 19-20; using econometrics to disaggregate, 17; essential features of, 40-41; explanation of economic growth of, 23; Harrod-Rymes variant, 24; innovation component of, 17-18; in neoclassical growth models, 23-24; New Growth Theory challenges to, 22; quality change effect on, 29-31; as rate of growth, 18; top-down approach for firms and industries, 35-38
Total resource productivity (TRP): agricultural sector, 599; application of formula to U.S. expansion of TFP to, 587; measurement of, 587, 606-8; producer-based model of, 589-94, 606; welfare-based model of, 594-98, 606
Trade theory: capital mobility, 469; neoclassical, 468; Ricardian, 468

Transportation, public: comparison of productivity in, 440-46, 456-57
TRP. *See* Total resource productivity (TRP)
U.S. Department of Agriculture: Economic Research Service, 599; National Agriculture Statistics Service (NASS), 570; National Resource Inventory (NRI), 569, 571
U.S. Department of Labor: Bureau of Labor Statistics (BLS), 21, 55, 66-74, 78-79; Mine Safety and Health Administration (MSHA), 373
Utilization: different concepts of, 250-51

Value added: from Domar weighting, 264-65; firm-level, 257, 263; growth of, 258-59, 263; as national accounting concept, 259; as service sector output measure, 420-21; used as production measure, 257
Vintage accounting system: for human and nonhuman capital, 531-32
Vintage effects: definition of, 506-7

Wage inequality: with slow down in labor productivity growth (1970s), 199-204
Welfare: measurement of, 515-16; in normative productivity analysis, 230; productivity as, 279-81
Welfare change: aggregate Solow residual as measure of, 280; measurement of, 230, 279